The New England Wild Flower Society
GUIDE TO GROWING AND PROPAGATING WILDFLOWERS
OF THE UNITED STATES AND CANADA

THE NEW ENGLAND
WILD FLOWER SOCIETY

Guide to Growing and Propagating

WILDFLOWERS

of the United States and Canada

WILLIAM CULLINA

A FRANCES TENENBAUM BOOK

HOUGHTON MIFFLIN COMPANY

BOSTON   NEW YORK

2000

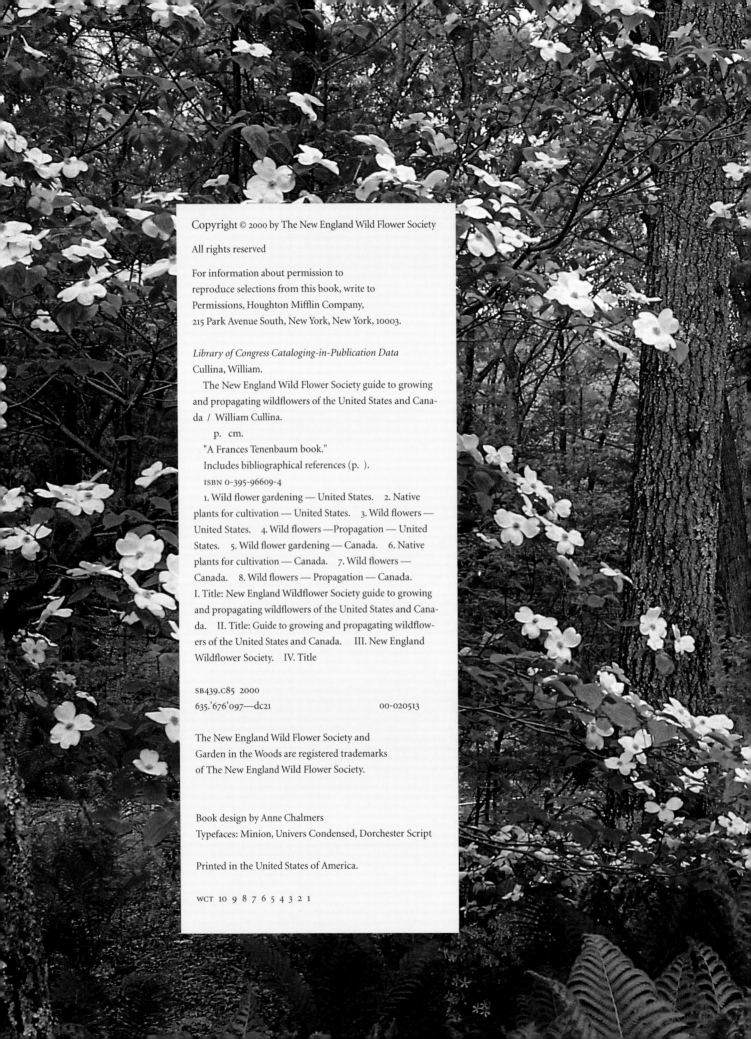

For information about permission to
reproduce selections from this book, write to
Permissions, Houghton Mifflin Company,
215 Park Avenue South, New York, New York, 10003.

Library of Congress Cataloging-in-Publication Data
Cullina, William.
    The New England Wild Flower Society guide to growing
and propagating wildflowers of the United States and Cana-
da / William Cullina.
        p. cm.
    "A Frances Tenenbaum book."
    Includes bibliographical references (p.   ).
    ISBN 0-395-96609-4
    1. Wild flower gardening — United States.   2. Native
plants for cultivation — United States.   3. Wild flowers —
United States.   4. Wild flowers —Propagation — United
States.   5. Wild flower gardening — Canada.   6. Native
plants for cultivation — Canada.   7. Wild flowers —
Canada.   8. Wild flowers — Propagation — Canada.
I. Title: New England Wildflower Society guide to growing
and propagating wildflowers of the United States and Canada.   II. Title: Guide to growing and propagating wildflowers of the United States and Canada.   III. New England
Wildflower Society.   IV. Title

SB439.C85 2000
635.'676'097—dc21   00-020513

The New England Wild Flower Society and
Garden in the Woods are registered trademarks
of The New England Wild Flower Society.

Book design by Anne Chalmers
Typefaces: Minion, Univers Condensed, Dorchester Script

Printed in the United States of America.

WCT 10 9 8 7 6 5 4 3 2 1

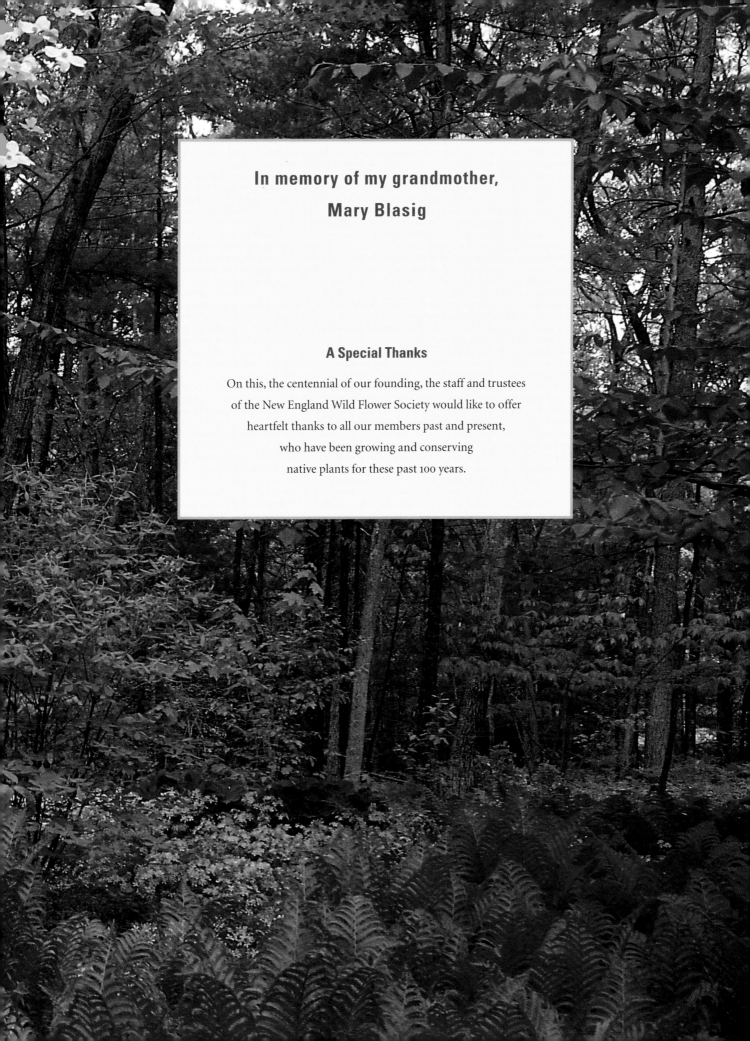

In memory of my grandmother,
Mary Blasig

A Special Thanks

On this, the centennial of our founding, the staff and trustees
of the New England Wild Flower Society would like to offer
heartfelt thanks to all our members past and present,
who have been growing and conserving
native plants for these past 100 years.

CONTENTS

PREFACE

I am much more comfortable talking about plants than about myself, but since this is a personal work, I suppose some context is appropriate. Thinking back, I realize I have always been a student of Life with a capital *L*. I spent my youth pouring over old *National Geographic*s and nature guides, fishing and wandering in marshes, learning the names of trees and snakes, dreaming of a career as a veterinarian, and growing all manner of plants. My mother grew up on a farm, so we always had a vegetable garden—though in the shade we could never produce much more than lettuce, beans, and small green tomatoes. My grandmother was a true horticulturist before there was a term for it, and she recognized the calling in me, beginning to give me divisions of her houseplants and perennials when I was seven or eight. By the time I was in high school I was collecting cacti, bromeliads, and palms, growing trees from seed, and preparing for a career in biology. My plans changed soon after starting college, though, as chemistry and biostatistics quickly dampened my enthusiasm for life as a Man of Science. Maybe I am only rationalizing my own shortcomings, but looking back on it, the textbooks and exams seemed to drain much of the joy and wonder out of Life and left me wanting more. I have a deep respect for science and the scientific method—much of my view of the world and its workings has been derived from it—but the study of life has meant much more to me than mere data sets and the laws of probability. In this sense I admit to being somewhat of a Romantic in the tradition of Jean Jacques Rousseau. He wrote something that resonates with me and captures my own sentiments perfectly: "Sometimes, in the privacy of my study, with my hands pressed tight over my eyes or in the darkness of the night, I am of the opinion that there is no God. But look yonder: the rising sun, as it scatters the mists that cover the earth, and lays bare the wondrous glittering scene of nature, disperses at the same moment all cloud from my soul. I find my faith again." So, I find myself closer in spirit to the nineteenth-century naturalists and transcendentalists like Thoreau and Muir than to a modern-day horti-culturist or ecologist. Like them, I spend most of my time observing nature with a mix of reverence and empiricism all the while attempting to piece together what I see into meaningful patterns. Necessarily, much of the information in this book is based on my experiences and friendships with the plants around me. Some is anecdotal, and I cannot expect it always to agree with your own experiences. However, I hope you will take my words as they were intended: a mix of science and poetry, fact and intuition, content to celebrate the remarkable, mysterious web of life that surrounds us all—Life that is completely accessible if we only take the time to stop and smell the wild-flowers.

It is absolutely true in horticulture, as with anything, that the more I learn, the less I know. It is hard to get a swelled head when you work with plants—they have a way of keeping you honest. No sooner have I looked with pride upon the glorious flowering of some rare treasure I have coaxed to bloom than it is a withered pile of sodden leaves mocking my insolence from the great beyond. When people hear that I am a professional horticulturist, they are usually embarrassed to let me into their homes, sure I will be disgusted at the sorry state of their houseplants or languishing gardens. My honest response is not to worry, for I have personally killed more plants than they could possibly imagine. That is the dark and secret truth of the professional horticulturist. However, each time a plant rots away under my care, another small thorn jabs my heart and I think again, "Okay, well that's the last." I hate to see plants suffer, just as I hate to see children or animals suffer, so I have spent much of my life attempting through trial and error to understand their needs and wants so that if I am to grow them, at least I can grow them well. I know that everyone that grows plants wishes the same; it is the bond we share as gardeners, so it is in this spirit that I present this book to you. I hope only that you may glean some truths from my triumphs and failures and come away in the end sharing my deep respect and love for all things green.

ACKNOWLEDGMENTS

I **would like** to extend a special thanks to Tom Fischer of *Horticulture* magazine for supporting this project, and my wonderful editor Frances Tenenbaum, for her vision, help, and encouragement along the way. I am also indebted to David DeKing, the director of the New England Wild Flower Society, for his patience and support, and Barbara Pryor, our public information director and the tireless slide editor of this book, for her guidance, keen eye, and unflagging enthusiasm. Special thanks as well to my sister and barrister, Susan Cullina, for her peerless legal advice and moral support, Lisa White of Houghton Mifflin, for her editing skills and good humor, and my colleagues: Cheryl Lowe, Chris Mattrick, and Pattie Scheuring, as well as my assistants, Kerry Norlin and Marion Murray, for picking up the slack so seamlessly while I took time off to write. I also want to thank Kerry for all her help checking and proofreading plant names and assembling the nursery sources section. My thanks as well to our librarians, Mary Walker and John Benson as well as the NEWFS Library Committee: Ruth Nastik, Margaret Flannagan, and Nancy Webb for assembling and maintaining such an outstanding reference collection that made my research incalculably easier, thorough, and fun. Thanks also to the Visual Images Committee for assembling such a vast collection of wonderful slides, David Heppert of CenterMedia for donating reproduction services, and the many talented photographers who have donated their work to us over the years. I am especially indebted to

Dorothy Long and John Lynch as well as Frank Bramley, Hal Horwitz, William Larkin, Albert Bussewitz, Walt and Louiseann Pietrowitz, Arieh Tal and Adelaide Pratt—all wonderful, generous artists whose images are as important to this work as my words. It is unquestionably one of the most rewarding parts of my job to work with a group of dedicated and supremely knowledgeable volunteers that share with me this process of horticultural discovery. Thanks to Helga Andrews, Christine Cofsky, Susan Dumaine, Carol Fyler, George Hibben, Lynn Luck, Sheila Magullion, Shari Michals, and Sara Silverstein. I have a special debt to my teachers and mentors at the University of Connecticut, including: Drs. Gustav Mehlquist and Pat Carpenter, who are sadly no longer with us, Drs. Mark Bridgen and Mark Brand, Professors John Alexopolos and Cathy Johnston, and Drs. Greg Anderson, Terry Webster, and the staff at the Ecology and Evolutionary Biology Greenhouses. Thanks also to Kim Hawks and all my friends at Niche Gardens for helping to make my time in North Carolina so rewarding.

Finally a personal thanks to my parents, Trudy and William Cullina, for their love and support, my friends and horticultural co-conspirators: Naomi Chin-Shong Blumenthal, Kai Hinkaty, Paul Morgan, and Carol Yee for their comradery, Tracy Brown for her years of companionship and encouragement, and Buddy the Cat for his company during the long hours at the computer.

THE NEW ENGLAND WILD FLOWER SOCIETY

Established in 1900, the New England Wild Flower Society is the nation's oldest organization dedicated to the conservation of wild plants. Its founders were part of the burgeoning turn-of-the-century "wilderness" and "return to nature" movement that sparked the campaign for a national park system and nurtured the fledgling conservation movement. In its early years, the Society focused on educating the public (through a series of publications and lectures) about our native plants and the disastrous effects large-scale wild collection combined with habitat distruction was having on wild populations.

Although the Society's principal conservation interests are in New England, many people are surprised to learn that our mission is to promote the conservation of all temperate North American flora through education, research, horticulture, habitat preservation, and advocacy. To further these goals, the Society manages four nationally recognized programs.

EDUCATION PROGRAM IN NATIVE PLANT STUDIES. Through courses, field trips, garden tours, teacher training, family programs, and publications, the Society teaches thousands of people every year about native plants and their habitats. No other botanical organization or university in the country offers such an array of educational opportunities on the topic of native plants. The Society's award-winning Certificate Program attracts hundreds of continuing education students to study field botany, ecology, and native plant conservation.

GARDEN IN THE WOODS. The Society owns and operates Garden in the Woods, the largest landscaped collection of wildflowers in the Northeast, as its botanical garden and living museum. Garden in the Woods was founded in 1931 by Will C. Curtis and Howard O. Stiles to research the science and practice the art of growing native plants. Curtis and Stiles cultivated their Garden for nearly 35 years. In 1965, they entrusted it to the Society. Individual gardens include Woodland Groves, a Lily Pond, Pine Barrens, and a Western Garden. The Garden is a center for conservation horticulture, propagation, and cultivation research. Today, our nursery offers the largest selection of propagated native plants in New England.

NEW ENGLAND PLANT CONSERVATION PROGRAM (NEPCoP). The Society founded and administers this program, a collaboration among botanists, federal and state agencies, and conservation orga-

nizations throughout the New England states. As one of the leading plant conservation collaborations in the United States, NEPCoP's activities include rare plant monitoring, rare plant reintroductions, invasive exotic plant control, habitat restoration, and habitat management.

PLANT CONSERVATION VOLUNTEER CORPS. The Society's Volunteer Corps surveys, monitors, and acts to preserve New England's native plant communities. These well-trained, knowledgeable volunteers assist conservation organizations, such as state heritage programs and land trusts, as they strive to manage plant populations on public and private lands. The Plant Conservation Volunteer Corps is part of the Society's ambitious strategy to revive interest in amateur field botany as a passion and pastime.

Nationally, the Society has a long history of collaboration and leadership in order to promote the conservation of native plants. We were one of the original institutional sponsors of the Center for Plant Conservation, a collaboration of more than 30 botanical institutions in the United States dedicated to preventing the extinction of native plants. Also, the Society is an active member of the American Association of Botanical Gardens and Arboreta.

We believe that one of the first acts of conservation that people can do is to nurture native plants in their own gardens. The personal experience of growing native plants seems to stimulate the desire to conservation them in their native habitats. Gardeners make some of the best conservationist.

We invite you to enjoy the exciting experience of cultivating native plants in your garden and to support plant conservation efforts in your region or state. For more information on the Society please visit our Web site or write us at our Massachusetts headquarters.

New England Wild Flower Society
180 Hemenway Road
Framingham, MA 01701-2699

Phone: (508) 877-7630
Fax: (508) 877-3658
e-mail: newfs@ newfs.org

Web site: www.newfs.org

The New England Wild Flower Society
GUIDE TO GROWING AND PROPAGATING WILDFLOWERS OF THE UNITED STATES AND CANADA

Introduction

Plants are wondrous things. They feed, clothe, and shelter us, fill our lives with color, fragrance, and beauty, and need nothing in return but a patch of soil and a place in the sun. Our once vast world is shrinking, though, and as we enter the twenty-first century, it is becoming increasingly difficult for plants to find the space they need to grow. What I hope to emphasize throughout this book is that gardening with native plants is not only fun and easy, it also fosters a genuine connection with the region you live in and the lives you share it with. Think of your garden not just as an extension of your house — a series of outdoor rooms, to use the current parlance — but as a *habitat* shared by you, plants, and the animals that depend on them for food and shelter. For every oak tree you transplant or meadow you seed, you create a home for dozens if not thousands of creatures that have evolved with them over time. Native plants are often promoted as low-maintenance, problem-free alternatives to finicky garden hybrids. While it is absolutely true that a plant that has evolved in your particular climate and soils will be hardier and more adaptable than many exotics from half a world away, it will likely be eaten by more types of insects, mammals, and birds than a plant growing far from its native home, and others, in turn, will eat them. This is precisely the point. While you may have to learn to live with some tattered leaves and blemished flowers, you can also free your garden and yourself from the pesticides that are undeniably and needlessly polluting our soil, air, and water while at the same time promoting a bit of ecological balance. Environmentalism need not be limited to mountaintops and rain forests. None of us can solve all the problems in the world, though in a small but very real way, whether you garden in window boxes in the city or acres in the country, you *can* put something back. There is value in preserving wilderness, but there is equal value in restoring the

(**BELOW**): Disporum maculatum. *It is the purple speckling on the flowers that gives Spotted Mandarin its common name. When these stately plants are in bloom, the air around them is redolent with a delicious, musky-sweet perfume.*

(LEFT): Aconitum uncinatum. *A picture is sometimes worth a thousand words. This cluster of Wild Monkshood looks for all the world like a group of penitent monks dressed in royal purple robes who have just stepped outside to chat and enjoy a bit of warm summer sunshine.*

(RIGHT): Echinacea purpurea. *The central "cone" of each coneflower bloom is a gradually expanding cluster of the fertile, purple-brown disk flowers that are highlighted with orange-tipped spines (the Latin root* Echin *means "beset with prickles," and this refers to the spines that guard the flowers/seeds). The newest flowers are found near the center of the cone, and this is where the skipper prefers to feed.*

suburbs and cities where most of us live to something closer to balance—for our children's sake and the sake of all the other species around us.

What Is a
Native Plant?

For the purposes of this work, *native* means plants growing in North America prior to European settlement, and the term *wildflower* indicates simply native herbaceous perennials excluding grasses and sedges, as well as ferns and other bryophytes. The use of native plants has become very politicized in recent years, and this is unfortunate. Like the noted writer-philosopher Wendell Berry, I am suspicious of Movements and do not want to see the enjoyment and appreciation of our wonderful flora needlessly polemicized under the auspices of a native plant *movement*. Therefore, I think both the term *native* as well as some of the reasons for choosing to grow these plants need further clarification.

It is natural for us humans to think of time in terms of our own life spans, and if we grant things that live and die over longer intervals an air of permanence it is certainly understandable. A Douglas-fir that has lived 1,000 years is incomprehensibly old to us, so to then think of the land itself as having a life span as well is nearly impossible. In geological time, 1,000 years is roughly equivalent to 10 minutes in the life span of a person. In this sort of relative time, it has been about two years since the age of the dinosaurs and about two hours since the last Wisconsin glaciers retreated north. If we could only view

the earth with some sort of super time-lapse photography for a few minutes, geological time would be understandable as the powerful dance of continents, mountains, ice, and water, where forests ebb and flow like waves on a beach and ancient trees are mere momentary bubbles in the changing surf. With this sort of perspective it becomes clear that what we see in the wilds at this particular moment in time is but a split-second freeze-frame in a much larger process, and to draw too many conclusions about particular elements in this composition without putting them into a geological context is a dangerous proposition. This becomes particularly important when one is discussing rarity and extinction or even the concept of what is a native plant. In geological time, a plant is only native somewhere as an airplane's transient vapor trail is native to a particular place in the atmosphere. Species are always in a state of flux, advancing and receding, evolving and disappearing, their presence in any one place only transitory. Even the land itself is constantly moving, shifting, and recombining. How can we then say that anything is native anywhere? It is equivalent to taking a photograph of a busy street and from then on assuming that these people caught in midstep have always resided on this bit of pavement and will always continue to, unless some great catastrophe intervenes. To argue this point would be an exercise in futility.

The important point, then, is not simply what it means to be *native*, but what possible consequences displacing a particular species from a particular place may have on the ecosystem as a whole. This is the key argument for what ecologists call *preservation of biodiversity.* Individual species do not exist in a vacuum—the actions of one species radiate out-

Chelone lyonii. *Pink Turtlehead is but one of the many beautiful wildflowers native to our disappearing wetlands. Half of our turtlehead species are considered rare or endangered, but all are easy to establish in a damp, sunny area.* Chelone *is one of only two larval food plants for the Baltimore Checkerspot butterfly, and the flowers are an important nectar source for late-season foragers.*

ward like ripples on a pond, affecting many others. For example, say the eggs of an insect that feeds on Hemlock trees are transported halfway around the globe by some freak weather event. The Hemlocks in this region have never experienced this pest, have no defenses against it, and begin to die out over much of their former range. As the range of the Hemlock recedes, so too do those of the fungi that feed on its wood, the birds that feed on its seeds, the caterpillars that consume its needles, etc. The gap left in the forest by the death of these trees allows the advance of other trees that could not grow in the shade of the Hemlock, and as this may well have been the climax tree in the forest succession of the region, the whole life cycle of the forest itself is altered. Should the diversity of life be high enough, other organisms that depend on these advancing species will move forward as well, and a few may eventually adapt to feed on the Hemlock pest itself, reversing the tide and restoring some kind of balance. In a healthy ecosystem, such disturbances can actually increase biodiversity over time, and the more species there are in a particular region, the more flexible and proactive the whole will be. Just as it is easier to write poetry with a vocabulary of 10,000 words as opposed to 200, so too will a large number of species be more responsive to change and able to restore balance after disturbance or insult. The elimination of biodiversity dams this flow, so to speak—the water still trickles by, but the salmon cannot swim and the bears cannot feast, the dragonfly nymphs have less to feed on, and it is hard to say if even the quality of the mud doesn't change for the worse. More than any other species on the planet, we have the ability to shape our environment.

I firmly believe that if we all decide to make an effort to restore some of the local plants to our landscapes, we will in no small way help make our own piece of the world a richer, more diverse, and, by consequence, a healthier place. This is not politics, it is simple truth.

How to Use This Book

It has become very clear to me as I work with and teach about native wildflowers that there is a real need for a comprehensive guide to their culture, personalities, and propagation. So, I have written a book that I hope will be useful for the novice and the expert alike, with information presented in a style that is approachable and easy to read, but still informative and accurate. The plants are arranged alphabetically by genus, each entry beginning with an overview that includes anecdotes and relevant information to serve as an introduction to the group. This is followed by notes regarding basic cultural advice, garden uses, and, if relevant, the plant's importance for particular wildlife. Each entry concludes with a list of representative species and their particularities. Detailed notes on propagation are in a separate section at the end of the book.

I have sought to include plants from all of temperate North America so that you may select species that are well suited to your individual climate, light conditions, and soil. While I encourage you to grow and appreciate the plants of your area, I know that we all as gardeners like to seek out the challenge of something new and different, so whenever possible I

Meadow in summer. Echinacea purpurea and Rudbeckia fulgida var. sullivantii (seen here in a meadow planting at Garden in the Woods) are both composites—members of the glorious Aster family. The Aster family is one of the three most successful plant families alive today and provides the wildflower gardener with myriad variations on a theme. There are roughly 1,000 genera and 20,000 species in the family worldwide—a remarkable diversity rivaled only by the Orchid family (Orchidaceae) and Grass family (Poaceae).

have included information to aid you in growing a particular plant successfully outside its native range.

Latin Names: Family, Genus, and Species

I realize that Latin is no one's first language and can be a bit ponderous to use if you are not accustomed to it. I have used Latin liberally in the text, not to be pompous, but because it really is valuable to know the Latin names and become comfortable using them for two reasons. First, common names are often wonderful and poetic, but many common names, such as bluestar, are generic, so it is difficult to know which plant someone is referring to. Even more confusing are names like mayflower or paintbrush, which are applied to multiple genera. Second, binomial Latin names can tell you a great deal about a plant because they represent a system of classification based on a plant's familial or evolutionary relationships and individual characteristics. Plants have been split into a series of categories and subcategories using characteristics of their vasculature, seeds, reproductive structures, etc., starting with the most global categories and working to the most specific. To briefly put this in perspective, this classification system works as follows:

There are two **divisions** in the plant **kingdom.** The first, **Pteridophyta,** includes all the things like

ferns and mosses otherwise known as bryophytes. These are plants that reproduce without flowers or seeds, relying instead on spores. The second division is the **Spermatophyta,** or seed plants, which make up by far most of the plants now on earth and are more recently evolved than the Pteridophyta. The Spermatophyta are divided next into **Gymnosperms,** which means naked seed, as the ovules or eggs are not enclosed in an ovary. This includes all of the conifers and a few related plants. The other subdivision of Spermatophyta is the **Angiosperms,** meaning in effect covered seed, as these evolved coverings or fruits for their ovules or seeds. This is the biggest group of plants alive today, and all the species covered in this book are Angiosperms. The Angiosperms are next divided into two **classes:** the **monocots,** or plants with only one cotyledon (the first or embryonic leaf), and **dicots,** which have two cotyledons. Monocots include grasses, lilies, orchids, irises, palms, bromeliads, sedges, and a few others, so they are pretty successful evolutionarily and a personal interest of mine. However, most of the plants we work with are dicots—it is a large and highly successful group.

Both the monocots and dicots are split into a series of **families.** A family is a fairly manageable grouping of plants that share certain recognizable characteristics. For example, the Orchid family are

(LEFT): Asclepias tuberosa. *It is hard to mistake Butterfly Weed for any other wildflower. Even from a distance, the intensity of the orange-red blooms is simply stunning.*

(RIGHT): Wyethia amplexicaulis. *The vibrant golden flowers of Mule's Ears are a true harbinger of spring in the high mountain meadows and pastures of the West, quickly blooming and setting seed before the summer drought forces them to retreat underground for the year.*

monocots with the sexual parts united into a structure called a column, and the Composites (Asteraceae) are dicots with flowers aggregated into distinct daisy-type inflorescences. It is very helpful to know which family a certain plant belongs to, as it gives many clues, especially regarding its propagation and habits. Certain families, such as the Ranunculaceae and Liliaceae, have a disproportionate number of wonderful garden plants, and knowing this helps you narrow your search for new possibilities. All family names end in "aceae." This is a nomenclatural convention that makes it easy to tell a family name from a genus or species.

Families are further split into **genera** (**genus** is singular). A genus is a smaller grouping of plants with very similar characteristics. True geraniums are all in the genus *Geranium,* lilies in *Lilium,* and black-eyed Susans in *Rudbeckia.* (Though they are both in the Lily family, trilliums have been split into a genus separate from true lilies, because they differ enough anatomically and cannot interbreed.) Conveniently, plants within a genus share many of the same characters, so I have used this as the organizing principle of the book. Genera are further divided into **species.** A species is a group of genetically very similar plants, which are distinct and interbreed. Humans are a species—*Homo sapiens*—which is distinct from other (now extinct) species in the genus *Homo,*

like *Homo erectus.* This binomial system is the standard way of writing out the Latin name of a species —the genus (capitalized) and the specific epithet (lowercased), all of it italicized. It is sort of like phone numbers with area codes and exchanges in that it allows for many more possible combinations than does one word alone. Thus *Oncidium maculatum, Hieracleum maculatum,* and *Phlox maculata* are three very different plants with basically the same specific epithet. Knowing that *maculate* means spotted tells you something about them too. With plants, the lines that separate one species from another are usually more blurred than with animals, so you can't say, well, if two plants produce a fertile offspring, then they are of the same species. Though you can tell from just looking that *Trillium grandiflorum* is different from *Trillium erectum,* species is an artificial construct, and plants are always in a state of flux and evolution. When a plant occurs over a wide range or in geographically isolated areas, often there are distinctive races, called *subspecies* (abbreviated ssp.), which are felt to be too close to be separate species, but are distinct enough from each other to be recognizable. *Erigeron chrysopsidis* ssp. *brevifolius* (meaning short-leaved) is slightly different from *E. chrysopsidis* ssp. *austiniae.* More commonly, there can be minor variations within a species, like flower color, size, or level of hairiness, not extreme enough

(LEFT): Cypripedium pubescens. *Large Yellow Lady-slipper used to be called* Cypripedium calceolus *var.* pubescens, *a large-flowered North American version of the European* C. calceolus *(the name refers to the plant's preference for limestone). However, it is now considered distinct enough from both the European species and the Small Yellow Lady-slipper (formerly* C. calceolus *var.* parviflorum, *now* C. parviflorum*) to be classified as a separate species—* Cypripedium pubescens.

(BELOW): Cypripedium reginae. *Showy Lady-slipper in the wilds of Vermont.*

to be given a subspecies designation. These are noted as *varieties* (abbreviated var.). Botanically speaking, varieties represent some consistent natural and minor variation that occurs within a given population of the species. In practice, the term variety is often confused and applied to all sorts of things, both horticultural and botanical. *Trillium grandiflorum* var. *roseum* is a pink-flowered form found growing with populations of white-flowered forms. There is *Chrysogonum virginianum* var. *australe*, which is a larger, clumping type of the species. The key here is that a variety is something that differs from the "typical" species in some relatively minor way, like people with red hair could be *Homo sapiens* var. *aurantiaca* (meaning orange). Except for this minor difference, they are just like everyone else in the species. Variety was intended to refer to natural or wild variants, but began to be used by horticulturists to refer to cultivated strains that appeared or were bred in gardens. To keep wild and human selected variations separate, the term cultivar was developed. A cultivar is a clone or seed strain selected for a particular trait or traits. It's written capitalized, unitalicized, and in single quotes, i.e., *Trillium grandiflorum* 'Rosalie'. There can be cultivars of a variety or subspecies, too, like *Homo sapiens* var. *aurantiaca*

'Woody Allen' or *Chrysogonum virginianum* var. *australe* 'Allen Bush', which is a cultivar of the variety *australe* selected for vigor and long bloom. The key is the quotes, so when you see *Chrysogonum* 'Allen Bush' in a catalog, you know that this is shorthand for the particular clone I just mentioned and will be exactly like all the other 'Allen Bush's' out there—unless a careless nursery person mixed up their labels or used open-pollinated seed.

When two species hybridize or interbreed naturally in the wild, the offspring's binomial is written with an × signifying that it is of hybrid origin. So, *Aster macrophyllus* and *A. spectabilis* will sometimes hybridize and produce *Aster × herveyi*. Hybrids made by people are not usually given a new species name, but are still written with an ×, like *Coreopsis ×* 'Moonbeam', a cultivar of hybrid origin.

Taxonomy

Taxonomic name changes are a common and often (to gardeners) frustrating result of ongoing research in the field of plant classification. I understand that the system of plant classification is in a constant state of flux as old information is clarified and new research tools uncover hidden relationships or differences. However, I am cognizant as well of the importance and meaning names take on beyond the confines of taxonomic research. Names, like all language, are conventions that allow us to share ideas and concepts, and thus take on a life of their own that should not be minimized. Therefore, while I sympathize with the goals of taxonomists, I am reluctant to embrace every new name change and revision that comes along, because I think these need time and debate within the professional botanic community before they are accepted, and even more time in the horticultural community before they are wholly adopted. I have tried to indicate where I have used a new name as well as where I have declined to—not out of obstinacy, but out of a desire for clarity borne from consensus and tradition.

The primary authorities I used for both Latin and common names are *Flora of North America, Manual of Vascular Plants of Northeastern United States and Adjacent Canada, A Synonymized Checklist of the Vascular Flora of the United States, Canada, and Greenland,* and *A Flora of the Pacific Northwest.*

Pronunciation

Words communicate information, and I believe there is no right or wrong way of pronouncing them, as long as the information comes across. Latin, like any language, has certain rules of grammar, and botanical Latin has evolved from it. However, whether you pronounce *Echinacea* ek-in-ay-SHAH or ek-in-AY-she-ah, people will understand, rules or no rules. So, with this in mind, I have given suggest-

ed pronunciations (based on horticultural convention) in parentheses for each genus, with the accented syllable in uppercase letters.

Disclaimer

Many of the plants covered in this work have a long and rich history as medicinals, and I have provided information where appropriate because I think it adds a great deal of human context. However, this information is provided for historical purposes only, and neither I, the New England Wild Flower Society, or the publisher in any way recommend or endorse the use of any of the plants here described for medicinal, culinary, or herbal use.

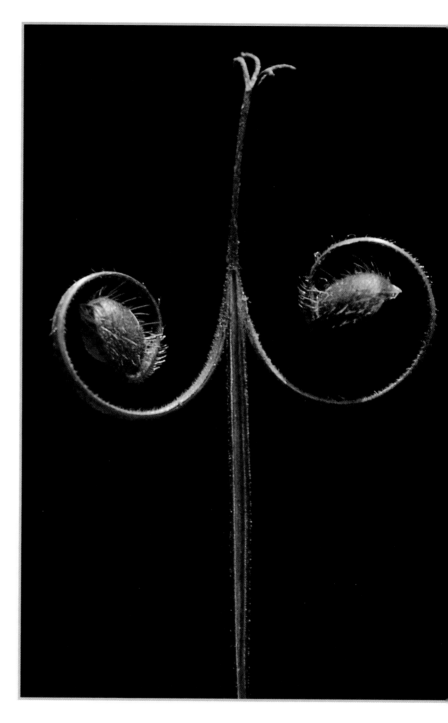

Geranium maculatum. *The MAR-vell-us coiled catapults of jerr-AYNE-ee-um mack-yule-ATE-um remain on the plant after they have sprung and shot out their seeds (see page 112 for details).*

Cypripedium pubescens *and* Phlox divaricata. *Garden in the Woods sits squarely within the eastern deciduous woodland floristic province, so, not surprisingly, it is famous for its displays of spring ephemerals. Though we grow a wide range of species from across North America in the Garden, the plants from our own region are usually easiest for us to grow.*

Each species entry includes the following:

HARDINESS RANGE:

I have based winter hardiness on the revised USDA Plant Hardiness Zone Map (pp. 298–299). The map breaks down North America into a series of zones experiencing gradually colder average minimum winter low temperatures. Hardiness zones indicate areas where the average minimum winter temperatures in a given year fall between a certain range. For example, Garden in the Woods lies in USDA Zone 6, where average winter minimums are –5° to –10°F, though many years we have lows well above zero and once in a great while there are years where they fall below –10°F. For each of the featured species, I have included a hardiness range that I have arrived at

based on personal experience, references, and the natural range of the plant. I include an upper and lower zone limit for each plant, the lower limit (smaller number) being the coldest zone in which it will grow and the upper being the warmest limit it can tolerate. This warmer limit needs further explanation. When I state a plant's range as Zones 4–7, I mean to indicate not only its cold tolerance, but also its unsuitability for gardeners in most of Zones 8–10, where summers are too long and warm for the plant to thrive (the exception being gardeners along the Pacific coast, who benefit from a cool maritime climate where both winters and summers are mild).

I have found hardiness ratings to be a useful general guide when selecting plants to try, but please take this information with a grain of salt. There is much more to determining a plant's hardiness in a particular situation than simply its tolerance of cold. Other climatic factors such as the amount of annual solar radiation, altitude, average relative humidity, patterns and amounts of rainfall and snowfall, reliability of snow cover, average summer high and low temperatures, and length and severity of extreme hot and cold temperatures (prolonged temperatures below 20°F or above 90°F are much harder for many plants to endure than a brief chill or heat wave). Furthermore, factors such as windiness of the site, freeze-thaw patterns and depth of soil frost, and seasonal day length at a particular latitude all play a part in determining a plant's hardiness. So even though Sable Island, Nova Scotia; Cape Cod, Massachusetts; Raleigh, North Carolina; Albuquerque, New Mexico; and Juneau, Alaska, are all within USDA Zone 7, they have vastly different climates, and it is rare to find a plant that will thrive in all of them. It is a subject on which I could easily write a book, but rather than developing more sophisticated hardiness ratings, I think it is far less complicated to grow the plants native to your area whenever possible and to seek out genotypes that originate nearby if you can. A *Veronica hastata* from Delaware will likely grow better in New Jersey than one originating in Arizona. If you want to grow plants from farther afield, look first for species with ranges that come close to yours in latitude or longitude. A plant from southern New Mexico will have a better chance in Georgia than in Wisconsin, and a gardener in Alberta will be more likely to overwinter plants from Saskatchewan than from New Brunswick. Pay close attention to soil recommendations, and remember that a healthy, established plant has the best chance of survival.

With this in mind, I have included a map of the floristic provinces of North America (p. 22) that are based on Bailey's Ecoregions maps[1] and Barbour and Billings's map of major plant formations.[2] It is meant to be used in conjunction with the range information given for each species, so states and provinces are indicated. Ecoregions, or floristic provinces, are simply regions with broadly similar climate and dominant vegetation that has adapted to it. In many ways, I find such a map more useful in determining a particular plant's suitability to my garden than the most detailed hardiness zone map. While the nine provinces indicated here are necessarily broad, each does have an undeniable ecological as well as sociological identity. Ask most people what comes to mind when they picture the Pacific Northwest and they will likely say green and wet. Ecoregions can be used as a guide in design as well, to create gardens that celebrate your region's uniqueness.

LIGHT:

The information after the hardiness zone is the preferred sun exposure for the species in question. *Sun* means full sun, or at least six hours of direct sun daily in midsummer. *Part sun* means two to five hours of direct sun and the rest of the day in shade (this sun does not have to come all at once, as long as the total exposure is at least two hours), and *shade* means less than two hours of direct sun. Granted, sunlight is difficult to quantify so simplistically. As you get closer to the equator, the sun becomes more intense, so gardeners in the Deep South can accommodate plants in shade that can grow happily only in full sun in the North. Where I have given a range, say from sun to part sun, assume that if you garden in southern Mississippi the plant may benefit from some afternoon shade while in Quebec, it will likely require full sun. Shade is even more difficult to quantify, as it represents a whole range of light from nearly full sun to almost darkness. There are few plants that will grow in what I call heavy shade—that found beneath dense evergreens or the small spaces between tall buildings. By *shade* I mean to indicate "high shade"—the kind you find on the north side of a building open to the sky or under a broken forest canopy where the tree limbs begin 20 to 30 feet above the ground. At this level of shade, if you pass your hand over the plant it should cast a visible shadow. We regularly limb up the trees in our woodland—raise the roof, so to speak—as this favors the growth of most shade plants. Sometimes I have used the term *light shade,* and by this I mean a spot that receives maybe an hour or two of direct sun or dappled sun for most of the day.

SOIL:

In many ways, finding plants to suit your soil (or vice versa) is the key to successful gardening. Most horticultural works, including this one, greatly simplify the classification of soils for the sake of brevity and, frankly, because we have much to learn about the interrelationship of plants and soil. In the wild, certain species are often associated with particular soil types, like sands or clays, or soils derived from certain minerals such as serpentine or limestone rock.

Other plants are generalists, found on a wide variety of substrates. Fortunately, most wildflowers are fairly accommodating in the garden if you can provide a soil within a certain range of water-holding capacity, pH, and fertility. The soil entry for each featured species provides basic moisture ranges as follows:

Wet means a soil with a high water table, where standing water is visible within 1 foot of the surface when you dig down with a shovel. Typically, the water table fluctuates during the season, and periodic standing or surface water is tolerated by most wetland plants. Obviously, wetlands are sensitive ecosystems important to wildlife as well as to many plants, so if you have this type of soil, be aware that your state and/or local authorities may have strict regulations and guidelines regarding wetland disturbance

Sarracenia purpurea and Ledum groenlandicum. *Bogs are a specific type of wetland with very poor, highly acidic soils and a high water table (see Bog Garden on page 185). Pictured here are Labrador Tea (in flower) and Common Pitcher Plant (foreground).*

Stylophorum diphyllum *and* Phlox stolonifera. *Woodland soils tend to be moist in spring but gradually dry out in summer as trees and warmer temperatures draw off more water than can be replaced by rainfall. Celandine Poppy blooms early when conditions are favorable, then dies back to a thick rootstock to wait out the dry season. Many wildflowers can take moderate drought during part of the year, provided the soil is moist during their growing season. Matching a plant as closely as you can to its natural habitat will help ensure success in the garden.*

or alteration. With this in mind, restoring damaged wetlands with native flora is one of the most satisfying and beneficial things you can do for your local ecosystem.

Moist refers to soil where the water table is at least 1 foot below the surface, but that never dries out completely (the soil 2–6 inches below the surface should be cool and damp to the touch) or for only brief periods. Obviously, this is an ideal soil for most plants and one that in practice is difficult to find. We all have wet and dry years, but think of this as an average condition. Many gardeners rely on occasional supplemental irrigation to keep soils evenly moist, but please consider more drought-tolerant alternatives if you find you need to constantly water. The addition of organic matter and a good layer of mulch will help hold water and cool the soil as well.

Dry or *droughty* soils feel dry to the touch a foot or more below the surface for at least part of the year. Often these soils are moist or wet in winter and spring and dry over the course of the summer. This is a common condition in many gardens, and fortunately there are a host of native wildflowers adapted to dry soils that are excellent alternatives to a dependence on irrigation.

Well drained. Plant roots need oxygen, as we do, and certain plants, especially those from dry, sandy soils and alpine environments, will easily suffocate if a soil holds too much water. A well-drained soil contains a high percentage of sand or gravel, which promotes air exchange and sheds water quickly.

Moist, well-drained soils strike a balance between air exchange and water retention. They have a good balance of organic material and grit but require regular rainfall or irrigation. *Dry, well-drained* soils are gritty enough to shed water even during times of rain. A heavy clay or gumbo soil would not be considered well drained, even if it is dry.

Acidic or alkaline. I have gone into pH more thoroughly in the section on ecological gardening, but by acid or acidic I mean soils with a pH under 5.5, and alkaline a pH above 6.5. Most wildflowers can be accommodated in soils with a pH between 5.5 and 6.5, so I have mentioned only the exceptions.

For detailed coverage of soils, please refer to "Ecological Gardening," p. 13.

HABITAT, RANGE:
The first line indicates the typical habitat this partic-

ular species prefers, such as swamps and wet prairies, to give you clues as to where you can best accommodate it in your own garden. I find this information extremely valuable when trying to place a plant or choose species for a given location. The second section, such as Wisconsin to Alberta south to Texas and Missouri, is meant to be a very generalized range limit for the plant in question. If you drew a box on a map of North America connecting these states or provinces, it would roughly contain the range of the species. Therefore, in this example, you might expect to find the plant in a suitable habitat in Minnesota and Oklahoma, but not New Mexico or Nova Scotia. Of course this does not necessarily mean that the plant would not thrive in a garden in Nova Scotia or New Mexico or that it occurs within every state within in the range box.

I compiled habitat and range information from a number of the sources in the bibliography, especially: Gleason and Cronquist's *Manual of Vascular Plants of the Northeastern United States and Adjacent Canada*, Hitchcock and Cronquist's *Flora of the Pacific Northwest*, Radford, Ahles, and Bell's *Manual of the Vascular Flora of the Carolinas, Flora of North America, vol. III*, Cronquist et al.'s *Intermountain Flora*, Steyermark's *Flora of Missouri*, Martin and Hutchin's *A Flora of New Mexico*, Munz' *A California Flora, Hortus Third*, and the Great Plains Flora Association's *Flora of the Great Plains.*

SIZE:

The first number is the average height under cultivation. When there is a large range in height, say, 12–24 inches, this indicates that either the plants are variable, depending on conditions, or that the flower spikes are markedly taller than the foliage. The second number (in parentheses) indicates the expected width (for clumping plants) or spread (in the case of running plants and ground covers) of the plant after three years in the garden so as to give an idea of necessary spacing.

COLOR, BLOOM:

Although you may disagree with my color perception, I have tried to get as detailed as I can about a particular flower. Many entries have a range, say, from violet to purple or white that you may expect to find over a species range, but not necessarily in a particular batch of seedlings. As for flowering season, I have given time of year rather than specific months since this varies greatly from region to region. If your spring lasts from early March until late May (aren't you lucky) then a flowering time of late spring would be the mid- to later part of May.

Dalea purpurea. *Purple Prairie Clover ranges from Wisconsin northwest into Alberta then south to New Mexico and sporadically as far east as Alabama. The range of this grassland legume approximates the range of the Great Plains floristic province, but its occurrence in the hot, humid Southeast would suggest to me that it will also grow well in wetter climates (which in fact it does).*

Statement on Wild Collecting

THE NEW ENGLAND WILD FLOWER SOCIETY originated in response to unrestrained plant collecting that was devastating populations of certain vulnerable ferns, club mosses, and woodland wildflowers, and it is still our policy today to not condone any wild collecting of plants or plant parts with the exception of seeds. Our planet is just too small to sustainably wild harvest anything anymore, and people who argue differently must have their heads in the sand. We have had to resort to growing even trees and fish in farms—two "resources" we have until recently freely wild collected and thought limitless, so how can we think that it could be any different with wildflowers? If an occasional person dug up a few plants of some fairly common plant, the effect would be negligible, but wildflowers are too popular, and the desire for profit at any cost too strong. Just as a rise in the demand for fish has nearly exterminated all the commercial fish species of the North Atlantic, so, too, the increasing popularity of wildflower gardening threatens the health and stability of wild populations everywhere. Certainly, the vast majority of plants sold today are nursery-propagated (grown from seed or cuttings or divisions of nursery stock), but it is the slow-growing woodland and bulbous species that are at once especially vulnerable and still harvested in uncon-

scionably high numbers. These include many of the lilies and lily relatives like trilliums, calochortus and erythroniums, as well as bloodroot, bluebells, hepaticas, lady-slippers, and gingers to name a few. The only way to stop this depredation is to eliminate the demand. When buying woodland wildflowers, ask your supplier about their source. If they are unsure or if the price seems too good to be true, look somewhere else. Most important, be very suspicious of vendors selling cheap, bare-root woodland wildflowers by the half dozen or hundred. No one who has put four to ten years into growing a lady-slipper from seed is going to sell it bare-root for pennies. You will certainly pay more for nursery-propagated material, but it is the only way that the practice of large-scale wild collecting will end. Be skeptical of supposedly "rescued" plants (plants dug from areas about to be developed or paved over). I know from personal experience of unscrupulous collectors who market supposedly rescued plants that were dug from safe, healthy populations. While I hate to see plants being destroyed under a bulldozer, the term "rescued plants" is too open to interpretation and abuse at this point to be anything more than a loophole for disreputable collectors.

Ecological Gardening

The term *ecological gardening* is becoming popular these days as a way of describing a more environmentally friendly way to grow plants. Traditional gardening can involve tremendous labor and expense to modify an existing site to accommodate unsuitable plants and equally large amounts in maintenance to keep the plants going. Granted, all gardens need at least a little annual care—that is precisely what makes them gardens and not wild areas. However, there is no question that it is far easier in the long run on both you and the environment if you make it a policy to find plants to fit the site whenever you can.

The central purpose of this book is to show you the possibilities that abound in our native flora so that you can choose plants that are both appealing *and* adapted to the climate and soils of the region in which you live. I have been frustrated myself by the lack of good information available on native perennials. With few choices, you inevitably have to spend time and expense modifying your site to fit their needs. Of course, if you have a place where "absolutely nothing will grow," do not expect wildflowers to fare any better. Fortunately, such situations are rare if you take the time to consider your conditions and plan accordingly.

I think a basic understanding of the fundamental, interrelated environmental factors that determine which plants will grow where, combined with the ability to recognize and choose plants accordingly, is all you really need to be an excellent horticulturist. Consequently, this brief section on cultivation is more about the fundamentals of plant biology and

ecology than are the paragraphs on cultivation included with each genus. I intend it as a sort of prologue as well as an attempt to explain some of the reasons *behind* typical gardening advice. There are many good books available that cover the basics of soil preparation, transplanting, watering, etc., and I do not think I need to cover these in detail here.

Plants live under the restraints of their environment just as we all do. The important limiting factors for plant life are the availability and quality of light, soil (which includes its physical structure, fertility, and moisture-holding capacity), water, and temperature. Matching plants to a particular set of these conditions is the essence of good gardening, whether you choose to call it *ecological* or not.

Certain plants are especially good at growing in a specific combination of environmental constraints, for example: full sun in sandy, dry soils with temperatures that are hot during the summer and mild during the cloudy winter, when most of the rainfall occurs. This combination is a fairly harsh one for plant life, and those species that can survive do so mainly by becoming *specialists* with a physiology, anatomy, and life cycle finely tuned to get the most out of a limiting environment. For example, cacti have been able to thrive in such environments by losing their leaves and evolving water-holding stems and deep roots. They are limited to certain rigid sets of environmental conditions by this, but within them, they compete exceedingly well. If you find these conditions in your garden, certain cacti would be obvious, low-maintenance choices. Other plants, considered *generalists,* adapt to a range of condi-

Cornus florida, Phlox divaricata, Matteuccia struthiopteris. Notice the high, open shade in the foreground as opposed to the dense shade under the low branches of a beech grove in the background. Shade is a matter of degrees, and while understory plants such as Flowering Dogwood, Wood Phlox, and Osmunda Fern thrive in the filtered light of oaks that have been limbed up 30 feet, they would fail to grow under the dense canopy of the low-branched beech.

tions, for example: sun to shade in silt or clay soils of moderate fertility and moisture content, consistent rainfall, and temperatures that are moderate in the summer and cold in winter. They have evolved to grow moderately well in a wider range of environmental conditions, but still, they cannot grow simply anywhere. Most popular garden plants are generalists to some degree, thus we can say on the labels "grow in sun to shade, moist to dry soils, Zones 3–10." However, if you limit yourself to these "easy" or adaptable plants, you are ignoring a host of wonderful wildflowers that are more exacting in their requirements, but not difficult if they are chosen carefully and sited correctly. When considering the plants in this book, keep this in mind and look at the constraints present in your own garden as opportunities to grow some wonderful specialist plants exceedingly well.

Light

Obviously, plants need light to grow. The ability to transform the energy in sunlight into stored chemical energy is the fundamental miracle of life that makes *everything* else possible. The intensity and duration of sunlight that strikes a particular spot is easy to quantify in a lab. One of my more interesting laboratory tasks when I was working in horticultural research was to collect the printouts from a machine set up at the experimental farm that plotted the intensity and duration of solar radiation from day to day on a graph. Sunny days showed up as even bell curves peaking around noon. Partly cloudy days looked like jagged mountain peaks because the intensity would vary abruptly as the sun came and went, and cloudy days resembled low, rounded hills. We measured the light from spring until fall, and we could see marked differences in the height and width of the curve between readings taken in late June and those taken in the waning days of September. After I had the graphs for the season, I carefully cut out the bells, craggy mountains, and low hills with a razor knife and put them in a machine that measures surface area. By using some mathematical calculations I have since forgotten, so many square inches of graph paper equaled so much solar radiation and I had neatly quantified the total amount of sun that had

shone on that particular spot during the growing season. I know there are computer programs that can collect and output this data more easily, but somehow cutting out those little blobs made the whole thing more real.

My point here is that it is helpful to think of sunlight as a quantity just as it is easier to think of rainfall as a number of inches or fertilizer as a number of pounds. Certain plants need a specific quantity of sunlight both daily and over the course of the season to grow their best, and you need to consider this when siting them in the garden. A beardtongue from 12,000 feet in the Colorado Rockies receives huge amounts of sunlight, say 40 buckets a day (this is an artificial unit of measurement I've made up for convenience) during the growing season because the days are long and the sun has not had to pass through much light-refracting atmosphere. However, the growing season is short at this altitude, so the plants quickly accumulate their necessary 1,600-bucket yearly quota and go dormant. A coneflower growing on the cloudless plains of Kansas may receive an average of 30 buckets of sun daily, but over a longer growing season, this could amount to a whopping 3,000 buckets—a quantity it needs for stocky growth, prolific flowering, and long life. A trillium from western Virginia may receive 20 daily sun buckets for a few weeks in spring before the trees leaf out then only about 3 buckets for the rest of the long season, for a total of only 900 buckets, even though it may ideally prefer 1,200 for flowering and seed set. It has adapted as best it can by emerging early and getting as much growing done as possible before the light dims. All of these species will grow best when they receive both the daily intensity and seasonal totals they were designed for. If you grow an alpine beardtongue at sea level in Seattle, it may not get the strong sun it needs unless it is sited very carefully, and the long growing season will likely "burn its candle at both ends" so to speak, shortening its life in cultivation. Alternatively, the trillium from the Appalachians will likely thrive in the longer growing season on Puget Sound, which allows it to come closer to its ideal 1,200 sun buckets annually.

One final point to consider is day length. Plants are able to sense day length and use it to tell time. Many plants grow and bloom based more on the length of the day than the air temperature or availability of water. Between March 21 and September 21, northern latitudes have increasingly then decreasingly longer days than southern latitudes. Many late-blooming plants such as asters time flowering to a particular day length. A September-blooming Prairie Aster from northern Illinois begins to initiate flower buds in August when the days are, say, 14½ hours long. The same species in southern Louisiana has its internal clock set for August days that are only 13½ hours long. Grow the Illinois plants in Louisiana and

they may bloom in July while the southern plants transplanted near the Great Lakes might not bloom at all because by the time the days get short enough to trigger flowering, cold has set in. Adaptation to day length is important to consider when you are choosing plants from a markedly different latitude.

Soil

O**ne of the** hardest aspects of plant cultivation to grasp—and yet perhaps the most vital to understand—is the concept of soil. We cannot see what happens underground, so it is more difficult to determine what might be going wrong down there

Delphinium tricorne. *Dwarf Larkspur is a charming spring ephemeral that begins growth very early, when the trees and shrubs that will later shade it have yet to leaf out. It is able to flower, set seed, and accumulate enough stored sugars for its long dormancy in only six weeks.*

Anemone patens var. multifida. Pasqueflower is well adapted for life in a gritty soil. The large particle size of sandy, rocky soil means there is plenty of air space and poor water retention in this type of substrate. Accordingly, the Anemone is fairly tolerant of drought, but very intolerant of anaerobic or low oxygen conditions around its roots.

when a plant is declining. I realize that out of sight, out of mind applies here, but before you doze off or skip to the next chapter, remember that understanding some of what goes on below ground is really the key to successful gardening. For ease of discussion, I have broken up this section into soil's physical structure, fertility, and pH, but really these are three facets of a larger whole, one influencing the others and vice versa.

Soil's Physical Structure: the Mineral Component

Soil is a mixture of minerals and the recycled remains of plants and animals that serves to anchor a

plant in place and hold reserves of water and nutrients vital for growth. The mineral component comes from eons of weathering which has broken down parent rock—anything from limestone to granite or volcanic ash—into tiny pieces of sand, silt, and clay. Soils are classified based on particle size, with sand particles the largest, then silts, and finally clays. The type of parent rock is important in determining the types and concentrations of different minerals in the soil and thus its fertility, but not its size classification. In other words, quartz sand and granite sand have different chemical properties, but they hold and shed water the same way. Take a minute to think about this process of weathering. Imagine taking a rock and splitting it into four chunks with a hammer just as rain and frost slowly wear away mountains. You have revealed what was formerly interior rock and thus have created more exposed surfaces than it had before. As you continue to break it down into smaller and smaller pieces (wear eye protection and sing prison work songs when you are doing this), the volume of rock has changed very little, but more and more interior surface is exposed. Water is an electrically charged molecule that clings to the surfaces of these particles just as it does to your skin after a shower, so the smallest particles—which have the greatest surface area for a given volume—will hold onto the most water. The gaps or pores between the particles get smaller as the particles themselves decrease in size. These pores are important channels that allow air exchange in the soil. Sandy soils have large pores and thus abundant airflow. Their large pores are also harder for water to "fill up." A fine clay soil has a tremendous surface area that can hold much more water, and furthermore, its pores are smaller, so the water routinely fills up all the pores in the fine soil, preventing oxygen from entering and fostering a condition known as saturation. (One of the ways that scientists classify wetlands is by the level of oxidized iron or rust present. Waterlogged soils are typically gray, not brown, in appearance because iron cannot oxidize to the familiar rusty brown without free oxygen.) Roots need air to breathe just as we do, and waterlogged, heavy soils can suffocate them. Plants like Skunk Cabbage and Marsh Mallow are adapted to waterlogged soils, so they have roots that can "hold their breath," so to speak, and so are good choices for places with high water tables and wet, clay soils (however, they are intolerant of droughty soils). Plants adapted to coarse soils, like wild buckwheat and prickly pear, will quickly suffocate in a heavy, wet soil, though. Conversely, sandy soils (which have less surface area so hold less water) often have too little water for many plants, and it is only those with deep roots (like wild buckwheat) or water storage capacity (like prickly pear) that thrive.

Accordingly, as a gardener you need to either stick with plants that are adapted to your soil's physical type and water table or modify the soil to suit the plants. Take a pinch of soil and hold it between your thumb and forefinger, then dip the lot in a glass of water. Now rub the moistened soil between your fingers. Does it feel gritty or very smooth and sticky? Is the color brown or gray? Gritty soils are more sandy; sticky smooth are clay. Silts fall in between. Although you cannot easily change the water table, you can make a heavy clay soil more aerated by adding sand and a sandy soil hold more water by adding silt or clay.

Soil's Organic Component

Between 2 and 15 percent of a soil's volume is made up of organic matter — plant and animal remains in various states of decay. Organic matter has important effects on a soil's physical structure, water-holding capacity, and fertility. Organic compounds stain soils deep brown or black, and it is no wonder this is the color we associate with fertility (and the makings of a good chocolate layer cake). Added organic material in the form of leaf and bark mulches, tilled cover crops, or composts will act like a sponge in sandy soils, allowing them to hold more water. In clay soils, the organic material will actually open up and aerate the soil by gluing the small particles together into larger ones, so either way it is a key component for creating an ideal rooting environment. In all soils, organic as well as clay colloids (decay-resistant particles with electrically charged surfaces and large surface area) are vital in what is called cation exchange. The nutrients a plant needs are available to it only in their ionic or soluble form (for example: table salt, when dissolved in water breaks up into the sodium ion Na+ and the chlorine ion Cl- which can be absorbed through cell membranes). These ions would be easily washed out of the soil in rainwater except that they are held by the electrically charged colloids like books in a library until a plant needs them.

To add organic matter to a new planting, spread 3–4 inches of well-rotted compost (meaning you do not see big chunks of identifiable leaves, wood, dung, etc. in the material and it is not hot to the touch) and mix it in thoroughly before planting. We also put down a mulch of shredded leaves and/or aged pine bark or wood chips every spring on established beds. Over time, worms, fungi, and other creatures mix this mulch with the lower layers, creating a deep, dark, rich topsoil that is perfect for most plants.

One brief comment about earthworms. Earthworms are like little pellet factories, breaking down organic material and extruding the remains in the form of dung or castings rich in fertilizer salts. They "till" under vast quantities of organic material annually. However, most people do not realize that all the worms in northeastern and central North America are introduced species brought here accidentally from Europe. They have rapidly taken over habitat left worm-free for millennia when the native species were driven south by the glaciers and had yet to return. These are aggressive, voracious scavengers, and it is difficult to say what effect they might have on plants and ecosystems not adapted to their presence. They are even displacing the less noticeable native worms in the southern United States. Worms have come to be seen as benign and friendly creatures that help the soil and feed wildlife. They are certainly welcome in the disturbed, heavily cropped soils of vegetable gardens, but I suspect that in undisturbed, stable forest communities, exotic worms can have negative effects. In the rich, organic soil we have built up at Garden in the Woods, worms transform the yearly mulch of leaves mixed with topsoil into a 6-inch layer of spongy pellets that fine-rooted plants are simply unable to root into. I am guessing that the fine sandy soil we have is especially good for making worm castings, and the upshot is that many plants have become difficult to grow well. I have been adding builder's sand to new plantings, which I think is too coarse to pass through the worms and so is not pelletized, and the results have so far been encouraging. Nevertheless, our resident crows are quite happy with the writhing abundance of worms. They come in when the trails close at 5:00 P.M. every day to rake though the mulch and get quite upset with me when I work late and interrupt their dinner.

Soil Fertility

Plants need minerals in their diet just as we do. Whereas we take a mineral supplement when our diet does not provide enough of certain nutrients, we give plants fertilizers. Look on a vitamin label and compare it to a fertilizer label. You will likely see potassium, phosphorus, magnesium, boron, calcium, and iron, among others. Think of fertilizing as providing mineral supplements to plants growing in soils depleted by improper care or outright abuse. Giving plants fertilizers in moderation to supplement what is lacking in the soil will make them grow better and help them fight off the effects of stress and disease. All successful gardeners learn to recognize the importance adequate fertility plays in helping a garden really shine. However, you can easily have too much of a good thing with fertilizer, so aim toward eventually building a healthy, stable soil that recycles all the nutrients plants need with little supplementation. While they are useful tools when properly applied, too much fertilizer can be toxic, and just as there are USDA daily allowances for vitamins and minerals, there are manufacturer recommendations for fertilizer rates that should not be exceeded. Plants that evolved in nutrient-poor environments such as bogs are especially prone to fertilizer poisoning. Inorganic or chemical fertilizers especially are basically just salts that can literally suck the water out of roots just as salt dries fish. Overabundance can also affect internal processes and cause distorted or unseasonably late growth. Excess nutrients that are not taken up by plants leach into water systems and cause further problems for humans and wildlife. I always recommend that you have your soil tested by a lab so that you will have a baseline and recommendations about how much fertilizer to add before beginning a new garden and every few years to monitor existing ones. Call or write to your local agricultural extension office for the soil testing lab nearest you.

Remember that all fertilizers are not created equal. Most agricultural fertilizers contain the big three—nitrogen, phosphorus, and potassium— which are given as a percentage of the gross content of the bag. A 20-10-10 fertilizer contains 20 percent nitrogen, 10 percent phosphorus, and 10 percent potassium by weight, with the rest consisting of other nutrients, fillers, and impurities. Certain inorganic or chemical fertilizers are incomplete, that is they contain adequate levels of only the three major nutrients and little or none of things like boron and molybdenum (two of a dozen "minor" nutrients needed in smaller amounts). Other products, such as lawn fertilizers, contain large amounts of one nutrient (in this case nitrogen) that can be toxic to plants other than those for which they were designed. Inorganic fertilizers, like 10-10-10 or the common liquid plant foods, are largely water soluble, meaning most of the nutrients can be taken up quickly by plants but are also easily washed out of the soil by rain or irrigation and drain into water supplies. These are manufactured in the form of salts like potassium nitrate and ammonium nitrate. They cause rapid greening and lush growth, but need frequent replenishment —metaphorically it is like living on a diet of candy. Organic fertilizers, which range from manure composts to dried and bagged products containing such things as cottonseed meal, crab meal, bonemeal, and dehydrated manure, have a greater percentage of their nutrients in nonsoluble form. These compounds must be broken down by microorganisms over time before they can become soluble and thus available to plants, just as the complex sugars or starches in a potato are released more slowly into our systems than are the simple sugars in a candy bar. This means organic fertilizers are in a sense "time-released," so they do not overwhelm and poison the plants or wash away as quickly as inorganic fertilizers do. We prefer organic fertilizers at Garden in the Woods for this reason and also because they are fairly complete, containing a good balance of the necessary minerals. Furthermore, they promote the growth of soil microflora (bacteria, fungi, earthworms, and insects), which feed on and break down the organic materials. A soil without a healthy microflora can be thought of like a person who has just taken a course of antibiotics. The system is a "blank slate," more easily colonized by pathogenic organisms because the benign inhabitants have been killed off. We use primarily blended granular organic fertilizers with an analysis approximating 5-5-5 applied in spring before growth begins and occasionally reapplied in early summer. Fertilizing perennials after midsummer, especially with nitrogen, is not a good idea unless they are severely deficient, as this can lead to prolonged growth that leaves them vulnerable to early cold snaps. When planting in fall, it is a good idea to amend the area with well-rotted compost, as this will provide a bit of fertilizer to help them establish without forcing new growth. Composts, especially properly prepared manure composts, are excellent sources of both organic matter and nutrients, and they are the best way to build a healthy, fertile soil over the long term. These are best applied to existing plantings as a spring mulch which will be slowly incorporated into the soil over the season. A healthy soil is a fragile thing, but annual additions of compost and careful and judicious use of fertilizer, combined with perennial plants to prevent erosion, will restore just about any ravaged soil in three to five years.

Recently there has been much talk about mycorrhizae and the supposed benefit of products that contain these beneficial fungi. Most plants form mutually beneficial associations with specific species of mycorrhizal fungi. The fungi are present in healthy soils and penetrate or envelop a seedling's feeder roots. These infected roots develop swollen or highly branched shapes and it is this hybrid plant-fungus root that is technically what is called the mycorrhizae. The fine, threadlike hyphae that these fungi produce in effect vastly increase the surface area of a plant's root system and aid in the uptake of certain nutrients, primarily phosphorus as well as copper, manganese, and zinc. Additionally, plants in the Rhododendron family have well-developed mycorrhizae that efficiently scavenge nitrogen in the nutrient-poor, acid soils they frequent. One of the best known mycorrhizal fungi is the truffle of gourmet fame, which infects the roots of oaks and hazels.

While mycorrhizae are of obvious value in nutrient-poor environments, I am very skeptical of the efficacy of so-called mycorrhizal supplements that are sold as growth-boosting magic bullets. In rare cases, such as when re-vegetating strip mine tailings or other sterile "dead" soils, inoculating transplants has been shown to improve growth. However, a typical garden soil should already contain a host of mycorrhizae, and further, their benefit is negligible if the soil is fertile. (I have even seen mycorrhizae develop on bearberry plants grown in a soilless potting mix in our nursery that likely blew into the pots as spore.) Finally, certain fungi are hosted by specific groups of plants, and a purchased mix is not guaranteed to match the plants you are growing. Unless you are involved in land reclamation, I think you would be better off putting your money into a good, yearly shot of compost and leaving the rest to Mother Nature.

Soil pH

Certain types of rock contain high levels of calcium and/or magnesium, two important plant nutrients that also affect the soil's chemistry. Limestone rock, which originates from marine deposits of coral reefs, shells, and the like, is very high in these nutrients, and ground limestone is an important fertilizer for several reasons. Calcium is not added to many pre-mixed fertilizers because it affects the solubility of other components. However, calcium and magnesium are two of the most soluble and thus easily rain-leached minerals. In wet climates they become quickly scarce in soils not derived from limestone rock and so have to be supplemented with dolomitic limestone (a type that contains both calcium and magnesium). The nutrients in limestone are important for plant growth, but they also affect the soil's chemistry (pH), making certain other nutrients more or less available depending on their levels. pH is a measurement of the relative abundance of hydrogen (H+) ions and hydroxyl (OH-) ions in the soil solution. It is measured on a scale from 1–14 with 1 being most acid and 7 being neutral; soils typically range in pH from 4.0 to 8.0. Remember that when a molecule (in this case water, H_2O) is dissolved, its components split apart into electrically charged ions —the form that can be absorbed by cells. At a low pH, there are more hydrogen ions floating around than hydroxyl ions, and at a high pH, the situation is reversed. Adding limestone raises the pH of the soil, by displacing hydrogen ions in the soil solution and replacing them with calcium. Certain minerals become more soluble in the company of H+, while many others become more soluble around OH-. Iron, which is abundant in all soils, is only readily soluble at a low pH. Phosphorus is more soluble and thus available to plants at a higher pH. Acid-loving plants do not really love acids; they have evolved on a diet rich in iron but low in most other nutrients so they are "lazy" about scavenging iron but very efficient at gathering up nutrients such as phosphorus. When you grow an acid-loving plant in alkaline soil, it cannot gather the necessary iron it needs, so it develops a deficiency. (Fertilizers sold to "rescue" iron-deficient, acid-loving plants contain the mineral in *chelated* form, meaning it has been combined with an agent that makes it soluble at higher pH.) Furthermore, since acid-loving plants are adapted to a life of scarcity when it comes to most other nutrients, they can be easily overwhelmed by excess. At a higher pH, most of the important nutrients become more soluble, and like humans exposed to a high-fat diet, they accumulate too much in their tissues, which can be toxic. Conversely, lime-loving plants evolved in basic soils under conditions of relative

abundance, and they quickly suffer deficiencies when the soil is too acidic.

In the wild, the availability of calcium and magnesium—and thus the pH—is one of the key factors determining the plants that grow in a particular place. Subtle changes in a soil's chemistry tip the balance to certain plants that are best able to cope with the particular abundance or lack of nutrients. If you are naturalizing plants in a meadow or woodland or restoring an area disturbed by human activities, it is important to pay attention to this and select species that are best suited to the site. In a garden situation, though, where small competitive advantages are not so important, suffice it to say that a nearly neutral to slightly acid pH (5.5–6.5), combined with good, balanced fertility will be suitable for most of the plants in this book. A soil test will measure your pH and give recommendations for adjusting it accordingly.

Lupinus texensis *and* Castilleja coccinea. *Texas Bluebonnet is native to dry, limestone-rich prairies in central Texas, so in cultivation it prefers a soil with a nearly neutral to slightly alkaline pH (6.0–7.5). The Painted Cup is more adaptable, able to grow in fairly acidic to neutral soils with a pH between 5.0 and 7.0. In the garden, both can be accommodated if you aim for a pH of 6.0–6.5.*

Temperature

Effects of Cold

In the scope of possible temperatures found in the universe, life as we know it can exist in only a very small range. While some plants can survive periods of temperatures below zero or above 100°F, most require a range of about 45°–85°F to grow and reproduce. Plants are not warm-blooded as we are, so the dangerous effect of cold involves the disastrous consequences that expanding, piercing ice crystals can have on cell membranes. Winter-hardy plants have ways of decreasing their relative water content and concentrating solutes in their tissues to act as antifreeze. This is a metabolically costly process, so plants produce only the minimum amount of antifreeze they need to endure the conditions in which they evolved. A Red Maple from the moderate climate of Florida will likely perish if planted in Quebec, while local Red Maples come through the winter fine. Cold hardiness is primarily genetically predetermined and varies moderately from plant to plant and tremendously from species to species. This is another reason why provenance is important when selecting garden plants. Fortunately, many plants, *Amsonia rigida,* for example, are much hardier than their native range would suggest because they have a genetic capacity for antifreeze production that is likely a holdover from colder times. Further, if you raise your own plants from seed, you can often select certain ones that are a little hardier and over time better the odds a bit.

Root hardiness, like stem hardiness, has to do with preventing ice formation. The earth holds tremendous quantities of heat through the winter and is slow to warm in summer, so soils rarely suffer the extremes of temperature found aboveground. Roots are therefore less cold-hardy than tops, and this is why even winter-hardy plants in unprotected pots rarely survive a cold winter. Mulch acts like a blanket that helps to retain heat in winter, so mulching is a good practice in cold, snowless climates (snow is an excellent insulator, as most gardeners know). In moderate climates, even subtropical plants will prove winter-hardy through occasional cold snaps if the ground remains unfrozen. Since lower water content equals higher levels of antifreeze, well-drained soils help many marginal plants survive the winter.

Effects of Heat

All chemical reactions speed up and slow down exponentially at different temperatures. Plants, like animals, use enzymes to catalyze or "manage" the chemical reactions needed to produce and use energy, and enzymes are designed to work most efficiently in a certain range of temperatures. Plants from cool climates have enzyme systems that operate well at lower temperatures, but if they're brought into warmer conditions, enzyme activity accelerates exponentially until it may simply cease, leading to a slow loss of vigor and death (the plant literally burns itself out). Conversely, plants from hot climates have metabolisms that can become sluggish when they are grown too cool, failing to bloom or store enough food reserves to survive a long winter. While a healthy individual can usually tolerate occasional fluctuations from its ideal range, in the long term this can translate into a failure to thrive. Night temperature is almost more important than day temperature in terms of enzyme function, since many metabolic processes involved in energy production happen only during the night.

Diseases

I have not discussed diseases and pests in any great length in this book for several reasons. This is not because native plants are problem-free — on the contrary, they are fed on by a host of organisms, most of whom have coevolved in the rich web of checks and balances of the local ecosystem. Most plants are attacked by something, and we should thank God for that as it is all that prevents them from running amuck. I believe focusing on disease is an easy way to get Medical Schoolitis, when you start to think you have every affliction you have studied. If you can minimize environmental stress by choosing plants suitable for the light, soil, and temperature conditions you have, most of them should grow reasonably well, and if not, try them in another spot or get something else. I firmly believe there is no plant worth growing if it must be maintained by applications of poisons. Please, do not needlessly expose yourself and your children to these chemicals. Find your tolerance for what might be called acceptable damages, and if the plant exceeds it, pull it out, period. I have run my nurseries and gardens with few pesticides by practicing good housekeeping, selecting resistant plants, and letting natural predators do the work. It is almost shocking after decades of overreliance on pesticides to discover that plants are not intensive-care patients in need of a constant chemical barrage to survive. Much as to most people 10 years ago an organic apple meant a small, arthritic lump riddled with worm holes, it is easy to envision an organic garden as a place overrun with pests, where a few pitiful blooms attempt to open through a net of spider mites, and leaves disappear under a barrage of fungi and bacteria like targets at a shooting gallery. Not true — believe me, really not true. An organic garden is a place buzzing with life.

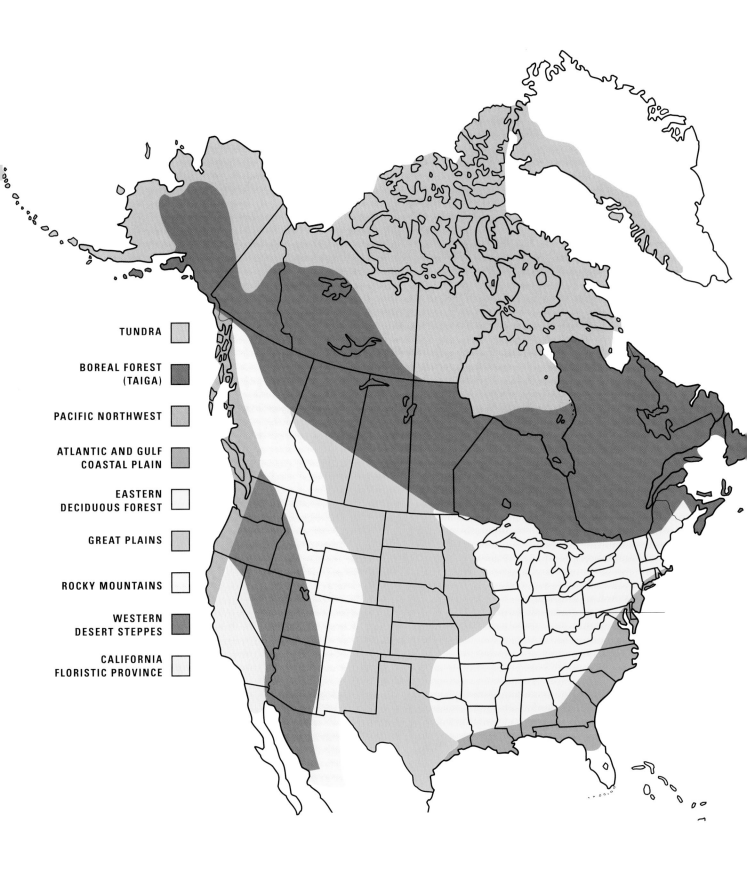

TUNDRA

BOREAL FOREST
(TAIGA)

PACIFIC NORTHWEST

ATLANTIC AND GULF
COASTAL PLAIN

EASTERN
DECIDUOUS FOREST

GREAT PLAINS

ROCKY MOUNTAINS

WESTERN
DESERT STEPPES

CALIFORNIA
FLORISTIC PROVINCE

Map of the Floristic Provinces
of North America

Floristic Provinces
of North America

Tundra

While I do not foresee tundra gardening becoming the next horticultural craze, the polar region of North America does harbor a surprising diversity of plants adapted to growing in one of the worst climates on earth. Life proceeds slowly and deliberately here, but it proceeds nonetheless. Tundra communities are composed mainly of sedges and grasses, with a scattering of heaths (plants in the Rhododendron family such as Mountain Cranberry, *Vaccinium vitis-idaea,* and Labrador Tea, *Ledum palustre*) and cushion plants similar to those found in the alpine zones of lower latitudes. In more sheltered areas, shrub willows and alders dominate. In all, there are about 700 species of plants native to this zone. Most tundra plants are circumpolar in distribution, occurring throughout the northern polar regions of the world.

The climate of the Arctic is dominated by the blocking effect of the cold polar high, a huge air mass occasionally felt as far south as Florida in winter, that keeps precipitation in the Arctic down to nearly desert conditions. An average of 10 inches of precipitation falls over the area every year, mostly in the summer when the polar high weakens and storms can move in off the oceans. Yet, ironically, the tundra is dominated by wetlands, a contradiction explained by the other dominant factor in Arctic ecology — ice. The warm season is so short in this area that the ground never completely thaws each year, and in fact the frost travels deeper and deeper each winter. Through much of the Arctic, the ground is frozen

1,000 feet deep, a remarkable deep freeze called permafrost. Each summer, only the top 6–24 inches of soil thaws, so rainfall cannot percolate down and accumulates on the surface in vast marshes and pools.

As the ground surface thaws in June and the brief two-month growing season begins, plants explode into growth. Nearly continual daylight during this time of the year helps plants take full advantage of this short window. Many tundra wildflowers have a cushion or bun shape, which traps the sun's heat inside like a greenhouse, elevating it as much as 50 degrees above the ambient temperature (and partially explains why these cushion plants simply "burn up" when grown in warm climates). Because decomposition and nutrient cycling is very low in the cold soils, Arctic plants subsist on a spartan diet. Many are at least semievergreen, which gives them a jump on the short season but also minimizes nutrient loss through leaf fall.

Boreal Forest (Taiga)

To the south of the Arctic tundra stretches a vast, nearly unbroken belt of coniferous forest and moss typically called the boreal forest or taiga. This is a land of long cold winters and cool, even occasionally hot, summers. Because of the dominance of polar high pressure, precipitation is concentrated in the summer months, and though averaging only about 17 inches annually, little evaporates and little drains

Tundra. High alpine areas of both our eastern and western mountains have much in common with the true tundra far to the north. A short, cool growing season, poor soil, and extreme winter temperatures limit most plants to a dwarfed, cushion habit—basically shrunken versions of their lower elevation relatives. One important difference between alpine and tundra conditions is the much higher level of solar radiation found at high elevations.

(ABOVE): *Fire is an important source of renewal in the boreal forest.*
(BELOW): *Glacier-fed stream in the Cascade Range.*

away because of the permafrost layer a few feet down. Consequently, the three-month growing season is damp and humid. Cold soils are slow to recycle nutrients, and the abundance of water leaches out much of what could be available, so the soils tend to be infertile and highly acidic — perfect places for mosses and lichens to flourish. The understory in these forests is an almost continual layer of feather and sphagnum mosses and their kin.

Surprisingly, the boreal forest is markedly less diverse than the tundra to the north. Here White and Black Spruce *(Picea glauca* and *P. mariana)* mix with Balsam fir *(Abies balsamea)*, Tamarack *(Larix laricina)*, birch, and aspen to create conditions less favorable for wildflowers than the colder grasslands closer to the pole. As the trees grow and shade the soil, it cools and thaws more shallowly in summer. Evergreen trees are also adept at scavenging nutrients and holding them in older leaves, so fertility decreases. Mosses flourish under the trees, further insulating the soil and helping to create a thick layer of acidic, organic peat. The cool, peaty soil and shallow permafrost also decrease evaporation and runoff, and forest soils become waterlogged. Ironically, the conditions created by the trees are the seeds of their own undoing. The increasingly cool, waterlogged, and nutrient-poor soils may lead to a forest's decline, and the dead and dying hulks are perfect fodder for the occasional fires that sweep through in summer. Fire signals liberation and renewal, and the process can begin again.

The few wildflowers that inhabit this hinterland are well adapted to the cold, nutrient-poor acid soils, bitter winters, and continual shade. Water is plentiful, so most are ill-prepared for drought. If grown in warmer climates, they need the kind of cool, damp soil found in bogs and low woods and are difficult to accommodate in the open garden.

Pacific Northwest

The **Pacific Northwest** province stretches from northern California to coastal Alaska in a narrow band never more than 120 miles from the Pacific Ocean. It is a land of cool, wet winters and mild, dry summers where coniferous forests reach unparalleled development. Several mountain chains running north to south bring an added level of environmental complexity to the region as well. The upper airflow in the northern hemisphere moves west to east, and for half of the year the strongest of these winds, the jet stream, flows incessantly over the area, bringing wave after wave of mild, moist, Pacific storms slamming into the Coast and Cascade Ranges. From September to April the Pacific Northwest receives roughly 75 percent of its annual precipitation. During the warmer months, the jet stream moves north and the region experiences several months of drought that is moderated by cool temperatures and fog rolling in off the cold waters of the Pacific. Drought is most pronounced in the southern half of the province, farthest from the summer storm track.

Evergreens have an advantage in this type of climate. The mild, wet winters allow them to continue photosynthesizing and storing energy that can be used to get a jump on deciduous species that have only the drier summer months to trap the sun's energy. Conifers like *Pseudotsuga menziesii* (Douglas-fir), *Tsuga heterophylla* (Western Hemlock), and *Thuja plicata* (Western Redcedar) dominate the forests, and it is only in specialized habitats such as along streams where deciduous trees like maple and alder can get the summer moisture they need to compete. The conifers in these forests reach enormous heights and live for centuries — far longer than related species in other regions. This is due primarily to the gentle climate and the infrequency of disturbances such as windstorms and fire which shorten life spans in other more environmentally rigorous places.

Wildflowers of the northwestern forests are also adapted to the unique rhythms of its climate. Many begin growing early in spring, rest in the summer, and then put out another flush of growth in fall. This presents a challenge to gardeners in other parts of the country where early and late frosts can take their toll. Even the alpine and subalpine areas in the region are mild by mountain standards, but they receive huge amounts of snow in winter, which persist as lingering snowpack long into summer. It is routine for spring to come to the glorious wildflower meadows in the subalpine parklands of the Cascade and Olympic Mountains as late as mid-August and for winter to return again two months later. It is the lingering snow and not extreme cold that limits tree growth in these spectacular mountain glades.

Rocky Mountains

The **Rocky Mountains** are both a looming barrier to the east-west migration of plants and a vital link between the boreal forests of the north and the Mexican deserts of the south. It is often said that mountains create their own weather, and nowhere is this more evident than in the Rockies. In general, with every increase in elevation, there is a corresponding increase in precipitation, wind, and solar radiation and a decrease in temperature and the length of the growing season. As air is driven up the western slopes of the Rockies by the prevailing winds, it becomes less dense as it moves farther from the influence of the earth's gravity. Like people leaving a hot and crowded room, air molecules spread out in the higher atmosphere, and the resulting cooling causes water to condense as rain and fog. The higher west-facing slopes receive up to four times the precipitation of the lower valleys (40 inches annually versus

only 10), much of it coming as snow in winter. As the air crests the mountains and descends, it warms and dries again, producing a pronounced rain shadow (a zone of lower precipitation) on east-facing slopes. Denver, which sits at the base of the eastern slopes, receives only 10 inches of precipitation annually, mostly in thunderstorms during the summer monsoon season.

The thinner air at high elevations obstructs less of the sun's radiation, as anyone who has skied in the Rockies without good sunglasses and sunscreen can attest. Plants that grow in the high mountains have thick, semitranslucent leaves and often a covering of down to protect them from its rays. The thin air is also a poor insulator, so although it can warm up quickly during the day, it cools readily at night. Thus, the mountains are characterized by large diurnal

Heavy, persistent snow pack in the Cascades limits tree growth in subalpine areas and allows space and light for wildflowers to flourish. The slopes below Mount Rainer are dominated by the glowing pink Magenta Paintbrush (Castilleja parviflora var. oreopola) for a few weeks in late summer when the snow finally melts.

fluctuations in temperature, warm summer days, cool summer nights, and long cold winters with snowpack persisting until June or July above 10,000 feet.

One of the unique features of long north-south mountain ranges is that similar vegetation can be found at higher and higher altitudes as one moves closer to the equator. It is easy to drive 40 minutes from the warm plain of Albuquerque, New Mexico, with its characteristic high desert vegetation up to 13,000 feet into the Sangre de Cristo Mountains, where boreal fir forests much like those 1,000 miles to the north dominate the peaks. In this way the Rockies provide a route for the north-south migration of plants, and many familiar wildflowers of the eastern forests, such as *Smilacina racemosa* (False Solomon's Seal) and *Cypripedium parviflorum* (Small Yellow Lady-slipper) reach the southwestern limits of their ranges in the higher elevations of Arizona and New Mexico. Concurrently, some of the characteristic plants of the southwestern deserts, such as *Echinocereus* and *Opuntia* cacti, have pushed

their ranges north on the warmer, drier eastern slopes. In a small zone along the United States-Canada border in Idaho, Montana, and British Columbia, where Pacific moisture reaches far inland, flora of the Pacific Northwest like *Thuja plicata* (Western Redcedar) and *Cornus nuttallii* (Western Dogwood) can be found several hundred miles east of their last outposts in the Cascades of western Washington. These eastern and southern outliers provide horticulturists in colder areas such as the Northeast with winter-hardy stock for gardens and hint at the remarkable diversity of this region.

Alpine vegetation (plants growing above treeline) is more extensive in the Rockies than anywhere else in North America except northern Canada and Alaska. Alpine plants share many similarities with their cousins from the tundra, but experience generally warmer, brighter days during the growing season. They typically have compact or tufted habits and large flowers that make them irresistible to many gardeners, but they require exacting conditions that are difficult to reproduce closer to sea level.

Rocky Mountain valley, Telluride, Colorado. The Rocky Mountains are real weather makers. Thunderstorms are a common occurrence in the summer, as warm, unstable air rises up and over the peaks.

California

Although it occupies a relatively small area of North America, this province is home to nearly one quarter (about 6,000 species) of our native plants, many growing nowhere else. What makes California so diverse? A combination of complex topography, soils, and climate. The northwestern part of the state falls just within the Pacific Northwest because enough summer moisture and fog dampen the effects of the dry summers that pervade the rest of the state. Most of California has a Mediterranean climate, characterized by cool, wet winters with little if any frost and hot, dry summers with daytime temperatures regularly above 100°F away from the moderating effect of the ocean. Like the Pacific Northwest, most of California's yearly rainfall comes between October and March. The heat and drought of summer encourages frequent fires that (before they were controlled by people) promoted the growth of summer-dormant shrubs and wildflowers that form characteristic landscapes of grassland and chaparral (dense shrubland). The climate also favors annual plants that can lay dormant as seed during dry years and burst into bloom quickly in times of watery abundance. Bulbs thrive in a Mediterranean climate, and California has the richest variety of Wild Onions, Mariposa, and true Lilies, among others, to be found anywhere in North America.

The Sierras and to a lesser extent Coast Ranges affect local climate much like the Rockies, (an increase in elevation brings cooler temperatures and higher annual precipitation, mostly as winter snow) but even the highest elevations rarely experience severe cold. Eastern slopes are warm and dry, with desert vegetation characteristic of the Great Basin to the north and the warm Mojave Desert to the south. These deserts, along with the Colorado Desert (an extension of the rich Sonoran Desert of Mexico and Arizona), comprise one of the richest desert systems in the world, home to over 2,000 species of plants — more than occur in all of New England.

A diversity of soils combine with geography and weather to give California its uniqueness. The state is a rocky smorgasbord of pieces of continents and seafloor that have drifted west and slammed into the coast over the millennia. Volcanic activity has combined with tectonic drift to complete the picture. Rock containing different kinds and levels of minerals weathers to create a tapestry of soil types. One of the most unusual of these is serpentine, derived from serpentine rock, an uncommon type of mineral relatively abundant in California. Serpentine differs from limestone in its low concentration of calcium and very high levels of magnesium and certain heavy metals that, combined, are very toxic to most plants. Certain species have evolved a tolerance to serpen-

tine and grow nowhere else. These serpentine endemics make up a large percentage of California's rare, unique flora.

Western Deserts and Steppes

Sandwiched between the Sierra and Cascade Mountain ranges to the west and the Rockies to the east is the great expanse called the Great Basin or intermountain cold desert. It lies in the rain shadow of the mountains to the west, and the Rockies block any limited summer moisture coming from the east. Most of the 5 to 20 inches of annual precipitation falls in winter as snow. Because the area is really a high plateau mostly 2–3,000 feet above sea level, winters are long and cold and summers are hot during the day and rather cool at night. Little of the precipitation that falls actually drains off to the sea. Most evaporates under the strong sun, so strongly alkaline and salt-laden soils frequently develop in low-lying areas. The Basin is bounded on the south by the subtropical Sonoran and Chihuahuan Deserts — areas of incredible diversity and beauty which, alas, are beyond the scope of this book.

The Great Basin is technically a semidesert or desert steppe, dominated by bunch grasses and sagebrush (*Artemisia* species). Sagebrush has an advantage in that its deep roots can tap the last of the percolating snowmelt and its woody stems are ready to leaf out quickly during the brief spring growing window. Grasses dominate only on better sites and have been further displaced by cattle grazing, which favors the unpalatable shrubs. The Great Basin is the only region of the United States where human population density falls below two people per square mile (comparable only to northern Canada), and for good reason — this is a harsh climate for people as well as plants. However, certain plants, such as milkvetch (*Astragalus* species) and the ubiquitous Sagebrush (*Artemisia tridentata),* thrive in this floristically diverse region. The slow snowmelt in spring dampens the ground for a few months, bringing an explosion of growth and flowering followed by a long dormancy during summer, fall, and winter. Dry-land plants can cope with moisture and heat, but not in combination, which makes them difficult to cultivate in less arid parts of the United States and Canada. However, as more and more people move to the semi-arid parts of the United States for the dry air and sunshine, the Great Basin's botanical riches offer wonderful replacements for the water-hungry trees and lawns of eastern suburbia.

Great Plains

To the east of the Rocky Mountains lies another great expanse of treeless country that, like the Great Basin, lies in the rain shadow of the mountains to the west, but close enough to the Gulf of Mexico to draw some of its moisture. Here, with the slightly higher precipitation than occurs in the Great Basin — especially in summer — grasses have the advantage over sagebrush and formed the backbone of the boundless prairies of these Great Plains before their conversion to agriculture. The climate on the Great Plains is characterized by cold, windy, and dry winters, a moist spring and early summer, and heat and drought late in the summer. A combination of drought late in the growing season and frequent spring and fall fires prevents forest from invading, with fire more important than drought in maintaining prairie vegetation the farther east you go.

Prairie is grassland by definition, with grasses and sedges comprising about 75–80 percent of the biomass. The prairies of the Great Plains have been divided into shortgrass and tallgrass types which blend in a central zone called the mixed-grass prairie. Shortgrass prairie is the most drought-tolerant, so it is found in the driest areas (the rain shadow

of the Rocky Mountains and western Texas). This is the region that became the great dustbowl in the 1930s, when overcultivation, combined with a succession of dry springs, left the fragile topsoil to blow away in the wind. To the north and east is a large zone of mixed prairie, with taller species on wetter and less grazed sites and short grass on marginal soils. This is the great wheat-growing region of North America, often called the breadbasket of the world. Finally, along the eastern fringe of the plains lies a belt of what was once pure tallgrass prairie, dominated by grasses that grow 2–4 feet in height, now primarily planted with corn and soybeans. The tallgrass prairie receives up to 35 inches of rain a year, three or four times the amount that falls in the western parts of the plains — certainly enough to sustain forests — but here fire combines with late-summer drought to kill off woody species that would otherwise predominate.

The same conditions that prove ideal for agriculture — deep, fertile, neutral to slightly acidic soils; a relatively long growing season; and spring and summer rains — are ideal for many wildflowers. Virgin prairie is a rich tapestry of grasses punctuated by plants in the Daisy family such as blazing stars (*Liatris* species), coneflowers (*Echinacea* and *Ratibida* species), and black-eyed Susans (*Rudbeckia* species)

Greene Prairie, University of Wisconsin Arboretum, Madison, Wisconsin. The wonderful restored prairie at the University of Wisconsin has been an important research site for grassland ecology for over fifty years. In midsummer, Purple Coneflower, Rattlesnake Master, and Flowering Spurge bloom under the towering spikes of Prairie Dock and Compass Plant.

as well as lupines, butterfly weeds, and myriad others enjoyed by gardeners around the world.

Eastern Deciduous Woodlands

From the Mississippi River drainage basin east toward the Atlantic and Gulf coastal plains and north up to the Canadian border is the heavily forested region known as the eastern deciduous woodland. This is an area characterized by warm to hot, humid summers and cool to cold, snowy winters. Rainfall is relatively high (from 35–80 inches annually), and importantly, it is distributed evenly throughout the year. The region receives precipitation both from eastward-moving fronts tapping moisture from the Gulf of Mexico, summer thunderstorms, and strong ocean cyclones moving north and west from the Atlantic Ocean. With a long growing season and even rainfall — especially in summer — deciduous trees (broadleaf species that lose their leaves in winter) are able to gain the advantage over the conifers and grasses that dominate most of the West. In the East, permanent grasslands are rare and usually only a successional stage present for a few years after fire or abandonment by agriculture. These meadow communities differ from the prairies farther west in that they lack deep, well-developed grassland soils (mollisols), rich species diversity, and subjection to occasional fire. Unless maintained by mowing, meadows in the East return quickly to forest. Soils over most of the rainy, humid eastern deciduous forest are slightly to highly acidic, with limestone soils present mostly in a few areas of the Appalachian Mountains and the Great Lakes.

The deciduous forests have a rich variety of tree species not typically found in the northern and western coniferous forests. Oaks and hickories dominate the poorer soils and uplands while maples, basswood, ash, tulip poplar, and others thrive on richer sites. Unlike evergreen, coniferous forest floors, which are relatively shaded throughout the year, from late fall until midspring the forest floor in these woodlands receives nearly full sun. This has resulted in the development of a rich herbaceous layer that takes advantage of the brief window in early spring between thaw and the leafing out of the canopy to burst into growth and bloom. These wildflowers, often called spring ephemerals because of their vernal impermanence, put on a glorious display for a few colorful weeks then quickly wither and go dormant as the canopy leafs out in late spring.

The Appalachian Mountains are the major eastern mountain chain, running from eastern Canada to northern Georgia. Because this region receives rain from both east and west, there is no rain shadow

on the eastern side of these mountains (a feature that allows easy east-west migration of plants). Like the Rockies, the Appalachians have been important routes for plant migration from north to south. The northern section of this forest was heavily glaciated in the last 20,000 years, and the glaciers drove many species south along the mountains where many subsequently were able to return after the glaciers receded. However, the southern Appalachians remain far richer in floral diversity than their counterparts in the north. In fact, the mountains of Virginia, the Carolinas, and northern Georgia have the richest assemblage of woodland wildflowers in North America. Interestingly, you have to journey to China and Japan to find the nearest relatives of many of these species, like *Diphylleia cymosa* (Umbrella Leaf) and the various *Hexastylis* species (evergreen gin-

Prairie in summer. Wild Bergamot, Prairie Blazing Star, Compass Plant, and Purple Coneflower combine in this beautiful natural mosaic. This prairie planting at Prairie Moon Nursery in southern Minnesota was seeded seven years previously and is just beginning to come into its own. The plot is burned about every two or three years to discourage woody plants and release nutrients as ash.

gers). The similarity in the floras of eastern Asia and the eastern United States is no accident, for they were once connected in a large belt of temperate, deciduous woodland that stretched around the world.

Atlantic and Gulf Coastal Plains

The **Appalachian Mountains** are one of the oldest mountain chains in the world and have been slowly eroding and washing toward the sea for millennia. The sands and gravel that once formed the backbone of mountains as tall as some of the Himalayas now lies in a skirt 20 to 100 miles wide along the Atlantic and Gulf Coasts. This sandy, flat coastal plain has a flora very different from the broadleaf forests that blanket most of the East. Most of the coastal plain is subtropical, with hot, humid summers and mild, wet winters. The warm Atlantic Gulf Stream passes near the coast in the Carolinas, and this helps moderate the climate along the coast in winter. Only the small strip from New Jersey to Cape Cod has a more temperate climate, with cooler summers and moderate winters — in part because of the more northern latitude and also because the Gulf Stream veers farther offshore as it heads for northern Europe. Even though the area receives ample rainfall (40–60 inches a year), the well-drained soils do not retain moisture consistently during the hot summers, so warm-season lightning fires are commonplace. The sandy, heavily leached soils are also very infertile, and this, combined with late-summer drought and fire, gives an advantage to several species of pine, including Longleaf Pine *(Pinus palustris)*, Loblolly Pine *(P. taeda)*, and Slash Pine *(P. elliotii)*, that often form almost pure stands on burned sites. Like the conifers of the Pacific Northwest, pines can take advantage of the mild, wet winter to continue photosynthesizing, and thus can grow extremely fast.

Interlaced with these sandy pinelands are vast wetlands — both tidal wetlands and wetlands along the floodplains of the great rivers that drain from the north and west. Swamps, marshes, and wire grass savanna carpet huge areas of the Southeast and provide habitat for many unusual and rare plants such as pitcher plants *(Sarracenia* species) and Venus-flytraps *(Dionaea muscipula)*. Lowland swamp forests that are too wet to burn contain such majestic trees as Bald Cypress *(Taxodium distichum)* and Tupelo *(Nyssa sylvatica)*.

From New Jersey north to Cape Cod, most of the coastal plain is pine barrens, with even poorer, coarser soils and an open canopy of Pitch Pine *(Pinus rigida)*, oaks, and often a dense shrub layer.

(OPPOSITE):Trillium grandiflorum *woodland in Vermont. The herb layer is particularly well developed in the eastern deciduous forest, especially on richer soils. Spring ephemerals such as Showy Trillium take advantage of the window in spring between ground thaw and leafing out of the canopy to grow and bloom.*

(BELOW):*Coastal scrub forest, Cape Cod. The Atlantic coastal plain narrows to a thin strip in the north. Here Pitch Pine, Scrub Oak, and various members of the Ericaceae, like Bearberry* (Arctostaphylos uva-ursi) *and Lowbush Blueberry* (Vaccinium angustifolium), *dominate the landscape.*

Encyclopedia of Plants

Aconitum uncinatum

Aconitum (ack-on-EYE-tum)
Ranunculaceae
Monkshood

Monkshoods are at their most diverse in the cool, misty mountains of Europe and Asia, and most of the familiar garden species come from the Himalayas and the European Alps. They produce richly colored, hooded blossoms on stout stems above clumps of deeply lobed leaves. In North America there are five species, with two restricted to Alaska and northern British Columbia. While admittedly not as dramatic as some of their Eurasian counterparts, the long-lived native monkshoods have lovely foliage and a quiet charm that makes them well worth growing as accent plants in the wildflower garden. The arching stems begin to bolt early in the season and continue to lengthen through the spring and early summer, growing long and often climbing through neighboring vegetation for support. In this way they can go relatively unnoticed until one day drawing your attention with terminal clusters of vibrant flowers.

CULTURE: The plants grow in moist to wet locations in the wild, usually in cool, lightly shaded spots. Ideally, site them in a place that receives a few hours of sun, but does not get excessively hot or dry. All monkshoods contain several toxic alkaloids that were used as medicines and poisons until recently. As a precaution, wear gloves when handling bruised or broken stems and roots. It is possible to divide the plants in spring, but I prefer to scratch a handful of seeds in places where I wish the plants to grow or move self-sown seedlings in early spring. *Aconitum*s are prone to drought stress as they come into flower; in a dry year they turn yellow and wither as if diseased, but return fresh and vigorous the next season.

USES: Late blooms add interest to shade gardens, and the arching stems and intricate leaves look lovely as an accent amid ground covers. The plants can be trained through shrubs or allowed to trail.

PROPAGATION: Easy to moderately difficult with fresh seed. See p. 245.

Aconitum columbianum
(Western Monkshood)

ZONES: 3–7; part sun, shade
SOIL: evenly moist
NATIVE TO: bogs, seeps, wet meadows, mainly in the mountains; Alberta to British Columbia north to Alaska and south to New Mexico
SIZE: 3–8 feet (2–3 feet)
COLOR: violet to purple (occasionally white); **BLOOMS** in summer

Western Monkshood has an interesting range, growing in local populations through much of mountainous North America, then occurring in small relict populations in the Northeast (often listed as a separate species, *A. noveboracense*) that have survived in cool microclimates since the last glaciation. The lower leaves are as intricately cut as the finest paper snowflakes.

Aconitum reclinatum
(Trailing Wolfsbane)

ZONES: 4–7; part sun, shade
SOIL: evenly moist
NATIVE TO: shaded ravines, primarily in the Appalachian Mountains; Pennsylvania and West Virginia to North Carolina
SIZE: 3–5 feet (2–3 feet)
COLOR: white or cream; **BLOOMS** in late spring, early summer

Trailing Wolfsbane differs from the other species in the narrow, elongated hood and typically white flowers. The sprawling stems send up small blooming side branches that give it a wild, brambly look. The 8-inch-wide lower leaves of a well-grown specimen are quite striking when they emerge in spring and are probably its most ornamental feature. It is interesting botanically because it is more closely allied to some of the Eurasian species than to the other natives and is possibly a stranded relict of past continental drift.

Aconitum uncinatum
(Southern Monkshood, Wild Monkshood)

ZONES: 5–8; part sun, shade
SOIL: evenly moist
NATIVE TO: moist to wet areas, woods and clearings; Pennsylvania to Indiana south to Kentucky and Georgia
SIZE: 2–5 feet (2–3 feet)
COLOR: violet to purple; **BLOOMS** in mid- to late summer
A lovely and vigorous species well suited to gardens. The flowers are often a rich shade of royal purple,

Aconitum uncinatum. The long arching stems of wild Monkshood often rely on neighboring vegetation for support, drawing little notice until they erupt into bloom.

Actea rubra. *Do not let the poisonous reputation of baneberries prevent you from enjoying these carefree, long-lived woodlanders in your garden. The striking, glossy fruit of Red Baneberry is a welcome addition to the pervasive green of the summer shade.*

and the lacy leaves have a solid, emerald green sheen with a bit of a burgundy flush in the sun. Like all *Aconitums*, the hood formed by the sepals is designed to channel pollinating insects as they search for the nectar produced in coiled spurs formed by the petals.

Actaea rubra

Actaea (ack-TAY-ah)
Ranunculaceae
Baneberry

The sanguine red or shocking white fruits of the baneberries are impossible to miss among the various shades of green that dominate the summer woodland. Their weight tests the strength of the long flowering stems, which arch laboriously above delicate compound foliage. It seems the perfect invitation to some passing bird to stop and dine, but rarely are the fruits eaten. Baneberries have a reputation for being poisonous, or at best unpalatable, and this may be the reason. In 1903, Alice Bacon boldly decided to find out for herself what the effects of ingesting Red Baneberries would be and wrote about her experiment in charming Victorian prose:

In the fear that children, attracted by the beauty of the fruit, might eat to their own undoing, an experiment in the qualities of the berries was entered upon with the following result.

A small dose was taken after the mid-day meal, as caution seemed advisable; but the only effect noted was a slight burning in the stomach.

The question, however of children eating the forbidden fruit was definitely settled once and for all, as no child, youth, sane adult, not even a hungry schoolboy would ever devour it from deliberate choice: the taste is most nauseous, bitter, puckery; indeed, several even more drastic adjectives might be applied with perfect truth.

After ingesting twice the initial dose two days later and experiencing only slightly more exaggerated symptoms, Ms. Bacon decided to double the amount once again (6 berries):

Half an hour afterward all curiosity on the subject of Red Baneberry was abundantly satisfied, for this one experimenter at least . . . suddenly the mind became confused and there was a total disability to recollect anything distinctly or arrange ideas with any consistency . . . words seemed to utter themselves independently . . . For a few minutes there was great dizziness, the body seeming to swing off into space, while the blue spots [she describes these as an initial visual hallucination] changed to dancing sparks of fire. The lips and throat became parched . . . swallowing was difficult; there was intense burning in the stomach with gaseous eructations, etc.[3]

In three hours she had recovered — sufficiently frightened by her last experience to discontinue experiments further, and settling the question once and for all.

Baneberries are a wonderful addition to the shade garden, where they prove to be long-lived and carefree plants. In northeastern North America, the ranges of the two species overlap, and interesting natural hybrids can occasionally be found (usually Doll's Eyes flowers a week or two later, making hybridization more difficult). I have seen plants of a lovely pink-fruited form that is probably one of these. The thin flower spikes of *Actaea* do not get as much attention as the berries, but are attractive in their own way. The small white petals and cloud of delicate anthers emit a musky sweet perfume that is pleasant but hard to describe.

CULTURE: Transplant in spring and site in a lightly shaded spot. Baneberries are easy, long-lived plants that will continue to improve over the years. They grow from a swollen rootstock, which makes division nearly impossible, but if you scatter the fruits around in the garden, new recruits will eventually appear. In damp summers, the foliage can blacken and die prematurely, which makes the remaining fruit clusters look a little sad or awkward, but this should not cause permanent harm to the plants.

USES: Most at home in the woodland garden, as a focal point among low ground covers, or massed for effect.

PROPAGATION: Slow but easy with fresh seed. See p. 245.

Actaea pachypoda (syn. A. alba)
(Doll's Eyes)

ZONES: 3–8; part sun, shade
SOIL: moist
NATIVE TO: rich woods; Nova Scotia and Quebec to Minnesota south to Oklahoma and Georgia
SIZE: 20–30 inches (12–16 inches)
COLOR: creamy white; **BLOOMS** in spring

Doll's Eyes is named for the prominent dark eye spot formed at one end of the chalky white fruit by the persistent stigma. The contrast of the fruits with the grape juice–colored pedicel is striking. There is a red-fruited form (f. *rubrocarpa*) that comes about 50 percent true from seed and may represent a hybrid with *A. rubra*. The fruit is effective for four to six weeks in late summer to fall, and the foliage is a bit more finely cut than the next species.

Actaea rubra
(Red Baneberry)

ZONES: 2–8; part sun, shade
SOIL: moist
NATIVE TO: rich woods; Newfoundland across northern Canada to Alaska south to California and Maryland and in the Rockies to Arizona and New Mexico
SIZE: 24–32 inches (16–18 inches)
COLOR: creamy white; **BLOOMS** in spring

A wide-ranging plant very similar to its European cousin *A. spicata* (the western North American form is sometimes listed as *Actaea arguta*). The brilliant, glossy fruit is effective from mid- to late summer, and now we know why. A white-fruited form is fairly common and lacks the eye spot of Doll's Eyes. A few of these white-fruited plants blended with the red is very pretty in an overstated sort of way (it has an effect like one of the red and white bobbers used in bait fishing—easy to see).

Agastache (ag-OST-ach-ee)
Agastache rupestris
Lamiaceae
Wild Hyssop

The wild hyssops are on the whole rather large, coarse plants, especially the eastern species, but several have great merit as garden plants where they grow well. As is typical in the Mint family, the sepals of the flower are united into a cup-shaped calyx that remains after the petals are shed, protecting the seeds inside. The calyx is often attractively colored in shades of pink and purple, which contrasts subtly with the petals and continues to provide interest after the petals have fallen.

All the eastern representatives and some from the West are completely herbaceous, growing rapidly in spring and summer on tall stems lined with pairs of oval, fragrant leaves. Flowers are borne in dense spikes atop the foliage late in the summer. These are prolific seed producers, and while a few of the larger plants can quickly add some height to plantings, a garden can easily be overrun with the progeny from just one Anise Hyssop (*Agastache foeniculum*) gone to seed. Removing the spent heads before they drop their seed is recommended, but keep in mind that the calyx will remain beguilingly colorful for several weeks after flowering, making it tempting to delay pruning until it is too late and the seeds have been shed (they have fooled me more than once).

There is also a group of highly ornamental species from the mountains of the Southwest and Mexico (formerly split into the poetically named genus *Cedronella*), similar in many respects to the salvias in habit. They grow from a central, woody base and are covered over a long season with vibrant flowers the colors of a desert sunset. The flowers are large, narrow, and more widely spaced on long successionally flowered racemes, again closer in appearance to *Salvias* than to their herbaceous cousins. They do not seed as aggressively, and although they perform well in the humid summers of the Southeast, the woody stems are vulnerable to the cold and wet of northern winters, making most of them unreliably perennial north of Zone 7 (but easily grown as annuals).

Agastache rupestris. *Softly tinted, gray-green foliage provides a beautiful foil for the salmon-orange flowers of Sunset Hyssop. The dark, colorful calyxes, clearly visible in this slide, add color and contrast after the flowers fall.*

Allium cernuum. The curious shepherd's crook flower stems of Nodding Onion set it apart from others in its tribe. Bees flock to the blooms and hang upside down, clutching the petals to gather nectar while ingeniously long anthers dust pollen on their furry bellies. Individual flowers expand successively from the center, each yielding eventually to a rice-papery capsule that can barely contain its cluster of glistening black seeds.

CULTURE: The herbaceous species are easily accommodated and adaptable. The woody types are deep-rooted plants best grown in freely drained soils. All are very drought-tolerant and generally trouble-free.

USES: Herbaceous types: meadows and borders. Woody types: massing, borders, hedges, xeriscaping.

WILDLIFE: Excellent nectar plants. The eastern species are valued by beekeepers. *A. barberi* and *A. rupestris* are a favorite of hummingbirds.

PROPAGATION: Easy from seed or cuttings. See p. 245.

Herbaceous Types

Agastache foeniculum
(Lavender Giant Hyssop, Anise Hyssop)

ZONES: 3–9; sun, part sun
SOIL: moist to dry
NATIVE TO: upland woods and dry prairies; Wisconsin to Manitoba south to Alberta and Colorado
SIZE: 3–5 feet (2 feet)
COLOR: blue-violet ; **BLOOMS** in late summer

A robust and widespread herbaceous species with distinctive anise-scented foliage used to make tea. The plants form several strong central stems with regular side branches, and the dense 2–4-inch flower heads concentrate near the tops of the higher stems. Calyx tubes are tinged rose purple. *A. urticifolia* (Nettle-leaf Giant Hyssop) is its western counterpart, and *A. scrophulariaefolia* (Purple Giant Hyssop) is a tongue twister from farther east with a less colorful calyx.

Agastache nepetoides
(Catnip Giant Hyssop, Yellow Giant Hyssop)

ZONES: 3–9; sun, part sun
SOIL: moist to dry
NATIVE TO: woodland gaps; Vermont to Minnesota south to South Dakota, Oklahoma, and Georgia
SIZE: 3–8 feet (2–3 feet)
COLOR: light yellow to yellow-green; **BLOOMS** in late summer

Yellow Giant Hyssop is not particularly striking in flower, but it is a remarkably strong grower, easily reaching towering heights in the garden and possibly worth growing for this reason. It is much like Anise Hyssop in branching habit and flower arrangement.

Woody Types

Agastache barberi
(syn. *A. pallida*)
(Giant Hummingbird's Mint)

ZONES: 7–9; sun
SOIL: well drained (very drought tolerant)

NATIVE TO: lower mountain slopes; Arizona to Mexico
SIZE: 2–3 feet (2 feet)
COLOR: rose to purple; **BLOOMS** summer to fall

A shrubby, woody-stemmed plant with gray-green triangular leaves and loose, terminal spikes of 1-inch tubular flowers. The species is grown less than its hybrids with *A. mexicana*, which are available in a range of oranges and purples that are popular perennials in the warmer parts of the United States. The foliage of the hybrids can have an interesting fragrance variously suggesting ripe fruit or old-fashioned floor polish.

Agastache rupestris
(Sunset Hyssop)

ZONES: 5–9; sun
SOIL: well drained
NATIVE TO: mountain slopes (5–7,000 feet); New Mexico and Arizona
SIZE: 16–24 inches (16 inches)
COLOR: rose to orange and purple; **BLOOMS** from late summer to fall

Probably the hardiest of the woody types and a wonderful perennial, blooming over a long season and aptly named for the orange and purple effect of the petals and calyx. The gray-green minty foliage is variably covered with white hair, giving the plants a lovely silver cast that contrasts beautifully with the blooms. Cut back lightly in late summer for repeat flowering. I was skeptical about this plant's winter hardiness, but it has performed well in the Northeast in a gritty soil.

Allium ce

Allium (AL-ee-um)
Liliaceae
Wild Onion, Allium

Do **not** let tearful kitchen memories of slicing onions deter you from growing a few of the dozens of lovely allium species native to North America. The distinctive smell is noticeable only when the stems are crushed or bruised. The onion's bulb stores water, nutrients, and energy for the plant during dormancy, and this makes alliums well suited to soils that are moist in winter and spring but dry in summer. It is not surprising, then, that California is home to many of our wild onions, but there is at least one species in every other state in the United States and much of Canada as well. Except for *A. canadense,* the familiar Wild Garlic, these are not aggressive plants and make fine, carefree additions to the rock garden and, in a few cases, the perennial border as well. Flowers come in many shades, from pink and violet through yellow and white. They are borne in umbels either above or among the leaves. Some species bloom when the foliage is dormant, which is a bit disconcerting to me (the bare stalks seem strangely disembodied), but a good strategy for conserving water and at the same time making flowers available when pollinators are particularly active or other nectar sources scarce.

With such a large group, it is difficult to pick a few to discuss, but I have tried to choose a representative selection from different parts of the continent and encourage you to discover some of the others for yourself.

CULTURE: Most *Allium* bulbs, even the small species, should be planted 3–4 inches deep, and this makes it imperative that a gritty, well-drained soil be used for the dryland types. Mark the location and you can easily dig and divide the bulbs when they are dormant. Wild onions do self-sow, though in my experience the native species are on the whole much less rampant than many of the European types more common in garden centers. They are easily accommodated, drought-tolerant, and generally trouble-free.

USES: Many wild onions are suitable for the rock garden. Because many go dormant after flowering, they are best interplanted with ground-covering plants such as the low *Penstemon*s, *Eriogonum*s, and *Antennaria*s. Larger summer-blooming types, such as *A. cernuum,* can be effective en masse in the border, meadow, or wild garden. These retain their foliage well after blooming. *A. tricoccum* is a good spring accent in the woodland garden.

PROPAGATION: Easy to moderately difficult from seed; easy from division. See p. 245.

Allium acuminatum

(Tapertip Onion, Hooker Onion)

ZONES: 3–9; sun
SOIL: moist in spring, dry in summer
NATIVE TO: dry prairies and hills; Wyoming to British Columbia, south-central California, Arizona and Colorado
SIZE: 8–12 inches (6 inches)
COLOR: pink to lavender; **BLOOMS** in early summer

A common species in the Northwest, preferring dry, open habitats and occasionally becoming a weed in wheat fields. The large vibrant pink flowers are held on scapes taller than the few, thin leaves, and the plants go dormant quickly after flowering. We have one planted with a clump of Yellow-eyed Grass, which comes up late and takes over after the onion retreats underground for the summer.

Allium brandegei

(Brandegee Onion)

ZONES: 4–8; sun
SOIL: sandy, well drained
NATIVE TO: dry montane meadows; Wyoming to eastern Oregon south to Utah and Colorado
SIZE: 6–8 inches (6 inches)
COLOR: white, light pink; **BLOOMS** in early summer

This small onion is one of the wider ranging members of a large group centered in California and the Great Basin that have flowering stems shorter than the leaves. The dense, tufted effect of the blooming plants is really charming.

Allium canadense

(Wild Garlic)

ZONES: 3–8; sun to shade
SOIL: wet to dry
NATIVE TO: woods, waste places, prairies; New Brunswick to North Dakota south to Texas and Florida
SIZE: 12–16 inches (1–2 feet)
COLOR: white ; **BLOOMS** in early spring

Wild Garlic commonly produces a cluster of small bulblets in lieu of flowers and seeds, and these send out a leaf, then drop and quickly root. This, combined with a strong root system, makes them invasive, difficult to control, and thus not a good subject for the garden. This common eastern plant has strongly flavored leaves that can be used like chives in cooking.

Allium cernuum

(Nodding Onion)

ZONES: 3–9; sun, part sun
SOIL: moist to dry
NATIVE TO: woodlands, prairies, and rocky outcrops; New York to Michigan and British Columbia south to Arizona and northern Georgia
SIZE: 12–16 inches (1 foot)
COLOR: medium pink; **BLOOMS** in summer

Nodding Onion remains remarkably consistent over its wide range and is one of the best for general garden use. The plants form thick stands of persistent foliage that give rise to slightly taller flower stems of cupped flowers. The stem bends just before the flower cluster, hence the common name (this makes

Amsonia tabernae-montana. *Their iron-clad constitution and the ethereal blue color of their blooms have made the aptly named bluestars a favorite among gardeners. The plants in this photograph are part of a stunning mass planting at Garden in the Woods, where they provide a lovely transition between a shrub border and a mixed planting of ground covers. The image captures the plants as they are half expanded in spring. Eventually the foliage will overtop the fading blooms.*

Nodding Onion easily recognizable). *A. stellatum* (Prairie Onion) is a similar plant from the Great Plains with straight flower stems.

Allium tricoccum
(Ramps, Wild Leek)

ZONES: 3–8; part sun, shade
SOIL: moist (at least in spring)
NATIVE TO: rich, deciduous woods; Nova Scotia to South Dakota south to Missouri and northern Georgia
SIZE: 6–12 inches (8 inches)
COLOR: white; **BLOOMS** in summer

Wild Leek has long been harvested for its strong-flavored bulbs, but the plants are rather slow-growing, and it is hard to say what effect this has had on their populations. The paired leaves of this species are unusually broad, resembling Lily of the Valley when they emerge in early spring. The foliage dies back in early summer, and just when one has forgotten them, the flower stalks appear from nowhere, bloom, and set seed.

Allium validum
(Swamp Onion)

ZONES: 3–7; sun
SOIL: moist to wet
NATIVE TO: swampy meadows at medium to high elevations; Idaho to Washington, south to California and Nevada
SIZE: 14–24 inches (8 inches)
COLOR: pink; **BLOOMS** in summer

A plant of wet mountain soils in the Sierras of the West. Notable for its thick, abundant foliage and unusual irislike rhizome with old bulbs arranged in a row. *A. brevistylum* is a hot pink–flowered Rocky Mountain relative also found in wet soils.

They are strongly clump-forming, and old plants have incredible woody rootstocks (anyone who recommends division of these plants must be comfortable with a chainsaw). The larger species of this North American genus can become very shrublike by the end of the growing season, and their foliage remains in perfect condition until it blazes glorious yellow or orange in the fall. In part this is because, like many plants in the Dogbane family, bluestars have a poisonous white latex sap that is a strong deterrent to pests. The sap can be a mild skin irritant.

CULTURE: *Amsonia*s take a year or two to settle in to a new location. Though they are not easy to divide, older crowns tend to break apart in a few places, and these can be separated in fall as the foliage withers. As a group, bluestars are not fussy about location, tolerating a wide range of moisture and light conditions.

WILDLIFE: A favorite nectar source of Mourning Cloaks and other early butterflies.

USES: Their long season of interest makes bluestars invaluable in the perennial border, wild garden, and wildlife garden. While many of the species grow in moist to wet locations in the wild, they are all reasonably drought-tolerant once established. Their shrubby habit and clean foliage is especially good for massing in larger plantings.

PROPAGATION: Easy from seed. See p. 245.

Amsonia ciliata
(Narrow-leaf Bluestar)

ZONES: 5–9; sun, part sun
SOIL: dry, well drained, tolerates but does not require lime
NATIVE TO: sand hills, sandy woodland, limestone balds and prairies; North Carolina to Missouri south to Texas, Mexico, and Georgia
SIZE: 14–20 inches (12–16 inches)
COLOR: pale blue; **BLOOMS** in spring

Amsonia tabernaemontana

Amsonia (am-SOWN-ee-ah)
Apocynaceae
Bluestar

The bluestars are all lovely variations on a theme. The flowers are similar in shape from one species to the next—an ethereal, forget-me-not blue that is simply irresistible—but the plants come in a range of sizes and leaf shapes that can fill many a garden need. They are remarkably long-lived, coming back year after year even long after a garden has been without a gardener. The flowers begin to open when the stems have only just emerged in spring and ride atop them triumphantly as both continue to expand.

A wide-ranging, refined plant with very narrow, linear leaves and a small stature. It looks in some respects like a small *A. hubrichtii*, and in fact the two were once lumped in together as varieties of the same species. Narrow-leaf Bluestar is somewhat slow-growing and slow to establish at first, but very drought-tolerant and well worth seeking out for the rock garden or low border.

Amsonia hubrichtii

(Hubricht's Bluestar)

ZONES: 5–9; sun, part sun
SOIL: moist
NATIVE TO: sandbars and bottomlands; western Arkansas and eastern Oklahoma
SIZE: 30–40 inches (36 inches)
COLOR: light blue; **BLOOMS** in spring

Hubricht's Bluestar is a striking garden subject that has taken the gardening world by storm in the last few years. Narrow, filiform leaves lend a soft, billowing texture to plantings, turning a beautiful apricot color in fall. It is best massed in groups of at least three to five for a dramatic effect.

Amsonia illustris

(Ozark Bluestar)

ZONES: 4–9; sun to light shade
SOIL: moist
NATIVE TO: moist sandy soils, gravel bars along streams; Missouri to Kansas and Texas
SIZE: 30–40 inches (30 inches)
COLOR: light blue; **BLOOMS** in spring

Much like Common Bluestar, *A. tabernaemontana*, with shinier leaves.

Amsonia jonesii

(Jones' Amsonia)

ZONES: 5–9; sun
SOIL: dry, well drained
NATIVE TO: sandy or gravelly soils in pinyon pine–juniper desert; Colorado to Utah, and Arizona
SIZE: 16–28 inches (18 inches)
COLOR: steel blue; **BLOOMS** in spring

A western desert counterpart to Common Bluestar. Will succeed as a rock garden subject in the East.

Amsonia ludoviciana

(Louisiana Bluestar)

ZONES: 6–9; sun, part sun
SOIL: sandy, moist
NATIVE TO: gravelly soils; Gulf Coast of Louisiana
SIZE: 24–30 inches (24 inches)
COLOR: light blue; **BLOOMS** in spring

This bluestar is very restricted in the wild and notable for the gray-green downy pubescence on the underside of the oval leaves. This shows to advantage as the stems emerge in spring with the foliage pressed up against the stem. The woolly leaves are a lovely counterpoint to the steel blue flowers.

Amsonia rigida

(Stiff Bluestar)

ZONES: 5–9; sun, part sun
SOIL: moist
NATIVE TO: sandy, wet soils; Georgia and northern Florida
SIZE: 20–24 inches (24 inches)
COLOR: light blue; **BLOOMS** in spring

Stiff Bluestar is notable for its distinctive wide, rounded leaves and stems that emerge with a dark purple cast. The leaves arrange themselves on the upper stems in a semicircular fashion. Smaller in stature than many of the others, at least in the North.

Amsonia tabernaemontana

(Common Bluestar)

ZONES: 3–9; sun to light shade
SOIL: moist to dry
NATIVE TO: moist to wet woods, along streams; New Jersey to Virginia, Illinois, and Kansas, south to Texas, and Florida
SIZE: 36–40 inches (36 inches)
COLOR: light blue; **BLOOMS** in spring

A wide-ranging and adaptable species and for many years the only bluestar used in gardens (the commonly available var. *salicifolia* has narrower leaves). Common Bluestar is a large carefree plant and surprisingly shade-tolerant.

Amsonia tomentosa

(Wooly Bluestar)

ZONES: 5–9; sun
SOIL: well drained
NATIVE TO: sandy soils, banks of seasonal streams in sagebrush desert; Utah to California, Nevada, and Mexico
SIZE: 12–28 inches (12–16 inches)
COLOR: steel blue; **BLOOMS** in spring

A lovely desert species with gray woolly leaves, loose panicles of flowers, and seedpods that are constricted like string beans. *A. eastwoodiana* is a glabrous relative with narrower leaves.

Anemone canadensis. *Glistening white upward-facing flowers set with a puff of yellow stamens are the hallmark of many windflowers—none more sumptuous in bloom than the Canada Anemone. While it can become rampant in fertile soil and sun, I have found that in light shade it scatters itself around more discreetly. I first became acquainted with this plant about twelve years ago through the generosity of a gardening friend who noticed me admiring the plants in her woodland and promptly dug up a clump for me. It has been happily growing along a dappled path in the company of Wild Geranium ever since.*

Anemone canadensis

Anemone (ann-NEM-own-ee)
Ranunculaceae
Windflower, Pasqueflower, Anemone

The **windflowers** are a large and heterogeneous genus in North America, even more so in recent taxonomic treatments that have lumped *Hepatica* and *Pulsatilla* into *Anemone* as well. (Just for the sake of comprehensibility, and maybe a subconscious wish to not let them slip into taxonomic obscurity, I am going to consider *Hepatica* separately.) The name stems from Greek mythology. The nymph Anemone was turned into a flower, forever at the mercy of the cold north wind, by a jealous goddess.

Anemones can be divided horticulturally into two groups: those that form spreading, fleshy, underground rhizomes and those that grow from a woody caudex or tuber. The rhizomatus species are delicate-looking woodland plants. Aerial shoots rise up at intervals from the buried, creeping rhizome, making each flowering stem appear to be a separate plant. A single diaphanous flower sits above a whorl of 3 leaflets which are in turn divided into 3–5 lobes. The plants form small colonies that emerge with the warm spring rains and quickly go dormant in the heat of summer.

The caudex types are for the most part larger plants, the leaves and flowering stems growing separately from the crown. Most of these have a rather coarse appearance and small flowers and so are sel-

dom grown, but the large-flowered pasqueflower (formerly *Pulsatilla*) is one of our most charming early-season wildflowers. There is a tuberous group as well, found in dry, rocky places, primarily in Texas and the central plains.

CULTURE: Woodland anemones are easily moved in late summer when the plants are dormant. Mark their location in spring and later gently dig the area with a spading fork, lifting out the brittle brown rhizomes and transplanting them to a spot with dappled shade and organic soil. The caudex species are easily transplanted from containers in spring, but, with the exception of *A. canadensis*, difficult to divide. Blister Beetles find anemones very attractive, but these are active late in the season, so damage is not serious. If you see any of the large gun metal blue insects with swollen abdomens lolling about on your plants, do not pick them off by hand, as they exude a bright yellow liquid from glands on their legs that can cause painful blisters on bare skin. The plants themselves also contain a chemical called Protoanemonin that can cause skin irritation, so wear gloves when contact with the sap is likely.

USES: Woodland, meadow, or rock garden, depending on species.

PROPAGATION: Easy to difficult from seed and division. See p. 245.

Rhizomatous Species

Anemone oregana
(Western Wood Anemone)

ZONES: (6)7–8; part sun to shade
SOIL: moist
NATIVE TO: damp woods, alpine meadows; from western Washington to California
SIZE: 3–8 inches (1–2 feet)
COLOR: shades of blue, purple, pink, sometimes white; **BLOOMS** in spring

Much like the eastern Wood Anemone, *A. quinquefolia*, in appearance, except for the color of the flowers. This species does not grow well outside of its native range, but it is a beautiful plant for shade gardeners in the Pacific Northwest. *A. lyallii* is its white-flowered counterpart, occurring over much the same range and into British Columbia.

Anemone piperi
(Piper's Anemone)

ZONES: 4–7; shade
SOIL: moist
NATIVE TO: moist woods; west of the Cascades in northern Idaho and eastern Washington and Oregon with outlying populations in Utah
SIZE: 6–10 inches (1–2 feet)
COLOR: white, rarely light rose; **BLOOMS** in spring

A robust species related to *A. oregana* found mostly in and around the Idaho panhandle. It looks much like the European species *A. nemerosa*, and while it is not presently cultivated, it is a lovely plant that I feel has the most potential among the woodland species for general garden use.

Anemone quinquefolia
(Wood Anemone)

ZONES: 3–8; shade
SOIL: moist
NATIVE TO: damp woods; Quebec to Manitoba south to eastern Iowa and Maryland and in the mountains to Georgia
SIZE: 3–6 inches (1 foot)
COLOR: white, the backs of the sepals sometimes blushed pink; **BLOOMS** in spring

Certainly the most adaptable of this group, and a good candidate for the informal woodland garden. Because it goes dormant quickly, it should be interplanted with more persistent species. The plants are small and frail looking, but can form vast colonies in fertile woodland soils that are quite lovely in bloom. Several varieties have been recognized from the southern Appalachians: var. *minima* is as it sounds, a miniature version, and var. *lancifolia* (also listed as a separate species) is slightly larger in height and flower than the typical form and has narrower leaves.

Tuberous and Caudex Types

Anemone canadensis
(Canada Anemone)

ZONES: 2–9; sun to shade
SOIL: moist to dry
NATIVE TO: moist to wet meadows, shores and prairies; Quebec to Alberta, south to New Mexico, Missouri, and Maryland
SIZE: 1–2 feet (3–6 feet)
COLOR: white; **BLOOMS** in early summer

Crystalline white, upward-facing flowers with bright yellow centers adorn the deeply dissected foliage of Canada Anemone. Individual crowns grow intermittently from an aggressive threadlike rhizome making it difficult to eradicate once established. Although this is one of the most ornamental species, it is best reserved for wild gardens. Shade tempers its aggressiveness considerably.

Anemone caroliniana
(Prairie Anemone, Carolina Anemone)

ZONES: 4–9; sun
SOIL: dry, well drained
NATIVE TO: dry prairies and balds; Wisconsin to South

Dakota south to Texas and Louisiana. Occasionally in North and South Carolina and Georgia.
SIZE: 10–14 inches (12–18 inches)
COLOR: ranges from white through pinks and purples to intense deep blue; **BLOOMS** late winter to early spring

Carolina Anemone does actually grow in the Carolinas, but it is much more common in the West. It is the easternmost of the tuberous types and one of the easiest to grow. In the Southeast, it is limited to dry rocky barrens, but in the Great Plains, it is found in dry prairies and pastures. The foliage emerges from the summer-dormant tubers in fall and persists through the winter. Flowering begins as soon as the first warm weather returns in spring. The plants form new tubers from spreading rhizomes and in this way eventually become small colonies. There are forms with flowers of a stunning, deep blue that are a joy to behold. It is a plant that should be more widely grown in the drier regions of North America.

Anemone multifida
(Cut-leaved Anemone)

ZONES: 1–8; sun, part sun
SOIL: moist to dry, well drained
NATIVE TO: boreal forests, rocky mountain slopes, and prairies; Newfoundland to Alaska south to California, New Mexico, New York, and Maine and in the Andes of South America
SIZE: 12–30 inches (12 inches)
COLOR: ranges from green to yellow, red, blue, and white; **BLOOMS** in summer

Another incredibly wide-ranging and variable anemone. The flowers are usually small, but the best blue color forms are simply stunning. The finely cut

Anemone patens *var.* multifida. *The seed clusters of Pasqueflower have a sparkling, frenetic energy about them, like hair tousled by the wind. This globe trotting native is common in the mountains of Europe as well, where its windblown look and ability to bloom defiantly in the cold winds of the early alpine spring inspired the name Anemone— daughter of the wind.*

Anemonella thalictroides. Amid certain populations of normally white-flowered Rue Anemones you may occasionally stumble upon a plant that carries the rosy blush of its buds through as a faint wash of pink in the expanded flowers. If you fancy pink over white, try growing up a few seeds from the plant and gathering seed from the darkest offspring over several seasons. Within a couple of years you will likely have a nice patch of the dark pink variety rosea *gracing your spring woodland.*

foliage persists after flowering, and the plants are not difficult to grow in cool climates. Like most of the group, flowers are followed by strawberry-shaped seed heads that disintegrate when ripe into a tuft of feathery down.

Anemone (Pulsatilla) patens var. *multifida*

(Pasqueflower)

ZONES: 2–9; sun, part sun
SOIL: moist to dry; well drained
NATIVE TO: prairies, rocky outcrops; Minnesota north through Canada to the Northwest Territories and Alaska, south to Idaho, New Mexico, and Illinois
SIZE: 4–8 inches, (6–8 inches)
COLOR: pale to dark violet or lavender, occasionally white; **BLOOMS** in early spring

Pasqueflower is a charming—you could almost say cuddly—little species with finely cut leaves and huge satiny blooms. The plants are entirely covered in white silky hair that protects them from late-season frosts and gives them a lovable, puppy dog quality. Pasqueflower is an easy and lovely plant for a well-drained, sunny spot. The blooms begin to appear as soon as the snow melts (the common name is from the French for Easter flower, referring to the time of bloom) and open fully only in the warmth of the sun. The flowers give way to attractive seed heads with long shaggy tails. They go semidormant in summer, but the foliage persists and often offers up a few late-season blooms in the early days of autumn. Var. *multifida* is the North American representative of this wide-ranging plant, but most of the plants available in nurseries are probably from European strains of *A. patens,* which was long used as an herbal remedy to treat cramping and premenstrual pain.

Anemone virginiana

(Thimbleweed)

ZONES: 2–9; sun to shade
SOIL: moist to dry
NATIVE TO: open woods, dry meadows; Quebec to North Dakota south to Arkansas and Georgia
SIZE: 12–30 inches (12–16 inches)
COLOR: white; **BLOOMS** in summer

Not a very showy species in flower, but the thimble-shaped seed heads are somewhat ornamental.

Anemonella thalictroides

Anemonella thalictroides

(ann-emm-on-ELL-ah)
Ranunculaceae
Rue Anemone

ZONES: 4–9; part sun, shade
SOIL: moist but well drained, slightly acid to neutral
NATIVE TO: deciduous woodlands; New Hampshire to Minnesota and Kansas, south to Arkansas and Florida
SIZE: 4–8 inches (8–12 inches)
COLOR: white, occasionally rose pink; **BLOOMS** from spring to early summer

Rue Anemones offer the gardener a perfect combination of fine, fernlike foliage and crystalline white, upward-facing flowers. The flowers are borne in spoked clusters of 1–6 from the center of each leaf; the leaves in turn are divided into several soft green leaflets and provide a lovely background for the blooms. Our single species is very closely related to meadow rues and is sometimes listed as *Thalictrum thalictroides. Anemonella* grows from a cluster of tubers that in young plants are united in one crown but with age break into several distinct ones. A very desirable, rose pink form (var. *rosea*) has been occasionally found, mainly in the upper Midwest, and it comes true from seed. There are several exquisite, double-flowered clones in cultivation; the many-petaled (technically many-sepaled) blooms continue to expand for a week or more. Rue Anemone is a reluctant spring ephemeral, ready to go dormant when summer heat arrives, but willingly continuing to bloom if the soil is damp.

CULTURE: The plants are easy to please and will continue to flower well into early summer if provided with sufficient moisture. They do suffer from crown rot if soils remain too wet in summer and fall, but any remaining tubers will resprout, so the plants will not be entirely lost. Best planted in a well-drained spot with a few hours of sun. They appreciate a dusting of limestone every year or two.

USES: At home in the shade garden, in drifts among rocks, or as an underplanting beneath deciduous shrubs. Lovely interplanted with Creeping Phlox (*Phlox stolonifera*) or other low ground covers that will fill the gaps when *Anemonella* goes dormant in summer.

PROPAGATION: Moderately difficult from seed and root cuttings. See p. 245.

Antennaria rosea (syn. *microphylla*)

Antennaria
(ann-ten-AIR-ee-ah)
Asteraceae
Pussy-toes, Everlasting

Pussy-toes get their name, as far as I can determine, from the slight resemblance of the inflorescence to the paws of a cat. Although you might easily overlook these diminutive plants in the wild, several of the species form wonderful, semievergreen mats of low rosettes in the garden, covering the ground and the spaces between larger plants. Botanically, they are interesting examples of apomictic reproduction, where seeds are set without sexual recombination. Since all the genes are inherited from one parent in this type of reproduction, new races and subspecies can be easily formed. This has led taxonomists to name hundreds of species over the

years, the vast majority merely geographic varieties of the more common plants. Male plants are usually much less common in any given population, which is to be expected when their services are less than necessary. (I will resist social commentary on this point.) I was alarmed one spring day as I was admiring a carpet of dusty gray *A. rosea* to find it overrun with bristly, velvety black caterpillars that turned out to be the larvae of the American Lady butterfly, looking much more forbidding without their makeup. It was certainly a challenge to my budding ecological sensitivity to not dispose of the caterpillars immediately, but I left them alone, and in two weeks they were gone and the plants quickly recovered.

The flowers themselves are fairly inconspicuous and rise from the center of older rosettes on leafy stalks in spring. The bracts that surround the flowers are sometimes attractively colored. As the flower stems age and go to seed, they have a somewhat rank appearance and can be sheared just above the rosettes (the name *Antennaria* refers to a fancied resemblance of the pappus, or parachute of the seed, to an insect's antennae).

CULTURE: Pussy-toes grow well in a range of soils, and thrive in dry, well-drained locations. Their main requirements are a soil that is freely draining and a spot where they will not be overrun and shaded by larger plants. The mountain species are not suited to hot, humid climates. Sections are easy to lift and move to a new location after new rosettes have begun rooting (four weeks after flowering ends).

WILDLIFE: Larval food of American Lady butterfly (*Vanessa virginiensis*).

USES: Excellent ground cover for sunny, dry areas, between paving stones, or among rocks. Their strong root system helps stabilize banks.

PROPAGATION: Easy from seed and division. See p. 246.

Antennaria alpina
(Pussy-toes)

ZONES: 2–7; sun to part sun
SOIL: well drained
NATIVE TO: alpine screes and rocky outcrops, often on limestone, circumboreal; in North America confined to the high elevations in the Rocky and Cascade Mountains
SIZE: 2 inches (12 inches)
COLOR: white; **BLOOMS** in spring
A tight, mat-forming species, much like *A. rosea* in effect.

Antennaria luzuloides
(Woodrush Pussy-toes)

ZONES: 5–8; sun
SOIL: well drained

Antennaria rosea (syn. microphylla). Low carpets of Pussy-toes are a common site in alpine areas of the West. This particular patch was growing in the Uncompahgre Mountains of southwestern Colorado along the edge of a beautiful alpine meadow that doubled as a ski slope in winter. The silvery soft foliage of this charming species forms a dense, interwoven blanket only 2 inches high.

Aquilegia canadensis. *Columbine petals remind me of the little juice-filled wax bottles I would buy at the candy counter as a child. If you silhouette the flowers in strong light, you can see the rich pool of sugary nectar that waits at each spur tip for a passing hummingbird or bee. Canada Columbine is the only eastern species, but it has many red-drenched relatives throughout the West. It will gently self-sow around the garden if you scatter the seeds when the capsules dry and crack open.*

NATIVE TO: damp but well-drained soils at lower to mid-elevations in the mountains; British Columbia south to California

SIZE: 4–8 inches (6 inches)

COLOR: white (bracts sometimes tinged pink); **BLOOMS** in early summer

Woodrush Pussy-toes is a clumping, tufted, nonrunning species with 2–3-inch narrow leaves that grow from a woody caudex. *A. argentea* (Silvery Pussy-toes) is a related plant from Oregon and California that runs to form loose mats of spoon-shaped, intensely silvery foliage in small rosettes.

Antennaria parlinii ssp. *fallax* (syn *A. plantaginifolia*)
(Plantain Pussy-toes)

ZONES: 3–9; sun, part sun

SOIL: moist to dry

NATIVE TO: open woodland, dry slopes; New Brunswick to North Dakota, south to Texas and Georgia

SIZE: 3–6 inches (24 inches)

COLOR: white; **BLOOMS** in spring

A robust and vigorous ground cover useful for covering large areas. Plantain Pussy-toes is larger than the others covered here and the best choice for gardeners in the Southeast. The leaves are gray-green above, silvery gray below, and form rosettes 4–6 inches across.

Antennaria rosea (syn. *microphylla*)
(Rosy Pussy-toes)

ZONES: 3–8; sun, part sun

SOIL: moist to dry, well drained

NATIVE TO: plains, mountains, subalpine woods; throughout the mid- and higher elevations of the Rocky, Cascade, and Sierra Mountains

SIZE: 1–3 inches (12–16 inches)

COLOR: white (bracts rose); **BLOOMS** in spring

One of the best garden subjects. Leaves are covered in a matted gray wool that wears away as they age, which gives the carpet a two-toned appearance. *A. parvifolia* (Plains Pussy-toes) is a related species with a distribution centered in the Great Plains.

can easily envision dancing ballerinas or Luna Moths perched on a twig when I meditate on these complex flowers. Columbine petals form long tubes or spurs that contain large reservoirs of nectar at their tips. *A. longissima* from the southwest United States and Mexico takes this to an extreme, with spurs up to 6 inches long! Many of the native species are hummingbird-pollinated and advertise this with bold red flowers. *Aquilegia* species are very interfertile (different species can cross to form fertile offspring), and this has been used to advantage by plant breeders, who have crossed our species with each other and with Eurasian varieties to produce a wealth of garden hybrids. In fact, if you grow seedlings from a mixed population of columbines, you will likely get a wonderful range of colors and forms. The only way to guarantee you will get the true species is to grow wild-collected seed.

All the columbines have divided, fine-textured foliage that is a perfect foil for the delicate flowers that dance above on thin stems. Most of the species flower heavily in spring, set seed, and then go semidormant during the heat of the summer. In the garden, they are best used as accents, allowed to self-sow here and there. They will often pop up in surprising places, and this informality is a large part of their charm. Division and transplanting of established plants should be avoided.

There are many localized species in the southwestern and central United States. These often grow in restricted or isolated habitats that have allowed them to become subtly distinct from the more widespread columbines.

CULTURE: In cultivation, most of the native species are short-lived, which may have more to do with improper growing conditions and predation than genetics. In the wild, columbines are found mostly in places that have abundant moisture in spring but go dry in summer. In the garden, they suffer from crown rot and leaf spot if watered too heavily during midseason's heat. The woody rootstock can also be attacked by root or crown borers, which produce the same rapid collapse. Columbine Leaf

Aquilegia canadensis

Aquilegia (ah-quill-EE-gee-ah)
Ranunculaceae
Columbine

The name "columbine" comes from the Latin for *dove*. While I can see no obvious physical similarities between flower and bird, there is a poetry to the intricate blooms that certainly inspires metaphor. I

Miners also regularly leave their trails in the leaves. After flowering, the plants die back to a few basal leaves for the summer, so interplant them with more substantial companions.

USES: Columbines are well suited to naturalizing in the rock garden. *A. canadensis* and *A. formosa* are the most adaptable species in the genus and will seed about in borders or woodland gardens as well.

WILDLIFE: Nectar source for hummingbirds and butterflies. *Aquilegia* is the only food for the larvae of the Columbine Duskywing *(Erynnis lucilius)*. These pale green caterpillars may totally defoliate the plants in late spring, but will leave the flowers alone.

PROPAGATION: Easy to moderately difficult from seed. See p. 246.

Aquilegia canadensis
(Canada Columbine)

ZONES: 3–9; sun to light shade
SOIL: well drained, slightly acid to neutral
NATIVE TO: ledges, woods, and cliffs; Quebec to Manitoba south to Texas and Florida
SIZE: 10–24 inches (8–12 inches)
COLOR: scarlet to pale orange-red (pale yellow and white forms exist); **BLOOMS** in late spring

The only eastern species, often found on limestone, but very adaptable in the garden. A favorite of many eastern wildflower gardeners and one of the best for the Southeast.

Aquilegia chrysantha
(Yellow Columbine)

ZONES: 3–8; sun, part sun
SOIL: well drained, moist in spring
NATIVE TO: damp microclimates in desert canyons; Colorado to Utah, south to Arizona and Texas
SIZE: 18–24 inches (12–16 inches)
COLOR: pale to golden yellow; **BLOOMS** in late spring, early summer

A robust species found along moist waterways at moderate elevations in the mountains of the Southwest. The upward-facing, long-tailed, elegant flowers are striking. Needs excellent drainage in humid summers, but is not really difficult. Yellow Columbine is hybridized with Colorado and Canada Columbines to produce the popular, long-tailed garden hybrids.

Aquilegia coerulea (caerulea)
(Colorado Columbine)

ZONES: 3–8; sun, part sun
SOIL: well drained
NATIVE TO: rocky slopes and near streams; Colorado, Wyoming, and Montana to Idaho south to Nevada and New Mexico
SIZE: 18–30 inches (12–16 inches)

COLOR: sepals blue or violet, petals either white or violet; **BLOOMS** in late spring

Colorado Columbine is a stunning plant with impossibly huge but perfectly proportioned flowers over blue-green leaves. Found above and below timberline throughout its range. Seed is often available, and it is easy to raise, which is fortunate, for like any of the alpines, it can be short-lived in cultivation.

Aquilegia elegantula
(Red Columbine)

ZONES: 4–8; sun, part sun
SOIL: moist, well drained
NATIVE TO: montane, moist coniferous woods, streambanks; Colorado to Utah south to Arizona and New Mexico
SIZE: 4–16 inches (8–12 inches)
COLOR: sepals yellow-green to red, petals same; **BLOOMS** from late spring to summer

One of the red- and yellow-flowered, *A. canadensis-formosa* group. Smaller in all respects, with narrow flowers and nonflaring petals. It is a common sight in the alpine meadows of the Rocky Mountains, with flowers mirroring in color those of the Rhexia-leaved Indian Paintbrush *(Castilleja rhexifolia)*.

Aquilegia formosa
(Red Columbine, Sitka Columbine)

ZONES: 4–8; sun to part sun
SOIL: moist
NATIVE TO: rich woods, moist meadows; Wyoming and Alberta to British Columbia and along the coast to southern Alaska south to California and Utah
SIZE: 16–30 inches (12–16 inches)

Aquilegia coerulea (caerulea). *The stunning bicolored flowers of Colorado Columbine are an unforgettable sight in the wild, and equally memorable in the garden. The upward-facing, long-tailed blooms have been popular with plant breeders, who have crossed them with Yellow Columbine to produce large-flowered hybrids in every color of the rainbow except (thankfully) green.*

Arisaema triphyllum. Jack at home in his covered lectern, preaching about plant conservation to the gathered minions. This is the variety stewardsonii, showcasing deep burgundy and lime zebra stripes that make it a treasured addition to the woodland garden. The spadix releases a musky perfume that draws amorous flies who descend it to the fertile zone at its base. In their spadix-hopping reproductive frenzy, they transfer pollen from male plants to the more robust females such as this.

COLOR: sepals pale to deep red, petals orange to yellow; BLOOMS from mid- to late spring

Much like the Canada Columbine in appearance, but larger in all respects. They are sold interchangeably in the trade, but Red Columbine is typically darker in flower and blooms one to two weeks earlier.

Aquilegia jonesii
(Limestone Columbine)

ZONES: 3–7; sun
SOIL: well drained, limestone
NATIVE TO: rocky, limestone soils in the subalpine zone; Wyoming, Montana, and Alberta
SIZE: 1–4 inches (2–3 inches)
COLOR: deep violet-blue; BLOOMS in spring

This species is a perfect combination of congested, tufted blue-gray foliage and large, nearly stemless, short-spurred flowers, but it's unfortunately a challenge to grow and bloom. Needs excellent drainage and a limestone crevice. *A. scopulorum* from Utah and Nevada has a similar habit, but is larger, with lighter, long-spurred flowers like a miniature Colorado Columbine.

Aquilegia pubescens
(Pale Columbine)

ZONES: 4–8; sun, part sun
SOIL: well drained
NATIVE TO: rocky meadows—alpine to subalpine; Sierra Nevadas of central California
SIZE: 18–30 inches (12–16 inches)
COLOR: cream to pale violet and white; BLOOMS in late spring

In many respects an evocative, pale-flowered form of *A. caerulea*. The flowers can have a beautiful sunset hue.

Arisaema triphyllum

Arisaema (air-iss-EE-ma)
Araceae
Jack-in-the-pulpit

One of my early botanical memories involves learning the story of Jack-in-the-pulpit from my mother after we had discovered the fantastic flowers in the swamp behind our house. There was the little preacher—really the spadix of the flower—standing proudly under his covered lectern, preaching to the faithful. The unusual flowers of *Arisaema* do capture the imagination, but they are really designed to capture the attention of small flies, who crawl down the spadix and over the flowers, pollinating them as they go. About halfway down the spadix is a ring of male flowers, and below them the females. On young or weakened plants, only the male flowers are fertile, and on older, vigorous individuals, it is only the females that are active. Not only is self-fertilization prevented, there is also the assurance that only the plants that can most afford it will have to expend the considerable resources necessary to form fruits and seeds. The flowers are protected from the elements by a spathe (the pulpit of the story), which begins to dry and split as the clusters of seed swell inside. *Arisaema triphyllum* is an adaptable plant, at home in a variety of soils, but reaching prodigious proportions in very moist, organic conditions. The single or paired 3-parted leaves are a bold addition to the shade garden, and the scarlet fruits—arranged like corn on the cob—are an added bonus in late summer.

CULTURE: With time, Jack-in-the-pulpits form a large flattened corm that reminds me of those holiday cookies with the chocolate kiss pressed into the middle. Small offsets are produced around the rim, and these eventually detach and grow on their own. In this way one plant can become a small colony in a few years' time. The corm completely sheds its outer skin and entire root system every fall and so is easy to move when it's going dormant. Carefully dig yellowing plants to find the corms, which are up to 12 inches deep. Small ones are teardrop-shaped and easy to overlook. Replant them 6 inches deep in rich, acid soil. There is a rust disease that affects the native *Arisaema*s and can quickly spread if not controlled. The disease is even more of a problem for the many

Asian species now being grown in our gardens. Infected plants develop cupped, misshapen leaves that erupt with rusty brown spores in spring as the plants are blooming. Remove and destroy infected plants.

USES: Specimens in the woodland garden, naturalizing in wooded wetlands.

PROPAGATION: Slow but easy from seed; easy from division. See p. 246.

Arisaema dracontium
(Green Dragon)

ZONES: 4–9; shade
SOIL: moist, organic
NATIVE TO: damp woods, wooded floodplains; Quebec to Minnesota, south to Texas and Florida
SIZE: 1–3 feet (12–16 inches)
COLOR: green; **BLOOMS** in late spring

Green Dragon gets its name from the long thin spadix, which coils serpentine and tonguelike from the narrow, green spathe. Certainly not nightmarish, but suggestive to the mythologically inclined imagination. The plants appear late in the spring, first the small offsets, then the largest adults sending up a sharp-pointed spear. This splits from the pressures of the expanding leaf, which emerges like a butterfly from a cocoon: an elegant semicircle of 7–15 narrow leaflets atop a tall petiole. The number and arrangement of the leaves is very different from the more common *A. triphyllum*.

Arisaema triphyllum
(Jack-in-the-pulpit)

ZONES: 3–9; shade
SOIL: moist, organic
NATIVE TO: moist woods; Nova Scotia to North Dakota south to Texas and Florida
SIZE: 12–28 inches (12–16 inches)
COLOR: green and brown or mahogany; **BLOOMS** in spring

Jack-in-the-pulpit springs from a pointed, warty sheath that protects the paired, 3-parted leaves as they come from the ground. There is some variability to the shape of the leaflets and color of the spathe, which has led intrepid botanists to name several varieties. There are forms with strong burgundy stripes on the inside of the spathe labeled var. *stewardsonii* that are very elegant in flower.

Aruncus dioicus

Aruncus dioicus
(air-UN-kiss)
Rosaceae
Goat's Beard

ZONES: 4–8; part sun, shade
SOIL: moist
NATIVE TO: rich woodland; Pennsylvania to Indiana south to Arkansas and North Carolina and in the west from British Columbia to Alaska south to California and Oregon
SIZE: 3–6 feet (3 feet)
COLOR: creamy white; **BLOOMS** from late spring to early summer

The flower plumes of a well-grown Goat's Beard have a soft, atmospheric effect that can be simply stunning in the dappled shade of early summer. The plants are a tremendous source of pollen and nectar and, from a distance, the flowers appear to be trembling from the accumulated buzzing of myriad bees, beetles, and flower flies. One should not be deterred by the prospect of attracting 6-legged wildlife—many of these insects prey on pest species as juveniles, and few will bother humans. Providing rich sources of nectar for these predators through the season is one of the best ways to naturally manage pests. Goat's Beard is dioecious—that is, male and female flowers are found on separate plants. The male flowers are a little larger, and the yellow anthers combine with this to make them a bit showier in bloom. However, plants are never sexed before being sold, and females have their own advantage, as the heavy clusters of developing seeds hang from the tops of the plant in golden green chains and provide interest into the fall. The plants are robust, with attractive compound leaves much like *Astilbe* that zigzag on strong stems. The woody crown of a mature specimen will send out 6–8 of these stems in

Aruncus dioicus. A large Goat's Beard in full bloom hosts a remarkable assemblage of bees, wasps, beetles, and flies relishing the wispy blossoms and too busy with their work to be bothered by a human observer. Large stands are a common sight along mountain roads in the Appalachians and Cascades.

Asarum canadensis.
Wild Ginger is one of my favorite ground covers, because the clean, confident foliage blends beautifully with so many other woodlanders. New leaves emerge in a flush in spring, all stretching their petioles for a place in the light, and the layered effect that results is part of its charm. Jug-shaped flowers are visible as the leaves just begin to expand, but then become quickly obscured by the foliar canopy.

a loose clump. The 12-inch plumes concentrate at the tops of these stems, lending a nice contrast of airy white over the deep green of the leaves.

Plants from the West are sometimes listed as *A. dioicus* var. *pubescens* or *A. sylvester.* Hybrids with the tiny Korean *A. aethusifolius* sometimes occur spontaneously when the plants are grown together, yielding a range of offspring of intermediate characteristics and size.

CULTURE: Grows best in a rich, moisture-retentive soil, but performs well anywhere the soil does not dry severely. To prevent scalding of the foliage, dappled shade or morning sun is best, especially in warmer regions. Clip off the spent male flowers after bloom. The plants self-sow and in perfect locations can be a problem unless the females are cut back as well.

WILDLIFE: Excellent nectar plants.

PROPAGATION: Moderately difficult from seed. See p. 246.

Asarum canadense

Asarum (ass-ARE-um)
Aristolochiaceae
Wild Ginger

One of my favorite natural foliage combinations is Maidenhair Fern underplanted with Wild Ginger. There is no mystery why these two work so well together—though their color is nearly the same, it is the strong contrast of the fine-leaved maidenhair with the low, broad foliage of the ginger that is so pleasing to the eye. Bold, distinctively heart-shaped foliage is the main attraction of *Asarum* for gardeners. The modest flowers of Wild Ginger sit resting like little knocked-over pots on the ground under the leaves. The sepals unite to form a swollen tube with a small opening that is more or less covered with red

or brown hairs. These evolved to attract small pollinating flies, but at this point they are mostly self-pollinating. It is possible that the necessary flies have either gone extinct or have not followed the plants north after the last ice age. *Hexastylis* (see p. 119), the group of evergreen gingers from the southeast United States, are not self-pollinating, and when taken outside of their native range, away from their pollinators, they do not set seed reliably.

All parts of the ginger plant, but especially the rhizomes, contain volatile oils that have the odor of the culinary ginger, *Zingiber officinale,* a tropical plant related to bananas. Although used historically as a medicinal, wild ginger should not be eaten, as it contains several possibly poisonous compounds. The leaves have been known to cause occasional dermatitis in sensitive people.

CULTURE: *A. canadense* and its western counterpart *A. caudatum* are easily grown in organic soil in the shade garden. Over time, the rhizomes form a dense tangled mat that can be dug and divided after the new leaves have expanded in spring (this is the time when new roots form). The gingers are strongly determinate—that is, they put out only one flush of leaves a season—so they will look a little tattered the first season after transplanting. Fortunately, except to multiply the plants, dividing is rarely necessary, and the clumps will expand about 6 inches in all directions each year. The evergreen *A. hartwegii* and its close relative *A. marmoratum* from the mountains of California and southern Oregon have beautiful, silver-mottled leaves like many of the *Hexastylis,* but they languish in both the cold and heat found outside their native range.

USES: Outstanding ground covers for shade. Only *A. canadense* is truly deciduous, but the others die back in very cold weather.

WILDLIFE: *A. canadense* is an alternate food source for the beautiful Pipevine Swallowtail butterfly (*Battus philenor*) and likely helps extend the range of this species north of its main food source, the Dutchman's Pipevine (*Aristolochia macrophylla* and *A. serpentaria*). The caterpillars are brown-black with small orange spots in 2 rows down their back.

PROPAGATION: Moderately difficult from seed; easy from division. See p. 246.

Asarum canadense
(Wild Ginger)

ZONES: 3–8; shade
SOIL: moist
NATIVE TO: rich woodland; New Brunswick to Alberta south to Louisiana and Georgia
SIZE: 6–8 inches (12–16 inches)
COLOR: yellow-brown; **BLOOMS** in spring
An indispensable plant for shade gardens, durable and carefree. It is a moderate spreader, and can over-

whelm delicate companions. Wild Ginger can tolerate moderate drought, flopping over when dry but quickly recovering after rain or the gentle shower of a passing hose.

Asarum caudatum
(Western Wild Ginger)

ZONES: 5–8; shade
SOIL: moist
NATIVE TO: moist, coniferous woods; British Columbia south to California and Oregon
SIZE: 5–7 inches (14 inches)
COLOR: burgundy; **BLOOMS** in spring

Slightly smaller in stature than Wild Ginger, with shinier, evergreen leaves and fascinating, long-tailed flowers. *A. lemmonii* is a relative from the central mountains of California with flowers that hang down, but is otherwise similar.

Asarum hartwegii
(Cyclamen-leaf Ginger)

ZONES: 6–8; shade
SOIL: moderately moist, well drained
NATIVE TO: rocky slopes in the montane conifer forests of the California Sierras
SIZE: 6 inches (8–12 inches)
COLOR: red-green; **BLOOMS** in spring

An enchanting ginger, with strong silver mottling along the veins of each leaf. In other ways similar to *A. caudatum,* but slower growing. A very desirable plant where it can be grown. Will survive but not thrive in the Northeast and the South.

Asclepias incarnata

Asclepias (ass-KLEP-ee-ass)
Asclepidaceae
Milkweed, Butterfly Weed

Milkweeds are synonymous in many gardeners' minds with the remarkable Monarch butterfly, which follows the blooming of various *Asclepias* from its wintering grounds in California and Mexico across all of North America. Successive broods hatch and continue to fly farther north, the last arriving in southern Canada in late summer. This last brood then flies thousands of miles back to its small forested winter grounds to wait out the cold before beginning the march north again the following spring. This incredible navigational feat is a potent antidote for human hubris and one of the most poetic examples of insect-plant interdependence that one could hope for. The Monarch is a tropical species that has vastly extended its range by migrating north in sum-

mer, exploiting the widespread and adaptable temperate milkweeds as a virtually untapped food source. The familiar white-, yellow-, and black-striped caterpillars are well known for concentrating several toxic glucosides from the plant's milky sap in their skin, making them unpalatable to predators. The plants do contain several physiologically active chemicals that were once used by Native Americans and colonial herbalists. An alternative name for Butterfly Weed, Pleurisy Root, comes from its once common use to treat lung problems. During World War II, milkweeds were grown in quantity for the downy parachutes that are attached to each seed. The down is six times more buoyant than cork and five times as warm as wool. The fibers from the cambium of several species yield strong fibers that have been used in textiles and for making strong rope and twine. My fondest milkweed memories are of collecting the large teardrop-shaped pods in the late fall with my mother; elaborately decorating them with gold paint, felt, and sequins; and hanging them on our Christmas tree.

The genus is also interesting for the devious way it accomplishes pollination. The petals of each flower are shaped into hoods, often with a prominent horn in the center. An insect that alights looking for

nectar will often find its proboscis or one or more legs slipping into the waxy hoods, where it becomes trapped as a structure called the corpusculum at the base of the flower snaps shut on the body part so inserted. In struggling to free itself, the insect dislodges the two pollen sacs (pollinia) which sit in the anthers at the base of the hood. The pollinia are attached by threads to a sticky structure with a great name—the translator. The insect eventually struggles free, and the translator dries and pivots the pollinia so that they fit like a key into the stigma of the next flower visited. The next time you think you

Asclepias incarnata.
Like many wetland plants, Swamp Milkweed will grow happily in drier soils. Its rounded clusters of bright rose flowers are some of the showiest in the genus, and its clumping habit makes it easier to accommodate in gardens than some of the aggressively spreading species.

Asclepias purpurascens. One hundred years ago, Purple Milkweed was fairly common in New England, so its present rarity is a curious mystery possibly due to changing land use that has eliminated the open pastureland that dominated the landscape in the nineteenth century. It is a favorite nectar plant of the Great Spangled Fritillary, whose larvae feed on violets. If you look carefully, you can see this one's right foreleg is trapped in the hood of a flower.

are stealthily sneaking up on a seemingly unsuspecting butterfly perched elegantly on a milkweed bloom, remember it may merely be temporarily trapped.

CULTURE: Milkweeds have thick, tuberous roots that can get infected easily if they are damaged. It is certainly possible to transplant them, but they really never need dividing. It is best to start with healthy container plants and plant them in a permanent location. The plants can look pretty tattered after flowering, but it is best to let them die back naturally. Crown rot is a problem for the dryland species only if the soil is consistently wet.

USES: Border, wildlife garden, rock garden, meadow. The bold foliage and intricate, showy flowers of many species, combined with their wildlife value, make the milkweeds indispensable in sunny gardens.

WILDLIFE: Excellent nectar plants. Food for the larval stage of the Monarch and Queen butterflies (*Danaus plexippus* and *D. gilippus*).

PROPAGATION: Easy from seed. See p. 246.

Asclepias cryptoceras
(Pallid Milkweed)

ZONES: 4–7; sun
SOIL: dry, well drained
NATIVE TO: dry clay hillsides; Colorado to Washington south to California and Nevada
SIZE: 6–14 inches (8–12 inches)
COLOR: lime green and rose; BLOOMS in spring

An utterly charming, large-flowered rock-garden species from hot, dry badlands. The rose-purple hoods contrast with the pale yellow sepals, almost

obscuring the few round leaves. Outside of its range for the specialty grower only. The clumping plants need excellent drainage and are best sown directly in lean soil.

Asclepias exaltata
(Tall Milkweed)

ZONES: 3–8; sun, part shade
SOIL: moist
NATIVE TO: moist, upland woods and openings; Maine to Minnesota and Iowa, south to Tennessee and Georgia
SIZE: 2–5 feet (2 feet)
COLOR: green and white; BLOOMS in late spring to early summer

The long tapered leaves of Tall Milkweed bear elegant drooping clusters of flowers in their upper axils. It is one of the earliest of the eastern species to bloom. Clumping, with large oval leaves like the Common Milkweed.

Asclepias humistrata
(Sandhills Milkweed)

ZONES: 6–9; sun
SOIL: dry
NATIVE TO: dry sandy woods, sandhills on the coastal plain from Georgia to Mississippi
SIZE: 1–3 feet, (1–3 feet)
COLOR: rose; BLOOMS in early summer

A dramatic foliage plant that is unfortunately hard to find in the trade. The large blue-gray leaves have strong pink veins. They are sessile and flat at the base, so they appear perfoliate and are a lovely contrast to the flowers. Clumping.

Asclepias incarnata
(Swamp Milkweed)

ZONES: 3–9; sun, part shade
SOIL: moist to wet
NATIVE TO: swamps and low meadows; Nova Scotia to Saskatoon, south to Utah, New Mexico, and Florida
SIZE: 2–4 feet (2 feet)
COLOR: white and pink; BLOOMS in summer

One of our widest-ranging and showiest species with flattened, brightly colored flower heads at the tips of tall stems. Although found in wet soils, it will thrive in the garden if soil is not droughty. Strongly clumping.

Asclepias purpurascens
(Purple Milkweed)

ZONES: 3–9; sun, part sun
SOIL: moist to dry

NATIVE TO: dry soils, mainly in the prairies; New Hampshire to Wisconsin and Kansas, south to Oklahoma and Virginia

SIZE: 2–4 feet (2 feet)

COLOR: rose purple; **BLOOMS** in summer

A good noninvasive substitute for the Common Milkweed, *A. syriaca*, in the garden. It has the same broadly elliptic leaves and showier, darker flowers. (*A. speciosa*, Showy Milkweed, is a similar, western species with felted gray leaves.)

Asclepias syriaca
(Common Milkweed)

ZONES: 3–9; sun, part sun

SOIL: moist to dry

NATIVE TO: fields, meadows, waste places; New Brunswick to Manitoba south to Nebraska, Oklahoma and Virginia

SIZE: 2–4 feet (3–5 feet)

COLOR: green and purple; **BLOOMS** in summer

A familiar roadside plant in the East, but too aggressive for garden situations. The plants form extensive colonies from a wide-spreading root system. New stems can spring up at great distances from the original plant.

Asclepias tuberosa
(Butterfly Weed)

ZONES: 3–9; sun, part sun

SOIL: well drained

NATIVE TO: sandy soils, upland woods; New Hampshire to South Dakota, south to Arizona, Mexico, and Florida

SIZE: 1–3 feet (2 feet)

COLOR: orange to red-orange or yellow; **BLOOMS** in summer

One of our most recognizable wildflowers. The bright orange color of the flowers is truly striking. The narrow leaves are a rich, glossy green and alternate thickly up the stems. Best in lean soils, but I have seen it thrive in the heavy clays of the South.

Asclepias variegata
(White Milkweed)

ZONES: 4–9; sun, part sun

SOIL: moist

NATIVE TO: openings in upland woods; Connecticut to Illinois south to Texas and Florida

SIZE: 1–3 feet (2 feet)

COLOR: white; **BLOOMS** in early summer

Notable for its pure white, waxy blooms, clustered, like most milkweeds, near the top of the plant. A beautiful plant if it can be located.

Asclepias verticillata
(Whorled Milkweed)

ZONES: 3–9; sun, part sun

SOIL: moist to dry

NATIVE TO: fields, open woods, and prairies; Massachusetts to Saskatoon, south to Arizona and Florida

SIZE: 1–2 feet (16 inches)

COLOR: white or pale green; **BLOOMS** in summer

Differs from all the others covered here in the very narrow, linear leaves in whorls of 3–6. A very soft-textured plant, but the flowers are not too dramatic.

Aster concolor

Aster (ASS-ter)
Asteraceae
Aster

Aster concolor. *Eastern Silvery Aster gets its name from the covering of long silvery hairs that decorate the leaves—especially the winter rosettes. Low clusters of shimmering oval leaves persisting through the cold are one of its most ornamental features.*

Few plants are so readily identified with the archetypal wildflower of the imagination as the native asters. Maybe they foster a romantic nostalgia for a simpler time, when horse-drawn wagons trailed slowly down rutted paths bordered with colorful daisies and the air was sweetened with the sound of birdsongs. Maybe it is the uncomplicated elegance of the genus that belies a dogged adaptability for the myriad conditions this hemisphere has to offer. Whatever the reason, this is a group no wildflower gardener can in good conscience ignore.

So identified with North America are the asters that is easy to forget that this is a cosmopolitan genus, with representatives through South America, Europe, and Asia. There are many to choose from among the natives, and I have tried to pick just a representative sample of the many species available. Our plants are mostly fall bloomers and range from tiny alpine endemics 2 inches high to towering 8-foot *Aster puniceus* and the shrubby, vining *A. carolinianus.*

As every intrepid student of botany will remember, the "flowers" of plants in the Aster family are really groups (inflorescences) of small fertile flowers called disk flowers, which form the center of the daisy, and sterile ray flowers which are the "petals." To make it easier on all of us, though, I will refer to these as flowers rather than inflorescences.

CULTURE: For the most part, asters are easy-to-grow perennials, and one can be found for just about every garden situation. They are easily moved in spring or fall, and the taller types will benefit from tip pruning in late spring to keep them from getting leggy. Asters are susceptible to many leaf spots, rusts, and mildew, which will often leave the lower leaves in pretty bad shape by flowering, but usually do no permanent harm. In formal situations, it is a good idea to screen the bottom half of the taller species with more diminutive foliage (ornamental grasses are particularly appropriate for this). Most asters benefit from division every four to five years. They typically spread out in all directions from their base, so the centers tend to die out with time. It is a good idea to deadhead the plants after flowering unless you want them to naturalize, as they easily self-sow.

WILDLIFE: Asters are one of the most important fall nectar plants, and a patch of flowering plants seems to attract any and all of the pollinators in the area, frantically trying to gather the last of the season's bounty. A number of asters are also important food plants for butterfly larvae. Many of the crescents feed on asters, including Pearl Crescent (*Phyciodes tharos*), which favors *A. novae-angliae.* Tawny Crescent (*Phyciodes batesii*) relies on *A. undulatus,* and Field Crescent (*Phyciodes pratensis*) feeds on *A. foliaceus*—its range coincides with the range of the plant. A similar situation is found with Harris' Checkerspot (*Chlosyne harrisii*), which feeds on *A. umbellatus.* The distinctive orange-and-black-striped caterpillars can be found on the plants in summer. Other checkerspots that feed on asters include *Chlosyne neumoegeni,* a western species that feeds on several, including *A. tortifolius.*

PROPAGATION: Generally easy from seed. See p. 247.

Aster alpiginus

(Alpine Aster)

ZONES: 4–7; sun
SOIL: gritty, well drained
NATIVE TO: alpine meadows; mostly in the Cascades of Oregon and Washington
SIZE: 4–10 inches (6 inches)
COLOR: violet; BLOOMS in late summer

One of the many alpine asters, this is a fairly adaptable plant for the rock garden, with narrow, tufted foliage and large flowers held just above. It is a major component of the celebrated wildflower displays in such places as Mount Rainier National Park.

Aster azureus

(Prairie Heart-leaved Aster)

ZONES: 3–9; sun
SOIL: moist to dry
NATIVE TO: prairies and dry woods; New York and Ontario to Minnesota, south to Texas and Mississippi
SIZE: 1–3 feet (1–2 feet)
COLOR: blue to blue-violet; BLOOMS in fall

Although I would not call the color of the flowers sky blue, they are certainly a beautiful, strong blue-violet. The lower leaves are typically heart-shaped, much like *A. cordifolius.* Often sold as a component of wildflower meadow seed mixes. It is a drought-tolerant, adaptable plant.

Aster carolinianus

(Climbing Aster)

ZONES: 6–9; sun, part sun
SOIL: moist to wet
NATIVE TO: margins of swamps, wet woods and thickets; North Carolina to Florida on the coastal plain
SIZE: 4–7 feet (3–4 feet)
COLOR: violet; BLOOMS in late fall

This unusual plant is not truly a vine, but has the habit of many roses in that it grows long weak stems that weave through the surrounding vegetation. The leaves look much like New England Aster in shape. Truly a glorious sight when trained to a wall or support. The plants are obscured by the many large flowers that grow in masses from the end of each stem.

Aster coloradoensis

(Colorado Aster)

ZONES: 3–6; sun
SOIL: gritty, well drained
NATIVE TO: alpine meadows and outcrops; Colorado
SIZE: 2–6 inches (3 inches)
COLOR: pink; BLOOMS in summer

A wonderful tufted miniature for the rock gardener from the high Rockies. Blooms for a long season with flowers held just above the leaves. Needs scree soil and cool conditions.

Aster concolor
(Eastern Silvery Aster)

ZONES: 5–9; sun

SOIL: dry, well drained

NATIVE TO: sandy soils, mostly along the southern coastal plain; Massachusetts to Florida and Louisiana

SIZE: 1–3 feet (12 inches)

COLOR: violet; **BLOOMS** in fall

The first time I saw this species along a roadside in North Carolina, I thought it was one of the blazing stars that populate the area. The flowers grow in tight clusters from the top third of nonbranching stems, which arch like wands from their accumulated weight. I was so impressed that I returned later to collect seed and we began offering it at the nursery. The leaves are small, oval, and covered with long silky hairs that give it a silver appearance. As with many asters, the leaves grow progressively smaller later in the season, so that those near the top are nearly reduced to scales. Western Silvery Aster, *A. sericeus,* has similar leaves, but the flowers are borne on branched stems. It is a native of dry prairies.

Aster cordifolius
(Blue Heart-leaved Aster, Blue Wood Aster)

ZONES: 3–8; sun to shade

SOIL: moist to dry

NATIVE TO: woodlands; Nova Scotia to Minnesota, south to Missouri and Virginia

SIZE: 2–3 feet (18 inches)

COLOR: violet; **BLOOMS** in fall

My favorite aster for the shade garden. Puts up clouds of small flowers on arched, branching stems lined their lower length with pointed, heart-shaped leaves. It can seed abundantly if not deadheaded. (I forgot to cut back the plants at the edge of the nursery and we were pulling seedlings out of containers all spring.)

Aster divaricatus
(White Wood Aster)

ZONES: 3–8; sun to shade

SOIL: moist to dry

NATIVE TO: woods; New Hampshire to Ontario, south to Ohio and Maryland and in the mountains to Georgia

SIZE: 1–2 feet (12–18 inches)

COLOR: white with rose disks; **BLOOMS** in fall

A common, almost weedy species in the Northeast, but one can forgive its aggressiveness for the masses of small white flowers it freely produces in the harshest of conditions. Spreads moderately to aggressively, so should be deadheaded to prevent self-sowing in the North.

Aster fendleri
(Fendler's Aster)

ZONES: 4–9; sun

SOIL: dry

NATIVE TO: dry prairies and sandy soils; Nebraska and Kansas to New Mexico and Texas

SIZE: 6–14 inches (6–10 inches)

COLOR: blue-violet; **BLOOMS** in late summer

A low, clumping plant of the drier prairies, often found in pastures as well. The plants grow from a woody base and form a mound of foliage and flowers.

Aster laevis
(Smooth Aster)

ZONES: 3–9; sun, part sun

SOIL: moist to dry

NATIVE TO: fields, dry woods, prairies; Quebec to British Columbia south to New Mexico and Georgia

SIZE: 1–3 feet (12–16 inches)

COLOR: violet; **BLOOMS** in fall

A tough, adaptable species with lovely blue-gray leaves that are long and tapered and gradually reduced in size up the stem. The 1-inch-wide flowers emerge from a loose panicle. I would rate it as one of the best for gardens. It has a neat habit, rarely needs staking, and is very drought-tolerant.

Aster cordifolius. *This species grew abundantly around one of my first apartments in rural Connecticut, and to this day it remains one of my favorite asters. Even though the foliage begins to look tired by fall, thick panicles of violet on tall arching stems are a lovely swan song to another growing season in the woodland garden.*

Aster macrophyllus
(Big-leaved Aster)

ZONES: 3–8; part sun, shade

SOIL: moist

NATIVE TO: woods; Nova Scotia and Quebec to Wisconsin, south to Pennsylvania and Kentucky and in the mountains to Georgia

SIZE: 6–30 inches (16–24 inches)

COLOR: light violet; BLOOMS in fall

Big-leaved Aster has large heart-shaped, fuzzy foliage that has given it the alternative name Lumberjack Toilet Paper. It forms a dense, spreading ground cover in rich woodlands, punctuated in fall by occasional spikes of flowers. Some clones appear to flower more heavily than others. It hybridizes occasionally with *A. spectabilis* to produce *A. × herveyi*, an excellent garden plant with the large spreading leaves of Big-leaved Aster and showier flowers.

Aster novae-angliae. Aster "flowers" are really assemblages of many small flowers. The colorful but sterile violet ray flowers of this New England Aster pass for its petals. Notice the 4 slight folds in each of the rays. These are the seams along which its 5 petals have been fused into 1 large "unipetal." Fertile yellow flowers grow in an expanding disk in the center.

Aster novae-angliae
(New England Aster)

ZONES: 3–9; sun, part sun

SOIL: moist

NATIVE TO: moist meadows, open woods, fields; Massachusetts and Vermont to North Dakota and Wyoming, south to New Mexico and Virginia at higher elevations

SIZE: 2–6 feet (2–3 feet)

COLOR: violet to purple or rose; BLOOMS in fall

One of the showiest and most often cultivated of the larger asters. Narrow, 3–4-inch leaves alternate all the way up the tall stems crowned in fall with rounded heads of 1-inch blooms. Forms a thick clump after a few years. Swamp Aster, *A. puniceus,* is an even larger cousin, with stems to 8 feet and open heads of violet flowers. It needs a wet spot to thrive, and the stems may need staking as they tend to bend under the weight of the flowers. Aromatic Aster (*A. oblongifolius*) is a later blooming, drought-tolerant relative from the Southeast, as is Big-headed Aster (*A. grandiflorus*), which tends to replace New England Aster at lower elevations in North Carolina and makes a good choice for southern gardens. Regrettably, this group suffers from leaf blights that leave their lower stems bare by blooming time, which limits their usefulness in formal situations.

Aster novae-belgii
(New York Aster)

ZONES: 3–9; sun, part sun

SOIL: moist

NATIVE TO: salt marshes, sea cliffs, moist meadows; mostly on the coastal plain from Newfoundland to South Carolina

SIZE: 1–3 feet (2 feet)

COLOR: violet to purple, rose, or white; BLOOMS in fall

New York Aster is a bushy, slowly spreading species with smooth, lance-shaped medium green leaves. Its habit and floriferousness have made it one of the most popular garden asters in Europe and it has been hybridized with *A. novae-angliae, A. laevis,* and others. The plants are prone to leaf diseases, especially when stressed by lack of moisture.

Aster turbinellus
(Prairie Aster)

ZONES: 3–9; sun, part sun

SOIL: moist to dry

NATIVE TO: moderately dry prairies and open woods; Illinois to Kansas south to Louisiana

SIZE: 2–4 feet (18–30 inches)

COLOR: strong violet, centers yellow-green; BLOOMS in fall

Amidst the bewildering variety of this genus, if I had to pick one of the taller violet species for general garden use, it would be Prairie Aster. The plants leaf out early, first producing a large tight clump of smooth, dark green leaves with rounded tips, then strong leafy stems that branch heavily to produce a veritable cloud of flat 1-inch daisies on stiff, leafless branchlets. The foliage is relatively blemish-free and stays on the plants until after flowering. Its one drawback is a tendency to flop under the weight of the developing blooms.

Aster umbellatus
(Flat-topped Aster)

ZONES: 3–9; sun, part sun

SOIL: moist

NATIVE TO: moist meadows and ditches; Newfoundland to Minnesota south to Kentucky and Virginia and in the mountains to Georgia

SIZE: 3–7 feet (3–4 feet)

COLOR: white, with yellow-green centers; **BLOOMS** in fall

An imposing plant with towering stems and flat or rounded clusters of ¾-inch flowers at the tips that are reminiscent of Joe-Pye Weed flowers in shape. Needs room and tends to flop in flower.

Astragalus crassicarpus

Astragalus
(ass-TRAG-all-us)
Fabiaceae
Milkvetch

There is something of a life lesson in the story of the milkvetch. These seemingly unassuming legumes are so well adapted to the generally inhospitable dry steppes and mountains of the world and they have prospered to such an extent that they may be the largest genus of flowering plants in the Northern Hemisphere, with anywhere between 1,000 and 2,000 species worldwide. They are nitrogen-fixing legumes like peas and beans, able, with the assistance of certain bacteria that flourish in special nodules on their roots, to convert abundant but biologically useless gaseous nitrogen into fixed, or nitrate, form, which is then available for use by the plant.

This, combined with deep taproots and tough, often woolly leaves, helps them compete admirably in environments fairly hostile to plants. Many of the species contain powerful alkaloids that are a problem for grazing livestock. The chemicals cause a slow neurological deterioration combined with an addiction so powerful that the affected animals will eat little else, and eventually die (the effect is in many ways similar to that of chronic opium use). *A. mollisimus,* the Wooly Locoweed, is a particular problem in rangelands, and in the 1880s bounties were paid for its extermination.

Fortunately for the dryland gardener, there are many absolutely beautiful, nonweedy species that thrive in sun and poor soils and reward you with brilliant pealike flowers in a range of colors. The pinnate foliage is equally beautiful on many species, as are the large inflated pods, which remind me variously of bedroom slippers or miniature melons hanging in small clusters from each stem. The plants grow from a thick, woody crown and taproot. Old stems do not die completely back, and new ones arise from their bases. There are a few species from eastern North America, but these are rather lax plants with small flowers of interest more to the botanist than the gardener. It is the harsh conditions of the dry West that have produced the most ornamental species. Tight mounds of soft gray foliage are covered for a time with masses of the intricate flowers, which look for all the world like a flock of brightly colored birds perched for a rest on the little plants. Do not let their difficult reputation scare you from giving a place to this wonderful genus. Although the plants do not take well to container culture and so are rarely found in commercial nurseries, they are easy for the home gardener to accommodate if a few needs are met.

Oxytropis is a closely related genus that contains a few species easily accommodated in the rock garden. *O. lambertii* (Purple Locoweed) is a wide-ranging prairie plant with purple flowers on 8–10-inch spikes above gray-green foliage. *O. sericea* is a similar plant with white flowers.

CULTURE: For the most part, milkvetches are xeric plants, needing very well drained, dry soils and full sun to thrive. Out of their native range, the cushion types can be grown successfully in the rock garden scree or sand bed provided they receive all-day sun. The deep taproots of *Astragalus* are notoriously resentful of disturbance, and this is the main reason they are not more commonly available in nurseries. However, with the success of specialty seed companies, it is easy to find the seed of a number of plants. Once established, the plants are very long lived, and although it takes them several years to become established, they continue to improve in size and quantity of flower every year. It is often recommended to sow the seed directly into the selected location in the garden, and as it germinates quickly, this method will work well. Alternatively, I have successfully transplanted first-year seedlings grown in deep containers, provided I was careful to limit disturbance of the root ball when it was planted in the garden.

USES: Xeriscaping, rock gardens. In the wild, the plants are found as scattered individuals forming

*Astragalus crassicarpus.
The less common pale yellow-flowered form of Ground Plum attracts the attention of visitors every spring when it bursts into bloom in Garden in the Wood's dry-land garden. Pinnately compound leaves are a common adaptation among the nitrogen-fixing members of the pea family.*

·N₂ Fixation·

It is impossible to overstress the importance of nitrogen fixation for life on earth. Nitrogen is an essential component of proteins and amino acids, including chlorophyll—without it, life here would cease to exist. Nitrogen gas is abundant in our atmosphere. However, much like the old adage of the shipwrecked sailor floating on the ocean, "water water everywhere but not a drop to drink," nitrogen as a gas is biologically useless. It is only in its reduced form, a single N atom bound with hydrogen as ammonium or oxygen as nitrate that nitrogen can be used by plants and animals. Availability of this chemically fixed nitrogen is the main limiting factor to plant growth worldwide. As organic material is broken down, nitrogen is constantly being lost back to the atmosphere and must be continually replaced. This responsibility falls mainly to a few groups of bacteria, which can catalyze the fixation of nitrogen with the help of a special enzyme called nitrogenase. The most important nitrogen-fixing bacteria for land plants are in the genera *Rhizobium* and *Bradyrhizobium,* which infect the roots of legumes. They are free-living in soils where legumes are present, but in this state, they cannot catalyze the reaction. When they come into contact with the root hairs of a developing legume seedling, they attach to it, causing it to curl inward and form a tumorlike growth (nodule). Inside the nodule, the flourishing bacteria find the specific conditions they need to successfully fix nitrogen. This process requires a great deal of energy, which the plants provide them in the form of sugars, and also requires a carefully controlled, low-oxygen environment (too much oxygen destroys the nitrogenase enzyme). In return for this, the plants siphon off the resulting nitrogen compounds for use in protein synthesis, etc. Plants that have developed these symbiotic relationships with bacteria have a tremendous advantage over those that do not, especially in infertile soils where nitrogen is scarce. There are specific species of *Rhizobia* that associate with different genera of legumes, and many native seed nurseries will sell innoculants for specific plants that can be used to establish colonies on the roots of your seedlings.

loose colonies, but show to best effect if planted in groups of 3 or more.

WILDLIFE: Larval host plants for several species of butterflies, including the Melissa Blue (*Lycaeides melissa*) and Acmon Blue (*Plebejus acmon*).

PROPAGATION: Moderately difficult from seed. See p. 247.

Astragalus aretiodes
(Cushion Orophaca)

ZONES: 3–7; sun
SOIL: gritty, dry
NATIVE TO: poor, stony soils at moderate elevations, short-grass prairie or sagebrush; Idaho to Washington and Oregon
SIZE: 3 inches (1 foot)
COLOR: lavender to violet; **BLOOMS** in summer
Tiny mat-forming plant with downy, silver foliage and relatively large flowers.

Astragalus crassicarpus
(Ground Plum)

ZONES: 3–8; sun
SOIL: well drained
NATIVE TO: dry prairies and bluffs; Illinois to Alberta south to New Mexico and Texas
SIZE: 6 inches (12 inches)
COLOR: pale violet (rarely yellow); **BLOOMS** in spring
Ground plum is so called for its large round pods. The plants are attractive in flower, and their more easterly range makes them more adaptable to Northeastern gardens than other species.

Astragalus detritalis
(Debris Milkvetch)

ZONES: 4–7; sun
SOIL: dry
NATIVE TO: shale and clay soils; locally in Utah and Colorado
SIZE: 8–12 inches (12 inches)
COLOR: vivid purple-pink; **BLOOMS** in spring
A stunning species in flower. The large brightly colored blooms are visible from a great distance. The pinnate leaflets are thin and stiff. *A. spathulatus* is a similar, widespread species with smaller flowers and softer foliage.

Astragalus kentrophyta
(Thistle Milkvetch)

ZONES: 3–8; sun
SOIL: well drained
NATIVE TO: dry prairies to alpine meadows; Manitoba to British Columbia south to California and New Mexico
SIZE: 3–4 inches (1–2 feet)
COLOR: white or pink to purple; **BLOOMS** in summer
A wide-ranging and adaptable dryland plant, forming low, spreading mats of prickly foliage decorated with large flowers over a long season.

Baptisia alba

Baptisia (bap-TIS-ee-ah)
Fabiaceae
Wild Indigo, False Indigo

The wild indigos have an easy-to-please disposition that has made them one of the most popular natives for general garden use. The Blue False Indigo has long been a staple of perennial gardens, valued for its ease of culture, proud spikes of pea flowers, and longevity. I once lived in a house where the remains of a long-abandoned garden were marked only by several peonies and a large healthy *Baptisia australis,* sole survivors of a once extensive planting. Recently, several additional southeastern and prairie species have become widely available, which has rekindled interest in this entirely American genus.

As is true with many things that choose calm longevity over a frenzied yet fleeting life, *Baptisias* take their time to mature. You must be willing to give them two or three years in the garden to become sizable, and even longer to reach their full potential. They grow from a thick, woody rootstock, and the first few seasons are devoted to underground development. The plants typically have 3-parted leaves alternating from a many-branching central stem. They bloom as the main stems are still maturing, giving them a strongly vertical look at this stage. The blooms themselves are carried in the fashion of the familiar garden lupine. After flowering, the plants continue to branch and produce new leaves, becoming bushier and more rounded in effect. For this reason, they should not be crowded, although ground covers are effective planted around their bases to hide the bare lower stems. While the flowers are only in bloom for a few weeks, the decorative foliage continues to look good most of the season.

There are several natural hybrids recorded between the white, violet, and yellow *Baptisias.* The colors of these hybrids range from muddy brown to pale violet and pink-lavender. Selection of superior forms seems like a good project for an intrepid backyard hybridizer.

CULTURE: Wild indigos really never need dividing and resent root disturbance. Buy container-grown material and pick a spot where they can grow unmolested. High pH soils can be a problem and may make them unsuitable to areas with soil pH over 6.5. (Our well water is high in lime, and the *Baptisias* resent it. I have to lower the pH of our standard container soil mix to keep them from looking stunted and yellowed.) Other than this, they are fairly adaptable and tolerate a range of moisture levels from dry to moist. Full sun will produce the best growth, but they can tolerate some shade, especially in the Deep South.

USES: Particularly effective when combined with low-growing ground covers or in the mixed perennial border. The blue-green foliage of the taller species is a fine backdrop for summer-blooming perennials. I recommend planting them in clumps of no more than three, as they can be a bit overpowering en masse.

WILDLIFE: The only known food of the larval stage of the Wild Indigo Duskywing *(Erynnis baptisiae),* a small eastern butterfly.

PROPAGATION: Easy from seed; difficult from cuttings. See p. 247.

Baptisia alba (syn. *pendula)*
(White Wild Indigo)

ZONES: 5–9; sun to light shade
SOIL: moist to dry
NATIVE TO: dry, open woods, clearings; Virginia to
     Tennessee south to Georgia and Florida
SIZE: 3 feet (3 feet)
COLOR: white with a hint of violet; **BLOOMS** in spring
A very elegant false indigo with a compact, rounded habit and chocolate-colored stems that contrast beautifully with the blooms. Easy and adaptable.

Baptisia australis
(Blue False Indigo)

ZONES: 4–9; sun, part sun
SOIL: moist to dry
NATIVE TO: moist woodland margins and prairies;
     New York to Nebraska south to Texas and Georgia
SIZE: 3–4 feet (3 feet)
COLOR: violet blue; **BLOOMS** in spring
The most familiar and wide-ranging species. *B. australis* var. *minor* is the western form, with smaller

Baptisia alba. Charcoal-colored stems add charm and visual complexity to the delicate spires of White Wild Indigo in full bloom. It takes three or four years for a plant to attain this size, but I think it is well worth the wait.

Boltonia asteroides. *A stand of 'Snowbank'—a cultivar of False Aster discovered in a friend's garden and introduced into cultivation by Will Curtis, the creator of Garden in the Woods—in all of its lusty, daisy white splendor. Imagine it interplanted with clumps of violet asters or as a background for a flock of pink polyethylene flamingos.*

habit and larger flowers, making it an excellent garden subject when it can be found. Both are vigorous, adaptable, and the fastest to mature from seed.

Baptisia bracteata var. *leucophaea*
(Cream Wild Indigo)

ZONES: 4–9; sun, part sun
SOIL: well drained
NATIVE TO: prairies and open woods; Michigan to Nebraska south to Texas and South Carolina
SIZE: 18–24 inches (2 feet)
COLOR: creamy white; **BLOOMS** in spring

A distinctive and very ornamental plant with low arching stems and flowers. The blossoms are large and a lovely, soft white and the leaves are stiff and gray-green. Needs a well-drained soil and full sun to thrive.

Baptisia leucantha
(Prairie False Indigo)

ZONES: 4–9; sun, part sun
SOIL: moist to dry
NATIVE TO: prairies, dry slopes, and in moist places along streams; Ontario to Minnesota and Nebraska south to Texas and Mississippi
SIZE: 3–4 feet (3 feet)
COLOR: white; **BLOOMS** in spring

Prairie False Indigo is a stately plant. Its thick stems hold the plant stiffly upright through the season, making it one of the best for underplanting. Think of it as a larger, more upright *B. alba*. In the tall-grass prairies, this false indigo towers over its companions like the emergent trees of the rain forest canopy. Also listed as *B. lactea* and *B. alba* var. *macrophylla*.

Baptisia perfoliata
(Eucalypt Wild Indigo)

ZONES: 7–9; sun, part sun
SOIL: moist, well drained
NATIVE TO: sandhills and open woods along the coastal plain; South Carolina to Florida
SIZE: 2–3 feet (2 feet)
COLOR: bright yellow; **BLOOMS** in spring

The distinctive, stiff, glaucous leaves are perfoliate, closely resembling the juvenile foliage of the Bluegum Eucalyptus used in flower arrangements. A valuable species for foliage effect, but the small flowers are ornamental as well. *B. arachnifera*, an endangered species from a few counties in southeast Georgia, is a fascinating plant. It is much like *B. perfoliata*, but the leaves are covered with flattened gray fur. Neither grows quickly, so keep them free of competition for a few years until established.

Baptisia sphaerocarpa (syn. *B. viridis*)
(Yellow Wild Indigo)

ZONES: 5–9; sun
SOIL: moist to dry
NATIVE TO: prairies and roadsides; Missouri to Oklahoma south to Texas and Louisiana
SIZE: 2–3 feet (3 feet)
COLOR: bright yellow; **BLOOMS** in spring

Probably the loveliest yellow-flowered species. The blooms are large and hold up well above the foliage. It can be distinguished from other taller species by the uppermost leaves, which are single rather than 3-parted. The round, marble-sized pods are also easy to recognize.

Baptisia tinctoria
(Wild Indigo, Yellow Wild Indigo)

ZONES: 3–9; sun, part sun
SOIL: moist to dry
NATIVE TO: poor soils—open woods, fields, clearings; Maine to Michigan south to Tennessee and Georgia
SIZE: 2–3 feet (2–3 feet)
COLOR: yellow; **BLOOMS** in summer

A dye made from the plant was used as an inferior substitute for true indigo, obtained from *Indigofera*, a tropical shrub. Not as showy in flower as many of the others, but its late bloom and rock-hard disposition make it valuable for tough situations. I have even seen it thriving in cracks of shear rock faces.

Boltonia asteroides

Boltonia (bolt-OWN-ee-ah)
Asteraceae
False Aster

You have to meet some plants in "person" to really appreciate them—descriptions will not do them justice. False Aster is one of those plants. Even the name connotes something inferior or second-rate. I would like to name them something like Clouds of Joy instead, because a grouping of the blue-gray *B. asteroides* covered with white, yellow-centered daisies will bring a smile to your lips and a song to your heart. There are several species, all from the eastern United States, but this is the one most frequently grown, and for good reason. Even though it inhabits wet meadows and swamps in the wild, False Aster is rugged and adaptable, tolerating a range of soils and moisture conditions. It is a perfect companion to true asters, goldenrods, grasses, and other staples of the fall perennial garden. Virtually all the plants of the typical variety available in the trade are the cultivar 'Snowbank', which was introduced by the New England Wild Flower Society for its more compact habit, reducing the need for staking.

CULTURE: False Aster is easily accommodated in the perennial garden. It will grow in heavy clay or sandy soils and tolerates wet as well as moderately dry conditions. The plants grow from a slowly expanding rhizome, which makes division in spring an easy task. Like the true asters, they benefit from division every three to five years to keep the clumps full and robust. Even the cultivar 'Snowbank' will flop in shade or rich, wet soils, but it can be pinched back in early June if this is a problem.

USES: Effective massed as background plants for the perennial garden or naturalized in the meadow.

PROPAGATION: Easy from viable seed and from cuttings. See p. 247.

Boltonia asteroides
(False Aster)

ZONES: 4–9; sun, part sun
SOIL: wet to dry
NATIVE TO: wet prairies, marshes, and meadows; New Jersey to North Dakota south to Texas and Florida
SIZE: 3–4 feet (3 feet)
COLOR: white, occasionally pink; BLOOMS in fall

Boltonia asteroides var. *latisquama* has slightly larger flowers that are more darkly colored than the typical variety. There is a compact form (var. *nana*), but it lacks the vigor of the straight species. *B. caroliniana* is a similar plant from the southeastern coastal plain distinguished by its clumping rather than spreading habit; smaller, more numerous flowers; and greener leaves.

Boltonia decurrens
(Decurrent False Aster)

ZONES: 4–9; sun, part sun
SOIL: wet to moist
NATIVE TO: wet soils along rivers; Missouri and Illinois
SIZE: 3–6 feet (2–3 feet)

COLOR: white to violet or pink; BLOOMS in fall

This is a tall, wetland species becoming rare in its native haunts. The foliage is medium green, and the leaves have prominent stipular wings ("earlobes") that line the stem. Its size and intolerance of drought make it of more limited use.

Calla palustris

Calla palustris (CAL-la)
Araceae
Water Arum

ZONES: 3–9; part sun to shade
SOIL: wet to flooded
NATIVE TO: bogs, swamps, and pools; New Brunswick to Manitoba south to Iowa, Indiana, and Maryland
SIZE: 12 inches (16–20 inches)
COLOR: white and green; BLOOMS from late spring to early summer

The Water Arum is a widespread but modest relative of the voluptuous, tropical Calla Lily popular with florists. *Calla palustris* is native to bogs and swamps through much of North America and parts of Europe and Asia. The flowers are the familiar shell-like spathe and spadix design of the Arum family. The spathe is glistening, pure white (much like the familiar Peace Lily, *Spathiphyllum,* in size and shape) with a knobby green spadix in its center — it has an unquestionable purity pleasingly at odds with the muck and mire that surrounds it. The flowers appear intermittently among the leaves in late spring

Calla palustris. Water Arum is happiest wading in the muck of vernal pools and swamps, its broad leaves an excellent stage for nightly concerts of peepers and wood frogs. Primeval ooze is a fitting habitat for such a suggestively tropical wildflower as this.

Callirhoe triangulata.
Clustered Poppy-mallow blooms are more open and appear in a more concentrated burst than other members of the genus. Its strong stems remain upright without staking or training, and its deep taproot allows it to survive rain-starved summers.

to early summer—never in large quantities. *Calla* has deep green, 4 × 6-inch, oval leaves with a thick, waxy substance. They grow from a creeping rhizome that lies close to the surface of the mucky soils this species prefers, forming loose, patchy colonies with time. Red berries follow the flowers in cone-shaped clusters, much like the familiar Jack-in-the-pulpit.

CULTURE: Ideally sited in a wet, swampy or boggy location. Often found in vernal pools that flood in spring but dry out on the surface during the summer. It will grow in standing water as well. It is usually found in rather shady spots, but I have found it grows and blooms more robustly with two to four hours of sun. Plants in too much shade get lanky and weak. The jointed rhizomes are often visible at or near the soil surface late in the season. These can be divided and moved easily in early spring or fall. Even older, eyeless rhizomes may rejuvenate after you remove the newer leads.

USES: Not a show-stopper, but the bold foliage and exotic flowers are a nice addition to water gardens, especially where shade is a problem.

PROPAGATION: Moderately difficult from seed and division. See p. 247.

Add to this the key phrases "long-blooming" and "drought-tolerant" and, why, it's irresistible (unless of course you hate magenta, but then we can find you one in soft rose or white). The downside to this sort of point-of-purchase description is that it leaves out a few important details, namely that the plants are—how can I put this nicely—rather informal growers. The lax stems and widely spaced leaves are designed to trail vinelike over the ground or form loose, bushy clumps that can lean on stouter neighbors when gravity overcomes them. While this is not necessarily a drawback, it does demand that you carefully consider how to place *Callirhoes* to advantage. Merely plunking one or two in the perennial border will not create much of an impression, but a full-blooming *C. involucrata* left to trail over a wall or rocks in a hot, sunny location is a beautiful sight. Poppy-mallows are in the Mallow family and have the same sort of flower as the familiar tropical hibiscus—a collar of bright yellow anthers beneath a star-shaped cluster of stigmas sitting in the center of 5 overlapping petals.

CULTURE: Easily grown in well-drained soils and full sun. The plants produce deep taproots and are thus very drought-tolerant once established. They are best left undisturbed when older, but self-sown seedlings can be moved with care when young. Japanese Beetles can be a problem. Flowers are continually produced from the tips of the stems, especially if the plants are occasionally deadheaded during the season.

USES: *C. involucrata* is effective cascading over walls, paving stones, and banks. *C. triangulata* is more strongly upright and therefore more suited to borders. The others are effective in the border if staked or caged (perish the thought).

PROPAGATION: Easy from seed. See p. 247.

Callirhoe triangulata

Callirhoe (cal-eh-ROW-ee)
Malvaceae
Poppy-mallow, Wine Cups

When the weather warms in spring and we winter-weary gardeners flock to our local nurseries to pore over the newest crop of promising perennials, there is usually not much to go by but colorful tags and sometimes equally colorful descriptions. In this respect, Wine Cups are a marketer's dream. Imagine this evocative common name paired with a picture of a glowing, 5-petaled, satiny bloom in a clear, vibrant magenta splashed with white in the center that practically screams "here, look at me."

Callirhoe digitata
(Finger Poppy-mallow)

ZONES: 4–9; sun
SOIL: well drained
NATIVE TO: rocky prairies, mainly on limestone; Arkansas to Missouri, Oklahoma and Kansas
SIZE: 3–5 feet (2 feet)
COLOR: deep rose to wine red with white at base; **BLOOMS** in summer

Finger Poppy-mallow can grow quite tall, but the finely dissected, widely spaced foliage gives it a see-through effect. The thin stems tend to lodge as they get taller, but I have seen it effectively contained in a tomato cage. *C. alcaeoides* (Pale Poppy-mallow) has much the same leaf shape, but most of the foliage is basal, with tall flowering stems and clustered flowers much like *Geranium*. It occurs over much the same range as Finger Poppy-mallow.

Callirhoe involucrata
(Purple Poppy-mallow, Wine Cups)

ZONES: 4–9; sun
SOIL: well drained
NATIVE TO: open places, dry prairies; Illinois and southern Minnesota to Wyoming south to New Mexico, Texas, and Arkansas
SIZE: 12–16 inches (3 feet)
COLOR: deep pink to wine red with white at base; **BLOOMS** in summer

Two-inch bowl-shaped flowers stand above the dissected, trailing foliage on long thin stems. New flowers are continually produced as the stems grow through the season.

Callirhoe triangulata
(Clustered Poppy-mallow)

ZONES: 4–9; sun
SOIL: well drained
NATIVE TO: sandy prairies, rocky clearings, commonly on acid soils; Illinois to Wisconsin and Iowa south to Missouri and occasionally to Mississippi, Georgia, and North Carolina
SIZE: 1–3 feet (2 feet)
COLOR: deep wine red with white at base; **BLOOMS** in summer (blooms more heavily but over a shorter period than the others)

Distinct because of its densely hairy, undivided, triangular leaves and stronger, upright stems that do not usually require staking. The flowers appear in one flush from the tips of the stems.

Calopogon tuberosus

Calopogon tuberosus (cal-oh-POE-gone)
Orchidaceae
Grass Pink

ZONES: 3–10; sun, part sun
SOIL: moist to wet, boggy
NATIVE TO: acid swamps, bogs, and wet meadows; Newfoundland to Manitoba south to Texas and Florida
SIZE: 1–2 feet (6 inches)
COLOR: typically bright lavender; **BLOOMS** in summer

The sugary nectar that most insect-pollinated plants offer to their emissaries is not only a reward, it is a distraction, too. Insects busy gathering nectar are less likely to gather valuable pollen as well. Some insects, however (bees, for example), will collect pollen as a protein source for developing young. This has obvious disadvantages for the plant, because pollen that is consumed cannot fertilize ovaries and produce seed. The orchids, which have elevated insect pollination to high art, have come up with a deviously effective way of preventing this thievery. In orchids, the pollen is concealed in 2 waxy sacs, called pollinia, which sit hidden under a special trap-door cap. Insects visiting the flowers trip open this anther cap, exposing the pollinia, which have adhesive discs on them that adhere to the animal's head or abdomen—frustratingly out of reach of hungry jaws. A hapless bee that has visited several flowers begins to look a little ridiculous with pairs of the bright yellow sacs stuck to its head.

Different orchid species have flowers tailored to fit the dimensions of a certain insect, so that the pollen can be applied in a good spot and successfully transferred to another flower. The Grass Pink is particularly clever in this regard. All orchid flowers are composed of 3 sepals and 3 petals. One of the petals has been modified into what is called a lip, usually colorfully marked and shaped to provide a place for the pollinator to land. Because the lip develops from the upper petal, these "landing pad" types must twist

180 degrees as they develop (a process called resupination) so that the lip faces down. In the non-resupinate Grass Pink, however, the lip is not a landing pad. Its base is ringed in a beard of yellow-tipped hairs made to resemble the anthers of a conventional flower. The column on which the pollen sits hidden faces down and is tipped with a flat landing surface instead. As the insect lands, fooled by the faux anthers, the pollen is unceremoniously glued to its rear end. The insect receives nothing more for its trouble than this small humiliation.

Calopogon tuberosus. *In the wild, Grass Pink grows typically as scattered individuals or in loose colonies in open, boggy ground. This particular bog is beginning to fill in with woody shrubs such as Labrador Tea* (Ledum groenlandicum), *Field Juniper* (Juniperus communis), *and Leatherleaf* (Chamaedaphne calyculata), *so the orchids will soon be forced out. The beard of false anthers designed to fool pollinators can be easily seen jutting out from the lip at the top of the flower.*

Caltha palustris. Stumbling upon a large patch of Marsh Marigold in full bloom is a real treat for the winter weary. Like many spring ephemerals, Caltha takes advantage of the window in early spring when the ground thaws but the tree canopy has not leafed out. Though in nearly full sun now, in six weeks this colony will be plunged into heavy shade—a signal that it is time to retreat underground until next year.

The Grass Pink is a striking orchid of wet meadows and bogs. A single irislike leaf gives rise in summer to 2–6 of the lovely flowers on a wiry stem. The plants usually go unnoticed among the grasses and sedges until they bloom, so it is quite startling to come upon a colony of the flowers in what had only a week previously looked like merely a patch of grass.

I hesitated to include this wonderful plant here because I do not want to encourage its wild collection, but as with many of our native orchids, recent advances in propagation are making nursery-grown plants increasingly available.

CULTURE: Grass Pinks are easily accommodated in wet, sunny meadows or bog gardens. The plants grow from a small corm that can be moved easily when the plants are dormant. Plant the corm 2 inches below the surface. They seem to tolerate competition from neighboring plants fairly well, but if given a little room and dilute fertilizer, they will double in size and number of flowers. They do not appear to be too fussy about soil type, provided it remains moist to wet through the year. In sphagnum bogs, the corms grow in the light layer of half-dead moss just below the surface. Removing the spent flowers is a good idea, because they put a great deal of energy into forming seeds otherwise.

USES: Best naturalized in a suitable site in the garden.

PROPAGATION: Difficult from seed and division. See p. 247.

Caltha palustris

Caltha (CAL-tha)
Ranunculaceae
Marsh Marigold

The familiar Marsh Marigold delights eyes weary of the drab grays and browns of winter with vibrant golden yellow blooms—a color that seems all too

common by late summer, but in early spring it is a joy to behold. The yellow species is joined in the West by a smaller, white-flowered alpine plant, *C. leptosepala*. The flowers are produced sequentially from a branching stem for about three weeks in spring. Each flower is a skirt of petallike sepals with a soft yellow tuft of stamens in the middle. Because the plants bloom before the trees leaf out, the glowing flowers can be seen from a great distance, even drawing the eye of harried motorists on highways and byways that bisect the plants' swampy homes. The leaves are bold and attractive until the seeds ripen in early to midsummer, when the whole plant yellows and goes dormant for the year.

CULTURE: Easily transplanted in spring. The thick white roots quickly anchor the plants in place, so they can be established beside streams or ponds. They will grow in shallow water as well (less than 4 inches), or anywhere the soils are not droughty—especially in spring. Although they are often found under deciduous trees, they bloom most profusely in full sun.

USES: Excellent beside water, naturalized in wetlands, boggy spots.

PROPAGATION: Moderately difficult from seed. See p. 248.

Caltha leptosepala
(Elkslip)

ZONES: 2–6; sun, part sun
SOIL: moist to wet
NATIVE TO: alpine and subalpine wet meadows and seeps; Montana to Alaska south in the mountains to California and New Mexico
SIZE: 6–14 inches (6–12 inches)
COLOR: white to greenish white, blush pink, or pale blue; **BLOOMS** in spring (snowmelt)

Smaller in all respects than the Marsh Marigold, with narrower, paddle-shaped leaves (plants from the Pacific coastal regions have wider leaves and 2-flowered inflorescences and are sometimes described as *C. biflora*). The many-sepaled, pure white flowers are a lovely sight emerging through lingering snows along high mountain streams in the Rockies. Some plants within a population have sepals colored blue-violet or pink on the reverse, especially as they age, which gives them an icy appearance so fitting to their habitat. Not nearly as adaptable to garden culture as its cousin, because it needs a cool root run to thrive.

Caltha palustris
(Marsh Marigold)

ZONES: 1–8; sun to shade
SOIL: moist to wet (standing water is tolerated in spring)
NATIVE TO: wet woods, swamps, shallow marshes;

Newfoundland to Manitoba, south to North Dakota, Illinois, and North Carolina, then also in the Northwest Territories and Alaska south to British Columbia

SIZE: 1–2 feet (1 foot)

COLOR: golden yellow; **BLOOMS** in early spring

C. palustris is a fine garden plant, growing into large clumps of shiny, rounded leaves finely toothed around their margins like the blade of a carpenter's saw.

Camassia leichtlinii

Camassia (cam-ASS-ee-ah)
Liliaceae
Camas Lily, Camas

Visitors to Garden in the Woods are awed by the stunning spires of rich blue-violet flowers of *C. leichtlinii* ssp. *suksdorfii* growing in large clumps by our pond. Its tepals are thin and set evenly apart to form a 6-pointed star, and each cradles a large golden orange anther that contrasts beautifully with the base color of the flower. The flowers open sequentially up the stalk over a period of ten days, each fading bloom producing a fat, 3-chambered seedpod filled with shiny black seeds about the size of a BB. Because they are slow from seed and offset, they have remained in relative obscurity, at least in much of this country, until recently, when skillful Dutch bulb growers started mass-producing them for sale as fall bulbs. I am very happy to see these beautiful native lilies finally coming into their own as garden plants par excellence.

The western camas were an important food source for Native Americans until Europeans introduced hogs (which relish the bulbs) and converted much of the rich grassland where they grow to agriculture. The sweet bulbs can be eaten raw and are an excellent source of starch when slow-cooked, with a creamy texture and a taste described like that of a chestnut. They begin growing with abandon as soon as the weather moderates in spring, putting up whorls of strap-shaped leaves with a flower spike emerging from the center when the leaves are two-thirds expanded. After flowering, the leaves remain green until the seed is mature, then they go dormant for the year.

CULTURE: *Camassia*s grow from a squat bulb that is much like a tulip bulb in size and shape. They are best purchased as dormant bulbs in the fall and planted immediately so that their roots can get established before winter (plant them four times as deep as the bulbs are tall). A site that is moist to wet in spring but dries somewhat in summer is ideal. I have read that wet soils in winter are a problem, but our plants are nearly submerged just about every year without any apparent problems.

USES: Accent near water, naturalizing for the smaller species. Because they are summer-dormant, *Camassia*s need to be grouped with other plants for best effect. Royal fern, *Osmunda regalis*, is a particularly effective companion. Plant bulbs of the smaller species in groups of 5–7 as they can get lost as individuals.

PROPAGATION: Difficult from seed; moderately difficult from division. See p. 248.

Camassia cusickii
(Cusick's Camas)

ZONES: 5–8; sun, part sun

SOIL: moist (wet in spring)

NATIVE TO: moist slopes along mountain rivers; Oregon

SIZE: 2–3 feet (16 inches)

COLOR: pale blue; **BLOOMS** in spring (a week later than *C. leichtlinii*)

The largest species, forming thick clumps of wide, straplike basal leaves and dense racemes of 1½-inch flowers. It produces offsets more quickly than most of the others, and for this reason I suspect that some plants sold in the trade as *C. leichtlinii* are actually this species.

Camassia leichtlinii
(Leichtlin's Camas)

ZONES: 4–8; sun, part sun

SOIL: moist in spring

NATIVE TO: meadows and prairies with spring moisture; British Columbia south to the California Sierras

Camassia leichtlinii. The refined beauty of Leichtlin's Camas speaks for itself. Pictured is the subspecies suksdorfii, *a large dark-flowered form that is particularly desirable for gardens.*

Campanula rotundifolia. *The irrepressible Harebell seems to be nearly always in bloom in our gardens. While individual plants go through periods of blooming followed by seed set, a brief rest, then repeat bloom, there are enough self-sown plants about that it is always possible to find one in flower — be it spring, summer, or fall.*

SIZE: 24–30 inches (12 inches)

COLOR: pale to dark violet-blue; **BLOOMS** in spring

The large dark flowers of the subspecies *suksdorfii* are particularly lovely. A fine garden plant similar in size to Cusick's Camas but tending to remain as single plants or small clumps.

Camassia quamash

(Common Camas)

ZONES: 4–8; sun, part sun

SOIL: moist to wet in spring

NATIVE TO: meadows, open areas with spring moisture; Montana to British Columbia south to California and Utah

SIZE: 12–18 inches (8 inches)

COLOR: pale to dark violet-blue; **BLOOMS** in spring (about a week later than *C. leichtlinii*)

Smaller in all respects than *C. leichtlinii*, with narrower leaves. This was the primary species gathered for food by Native Americans and later by European settlers, and the most widespread in the West. Quamash or Camas are the Native American names for the plants. There are a number of named varieties, including a larger form with blue anthers called var. *utahensis* and a dark violet phase with large flowers called var. *maxima*.

Camassia scilloides (syn. *esculenta, angustata*)

(Wild Hyacinth)

ZONES: 3–9; sun, part sun

SOIL: moist

NATIVE TO: meadows, prairies, and open woods; Pennsylvania to Ontario and Wisconsin south to Texas and Georgia

SIZE: 12–16 inches (6–8 inches)

COLOR: pale blue-violet or white; **BLOOMS** in spring

The only eastern species and one of the smallest. It does not have the garden presence of *C. cusickii* or *leichtlinii*, but its loose racemes of thin-tepaled flowers and agreeable nature make it a good choice for naturalizing. Plants of Common Camas are sometimes listed as *C. esculenta*, but this is correctly a synonym for Wild Hyacinth.

Campanula rotundifolia

Campanula

(cam-PAN-yule-ah)

Campanulaceae

Harebell

There are few people who can resist the quiet charms of the little harebells. There are hundreds of species in Europe and Asia, with a few that inhabit rocky and mountainous country in North America. Some of our native *Campanula*s are excellent choices for the rock garden, while others are too refractory for any but the specialist to experiment with. All have flowers in the blue-violet range, typically bell-shaped in form, but some of the western species have open, star-shaped blooms. They have tiny seeds (up to 1 million per ounce) and will self-sow when content with their surroundings, moving here and there from year to year as microclimates in the garden change. The widespread *C. rotundifolia* is especially long-blooming, often, I fear, overextending itself at the expense of a long life. Fortunately, even though an individual plant may last only a few seasons, new seedlings will constantly spring up to replace it. This sort of migratory nature is perfect for those with a naturalistic gardening bent, but if you like plants with a sense of constancy, harebells may be subtly disconcerting.

The related *Campanulastrum americanum* (Tall Bellflower) is a biennial from moist meadows and woodlands in east-central North America. The first year it remains a tight rosette of triangular leaves that bolts the following spring to form tall stems somewhat like *Lobelia*. One-inch, flared, blue-violet flowers are produced in small clusters from the upper leaf axils for four to six weeks in summer. They are a good choice for naturalizing among plants like *Aster cordifolius* in part sun or light shade.

CULTURE: The strictly alpine western species are best accommodated in rock garden screes. The more adaptable *C. rotundifolia* and the eastern *C. divaricata* will adapt well to a variety of garden conditions. Most of the species covered here grow from a central woody crown, which makes division risky. Instead, collect the seed and disperse it where you want to establish new plants. If sited properly, they require little if any maintenance.

USES: Rock gardens, naturalizing.

PROPAGATION: Easy from seed. See p. 248.

Campanula divaricata
(Southern Harebell)

ZONES: 4–9; sun to light shade
SOIL: moist to dry
NATIVE TO: clearings and rocky woods, mostly in Appalachian Mountains; Maryland to Kentucky south to Alabama and Georgia
SIZE: 10–16 inches (1 foot)
COLOR: blue-violet; BLOOMS from late summer to fall

An enchanting plant, producing a haze of ¼-inch bell-shaped flowers on thin stems late in the season. I will always remember first seeing drifts of these harebells blooming in perfect scale with *Sedum telephioides* in a rocky pasture in the Blue Ridge Mountains. Narrow, toothed leaves alternate up stiff stems that originate from a narrow base.

Campanula lasiocarpa
(Alaskan Harebell)

ZONES: 3–7; sun, part sun
SOIL: moist, well drained
NATIVE TO: gravelly alpine slopes; Alaska
SIZE: 3–6 inches (6–8 inches)
COLOR: blue; BLOOMS in summer

Long-blooming, tufted plants make a neat cushion of narrow leaves. Best in a scree soil protected from summer heat. For the specialist outside of its native range.

Campanula parryi
(Parry's Harebell)

ZONES: 3–7; sun, part sun
SOIL: moist, well drained
NATIVE TO: alpine, rocky slopes and crevices; Wyoming and Utah to Arizona and New Mexico
SIZE: 12 inches (8 inches)
COLOR: blue-violet; BLOOMS in summer

Similar to *C. rotundifolia,* but with typically darker flowers that face upward rather than nod. A plant for the scree garden.

Campanula rotundifolia
(Harebell)

ZONES: 3–8; sun to light shade
SOIL: moist to dry
NATIVE TO: rocky places, crevices, sandy shores, mostly in the mountains; Newfoundland to British Columbia south to Mexico, Indiana, and New Jersey
SIZE: 8–14 inches (8 inches)
COLOR: blue-violet; BLOOMS from summer to fall

C. rotundifolia winters as a rosette of small round leaves that send up wiry flowering stems with long narrow foliage that look like they belong to something else. Bell-shaped flowers are ½-inch long. Tends to bloom in spurts over the season and is an easy plant for the garden. Most of the plants in the trade are selections of European forms of the species with larger or darker flowers.

Castilleja integra

Castilleja (cast-ill-AY-ah)
Scrophularaceae
Paintbrush, Painted Cup

No one who has seen paintbrush in the wild can easily forget the sublime sunset hues of their intricate flowers. The colorful bracts that surround the blooms mirror the rocks and sky of desert and mountain so perfectly that their photographs are in practically every wildflower calendar and book. There are at least 150 species in western North America, so widespread and common that they are practically synonymous with the West, but few are grown in gardens. Why? Like many in the Figwort family, paintbrushes are hemiparasites, that is their roots attach themselves to the root systems of other plants with specialized structures, called haustoria, that divert water and possibly nutrients and carbohydrates from the host plant. They come in many shades of red and orange (these are hummingbird-pollinated), as well as yellow and green. The flower bracts and at least the upper leaves of many species have a distinctive bird's-foot shape that makes them easy to recognize even out of flower. Except for color, there is usually no clear demarcation between the leaves and floral bracts, so it is easy to imagine them simply with their tops dipped in paint. (It is the bracts that are the colorful part of the inflorescence; the flowers themselves are small and cream or green —for this reason, the blooms remain colorful for long periods.) The plants hybridize freely, and many intermediate polyploid forms exist that often make exact identification difficult.

Castilleja integra. *This paintbrush has been one of the easiest ones for me to cultivate, so though it is still a bit of a challenge, you'll be well rewarded for attempting to grow it.*

CULTURE: This unusual adaptation raises several hurdles for the horticulturist. Aside from the obvious psychological aversion that we humans have to the term *parasite,* there is the problem of finding and cultivating a suitable host plant for the paintbrush to grow with. Regarding the first, one must dispel any nightmarish images of paintbrushes run amuck, draining the life's blood from your garden like a thirsty vampire. Available evidence suggests that the amount of damage to host plants is slight and really only a possible problem in marginal conditions. Its seems that *Castilleja* relies on a host primarily to aid water uptake (much the same as many plants rely on mycorrhizal fungi for nutrient absorption). As for host specificity, there has been some research, but most information is merely speculation based on sympatric plants. Suggested hosts include *Penstemon*s, *Eriogonum*s, and native bunch grasses including Little Bluestem *(Schizacyrium scoparium).* It is not clear just how important host plants are for the paintbrushes under cultivation. I have grown and flowered both eastern and western species in containers without any host species, but less successfully in the garden. Take *C. chromosa,* for example. Seedlings of this and most of the species germinate readily after three months of stratification. A 4-inch pot of seedlings will begin to thin out after a few weeks, but if kept evenly watered and fertilized, 10–20 percent will survive and become 2–3-inch plants the first season. If left in the containers the following spring, the plants will grow and some will bloom, but generally they'll appear stunted and go dormant quickly. I have had excellent results transplanting the one-year plants into a mixed trough containing a gritty soil and plants such as *Penstemon, Sisyrinchium, Eriogonum,* and *Draba* (all genera that grow in the same areas as *Castilleja).* Whether it is the fresh soil and more even moisture in the troughs or parasitism is hard to say, but the trough plants grow and flower much more robustly. Year-old plants interplanted with similar species in the scree garden grew for a time but then died, which leads me to suspect that they are very sensitive to drought before they are established, and need careful watering the first season after transplanting. Of course, if you have access to a good amount of local seed, scattering it around in the rock garden may produce good results in time.

The perennial species grow from a woody crown that puts up one to many leafy flowering stems topped with the showy inflorescence. The plants go dormant quickly after flowering, dying back to small leafy buds at or below the soil surface.

USES: Striking plants for naturalizing where they are native. More research needs to be done on their complex biology.

WILDLIFE: Paintbrushes are larval food plants for a number of checkerspot butterflies (*Chlosyne* and *Euphydryas* spp.) and are excellent nectar plants for adult insects and hummingbirds.

PROPAGATION: Difficult from seed. See p. 248.

Castilleja chromosa
(Desert Paintbrush)

ZONES: 4–9; sun
SOIL: dry, well drained
NATIVE TO: sagebrush desert and open, pinyon-juniper woodland; Wyoming to Oregon south to California and New Mexico
SIZE: 4–8 inches (8 inches)
COLOR: crimson to scarlet red; **BLOOMS** in summer

A widespread and somewhat variable species, associated with and maybe dependent on Sagebrush (*Artemesia tridentata*). It is a consummate paintbrush, with compact habit and dense, large-bracted heads. Desert Paintbrush is good species to try in dryland gardens.

Castilleja coccinea
(Painted Cup)

ZONES: 4–9; sun, part sun
SOIL: moist
NATIVE TO: damp meadows and prairies; Massachusetts to Manitoba south to Oklahoma and South Carolina
SIZE: 1–2 feet (4–6 inches)
COLOR: scarlet with yellow and white; **BLOOMS** in summer

Biennial. The first year the plants form small flattened rosettes of rounded leaves that bolt the following year. Leaves along the flowering stem have the characteristic bird's-foot shape. A striking plant to find in the wild, but difficult to establish permanently in cultivation. Some success may be had sowing seed directly in a moist meadow where competition is not too thick. One of only three eastern species. *C. sessiliflora* is a plains species that gets as far east as Illinois. It is not as showy in flower, with yellow-green bracts tinged pink and gray-green and narrow leaves, but it is a perennial species that is easier to grow under average garden conditions.

Castilleja flava
(Yellow Paintbrush)

ZONES: 3–9; sun
SOIL: dry, well drained
NATIVE TO: sagebrush and dry, lower montane slopes; Montana to Oregon south to northern Utah and Colorado
SIZE: 4–16 inches (6–8 inches)
COLOR: yellow; **BLOOMS** in summer

One of a number of yellow-flowered species. The inflorescence is typically branched, open, and set above long thin leaves, the upper ones 3-forked. It is a tetraploid species, suggesting a hybrid origins.

Castilleja integra
(Paintbrush)

ZONES: 4–8; sun, part sun
SOIL: well drained
NATIVE TO: dry plains and open mountain woodland, at moderate elevations; Colorado to Arizona south to Mexico and Texas
SIZE: 3–8 inches (6 inches)
COLOR: red-orange; **BLOOMS** in summer

A close, perennial relative of *C. coccinea*, with undivided leaves; rounded, barely 3-lobed bracts; and bright but few-flowered racemes. Another good species to start with.

Castilleja miniata
(Great Red Paintbrush)

ZONES: 3–8; sun, part sun
SOIL: moist
NATIVE TO: moist timberline meadows, slopes, and streams, mostly in the mountains; North Dakota to Alaska south to California and New Mexico
SIZE: 1–2½ feet (8–12 inches)
COLOR: red-orange; **BLOOMS** in summer

The most widespread paintbrush, seen commonly in moist places in the Cascade and Rocky Mountains. The plants can be quite tall, with long branched inflorescences with sharply pointed bracts and undivided, typically shiny green leaves. Fairly adaptable to cultivation if drought can be avoided. Rhexia-leaved Paintbrush (*C. rhexifolia*) is a somewhat shorter relative common at higher elevations of the western mountains with bracts ranging from scarlet to crimson, purple, and rose. The sympatric yellow-flowered *C. sulphurea* is indistinguishable from it when not in bloom but prefers more exposed sites. It has unlobed bracts.

Blue **Cohosh** emerges like some subterranean forest spirit stretching its arms in the warmth of the spring sun. The new growth is stained an extraordinary violet-gray—at first with compound leaves tightly curled as they are forced through the soil and then gradually lengthening and unfurling on sinuous stems. As the leaves fully expand, they fade to a less radical blue-green shade, setting the stage for the starry flowers that are borne in short clusters where the leaflets join the stem. Marble-sized seeds follow in summer—at first waxy green, then turning a deep blue-black when ripe. The foliage effect is akin to a giant columbine and lends an airy touch to woodland plantings, but I would grow it for the emerging leaves alone, so striking is their color. Cohosh is a Native American word for the plant, which was an important medicinal used to treat a wide variety of problems, especially those surrounding pregnancy and childbirth (another common name is Papooseroot, a reference to its use in inducing labor). Some authors segregate *C. giganteum* as a separate species. It has larger leaves and dark purple flowers and blooms two weeks earlier.

CULTURE: Grow in a rich, woodland soil with adequate moisture through the season. The plants are found abundantly in limestone soils, and although they will grow on acid soils, occasional liming improves overall color and vigor. Division of the woody rootstock is possible in spring or fall, but seldom necessary as the plants are fairly slow-growing and a large clump makes a much better impression.

USES: Background and accent in the shade garden.

PROPAGATION: Moderate to difficult from seed. See p. 248.

Caulophyllum thalictroides. *The violet-gray of Blue Cohosh's emerging foliage fades to a delicate blue-green as the leaves mature and will remain in good condition until after the seeds have turned deep blue-black. Each "fruit" contains only 1 large seed that will lay in the ground two or three years before sprouting as a vigorous seedling. Slow germination has made this plant uncommon in the nursery trade, but you can introduce it into your garden by scratching a few seeds here and there every year.*

Caulophyllum thalictroides

Caulophyllum thalictroides
(call-oh-FILL-um)
Berberidaceae
Blue Cohosh

ZONES: 3–8; shade
SOIL: moist, neutral
NATIVE TO: rich woods; New Brunswick to Ontario and Manitoba south to Missouri and South Carolina
SIZE: 2–3 feet (2 feet)
COLOR: white or ocher, more or less tinged blue or purple; **BLOOMS** in spring

Chamaelirium luteum

Chamaelirium luteum

(cam-eh-LYRE-ee-um)

Liliaceae

Devil's Bit

(ABOVE): Chamaelirium luteum. *Although it is difficult to tell sometimes whether a particular Devil's Bit is male or female, by the crowded inflorescence and lack of telltale yellow pollen spots, I would guess this is a female. A damp, open location allows the plants to really flourish.*

(RIGHT): Chelone lyonii. *It is clear how Turtleheads get their name, as the blooms do resemble the shell of a turtle hinged open, a timid yellow head just poking out. Frankly, the shape more readily suggests the head of a fish to me, though as a common name, Bass Mouth just doesn't have the same charm.*

ZONES: 4–9; sun to light shade

SOIL: moist to wet

NATIVE TO: moist woodland and bogs; Massachusetts to southern Ontario and Illinois south to Indiana, Arkansas, Louisiana, and Georgia

SIZE: 8–14 inches (6 inches)

COLOR: white; **BLOOMS** in early summer

Devil's Bit is a sublime little plant, probably not flashy enough for many gardeners, but really quite lovely in bloom when well grown. In New England it is a rare plant (though more common in the south), and I spent a day last summer with a group of botanists trudging around an old locality in a fruitless attempt to relocate it. (I fear that our two dozen well-meaning but nevertheless destructive boots may well have trodden any plants that were there.) However, in the woods behind my home in the Piedmont of North Carolina, the plants were fairly numerous on damp hillsides, growing with *Hepatica*s and Wild Gingers under oak and Loblolly Pines. Why they are so rare in the north of their range many be due in part to glaciation, but as the plants are dioecious, the romantic in me wonders if they might just have trouble finding the right partner (a dating service for *Chamaelirium*—now there's a novel idea). It was certainly valued by Native Americans for treating female disorders and to prevent miscarriage, but it was not ever collected in quantity like Ginseng or Goldenseal. The thick, dark green, spatulate basal leaves are tenacious, but usually succumb to cold by winter's end. In spring, a new crop unfurls from the short rhizome that looks like a ferruled caterpillar trailing behind the new growth

and roots. The biggest rhizomes produce a flowering stem hung with a few small leaves and crowned with a thin raceme of frilly white flowers. The male plants have longer, looser inflorescences than the females.

CULTURE: Devil's Bit will grow in a moist to wet, organic soil, either in light shade or full sun. It will suffer if the soil is droughty, and the few-rooted plants have a tendency to heave until well established. They need to be free from too much competition.

USES: Most effective massed in the shade or bog garden.

PROPAGATION: Difficult from seed; moderately difficult from division. See p. 249.

Chelone lyonii

Chelone (chee-LOAN-ee)

Scrophulariaceae

Turtlehead

I like to think that the fanciful common name turtlehead leaped from the fertile imagination of some long-forgotten child, who saw in the complex hooded flowers curious little turtles emerging cautiously from their colorful shells. It is not hard for us callous adults to see this clear resemblance in the blooms, which cluster like bunches of grapes late in the season on sessile stems among the topmost leaves. The plants spread by means of strong rhizomes that are not really invasive, but do allow them to compete well in the crowded, wet, open habitats that are so popular with many wildflowers.

Turtleheads, especially *C. lyonii,* are excellent garden perennials for a damp location. They form dense colonies of upright stems clothed in pairs of oval or lance-shaped, pointed leaves. The distinctive flowers appear in tight clusters on the tops of the plants late in the season. They are not seriously troubled by any pests or diseases, though rusts may spot some of the leaves in spring.

CULTURE: Although turtleheads are found in wet locations in the wild, they adapt well to average garden soils as long as drought can be avoided. They divide and transplant readily, and once established are virtually trouble free.

USES: Borders, wet meadows, beside water. Valuable plants for late-season color. The showy blooms are effective for several weeks and the strong stems and foliage are a good filler in the border. *Physostegia* and *Lobelia*s make excellent companions.

WILDLIFE: Nectar plants. White Turtlehead is one of two larval food plants for the lovely orange and brown Baltimore Checkerspot, *Euphydryas phaeton,* (the other is the native Honeysuckle, *Lonicera ciliata*). The black caterpillars are striped with orange and armed with fierce-looking black tubercles along the back.

PROPAGATION: Easy from seed or cuttings. See p. 249.

Chelone glabra

(White Turtlehead)

ZONES: 3–9; sun, part sun
SOIL: moist to wet
NATIVE TO: wet woods, swamps, and shores; Newfoundland to Minnesota south to Alabama and Georgia
SIZE: 3 feet (2 feet)
COLOR: white; **BLOOMS** from late summer to fall

The leaves of this species are narrowly lanceolate, making it readily identifiable out of flower. It has wide-ranging rhizomes, so it is difficult to maintain in neat clumps; it is less frustrating to let it naturalize among its companions.

Chelone lyonii

(Pink Turtlehead)

ZONES: 4–9; sun, part sun
SOIL: moist to wet
NATIVE TO: swamps and shores; mostly southern Appalachian, Virginia to North Carolina and Georgia
SIZE: 2½–3 feet (2 feet)
COLOR: rose pink; **BLOOMS** from late summer to fall

Of the two, Pink Turtlehead is a better garden plant overall, as it has broader, more lustrous foliage, denser inflorescense, and a more tightly clumping habit. There are two other species sometimes available: *C. cuthbertii* and *C. obliqua,* which differ from Pink Turtlehead in their narrower leaves closer in shape to *C. glabra.*

Chimaphila umbellata

Chimaphila

(kime-AH-phil-ah)
Pyroliaceae
Spotted Wintergreen, Pippsissewa

*C*himaphilas are distant relatives of the rhododendrons, and they share with their cousins a love of poor, acid soils and moist climates. They are diminutive evergreen plants with inquisitive underground stems that creep through the forest litter looking for gaps of light. Under the best conditions they can form a continuous ground cover, but more often they are found in scattered patches or loose colonies. Each flowering stem is composed of 3–8 thick, leathery, whorled leaflets gathered near the top and 1–5 intricate flowers on a stiff pedicel just above them. The flowers are one of those delicate jewels that you need to get down on your hands and knees to really appreciate. The 5 waxy petals appear as if carved from fine alabaster, with a ring of yellow or purple stamens pressed flat against them.

*Chimaphila*s appear to rely heavily on symbiotic, mycorrhizal fungi to help them gather water and nutrients in the poor soils they inhabit. Probably because of this, they are difficult to establish in areas where they do not normally grow. *Pyrola* (Shinleaf) is a related genus. Its culture and propagation are the same as for *Chimaphila.*

Chimaphila umbellata. *When you examine it closely, Pippsissewa's alabaster petals conceal a striking upside down green volcano (a.k.a. the stigma) ringed by an ocean of mauve. In western populations, the mauve often turns to a royal purple that stains the anthers and suffuses the petals.*

Chrysogonum virgini-
anum. The endearingly
disheveled blooms of
Gold-star begin to open
when still tightly tucked
among the expanding
rosettes in midspring.
Eventually the flower
stems stretch and erect
themselves well above
the leaves, but it is the
first precocious, stemless
daisies arrayed so opti-
mistically in the leaves
that I find irresistibly
cute.

CULTURE: *Chimaphila*s are best naturalized in dry, acid woodlands. They can be transplanted from containers in spring. A light topdressing of a granular, organic fertilizer early in the year will encourage thick growth and heavier flowering. They are gregarious little plants, and I have found that whenever they are naturally occurring on a site, they will gravitate toward cultivated areas in an innocuous way. Small sods will transplant if moved carefully in spring.

USES: Naturalizing in woodland/shade garden. Best interplanted with other ground covers. Good companions for *Gaultheria procumbens, Mitchella repens, Coptis* spp., and *Linnaea borealis.*

PROPAGATION: Difficult from seed; moderately difficult from cuttings. See p. 249.

Chimaphila maculata
(Spotted Wintergreen, Pipsissewa)

ZONES: 3–8; part sun, shade
SOIL: dry, acid
NATIVE TO: dry, acid woods, especially sandy soils; Maine to Michigan south to Alabama and Georgia
SIZE: 2–6 inches (12–16 inches)
COLOR: opaque white, sometimes with a pink tinge; **BLOOMS** in summer

This more southerly species has very pretty leaves that grow in whorls of 3–7 on short stems. The base color is a dark gray-green with hints of burgundy and there is a jagged, irregular patch of silver in the center of each, especially along the midvein.

Chimaphila umbellata
(Prince's Pine, Pipsissewa)

ZONES: 2–8; part sun, shade
SOIL: moist to dry, acid
NATIVE TO: dry to moist, acid woods, especially sandy soils, circumboreal; in North America from Nova Scotia to British Columbia south to California, Colorado, and Virginia
SIZE: 3–6 inches (12–16 inches)
COLOR: opaque white tinged burgundy; **BLOOMS** in summer

Pipsissewa has lustrous, shiny, deep green leaves that are finely toothed along the margins so as to appear spiny like an evergreen holly. Overall it is larger than the former species and can make an effective evergreen ground cover in the right situation. It also seems more adaptable to various soil conditions, growing in moist as well as dry soils.

Chrysogonum virginianum

Chrysogonum virginianum
(cry-SOG-on-um)
Asteraceae
Gold-star, Golden Star

ZONES: (4) 5–9; part sun to shade
SOIL: moist to dry
NATIVE TO: woodlands; Pennsylvania to Ohio south to Mississippi and Florida
SIZE: 6–12 inches (12–18 inches)
COLOR: golden yellow; **BLOOMS** in spring through early summer

There is something very endearing about Gold-star. Maybe it is the uneven size and arrangement of the ray petals that give it an unpretentious look, appearing a bit like they were drawn by the crayons of a child. It is certainly one of the most reliable and longest blooming native ground covers for shady spots. The flowers begin to appear among the leaves in midspring. At first they almost cover the plants, but as spring grows into summer, they appear more sporadically amidst a carpet of leaves. After flowering has peaked, the plants send out dozens of new shoots that run along the ground a few inches before taking root. In mild winters, the rough, hairy leaves are semievergreen, but die back to the ground in very cold weather.

There is some horticultural confusion regarding the two varieties of Gold-star. Var. *virginianum* has the wider distribution, a denser habit, and stems that spread underground (rhizomes). The flowering stems on this variety can become quite tall and branched as the season progresses, but the size of both the leaves and flowering stems is variable. Most of the plants available in the trade are this type. *C. virginianum* var. *australe* sends out long, above-ground stolons that form new rosettes at their tips, like a strawberry plant. Flowering stems are shorter. This is a more southern and coastal plant that is less winter-hardy north of its range.

CULTURE: *Chrysogonum* is adaptable to various soil types and responds very well to regular fertilization. While it will grow fairly well in dry shade, it is denser in both foliage and flower in partial sun and moist soil. Divide clumps every five years in early spring to keep the patch dense and vigorous.

USES: Ground cover, bank stabilization.

PROPAGATION: Easy from seed, cuttings, and division. See p. 249.

Chrysopsis falcata

Chrysopsis (cry-SOP-siss)
Asteraceae
Golden Aster

Chrysopsis are a group of drought-tolerant, mostly mounding plants in the Aster family that, admittedly, I used to dismiss as just another yellow daisy. However, they have grown on me (figuratively speaking) because of their toughness, neat habit and foliage, and cheerful blooms. Golden Asters are clumping to slowly spreading, taprooted plants found in dry soils. They need little care once established and are moderately long-lived.

CULTURE: Transplant as container-grown seed-

lings into well-drained soil and sun. They will usually self-sow where happy.

USES: Rock garden, xeriscaping, borders.

PROPAGATION: Easy from seed. See p. 249.

Chrysopsis (Pityopsis) falcata
(Sickle-leaved Golden Aster)

ZONES: 5–9; sun
SOIL: sandy, dry
NATIVE TO: sandy areas, dunes; coastal Massachusetts to New Jersey
SIZE: 4–8 inches (10–12 inches)
COLOR: yellow; **BLOOMS** in mid- to late summer

Sickle-leaved Golden Aster is endemic to the northern Atlantic coastal plain, where it grows abundantly as a low, mounded, silver-haired plant with long thin leaves. One-inch golden flowers decorate the plants late in the season. Quite attractive for foliage effect because the leaves interlock like three-dimensional lace.

Chrysopsis mariana
(Shaggy Golden Aster, Maryland Golden Aster, Broad-leaved Golden Aster)

ZONES: 5–9; sun, part shade
SOIL: well drained
NATIVE TO: sandy woods and barrens; southern Massachusetts to Ohio south to Kentucky and Florida
SIZE: 8–16 inches (12 inches)

(LEFT): Chrysopsis falcata. *Sickle-leaved Golden Aster is considered a rare plant, but in its habitat—sandy pine barrens of the northern Atlantic coastal plain— it is abundant. The problem is finding enough suitable places to grow, since the northern coastal plain is under great development pressure. Every year more and more sand plain grassland is converted to lawn and asphalt. While this* Chrysopsis *cannot survive in a manicured lawn, it thrives in a rough, low meadow so appropriate for the sandy soils of the coast.*

(RIGHT): Chrysopsis mariana. *In this photograph it is easy to make out the thin covering of gray hair that covers the leaves of Golden Aster. The rich yellow blooms complement fall blooming asters wonderfully.*

Cimicifuga racemosa. *The meandering, serpentine quality of Black Cohosh's impressive spires add a welcome note of drama to the summer woodland. Closely packed blooms are like dance floors for bumblebees, who perform elaborate jigs as they busily gather pollen. The plants take up considerable real estate when mature and will also self-sow if not deadheaded. In smaller gardens, the more diminutive Cimicifuga laciniata or C. rubifolia are better choices.*

COLOR: entirely golden yellow; BLOOMS late summer to early fall

A plant primarily of the coastal plain, *C. mariana* forms thick clumps of narrowly spoon-shaped leaves that are shiny dark green and sparsely covered in long gray hair (like a man in the late stage of baldness). Late in the season leafy stems crowned with branching clusters of golden flowers decorate the plants. It appears shorter-lived than the others, though I do not know if this is a cultural problem or a genetic predisposition. It does self-sow readily, however.

Chrysopsis villosa
(Hairy Golden Aster)

ZONES: 3–9; sun
SOIL: well drained, dry
NATIVE TO: dry, open, rocky or sandy places; Minnesota to British Columbia south to California and Texas
SIZE: 1–3 feet (1–2 feet)
COLOR: yellow; BLOOMS from summer to fall (depending on variety)

A very wide-ranging and variable species. The best for gardens are the smaller forms from the mountain and intermountain West, which form low clumps of stiff, leafy stems with clusters of flowers at the tips. The leaves are more or less silvery gray with undulating margins. We have grown a coarser form that is more likely the related *C. camporum* (Prairie Golden Aster). Reaching 4 feet in height, it blooms in fall and is a slow spreader rather than a clumper. It is becoming a weed in the South.

Cimicifuga racemosa

Cimicifuga
(sim-eh-seh-FUGE-ah)
Ranunculaceae
Bugbane, Black Cohosh

Cimicifuga is a plant whose list of descriptive names reflects a particularly rich history of human use. Snakeroot, Black Cohosh, Bugbane, Fairy Candles, Rattletop—who could ask for more? It's not surprising, though, that nurseries often refer to the plants only as Fairy Candles, as words like bug, black, and snake might frighten some sensitive consumers. (Speaking of names, a recent revision of the genus has lumped it in with *Actaea,* but I will leave them separate for convenience's sake.)

All the snakeroots are excellent foliage and background plants for the shade garden. They do become quite large after a few seasons, with a mound of dense, compound foliage that will crowd even the most stalwart companions if planted too thickly. They are particularly effective at the rear of the shade border, where the fine-textured foliage and soaring flower spikes make the perfect backdrop for ferns and ground covers.

Like *Actaea* (Baneberry) and *Caulophyllum* (Blue Cohosh), the pinnately compound leaves arise from a thick central crown. The wandlike flower spikes emerge late in the season and continually reorient to the vertical as they grow, giving them a vaguely serpentine quality. The flowers are mainly clusters of stamens that develop like rows of beads along the top foot or so of stem and open from the bottom up in little pyrotechnic bursts of white and gold. The flowers are excellent pollen and nectar sources and are always abuzz with all kinds of pollinators.

CULTURE: Bugbanes transplant easily into moist, slightly acid, well-drained soils. They will grow in sun provided the soil never dries excessively, but are more drought-tolerant in shade. The flowers may abort if the plants get too dry. They are long-lived, dense-rooted plants that can be divided in spring, though this is seldom necessary. *C. racemosa* is particularly promiscuous, and we routinely deadhead most of our plants to prevent unwanted seeding. Leaf-spotting is sometimes a problem in humid weather, so try to avoid watering in the evening. Like many of the Ranunculaceae, limestone is appreciated but not strictly necessary unless the plants appear pale green in color. Even *C. rubifolia,* which is a limestone endemic, grows well in soils with a pH of 5.0–5.5.

USES: Borders, screening, background, massing. The plants bloom in the summer and fall, and so are valuable for late-season flower effect in the shade garden.

WILDLIFE: *Cimicifuga racemosa, C. elata*, and *C. laciniata* are great for providing nectar during the summer lull.

PROPAGATION: Moderately difficult from seed. See p. 249.

Cimicifuga americana
(American Bugbane)

ZONES: 4–8; part sun to shade
SOIL: moist
NATIVE TO: moist, wooded coves in the southern Appalachians; southwestern Pennsylvania to northern Georgia and Tennessee with an outly-ing population in northern Illinois
SIZE: 3–4 feet (3 feet)
COLOR: white; **BLOOMS** in fall

American Bugbane is like a fine-leaved Black Cohosh, but it is valuable in the garden as it blooms much later and lacks the pungent aroma when in flower. Because of its late bloom, I get viable seed only one year out of five when we have a particularly long, mild fall. This is a problem we encounter with many late-blooming southern plants in the North.

Cimicifuga elata
(Tall Bugbane)

ZONES: 6–8; part sun to shade
SOIL: moist
NATIVE TO: rich, open to dense coniferous forests; Oregon and Washington to extreme southern British Columbia
SIZE: 3–5 feet (3 feet)
COLOR: white sometimes blushed pink; **BLOOMS** in summer

Tall Bugbane is a robust, early-blooming species with foliage that is divided into a few large leaflets. I was growing a nice specimen for several years but it was "borrowed" and never returned. The plants are restricted to low-elevation temperate rain forest west of the Cascades and are becoming rare because of habitat loss.

Cimicifuga laciniata
(Cut-leaved Bugbane)

ZONES: 5–8; part sun to shade
SOIL: moist
NATIVE TO: rich, open woods, steamsides, margins; northwestern Oregon
SIZE: 3–4 feet (2–3 feet)
COLOR: white; **BLOOMS** in summer

Until recently, this species was known only from Lost Lake on Mount Hood, making it a very rare plant. More populations have now been located, so even though it is restricted in range, it is no longer consid-ered endangered. As a garden plant it has performed well in the Northeast, but I suspect given its prove-nance, it is intolerant of excessive summer heat. Cut-leaved Bugbane is notable for blooming earlier than any of the other species. The heavily lobed and divid-ed foliage is much like that of *C. americana*.

Cimicifuga racemosa
(Black Cohosh)

ZONES: 3–9; part sun to shade
SOIL: moist
NATIVE TO: rich woods; Massachusetts to Indiana south to Missouri and Georgia
SIZE: 3–5 feet (3– 4 feet)
COLOR: white; **BLOOMS** in summer

A robust and easy species that blooms much earlier than any of the others. Its one drawback is the odor of the blooms, which has the sour, musky smell I associate with overly territorial male cats but which probably serves to attract pollinating beetles. In hor-ticultural publications var. *cordifolia* is sometimes listed, but the plants are likely *C. rubifolia*. To con-fuse things more, the epithet var. *cordifolia* is really a synonym for *C. americana* that has been hopelessly misapplied.

Cimicifuga rubifolia
(Appalachian Bugbane)

ZONES: 4–9; part sun, shade
SOIL: moist, neutral
NATIVE TO: wooded slopes and coves, riverbanks, mostly on limestone; scattered populations in Virginia and Tennessee as well as Illinois, Indi-ana, Kentucky, and Alabama
SIZE: 3 feet (2–3 feet)
COLOR: white; **BLOOMS** in fall

A very attractive species with 3–9, maplelike leaflets and late-blooming, faintly sweet-smelling flowers. The plants are also more compact in all respects than many of the others. In many ways this plant is indis-tinguishable from some forms of the Japanese *C. japonica* var. *acerina*.

Claytonia virginiana

Claytonia (clay-TONE-ee-ah)
Portulacaceae
Spring Beauty

Claytonia virginiana. *Spring beauties form ephemeral carpets in the woodland garden, for a few weeks covered in charming pink-veined flowers. I especially like the unusual bubble gum pink anthers that flatten out against the petals.*

Spring beauties epitomize the unsullied grace of the spring ephemerals, carpeting low woodlands for several weeks with candy-striped little flowers on meandering stems. The flowers open sequentially, reminding me of a line of skiers waiting below the gates for a chance to go up and over the hill. Soon after the snow melts, the plants put up a few long succulent leaves from a deep underground corm. The leaf petioles must fight their way through 6 to 8 inches of soil and stones, so that different pairs of leaves and flowering stems appear distant and unconnected to others that originate from the same corm. Spring beauties seed and form offsets readily, so in time they can form large patches that blend beautifully with other spring ephemerals. As the warmth of summer draws near, they quickly yellow and die back for the year.

CULTURE: *Claytonia*s are easily moved when dormant, as most of the roots are shed with the leaves, leaving only a reddish brown, pea- to marble-sized corm. They are impossible to find once completely dormant, however, so it is best to wait until the leaves are yellowing in late spring, then, using a spading fork, gently dig and trace the leaves back to the deep corm. Choose stems that have flowered, as these will be larger and easier to find. Remember that the leaves may emerge some 3–4 inches from the corm, so dig carefully. Spring beauties (with the exception of *C. megarhiza*) are at home in moist but well-drained, slightly acid to neutral soils. They can take considerable drought when dormant in summer, as long as moisture returns for a fall flush of root growth.

USES: Naturalizing in the woodland or shade garden. Spring beauties are a perfect candidate for sequential planting schemes as they bloom and die back quickly. Drifts look especially lovely interplanted with *Dicentra, Asarum,* Creeping Phloxes, *Sanguinaria,* and *Tiarella.*

PROPAGATION: Moderately easy from seed; easy from division (except *C. megarhiza*). See p. 249.

Claytonia caroliniana
(Spring Beauty)

ZONES: 3–9; part sun, shade
SOIL: moist in spring
NATIVE TO: moist woods; Nova Scotia to Minnesota south in the mountains to Tennessee and Georgia
SIZE: 3–6 inches (6 inches)
COLOR: white stained pink to strong pink; **BLOOMS** in early spring

Much like *C. virginiana* except the leaves are broader and more paddle-shaped. The flowers in the populations I have seen also tend to be slightly darker colored as well.

Claytonia lanceolata
(Western Spring Beauty)

ZONES: 4–8; part sun, shade (grows in full sun at alpine elevations)
SOIL: moist in spring
NATIVE TO: dry to moist sagebrush and pinyon-juniper woodlands to gravelly and rocky alpine slopes and meadows; Alberta to British Columbia south to California and New Mexico
SIZE: 3–8 inches (4–6 inches)
COLOR: light to dark pink, very rarely yellow; **BLOOMS** in spring

The western equivalent of *C. virginiana*, growing in a wide range of habitats, but in general more sun- and drought-tolerant than the eastern plants and needing a pronounced dry summer rest to prevent rotting at lower elevations.

Claytonia megarhiza
(Alpine Spring Beauty)

ZONES: 2–7; part sun
SOIL: gravelly, well drained but moist in spring
NATIVE TO: gravelly or rocky soils, crevices, talus slopes above 10,000 feet; Alberta to British Columbia south to Oregon and New Mexico
SIZE: 2–4 inches (6 inches)
COLOR: light to dark pink; **BLOOMS** in spring

Very different from the others, having evolved in the harsh alpine environment of the high western mountains. It puts out a thick rosette of overlapping leaves from a fleshy rootstock, much like *Lewisia* or *Sempervivum.* The flowers sit on stems just longer than the leaves, forming a ring around the rosette— the effect is quite charming. The plants are at home wedged in rock crevices at very high altitudes. It is a very challenging plant to grow, especially for areas with warm, humid summers.

Claytonia virginiana
(Spring Beauty)

ZONES: 3–9; part sun, shade
SOIL: moist in spring
NATIVE TO: rich woods and bottomlands; Quebec and Ontario south to Georgia
SIZE: 4–6 inches
COLOR: white stained pink, rarely yellow; **BLOOMS** in spring

A wide-ranging plant with narrow, linear leaves and a sunny disposition. There is a rare yellow form that occurs occasionally in the central part of its range. I have grown plants from New Jersey labeled as f. *hammondiae* and they are indeed true yellow, a striking contrast in such a strongly pink-flowered genus.

Clematis ochroleuca

Clematis
(KLEM-a-tiss)
Ranunculaceae
Virgin's Bower, Leather-flower

I have to confess I am attracted to the Victorian opulence of the cultivated clematis, but I do so with the guilt of the health food practitioner who admits an occasional indulgence in greasy fast food. There are quite a few native *Clematis* in North America, but none have the in-your-face boldness of many of the garden hybrids. So I appreciate both groups—one for its casual charm, the other for its florid excess. Likewise, I encourage you to put your preconceptions about the genus aside and enjoy what are some of the most graceful and seductive wildflowers we have the pleasure of sharing the continent with.

There are broadly two types of native *Clematis*. The first group are the more familiar vining types, climbing by means of nimble petioles that curl around any object nearby. Then there is a group that forms dense, nonvining clumps of stiff, self-supporting stems. These are easily accommodated in the perennial border or mass planting.

The showy parts of the *Clematis* flower are the sepals, which in many of the species are fused together about half their length into a little urn or bell. Only the tips of the sepals reflex back so as to advertise the opening to any would-be pollinators who happen by. There are a few with larger, more diaphanous flowers that are not fused but still never fully open—adorably circumspect about their considerable beauty.

Almost more wonderful than the flowers are the exquisite downy tails or beaks that decorate each seed. On some species this down can have the look and luster of spun gold glinting in the sun. Others have hair of a duller silvery gray, but produce seed in such abundance that the plants seem covered in frost when fruiting.

CULTURE: The wild *Clematis* share a resentment of disturbance with their cultivated cousins and take a year or two to acclimate after transplanting. The vining types especially have brittle stems that are easily snapped when handled during transplanting. The fibrous bark and cambium remains intact when this happens, so it is difficult to tell that damage has been done until the sections above the break begin to yellow and wither. It is therefore best to handle the plants only when they're dormant or in soft new growth and to provide accessible support for the emerging stems so they will not be broken by heavy rains or wind. Fortunately, strong plants will send up new growth from below the break and will not be set back permanently. The plants never need dividing and should be placed in a spot where they can be enjoyed for years to come. I have not had a problem with *Clematis* wilt, but this could potentially be a problem if the disease has been introduced into your garden on infected cultivated plants. In general, the vining species like moist to wet, fertile soils, while the shrubby types prefer somewhat less moisture and better drainage.

USES: Vines are effective trained to fences or trellises, but they will also scramble through shrubs and rocks. The shrubby types are good subjects for massing, perennial borders, rock gardens, and the like.

PROPAGATION: Slow and moderately difficult from seed and cuttings. See p. 250.

Clematis crispa
(Blue Jasmine)

ZONES: 5–9; sun to part sun
SOIL: moist to wet
NATIVE TO: low woods, swamps and marshes; Virginia to southern Illinois south to Texas and Florida
SIZE: 6–10 feet (2 feet)

Clematis ochroleuca. *The remarkable spun-gold tails that festoon the seeds of the aptly named Curly-heads are its most ornamental feature. When the seeds ripen in late summer the golden hairs fade to tan and puff out like the tail of a frightened cat, signaling that they are ready to collect. Unlike the familiar garden* Clematis, *this is a bushy, clumping wildflower that carries its flowers and seeds in a crown at the top of the stems.*

COLOR: violet with cream interior; BLOOMS in early summer

I was very impressed with the flowers of the Blue Jasmine vine when I gave them a close inspection. They are 1½ inches or so across and of the same heavy substance as the other leather flowers, but the ridged and furrowed sepals roll far back to reveal a shell-like interior. The whole reminds me in color and texture of the frosted ornaments on a violet wedding cake. The leaf segments are very long and narrow. Blooms on new wood.

Clematis hirsutissima
(Sugar-bowls)

ZONES: 4–7; sun, part sun
SOIL: moist, well drained
NATIVE TO: meadows and open mountain woodland; South Dakota and Wyoming to Washington south to Oregon, Utah, Arizona, and New Mexico
SIZE: 10–12 inches (12–14 inches)
COLOR: gray-violet to dark violet; BLOOMS in early summer

In habit, this shrubby mountain species is similar to Curly-heads, *C. ochroleuca*, but the fine leaves are pinnately compound and covered with dense hair to protect them from frost and strong sun. It is a great little foliage plant for the rock garden, and the small flowers are somewhat showy.

Clematis occidentalis var. occidentalis
(Purple Clematis)

ZONES: 3–8; part sun
SOIL: moist, neutral
NATIVE TO: rocky woods and ledges, often over limestone; New Brunswick to Ontario south to Illinois, New York, and North Carolina
SIZE: 4–6 feet (2 feet)
COLOR: violet; BLOOMS in spring

A lovely plant with large drooping, satiny flowers and a vining habit. The size and shape of the flowers is closest to those of the garden hybrids. It is a rather weak grower, unfortunately. The northwestern variety *grosseserrata* has been easier for me in cultivation as has the closely related *C. columbiana* from the Rockies. Do not cut it back in spring, as it blooms from old wood.

Clematis ochroleuca
(Curly-heads)

ZONES: 5–9; sun to light shade
SOIL: moist to moderately dry
NATIVE TO: upland woods and gaps; southeastern New York to Georgia, mostly along the coast

SIZE: 12–18 inches (16 inches)
COLOR: ocher yellow with violet overtones; BLOOMS in spring

This is one of the best of the shrubby types, with large undivided oval leaves on upright stems. The flowers are somewhat ornamental, but the golden tails of the seed heads are the real joy to see. *C. albicoma* is a smaller version from a few shale barrens in Virginia that blooms two weeks later and *C. fremontii* is another close relative from limestone prairies in Kansas and Missouri.

Clematis reticulata
(Fine-veined Leather-flower)

ZONES: 5–9; sun, part sun
SOIL: moist to moderately dry
NATIVE TO: dry woods and openings in sandy soil; South Carolina to Alabama and Arkansas south to Texas and Florida
SIZE: 4–10 feet (3 feet)
COLOR: pale violet; BLOOMS in early summer

A vigorous vining plant with doubly-pinnate, rounded leaflets in the urn-flower group. *C. pitcheri* is a relative from limestone woods in the central United States with slightly more open flowers. Both bloom on new and old wood.

Clematis texensis
(Scarlet Clematis)

ZONES: 5–9; sun, part sun
SOIL: moist to dry, neutral
NATIVE TO: limestone woodlands and cliffs in a small area of south-central Texas
SIZE: 4–8 feet (2–3 feet)
COLOR: red to red-purple; BLOOMS in spring

A stunning relative of *C. viorna* with bright red urn-shaped flowers and stiff blue-gray leaves and a very limited natural distribution. It has been used extensively by European breeders to give red color to hybrids, and often catalogs that list *C. texensis* are really selling one of these. The plant needs a warm microclimate to thrive north of Zone 7, but it is well worth the effort.

Clematis viorna
(Leather-flower)

ZONES: 4–9; sun to part sun
SOIL: moist
NATIVE TO: moist woods, slopes, and streambanks; Pennsylvania to Illinois south to Arkansas, Alabama, and Georgia
SIZE: 4–10 feet (2–3 feet)
COLOR: pink and green; BLOOMS in summer

You have to search a little to find the flowers on this plant, but they are quite striking even though small,

❧ **Contractile Roots** ❧

Plants that concentrate stored reserves in fleshy bulbs, corms, rhizomes, or tubers provide a potentially rich source of food for hungry animals, who can wipe out an entire colony during one winter's foraging. Many of these plants respond to the threat by lacing their tissues with toxic or bitter chemicals to deter herbivory, but this is not always successful. (The onion's acrid, sulfurous aroma is certainly little deterrent to most humans.) Others simply grow deeper every year, eventually reaching depths that many animals will not dig to. Some plants, such as *Erythronium americanum* and *Arisaema dracontium,* send out long bur-

rowing stems each year that deposit the new corms ever deeper in the earth. But perhaps the most ingenious strategy that I know of is used by wildflowers without the benefit of such tunneling stems. Species such as most of the trilliums have roots that begin life by snaking their way deep in the soil in spring, then, once they have a secure hold, they contract like an accordion's bellows, pulling the rhizome ever deeper into the soil. Thus a seedling that may germinate only ½ inch down in the soil can by maturity be 6–12 inches deep.

---

with a purplish pink base and abruptly yellow-green tips. It is a fairly vigorous but noninvasive plant with typical, pinnate leaves that is as happy trailing through brush as it is climbing a trellis. New flowers appear from the growing tips over much of the summer.

Clematis virginiana
(Woodbine, Virgin's Bower)

ZONES: 3–9; sun to part sun
SOIL: moist
NATIVE TO: streambanks, moist fields, fencerows; Nova Scotia to southern Manitoba south to Iowa, Texas, and Florida
SIZE: 3–8 feet (3–5 feet)
COLOR: white; **BLOOMS** in late summer

A rampant, vigorous species that spreads from root sprouts and seed (in effect it is much like the Asian Sweet Autumn Clematis, *C. terniflora*). The seed heads are ornamental when hung in masses from all neighboring vegetation, but it is too aggressive for most gardens. *C. ligusticifolia* is its more drought-tolerant twin from west of the Rockies.

Clintonia uniflora

Clintonia (clin-TONE-ee-ah)
Liliaceae
Bluebead Lily

Bluebead lilies are superbly well adapted for life on the dim forest floor. Their large, flat, tongue-shaped leaves array themselves like emerald green solar collectors, efficiently gathering whatever weak light might penetrate the dense canopy above. This ability makes them particularly suited to life under

conifers, and they are at their best in the cool, mossy forests of the Cascades and Appalachians. They are slow growers, but the bold, glossy foliage is a striking presence in the shade garden and well worth your patience. From the center of each set of 2–6 leaves arises a stout stalk of 1–5 pendent flowers that are miniature copies of the familiar florist's lily. These are followed in fall by large deep-sea blue fruits each containing a bundle of seeds. Given time, each plant forms a cluster of several crowns that look great scattered or in drifts among other woodland wildflowers.

Clintonia uniflora. *The large white flowers of Bead-lily seem especially radiant smiling up at you in the dim light under a canopy of fir and hemlock. It is often found in the company of Trefoil Foamflower, whose cloudlike inflorescences weave among the slaphappy strap-leaves of* Clintonia *in perfect complement.*

*Conradina verticillata.
A fine crop of
'Snowflake', a white-
flowered cultivar of
Cumberland Rosemary
grown from cuttings in
the nursery. Fortunately,
many rare species are
easy to propagate in a
nursery setting, making
them readily available to
gardeners and taking
some of the pressure off
of fragile wild popula-
tions. I took the cuttings
in late June, about four
weeks after flowering,
and potted up the rooted
transplants three weeks
later. Pictured here the
following spring, they
have filled out and are
blooming spectacularly.*

CULTURE: Shade and cool, moist, acid soils rich in humus are ideal. Of the four, *C. umbellulata* is the most tolerant of heat and drought, so makes the best subject for most gardens and should be more widely grown. The others are more finicky outside their native haunts, but certainly not impossible to grow. They are best moved in fall as the leaves are withering. The plants consist of thick, jointed, short-branched rhizomes with a tangle of fleshy roots attached. The rhizome can be carefully severed after the plants are lifted and then teased into several clumps. It will usually take a year for the transplants to recover, but all in all they are not too difficult to move. I have also dug them as the leaves are emerging in spring, but the plants are set back more severely.

USES: Lends a bold textural effect to shade plantings. Useful as scattered clumps intermixed with finer-leaved plants or massed as a ground cover. I realize that they are not always easy to come by, but they are certainly worth searching for. Good companions include *Asarum, Trillium, Adiantum, Phlox,* and *Medeola.*

PROPAGATION: Difficult from seed; easy from division. See p. 250.

Clintonia andrewsiana
(Red Clintonia)

ZONES: 8–9; shade
SOIL: moist, acid
NATIVE TO: damp, coastal coniferous forests in the Redwood belt; Northern California to south-western Oregon
SIZE: 12–18 inches (16–18 inches)
COLOR: deep rose purple; **BLOOMS** in spring
A striking plant in flower, but, alas, not very hardy outside its cool, moist home in the Redwood belt along the central Pacific coast. Each one of a cluster of 5–6 leaves can reach a foot or so in length, and the ½-inch flowers are arranged in umbels of 10 or more on a stiff, 12–18-inch stem.

Clintonia borealis
(Bluebead Lily)

ZONES: 2–6; shade
SOIL: moist, acid
NATIVE TO: moist, shaded, cool woods and bogs; Labrador to Manitoba south to northern Indiana and New Jersey, then in the mountains to Tennessee
SIZE: 8–12 inches (12 inches)
COLOR: yellow; **BLOOMS** in spring
Bluebead Lily is a common understory species at higher elevations in the Appalachians and north into the boreal forests of Canada. While it will grow in lowland conditions, it has a tendency toward early

dormancy. The marble-sized deep blue fruits are quite beautiful.

Clintonia umbellulata
(Bead-lily, Speckled Wood Lily)

ZONES: 4–8; shade
SOIL: moist, acid
NATIVE TO: rich mountain woods; New York and Ohio south in the mountains to Georgia
SIZE: 12–14 inches (12 inches)
COLOR: white; **BLOOMS** in spring
This is perhaps the best *Clintonia* for the garden, as it holds up well in heat and moderate drought. The flowers are smaller and more numerous than *C. borealis,* and the fruits are pea-sized and blue-black in color.

Clintonia uniflora
(Bead-lily, Bride's Bonnet)

ZONES: 6–8; shade
SOIL: moist, acid
NATIVE TO: damp coniferous forests; southwestern Alberta to British Columbia and Alaska south to California and eastern Oregon
SIZE: 6–12 inches (12 inches)
COLOR: white; **BLOOMS** in spring
The western counterpart to *C. borealis,* with large, luminous single flowers, but otherwise similar in habit and requirements. It spreads fairly quickly to form patches.

Conradina verticillata

Conradina (con-rad-EEN-ah)
Lamiaceae
Wild Rosemary

The wild rosemarys are an interesting and little-known group of aromatic evergreens that inhabit the sandy coastal plain of the southeast United States.

One outlying species is restricted to gravel sandbars in only a few small areas on the Cumberland Plateau of Kentucky and Tennessee. Lovely additions to the herb or rock garden, most are rare in the wild, but easy to propagate from seed or cuttings. Only *C. verticillata* is hardy north of USDA Zone 7, but they all perform well in the heat and humidity of the Southeast. The plants do somewhat resemble the cultivated rosemary in habit, forming small woody shrubs with branching stems of narrow needlelike leaves. Large pink flowers near the stems' tips have the typical asymmetrical bilabiate (2-lipped) mint shape. The leaves even smell just like the true *Rosmarinus,* but I cannot vouch for their edibility. Certainly in many ways they seem as if they would be more at home in the Mediterranean climate of southern California than the humid South, and they may be relicts of a time when the Southeast was higher and drier than it is at present.

CULTURE: *Conradina*s thrive in poor, sandy, acid soils and full sun with moderate spring fertilization. (Root rots can be a problem if soils are too heavy and wet.) They transplant well in spring, but should have some supplemental water to get them through the first summer. A light pruning after flowering helps keep them from getting too rangy looking. Overall they are undemanding, problem-free plants that will reward you with lovely flowers and neat foliage.

USES: Herb and rock garden, seashore garden. *C. verticillata* acts more like a trailing ground cover and works well on slopes or intermixed with other low evergreens such as *Arctostaphylos uva-ursi.*

PROPAGATION: Easy from seed and cuttings. See p. 250.

Conradina canescens
(Gray Wild Rosemary)

ZONES: 7–9; sun to light shade
SOIL: sandy, moderately moist to dry
NATIVE TO: sandy soils on the coastal plain; Florida
SIZE: 1–2 feet (1 foot)
COLOR: violet; **BLOOMS** in early summer

The whorled, needlelike foliage of *C. canescens* is covered by a woolly pubescence that is more of a warm gray than silver. The first time I saw it growing I was impressed by the hazy, soft look the plant has as a whole. It becomes a small woody shrub much like Lavender or true Rosemary.

Conradina verticillata
(Cumberland Rosemary)

ZONES: 6 (5)–9; sun to part sun
SOIL: moist, well drained
NATIVE TO: sandbars along rivers; Cumberland area of Tennessee and Kentucky
SIZE: 4–8 inches (1–2 feet)

COLOR: violet, occasionally white; **BLOOMS** in early summer

This rare species has deep, glossy green foliage and trailing woody stems that can grow 6 feet or more from the crown with time. It grows on sandbars along a few rivers in the Cumberland Plateau of Tennessee and Kentucky — constantly under threat from flooding and inadvertent, aqueous relocation.

Coptis trifolia ssp. *groenlandica*

Coptis (COP-tis)
Ranunculaceae
Goldthread

Goldthreads are another denizen of the deep cool forests of the North and Pacific West. Their lyrical common name refers to the mustard yellow color of the roots and rambling underground stems that carry these little evergreens gently about the forest floor. The rhizomes terminate in small crowns of one to several shiny, lobed leaves that send up thin, upward-facing, 5-petaled flowers on slightly taller stalks. On the whole, the plants remind me of refined wild strawberries in appearance. The flowers give way to curious seed capsules that array themselves like daisywheels one to a stem. Each capsule is made of 2 papery, boat-shaped wings. The upper wing is overturned and sets inside the other, forming a little container for the seeds. The wings are hinged where they attach to the stem so that a drop of rain landing on the protruding lower part forces it down, releasing a seed and catapulting it skyward like a jai alai ball from a cesta.

Coptis trifoliata ssp. groenlandica. *Native to Greenland (or Groenland) and most of the boreal forests around the globe, this dainty little Goldthread is happiest in the damp, peaty soils of shaded evergreen forests. In cool, moist climates it also ventures forth into the stronger sun of mossy bogs. Flowers yield to curious wagon-wheel seed capsules that use the energy in falling raindrops to launch their seeds.*

Coreopsis lanceolata. The "torn jeans" appearance of tickseed's rough-cut petals is part of their charm. Longstalk Tickseed is native to the Great Plains, but it is used extensively in wildflower seed mixes along highways and can now be found naturalized in parts of the East. Though its bloom period is short by Coreopsis standards, the size and sheer quantity of flowers it produces in one spectacular explosion more than compensates for its floral brevity.

CULTURE: Goldthreads are relatively easy to establish in cool climates and damp, acid soils under deciduous or evergreen trees. They put up only one flush of leaves in the spring, so do not worry if your transplants just sit there the first year—underground, they are sending out new rhizomes and roots and should triple in size the following year. Of the three, I find *C. laciniata* to be the most adaptable and vigorous, and its beautiful, deeply cut evergreen leaves certainly make it a worthy addition to the shade garden. In time it will form a solid ground cover if competition is not too severe.

USES: Ground cover in the shade garden mixed with *Dalibarda, Linnaea, Clintonia, Oxalis*.

PROPAGATION: Moderately easy from seed; fairly easy from division. See p. 250.

Coptis asplenifolia

(Spleenwort-leaved Goldthread)

ZONES: 4–8; shade
SOIL: cool, moist, acid
NATIVE TO: moist coastal forest; British Columbia to central Alaska along the coast
SIZE: 2–3 inches (6–12 inches)
COLOR: white; BLOOMS in spring

Much like *C. laciniata*, but with less finely toothed leaves. It has performed well for many years in our garden, though it is slower growing and more drought sensitive than its cousin.

Coptis laciniata

(Oregon Goldthread, Cutleaf Goldthread)

ZONES: 5–8; shade
SOIL: moist, acid
NATIVE TO: moist coniferous forest; northern California to Washington
SIZE: 2–3 inches (6–12 inches)
COLOR: white; BLOOMS in spring

The 3-lobed leaves are deeply dissected and toothed on their margins, giving the 2½-inch leathery, glossy leaves a lacy appeal. A common ground cover in the fir forests of the Pacific Northwest and the best overall for gardens.

Coptis trifolia ssp. groenlandica

(Goldthread)

ZONES: 2–7; shade
SOIL: moist, cool, acid
NATIVE TO: damp forests and bogs, circumboreal; Greenland to Alaska south to British Columbia, Iowa and New Jersey and in the mountains to North Carolina
SIZE: 1–2 inches (6–8 inches)
COLOR: white; BLOOMS in spring

This goldthread has glossy, dark green leaves shaped like a 3-leaved clover, and it usually grows scattered in loose mats among moss in damp to boggy spots. Admittedly, it is a little small to make much of a garden impact.

Coreopsis lanceolata

Coreopsis (core-ee-OP-sis)
Asteraceae
Tickseed

Tickseeds are indispensable wildflowers for the sunny garden. They are easy, undemanding plants that come in a range of sizes and seasons of bloom, making it possible to have at least one in flower from spring through late fall. The dominant colors of the group are yellow and gold, but there are reds, pinks, and oranges as well. It is hard to generalize beyond that, so I will cover the individual species in greater detail.

CULTURE: Easily transplanted into average garden soils throughout the growing season. Most grow from short rhizomes that make clumps easy to divide in spring, and they benefit from occasional division (every three to five years) to keep them vigorous. There are a number of annual species, such as the dark red-centered *C. tinctoria* and the yellow and brown *C. cardaminifolia*, that are sometimes sold unwittingly as perennials. They are occasionally seen in seed meadow mixes as well. Certainly they are fine plants as long as you know not to expect them to return.

USES: Borders, meadows, massing—combine with *Aster*, ornamental grasses such as *Sporobolus*, and with *Andropogon, Heuchera, Boltonia*, and *Rudbeckia* to name just a few.

PROPAGATION: Easy from seed or cuttings. See p. 250.

Coreopsis atkinsoniana

(Columbia Coreopsis)

ZONES: 6–8; sun
SOIL: moist

NATIVE TO: riverbanks; Saskatoon to British Columbia and Arizona
SIZE: 2–3 feet (12–18 inches)
COLOR: bright yellow petals with brown base and brown disk; **BLOOMS** in summer

A biennial or short-lived perennial species with large lacy, divided leaves and colorful flowers. Self-sows much like *Rudbeckia triloba*, so it will persist in a naturalized situation.

Coreopsis auriculata
(Lobed Tickseed)

ZONES: 4–9; sun to light shade
SOIL: moist in spring
NATIVE TO: woods; Virginia and Kentucky to Louisiana
SIZE: 3–18 inches (12–16 inches)
COLOR: golden orange; **BLOOMS** in late spring

The variety *nana* (Dwarf Lobed Tickseed) is most often available, and it is a superior plant for early-season color, forming low spreading clumps of semievergreen, oval, basal foliage on long petioles and wiry stems of absolutely vibrant flowers with toothed ray petals. It goes into a semidormancy after flowering, not really dying back, but fading into the background.

Coreopsis integrifolia
(Tickseed)

ZONES: 6–9; sun
SOIL: moist to wet
NATIVE TO: wet meadows, bogs; endemic to northern Florida
SIZE: 1–2 feet (2 feet)
COLOR: golden yellow; **BLOOMS** in fall

An endangered species notable for its leathery, glossy leaves and very late flowering (it is one of the last plants to flower at Garden in the Woods). Needs a fair amount of moisture to thrive. It has a spreading habit and 3-inch oval, opposite leaves on thick stems. The flowers are borne on long peduncles at the top of the stems.

Coreopsis lanceolata
(Longstalk Tickseed, Lance-leaved Coreopsis)

ZONES: 3–9; sun, part sun
SOIL: moist to dry
NATIVE TO: sandy, dry prairies and shores; Michigan south to New Mexico and Florida (naturalized elsewhere)
SIZE: 18–30 inches (2 feet)
COLOR: golden yellow; **BLOOMS** in early summer

Lance-leaved Coreopsis is a tough, vigorous plant that is often used as a component of wildflower seed mixtures. It has a fairly short blooming season and a habit of seeding prolifically, so it is perhaps best reserved for naturalizing and meadow gardens. The plants form thick clumps of coarsely hairy, basal leaves with flowers on branched stems above. *C. grandiflora* (Big-flowered Tickseed) from the Southeast is very similar, but it has finer, divided cauline or stem leaves. The ray petals have the same ragged, toothy appearance and radiant golden color. It is an excellent border perennial, and selections such as 'Flying Saucers' are available with especially large, flat blooms.

Coreopsis rosea
(Pink Coreopsis)

ZONES: 4–8; sun, part sun
SOIL: moist to wet
NATIVE TO: wet, sandy, acid soils and pond shores along the coast; Nova Scotia sporadically to Georgia
SIZE: 1 foot (1 foot)
COLOR: soft pink with a yellow eye; **BLOOMS** in summer

A cute little species that was for a time marketed as a pink version of the popular *Coreopsis* × 'Moonbeam', which it resembles somewhat in habit. The plants form dense stands of thin stems covered with needlelike, whorled leaves. The ½-inch pink daisies appear from among the foliage for about four weeks in summer. Its biggest drawback is that the thin stems tend to flop and mat down after a heavy rain. Pink Coreopsis is a threatened species in the wild.

Coreopsis tripteris
(Tall Tickseed)

ZONES: 3–9; sun, part sun
SOIL: moist to wet
NATIVE TO: low woods and clearings; Massachusetts to southern Ontario and Wisconsin south to Texas and Florida
SIZE: 3–6 feet (3 feet)
COLOR: light to medium yellow; **BLOOMS** in mid- to late summer

Tall Tickseed is an impressive plant, with thick stems clothed in 3-lobed, opposite leaves that produce clouds of airy yellow flowers from their upper third. It makes a good back-of-the-border or tall-grass meadow addition, but deadhead it after flowering as it seeds prolifically.

Coreopsis verticillata
(Threadleaf Tickseed)

ZONES: 4–9; sun, part sun
SOIL: moist to moderately dry
NATIVE TO: dry woods and clearings along the coastal plain; Maryland to South Carolina

SIZE: 12–26 inches (12 inches)

COLOR: light yellow to gold; **BLOOMS** in summer

The species is not grown nearly as often as its hybrid *C.* × 'Moonbeam', which has proven to be a consistent favorite with gardeners. It has soft, pale yellow blooms that seem to be floating above the fine leaves. It is sterile, never setting seed, and blooming from early summer almost to frost. Its color blends with just about everything. Suprisingly, given its parents' native range, 'Moonbeam' does not seem to perform as well in the Southeast as other species. Other excellent, widely available cultivars of the straight species include 'Zagreb' and 'Golden Showers'.

Cornus canadensis

Cornus (CORE-nuss)
Cornaceae
Bunchberry

Cornus canadensis. *It becomes clear when you look at the shape and arrangement of the white bracts that surround each cluster of Bunchberry flowers that they are indeed really leaves that have been merely modified in shape and in color. Under optimal conditions (a cool, damp soil and a few hours of sun), each knot of flowers will develop into a bunch of striking scarlet berries each containing a hard seed surrounded by a tough, fibrous pulp.*

I have always been fascinated by the little ground-covering Bunchberry. A patch of it in flower appears for all the world like a Flowering Dogwood (*Cornus florida* or *nuttalii*) that has been buried up to its outermost twigs by some silent, serious landslide. Really, though, they are as close to a herbaceous perennial as any dogwood could hope to be, with soft, spreading rhizomes that are constantly branching and sending up the unmistakable aboveground stems. Each stem has 2–3 sets of overlapping, opposite leaves at its tip, set so close together as to appear whorled. From the center of this leafy conglomeration comes the 'flower,' really a ball of small flowers on a short stem surrounded by 4 showy, pointed bracts. Like poinsettias, these showy bracts hang on colorfully for a while after the small flowers have come and gone, eventually yielding to a cluster of berries that turn regal scarlet red when ripe.

This plant has always been an uncomfortable enigma for taxonomists. At times it has been placed in its own genus and at others split into several regionally distinct species. I will cover one of these regional forms separately, but in habit and culture they are similar, and I almost prefer to look at the plant as one wide-ranging and variable species—the bunch-buried dogwood, so to speak.

CULTURE: Bunchberries are northern plants that prefer cool, moist soil and chilly nights. If summer night temperatures do not routinely fall into the 50s and low 60s, little seed will be produced, but the plants will otherwise grow well. I would not recommend them for the Deep South, however. They can take considerable sun in the North, especially where the soil is very moist, and form dense patches along roadsides in northern New England, where occasional mowing keeps competition in check. They also grow well in the shade, but growth is more sparse and patchy. They respond well to light fertilizing.

In fall, a cluster of 1–10 little buds are set at the base of each withered flowering stem, and others form at intervals on the spreading rhizomes. It is fairly easy, before growth begins in spring, to carefully lift a few of these pieces to spread them about.

USES: Ground cover for moist shade.

PROPAGATION: Moderately difficult from seed. See p. 250.

Cornus canadensis
(Bunchberry)

ZONES: 2–6; part sun, shade (grows well in full sun in the North)

SOIL: moist, acid

NATIVE TO: moist forests, bogs and streambanks, circumboreal; Greenland to Alaska south to British Columbia, Minnesota, and New Jersey and in the mountains to California and Virginia

SIZE: 3–6 inches (12–16 inches)

COLOR: bracts are white, flowers yellow or green; **BLOOMS** from late spring to early summer

Cornus suecica
(Swedish Cornel)

ZONES: 1–4; sun to shade

SOIL: moist, acid

NATIVE TO: wet boreal forest; south in North America to Newfoundland, Nova Scotia, and Quebec

SIZE: 2–3 inches (6–12 inches)

COLOR: bracts are white, flowers deep blue purple; **BLOOMS** from late spring to early summer

A circumboreal species that differs from *C. canadensis* in the deep blue-violet color of the flowers which cast their glow on the white bracts and give the whole an eerie, bluish hue. Smaller and less vigorous in cultivation south of its native range.

Cypripedium acaule

Cypripedium

(sip-re-PEE-dee-um)

Orchidaceae

Lady-slipper

I have a special fondness for orchids, and of the group, lady-slippers are one of my favorites. The complex flowers possess a veneer of tremendous embellishment that hints as well at a deeper clarity of design. The slipper orchids differ from most in this vast family in that they have 2 pollinia rather than 1 (see *Calopogon* for an explanation), located on either side of the column. They are a divergent or perhaps more primitive line within the family, but primitive in this group is pretty sophisticated indeed. The exotic pouch formed by the flower's lip is an ingenious trap that lures in unsuspecting bumblebees with the empty promise of a nectar treat. The entrance narrows inside the pouch, functioning like a lobster trap—easy to enter but impossible to exit. With this escape unavailable, the bee must crawl up the back of the flower, using carefully placed hairs as a ladder. As it climbs, it must first squeeze by the female stigma, then past one of the pollinia, which adheres safely to its back. Should the bee enter another flower, this pollen will be deposited on its stigma before the bee picks up more of the sticky yellow stuff. Unfortunately for the plants, bees are quick learners, and with no nectar to reward them for their troubles, they quickly tire of the game, so few of the flowers are pollinated each season.

Lady-slippers store food reserves in a thick nest of roots and with time can support large clumps of 20 or more flowering stems. They are long-lived as well —certain Yellow Lady-slippers have been growing at Garden in the Woods for more than 50 years. There is an air of mystery surrounding these plants, in part because their unique germination requirements have made them relatively unavailable except as sadly depleted, dehydrated plants collected from the wild and barely clinging to life. That these perish soon after planting in the garden is no surprise and should be attributed to rough treatment rather than some other mysterious deficiency. I feel confident, however, that advances in laboratory techniques will soon make them much more widely available, and healthy, nursery-raised seedlings are overall much easier to handle than near-dead, recently wild plants.

Except for *C. acaule,* the plants are composed of stout stems of a few alternating leaves with distinctive pleats along the veins. Flowers appear at the ends of the expanding growths in spring.

CULTURE: Overall, the lady-slippers require a soil that is consistently moist yet well aerated. A mix of humus, loam, and sand will usually suffice. The wetland types can be grown in a lined artificial bog (as described for *Sarracenia*). The plants are best moved and divided before growth begins in spring or in early fall. Be careful not to damage the all-important roots. *Cypripedium* roots cannot grow a new tip should theirs be injured. Many of the species are lime-lovers, and a yearly topdressing of dolomite is beneficial should the leaves begin to look pale. Sprinkle a handful of a granular organic fertilizer around the plants in spring.

USES: Specimens in the shade or wetland garden.

PROPAGATION: Difficult from seed; moderately difficult from division. See p. 251.

Cypripedium acaule

(Pink Lady-slipper)

ZONES: 3–8; light shade

SOIL: poor, acid humus

NATIVE TO: acid, upland woods and sphagnum bogs; Newfoundland to Alberta south to Indiana and New Jersey then along the coast and mountains to Georgia and South Carolina

SIZE: 1 foot (1 foot)

COLOR: pink, occasionally white; **BLOOMS** in spring

The familiar, pleated basal leaves and elegant single flower of *C. acaule* are a much loved, fairly common sight in eastern woodlands, but the plants really do not adapt well to cultivation. I suspect they are very particular about soil moisture and chemistry, and I would strongly recommend trying one of the other species in the garden and just enjoying these in the wild.

Cypripedium acaule. Tough, drought-tolerant Pink Lady-slippers can survive in places few other wildflowers dare to root. This graciously circumspect specimen appears promptly every spring in between the twin trunks of a Black Oak (Quercus velutina) behind my office. Of all the lady-slippers, this one is the most recalcitrant in cultivation, requiring just the right balance of soil, moisture, and light to persist for more than a few years in the garden.

Cypripedium aretinum
(Ram's-head Lady-slipper)

ZONES: 2–6; part sun, light shade
SOIL: evenly moist
NATIVE TO: moist, acid, coniferous woodland and
bogs; Quebec to Manitoba south to Minnesota
and Massachusetts
SIZE: 8–12 inches (1 foot)
COLOR: burgundy and white; BLOOMS in spring

A most unusual little plant from the cool north woods, with a pouch that reminds me of the jutting jaw of an unshaven Popeye the Sailor. It can be grown with some difficulty in moist, cool soils where summer temperatures remain moderate.

Cypripedium californicum
(California Lady-slipper)

ZONES: 6–8; part sun
SOIL: moist
NATIVE TO: moist soils along mountain streams;
northern California to southwestern Oregon
SIZE: 16–28 inches (16 inches)
COLOR: white lip and lime green petals/sepals; BLOOMS
in spring

An absolutely stunning plant in full bloom, as a healthy stem can produce six or more of the contrasting flowers. I have yet to try it in the open garden, but seedlings are growing well.

Cypripedium candidum
(Small White Lady-slipper)

ZONES: 3–8; sun, part sun
SOIL: moist to wet, calcareous
NATIVE TO: limestone fens, swamps, and wet prairies;
New York to North Dakota and Nebraska south
to Missouri, Ohio, and New Jersey
SIZE: 4–10 inches (6–8 inches)
COLOR: white lip with green petals/sepals; BLOOMS in
late spring

In habit this demure little plant is much like a reduced Yellow Lady-slipper, with lovely white flowers and 3–5 narrow, pointed leaves clothing a short stem. It needs a fair amount of sun and a damp, alkaline soil to thrive. Though it has been slow from seed (five-year seedlings have yet to bloom), it has not been difficult, at least in containers.

Cypripedium kentuckiense
(Kentucky Lady-slipper)

ZONES: 4–9; light shade
SOIL: moist
NATIVE TO: low woods and coves; scattered from Tennessee to Arkansas south to Oklahoma and
Louisiana
SIZE: 18–28 inches (16 inches)
COLOR: pale yellow lip and brown petals/sepals;
BLOOMS in late spring

Cypripedium pubescens. *Rising up from a patch of Big-leaved Aster and Bracken Fern* (Pteridium aquilinum), *a patch of Large Yellow Lady-slippers has an otherworldly quality. One of last year's seedpods, long ago disgorged of its contents, is still visible in the lower left. In the wild, large clumps like this may be anywhere from twenty to one hundred years old, but under careful cultivation, similar size can be attained in less than a decade. Its pollenia can be found on either side of the column, which sits behind a red-striped flap above the mouth of the pouch.*

Cypripedium Seed Germination

Orchid seeds are unique in that they have evolved a dependency on a symbiotic (meaning "to live together") relationship with certain groups of soil fungi. Orchid seeds are adapted to wind dispersal, so they are very lightweight and produced in huge numbers. The typical lady-slipper seedpod contains between 10,000 and 20,000 seeds! Orchid seeds are light because they lack the endosperm or food reserves that most seeds rely on for initial growth. Endosperm provides seedlings with the nutrients and energy they need to grow roots and leaves that will allow them to become self-sufficient (much as the egg yolk nurtures developing bird embryos). Without endosperm, orchid seeds cannot germinate unless they become infected by certain soil fungi, which the seedlings partially digest to obtain the sugars and nutrients necessary for growth. Once a seedling has chlorophyll-containing leaves and a few roots, it can begin providing these substances for itself and so becomes less and less dependent on the fungus for survival. In fact, research on mature Yellow and Showy Lady-slipper roots has turned up very little fungus infection, so it appears that—at least with these species—the fungus becomes much less important as the plants become older.

Orchid mycorrhizae, as these symbiotic fungi are called, are grouped mostly into the genus *Rhizoctonia.* It appears that there are hundreds of species and forms of *Rhizoctonia* that are capable of symbiosis with orchids. It does not appear true, as was once thought, that every species of orchid has evolved with a specific fungus, but rather that the orchid can rely on at least a couple of different fungi interchangeably. In fact, research has shown that a species of fungus isolated from a tree-dwelling tropical orchid is capable of successful symbiosis with the completely unrelated temperate species *Goodyera pubescens,* our Rattlesnake Plantain. Some species of fungus have worldwide distribution, while others are limited to local areas. What I find very interesting is that at least some species of *Rhizoctonia* are pathogenic or disease-causing when they infect nonorchidaceous species, such as members of the Mustard family. It may well be that in the distant past, these fungi were parasites on orchid seeds, but through time, the seeds developed ways to resist and eventually control this parasitism to their own benefit. In effect, the seeds have reversed roles, now becoming parasites of the fungus. It is not clear what benefit the fungi get from this relationship, although it may be that they receive certain enzymes or nutrients from the orchid. *Rhizoctonia* species are part of the soil flora, and most if not all are able to grow readily as saprophytes (living by breaking down nonliving organic matter). Thus you should normally find at least a few species in any soil that contains decomposing organic matter—whether orchids are present or not. It seems that some species are generalists—that is they are capable of growing in a variety of soils and organic materials—while others are specific to certain habitats.

There are still many unanswered questions about orchid fungi and their importance. Lady-slippers in particular have been associated with at least six species of *Rhizoctonia.* These fungi are present in soils where the orchids grow and are thus available to infect and aid in the germination of seedlings. *Cypripedium* seedlings have also been germinated in a lab using one of the most common and widespread species of orchid fungi, but it is not clear whether this particular species aids germination in the wild. Thus, even though orchids may not be growing on a particular site, it is likely that the soils contain suitable fungi that will allow germination if seeds are introduced.

Mature plants (those at or near flowering size) of some if not all of the species do not seem to be dependent on mycorrhizae to any great degree. The plants have large dark green leaves and a well-developed root system characteristic of species able to meet their needs independently. In my experience, adequate sunlight; moisture; and a well-aerated, good organic soil with adequate fertility is all adult lady-slippers need to grow well. In fact, even small seedlings that we have received in sterile bags (growing without mycorrhizae) grow on very well in a sterile, hydroponic mix. It seems clear that once the seedlings have passed out of the critical germination stage, they can grow well in cultivated conditions without mycorrhizae.

Cypripedium reginae. *The New England Wild Flower Society is now growing quantities of this peerless wildflower from lab-raised seed, produced without the benefit of mycorrhizal fungi.*

Dalea purpurea. *Native prairies are not uniform in size or in their distribution of species. Specific plants are often slightly more adapted to a particular microclimate's combination of soil, light, and wind conditions than competitors. Purple Prairie Clover prefers moderately dry sites, especially if they have recently been burned. Often it is abundant in one area, and only a few feet away it is completely absent. Such natural species mosaics are more difficult to establish in small prairie gardens, so do not expect that every seed you sow will do equally as well in your own little slice of grassland.*

Kentucky Lady-slipper was recognized as a distinct species only 15 years ago. It is a striking plant much like a very large *C. pubescens,* with enormous pale yellow flowers the size of a large hen's egg. The plants are very easy in the woodland garden and, though hard to find now, should be readily available in the near future as lab-raised seedlings are disseminated. I believe this is one of the best-kept secrets of our eastern flora — truly outstanding.

Cypripedium parviflorum
(Small Yellow Lady-slipper)

ZONES: 4–8; light shade
SOIL: moist
NATIVE TO: bogs and low woods; Newfoundland to British Columbia south to Washington, Utah, New Mexico, Texas, Ohio, and in the mountains to Georgia
SIZE: 10–14 inches (12 inches)
COLOR: deep yellow lip and dark brown petals/sepals; **BLOOMS** in spring

For many years this and *C. pubescens* were considered forms of the same species, but they are very distinct from one another. Small Yellow Lady-slipper blooms ten days later with 2–4 1½-inch flowers per spike. The lip is usually a strong chrome yellow. Quite dainty and enchanting, and one of my favorites.

Cypripedium pubescens
(Large Yellow Lady-slipper)

ZONES: 4–8; light shade
SOIL: moist, neutral
NATIVE TO: rich woodland; Nova Scotia to Maine and Minnesota south to Missouri, Alabama, and Georgia
SIZE: 12–18 inches (12–16 inches)
COLOR: light to medium yellow lip, green to brown petals/sepals; **BLOOMS** in late spring

We grow thousands of these plants at Garden in the Woods, but each spring when they bloom I am transfixed once again by their elegance and grace. The typical forms have lip pouches about half the size of a hen's egg and twisting petals and sepals that radiate from it like some glorious fantasy mustache. One of the easiest to grow in a moist, woodland situation.

Cypripedium reginae
(Showy Lady-slipper)

ZONES: 3–8; sun, part sun
SOIL: moist to boggy, neutral
NATIVE TO: fens, bogs and swamps in limestone areas; Newfoundland and Quebec to North Dakota south to Missouri and Georgia
SIZE: 14–28 inches (16–20 inches)

COLOR: light to dark pink lip and white petals/sepals; **BLOOMS** from late spring to early summer

Certainly a regal plant if ever there was one. Showy Lady-slipper is a remarkable plant to see in the wild, with a bubble-gum pink lip contrasting beautifully with the crystalline white petals/sepals. The leaves are covered in stiff hairs, giving the plants a silvery green sheen. I have heard reports of the hairs causing dermatitis much like poison ivy, though I have handled many without problem. It needs a fairly open, constantly moist spot with a neutral pH to thrive, but given this it is not too difficult.

Dalea purpurea

Dalea (Petalostemum)
(DALE-ee-ah)
Fabaceae
Prairie Clover

The delicate-looking *Dalea*s are important nitrogen-fixing legumes of the prairies that have yet to catch on with gardeners (partly because they do not look like much in containers, so growers avoid them). They are often sold as a component of meadow seed mixes, but they can be a nice addition to the perennial border as well. They form bushy, vase-shaped clumps of strong stems covered in very fine, pinnate foliage and adorned from every tip in summer with tight, cylindrical heads of tiny flowers. The heads open from the base toward the tip, the blooming flowers in a ring or crown that advances upward like some colorful Fourth of July sparkler going in reverse.

The genus is now lumped into the larger new world genus *Dalea,* but older horticultural sources still refer to them as *Petalostemum.*

CULTURE: Easily grown in moist to dry soils and full sun.

USES: Borders, meadows.

PROPAGATION: Easy from seed. See p. 251.

Dalea candida
(White Prairie Clover)

ZONES: 3–9; sun
SOIL: moist to dry
NATIVE TO: prairies and meadows; Wisconsin to Alberta south to New Mexico, Texas, and Tennessee
SIZE: 3–4 feet (16–18 inches)
COLOR: white; **BLOOMS** in summer
A tall plant that is not particularly showy in flower, but it has a place in the meadow garden.

Dalea purpurea
(Purple Prairie Clover)

ZONES: 3–9; sun
SOIL: moist to dry
NATIVE TO: prairies and openings; Indiana to Alberta south to New Mexico and Alabama
SIZE: 2–3 feet (14–18 inches)
COLOR: lavender; **BLOOMS** in summer
Probably the best of the genus for garden use. The compact habit and colorful flowers are quite attractive.

Darmera (Peltiphyllum) peltata (dar-MARE-ah)
Saxifragaceae
Umbrella Plant

ZONES: 5–8; part sun, shade
SOIL: moist to wet, acid
NATIVE TO: mixed evergreen forest along mountain streams; southwestern Oregon to northern California
SIZE: 3 feet (3–4 feet)
COLOR: pink; **BLOOMS** in spring

There is something absolutely unworldly about the fantastic Umbrella Plant. In early spring, big flower stems that remind me of extraterrestrial antennae (it's been a while since I've seen an extraterrestrial, but it's a sight you don't easily forget) sprout from a thick, leafless tangle of shallow rhizomes as big around as garden hoses left in a heap. The stems eventually produce a grapefruit-sized cluster (technically a cyme) of pretty, small pink flowers. Only after the flowers have had their moment in the sun do the huge parasol-like leaves begin to grow, eventually forming a bold and spectacular dome of foliage. The round, pleated leaves can be over a foot in diameter, forming a shallow cone with the leaf petiole attached in the center

beneath. If I miss the seed before it is shed, I can usually collect plenty that has been caught, like coffee in a filter, within the large leaves. There is a dwarf form, var. *nana*—about one-half the size of the species, that is readily available and a good choice for smaller gardens.

CULTURE: In the wild *Darmera* grows in wet soils along mountain streams, and it appreciates similar conditions under cultivation. A waterside or mucky spot is ideal, for although it will survive with average moisture, the plants will be stunted and tend to go dormant prematurely. Give Umbrella Plant room to spread, because the thick rhizomes are best left undisturbed once established.

Darmera peltata

USES: Can lend a bold, tropical look to gardens without becoming invasive. Waterside, moist to wet soils.

PROPAGATION: Moderately easy from seed and rhizome cuttings; fairly easy from division. See p. 251.

Darmera peltata. *The huge leaves of Umbrella Plant are without equal among the wildflowers for sheer show-stopping impact. That these giants spring from seeds smaller than a grain of salt makes them, in my mind, even more remarkable. By the time the leaves have fully expanded, the precocious flowers have long ago withered and begun to shed their tiny seeds. They do need a considerable bit of damp real estate—this plant is roughly 5 feet in diameter and stands 3 feet high.*

Delphinium cardinale. *Like many of the incredible wildflowers native to southern California's gentle climate, Scarlet Larkspur lacks the ability to withstand long periods of subfreezing temperatures. Even when crossed with hardier species, its tenderness is passed on to the offspring in direct proportion to its brilliant red coloring.*

Delphinium cardinale

Delphinium
(dell-FIN-ee-um)
Ranunculaceae
Wild Larkspur

Much like *Clematis*, there are a number of native delphiniums that are certainly modest in flower compared with the familiar garden hybrids sold in garden centers, but they make up in ruggedness what they might lack in flower size. California is the center of diversity for the genus in North America, with dozens of species, including the spectacular scarlet *D. cardinale* from the southern part of the state. (One of my mentors, who went to graduate school in California, thought it would be fun and easy to produce hardy red delphiniums by breeding with *D. cardinale*. Forty years went by and he still never got a good, hardy red delphinium!) The flowers are composed of 5 sepals that form a star that encloses the petals, which are more or less fuzzy and wrap around the sexual parts of the flower so that a pollinator must pry them apart to access the tasty nectar at the end of the long spur formed by the dorsal sepal. They remind me of little bearded gnomes with pointed caps. The flowers are borne on long branching racemes well above the leaves.

Wild larkspurs are on the whole opportunists, taking advantage of moisture and light early in the season to grow and bloom, then retreating below ground until the following spring. Because of its later bloom, *D. exaltatum* makes the most satisfying and enduring foliage plant. The others, though worth growing for their beautiful blue flowers, need to be integrated into mixed plantings that hide the gaps left by their rapid departure. Like their cousins, *Aconitums,* they are poisonous if ingested and have caused a number of livestock poisonings in the western rangelands (those cattle should know better). There are 60 or so species in our flora, many endemic to small areas of the West. I have chosen a few representatives from different regions and habitats.

CULTURE: Delphiniums grow from a gnarled, woody rootstock that fattens with time so that older plants have a number of eyes or crowns but younger ones are a bit thin looking. Just give them time. I do not recommend dividing plants, though they can be moved in early spring. Place them in a spot that receives adequate moisture through early summer. They are on the whole long-lived plants that require little care.

USES: Best reserved for accents in a mixed planting or naturalized in a meadow or grassland.

PROPAGATION: Moderately difficult from seed. See p. 251.

Delphinium bicolor
(Little Larkspur)

ZONES: 4–8; sun, part sun
SOIL: moist in spring
NATIVE TO: shortgrass prairies, dry meadows, open woodland; North Dakota to western Washington south to southern Idaho and northwestern Nebraska
SIZE: 4–16 inches (6 inches)
COLOR: deep blue to purple; **BLOOMS** from late spring to early summer

A small plant with relatively large, flat flowers. The few, rounded leaves are heavily divided and about 2 inches in diameter.

Delphinium cardinale
(Scarlet Larkspur)

ZONES: 8–10; sun
SOIL: moist in spring
NATIVE TO: steep slopes in chaparral; central California to Baja California
SIZE: 3–5 feet (12–16 inches)
COLOR: scarlet red; **BLOOMS** from spring to early summer

A spectacular, hummingbird-pollinated species too tender for most gardeners but mentioned as it is used extensively in hybridizing. Certainly it should be sought out where it can be grown.

Delphinium carolinianum
(Carolina Larkspur)

ZONES: 5–9; sun, part sun
SOIL: moist in spring

NATIVE TO: prairies and openings, limestone glades; South Carolina to Illinois south to Texas and Florida

SIZE: 2–4 feet (12–16 inches)

COLOR: pale to dark violet or blue; BLOOMS from spring to early summer

Carolina Larkspur has very thin, palmately divided foliage loosely clothing the tall flower stems. The flowers are moderately sized and flare open well. *D. virescens* (Plains Larkspur) is now considered a pale-colored form of this species.

Delphinium exaltatum
(Tall Larkspur)

ZONES: 4–9; part sun

SOIL: moist, calcareous

NATIVE TO: open woods, slopes, mostly on limestone; Pennsylvania to Ohio and Missouri south to Tennessee and South Carolina

SIZE: 3–6 feet (16–24 inches)

COLOR: lavender to greenish violet; BLOOMS in late summer

Tall Larkspur has grayish green leaves divided into 5 lobes that are in turn divided into 3 teeth at their tips. It is a large and vigorous plant with, unfortunately, rather small flowers. It blooms fairly late so the foliage remains in good condition most of the summer. *D. glaucum* is a related species from large areas of the West.

Delphinium menziesii
(Menzie's Larkspur)

ZONES: 5–9; sun, part sun

SOIL: moist in spring

NATIVE TO: meadows and midelevation, open woodlands; southern British Columbia to Oregon

SIZE: 1–2 feet (8–12 inches)

COLOR: blue-purple, occasionally pale yellow; BLOOMS in spring

Menzie's Larkspur is an adaptable and beautiful little plant with thin, ferny foliage and relatively large, vibrant flowers. The sepals sweep back as if the flowers are flying in a stiff breeze. *D. nuttallianum* is a widespread, slightly smaller-flowered relative that grows over much of the area west of the Rockies. The often stunted but vibrant purple or blue flowers are a lovely sight amid the lupines and paintbrushes of mountain meadows.

Delphinium tricorne
(Dwarf Larkspur)

ZONES: 4–9; sun to light shade

SOIL: moist to wet

NATIVE TO: moist, wooded slopes, prairies, thickets; Pennsylvania to Iowa south to Oklahoma and Georgia

SIZE: 8–14 inches (8–12 inches)

COLOR: light to dark purple, pink, or white; BLOOMS in spring

Dwarf Larkspur got its common name before the western flora was discovered. It is small compared to the other eastern species, with large glowing flowers and a habit of fading quickly once the blooms have been pollinated. A fairly common plant and a good choice for a damp spot that could use a splash of color.

Dentaria diphylla

Dentaria (Cardamine)
(den-TARE-ee-ah)

Brassicaceae

Toothwort

Toothworts have a calmly unassuming quality, comfortably taking second seat to the more flamboyant of the spring ephemerals. Nevertheless, no spring woodland is complete without a few of them scattering 4-petaled blooms in the dappled light. *Dentaria*s grow from brittle, fleshy rhizomes that form a matted tangle just below the soil surface. They have bumps or ridges on their surface that suggest teeth, hence the name. The deeply lobed leaves begin to appear soon after the snow melts and the stalks of flowers soon follow.

Toothworts go dormant in early summer, sometimes appearing briefly again in fall but often remaining underground until spring. Often I have

Dentaria diphylla. *Like Spring Beauties and Dutchman's Breeches, toothworts create a thick, if only temporary, carpet in the woodland garden, covering up the bare ground of early spring with a lush canopy of leaves. I like to use them with plants that are slow to emerge, such as Maidenhair Fern, Solomon's Seal, and Jack-in-the-pulpit. The early ground covers add beauty and interest elaborated on by the emergence of the more leisurely species that eventually take their place in the light.*

Dicentra formosa.
Western Bleeding Heart is an outstanding garden plant, continually producing fresh leaves and flowers as long as there is enough moisture and light. It is a fairly common plant in the Pacific Northwest, growing everywhere from the coastal lowlands up to subalpine meadows. The blue-green foliage seems particularly striking against these volcanic cliffs below Crater Lake in south-central Oregon.

dug into a patch of temporarily forgotten toothworts in the heat of summer as I was transplanting some new treasure, shattering the rhizomes to pieces. They just shrug off such rough treatment and return even more abundantly the following year. I would not consider them invasive, though, as their small stature and ephemeral habits make them good bedfellows for a host of woodland plants.

Dentaria has been included in the large cosmopolitan genus *Cardamine*, but at least horticulturally, I think they are distinct enough to be segregated. There are many weedy *Cardamine*s, but I have yet to meet a *Dentaria* that I feel does not have garden merit. I worry about them becoming smothered in mediocrity by association. Admittedly, some *Cardamines* (*C. douglasii*, for example) can make decent garden plants though their season of active growth is very short.

CULTURE: Adaptable, but best in a humusy, slightly acid soil. Summer drought is tolerable provided it is not too severe and moisture returns in fall. There is a fungus disease—possibly a rust, but I cannnot be sure—that infects the plants, causing blotchy leaves and weakened growth and visible as a white bloom on the undersides of the leaves when fruiting. Removing infected leaves or plants is about all you can do, but luckily it is not severe very often.

USES: Ideal for mixed woodland plantings and to fill gaps around late-emerging plants.

WILDLIFE: *Dentaria* is a principal food for the larva of two native White butterflies *Pieris napi* (Mustard White) and *P. virginiensis* (West Virginia White). They can do a fair amount of leaf damage, but appear late in the plant's growing season, so the effect is only transitory.

PROPAGATION: Difficult from seed; easy from division. See p. 251.

Dentaria diphylla
(Twin-leaf Toothwort)

ZONES: 3–9; shade
SOIL: moist to wet
NATIVE TO: rich, moist woods; New Brunswick to Minnesota south to Alabama and Georgia
SIZE: 4–6 inches (12 inches)
COLOR: white; **BLOOMS** in spring
A robust, broad-leaved species distinguished by the pair of opposite leaves on the flower stem. Forms large clumps quickly.

Dentaria laciniata
(Cut-leaf Toothwort)

ZONES: 3–8; shade
SOIL: moist
NATIVE TO: rich, moist woods; southern Quebec to Minnesota south to Oklahoma, Louisiana, and Florida

SIZE: 3–5 inches (8–12 inches)
COLOR: white flushed with pink; **BLOOMS** in spring
The leaves of this toothwort are divided into 5 narrow segments, and the margins of each are finely cut. A whorl of 3 sits on each stem, with a flower spike in the middle. A very beautiful plant but not as vigorously spreading as some of the others.

Dentaria maxima
(Three-leaved Toothwort)

ZONES: 3–9; shade
SOIL: moist
NATIVE TO: rich, moist woods; New Brunswick to Maine and Wisconsin south to Kentucky and West Virginia
SIZE: 4–6 inches (12 inches)
COLOR: white; **BLOOMS** in spring
This is thought to be a natural hybrid between *D. laciniata* and *D. diphylla*, as it has the jointed rhizomes of the former and broad leaves of the latter. It is an excellent garden plant—probably the best of the eastern species. The broad, clean leaves are deeply toothed, and it has the vigor of *D. diphylla*. The laciness of the leaves varies from plant to plant, some grading more toward *D. laciniata*. Though listed as sterile, I have obtained fertile seed from plants that were growing with one of the parents.

Dicentra formosa

Dicentra (dye-CENT-ra)
Fumariaceae
Bleeding Heart

The *Dicentras* are one of my favorite group of wildflowers, easily recognized by their soft mounds of finely pinnate foliage and delicate, complex flowers that hang like charm bracelets above the leaves. The flowers consist of 2 oddly shaped outer petals that together form the shape of a heart or bonnet and 2 beaked inner petals that surround the pistil and stamens. Only large long-tongued bees are usually able to pry open the petals to get at the sweet nectar inside. The four species described here form two morphological groups. The first are low spring ephemerals of eastern woodlands that spend the summer as dormant bulblets. The second two are larger plants, forming dense, leafy clumps and blooming over a long season in spring and summer.

CULTURE: *Dicentra*s thrive in moist, fairly rich soils. They require little care other than occasional fertilizing, and for the ephemerals, a topdressing of limestone every year or two. *D. eximia* and *D. formosa* seem equally content in sun or light shade, though bright light and summer moisture promote longer flowering.

USES: The larger species are very effective massed in borders, as edging, among rocks, or as specimens. The ephemerals are best naturalized in a woodland setting.

WILDLIFE: Good nectar plants for bumblebees. *D. formosa* is the larval food plant of the butterfly *Parnassius clodius* (Clodius Parnassian) in the Northwest.

PROPAGATION: Easy to difficult from seed; easy from division. See p. 251.

Dicentra eximia. *Like its western cousin, Wild Bleeding Heart is one of our longest blooming wildflowers. European breeders have crossed the two species to create a range of hybrids with brilliantly colored foliage and blooms. In fact, even though they're often labeled as* D. eximia *or* D. formosa, *most of the plants available in nurseries (such as 'Bacchanal', 'Luxuriant', and 'Stewart Boothman') are hybrids intermediate between the two.*

Dicentra canadensis
(Squirrel Corn)

ZONES: 3–8; part sun, shade
SOIL: moist in spring
NATIVE TO: rich, deciduous woodlands; Quebec to Illinois south to Kentucky and Virginia
SIZE: 3–5 inches (8–12 inches)
COLOR: white, sometimes tinged pink; **BLOOMS** in spring

Squirrel Corn forms a temporary ground cover of fine blue-green leaves and short arching spikes of fragrant, heart-shaped flowers. A fine plant to mix with other spring ephemerals. It blooms a week later than *D. cucullaria,* so combine them to extend the bloom period.

Dicentra cucullaria
(Dutchman's Breeches)

ZONES: 3–8; part sun, shade
SOIL: moist in spring
NATIVE TO: rich deciduous woodlands; Nova Scotia and eastern North Dakota to Oklahoma and Georgia
SIZE: 3–6 inches (6–8 inches)
COLOR: white to light pink; **BLOOMS** in early spring

Dutchman's Breeches can be distinguished from *D. canadensis* by the pointed rather than rounded lobes or shoulders of the outer petals and lack of fragrance. It forms spreading colonies, but tends to remain in discrete crowns rather than a uniform mat.

Dicentra eximia
(Wild Bleeding Heart)

ZONES: 4–9; sun to shade
SOIL: moist
NATIVE TO: rich woodlands, mostly in the Appalachian mountains; New Jersey and West Virginia south to Virginia and Tennessee
SIZE: 12–18 inches (18–24 inches)
COLOR: pink, occasionally white; **BLOOMS** in flushes from late spring until fall

A robust and beautiful plant, forming strong clumps of medium green foliage. It seeds readily, but the brittle seedlings are easy to remove where unwanted. There are several hybrids between this and *D. formosa* widely available in the trade. They are usually intermediate between the two, with glaucous foliage and a weakly to aggressively spreading habit.

Dicentra formosa
(Western Bleeding Heart, Pacific Bleeding Heart)

ZONES: 4–9; sun to shade
SOIL: moist
NATIVE TO: moist areas from coastal forests to timberline; British Columbia to northern California
SIZE: 12– 16 inches (2 feet)
COLOR: light pink to dark rose; **BLOOMS** from late spring to late summer

A valuable garden plant, with often vibrantly colored flowers. It has wandering rhizomes that are difficult to contain and best left to ramble around the garden at will. *D. formosa* ssp. *oregana* is localized along the California-Oregon border, with striking blue-gray foliage and cream to white flowers.

Diphylleia cymosa

Diphylleia cymosa

(dye-phil-AY-ah)
Berberidaceae
Umbrella Leaf

ZONES: 4–8; part sun, shade

SOIL: moist to wet

NATIVE TO: moist areas along seeps and streams; Blue Ridge Mountains from Virginia to Georgia

SIZE: 18–28 inches (24 inches)

COLOR: white; BLOOMS in spring

I **remember** when I first encountered this lovely plant on a perfect spring day in the Blue Ridge Mountains of North Carolina. The air was dense with green and the warm smell of life shaking off another evening rain. I was reveling in the beauty of a large swath of Canada Violets in bloom when I noticed some strange, bold leaves by a creek in the distance. Though I had never seen Umbrella Leaf, I did not know that the plant grew only in these blessed mountains from Virginia to Georgia. It was not until I came to Garden in the Woods that I began to grow and admire it as a garden plant. The large, sharply lobed leaves are cleft halfway down their middle, so as to appear like a pair of wings rather

than a single leaf. When emerging, the leaves have the same reddish brown coloration and closed umbrella appearance as Mayapple, and flowering growths produce an extra leaf along the stem. The plants take a few years to reach full size, but in a rich, moist soil they can eventually form large stately clumps with a bold presence that immediately sets my mind swimming with possible textural combinations. Small, 6-petaled white flowers grow in a flat cluster on a long arching stem that later supports blue fruits with lovely, contrasting red pedicels. If you squeeze one of the ripe fruits, out pops one of the most beautifully colored wildflower seeds I know. It is large, shiny, and a unique color somewhere between purple and crimson.

CULTURE: Grow in a rich soil that stays evenly moist. The plants take three to four years to reach their full size, so divide them only when absolutely necessary. They grow in tight, nonspreading clumps from a thick rhizome. For best effect, plant them in drifts of at least six or eight plants.

USES: For foliage effect in moist, shady spots.

PROPAGATION: Moderately difficult from seed. See p. 251.

Disporum maculatum

Disporum (diss-POUR-um)

Liliaceae
Fairy-bells

I **have** watched a fair number of greenhouses being constructed, and it always amazes me to see a pile of metal and glass transformed into soaring, complex architecture of delicate trusses and transparent skin. The result is refined yet predictable from one structure to the next, a poetic reliability of sorts. I see some of the same qualities in the vegetative architecture of the woodland fairy-bells. These lily relatives send up leafy stems of alternating, prominently veined leaves that begin to branch and split as they expand, creating a tree-shaped framework for the foliage to hang on. These stems are very consistent in size and shape from one to the next, so they are wonderful for adding some repetition to your planting designs, but delicate and complex enough that they are never tiring to look at.

Fairy-bells have small lilylike flowers that emerge with the expanding foliage like shells tossed in an emerald surf. We have a large bed of *D. maculatum* in the nursery, and when they are in bloom, the air is filled with a delightfully sweet, powerful perfume. All but *D. maculatum* form rich orange or red berries in the fall that hang in succulent candelabras from the branch tips. They usually hang on after the leaves yellow. When not in flower or fruit, the plants look very similar, and any of them make a welcome addition to the shade garden.

CULTURE: All the fairy-bells grow well in average woodland soils. The root systems form an impenetrable mass that resembles a heap of thick ramen noodles. While it is possible to divide them in early fall—and they transplant well—you will need an old saw or pruners to hack your way through the tangled clump. Be careful not to damage the tender buds that lie buried in the center.

PROPAGATION: Moderately difficult from seed. See p. 251.

Disporum hookeri

(Hooker's Fairy-bells)

ZONES: 4–8; shade
SOIL: moist
NATIVE TO: moist, rich woods; British Columbia to California, also isolated populations in Michigan
SIZE: 18–26 inches (16 inches)
COLOR: creamy white; **BLOOMS** in spring
One of a group of closely related, red-fruited species. Others include *D. trachycarpum* (Wartberry Fairy-bells), a similar species from much of the mountainous West with bright red, slightly wrinkled fruits. *D. lanuginosum* (Fairy-bells) is another related plant from rich woods over much of eastern North America that bears striking orange-yellow berries.

Disporum maculatum

(Fairy-bells, Nodding Mandarin)

ZONES: 4–8; shade
SOIL: moist
NATIVE TO: rich mountain woods, scattered; from Maryland to Ohio south to Alabama and Tennessee, also in Michigan
SIZE: 20–28 inches (16 inches)
COLOR: cream with purple spotting; **BLOOMS** in spring
Nodding Mandarin has relatively large (2 inches), wide-flaring flowers and 3-lobed fruits that are woody and yellow when ripe. It is the most ornamental for flower effect.

Disporum smithii

(Fairy-lantern)

ZONES: 5–8; shade
SOIL: moist
NATIVE TO: moist forests; Cascade Mountains from British Columbia to northern California
SIZE: 16–20 inches (16 inches)
COLOR: creamy white; **BLOOMS** in spring
Differs from *D. hookeri* in the larger, narrowly bell-shaped flowers.

Dodecatheon pulchellum

Dodecatheon
(doed-eh-KATHE-ee-on)
Primulaceae
Shooting Star

Shooting stars are much-loved wildflowers with intricate blooms that look for all the world like tiny umbrellas torn violently inside out by some silent tempest wind. The swept-back petals join in the center to form a circular ring from which protrudes a beaklike amalgamation of pistils and stamen. The blooms are borne like a complex, colorful chandelier on tall stems, which adds greatly to their charm.

*Dodecatheon*s are lovers of moisture when in active growth, drawing on spring rains and snowmelt to produce a flush of thin, succulent leaves in a basal rosette. They are spring ephemerals, quickly yellowing in the summer heat, and with such a short season of active growth, they are a little slow to mature. Patience will reward you, though, as an older

Dodecatheon pulchellum. *Shooting Star's fantastic flowers are reminiscent of the florist's Cyclamen, a fellow member of the fabulous Primrose family. Certain families, such as the Primrose, Lily, and Buttercup families have a preponderance of horticulturally outstanding species in their ranks, thus a basic knowledge of family relationships is helpful when trying to narrow down choices from seed and plant catalogs. Although rarely available at local garden centers, many different* Dodecatheon*s are available as seed from specialty firms.*

multicrowned plant in flower is a stunning sight.

There are a dozen or more very similar species, all native to North America. I have grown many from seed, but because they hybridize freely in gardens and are often difficult for all but the expert to distinguish in the wild, the seed is often mislabeled. Fortunately, there is no such thing as an ugly shooting star, and you may get some interesting surprises this way.

CULTURE: Shooting stars are easily grown in a variety of garden situations. They will grow equally as well in the lightly shaded woodland or the open garden as long as they have ready access to moisture in spring. I find it helpful to plant *Dodecatheon*s at the base of a large stone — in part so as to mark their location when dormant and also because such siting seems particularly appropriate as a backdrop for the flowers.

PROPAGATION: Moderately difficult from seed; easy from root cuttings. See p. 252.

Dodecatheon amethystinum (syn. *radicatum*)
(Amethyst Shooting Star)

ZONES: 4–9; sun to light shade
SOIL: moist to wet in spring
NATIVE TO: moist prairies and meadows; Pennsylvania to Wisconsin south to Missouri
SIZE: 8–14 inches (8–12 inches)
COLOR: light to dark pink; **BLOOMS** in spring
Basically a dark form of *D. meadia*, usually blooming a bit later but impossible to tell from it when not in flower (though supposedly the leaf bases of Amethyst Shooting Star are more heart-shaped).

D. pulchellum (Dark-throat Shooting Star) is another closely allied and widespread species from much of the West. Found growing everywhere from tidal wetlands to mountain seeps, its flowers vary from light to dark pink, though outstanding nearly red–flowered forms are sometimes available through specialty nurseries.

Dodecatheon clevelandii
(Cleveland's Shooting Star)

ZONES: (6) 7–9; sun, part sun
SOIL: moist in spring
NATIVE TO: grassy slopes, chaparral below 2,500 feet; California
SIZE: 12–20 inches (12 inches)
COLOR: white through magenta; **BLOOMS** in spring
This is a widespread, robust plant restricted to California. I have grown var. *insulare* and was impressed by its size and hardiness (given the moderate climate of its homeland). The leaves are 6–8 inches long and fairly broad, giving it a lettucelike appearance. The flowers are among the largest in the genus, measuring over an inch in length with wide petals.

Dodecatheon dentatum
(Dentate Shooting Star, White Shooting Star)

ZONES: 4–7; sun to light shade
SOIL: moist to wet in spring
NATIVE TO: wet places in the mountains; central Idaho to southern British Columbia south to Oregon
SIZE: 6–10 inches (8 inches)
COLOR: white; **BLOOMS** in spring
As you may have guessed from the name, this species has distinctly toothed, rounded to spade-shaped leaves on long petioles — quite attractive. The flowers are always white.

Dodecatheon hendersonii
(Sailor Caps, Mosquito-bills)

ZONES: 5–8; sun, part sun
SOIL: moist in spring, well drained
NATIVE TO: moist prairies and slopes; British Columbia to central California
SIZE: 12–14 inches (8–12 inches)
COLOR: pink to magenta; **BLOOMS** in spring
The leaves are rounded and thick, usually with a slight to prominent glaucous bloom. It is typically dark colored in flower and some forms are an absolutely delicious shade of red-purple. Sailor Caps is the first *Dodecatheon* to bloom in our gardens.

Dodecatheon meadia
(Eastern Shooting Star)

ZONES: 4–9; sun to light shade
SOIL: moist
NATIVE TO: woods and meadows; Maryland to Wisconsin and Iowa south to Texas, Alabama, and Georgia
SIZE: 8–14 inches (8–12 inches)
COLOR: pale to medium pink; **BLOOMS** in spring
D. meadia is primary eastern species and probably the best for shady situations. *D. frenchii* is a charming, compact, white-flowered relative from Kentucky and Illinois. It has leaves that are wider and of thinner substance as well.

Dodecatheon poeticum
(Narcissus Shooting Star)

ZONES: 6–8; sun, part sun
SOIL: moist
NATIVE TO: grassland and forests at moderate elevations, usally near seeps, streams; Washington and Oregon
SIZE: 14–20 inches (12 inches)
COLOR: rose to magenta; **BLOOMS** in spring
Admittedly I first grew this species just because I liked the name, but it is very distinctive. The downy leaves are large and paddle-shaped with long, stiff red petioles. At first I did not even recognize it as a

Dodecatheon, thinking I'd been sent the wrong seed (it looks very much like the Swamp Saxifrage, *Saxifraga pennsylvanica,* in leaf). *D. cusickii* (Sticky Shooting Star) is similar.

Echinacea purpurea

Echinacea (eck-in-AY-see-ah)
Asteraceae
Coneflower

Coneflowers lead a double life these days. They continue to be much loved as garden plants on the one hand while being embraced by the popular consciousness as an herbal remedy of unparalleled ability on the other. I have recently boarded the *Echinacea* train myself, but still I wonder—am I well because it worked or did it work because I am well? An egg is a chicken unless you drop it first. Regardless, they are indispensable plants in the summer garden, and they add welcome splashes of pink and purple to our prairies and meadows.

There are about half a dozen species, all native to North America. I have grown most of them and find that, though all have their charms, *E. purpurea* and *E. tennesseensis* make the best garden subjects overall. However, many are becoming very rare in the wild and, among other things, are suffering genetic homogenization from cross pollination with cultivated *E. purpurea*, so I would encourage you to seek out and grow your local species if you can. The central "cone" of each bloom is a gradually expanding cluster of the fertile, purple-brown disk flowers that are highlighted with orange-tipped spines (the Latin root *Echin* means "beset with prickles," and this refers to the spines that guard the flowers and seeds). The sterile ray flowers (petals) hold their color a long time, so the plants remain colorful for a month or two.

CULTURE: Easily grown in sunny situations. Different species can be selected for tolerance of both moisture and drought. Most of them grow from a forked taproot that forms multiple, leafy crowns which support the stout flowering stems. Aside from grasshoppers munching a few leaves, they are just about pest-free.

WILDLIFE: A favorite nectar plant for midseason butterflies. Goldfinches love to perch on the stems and devour the ripened seeds. They make a start in one of the cones and neatly eat the seeds row by row like corn on the cob. They get quite irritated when I disturb them to harvest some seed myself.

PROPAGATION: Easy from seed. See p. 252.

Echinacea angustifolia
(Purple Coneflower)

ZONES: 3–9; sun
SOIL: well drained
NATIVE TO: rocky prairies and plains; Minnesota to Montana south to New Mexico and Iowa
SIZE: 8–16 inches (12–14 inches)
COLOR: light to dark rose; BLOOMS in early summer
Small coneflower is adapted to life on the dry plains, with narrow, hairy leaves and short flower stems. The rays are also narrow and reflexed or drooping. It is one of the preferred medicinal species, grading into the taller, tetraploid *E. pallida* (Prairie Coneflower) as it moves into the eastern prairies. Another species, *E. simulata*, is intermediate in size between the two. It has proved to be the earliest-blooming coneflower I have grown, putting out its first dark, thin-petaled flowers in mid- to late spring. It is native to Missouri and adjacent states.

Echinacea laevigata
(Appalachian Coneflower)

ZONES: 5–9; sun, part sun
SOIL: moist
NATIVE TO: meadows on neutral soils; Virginia to Georgia
SIZE: 20–30 inches (16–18 inches)
COLOR: rose; BLOOMS in summer
An interesting plant with the broad, glossy leaves of *E. purpurea* and the tall stems and narrow rays of *E. pallida*. One of the most vigorous growers and a good choice for the perennial border if you want a lacier floral effect than can be obtained with Purple Coneflower. Sadly, it is either extinct or endangered in much of its former range, which was long ago converted to agriculture.

Echinacea paradoxa
(Yellow Coneflower)

ZONES: 4–9; sun
SOIL: well drained
NATIVE TO: limestone prairies and balds; Missouri and Arkansas
SIZE: 24–30 inches (16–18 inches)

Echinacea purpurea. *Rising like rosy-flushed badminton shuttlecocks from the boundless prairie or the garden border, the kinetic blooms of Purple Coneflower are something I cannot imagine any sunny garden being without. The disk or cone in the center of each daisy is a tightly packed, expandable spike of small fertile flowers that remains as a crib to contain the seeds and also a makeshift perch for ravenous Goldfinches to extract them.*

Echinocereus reichenbachii. *Lace Cactus wears a lovely coat of fine white spines and erects remarkable satin blooms for a few precious days each spring. The flowers close up at night to limit water loss, then quickly expand under the warmth of the sun. I grew this particular plant from seed while in college and hauled it and its siblings around unceremoniously for about five years before finally setting them in their permanent home, a raised bed covered with a carpet of Pussy-toes. The life of a vagabond can be as tough on the plants as it is on the gardener.*

COLOR: rays golden yellow, cone dark purple; BLOOMS in summer

In habit this plant resembles a shiny-leaved *E. pallida*, with narrow, basal foliage and tall arching stems each topped with a single bloom. The flower color is unique in the genus, but, like Pale Coneflower, the habit of the plant is rather lax and needs to be grown in full sun and a lean soil to stay compact. Rare or endangered throughout its limited range.

Echinacea purpurea

(Purple Coneflower, Broad-leaved Cone-flower)

ZONES: 3–9; sun, part sun
SOIL: moist
NATIVE TO: moist prairies and meadows and gaps in low woods; Ohio to Michigan and Iowa south to Oklahoma, Louisiana, and Georgia
SIZE: 26–40 inches (18–24 inches)
COLOR: rays typically dark rose, rarely white; BLOOMS in summer

An excellent and commonly available garden plant. It is the most robust, shade-tolerant, and moisture loving of the group, and many selections are available with broad, flat rays and deep color as well as compact habit. The white-flowered cultivars such as 'White Swan' are simply stunning. This is the only fibrous-rooted species, and it may be somewhat short-lived in meadow plantings.

Echinacea tennesseensis

(Tennessee Coneflower)

ZONES: 4–9; sun
SOIL: well drained
NATIVE TO: red cedar glades and balds; central Tennessee
SIZE: 12–20 inches (12 inches)
COLOR: rose; BLOOMS in summer

Another of the rare species, this Tennessee endemic is related to *E. angustifolia*, but, at least in the few I have seen, the ray flowers do not reflex (they are broad and flat like a small Purple Coneflower's), and the color is a vibrant deep rose. The foliage is also less hairy and more glowing green than is typical with Small Coneflower. It is a beautiful plant that, unfortunately, because of its endangered status, is not readily available, and since it crosses readily with other species, plants offered commercially are more often than not hybrids with *E. purpurea* or *E. pallida*. The hybrids with Purple Coneflower are certainly outstanding garden plants with a compact habit, narrow foliage, and large, flat, rose-colored flowers. They are also very drought-tolerant so by all means acquire some if you can.

Echinocereus reichenbachii

Echinocereus
(eck-eye-no-SEAR-ee-us)
Cactaceae
Hedgehog Cactus

It is one of the great ironies of nature that some of the most exquisite, opulent flowers imaginable are produced by the tough little barrel cacti of the American deserts and plains. It is an apparent paradox that such unassuming succulents put so much of their resources into producing glorious funnel-shaped flowers often larger than the plants themselves. However, it makes sense if you consider that the scattered plants are in bloom for only a few favored days each year and so must do all they can to attract any pollinators in the area. The silky, many-petaled flowers narrow into a tube packed with huge amounts of pollen to dab on any bird, bat, or bee that lands. They appear first as little nubs on the barrel above the previous season's spines and slowly swell and lengthen until one morning the warming sun spurs them to flare open triumphantly.

When not in bloom, the various hedgehog cacti are still highly ornamental, with fluted barrels and beautifully shaped and colored spines. While I do not foresee them replacing *Coreopsis* on any list of top ten perennials, they are certainly charming examples of adaptation to harsh environments, with a place in rock gardens and xeriscapes. As an interesting sociological aside, I have noticed that men seem especially fascinated by both cacti and carnivorous plants, though I won't hazard a guess as to why. Though chances are you will not find any at your local garden center, there are several specialty mail-order nurseries in the Southwest that focus on hardy cacti, offering plants and/or seeds.

CULTURE: Many hedgehogs are surprisingly hardy and easy to grow. In the wild they are commonly found under the light shade of grasses, shrubs, or rocks, and desert gardeners should try to duplicate these conditions to protect the barrels from scalding. They will also grow in the wetter parts of North America, provided they receive full sun and are in a gritty, well-drained soil (a scree mix is suitable). The plants survive freezing temperatures by shriveling to lower their water content in fall, but plump up quickly in spring.

PROPAGATION: Slow and moderately difficult from seed. See p. 252.

Echinocereus fendleri var. *fendleri*

(Fendler Hedgehog Cactus)

ZONES: 5–9; sun
SOIL: dry, well drained
NATIVE TO: sandy or gravelly soil in sagebrush grasslands to Pinyon or Ponderosa Pine forest; Colorado to Arizona south to Mexico and Texas
SIZE: 2–6 inches (6 inches)
COLOR: magenta; **BLOOMS** from spring to summer (after rains)

This hedgehog grows as individual stems to small clumps and coats itself with an impressive armament of 1-inch upward-curved spines surrounded by smaller spines that lay flat against the barrel in an interlocking fabric. The lovely spines are the main reason I grow it, as the plants seem to need more sun and heat than I can provide to produce their glorious magenta flowers.

Echinocereus reichenbachii

(Lace Cactus)

ZONES: 4–9; sun
SOIL: dry, well drained
NATIVE TO: rocky hillsides, mainly on limestone; Oklahoma to Colorado south to Mexico and Texas
SIZE: 4–10 inches (6–8 inches)
COLOR: bright pink to purple; **BLOOMS** in early summer

Lace Cactus forms fairly tall, single to several-stemmed clumps of 1–2-inch-diameter barrels covered in interlocking, flattened spines that suggest the common name. The spines are often white in color, which adds to the effect (the color and shape of the spines resemble the dreaded mealy bug—bane of my existence when I used to manage a research collection of various succulents under glass). It pro-

duces wonderful satiny pink flowers reliably each spring in my garden.

Echinocereus triglochidiatus

(Claret Cup Cactus)

ZONES: 5–9; sun
SOIL: dry, well drained
NATIVE TO: rocky or grassy hillsides, canyons, pinyon-juniper forest margins, up to 9,000 feet; South Dakota to Wyoming and Nevada south to Mexico and Texas
SIZE: 3–12 inches (8–12 inches)
COLOR: scarlet to crimson; **BLOOMS** from spring to early summer

Claret Cup Cactus is spectacular not only for the color of its flowers but also for the dense, many-stemmed clumps that develop over time. I have seen plants in New Mexico with more than one hundred 1 1/2-inch stems crowded like commuters on the five o'clock train in large domed cushions. (Plants of this size must be at least a century old, as its growth is certainly not rapid.) The most widespread type in this variable species complex is var. *melanacanthus*, which has long thin spines much like *E. fendleri* and grows throughout most of the central and southern Rockies. Var. *gonacanthus* is noticably different, with fewer but very thick spines. These are the hardiest varieties of this species and the only ones I have sucessfully grown.

Echinocereus viridiflorus var. *viridiflorus*

(Hedgehog Cactus)

ZONES: 4–9; sun
SOIL: dry, well drained
NATIVE TO: gravelly soils in grassland and forest edge from the plains to 9,000 feet in the Rocky Mountains; South Dakota to Wyoming south to New Mexico and Texas
SIZE: 2–6 inches (6 inches)
COLOR: green to chartreuse; **BLOOMS** from spring to summer (after rains)

This typically solitary-stemmed species is one of the hardiest. The barrels are a glossy, dark green, and the spines are fairly short and bright white. The small green flowers are not stunning, but the plants bloom pretty well for me.

Epigaea repens

Epigaea repens (ep-ee-JAY-ah)
Ericaceae
Trailing Arbutus, Mayflower

Epigaea repens. *A bee caught in an indelicate position gathering nectar from the redolent blooms of a blushing Mayflower. The flower buds formed the previous season and waited in tightly packed clusters for the first warmth of spring. On several occasions I have forced pots of the delicious plants in late winter by bringing them from the cold frame into a cool, sunny room. The flowers last for a week or two this way and provide a little taste of spring when I most need it.*

ZONES: 3–9; part sun, shade

SOIL: acidic, moist but well drained

NATIVE TO: sandy or humusy, acid soils, woodland and pine barrens; Newfoundland to Saskatchewan south to Iowa, Mississippi, and Florida

SIZE: 2–4 inches (12 inches)

COLOR: white to medium pink; BLOOMS in early spring

It is difficult to describe the delicate allure of the little Mayflower. In New England it is one of the few plants with a reputation and lore that is large enough to precede it so that many people not usually interested in wildflowers seek it out. Most are surprised when they meet one in person that the ragged little evergreen in front of them is the fabled Trailing Arbutus. It is a member of the Rhododendron family and shares with many in this blessed clan a reluctance to shed its leaves in autumn. These remain, tattered but still a rough, leathery green, until summer of the following year. This made it a favorite winter decoration in the nineteenth century, and alarm over its widespread harvest was a key issue galvanizing a group of Boston women to form the Society for the Preservation of New England Flora (later the New England Wild Flower Society) in 1900. In part as a result of their efforts, a law was passed making it illegal to commercially harvest the plants, and it was named the state flower of Massachusetts. Like its relative Wintergreen, *Epigaea* is a low, woody ground cover that sends out 1–3 whorls of new growth from the tips of the previous season's wood just after flowering. These trail a short way through the forest duff before unfolding a set of stiff, undulating, narrowly oval leaves. The leaves are held at a 45 degree angle to the ground in sun but lie flat to collect maximum

light in shade. The plants are slow growing and a bit particular about siting, but can form a lovely matted ground cover in time.

The true joy of Mayflower is the blooms—waxy little bells that form in bunches at the tips of the stems and release a glorious, heady perfume similar to jasmine that hangs heavily in the air during the first warm days of spring. This past spring I received a call from a well-known perfume designer who wanted to extract and synthesize this aroma for a line of beauty products. An assistant came out and bought a flat of blooming plants that she whisked away to a lab in New Jersey for analysis. I have not heard, but some day soon a line of Mayflower perfume based on our little plants may just appear on department store shelves.

In a wild population it is easy to discover flowers that range from white to light pink and occasionally darker pink as well. A double-flowered form 'Floraplena' with shell pink flowers and smaller leaves has been in the garden for many years. The flowers are quite showy but lack as strong a fragrance. Arbutus plants are dioecious, so male and female plants are necessary for seed.

CULTURE: *Epigaea* has a reputation for being difficult, which is partly deserved, but it can be very successfully grown in gardens if you consider its needs carefully. (We have a number of patches at Garden in the Woods that have been getting larger every year since they were planted by Will Curtis back in the 50s.) In the wild, I usually find the plants on north- or east-facing slopes or hillsides. The slope sheds many of the tree leaves that can smother the plants, and the aspect keeps more moisture in the soil during the growing season. They need a very acid, moist but well-drained soil liberally amended with humus and kept watered for the first two seasons after transplanting. Growth and flowering are better with a few hours of direct sun, though this may bleach the leaves somewhat. Do not try to dig mats from the wild. They grow out from a central, woody crown that is deep-rooted but easily damaged, and the fine feeder roots that grow along the trailing stems are not enough to support a large plant. Instead start with well-rooted container plants put out in spring. It takes a few years for the plants to form deep, woody roots, so they need careful watering for two seasons but eventually are very drought-tolerant. A light dressing of organic fertilizer and a mulch of shredded oak leaves or pine needles worked around the leaves is appreciated in spring.

USES: Evergreen ground cover.

PROPAGATION: Difficult from seed; moderately difficult from cuttings. See p. 252.

Epilobium angustifolium

Epilobium angustifolium
(epp-ee-LOBE-ee-um)
Onagraceae
Fireweed

ZONES: 2–8; sun, part sun

SOIL: moist

NATIVE TO: moist open areas, especially abundant two to three years after fire, circumboreal; in North America from Labrador to Alaska south to New Mexico, Nebraska, Ohio, and New Jersey

SIZE: 2–4 feet (2 feet)

COLOR: bright pink; **BLOOMS** in midsummer

I **will never** forget a summer canoe trip into the Quetico region of Ontario, north of Lake Superior, with its miles of unspoiled lakes and forest. Here, as in much of the North, the ubiquitous Fireweed decorates the summer landscape with bold spikes of its crepe paper–pink blooms. On this trip I brought an edible wild plants guide by a well-known enthusiast that recommended the pith of *E. angustifolium* as a tasty cooked vegetable treat. After an hour of painstaking work scraping the meager pith from a couple dozen stems I cooked the slimy, pea green mass with open mind and fading enthusiasm, but the first mouthful brought home to me the subtle difference between the words edible and palatable and put an end to my foraging on that trip.

Fireweed is a tall plant with many long narrow leaves. The flowers appear in long racemes at the top of the stems for several weeks. They are shaped like an evening primrose, with 4 nonoverlapping petals alternating with 4 narrow sepals.

There are many native *Epilobium*s, but as a whole they are weedy plants of disturbed areas with small flowers and cottony seeds that erupt from long thin pods and find their way everywhere. Besides *E. angustifolium*, the other best horticultural species are somewhat tender mountain plants best grown in scree. (These include *E. latifolium, E. obcordatum,* and *E. rigidum,* all showy, compact, less invasive species that hail from the mountains along the Pacific coast.)

CULTURE: Fireweed can be easily accommodated in a moist, sunny spot in the garden, The others need a gritty soil that is not too dry.

USES: Fireweed is an aggressively spreading plant that is probably best suited for naturalizing in the meadow or along the woodland edge.

PROPAGATION: Easy from seed. See p. 252.

(LEFT): Epilobium angustifolium. *In the few years after conflagration sweeps through forest or meadow, Fireweed puts on a spectacular show. It is unclear whether it is responding to nutrients or chemicals released by the fire or simply a reduction in competition.*

Eriogonum umbellatum

Eriogonum (air-ee-OG-on-um)
Polygonaceae
Wild Buckwheat

The **wild buckwheats** are widespread and common wildflowers in the dry and mountainous West. In general they form small rosettes of gray or silver, felted leaves, either in tight masses or loose colonies separated by woody, ground-hugging stolons or upright branches. The types most frequently grown are low, mat-forming plants or mounded subshrubs well suited to rock gardens or xeriscapes. Flowers are borne in dense, fluffy heads on stiff, forking stems above the rosettes. Their strawflower substance and myriad colors are a welcome addition to the summer garden. The bracts that surround the seeds remain colorful for quite a while, even changing color and persisting long after flowers have given way to seeds.

Of even greater importance to the ecologically minded horticulturist is their value as larval food plants for a bewildering number of butterflies throughout the West. Butterflies known to feed on *Eriogonum* include many lovely *Callophrys* spp. (hairstreaks), *Apodemia mormo* (one of the widespread metalmarks), many *Lycaena* spp. (cop-

(RIGHT): Eriogonum umbellatum. *Buckwheats are important food plants for many butterfly caterpillars. Sulfur Flower is one of the most common and a fairly easy plant in the rock garden. The color of the bracts that surround each flower is variable from plant to plant and often darkens as the flowers age and seed is set.*

pers), as well as *Philotes* and *Plebejus* spp. (blues). One can only imagine how many other less-studied insects rely on these plants as well. Temper this with the reality that 130 of the 200 or so native buckwheats are listed as rare or endangered in at least part of their range. Surely *Eriogonum*s should be at the top of every western butterfly gardener's plant list. There are many lovely species, though some are coarse or weedy, and I have chosen but a few of the more wide-ranging, easily cultivated types that should appeal to a large number of butterfly species.

CULTURE: Wild buckwheats should be sited in full sun in well-drained, droughty soils. It is best to start with healthy, container-grown seedlings, as the deep central taproot is easily damaged. Even though many of the species trail over the ground, they root only from the central crown, much as a low shrub like *Arctostaphylos uva-ursi* (Bearberry).

USES: Ground cover or low shrub — rock garden, xeriscaping, butterfly garden.

WILDLIFE: See notes above.

PROPAGATION: Easy from seed. See p. 252.

Eriogonum allenii
(Shale Buckwheat)

ZONES: 4–9; sun, part sun
SOIL: moist to dry, well drained
NATIVE TO: rocky shale barrens in the Appalachian Mountains, Virginia to West Virginia
SIZE: 8–16 inches (12–14 inches)
COLOR: bright yellow; **BLOOMS** in late summer
I include this larger species mainly for comparision, as it is one of only two eastern members of the genus. Loose, 10-inch rosettes of rather coarse, gray-green leaves with white felt underneath are topped with forked stems of sulphur yellow flowers late in the season. It is an unusual plant restricted to a small area in the Appalachians.

Eriogonum flavum
(Yellow Buckwheat)

ZONES: 3–8; sun
SOIL: moist, well drained
NATIVE TO: rocky, alpine and subalpine areas; Alberta to Alaska south to Oregon and Colorado
SIZE: 2–5 inches (12 inches)
COLOR: bright yellow, sometimes tinged pink; **BLOOMS** in summer
A mat-forming, congested alpine species with narrow, silvery leaves. Very pretty.

Eriogonum nudum
(Barestem Buckwheat)

ZONES: 4–8; sun
SOIL: dry, well drained

NATIVE TO: dry, rocky, open areas up to 8,000 feet; central California to Washington
SIZE: 8–24 inches (14–18 inches)
COLOR: variable — white through rose and yellow; **BLOOMS** in summer
A low shrubby form with round leaves on long petioles and branched, open spikes. Widespread and common through its range. It is very similar to and sometimes included with *E. latifolium*.

Eriogonum ovalifolium
(Cushion Buckwheat, Oval-leaved Buckwheat)

ZONES: 3–7; sun
SOIL: well drained, moist
NATIVE TO: rocky, alpine areas; Alberta to British Columbia south to California and New Mexico
SIZE: 1–4 inches (3–6 inches)
COLOR: yellow, white, or pink; **BLOOMS** in early summer
A very low, dense to loosely mat-forming plant with rounded leaves in small rosettes. Very cute. Various color forms are available from seed. The flower/seed heads tend to sprawl on the ground around the foliage as if too heavy for the weak stems.

Eriogonum umbellatum
(Sulfur Flower)

ZONES: 3–8; sun
SOIL: well drained
NATIVE TO: sagebrush desert to alpine scree and talus slopes; Montana and British Columbia south to California, Arizona, and Colorado
SIZE: 2–10 inches (6–12 inches)
COLOR: cream to yellow and orange, often tinged pink; **BLOOMS** in early summer
I find this open, mat-forming species to be one of the easiest to accommodate in the East. The leaves are paddle-shaped or rounded, ¼- to ½-inch wide, and variously tinted green, gray, and red.

from a thick taproot, producing deciduous crowns of sword-shaped gray-green leaves with a few token spines along the leaf margins. Each crown flowers only once, sending up a leafy stalk of spiny heads that are a lovely, hazy blue color when in bloom. After flowering, the stems wither but form new crowns around their base, so unlike many in the genus, it is reliably perennial in the garden. The colorful common name comes from its use as a remedy for snakebite, and it was also felt to have use in treating impotence and related male sexual problems.

CULTURE: Purchased container plants establish easily in a variety of soils, but it is best to leave established plants alone, as the root system resents disturbance. Self-sown seedlings can also be moved readily when small. Rattlesnake Master is a tough and easily pleased perennial that can be quite striking as a foliage plant when well grown, so give it some breathing room and a warm, sunny spot to really shine.

USES: Perennial border or perhaps best naturalized in meadow or prairie.

PROPAGATION: Easy from seed. See p. 252.

(LEFT): Eryngium yuccifolium. *Although I mostly grow Rattlesnake Master for its sword-shaped foliage, the unusual flowers are attractive in their own way. It is a common plant of tallgrass prairies, growing in the company of Flowering Spurge, Purple Coneflower, and Blazing Stars.*

Eryngium yuccifolium

Eryngium yuccifolium
(err-IN-gee-um)
Apiaceae
Rattlesnake Master

ZONES: 4–9; sun
SOIL: moist to dry
NATIVE TO: moist to dry open woods and prairies; Virginia and Minnesota to Kansas south to Texas and Florida
SIZE: 2–3 feet (12–16 inches)
COLOR: white to pale blue-violet; **BLOOMS** in summer

The *Eryngiums* are an odd bunch—somewhere between a yucca and thistle in appearance with the wide, strap-shaped leaves of the former and the bristling, violet flowers of the latter. They are not related to either, though, and betray their family ties to Angelica and others in the Carrot family through an affinity for water that seems at odds with their drought-tolerant appearance. Most of the native species grow in marshy or seasonally flooded areas along the East and West Coasts and so are of limited use in the garden. (The eastern *E. aquaticum* and the western *E. articulatum* and *E. alismaefolium* are sometimes available from aquatics nurseries and worth a try in larger water gardens.) Of the North American group, only the descriptively named Rattlesnake Master (*E. yuccifolium*) grows in drier soils, and it makes a distinctive though not stunning addition to the perennial border or meadow. It grows

Erythronium americanum

Erythronium (air-eh-THRONE-ee-um)
Liliaceae
Trout Lily, Fawn Lily, Dog-tooth Violet

North America is blessed with a rich complement of these wonderful little spring bulbs. There are two eastern species that form carpets of low, mottled foliage punctuated with occasional flowers (the reflexed tepals have a windswept look, as if being held out the window of a moving automobile). The gray, green, and brown patterning on the foliage suggests the markings on the side of a brook trout. This, along with a season of bloom that coincides with trout fishing season, explains the most widely used common name, Trout Lily. Along the Pacific coast

(RIGHT): Erythronium americanum. *Blooming Yellow Trout Lilies are two to three times the size of their sterile companions and hold their leaves in pairs instead of singly.*

there are more than a dozen exquisite species that populate forested mountain valleys and sunny alpine meadows. As a group these are larger plants in leaf and flower, with a clumping rather than a running habit. Unlike the eastern species, most of the bulbs flower each year, so they have a much stronger presence in the garden. Many of these have attractively patterned foliage as well, but the markings are more regular — a whitewashed or burgundy netting over a base of green.

All *Erythronium*s are spring ephemerals, happiest where they can take advantage of spring sun to grow and bloom and then going quickly dormant in summer. Typically, bulbs producing a pair of leaves will bloom that season, while single leaves are sterile. (If given time, these should eventually flower.) They are ideal interplanted with woodland ground covers that will hide the gaps they leave in summer.

Until recently these slow-growing lilies were unavailable except as wild-collected plants, but Dutch bulb growers are now mass-producing several of the western types, and they are available from bulb importers in the United States and Canada.

CULTURE: The bulbs (technically corms) are shaped like cloves of garlic, with a ring of roots at the base. They do not take dry storage very well, so if you are buying them bareroot, look for corms that are plump and unshriveled, with no sign of softness or mold (they are available from retailers in late September). Plant them immediately in a fertile, humusy but well-drained soil 2–3 inches deep. Potted plants are easy to transplant in spring.

About the time of flowering, *E. americanum* and *E. albidum* send out curious, stolonlike growths that seek out deeper territory, grow a new corm at their tip, then wither and fade like a spent umbilical cord. This makes them difficult to contain in a pot, as they often exit the drain holes and burrow into the ground beneath. It also makes them difficult to dig, as the larger corms are 6–12 inches deep. I usually dig up part of a stock bed in early spring as the leaves are emerging and carefully pot up or transplant the bulbs, setting them as deep as I can. The other species are easier, forming large corms that slough off in irregular sections, giving rise to new offsets that can be removed easily after the plants have gone dormant and lost most of their roots. All trout lilies respond to good soil and spring fertilization, and I have found this to be about the best way to coax more blooms out of the shy-flowering eastern species. (I have tried the supposed trick of planting *E. americanum* on top of a submerged, flat stone to contain it and theoretically produce more flowers, but I cannot say I noticed any difference.)

USES: Best in mixed or successional plantings in the shade or woodland garden.

PROPAGATION: Difficult from seed; easy from division. See p. 253.

Erythronium albidum
(Fawn Lily, White Dog-tooth Violet)

ZONES: 3–9; deciduous shade
SOIL: moist
NATIVE TO: moist wooded slopes; southern Ontario to Minnesota south to Oklahoma, Maryland, and in the mountains to Georgia
SIZE: 3–6 inches (6–12 inches)
COLOR: white with a bluish tint, especially as it fades; **BLOOMS** in early spring

Out of flower this looks much like *E. americanum,* although the leaves have a slightly grayer cast. The flowers are lovely, and it spreads less and blooms more heavily than Yellow Trout Lily in cultivation. More common in the western part of its range.

Erythronium americanum
(Yellow Trout Lily)

ZONES: 3–9; deciduous shade
SOIL: moist in spring
NATIVE TO: moist wooded slopes and bottomlands; Nova Scotia and Ontario south to Alabama and Florida
SIZE: 2–6 inches (6–12 inches)
COLOR: yellow with red-brown overlay on the exterior; **BLOOMS** in early spring

A common and much-loved eastern woodland plant. It appears that there are two forms of the species, one reproducing mostly vegetatively to form carpets of single leaves and seldom flowering, the other forming fewer stolons, emerging later and producing large, paired leaves and flowers. It is hard to say whether these are genetically distinct races or just a reflection of growing conditions. A nonstoloniferous form from the Southeast is sometimes listed as *E. umbilicatum.*

Erythronium citrinum
(Fawn Lily)

ZONES: 6–8; light shade
SOIL: moist in spring
NATIVE TO: coniferous forest; Siskiyou Mountains of southwestern Oregon and northern California
SIZE: 8–14 inches (6 inches)
COLOR: creamy white with a blotch of yellow in the throat and green at the base; **BLOOMS** in early spring

A beautiful plant with darkly mottled leaves and tall multiple-flowered stems.

Erythronium hendersonii
(Adder's Tongue)

ZONES: 6–8; light shade
SOIL: moist in spring

NATIVE TO: wooded slopes up to 5,000 feet; Siskiyou Mountains of southwestern Oregon and northern California

SIZE: 6–10 inches (8 inches)

COLOR: lavender to blue-violet; **BLOOMS** in spring

Dark green leaves with a milky overwash. The lovely flowers are bluish white variably tinged with darker violet, especially toward the base and tips. This plant is slow to multiply.

Erythronium revolutum
(Coast Fawn Lily)

ZONES: 6–8; shade

SOIL: moist

NATIVE TO: margins of swamps and streams in coniferous forests along the coast; Vancouver Island to northern California

SIZE: 8–16 inches (6 inches)

COLOR: light pink to white; **BLOOMS** in spring

Not as easy to cultivate, preferring cool, temperate spots very damp in spring then drier in summer. I mention it mainly because the outstanding cultivar 'White Beauty' is wrongly attributed to this species but is likely an *E. californicum* hybrid.

Erythronium tuolumnense
(Trout Lily)

ZONES: 5–8; part sun, light shade

SOIL: moist in spring

NATIVE TO: wooded slopes in the foothills of the Sierras; Tuolumne and Stanislaus Counties, California

SIZE: 12–14 inches (6 inches)

COLOR: bright yellow; **BLOOMS** in spring

A rare species from a small area of the California Sierras east of Santa Cruz. It has green leaves and up to 5 bright yellow flowers per stem. Unlike many of the western species, even though it is a shy bloomer, it multiplies by offsets fairly quickly. The free-flowering 'Pagoda' is an excellent and commonly available cultivar or perhaps hybrid.

Eupatorium perfoliatum

Eupatorium
(you-pat-OR-ee-um)

Asteraceae

Joe-Pye Weed, Boneset, Wild Ageratum

Several *Eupatoriums* make excellent garden plants, with interesting foliage and hazy masses of purple or white flowers that are absolute favorites of butterflies and bees. They are tough, easy plants for a

range of soils and uses, and no wildflower garden would be complete without one or two. Joe-Pye is one of my favorite summer wildflowers, with a size and presence that rivals any shrub and smoky lavender flower heads that can be as big as basketballs on 6-foot stems.

Boneset tea was once a very common herbal remedy for colds and fever, and when I was in college I collected some from the wet meadow behind my house, dried it, and stashed it away to try the next time I felt a cold coming on. My roommate had shown up that fall with a German shepherd puppy that he kept locked in our room while we were in class, and she had the habit of chewing things up to show her dissatisfaction with this arrangement. I came home one day to find the sheets ripped off my bed and a big tear in the center of my mattress which the puppy had used to extract great quantities of stuffing that now lay like movie snow in heaps all over the floor. She had also chewed through guitar cords, eaten an Areca palm, then somehow opened my drawers and pulled out my clothes along with the sandwich bag full of crushed Boneset leaves. She sampled the herb, and I'd like to think it made her nauseous or at least calmed her down, stopping her reign of terror in time to save my clothes from a toothy death. I never did attempt to try Boneset again. Other species have medicinal uses as well. Legend has it that Joe-Pye Weed was named after the Native American by the same name who taught the New England Colonists its use against typhoid fever.

Eupatorium perfoliatum. Boneset was such a common and foul-tasting remedy for colds during the eighteenth and nineteenth centuries that every child feared its name. Notice how the stem appears to pierce the leaves—a neat example of perfoliation. It is a good indicator for moist meadows and swamps, able to thrive in the stiff competition such habitats have to offer.

Eupatorium fistulosum. *Joe-Pye's developing inflorescences take on a silvery purple hue several weeks before the blooms actually open. I think of it as pre-publicity to alert all insects in the area that the feast will soon begin. Under good garden conditions, these heads can be up to 16 inches across, far larger than they typically get in the wild.*

Fresh *E. hyssopifolium* rubbed on the skin is said to take the sting from insect bites, but I have not tried it.

CULTURE: Easily transplanted in average garden soils in a sunny spot. All of the wetland species covered here will perform well in drier situations but are more robust with even moisture. Most of the species are late to emerge in spring, so do not be discouraged if the roots sit idle until the danger of frost has passed. They quickly make up for the late start with a rapid burst of growth. The larger types need a fertile soil and ample space to reach their full potential. The leaves of *Eupatorium*s are favored by grasshoppers, flea beetles, and sawflies, which can sometimes leave them looking a bit bedraggled in midsummer; otherwise they are trouble-free.

USES: Most are excellent in the summer perennial border or meadow.

WILDLIFE: Excellent nectar plants.

PROPAGATION: Easy from seed or cuttings. See p. 253.

Eupatorium capillifolium
(Dog Fennel)

ZONES: 5–9; sun, part sun
SOIL: moist to dry
NATIVE TO: fields, roadsides, pastures; New Jersey to Arkansas south to Texas and Florida
SIZE: 3–7 feet (2 feet)
COLOR: greenish white; **BLOOMS** in late summer
I was very impressed by this plant when I moved to North Carolina, but most locals consider it a weed. The small leaves are finely cut so that the plant has a soft, delicate look. The flowers are not too interesting, but the seed develops in wispy, ghostlike panicles similar to pampas grass in appearance. They are quite pretty on the tall, strong stems for about a month in fall.

Eupatorium coelestinum
(Mist Flower, Hardy Ageratum)

ZONES: 4–9; sun to light shade
SOIL: moist to wet
NATIVE TO: low woods and moist meadows; New Jersey and Illinois south to Texas and Florida
SIZE: 2–3 feet (3 feet)
COLOR: blue to violet; **BLOOMS** in late summer
Mist Flower is lovely in bloom, forming dense stands topped with soft, flat-topped heads. It is a rampant spreader, though, needing frequent division and thinning to keep vigorous. There are several compact forms available that will not flop (lodge) as easily as this species.

Eupatorium fistulosum
(Hollow-stemmed Joe-Pye Weed)

ZONES: 3–9; sun, part sun
SOIL: moist to wet
NATIVE TO: wet meadows and openings; Maine to Iowa south to Texas and Florida
SIZE: 3–8 feet (3–4 feet)
COLOR: white through mauve to red-purple; **BLOOMS** in late summer
An outstanding plant, but not for the faint of heart as it can reach prodigious size. The lanceolate leaves are arranged in whorls of 4–7 and topped late in the season with huge round-topped panicles that attract every swallowtail butterfly in the area. There are two related species: *E. maculatum* (Spotted Joe-Pye), with stems spotted and mottled with purple, and *E. purpureum* (Purple Joe-Pye) with solid pith. These both have fewer leaves to a whorl (3–4). The names are used interchangeably in the trade, and there is some confusion about the identity of several selected cultivars. 'Big Umbrella' appears to me to be a selection of *E. purpureum*, and 'Gateway' a selection of *E. maculatum*. All make excellent garden plants.

Eupatorium hyssopifolium
(Thoroughwort)

ZONES: 5–9; sun, part sun
SOIL: dry, well drained
NATIVE TO: poor, sandy soils near the coast; Massachusetts to Tennessee south to Louisiana and Florida
SIZE: 1–3 feet (16–24 inches)

COLOR: white; BLOOMS in late summer

A clumping species for sandy, dry soils, with very narrow, whorled gray-green leaves and large flat-topped inflorescenses up to a foot across. I like the fine texture and small stature of this plant but, admittedly, it is no show-stopper and looks a bit muddy when the inflorescences brown after flowering.

Eupatorium perfoliatum

(Boneset)

ZONES: 3–9; sun, part sun

SOIL: moist to wet

NATIVE TO: moist meadows and swamp margins; Nova Scotia and Quebec to North Dakota south to Texas and Florida

SIZE: 2–4 feet (2 feet)

COLOR: white; BLOOMS in late summer

Not a spectacular species, but interesting in the meadow for foliage effect. The opposite leaves are triangular, stretched to a long tapering point. The bases of each pair are fused, so it appears the stem perforates the middle like an arrow through felt. Loose, rounded heads of white flowers top the foliage late in the season.

Eupatorium rugosum

(White Snakeroot)

ZONES: 4–9; sun to light shade

SOIL: moist

NATIVE TO: woods; Nova Scotia to Saskatchewan, south to Texas and Georgia

SIZE: 2–4 feet (2–3 feet)

COLOR: white; BLOOMS in fall

White Snakeroot has toothed, ovate, opposite leaves on strong stems and aggressive rhizomes that can be invasive in moist, fertile soils. You will often see it colonizing woodland edges, and it is valuable for filling lightly shaded sites in the garden. The burgundy-leaved selection 'Chocolate' is a fine introduction. 'Chocolate' colors best in sun, and the snow white flowers are a pleasing contrast.

Euphorbia corollata

Euphorbia corollata

(you-FORB-ee-ah)

Euphorbiaceae

Flowering Spurge

ZONES: 3–9; sun, part sun

SOIL: dry

NATIVE TO: dry woods and prairies; New Hampshire to Minnesota south to Tennessee and Florida

SIZE: 2–3 feet (16–24 inches)

COLOR: bracts snow white, flowers green to yellow; BLOOMS in summer

*E*uphorbia is a huge genus, with upward of 1,500 representatives growing in every conceivable habitat around the world. Everything from the giant cactus-like plants of Africa to the florist's Poinsettia fall into this cosmopolitan group. There are a number of European and Asian species found in horticulture, but only one native, *E. corollata*, is really ornamental enough for garden use. It is a fine plant, with small, elliptical, dark green leaves on straight stems and densely branched panicles that have the cloudlike quality of Baby's Breath (*Gypsophylla*). Like Poinsettia, the showy parts are bracts, not petals, so they are effective for several weeks after the flowers are gone. The bracts form in rings of 5 around each flower and are a pure, flat white like the color you usually see only in a paint can. As an added incentive, the foliage turns Sugar Maple shades of orange and gold as the plants wither in the early fall. I have noticed a fair amount of variation in the height of different individuals and have easily selected a strain with a compact, floriferous habit and earlier bloom.

CULTURE: Flowering Spurge is adaptable to many soil types, and does very well in poor, droughty locations. The plants grow from a slowly creeping rhizome that forms fairly dense stands with time. They shouldn't be disturbed once they are established, but the plants will freely self-sow, and the distinctive seedlings are easy to dig and move. Be careful not to

Euphorbia corollata. *Flowering Spurge has it all (except maybe a flattering common name) —an ironclad constitution, lovely long-lasting blooms, and brilliant fall color.*

(LEFT): Filipendula rubra. *Queen of the Prairie is at its best in rich soils, and division and replanting every three years helps keep the clumps vigorous and contained. Ornamental grasses make excellent companions, as their foliage helps fill in for the Queen when she retires after flowering.*

(RIGHT): Gaillardia aristata. *Blanket Flowers grow robustly under the brilliant sunshine of a Colorado summer. They are used to full effect by the staff of the Denver Botanic Garden, both in formal plantings and naturalistic displays.*

get any of the white latex that oozes from damaged stems on your skin. It is mildly irritating and occasionally causes dermatitis in sensitive people.

USES: Dry borders, meadows.

PROPAGATION: Easy from seed. See p. 253.

Filipendula rubra

Filipendula rubra
(fill-eh-PEN-jew-lah)
Rosaceae
Queen of the Prairie

ZONES: 3–7; sun, part sun

SOIL: moist to wet

NATIVE TO: low woods, wet meadows and prairies; New York to Minnesota south to Kentucky and down the Appalachians through North Carolina

SIZE: 3–7 feet (3–4 feet)

COLOR: pink; BLOOMS in summer

Queen of the Prairie is certainly a regal plant, with tall zigzag stems of large deeply lobed leaves that form sizable stands in moist, fertile soils. Glorious, rich pink, cotton candy flowers that resemble the cultivated *Astilbe*s crown the plants in summer. It is one of the stars of the magnificent tallgrass prairies that once clothed large areas near the western Great Lakes, and it is well adapted for such a life. The plants send out vagabond rhizomes that spread far and wide in search of a place in the sun. For this reason, it is difficult to contain in an average perennial garden. If you can devote some time to keeping it corralled, it is certainly worthwhile in a more formal situation, as

masses of the flowering plants are an incredible sight. The plants die back somewhat after flowering, though, so make provisions for this in your design. It is certainly an excellent choice for naturalizing in the moist meadow, where it will blend with other species and act like an occasional exclamation mark when in bloom.

There are several European and Asian species that are commonly sold, including *F. ulmaria*, *F. vulgaris*, and *F. purpurea*.

CULTURE: Fertile, evenly moist, neutral soil and a cool climate are important for Queen of the Prairie to look its best. I have grown it in the heat of the South, and it survives, but remains stunted and sad. After flowering, cut back the plants and new sets of basal leaves will emerge. It is easy to dig and move the running crowns in spring before they begin to bolt (you may find it easier to sever the strong rhizome with a pair of pruners first).

USES: Borders, meadows.

PROPAGATION: Moderately difficult from seed. See p. 253.

Gaillardia aristata

Gaillardia (gal-LARD-ee-ah)
Asteraceae
Blanket Flower

Blanket flowers are daisies that are studies in burgundy, plum, orange, and gold—colors that reminded early settlers of the blankets woven by Native Americans. They are easy, vigorous plants, but have never really caught on with gardeners. I suspect the Halloween colors might be a little garish for some, but I think their lack of popularity can be attributed mostly to the commonly sold hybrid *G. × grandiflora*, a cross between *G. pulchella* and *G. aristata*. The first is a fast-growing, long-blooming annual that is often sold in wildflower seed mixes, the second a reliable, clumping perennial that blooms for a month or two in summer. The two have been crossed in an attempt to combine large brightly colored flowers and long bloom with a perennial nature. The hybrid is a showy plant that comes in a range of colors, but it is a short-lived perennial at best, and many gardeners become quickly disillusioned with its impermanence. This reputation has been unfairly transferred to *G. aristata*, which is a fine, long-lived and drought-tolerant perennial that is great incorporated into sunny borders and short-grass meadows. It forms leafy clumps of hairy, light green, basal foliage similar to that of black-eyed Susans that act as a good backdrop for the blooms. The flattened, central disk of all blanket flowers grows rounder as the ray petals fade, eventually shedding them to complete its evolution into a perfect sphere of ripening seeds.

CULTURE: Well-drained soil and full sun—all *Gaillardia*s will suffer in heavy soils. Deadhead the plants for longer bloom, but leave a few seed heads to allow them to self-sow.

USES: Borders, meadows, xeriscaping, butterfly gardens.

PROPAGATION: Easy from seed. See p. 253.

Gaillardia aristata
(Blanket Flower)

ZONES: 3–9; sun
SOIL: well drained
NATIVE TO: prairies; Alberta to British Columbia south to Arizona and New Mexico
SIZE: 12–16 inches (2 feet)
COLOR: disk plum, rays red or purple in center and yellow toward the edge; **BLOOMS** in early summer

The plants form crowns off a forking root, eventually becoming sizable clumps. The leaves are long, thin, and coarsely toothed. In typical plants, the ray petals are yellow with a narrow band of burgundy at the base where they meet the dark purple disk. In a given population, though, you can find individuals with more or less red banding in the flowers. *G. pinnatifida* is another perennial species with more heavily lobed foliage and small yellow flowers that make it of limited use in gardens.

Gaillardia pulchella
(Rosering Blanket Flower)

ZONES: 3–9; sun
SOIL: well drained
NATIVE TO: sandy soils, prairies and beaches; Missouri and Nebraska south to Mexico, also along the coast from Texas to Virginia
SIZE: 12–20 inches (12–16 inches)
COLOR: disk plum, rays mostly purple or burgundy with yellow tips; **BLOOMS** in summer

A showy annual. Adaptable but best in lean soils, even dunes, where it easily naturalizes.

Galax urceolata

Galax urceolata
(GAY-lax)
Diapensiaceae
Wandflower, Galax

ZONES: 4–8; shade
SOIL: moist, acid
NATIVE TO: moist deciduous woodlands, north-facing slopes at lower elevations; Maryland to West Virginia south to Georgia
SIZE: 12–16 inches (12–14 inches)
COLOR: white; **BLOOMS** from late spring to early summer

Galax is a magnificent, evergreen ground cover that forms vast, undulating carpets on the foothills and peaks of the southern Appalachians. It prefers the moist, acid humus that forms in cool, rainy climates and is abundant in the rhododendron glades of the Blue Ridge and Great Smoky Mountains. The plants grow from wiry, shallow rhizomes that spread from the older clumps, much like subterranean strawberry runners, and terminate in new crowns. The rich, glossy, dark green leaves are nearly round and produced in such abundance that they completely obscure the ground beneath. I would liken their effect to a verdant swath of waterlilies with leaves vying for a place in the sun. Without a doubt it is one of our finest ground covers, but like all members of this small family, *Galax* is slow to propagate and get established, so it remains a coveted rarity in gardens. Thin wands of filamentous white flowers

Galax urceolata. The incomparable luster of Galax leaves is as brilliant after a long winter as it was when they first emerged. It should be planted fairly thickly, as plants take several years to root in and become a solid ground cover. The delicate flowers give way to small pointed capsules that contain the tiny seeds. In the wild they usually germinate in patches of moss, and you can use this same technique to raise your own seedlings. Find a patch of moss that usually remains damp, and sprinkle the seeds into it as soon as they ripen in the fall. Small plants should be visible within a year and ready to move in two.

Gaultheria procumbens. *For reasons that are as yet unknown, Wintergreen seed rarely germinates in the wild, and most plants are single clones that have been slowly spreading a few feet every year, eventually carpeting areas as big as several acres. When cleaned from the berries, the small seeds sprout readily when sown on the surface of a damp potting mix and placed on a windowsill in a self-sealing plastic bag. They are slow-growing and delicate, however, with fine roots that need constant moisture.*

appear above the leaves in late spring for a charming contrast with the foliage. When frost nips the plants in fall, the leaves turn a shade of deep burgundy but remain perfectly evergreen. The leaves were once harvested in great quantities for holiday decorations and are still popular as greens in floral arrangements.

CULTURE: Grow *Galax* in an organic, acid soil that never dries severely. They can take an occasional dry period in the summer, but prolonged drought damages their threadlike root systems and they may lose some leaves. It is a very shade-tolerant plant, at home under acid-loving shrubs like azaleas and blueberries. It takes two to three years for plantings to fill in, but it is best used en masse as a border along paths or other places where a neat, permanent cover is needed. A light organic fertilizer is beneficial in spring. Once established, *Galax* is a long-lived, trouble free plant.

USES: Slow-growing, elegant ground cover for shade.

PROPAGATION: Difficult from seed; moderately difficult from rhizome cuttings and division. See p. 253.

For reasons that are not understood, wintergreen seed rarely germinates in the wild (though it sprouts easily under cultivation). It seems to reproduce solely by vegetative means, spreading far and wide on thin rhizomes that follow gaps in the forest canopy. It has proven to be a good indicator for past land-use patterns. Its absence in an otherwise suitable habitat usually indicates the area was once plowed and the plants have never been able to return.

Wintergreen is becoming a popular container perennial, and when grown confined in a rich mix with ample water and all the fertilizer it can stand, it forms a deceptively thick, inviting mass with grape-sized matte scarlet fruits. However, keep in mind that the habit of the plant in the ground is a rather loose colony, rarely a solid mat. The rhizomes put up individual flowering stems with 3–5 of the leathery, rounded leaves gathered near the top and a few delicate, bell-shaped flowers tucked between them.

CULTURE: In general, the plants want an acid, peaty soil that never dries severely and a fairly cool climate. *G. procumbens* is the most adaptable, tolerating more heat, humidity, and drought than the others, but it is still no plant for the hot Southeast. While all the species will grow in shade, the carpets will be much fuller and denser flowering with some sun and light fertilization in spring. It is best to start with small container plants set out early in the year. Typically, the plants put up just one flush of new growth aboveground in late spring and creeping underground rhizomes in summer. I planted 40 plugs of *G. procumbens* in some dry woods six years ago, and they have now nearly covered an area of about 200 square feet.

USES: Evergreen ground cover.

PROPAGATION: Difficult from seed; moderately difficult from cuttings and division. See p. 253.

Gaultheria hispidula
(Creeping Snowberry)

ZONES: 2–7; part sun, shade
SOIL: evenly moist
NATIVE TO: moist woods and bogs, often trailing on moss; Newfoundland to British Columbia south to Minnesota, New Jersey, and in the mountains to North Carolina
SIZE: 1–2 inches (6–10 inches)
COLOR: white; **BLOOMS** in summer

An interesting low ground cover forming a solid mat of alternating ¼-inch leaves that follows the contours of the ground. It needs a damp, acid site and cool climate to thrive, but is certainly worth a try if you have a proper spot. The leaves are light yellow-green in color, and the trailing plants really look more like a sedum than a wintergreen. The chalky white, pea-sized berries appear in summer perched on the foliage as if dropped from above.

Gaultheria procumbens

Gaultheria (gall-THAIR-ee-ah)
Ericaceae
Wintergreen, Checkerberry

There are three or four species of native *Gaultheria* that fall somewhat reluctantly into the category of wildflower, inhabiting that gray area between woody plant and perennial. Wintergreen oil is certainly very familiar to everyone as a flavoring in mints and toothpastes, but few people associate the taste with the diminutive evergreen ground cover that forms broken carpets through northern woodlands across the continent.

Gaultheria ovatifolia
(Slender Wintergreen, Oregon Wintergreen)

ZONES: 5–7; part sun, shade
SOIL: moist, acid
NATIVE TO: dry woods to moist subalpine forest; Idaho to British Columbia south to northern California
SIZE: 4–12 inches (12–16 inches)
COLOR: white tinged pink; BLOOMS in summer

A close cousin to *G. procumbens* and sometimes sold as a substitute as it has a larger, denser habit. It can be distinguished by the rusty hairs that cover the calyx. Red fruits persist from late summer through spring. *G. humifusa* (Alpine Wintergreen) is another westerner, from damp, alpine habitats — it is more difficult in cultivation. Give it a peaty spot with even moisture and it will make a dense, evergreen mat.

Gaultheria procumbens
(Checkerberry, Wintergreen)

ZONES: 2–8; part sun, shade
SOIL: moist to dry, acid
NATIVE TO: upland woods to margins of bogs; New-foundland to Manitoba south to British Columbia, Minnesota, and Virginia
SIZE: 3–6 inches (12 inches)
COLOR: white with pink tinge; BLOOMS in summer

The edible fruits are effective from summer until the following spring, as they do not seem to be too attractive to birds. (I like to pop a few in my mouth for the fresh minty taste.) This is the easiest and most drought-tolerant of the lot. One of the few plants that really relishes dry shade.

Gaura lindheimeri

Gaura (GWAR-ah)
Onagraceae
Gaura

Gaura is a genus of 20 North American annuals, biennials, and perennials related to evening primroses. Many of the group are coarse, weedy plants, but a few can be very attractive in flower, and one — *Gaura lindheimeri* — has become a popular, long-blooming, drought-tolerant border perennial. It forms bushy clumps of dark green leaves that get gradually smaller up the flowering stems. The orchidlike flowers are produced a few at a time in ever-lengthening racemes and continue until a hard frost. Another, *G. coccinea*, is a small, sometimes brightly colored plant with wandlike stems of small, narrow leaves that grows from a spreading, woody rootstock and produces a flush of flowers much like Fireweed (*Epilobium*). There is consensus that these plants need a

well-drained soil to be reliably perennial, but I have grown *G. lindheimeri* in almost pure sand and have still found it to be short-lived, though self-sown recruits have kept it spreading about the garden for 15 years now. I suspect that in areas with drier winters, the plants are longer-lived.

CULTURE: Well-drained, even droughty soils and full sun. *G. lindheimeri* is a good plant for the Southeast, but only in areas with sandy soils. Pruning back overly lanky, older flowering stems is a good idea to promote a new flush of flowers. Division or disturbance of these deep-rooted plants once established is not recommended.

USES: Borders, xeriscaping, meadows.

PROPAGATION: Easy from seed or cuttings. See p. 254.

Gaura biennis
(Biennial Gaura)

ZONES: 4–9; sun, part sun
SOIL: moist to dry
NATIVE TO: fields, disturbed habitats; Massachusetts to Nebraska south to Texas and North Carolina
SIZE: 2–4 feet (12 inches)
COLOR: white changing to pink; BLOOMS from spring to summer

A weedy biennial or annual species with tall spikes of small flowers. I include it not for beauty but because it sometimes appears as a component in wildflower seed mixes. Self-sows readily.

Guara lindheimeri. *Given the proper site, White Guara is almost always in bloom. The spikes continue to lengthen and bloom for months, eventually holding the fluttering flowers far off the ground on graceful, arching stems.*

Gentiana clausa. The flowers of Meadow Bottle Gentian are certainly lovely but seemingly impenetrable — they never open any more than this. However, bumblebees are remarkably adept at prying open the flowers at the tip and forcing themselves inside. Notice the pleats along the flower that act as expansion joints to accommodate the prodigious bees.

Gaura coccinea
(Scarlet Gaura)

ZONES: 3–8; sun
SOIL: dry
NATIVE TO: dry prairies, plains and slopes; Minnesota to Alberta south to California and Texas
SIZE: 1–2 feet (2 feet)
COLOR: white or pink changing quickly to bright or purplish red; **BLOOMS** in summer

A pretty little plant that has yet to catch on with growers and dry-climate gardeners, perhaps because of a spreading habit that makes it most suitable for naturalizing. One to eight stems appear in scattered clumps, and the flowering stem continues to elongate much like a miniature White Gaura.

Gaura lindheimeri
(White Gaura)

ZONES: 6–9; sun
SOIL: well drained
NATIVE TO: open, sandy places; Louisiana and Texas
SIZE: 2–3 feet (12–18 inches)
COLOR: typically white aging to pink, occasionally darker pink; **BLOOMS** from summer to fall

The best of the genus for gardens. Perennial retailers like it because it is fast-maturing and looks good in a container (sometimes better than it does in the ground). Most plants on the market are either the compact cultivar 'Whirling Butterflies' or the dark pink 'Siskiyou Pink'. Because the flowers develop on arching spikes well above the foliage, by late in the season they look like moths flitting above the grass.

Gentiana clausa

Gentiana (gen-tee-ANN-ah)
Gentianaceae
Gentian

The gentians offer us some of the most intense cobalt blues, the softest powder blues, and delicately ethereal blue-violets of any wildflowers. Most of the eastern species are of the closed or bottle type, with the 4 petals fused into an inflated, jug-shaped tube. It is an ingenious design to facilitate cross-pollination: a narrow opening at the top is just big enough for large, strong bees to stick their heads in and pry open the corolla so that they can crawl inside. The petals have extra folds along their seams, like the bellows of an accordion, that act as expansion joints to prevent the flower from ripping as the bee climbs inside (if only blue jeans had such devices). The bee squeezes down past the stigma on its way to the base of the flower to sip nectar, depositing any pollen it may have carried in before passing the anthers for anoth-

er dose. There are some western species as well, but they grow in specialized, typically alpine habitats that make them difficult to handle in cultivation.

All of our true gentians are perennial from thick white fleshy roots, but there is a related plant, the extraordinary *Gentianopsis crinita* (Fringed Gentian), that is a true biennial. It is certainly worth the trouble of growing for the huge, upward-facing tubular flowers that flare open about halfway up — 4 rounded petals bearded with a long delicate fringe along their margins. Fringed Gentian is a limestone species in the wild, though in cultivation it seems fairly adaptable, and this goes for some of the others as well.

CULTURE: All the species listed here bloom late in the season, providing welcome bursts of intense color as the days begin to cool. They have a reputation for being difficult to grow, stemming mostly from their resentment of root disturbance. Given that most perennials are grown and sold in containers these days, this is really not a problem. I have successfully dug and moved established garden plants even in the heat of summer, though I would not recommend it. No matter how you move them, be careful to keep them watered the first season even if they just sit there sulking.

They are best in a moist, fertile soil with at least a few hours of sun. Full sun may bleach or bronze some of the foliage on the bottle types, but otherwise the plants will survive.

USES: Effective scattered in the border. The bottle types will work massed or as edging in more formal plantings, and *Gentianopsis* will sometimes naturalize in moist meadows.

PROPAGATION: Moderately difficult from seed. See p. 254.

Gentiana autumnalis
(Pine-Barren Gentian)

ZONES: 5–9; sun, part shade
SOIL: moist, acid

NATIVE TO: moist pine barrens along the coast; New Jersey to South Carolina
SIZE: 8–18 inches (12 inches)
COLOR: cobalt blue, fading to pale green at base; BLOOMS in fall

Pine-Barren Gentian is a thin plant with stiff, narrow leaves and straight stems topped late in the season with a few spectacular deep, clear blue flowers that flare open much like *Gentianopsis*. It has proven elusive and difficult but not impossible to cultivate, needing a sandy soil with a fairly high water table. An easier species is *G. puberulenta* (Prairie Gentian). It has similar flowers and favors slightly drier habitats.

Gentiana clausa

(Meadow Closed Gentian, Meadow Bottle Gentian)

ZONES: 3–9; part sun
SOIL: moist to wet
NATIVE TO: moist woods, seeps, and thickets; Maine and Quebec south to Ohio and Maryland and in the Appalachians to Georgia
SIZE: 14–18 inches (24–30 inches)
COLOR: pale to deep blue-violet; BLOOMS in fall

In habit Meadow Bottle Gentian is a rounded clump of opposite, elliptical leaves with parallel veins. The stems begin upright, but usually lean over with the weight of the developing flowers. The distinctive flowers are cradled between the topmost leaves in a tight cluster. There are a number of closely related species. *G. andrewsii* (Prairie Bottle Gentian) is nearly identical, distinguished by a fine fringe on the petal tips around the opening and more common westward. *G. villosa* (Striped Gentian) is another relative. It is not a striking plant, with semitransparent greenish blooms striped with purple inside. *G. flavida* (Pale Gentian) is a midwesterner with pale yellow flowers.

Gentiana saponaria

(Soapwort Gentian)

ZONES: 6–9; part sun
SOIL: moist
NATIVE TO: moist woods and thickets; southern New York to Illinois south to Oklahoma, Texas, and Florida
SIZE: 14–18 inches (24 inches)
COLOR: light blue; BLOOMS in fall

Resembles other bottle types, but the leaves have a lighter, waxy cast; the flowers are more of a powder blue; and it blooms a week or two later than *G. clausa*. *G. catesbaei* (Coastal Plain Gentian) is similar, but with petals that flare open partially at the tips. They are typically darker color.

Gentianopsis crinita

(Fringed Gentian)

ZONES: 3–8; sun, part sun
SOIL: moist, neutral
NATIVE TO: moist or wet open places, usually on limestone; Maine to Manitoba, south to Iowa, South Dakota, and in the mountains to North Carolina
SIZE: 1–3 feet (8 inches)
COLOR: satiny blue-violet; BLOOMS in fall

Biennial. Truly spectacular—one of our most glorious wildflowers. The blooms are very large, with intricate fringes on the petals and held proudly above the small leaves on stiff stems. I have never been able to get a self-sowing population established in the garden, relying instead on the fish hatchery approach of growing the seedlings for a season in the nursery in small containers and planting them out late in the summer. They overwinter as rosettes that begin to bolt in midsummer. Larger, overwintered plants are harder to transplant and need careful watering to get established. It may seem like too much trouble—until they bloom!

Geranium maculatum

Geranium
(jerr-AYNE-ee-um)
Geraniaceae
Cranesbill, Wild Geranium

Geranium maculatum. The sight of Cranesbill always transports me back to childhood and the dozens of cheery pink flowers that decorated the woodland behind my house each spring. One of the true joys of wildflower gardening is the connection it can foster between you, the surrounding region, and the lives you share it with.

Cranesbill is a charming, modest wildflower found in moist woodlands and forest edges. It is far easier on the eyes than its distant cousins—the fluorescent red geraniums (*Pelargonium* spp.) sold as bedding plants. Cranesbills form a mound of deeply lobed medium green leaves that send up thin, leafy stems of 5-petaled flowers with a fine network of darker veins lacing the surface (looking remarkably like a *Geranium*'s version of a cardiovascular system). The blooms open sequentially over a few weeks in spring.

The name Cranesbill refers to a curious beaked structure formed by extensions of the carpels that surround the seeds. Think of this structure as a deep wooden spoon cupped around each seed, then picture five of these spoons standing upright back to back (spoon end down), their handles pressed together and the cups facing outward in a circle around the base. As the seeds mature, the beak lengthens, then begins to dry, and fibers inside each section (the handle of each spoon) start to coil. Great tension is generated by these coiling fibers, and eventually the base of the spoon snaps rapidly upward, catapulting its seed yards away. A patch of ripening *Geranium* seed heads is like Lilliputian artillery, and you can often hear the seeds being scattered around on a warm summer day. It should not be surprising that, like violets, *Geranium*s are good at gently naturalizing in moist situations. Several European species that have catapulted themselves out of gardens are becoming a problem in the wild—particularly in the Pacific Northwest where the climate especially suits them. *G. robertianum* (Herb Robert) is very troublesome in certain areas of both the East and West.

CULTURE: Cranesbills are adaptable plants. When I was seven, I transplanted a roughly dug plant from our back to front yard—the first successful transplant of my horticultural career and I suppose my introduction to gardening with natives as well. The plant flourished in its new home for about 15 years, and its offspring are still popping up here and there in the area. If a seven-year-old can do it . . . well, you know the rest. These *Geranium*s grow from a thick, woody caudex that stores reserves for summer dormancy, which helps to account for their resiliency. They will grow in sun or shade as long as the soil is moist in spring and of at least moderate fertility. The caudex begins to rot and break apart as it ages, so older plants can be separated into individual crowns in fall.

USES: Woodland gardens, naturalizing along forest margins.

PROPAGATION: Easy from seed. See p. 254.

Geranium maculatum

(Wild Geranium, Cranesbill)

ZONES: 3–9; sun to light shade
SOIL: moist, at least in spring
NATIVE TO: woods and clearings; Maine to Manitoba south to northeastern Oklahoma and South Carolina
SIZE: 14–18 inches (12 inches)
COLOR: pink, occasionally white; **BLOOMS** in spring
Wild Geranium begins the season as a cluster of medium green, palmately lobed leaves. Each of the 5–7 fingerlike lobes is toothed and divided at the tip. Stout, branched flower stems erupt from the clump in midspring, eventually bearing the blooms well above the leaves. The plants are troubled occasionally by a rust that disfigures the leaves but does not kill the plants. Goes semidormant after seed is shed.

Geranium oreganum

(Western Geranium)

ZONES: 5–8; sun to light shade
SOIL: moist
NATIVE TO: meadows and woodland, western Cascades; Washington to northern California
SIZE: 1–2 feet (16 inches)
COLOR: deep rose purple; **BLOOMS** in early summer
Similar to the above, with larger, darker flowers and leaves more deeply toothed and hairy.

Geranium viscosissimum

(Sticky Purple Geranium)

ZONES: 4–9; sun to light shade
SOIL: moist in spring
NATIVE TO: subalpine to alpine meadows and woodlands; Alberta to British Columbia south to California, Colorado, and South Dakota
SIZE: 10–26 inches (16 inches)
COLOR: pink to rose purple; **BLOOMS** in late spring
This is a wide-ranging, sprawling plant similar to Western Geranium and named for the sticky glandular hairs that cover the leaves and stems. Most of the plants I have seen have good, dark pink flowers and strong red pigment in the petioles and stems. It prefers damp, sheltered spots in the mountains, and it is one of the common understory plants of the beautiful aspen forests of the Rockies. *G. richardsonii* (White Geranium) is a more compact, white-flowered alpine relative found through much of the Rockies and west into California. *G. californicum* is a handsome but tender pink-flowered species found throughout the southern half of the California Sierras.

Geum rivale

Geum (GEE-um)
Rosaceae
Avens

The **avens** are a cold-loving race from the northern parts of the globe, with coarse rosettes of shaggy leaves that are pinnate in structure, with all but the terminal leaflets reduced to vestigial remnants that gradually enlarge as they approach the tip. For the most part they are not very showy in flower and/or a bit specialized in their habitats to be of general garden use, but the most adaptable, *G. triflorum*, is grown for the atmospheric effect of its thin, furry styles that continue to lengthen like little puffs of smoke from the centers of the faded flowers. The fine, long hair of the 2-inch dark red styles catch sunlight and refract it as if through frosted glass. This makeshift parachute enables the ripened seed to travel hither and yon on the strong prairie wind.

CULTURE: The native *Geum*s are a durable, pest-free group if you can provide the right habitat. Not surprisingly, Water Avens needs a moist to wet spot in the garden, while Prairie Smoke prefers a dry, gritty soil. The rosettes are easily dug and divided in spring.

USES: Wetlands or rock garden, xeriscaping.

PROPAGATION: Easy from seed. See p. 254.

Geum rivale
(Water Avens)

ZONES: 2–7; sun to light shade
SOIL: moist to wet
NATIVE TO: swamps and wet meadows, circumboreal; in North America from Newfoundland to Alberta south to California, Indiana, and New Jersey
SIZE: 16–24 inches (12 inches)
COLOR: purple-red; BLOOMS in late spring
The plants form spreading rosettes of clean foliage that produce bunches of bell-shaped flowers, the petals barely longer than the cupping sepals. Not a truly showy plant, but worth naturalizing within its range, as it looks interesting blooming among skunk cabbages and *Osmunda* ferns.

Geum triflorum
(Prairie Smoke)

ZONES: 3–9; sun
SOIL: dry, well drained
NATIVE TO: dry woods and prairies; Newfoundland to New York, Minnesota, and British Columbia south to California and New Mexico
SIZE: 10–16 inches (12 inches)
COLOR: pink; BLOOMS in spring
With time, Prairie Smoke forms mats of small hairy rosettes that send up stiff stalks with a cluster of cupped blooms on each. The ornamental seed heads are effective for about four weeks, and the plant doubles as decent semievergreen ground cover.

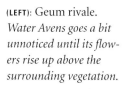

(LEFT): Geum rivale. *Water Avens goes a bit unnoticed until its flowers rise up above the surrounding vegetation.*

(RIGHT): Geum triflorum. *Fuzzy, ornamental styles begin to elongate as soon as Prairie Smoke flowers are pollinated.*

Helianthus divaricatus. Though less exuberant in flower than some of its relatives, Woodland Sunflower is very shade tolerant. It forms large colonies in rich soils along woodland edges and gaps, often visible as a speckle of yellow in the dappled sunlight along forest roads in midsummer. Its traveling rhizomes allow it to adapt to the changing position of light gaps from season to season.

Helianthus divaricatus

Helianthus
(heel-ee-ANN-thus)

Asteraceae

Sunflower

The perennial sunflowers are fantastic plants, the largest growing to 10 feet or more before exploding into glorious golden bloom as frosts cut down their less stalwart companions. I fear that most are just too big for many modern gardens, looking a bit like giraffes in a chicken yard unless given the space befitting their scale. Unlike the monsterous-flowered strains of the annual seed Sunflower (*H. annuus*), they produce clouds of small blooms in terminal panicles that give the plants a fine texture despite their size. There are also some shorter and earlier blooming species that are less visually dramatic but easier to accommodate.

CULTURE: All the perennial *Helianthus* grow from a creeping rhizome that in some species (*H. tuberosus*, for example) can be quite deep and aggressive, and I have indicated this in the descriptions. The best types for gardens have short rhizomes that are slow to spread and not hard to control by circling the clump in spring with a sharp spade, then pulling out any stems that have traveled too far afield. It is also easy to dig and transplant them in this way. The other thing to keep in mind is that all the *Helianthus* tend to lean over under the weight of their flowers after a rain, and a 10-foot-high *H. giganteus* clump can temporarily consume a fair amount of real estate when in flower. I have often thought that a little selection for seedlings with fatter stems could, in several generations, produce a stronger plant for the trade. The wetland types look wonderful in a ditch or low meadow, but suffer if the soil is droughty. Others are very drought-tolerant once established.

USES: Screening, rear of borders, meadows, butterfly gardens, and pond sides.

WILDLIFE: Nectar, also larval food for *Chlosyne nycteis* (Silvery Checkerspot butterfly), and *Chlosyne lacinia* (Bordered Patch butterfly)—sometimes a pest of cultivated sunflowers in the lower Great Plains. The seed heads are excellent for goldfinches and others.

PROPAGATION: Easy from seed or cuttings. See p. 254.

Helianthus angustifolius
(Narrow-leaved Sunflower, Swamp Sunflower)

ZONES: 5–9; sun, part sun
SOIL: moist to wet
NATIVE TO: mostly coastal swamps and wet meadows; southern New York to Florida and Texas
SIZE: 5–9 feet (3–4 feet)
COLOR: disk purple, rays yellow; **BLOOMS** in fall

One of the best garden plants, but it does need room. Its rhizomes are attenuated, so it remains in a gradually increasing clump. The long narrow leaves are distinctly dark green and glossy, and great numbers of black-eyed daisies are borne in clusters along the upper quarter of the stems. In my garden it is the last of the sunflowers to bloom.

Helianthus divaricatus
(Divaricate Sunflower, Woodland Sunflower)

ZONES: 3–9; sun to light shade
SOIL: moist to moderately dry
NATIVE TO: woods and openings; New Hampshire to Wisconsin south to Oklahoma and Florida
SIZE: 2–4 feet (3–6 feet)
COLOR: disk and rays yellow; **BLOOMS** in summer

A common plant in the East, providing welcome color to roadsides and clearings in summer. It has fairly broad, opposite leaves and flowers in small clusters along the upper stem. It is an aggressive spreader, best reserved for wild areas.

Helianthus giganteus
(Swamp Sunflower, Giant Sunflower)

ZONES: 3–9; sun, part sun
SOIL: moist to wet
NATIVE TO: swamps and wet meadows; New

Brunswick to Alberta south to Nebraska, Ohio, and Georgia

SIZE: 6–10 feet (4–5 feet)

COLOR: disk yellow, rays pale to strong yellow; **BLOOMS** in fall

A towering plant when full grown, with loose branching panicles of 2½-inch flowers topping rough, hairy stems. The leaves are lighter green and of thinner texture than those of Narrow-leaved Sunflower, and it blooms seven to ten days earlier. There are several stunning pale yellow cultivars, including 'Sheila's Sunshine', on the market. Their shade is close to *Coreopsis* × 'Moonbeam'.

Helianthus maximilliani
(Maximillian Sunflower)

ZONES: 3–9; sun, part sun

SOIL: moist to dry

NATIVE TO: moist to dry, often sandy prairies; Minnesota and Manitoba to eastern British Columbia south to Texas and Missouri

SIZE: 6–8 feet (3–4 feet)

COLOR: disk and rays yellow; **BLOOMS** from late summer to fall

A very coarse, rugged plant with large rough leaves to 10 inches long and thick, fleshy roots. Flowers on short stalks from the axils of the upper leaves. Drought-tolerant and nonrunning, but a bit rough in texture for my taste.

Helianthus microcephalus
(Small-headed Sunflower)

ZONES: 4–9; sun to light shade

SOIL: moist

NATIVE TO: woods and clearings; New Jersey to Minnesota south to Louisiana and Florida

SIZE: 3–6 feet (3–4 feet)

COLOR: disk and rays yellow; **BLOOMS** in late summer

An excellent garden species, with dark green, lanceolate leaves, short rhizomes, and a branching, bushy habit. Tolerates some drought and shade.

Helianthus mollis
(Ashy Sunflower)

ZONES: 4–9; sun, part sun

SOIL: moist to dry

NATIVE TO: dry prairies; Ohio to Wisconsin and Kansas south to Texas and Georgia

SIZE: 3–4 feet (2–3 feet)

COLOR: disk and rays yellow; **BLOOMS** in summer

A distinctive plant with broad, oval leaves covered with a coarse, matted pubescence that gives the plants an attractive, ashen look. It is a drought-tolerant midseason bloomer. The main drawback to *H. mollis* is that the plants tend to spread into wide, open clumps that are hard to accommodate in a more formal design.

Helianthus salicifolius
(Willow-leaved Sunflower)

ZONES: 4–9; sun, part sun

SOIL: moist to dry

NATIVE TO: dry prairies, often on limestone; Missouri and Kansas to Texas

SIZE: 3–5 feet (3–4 feet)

COLOR: disk purple, rays yellow; **BLOOMS** in fall

An unmistakable plant, with long thin leaves densely clothing the stems and appearing as a tuft from the growing tip. The effect reminds me of the jets of a fountain shooting into the air. Excellent for foliage effect, but the plants invariably lean and sprawl late in the season. The flowers are thin and small, certainly not its best attribute.

Helianthus tuberosus
(Jerusalem Artichoke)

ZONES: 3–9; sun, part sun

SOIL: moist

NATIVE TO: moist open areas, waste places; Quebec to Kansas south to Texas and Florida

SIZE: 4–6 feet (3 feet)

COLOR: disk and rays yellow; **BLOOMS** in late summer

Jerusalem Artichoke forms gnarled, edible tubers along its aggressive, spreading rhizomes. I would recommend it only if you want to grow the plants for food, and even then you must choose a spot that is isolated from other plants as they form large stands that are difficult to eradicate once established. *H. nuttallii* (Swamp Sunflower) hails from wet meadows from western Canada to California and Arizona. The narrow leaves look much like *H. angustifolius*, but it has the same aggressive nature as Jerusalem Artichoke.

(LEFT): Heliopsis helianthoides. *Long popular in Europe as a border perennial, Oxeye cultivars with two or three times the normal complement of ray flowers have been named and distributed. The extra ray petals of the plant in this photograph give the blooms a full, semidouble appearance. Heliopsis differs from the true sunflowers—and for that matter most of the Aster tribe—in that both its disk and ray flowers are fertile (capable of producing seed). Since there is no reproductive disadvantage to an Oxeye having extra rays, this mutation is fairly common in the genus.*

(RIGHT): Helonias bullata. *Swamp Pinks are a star attraction among the many beautiful wildflowers of high spring at the Garden in the Woods. The impressionist combination of pink and violet blue is as striking in nature as it is on a canvas by Claude Monet. It is one of the many rare plants the New England Wild Flower Society has on display to help educate visitors about our remarkable flora.*

Heliopsis helianthoides

Heliopsis helianthoides
(heel-ee-OP-sis)

Asteraceae
Oxeye

ZONES: 3–9; sun, part sun

SOIL: moist to dry

NATIVE TO: prairies, meadows, dry woods; Quebec to British Columbia south to New Mexico and Georgia

SIZE: 3–5 feet (3 feet)

COLOR: yellow to golden orange; **BLOOMS** in summer

Oxeye is somewhere between *Helianthus* and *Rudbeckia* in effect. It has the shrubby habit and yellow disks and rays of some sunflowers, but the blooms are produced in great quantities on thin stems above the foliage, much like *Rudbeckia*. It is one of the finest large summer bloomers for the garden, growing in a range of soils and forming thick, nonspreading clumps of branching stems, with toothed, opposite leaves that are a clean, medium green. The western variety *scabra* is most commonly grown. It has stiffer leaves and a neater, bushier habit. Var. *helianthoides* is the eastern form, with thin leaves and a taller, loose habit. Europeans have long appreciated the merits of Oxeye, and breeders have developed a number of compact, double, and large-flowered cultivars using the western form.

CULTURE: Transplants readily in a moist or dry spot. Grasshoppers can sometimes be a problem, but otherwise it is a carefree plant.

USES: Borders, meadows.

PROPAGATION: Easy from seed or cuttings. See p. 254.

Helonias bullata

Helonias bullata
(hell-OWN-ee-us)

Liliaceae
Swamp Pink

ZONES: 5–9; sun to light shade

SOIL: moist to wet

NATIVE TO: scattered swamps and bogs; New Jersey south to South Carolina on the coastal plain and in the Blue Ridge Mountains from Virginia to Georgia

SIZE: 10–16 inches (12–18 inches)

COLOR: pink, blue; **BLOOMS** in spring

The enigmatic Swamp Pink is a rare plant in the wild, living in scattered bogs and swamps from New Jersey to South Carolina, but nowhere is it common. In cultivation, though, it is easy and rewarding, provided it has a mucky soil and some elbow room. The 8-inch evergreen, strap-shaped leaves form tight rosettes (somewhat like a miniature yucca in effect) that blush burgundy and dry a bit at the tips in cold weather, but otherwise emerge from winter unscathed. As the air warms, fat, pointed buds that developed in the center of each crown the previous fall begin to swell, releasing a new fan of leaves, or, if you are lucky, a thick flower spike with a dense, drumstick head of remarkable, sweetly scented blooms. The tepals are bright pink, and the anthers hazy blue—a rare and striking color combination in the world of wildflowers. The plants form thick clumps with time, making a lovely ground cover beside water or mixed in a bog planting.

The New England Wild Flower Society has been propagating and distributing Swamp Pink for many years, and it is beginning to become more available in the trade.

CULTURE: Grow in a moist to wet, organic soil. The plants can take brief periods of drought, but they will look limp and tattered if their thick roots are deprived of moisture for long. It is easy and also a good idea to divide Swamp Pink every five years or so, as the offsets eventually become overcrowded and less likely to bloom. Divide them after they have flowered in late spring to early summer by gently teasing apart individual crowns or small clumps and resetting them.

USES: Pond sides, bog garden.

PROPAGATION: Difficult from seed; easy from division. See p. 254.

Hepatica acutiloba

Hepatica (heh-PAT-eh-cah)
Ranunculaceae
Hepatica

Life does not really stop in winter—the cold just slows things down to a pace that is hard for us to see. April is the time around Boston where things begin moving quickly enough again to notice. One of the early players in this budding vernal drama is hepatica. The first warmth of the month spurs its down-covered buds to reveal many-petaled flowers of an ethereal blue or dusky violet that might go unnoticed in the explosion of color and smell of high spring. In this time of sensory famine, though, they are a priceless gift. Taxonomists dispute the number of species in this small genus, but I prefer to think of them as one race that has ridden the tectonic elephants and glacial tides completely around the Northern Hemisphere. There are hepaticas in Europe and Asia that look only vaguely different

from our own. Only *H. transylvanica*, from the mountains of central Europe, is really distinct, with large felted leaves that are nearly circular in outline. The others have 3-lobed, leathery leaves that I prefer to call reluctantly deciduous, as they hang on, tattered, limp, and stained with burgundy by the cold until a new set begins to emerge. They give the plants a head start in spring, able to photosynthesize as soon as the snow clears and the soil warms without risking tender new leaves to lingering frosts. Hepaticas are tidy little plants—about the size and shape of African Violets. Though in the wild they occur as scattered plants each with only 2–4 leaves, in the good life of the garden they can become truly exuberant. A well-grown plant can have dozens of leaves and 40 or more flowers forming a bouquet in the center.

Both the Latin and common names refer to the plant's importance in the old European Doctrine of Signatures, which held that plants that resembled a body part or organ—in this case the leaves' resemblance to a liver—were useful in treating disorders of that organ.

CULTURE: Hepaticas are best sited in a spot that receives a few hours of sun and a soil that is moist and humusy. They are easily swamped by larger wildflowers, so plant them in drifts or among rocks where they will not get lost or smothered. They respond well to light fertilization in spring, and *H. acutiloba* appreciates a shot of limestone now and then. A bit of sun and good air movement helps prevent the leaf spotting that can sometimes plague them, and along with the occasional slug, blister beetles can do some damage in fall.

USES: Scattered or massed in the woodland garden.

PROPAGATION: Slow and moderately difficult from seed; easy from division. See p. 254.

Hepatica acutiloba
(Sharp-lobed Hepatica)

ZONES: 3–8; part sun, shade
SOIL: moist
NATIVE TO: rich woods and floodplains, often on limestone; Quebec to Minnesota south to Arkansas and northern Georgia
SIZE: 3–6 inches (8–12 inches)
COLOR: pale to dark violet blue or white; **BLOOMS** in early spring

This species has 3-lobed leaves with each lobe ending in a point. It favors sweeter soils than *H. americana*, and the flowers seem to be much more variable in color, with all shades of blues and violets, even pinks represented in a single large population. It is more prone to leaf spotting in my garden.

Hepatica acutiloba. *Though I have been accused of saying this too often, Hepaticas are absolutely one of my favorite wildflowers. This is partly because their little blue posies appear at a time when I am feeling acutely color deprived and partly because they respond so well to cultivation. It thrills me to see elegant clumps get bigger and bigger each year, to see them burst out in flower and then leaf, and know that next year they will be larger still.*

Heuchera 'Palace Purple'. 'Palace Purple' was one of the first Coralbell hybrids to become popular: not for the color of its flowers, but for the lovely burgundy shading of its leaves. It was discovered in one of the royal gardens in England and probably represents a hybrid between Heuchera micrantha *and* H. villosa. *Traditionally, Coralbells could be propagated easily only by seed, and when 'Palace Purple' is produced this way without careful culling and selec-*

Hepatica americana
(Round-lobed Hepatica)

ZONES: 3–8; part sun, shade

SOIL: moist

NATIVE TO: woodlands; Quebec to Minnesota south to Georgia

SIZE: 3–6 inches (8–12 inches)

COLOR: typically dark violet-blue; **BLOOMS** in spring

Round-lobed Hepatica has lobes with blunt tips and flowers about one week later. Both species can have some burgundy mottling and irregular silver patches over their primarily gray-green leaves, but this one can have a lovely, pronounced marbling, especially as the new leaves emerge (I have selected seed strains with good leaf color that come 100 percent true). The flower color of *H. americana* is a fairly consistent, stunning deep violet blue. I find it the better garden plant of the two, and it is one of my very favorite wildflowers, period.

new hybrids are rather drab, the evergreen foliage is outstanding and combines well with many other plants. *H. americana* has a particularly tall, awkward inflorescence that seems to dominate in hybrids, and I usually just clip them off as they appear. Hybrids involving *H. villosa* as well as *H. cylindrica* and some of the other western species can be quite lovely in flower, though, and worth keeping.

There are a number of dwarf alpine species that make fine additions to the rock garden, looking particularly good sandwiched in crevices between large rocks. All the alumroots produce neat mounds of rounded leaves on long petioles from a swollen caudex and tall stems of wispy little flowers, mostly in shades of white or green.

With a bit of garden sorcery, *Heucheras* have been crossed with *Tiarellas* (foamflowers) to create the hybrid genus × *Heucherella*. I was not impressed with the vigor of the first hybrids available, but recent efforts have yielded some fine plants that combine the foliage of coralbells with the large frilly flower spikes of foamflowers. The plants are sterile and so need to be propagated by division or tissue culture and need a bit more moisture than straight coralbells do. × *Heucherella alba* involves the clumping *Tiarella wherryii* and × H*eucherella tiarelloides* involves the running *T. cordifolia*.

CULTURE: The larger species and hybrids are drought-tolerant and adaptable, but do suffer root rots if the soil is heavy and wet. Many will grow in the shade, but the plants look thin and lax and coloring is washed out. In full sun, the foliage can bleach or bronze where it is particularly exposed. They are really at their best in part sun and rich, moist soil, producing thick clumps of stiff leaves often boldly colored and patterned. They are fairly heavy feeders, so topdress in spring and again a month later. The crowns are difficult but not impossible to divide in spring. Before cutting through the caudex, make sure both divisions will have roots.

USES: All except *H. sanguinea* are primarily excellent foliage plants, useful in borders, massed, or as edging in formal or informal plantings. The alpine species look good lodged in a crevice or wall. All the species look very natural planted in and around rocks.

PROPAGATION: Easy from seed. See p. 255.

Heuchera americana
(Common Alumroot)

ZONES: 3–9; sun to light shade

SOIL: moist to dry

NATIVE TO: dry woods; Connecticut to Ontario south to Oklahoma and Georgia

SIZE: 1–2 feet (12–16 inches)

COLOR: cream; **BLOOMS** in early summer

The round 3–4-inch foliage is typically dark green with irregular patches of red along the vein, and

Heuchera 'Palace Purple'

Heuchera (HUGH-car-ah)
Saxifragaceae
Alumroot, Coralbells

tion, the intensity of coloration tends to diminish in successive generations. Accordingly, most of the flood of new pattern-leaved alumroots that have become available recently are produced through tissue culture. The procedure is costly, but if done correctly, it assures consistency from one crop to the next.

Few wildflowers are as trouble-free and adaptable as coralbells. There are upward of 30 species, all North American, growing in a range of habitats across the continent. They readily interbreed, and it is the garden hybrids and not true species that are most commonly available. For many years the word coralbells was synonymous with the cherry pink– or red-flowered hybrids derived from the southwestern *H. sanguinea*. Recently, though, a range of new cultivars have flooded the market with dramatic, colorful foliage that shows the influence of the richly patterned *H. americana,* the burgundy-leaved *H. villosa* 'Atropurpurea', and the filagreed *H. micrantha,* among others. While the flowers of most of these forms have been selected that have both more pronounced burgundy veining as well as a silvery overlay. The flowers are borne on loose, few-branched panicles far above the leaves.

Heuchera cylindrica
(Roundleaf Alumroot, Lava Alumroot)

ZONES: 4–8; sun, part sun
SOIL: moist to dry
NATIVE TO: rocky woods and subalpine meadows; Alberta to British Columbia south to California and Nevada
SIZE: 8–24 inches (12 inches)
COLOR: cream to green; BLOOMS in late spring
The leaves of Roundleaf Alumroot are more or less hairy and finely toothed. In the plants I have grown, the dark foliage is noticeably scalloped like the shell of a giant clam, but I find little reference to this in the literature. (It may disappear upon pressing for herbarium specimens.) The flowers are congested into a tight raceme on a tall stem. *H. micrantha* is another attractive species from the Pacific Northwest with hairy, often undulating leaves streaked with gray and large open panicles of creamy flowers in late spring. The cultivar 'Palace Purple' is often attributed to *H. micrantha*, but in my opinion this widely available hybrid involves *H. villosa* 'Atropurpurea' in its parentage as well.

Heuchera parvifolia
(Small-flowered Alumroot)

ZONES: 4–8; sun, part sun
SOIL: moderately dry, well drained
NATIVE TO: rocky crevices and slopes, alpine to subalpine, often on limestone; Alberta south to Arizona and New Mexico
SIZE: 6–14 inches (6–8 inches)
COLOR: creamy white; BLOOMS in early summer
The small leaves of this species are covered in a fine pubescence, giving the plant a gray cast. Racemes are short and densely flowered, the flowers large for the plant and fairly attractive. There are other even smaller tufted plants that are true alpines, including *H. bracteata* from the central Rockies and forms of *H. rubescens* from much of the mountain West. They are all neat foliage plants for the rock garden or scree.

Heuchera sanguinea
(Coralbells)

ZONES: 6–9; sun, part sun
SOIL: moist, well drained
NATIVE TO: rocky, shaded places 5,000–8,500 feet; New Mexico and Arizona south to northern Mexico
SIZE: 8–16 inches (8–12 inches)
COLOR: pink to red; BLOOMS in summer
A lovely species in flower—it is the only one with brightly colored flowers that are doubtless a hummingbird adaptation. It is not too easy in cultivation, but its superlative hybrids, lumped under *Heuchera × brizoides*, are much more adaptable and have entirely supplanted it in gardens. These boast many racemes of red or hot pink flowers and small rounded leaves often overlaid with silver and burgundy (a contribution from *H. americana* and *H. micrantha*).

Heuchera villosa
(Maple-leaved Alumroot)

ZONES: 4–9; sun to light shade
SOIL: moist
NATIVE TO: moist rocky cliffs and outcrops; West Virginia to South Carolina and Tennessee, sporadically west to Arkansas and Indiana
SIZE: 10–18 inches (14–18 inches)
COLOR: white; BLOOMS in late summer
Unique with sharply pointed, lobed leaves and airy panicles of flowers that appear like a veil over the foliage late in the season. The burgundy-leaved form, usually listed as 'Atropurpurea', is particularly fine and has lent its color to many hybrids. This is the largest species I have grown, and with good culture, Maple-leaved Alumroot can become remarkably big, with 6-inch leaves in clumps a foot and a half high and wide. The related *H. parviflora* has rounded rather than pointed lobes.

Hexastylis minor. *One of the large clumps of Cyclamen-leaved Ginger in my North Carolina garden. It is one of two species common in the mixed pine-hardwood forests in the Piedmont region of the state. The silver mottling is highly variable, nearly lacking in some individuals and almost covering the leaves in others. Like Coralbells, these exquisite, slow-growing gingers are now being produced in tissue culture, which should greatly increase both their availability and popularity.*

Hexastylis minor

Hexastylis (hex-ah-STYE-liss)
Aristolochiaceae
Evergreen Ginger

The southeastern evergreen gingers are remarkable foliage plants, slower growing and more refined than their cousins the *Asarum*s. They are a group of ten species restricted to the Southeast United States, growing in mixed hardwood and coniferous forests.

They take advantage of increased light and moisture during the mild winters to continue photosynthesizing and storing energy for a flush of spring growth. Like Wild and Western Ginger, they grow from fleshy, aromatic rhizomes and roots and put up one set of new leaves a year. The flowers are superficially similar as well, but differ enough in the arrangement of the sexual parts (specifically the distinct styles, superior ovary, and connate or fused sepals, if you were wondering) that they have been segregated into their own genus. In the wild they grow as scattered plants, often with just 2 or 3 leaves on long petioles that are half buried in the leaf litter. Under cultivation, though, they form large clumps with dozens of leaves. All the species have foliage that is tough and leathery, usually dark green and either matte or glossy. Some have beautiful overlays of silver or cream, as either irregular blotches or regular patterning between the veins. This is variable within a population, and it was easy for me to find plants with nearly green as well as almost entirely silver coloration on a brief walk through the local woods near my house in Durham, North Carolina.

CULTURE: Fairly easy to establish in moist, acid, shaded sites, provided they can be kept well watered the first season. Newly divided individuals will flop and sulk the first year, but should put up a good new flush of leaves the following spring. They tend to root only on older sections of the branching, vertical rhizome, so divisions must be done with care to ensure that each has at least one fleshy root. Once established they are fairly drought tolerant, slumping and wilting temporarily if dry but quickly recovering after rain. The plants (except for *H. lewisii* and *H. shuttleworthii* var. *harperi*) remain as discrete clumps, so they are best used in threes and fives as a large massing looks as forced as a bad hair weave. They are very shade-tolerant, but make their best growth with dappled sun, and most are surprisingly cold-hardy. Slugs are the main enemy of the gingers, and these are no exception. They have the habit of chewing into developing leaves and flowers, permanently marring and disfiguring them. The mature leaves must be less tasty to a mollusk's delicate palate, as these are usually left alone.

USES: Best used as specimens or combined with other gingers or low ground covers like Creeping Phlox.

PROPAGATION: Difficult from seed; moderately difficult from division. See p. 255.

Hexastylis arifolia
(Arrow-leaved Ginger)

ZONES: 5–9; shade

SOIL: moist

NATIVE TO: wooded slopes; Virginia south to Louisiana and Georgia

SIZE: 3–10 inches (12 inches)

COLOR: yellow-green; **BLOOMS** in early spring

The most widespread *Hexastylis* and one of the easiest and robust in the garden. The triangular, pointed leaves and narrow, nearly closed bottle-shaped flowers are distinctive. The typical plant has an irregular blotch of silver between the veins near the base of the leaf, but this is variable.

Hexastylis heterophylla
(Evergreen Ginger)

ZONES: 4–9; shade

SOIL: moist

NATIVE TO: moist, acid woods; in the Appalachian Mountains from Virginia to Georgia

SIZE: 3–6 inches (8–12 inches)

COLOR: yellow-green; **BLOOMS** in spring

Typically this species has solid, shiny dark green, pointed leaves with prominent parallel veins, which distinguishes it from the sympatric *H. virginicum*.

Hexastylis lewisii
(Creeping Ginger)

ZONES: 5–9; shade

SOIL: moist

NATIVE TO: mostly lowland and floodplain forest; Virginia to North Carolina

SIZE: 3–5 inches (12 inches)

COLOR: yellow-green marked with burgundy; **BLOOMS** in late spring

A rare little ginger with traveling rhizomes and widely spaced leaves. This makes the plants easy to propagate through division, and it makes a better ground cover than most. In the few clones I have seen, the leaf is only slightly variegated with silver.

Hexastylis minor
(Cyclamen-leaved Ginger)

ZONES: 5–9; shade

SOIL: moist

NATIVE TO: mixed woodland on slopes or floodplains; the Piedmont area from Virginia to South Carolina

SIZE: 3–8 inches (8–12 inches)

COLOR: yellow-green more or less overlaid and infused with burgundy and white; **BLOOMS** in spring

A common, clumping, round-leaved plant of the southern Piedmont, often with very beautifully patterned flowers and leaves. Forms can be found with all degrees of silver variegation, and the flowers can be as intricately patterned as a paisley fabric.

Hexastylis shuttleworthii
(Mottled Wild Ginger)

ZONES: 4–9; shade

SOIL: moist

NATIVE TO: moist acid woods under rhododendron; Appalachian Mountains from Virginia to northern Alabama

SIZE: 3–5 inches (8 inches)

COLOR: yellow-green suffused with burgundy; **BLOOMS** in late spring

In leaf shape and habit, this plant resembles *H. minor*, but the leaves are a mat gray-green. The flowers are larger and appear later in the spring. Var. *harperi* is distinct because of its long creeping rhizomes — it is a rare plant found in a few bogs in Alabama, Georgia, and Mississippi and it is less hardy to cold. *H. virginica* (Virginia Wild Ginger) is another related plant with smaller flowers. It is one of the hardiest species, growing as far north as Maryland.

Hexastylis speciosa
(Showy Ginger)

ZONES: 5–9; shade

SOIL: moist

NATIVE TO: moist shaded forest; found only near Montgomery, Alabama

SIZE: 4–10 inches (12 inches)

COLOR: yellow-green with patches of dark burgundy and white on the flared sepal tips; **BLOOMS** in late spring

This rare species looks much like Arrow-leaved Ginger in leaf, but the relatively huge 1-inch flowers are unique and the last to open. The 3 rounded sepals flare open halfway up to reveal an intricately colored interior — certainly worth rummaging around in the leaves to see.

Hibiscus moscheutos var. *palustris*

Hibiscus (hi-BISS-cuss)
Malvaceae
Rose Mallow

Show **most people** a *Hibiscus* flower and they will likely be transported to the beach of some tropical isle where the rustle of palm fronds mixes with the sweet calls of colorful birds and the crash of a gentle surf. This is not surprising, because this is primarily a tropical genus of robust, ever-blooming shrubs loved by everyone for their large vibrant flowers — most only lasting a day but produced in such abundance that the plants are nearly always in bloom. In tropical areas they are popular as hedges;

they are sold in this country as house or patio plants. The few adventurous *Hibiscus* that have journeyed into North America have not strayed far beyond the warm, humid Southeast, growing mostly in the marshes and wet ditches that are the closest thing we have to the wet tropics. There are two that have even moved as far north as Massachusetts and Ohio, but they are the exception.

Although all the North American *Hibiscus* have been forced to retreat underground during the cold of winter, they grow extremely fast, and by late summer it is hard to believe that such large shrubby plants are truly herbaceous. While these temperate species do not bloom over a long season like their tropical cousins, when they do bloom it is quite a show. The huge 6-petaled crepe-paper flowers burst from the tips of the tall canes late in the summer, and though each lasts only a day or two, they appear in succession, so the plants stay colorful for several weeks. Breeders have crossed the red-flowered *H. coccineus* with the hardier *H. laevis* and *H. moscheutos* to get the outrageous dinner plate hybrids with flowers nearly a foot across (often seen in catalogs beside a small child for scale). While these "improvements" may not be to everyone's taste, few can object to the presence and grace of the smaller flowered but equally colorful wild species.

CULTURE: *Hibiscus'* stout stems grow from a huge fleshy rootstock that stores the energy they need for rapid summer growth. They are not difficult to transplant as container specimens, provided you

Hibiscus moscheutos var. palustris. *Only mallows and orchids have combined the sexual parts of the flower, the pistil and stamens, into one conglomerate structure called a column. Though not as complex as the column in orchids, this Rose Mallow's is clearly visible protruding from the center of the bloom. A pollinator coming from another flower will likely first brush the sticky female stigma at the column's tip, depositing any pollen it picked up at the last stop. As it heads down toward the petal bases to gather nectar, it may stop to gather a new load of pollen from the bottlebrush of anthers that line the lower shaft. Even though this bloom has only been open a short while, pollinators have certainly visited it, as evidenced by the dusting of pollen they have spilled on the petals.*

have a fairly rich soil that never dries terrribly in summer. While they do not require it, they can take a fair amount of wetness, even standing water in the spring. They are all slow to emerge in spring, so do not be alarmed if you see little sign of life until the warmth of early summer. *Hibiscus* are heavy feeders —they need to be to grow so quickly. The plants are long-lived, but it is very hard and seldom necessary to ever divide or move them once established. In marginal areas, a thick mulch will help the rootstock overwinter, because, even if the crown is killed, new buds can form deeper down on the roots to replace it. In areas where Japanese Beetles are plentiful, it is hard to grow these plants well. The beetles love them and devour both leaves and flowers. Fortunately, at least in eastern Massachusetts, this scourge has been much less severe than in the recent past, and we are again able to grow the *Hibiscus* well. (I have not found any scientific evidence for the decline in Japanese Beetle populations, but I can only hope some natural predator has finally begun to catch up with them.)

USES: Borders, pond sides, naturalized in marshes or swales.

PROPAGATION: Easy from seed or cuttings. See p. 255.

Hibiscus coccineus

(Scarlet Rose Mallow)

ZONES: 7–9; sun
SOIL: moist to wet
NATIVE TO: marshes near the coast; Georgia to Florida
SIZE: 6–8 feet (3 feet)
COLOR: deep red; **BLOOMS** in mid- to late summer
A spectacular species with deeply divided, almost compound leaves and brilliant red flowers.

Hibiscus laevis (syn. *militaris*)

(Smooth Rose Mallow, Halberd-leaved Rose Mallow)

ZONES: 4–9; sun
SOIL: moist to wet
NATIVE TO: wet soils and marshes, mostly along the coastal plain; Pennsylvania to Ohio and Minnesota south to Texas and Florida
SIZE: 3–7 feet (3 feet)
COLOR: pink with darker center; **BLOOMS** in late summer
Typically darker in flower than Common Rose Mallow, with a spadelike lobed leaf that resembles the blade of the sixteenth-century halberd spear.

Hibiscus lasiocarpus

(Downy Rose Mallow)

ZONES: 5–9; sun
SOIL: moist to wet
NATIVE TO: marshes; Illinois and Missouri south to Texas and Florida
SIZE: 4–8 feet (3 feet)
COLOR: pink with dark center; **BLOOMS** in late summer
Resembles *H. moscheutos* in form, but the leaves are covered with a downy pubescence that gives the plant a lovely gray-green aura.

Hibiscus moscheutos

(Common Rose Mallow, Swamp Rose Mallow)

ZONES: 4–9; sun
SOIL: moist to wet
NATIVE TO: marshes and shores; Massachusetts to Wisconsin south to Texas and Florida
SIZE: 4–7 feet (3–4 feet)
COLOR: white to pink with a darker center; **BLOOMS** in late summer
The most common and widespread rose mallow, with large rounded leaves. The typical plants have white flowers, but the darker flowered var. *palustris* (sometimes listed as *Hibiscus palustris*), is the most commonly cultivated and hybridized.

Kosteletzkya virginica

(Seashore Mallow)

ZONES: 6–9; sun
SOIL: moist to wet
NATIVE TO: marshes along the outer coastal plain; Virginia to Florida and Mississippi
SIZE: 3–4 feet (3 feet)
COLOR: pink; **BLOOMS** in late summer
A lovely, branching mallow producing dozens of 2½-inch soft pink flowers that remain half closed. The leaves are triangular in shape. The smaller leaves and flowers of this plant give it a finer presence in the garden.

Houstonia caerulea

Houstonia
(syn. *Hedyotis*)
(hoost-OWN-ee-ah)

Rubiaceae

Bluets, Quaker Ladies

We grow and sell bluets at Garden in the Woods, and one of my interns a few years back thought it preposterous that anyone would pay good money for such a "common" wildflower, no matter how well grown. We brought a couple of flats to the plant sale of an esteemed local institution that fall (under nursery culture the seedings bloom out of season their first year), and on a table full of rarefied treasures and opulent blooms, the little Quaker Ladies were the first to sell out! Bluets are one of those plants that everyone remembers fondly from childhood, gracing lawns and pathways with ankle-high bouquets of pale blue flowers on thread-thin stems. There are upward of 300 species in the genus *Hedyotis* (one of the reasons botanists have preferred to leave the *Houstonias* in their own, more manageable group). There are only a few North American species that are grown in gardens, more as naturalized wildlings than pampered pets, but they are charming nonetheless. There is some debate about the longevity of individual plants, but I have grown all the species listed here and have found them to persist at least two years, often more. They usually seed willingly as well, so once established they will likely stay.

CULTURE: First and foremost, bluets need a place where there is not too much competition, as they are easily smothered and sent packing. Good spots are the edge of gravel paths, in moss or bare soil, or thin spots in a lawn or dry meadow. They are tough little things, despite their delicate appearance, and need little care once established. Container-grown plants can be set out in spring, but you will be more likely to find seed, which can be scratched into a bare spot in fall. Learn to recognize the little rosettes of the plants in spring, as these can be moved fairly easily as well.

USES: Naturalizing along paths, in poor lawns or meadows.

PROPAGATION: Fairly easy from seed or division. See p. 255.

Houstonia caerulea
(Bluets, Quaker Ladies)

ZONES: 3–9; sun to light shade

SOIL: wet to dry

NATIVE TO: moist soil, meadows, lawns; Nova Scotia to Wisconsin south to Arkansas and Georgia

SIZE: 1–4 inches (3 inches)

COLOR: light blue with a yellow center; **BLOOMS** in spring, sometimes again in summer

Quaker Ladies grow from ground-hugging 1-inch-diameter winter rosettes of narrow, bluntly tapered leaves. These erupt in spring with dozens of wire-thin stalks that split in two and end in single 4-petaled flowers. The plants nearly disappear after flowering, but eventually more rosettes are formed from the creeping rhizome to take the plant through winter. In the Great Plains there is a more diminutive version, *H. crassifolia* (Small Bluets), that is an annual of dry, sandy soils. Confusion over the two species may in part explain conflicting information about the longevity of *H. caerulea*.

Houstonia longifolia
(Long-leaf Bluets)

ZONES: 3–9; sun, part sun

SOIL: dry, well drained

NATIVE TO: gravelly soil and barrens; Maine to Saskatchewan south to Arkansas and South Carolina

SIZE: 5–10 inches (6 inches)

COLOR: pale purple to white; **BLOOMS** in summer

Long-leaf Bluets form bunching stems of thin, opposite leaves crowned with clusters of small flowers in summer. It is a very tough, drought-adapted plant that can grow where others fear to root. *H. nigricans* and *H. nuttalliana* are larger relatives from similar habitats through the Great Plains.

Houstonia michauxii
(Mountain Bluets)

ZONES: 4–8; part sun

SOIL: moist

Houstonia caerulea.
The elegant simplicity of a clump of Quaker Ladies is hard to improve upon. The plants form hard mounds of tightly packed foliage in summer and fall, which carries them through the winter. When the clumps erupt into bloom in spring, the rosettes become a bouquet of threadbare stems. Bluets are opportunists, colonizing damp, open ground free of larger plants that would quickly shade them out. Consequently, they thrive in the rough lawns and pathways we create out of our own need for open space.

Hydrastis canadensis. The tempting fruits of Goldenseal are placed where a passing bird is most likely to see them. When unripe, the fruits are nearly indistinguishable from the green of the leaves, and I must collect what I need for propagation just as the berries begin to blush, for they are quickly devoured once the red light goes on. Though the seed takes two seasons to sprout, the plants grow rapidly, often blooming the following spring in the nursery containers.

NATIVE TO: moist, mossy spots in the southern Appalachians; from Pennsylvania to Georgia
SIZE: 1–2 inches (4–6 inches)
COLOR: light blue with a yellow eye; BLOOMS from late spring to early summer

A unique little species that creeps across moss and bare ground on prostrate stems like a miniature version of its cousin, Partridgeberry. The flowers are disproportionately large—as big as *H. caerulea* and of a similar hue.

Houstonia purpurea
(Purple Bluets)

ZONES: 4–9; sun, part sun
SOIL: moist to dry
NATIVE TO: prairies, barrens, and bottomlands; New Jersey to Iowa south to Texas and Georgia
SIZE: 6–18 inches (8 inches)
COLOR: light purple to white; BLOOMS from late spring to early summer

In habit this plant is like *H. longifolia,* with stiff stems branching near the top from a low overwintering rosette, but in this case the plants are more robust and the opposite leaves are ovate in shape.

Hydrastis canadensis

Hydrastis canadensis (hi-DRAST-is)
Ranunculaceae
Goldenseal

ZONES: 4–8; part sun, shade
SOIL: moist, slightly acid to neutral

NATIVE TO: rich deciduous woodlands; New Hampshire to Minnesota south to Kentucky and Georgia
SIZE: 6–8 inches (12–16 inches)
COLOR: white; BLOOMS in spring

The legendary reputation of Goldenseal began to coalesce in the nineteenth century, when pharmacology was an imprecise science and peddlers hawked every conceivable concoction for all manner of ailments. The plants have been harvested in large quantities for so long that it becomes difficult to assess the possible consequences on their numbers. The consensus is that Goldenseal is becoming rarer in the wild, and there is little doubt that the slow-growing plants are vulnerable to overcollection. However, a more insidious cause of their decline is the steady conversion of rich, primary deciduous forests to farms, suburbs, and woodlots. Whether it was ever very abundant over much of its range is hard to say. Certainly, it falls under the category of a slow-migrating woodland herb that does not easily or quickly recolonize disturbed sites, and it may have just been reestablishing itself after the last glaciation when humans arrived.

Goldenseal's primary medicinal use is for problems with the body's mucus membranes. While its physiological activity is poorly understood, it seems to have antibacterial, anti-inflammatory, and astringent properties so is used to treat a wide range of ailments—from common colds to gastritis and gynecological infections. Its medicinal properties aside, though, *Hydrastis* is a fascinating little plant, with paired, maple-shaped leaves on short stems and a raspberry-like fruit that sits down in the folds of the upper leaf as if it just dropped down from above and was caught there by chance. Its mass of thick roots and stocky rhizome are the color of hotdog mustard. The roots have the ability to sprout new rhizomes at intervals along their length, so eventually the plants form a dense little colony that makes a very attractive, bold-textured ground cover for the shade garden. The petalless white flowers appear as feathery tufts with the emerging leaves. The fruits are effective for two to three weeks in late summer if not eaten by squirrels first.

CULTURE: Goldenseal thrives in a cool, rich, organic, slightly acid to neutral soil with even moisture. It will reluctantly tolerate some dryness once established, but should be watered if it shows signs of wilting, as it can go into early dormancy otherwise. If there is adequate moisture, the leaves remain attractive into early fall. When I first grew *Hydrastis,* I was prepared to coddle it as a rare and difficult treasure, but was pleasantly surprised to find it an undemanding plant as long as its basic needs are met. It responds very well to moderate fertilization, which encourages large, deep green foliage and ample fruiting. I have had some problems with what I believe is a root infection in a marginal site that is probably too hot, sunny, and dry for its liking, and the rhizomes sometimes fall prey to hungry voles.

USES: Excellent as a woodland ground cover.

PROPAGATION: Slow but easy from seed; fairly easy by division. See p. 255.

Hydrophyllum occidentale

Hydrophyllum
(hide-ROE-phil-um)

Hydrophyllaceae
Waterleaf

The waterleafs are coarse, woodland perennials related to the borages, with pale blue-violet or white flowers in unfurling clusters just above the leaves. The petals are fused into a bell, and the anthers and stamens project out far from it, giving the blooms a hazy, soft appearance. Their main ornamental feature is the intricate silvery and gray waterspotting or variegation that develops as the leaves emerge in spring. Like the spots on a fawn, this fine, silver mottling fades as the leaves mature. They are for the most part strongly clumping perennials that can have a place in the mixed-woodland understory, but they are copious self-seeders and can become invasive if not deadheaded. The bold, hairy foliage remains in good shape for about half the summer before succumbing to mildew, at which time the plants can be cut back to the ground.

Also of possible interest to the wildflower gardener are the related *Phacelia*s, a large group of mainly annuals and biennials as well as a number of alpine perennials that are difficult to maintain in cultivation. Probably the best for general garden use is the Appalachian *Phacelia bipinnatifida* (Forest Phacelia), a biennial with rough-hairy leaves shaped like *Dicentra* that in their second season send up 1–2-foot branching stems of large, light blue flowers, and *P. fimbriata* (Blue Ridge Phacelia), an annual species with finer leaves and unfurling racemes of fringed white flowers. They grow and bloom quickly in the spring, temporarily turning large drifts of woodland white or blue, but they go through a protracted, withering death as they set seed—looking floppy and yellowed for several weeks in early summer—that makes them hard to incorporate in anything but a naturalized setting. Grow in fertile soil and deciduous shade and cut back only after seed has shed.

CULTURE: Easily accommodated in a lightly shaded spot. They are fairly drought-tolerant and pest-free.

USES: Scattered in informal woodland plantings.

PROPAGATION: Easy from seed. See p. 255.

Hydrophyllum canadense
(Maple-leaved Waterleaf)

ZONES: 3–8; part sun, shade
SOIL: moist
NATIVE TO: rich, moist woods; Massachusetts and Vermont to Wisconsin south in the Appalachians to Georgia
SIZE: 10–16 inches (12–16 inches)
COLOR: white to light purple or pink; **BLOOMS** in spring

Unique in the genus for its large maplelike leaves. The flowers are held in branched clusters just above the foliage. It is rare in New England, but after seeing it grow with abandon in the garden, I wonder why.

Hydrophyllum occidentale
(Western Waterleaf)

ZONES: 5–8; part sun, shade
SOIL: moist
NATIVE TO: rich mountain woods; Idaho to Oregon and California
SIZE: 1–2 feet (1 feet)
COLOR: white to blue; **BLOOMS** in spring

Attractive for its long pinnate leaves with rounded teeth (that are much like *Stylophorum* in shape) and the dense, ball-like inflorescence. Similar in both leaf shape and the ball-like cymes are the eastern *H. macrophyllum* (Hairy Waterleaf), with white to pinkish flowers, and the Pacific northwestern *H. capitatum* (Cat's Breeches), with white to blue flowers.

Hydrophyllum virginianum
(Eastern Waterleaf)

ZONES: 4–9; part sun, shade
SOIL: moist
NATIVE TO: moist to wet woods and openings; Quebec to North Dakota south to Oklahoma and in the mountains to Georgia
SIZE: 12–16 inches (12–18 inches)
COLOR: pale to deep violet; **BLOOMS** in spring

This widespread plant has coarsely toothed, pinnate foliage and especially strong markings in spring. If you can find it, the Appalachian var. *atranthum* is superior, with dark violet flowers. In the Pacific

Hydrophyllum occidentale. The emerging foliage of Western Waterleaf has a lovely irregular spotting, and the leaves themselves are pinnate in shape, much like a Jacob's Ladder. Admittedly, the flowers are not as richly colored as its cousin Hydrophyllum capitatum.

Northwest, this species is replaced by the similar *H. fendleri* (Fendler's Waterleaf) and the finer *H. tenuipes* (Slender-stem Waterleaf), which is the better of the two for gardens.

they are not harmed by drought. The small corms can be divided, preferably just as the plants are emerging in spring, and self-sown seedlings are usually abundant and easily moved.

USES: Massing, ground cover, rock garden.

PROPAGATION: Moderately difficult from seed or division. See p. 255.

Hypoxis hirsuta

Hypoxis hirsuta (hi-POX-is)
Liliaceae
Common Star Grass, Yellow Star Grass

Iris cristata

Iris (EYE-ris)
Iridaceae
Iris

(LEFT): Hypoxis hirsuta. *A large clump of Yellow Star Grass is usually surrounded by its offspring, as most of the seed falls close by. If given a few years and kept free of interlopers, Hypoxis can form a tidy little ground cover over a patch of sunny, open ground.*

(RIGHT): Iris cristata. *Crested Iris is another of my favorites. I love its little arching fans and the way they form a dynamic ground cover that plays off the fine-textured foliage of taller companions. The dainty flowers arise singly or in pairs from the terminal bud of each overwintering rhizome, so encouraging a dense mat will pay off in heaviest bloom.*

ZONES: 3–9; sun to part sun

SOIL: moist to dry

NATIVE TO: dry woods and openings; Maine to Manitoba south to Texas and Georgia

SIZE: 3–6 inches (6–8 inches)

COLOR: bright yellow; **BLOOMS** from late spring to summer

The diminutive *Hypoxis* is one of the longest blooming of wildflowers, producing 6-petaled (or more correctly—tepaled) little flowers amongst the thin grasslike foliage from late spring through summer with occasional pauses to gather itself together and set some seed. The plants grow from small corms that tend to multiply with time, and when combined with self-sown recruits, they can form a dense sod of deep green, stiff leaves. They are thought by some authors to be a possible ancestor to the orchids, though this is matter of some conjecture.[4]

There are a few very similar species from the southern coastal plain, including *H. micrantha* and *H. sessilis* that are generally smaller and fewer flowered.

CULTURE: Adaptable plants, growing happily in moist to dry soils but found in the wild in rather poor, open sites. They tolerate light shade, but best growth and blooming is in at least part sun. They will continue to flower as long as adequate moisture is available, but other than going partially dormant,

No garden would be complete without a few of this lovely genus, and our native species provide us a wide range of sizes and colors for both shade and sun, moist and dry soils. Irises have long been popular garden plants, and both the species and their hybrids have been split by horticulturists and botanists into twelve groups or series based on the features of flowers and seed capsules. It is a little ponderous to describe all of these series separately in a work like this, so I will lump the plants together here based more on cultural requirements and their natural range. If you are interested, there are several excellent books on the genus, as well as an International Iris Society devoted to their cultivation.

Iris flowers consist of 3 sepals, termed falls, that are borne horizontally, and 3 petals, or standards, that are held erect. Our native species typically have standards that are smaller and narrower than the falls, unlike the familiar Bearded Iris of gardens.

The most common garden irises are European and Asian in origin (the Bearded and Siberian Irises and Japanese Iris, its forms and hybrids). The California irises represent a group of lovely species from the Pacific Coast, with a range of colors from white through yellow and purple that have been used to advantage by hybridizers. Many grow in woodlands or meadows very near the ocean and so are difficult to grow in any but a mild, maritime climate. All the same, a few are adaptable garden plants for the cooler parts of the country.

Iris versicolor is a widespread eastern plant related to *I. ensata*, the Japanese Iris. I will include it and *I. prismatica* with the Louisiana irises as all are fairly robust, wetland species. There are two others—*I. missouriensis* and *I. setosa* that I will consider here as well.

Finally, (thank God, you say) there are three eastern and one western woodland species that are similar in size and cultural requirements. These are perhaps my favorites, possessing the qualities of a good ground cover and a smaller stature that makes them more accommodating in many gardens.

CULTURE: Most of the wetland species will tolerate drier soils but not drought, and *I. veriscolor* can even grow in shallow water. The California types want a well-drained, acid soil and some sun. They are difficult in both hot and cold climates. The woodland irises prefer a partly sunny to lightly shaded spot with a good, organic soil, but *I. cristata* is especially adaptable and will tolerate considerable summer drought when established. Iris borers are a potential problem, but I have had much less problem with these rhizome pests on native species. Irises can be infected with a mosaic virus that causes streaking and necrosis in the leaves parallel to the veins, as well as a decrease in vigor. There is no cure, so if you find an infected plant, discard it as the disease can be spread to others by insects or cutting tools. Slugs can be a pest, chewing long slits in the leaves parallel to the veins, and posing a real threat to the dwarf types. In general, though, they are easily grown, satisfying plants that are best divided every three to five years in spring or summer but otherwise need little care except fertilizing in spring. Plant the rhizomes at or just under the surface of the soil.

USES: Myriad—from formal borders to woodlands, meadows, and pond sides.

PROPAGATION: Easy to moderately difficult from seed; generally easy from division. See p. 255.

California Irises

Iris douglasiana

(Douglas Iris)

ZONES: 6–8; sun, part sun

SOIL: moist

NATIVE TO: meadows, fields, open woodland; central California to Oregon near the coast

SIZE: 1–2 feet (12 inches)

COLOR: ranges from cream to deep purple; **BLOOMS** in spring

An abundant species that crosses in the wild with other California irises. It has fairly wide, semievergreen leaves and, considering its native range, can be surprisingly adaptable and hardy in cultivation.

Iris innominata

(Golden Iris)

ZONES: 7–8; sun, part sun

SOIL: moist in spring

NATIVE TO: open or partially wooded slopes; northern California to southwestern Oregon

SIZE: 8–12 inches (8 inches)

COLOR: from pale to dark yellow with violet veining; **BLOOMS** in spring

A lovely evergreen with narrow, shiny leaves and beautiful pastel-colored flowers.

Iris tenax

(Oregon Iris)

ZONES: 5–8; part sun to light shade

SOIL: moist to somewhat dry

NATIVE TO: open woodland; western Oregon and Washington

SIZE: 10–14 inches (10 inches)

COLOR: typically violet or purple, occasionally yellow or white; **BLOOMS** in spring

A very attractive species and the hardiest of the group, growing well in Zone 5 but only reliably evergreen in Zones 7–8. The dark green leaves are very tough and arch out in grasslike tufts from a short rhizome. The falls are large and distinctly rounded.

Iris tenuissima

(California Iris)

ZONES: 7–8; part sun

SOIL: moist in spring

NATIVE TO: dry, sunny mixed evergreen woodland; northern California

SIZE: 10–12 inches (1 foot)

COLOR: cream with brown or purple veining; **BLOOMS** in spring

A small evergreen species with thin leaves and flowers in pairs above the foliage. Tender, but used in hybrids to impart its unusual coloration. *I. chrysophylla* (Slender-tubed Iris) from Ponderosa Pine forests in eastern Oregon into northern Califirnia is similar in appearance. It is hardier, but still somewhat difficult to grow, needing summer rest and good drainage.

Louisiana and Blue Flag Irises

Iris brevicaulis

(Lamance Iris, Zigzag Iris)

ZONES: 4–9; sun, part sun

SOIL: moist to wet

NATIVE TO: swamps and wet shores; Ohio and Kansas

Iris fulva. *Copper Iris is striking as a single clump, but a large swath like this is simply a marvel. The true species is less common in cultivation than are its hybrids, but it's worth seeking out from specialty catalogs.*

south to Kentucky and Louisiana
SIZE: 2 feet (2 feet)
COLOR: blue-violet to white; **BLOOMS** in early summer
The leaves of Lamance Iris are lax and arching, and the creeping rhizomes form matted clumps in wet soils. The flowers are produced on a zigzag stem down amongst the leaves. They are distinctive in that they have a triangular white patch. It is the last of the water irises to bloom in our gardens.

Iris fulva
(Copper Iris)

ZONES: 5–9; sun, part sun
SOIL: moist to wet
NATIVE TO: swamps and wet meadows; Pennsylvania and Illinois south to Missouri and Georgia
SIZE: 2–3 feet (2 feet)
COLOR: copper to brick red; **BLOOMS** in spring
In habit and cultural needs this plant is much like Northern Blue Flag, but it is unique in color and makes a striking accent in the wet garden when in bloom. Copper Iris has been used extensively in hybridizing among the Louisiana group to bring in bronze and red.

Iris missouriensis
(Western Blue Flag)

ZONES: 3–9; sun
SOIL: moist to somewhat dry

NATIVE TO: moist meadows and seeps to dry steppes, sagebrush, and open woodland; North Dakota to British Columbia south to California and New Mexico
SIZE: 10–16 inches (12 inches)
COLOR: pale to deep violet-blue; **BLOOMS** in late spring
Widespread in the West and the most drought tolerant of our species as long as there is moisture available in spring. It is a medium-sized iris, with stiff leaves and thin flowers held on strong stems just above. Western Blue Flag grows well in the East provided the soil is well drained.

Iris prismatica
(Slender Blue Flag)

ZONES: 3–9; sun, part shade
SOIL: moist to wet, acidic
NATIVE TO: bogs and wet meadows along the coast and in the Appalachians; Nova Scotia to Georgia
SIZE: 10–14 inches (1–2 feet)
COLOR: violet to rose; **BLOOMS** in early summer
A slender-leaved species with distinctive 3-sided pods and wide-spreading rhizomes that create loose colonies in peaty soil. Its spreading habit makes it a little difficult to accommodate in formal situations, but Slender Blue Flag is great for naturalizing.

Iris setosa
(Arctic Blue Flag, Beachhead Iris)

ZONES: 3–7; sun, part sun
SOIL: moist
NATIVE TO: rocky shores, headlands, beaches; Alaska in the West and Newfoundland to Quebec south to Maine in the East
SIZE: 10–16 inches (8–12 inches)
COLOR: violet-blue; **BLOOMS** in late spring
This is a northern plant that grows in moist spots along both coasts and through the Aleutians into northwestern Asia. It has stiff, upright leaves in a tight fan and pretty flowers just above. The smaller eastern form, Beachhead Iris, has been segregated as var. *canadensis.*

Iris versicolor
(Northern Blue Flag)

ZONES: 4–9; sun to light shade
SOIL: moist to wet
NATIVE TO: shores, swamps, and wet meadows; Newfoundland to Manitoba south to Minnesota and Virginia
SIZE: 3–4 feet (2–3 feet)
COLOR: blue-violet to purple; **BLOOMS** in late spring
A very robust plant, especially in shallow water, where the wide, arching blue-green leaves can reach 4 feet in height. Northern Blue Flag is an excellent

tropical-looking foliage plant beside a pond in that difficult transition between land and water. *I. pseudacorus* (Yellow Flag) is a huge, vigorous, Eurasian species introduced as a garden plant that has naturalized in North America and is potentially invasive —displacing *I. versicolor* in the wild.

Iris virginica
(Southern Blue Flag)

ZONES: 5–9; sun, part sun
SOIL: moist to wet
NATIVE TO: wet ditches, pond shores, and marshes; Maryland to Texas along the coast, and scattered inland from Ontario to Oklahoma
SIZE: 2–3 feet (2 feet)
COLOR: light to dark violet; **BLOOMS** in late spring
Southern Blue Flag is very similar in appearance to *I. versicolor*, but the flowers are held on shorter stems and the new growth emerges with a burgundy tinge that persists at the base of the leaves into summer. This is a very attractive feature and selections have been made with especially dark coloration. The typical variety is restricted to the Southeast coastal plain, but var. *shrevei* extends inland to the Great Lakes (it tends to have darker flowers and narrower leaves). Both are robust, spreading plants.

Dwarf, Woodland Irises

Iris cristata
(Crested Iris)

ZONES: 4–9; part sun, shade
SOIL: moist
NATIVE TO: rich wooded slopes and floodplains; Maryland to Oklahoma south to Georgia
SIZE: 4–8 inches (12 inches)
COLOR: violet or occasionally white; **BLOOMS** in spring
Crested Iris is a superlative woodland ground cover with broad, arching leaves from shallow, creeping rhizomes. The little flowers shoot up singly from buds along the previous year's growth. The common name refers to the elaborate, light-colored crest or keel on each fall. Crested Iris is an adaptable plant, but it is at its best in a fertile soil with a few hours of sun.

Iris lacustris
(Dwarf Lake Iris)

ZONES: 4–7; part sun
SOIL: moist, neutral
NATIVE TO: gravelly, calcareous lakeshores; locally around the western Great Lakes from Ontario to Michigan and Wisconsin
SIZE: 3–5 inches (8 inches)
COLOR: violet or occasionally white; **BLOOMS** in spring (seven to ten days earlier than *I. cristata*)
A charming smaller version of *I. cristata* with narrower leaves that are stiff, not arching. It is rare now in the wild, but grows well in cultivation planted in slightly acid to neutral soils, forming thick mats of light green foliage.

Iris tenuis
(Clackamas Iris)

ZONES: 6–8; part sun, shade
SOIL: moist
NATIVE TO: moist, shaded streambanks; Clackamas County, Oregon
SIZE: 4–8 inches (8–12 inches)
COLOR: white or light violet; **BLOOMS** in spring
A rare, western relative of Crested Iris and similar to it in size and habit. I have only recently acquired this plant, so I am not sure how adaptable it will prove to be, but it has done well in a moist, lightly shaded spot. In Massachusetts there is a pronounced summer dormancy with new growth beginning again in fall, but whether this is due to heat or an internal clock I am not sure.

Iris versicolor. *Blue flag and its cousins are as valuable for foliage effect as for bloom. In mucky soil and full sun, they can reach prodigious size. Flowers that are pollinated set pods about the size and shape of kiwi fruits that are tightly packed with large buoyant seeds. Peeling open a pod just as it begins to yellow will reveal ranks of the seeds arranged like segmented caterpillars as big as your thumb. The heavy pods usually drop to the ground as they develop, eventually spilling the seeds that can take root there or float to new territory during spring floods.*

plants bloom very early in the year, when pollinators are not very active. Whether the flowers are self-pollinating or the stealthy bees are quicker than I give them credit for, almost every flower sets a good crop of seed. I imagine that, like Bloodroot, Twinleaf blooms early in the season (a risky time, not only because of low pollinator activity, but also the good chance of a cold snap that could destroy the flowers or the plants themselves) so that it will have time to ripen its seed and send them on their way before the canopy closes over and the sunlight dims. The real beauty of these woodland plants is in their leaves—2-parted affairs that look like sets of butterfly wings floating above the ground on strong, nearly invisible petioles. The plants grow in impressive clumps from an impenetrable mass of roots, but if set a foot or so apart in drifts, they make a perfect, bold ground cover for a shady spot. The matte blue-green foliage emerges with the flowers—its wings folded like a resting butterfly and at first colored the same dusky violet as the new shoots of Blue Cohosh.

For the child in the family or in you, there is another surprise waiting among the leaves in midsummer. The large cinnamon-toned seeds develop in a very curious pod shaped like an urn with a pointed, hinged trash can lid. If you wait until the capsules start to yellow and grasp one below the cap between thumb and forefinger and squeeze . . . it opens up like a choking Pac Man just given the Heimlich maneuver and disgorges the seeds. I never get tired of it.

CULTURE: Twinleaf is fairly drought-tolerant, preferring a spot that is bright in spring but out of

(LEFT): Iris verna. *One of the joys of a lighthanded or naturalistic approach to gardening is the way plants left to their own devices will assemble in charming combinations. I would never have thought to plant Dwarf Iris in a bed of Sphagnum moss, but it moved down from higher on the slope on its own accord. This patch of moss, at the base of a north-facing slope fed by a spring, is a perfect seed bed for Galax, Wintergreen, and even Cinnamon Fern (Osmunda cinnamomea).*

(RIGHT): Jeffersonia diphylla *seed capsule. Twinleaf's marvelous seed capsule about to disgorge its basket of seeds. Each seed is tipped with a fleshy white elaiosome to attract the ants that disperse them.*

Iris verna
(Dwarf Iris)

ZONES: 5–9; sun to light shade
SOIL: moist, acid
NATIVE TO: shaded, sandy or peaty soils and cliffs; Pennsylvania to Kentucky, south to Mississippi and Georgia
SIZE: 6–10 inches (12 inches)
COLOR: deep violet blue or white; **BLOOMS** in spring

Very different from Crested Iris in appearance, with stiff, narrow, deep green leaves and flowers that appear before the foliage. The typical variety is a spreading, understory plant forming loose colonies in poor, acid soil. Var. *smalliana* is a better garden plant for most situations as it is strongly clumping.

Jeffersonia diphylla

Jeffersonia diphylla (jeff-er-SOWN-ee-ah)
Berberidaceae
Twinleaf

ZONES: 4–9; shade
SOIL: moist, slightly acidic to neutral
NATIVE TO: rich woodland, typically on limestone; New York and Minnesota south to Tennessee
SIZE: 12–16 inches (12–16 inches)
COLOR: white; **BLOOMS** in early spring

Flowering seems like something that Twinleaf would just as soon dispense with entirely. As it is, the pretty 8-petaled flowers last only a day or two. This is all the more surprising when you consider that the

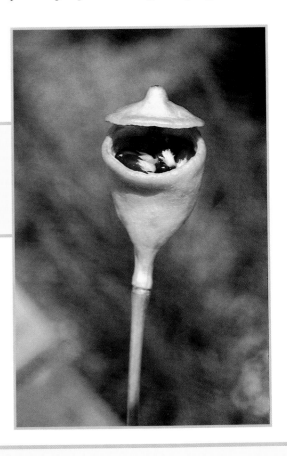

the summer sun. Ideally, site it in a moist spot with deciduous shade. It is found commonly in limestone soils, and an occasional dusting of dolomite will ensure the leaves are a vivid, deep blue-green. Dividing the crowns is a challenge and should be done with a sharp pair of pruners in early fall. Inevitably, I end up destroying as many of the crown buds as I save in this process, so I prefer to dig the self-sown seedlings that appear in time around the clumps instead.

USES: Excellent as a large ground cover or massed or scattered in the shade garden. The bold foliage combines well with ferns and other finer things.

PROPAGATION: Slow but easy from seed. See p. 256.

Lewisia cotyledon

Lewisia (lew-IS-ee-ah)
Portulacaeae
Lewisia, Bitterroot

Lewisias are perfectly adapted for life in a wet winter—dry summer climate, with thick, tuberous roots and ground-hugging rosettes of succulent leaves that can wait out the heat of the dry months then quickly burst into growth and spectacular bloom with the return of cool rains or snowmelt. The flowers of lewisias come in a remarkable range of colors, from pure white through all shades of pink and magenta to yellow, even apricot and orange. Some are candy-striped or fade from one color to another as they age. All are many-petaled affairs with a satiny, luminous quality and appear singly or in many-flowered, branched panicles above the leaves. The Achilles' heel of this group is that, although the roots are drought- and cold-hardy, they cannot stand excessive water—especially in the heat of summer—which can rot the tubers more quickly than you can say "pass the fungicide, please." Forms of *Lewisia cotyledon* are especially popular in Europe, and gar-

deners have selectively bred plants in a range of colors that are more tolerant of summer moisture. However, if you live in the East, most of the other species will prove to be short-lived unless you pamper them in a trough or alpine house. For gardeners from the Rockies and west, the lewisias are wonderful, much more amenable additions to the rock garden.

CULTURE: Plant lewisias in a gritty scree, ideally with the top inch of the taproot protruding or else cradled between a few stones. Some sun is necessary, but pick a spot out of noon sun. In wetter climates, placing the plants in a vertical wall or crevice or at the base of an overhanging stone can improve the chances of survival. I do not want to give the impression that the plants are extremely difficult, as they grow quickly from seed and with a little care in siting, they can be simply stunning. Even if they bloom for only one or two seasons, the effect is worth the trouble, and they are among the most cherished groups of rock garden plants and a personal favorite of mine. They are fairly heavy feeders when in active growth, and a rich but gritty soil of good compost, gravel, and sand is ideal. Many of the species are deciduous in summer, and even those that are evergreen need a pronounced dry rest in summer and a fair bit of moisture in spring.

USES: Rock garden, planted wall.

PROPAGATION: Generally easy from seed. See p. 256.

Lewisia brachycalyx
(Southern Lewisia)

ZONES: 5–8; sun, part sun
SOIL: gritty, well drained and moist in spring
NATIVE TO: seasonally wet meadows in the mountains 4,500–7,500 feet; Utah to California south to Arizona and New Mexico
SIZE: 2–4 inches (6 inches)
COLOR: white, often veined pink; **BLOOMS** in spring

The leaves of this species are flat and spoon-shaped, and the large frilly flowers sit flattened on top of the leaves on short stems. The effect of a big plant in bloom is like a rhododendron flower truss that's been stuck in the ground—very lovely and only moderately difficult in areas with summer rain. Deciduous.

Lewisia columbiana
(Columbia Lewisia)

ZONES: 5–8; part sun
SOIL: well drained
NATIVE TO: gravelly slopes and crevices; Idaho to Washington south to California
SIZE: 2–5 inches (4–6 inches)
COLOR: light to dark pink; **BLOOMS** in spring

A low evergreen with succulent, needle-shaped

Lewisia cotyledon. A first-bloom seedling Lewisia with candy stripe patterning. Though the candy stripe types are typically pink and white, the species can have blooms ranging from solid pink to orange, yellow, and white. It is a fairly easy plant to cultivate. This particular plant germinated in spring and was put out in the garden in late summer. Like many wildflowers grown under optimal conditions in the nursery, Lewisias will often bloom the first year from seed, albeit out of season. By the following spring, it will be back on its natural blooming schedule.

leaves and many-branched stems of small flowers. Not as showy in flower as some of the others, but a well-grown plant of the darker-flowered strains has a charming Baby's Breath quality. It is about the easiest, most moisture-tolerant species in cultivation.

Lewisia cotyledon

(Lewisia)

ZONES: 5–8; sun, part sun
SOIL: gritty, acidic, well drained
NATIVE TO: rocky slopes, 4,000–7,500 feet; Siskiyou Mountains of southwestern Oregon, northern California
SIZE: 3–8 inches (8 inches)
COLOR: typically pink, also white through orange, sometimes striped parallel to the length of the petals; **BLOOMS** from spring to early summer

The most widely cultivated and adaptable lewisia, with flowers that range from cream and apricot through pink and candy-striped. The flat, succulent leaves are evergreen, and the plant seems less stringent about a summer rest. There are a number of seed strains and colors available, though the typical pink forms are the most reliably perennial. Because the plants are easy to produce from seed and the seedlings grow vigorously in pots, this has become a popular container perennial in the industry. If sited well they are not difficult to grow and will reward you with a breathtaking spring display. Thank you Siskiyou Mountains for so many lovely plants.

Lewisia tweedyi. Sublimely beautiful flowers make Tweedy's Lewisia one of the most cherished wildflowers among rock gardeners. The Wenatchee Mountains are in the rain shadow of the taller Cascades to the west, so most of their precipitation falls in the height of the winter rainy season. Summers in the Wenatchees are warm and dry, so it is only heat in combination with moisture that makes them vulnerable to rot under cultivation.

Lewisia rediviva

(Bitterroot)

ZONES: 3–7; sun
SOIL: gritty, well drained
NATIVE TO: gravel or clay soils, sagebrush desert, and lightly forested foothills; Montana to British Columbia south to California and Arizona
SIZE: 2–6 inches
COLOR: white to rose; **BLOOMS** in spring

This rugged little lewisia was long prized for its edible root by the Native American tribes of the Northwest. The fleshy taproot remains in good shape for a year or more in storage and so could be cached as insurance against times of scarcity. Before being eaten, the dried roots were rinsed and boiled to remove bitterness and soften the flesh. The plants put up little tufts of fleshy leaves and beautiful sessile flowers that form a little posy much like *L. brachycalyx*. After flowering, the plants go completely dormant. They grow in places that are very dry in summer, and they need a similar situation in the garden to thrive.

Lewisia tweedyi

(Tweedy's Lewisia)

ZONES: 4–8; part sun
SOIL: moist in spring, gritty and very well drained
NATIVE TO: gravelly slopes and rock crevices in open pine woodland; restricted mostly to the Wenatchee Mountains of Washington
SIZE: 4–8 inches (8–12 inches)
COLOR: pale to dark apricot; **BLOOMS** in spring

Lewisia tweedyi is a remarkable plant in flower—the large flat leaves can form sizable rosettes and a healthy plant produces a dozen or more 2½-inch glowing satin blooms. The plants have the infuriating habit of rotting off just after flowering, and I wonder if water can enter the huge root through rotting flower stems and lead to their demise (or it may be that the plants expend so much energy in flowering that they are weak and prone to infection at this point). When I first became interested in this group I grew an enormous plant in a little scree I had fashioned out of gravel salvaged from old benches in the greenhouses where I worked. I think the stuff was laden with fertilizer salts. It bloomed magnificently the second spring (such was my excitement that I borrowed a video camera to document the occasion) but practically rotted that summer and never really recovered. Evergreen; best to grow it vertically as described above.

Liatris aspera

Liatris (lee-AH-tris)
Asteraceae
Blazing Star

I was familiar with blazing stars as a cut flower long before I knew them as garden plants. I remember as a kid being intrigued by the flowers' curious gravity- and convention-defying habit of opening from the top down along the spike. I have never been able to develop a satisfactory answer to why they bloom this way, and maybe there isn't one. Aside from their popularity as long-lasting cut flowers, *Liatris* are also one of the staples of the summer garden. Bold spikes of purple flowers combine with fine-textured foliage and a very hardy disposition to make them favorites both here and abroad.

There are basically two types of inflorescences among blazing stars. The more commonly available commercially are the spiking types like *Liatris spicata* and *L. pycnostachya*, with the blooms aggregated into dense broomstick racemes. The other is the button type, with the blooms spaced out farther on the stem in doorknob-shaped heads. There are many button species in the wild, and they are very charming in their own way, though less readily available in the trade. All *Liatris* produce strong stems with thin, closely set leaves whorled like pine needles up their length. The leaves become gradually shorter as they move up the stem in anticipation of flowering so that the plants have a vaguely conelike appearance. The fertile flowers emerge at the top first, then the lower ones open, moving as a ring of color down to the base of the spike over a period of several weeks.

In the Southeast there grows a related genus with the lyrical name *Carphephorus* (car-feh-FOR-us) that bridges the evolutionary gap between *Eupatorium* and *Liatris*. They differ from blazing stars in that the lavender, button-type flowers form not in spikes but in branching panicles akin to Joe-Pye Weed or Boneset. *Carphephorus* are not in cultivation as far as I know, but they should be. *C. tomentosus* and *C. bellidiflorus* are the most common, growing in sandy pinelands along the coastal plain from Virginia to Florida. I have searched in vain for a common name for this genus so I suggest we call them Blazing Joes.

CULTURE: *Liatris* grow from a bulbous, woody rootstock that forms as a cluster of spheres sitting just at or below the surface with finer feeder roots sprouting from their lower halves. Because the dormant tubers can take a fair bit of drying, they are sometimes sold as bulbs in mail-order catalogs. If you buy them bare root, plant the tubers so that they are just buried in the soil. Container-grown plants are also easy to handle. With a few exceptions, *Liatris* are very drought-tolerant plants that can grow in a wide variety of soils. They should be placed in a sunny location, as they can get lanky in the shade. Avoid overfertilizing for this same reason. They are long-lived plants that never need dividing, but the tubers can be separated to multiply them in spring or fall.

USES: Borders and meadows.

WILDLIFE: Excellent nectar plants for the butterfly garden; seeds are important food for birds.

PROPAGATION: Easy from seed. See p. 256.

Liatris aspera

(Rough Blazing Star)

ZONES: 3–9; sun, part sun
SOIL: moist to dry
NATIVE TO: sandy, dry prairies and openings; Michigan to North Dakota south to Oklahoma and Texas
SIZE: 3–5 feet (2–3 feet)
COLOR: pink-purple; **BLOOMS** in summer

A large button type. The buttons are big and showy and the plants are very tough and adaptable, but the tall stems have the habit of bending and flopping as they grow in the pampered soil of a garden, looking a bit unkempt and octopus-like but perhaps introducing some needed chaos in the formal border.

Liatris graminifolia

(Grass-leaved Blazing Star)

ZONES: 5–9; sun, part sun
SOIL: moist to dry
NATIVE TO: sandy or dry clay, acid soils; New Jersey south to Alabama along the coastal plain

Liatris aspera. This closeup of a Rough Blazing Star shows succinctly what I mean by a button-type flower, as opposed to the dense spikes of Prairie Blazing Star on the following page. Liatris have composite inflorescences like all members of the daisy family, but they lack the familiar ray petals of coneflowers and black-eyed Susans. It is clear, though, that each button is a cluster of small blooms arranged in what would be the central disk of plants like asters.

SIZE: 14–18 inches (12 inches)

COLOR: pink-purple; **BLOOMS** in summer

A smaller, very thin-leaved, spiking type common along dry roadsides in the Southeast, though admittedly the spikes are rather thin and the plants can get lanky. I grew a crop of these last year, and the bolting plants were so soft, grass green, and inviting that everyone who passed ran their hands over them fondly. Similar are *L. microcephala* from the Southeast—a better garden subject with fuller foliage and larger flowers (but only reliably hardy from Zones 6–9) and *L. cylindracea* from the Midwest.

Liatris punctata
(Dotted Blazing Star)

ZONES: 3–9; sun

SOIL: moist to dry

NATIVE TO: dry, sandy prairies; Michigan to Manitoba south to New Mexico and Arkansas

SIZE: 8–14 inches (8–12 inches)

COLOR: pink-purple; **BLOOMS** in summer

This is the westernmost blazing star, and it is an immensely attractive, drought-tolerant plant for a lean, gritty soil. It grows from a deep taproot instead of a tuberous crown and forms neat clumps of short stems, silvery gray-green leaves, and thin but dense wands of flowers. *Liatris squarrosa* (Plains Blazing Star) is a somewhat larger plant with narrow leaves and button flowers that ranges from the Mid-Atlantic to the foothills of the Rocky Mountains.

Liatris pycnostachya
(Prairie Blazing Star, Gayfeather)

ZONES: 3–9; sun, part sun

SOIL: moist

Liatris pycnostachya. Prairie Blazing Star *favors moist spots in the wild, and it grows robustly in the damper areas of the meadow at Garden in the Woods. It is a tall species with dense whorls of fine leaves on strong stems that do not need staking. Overall I think it is the best species for perennial borders and formal gardens.*

NATIVE TO: prairies and openings; Indiana to North Dakota south to Texas and Mississippi

SIZE: 3–4 feet (16–24 inches)

COLOR: pink-purple, occasionally white; **BLOOMS** in summer

An outstanding border or meadow plant for richer soils, forming tall, vigorous clumps of thin foliage and dense spikes. Gayfeather was rated very highly by the Chicago Botanic Garden for overall garden performance, and it is one of the stars of our moist meadow at Garden in the Woods.

Liatris scariosa
(Northern Blazing Star)

ZONES: 3–8; sun, part sun

SOIL: moist to dry

NATIVE TO: barrens, sandy prairies and openings; Maine to Michigan south to Missouri and in the Appalachian Mountains to Georgia

SIZE: 1–4 feet (12–18 inches)

COLOR: pink-purple; **BLOOMS** in summer

This is another of the button types, with fairly wide, lance-shaped lower leaves that narrow and shorten toward the top. Var. *novae-angliae* (New England Blazing Star) is the only blazing star native to New England, favoring sand barrens and plains near the coast where the stunted, 1-foot-tall plants give little cue to the stature they can reach in cultivation. *Liatris squarrulosa* (Southern Blazing Star) is a close southern relative, with larger basal leaves covered in a downy pubescence. There is a variety of *L. squarrulosa* sometimes listed as *L. earlei* that I grew from seed sent by the Shaw Arboretum, and it has proved to be a unique plant in this group with large, wide basal leaves and button spikes that appear later than any of the others I have grown (it should be called *L. lateii*, methinks). The plants are covered with stiff but sparse gray hair like the unshaven hero of an old western, and the flower stems have lovely, contrasting maroon color in strong light.

Liatris spicata
(Marsh Blazing Star, Gayfeather)

ZONES: 3–9; sun, part sun

SOIL: moist to wet

NATIVE TO: wet meadows; New York to Wisconsin south to Louisiana and Florida

SIZE: 2–4 feet (18 inches)

COLOR: pink-purple, occasionally white; **BLOOMS** in summer

This densely spiked wetland species is one of the most commonly available in nurseries, with several compact cultivars from European breeders. It is a fine garden plant that will tolerate more moisture than most of the others, but does fine in average soils as well.

Lilium canadense

Lilium (LIL-ee-um)
Liliaceae
Lily

I can't help but wax rhapsodic about the lilies; they are absolutely magnificent plants and I find it hard to contain my verbal enthusiasm. The largest are towering perennials, with stems reaching 7 or 8 feet and festooned along their upper third with colorful candelabras of red, orange, yellow, or white. Most of our species have the strongly reflexed tepals (the word for petals and sepals that resemble each other in shape and color) and whorled foliage of the familiar garden tiger lilies, though a few are more trumpetlike in character. On the whole they are smaller flowered and less flamboyant than the garden hybrids, and I think this adds greatly to their charm. In spring, thick spearlike stems shoot from the ground and grow rapidly with leaves unfolding like a chain of umbrellas at intervals along the way. This prodigious expansion is made possible by the lily's bulb, a loose cluster of scales vaguely resembling a small artichoke that is packed with stored sugars and nutrients. Sadly, these sweet bulbs are favorites of voles and other rodents, and they will seek out and destroy colonies with tactical precision. The lilies are not totally helpless, though. Each of the bulb's many scales has the ability to root and form a new bulb, and so any that were overlooked will start the colony anew.

Most of our two dozen species are of the Turk's Cap type, with orange-red to yellow flowers 3–4 inches across, spotted internally with combinations of brown, black, and maroon that hang pendently on short stems growing from the axils of the upper leaves. A few, like the wide-ranging Wood Lily, *Lilium philadelphicum*, have upward-facing flowers—usually 1 or 2 at the top of a stem—with gaps between the segments to let water drain out (that is my theory, anyway). Nearly half our species grow in California, many now becoming scarce because of

habitat loss. These are less often cultivated but certainly make wonderful plants for gardeners in moderate climes.

CULTURE: For the most part the larger lilies are wetland plants, reaching their fullest potential in evenly moist, slightly acid, fertile soil. Only *L. philadelphicum* and a few species from northern California are found in drier soils. If the soil dries too severely during their rapid growth, the plants will slow or even stop expanding and abort their flowers. This said, in general the native lilies will grow well in average garden soils and are not difficult to accommodate. Because they are tall but thin, they make excellent companion plants scattered through a moist meadow, near water, or in a mixed border. Where voles are a problem, you may need to resort to caging your plants, which is usually very effective. Because most of the plants form 2–6-inch rhizomes between each bulb, make sure the cage is big enough to accommodate a few years of growth. A more serious threat has just appeared recently in Massachusetts and is spreading rapidly in all directions. The Asian Lily Leaf Beetle (*Lilioceris lilii*) is a small red beetle, longer and narrower than a ladybug, that feeds solely on true lilies and related *Fritillaria*s. Both the adults and the larvae are voracious feeders and can quickly leave all the lilies in an area pitiful leafless stalks. I am hoping that some natural controls can be found for this insect, or the outlook for wild lilies is discouraging.

USES: Borders, meadows.

PROPAGATION: Slow and moderately difficult from seed or bulb scale division. See p. 256.

Lilium canadense
(Canada Lily)

ZONES: 3–8; sun to light shade
SOIL: moist to wet, acid
NATIVE TO: moist to wet meadows and openings; Quebec to Indiana south to Kentucky and western Virginia
SIZE: 3–5 feet (14–18 inches)
COLOR: yellow to yellow-orange; **BLOOMS** in summer
A familiar and adaptable eastern species. The tepals do not reflex severely so the flowers have a distinctive trumpet shape. *Lilium grayi* (Gray's Lily) is a related plant found only on a few misty mountain balds in the southern Appalachians. It is a smaller, deep red–flowered plant with copious purple speckling on the interior of the thick, waxy tepals—very lovely but not as easy in cultivation.

Lilium columbianum
(Oregon Lily)

ZONES: 5–9; sun to light shade
SOIL: moist

Lilium canadense. *Canada Lilies soar above their companions, festooning their tops with nodding bells of cantaloupe yellow for ten days or so in early summer. The plants are slow but not terribly difficult from seed, requiring five or six years to fully mature. You can knock a few years off the process by breaking apart the triangular scales of a mature bulb in autumn and replanting them. Each will form a new plant roughly the size if a two-year-old seedling.*

(**LEFT**): Lilium philadelphicum. *The distinctive gaps at the base of a Wood Lily's flower seem designed to let the rainwater that would otherwise fill the blooms and topple the plants drain off.*

(**RIGHT**): Lilium superbum. *The majority of our native lilies are of the Turk's Cap type, with reflexed, brilliant orange or red tepals heavily freckled with brown (like a fairskinned person too long in the sun).*

NATIVE TO: openings in coniferous woodland, along the coast and into the Cascade Mountains; Idaho to British Columbia south to northern California

SIZE: 3–4 feet (14–18 inches)

COLOR: yellow-orange; **BLOOMS** in summer

A widespread, small-flowered Turk's Cap in the Pacific Northwest and a good garden subject.

Lilium pardalinum

(Leopard Lily)

ZONES: 6–9; sun, part sun

SOIL: moist to wet

NATIVE TO: moist to boggy areas, often stream sides; southwestern Oregon to California

SIZE: 3–6 feet (2–3 feet)

COLOR: ranges from yellow to deep red-orange; **BLOOMS** in summer

A vigorous, spreading species in the Turk's Cap group forming large colonies in rich soils. Some plants in cultivation, such as the popular var. *giganteum* (Sunset Lily) may represent natural hybrids with other sympatric species like *L. humboltii*. This hybrid is listed as *L. harrisianum* in some references as well, and it is a superb but fairly tender plant for rich soil and a mild climate.

Lilium philadelphicum

(Wood Lily)

ZONES: 3–9; sun, part sun

SOIL: moist to dry, well drained

NATIVE TO: moist to dry, often sandy soils, meadows and clearings in woodland; New Hampshire to British Columbia south to New Mexico, Kentucky, and North Carolina

SIZE: 6–24 inches (8–12 inches)

COLOR: red to orange-red; **BLOOMS** in summer

Wood Lily is a striking little plant when one stumbles on a blooming colony, with staunchly upright flowers above a few whorls of leaves and stems that seem out of scale with the size of the bloom. It prefers a well-drained soil, even almost pure, acidic sand. I have seen plants on Cape Cod growing among the dunes within sight of the Atlantic that were barely 6 inches high. The form from west of the Appalachians has mostly alternate leaves and has been segregated as var. *andinum*. *L. catesbaei* (Leopard Lily) is similar, but with larger, even more widely spaced segments —quite an unusual stoloniferous plant found in bogs along the coastal plain from Georgia to Florida and Alabama and suitable for a Pitcher Plant bog, though it is rarely available. The first time I saw one of these large spidery flowers I was dumbstruck by its unearthly beauty.

Lilium superbum

(Turk's Cap, Turk's Cap Lily)

ZONES: 4–9; sun, part sun

SOIL: moist to wet

NATIVE TO: wet meadows and swamp margins; New Hampshire and Massachusetts south to Alabama and Georgia

SIZE: 3–8 feet (18–24 inches)

COLOR: orange to red-orange; **BLOOMS** in summer

A spectacular lily in bloom, and one of the easiest to

cultivate. A large plant can carry up to 30 of the bright, strongly reflexed flowers. *Lilium michiganense* (Michigan Lily) is a very closely related species, somewhere between Canada Lily and Turk's Cap in appearance. It ranges from New York and Manitoba to Tennessee and Arkansas, and the plants I have grown have all had luminous dark orange flowers that appeared two weeks earlier than *L. superbum*.

Lilium washingtonianum

(Shasta Lily, Washington Lily)

ZONES: 6–8; sun, part sun
SOIL: moist in spring
NATIVE TO: montane meadows and open woodland; Oregon to northern California
SIZE: 3–7 feet (2 feet)
COLOR: white changing to pink or purple with an overlay of pink or purple spotting concentrated in the throat; **BLOOMS** in summer

Surely this is one of the queens of the genus, with tall stems of up to 40 regal flowers. The throat is stained and spotted pink, and the whole bloom takes on a pinkish tinge as it ages. In their mountain haunts the air is hung with a sweet perfume when any are in flower. Needs a moist but well-drained soil and a cool climate to thrive. It has overwintered in the Northeast with winter protection.

ranean. Our species is perennial, growing from a fleshy taproot that sports a basal rosette of fleshy, undulating leaves with a protruding midvein, forming neat mounds to support the airy spikes.

CULTURE: If you do not have a salt marsh available, plant Sea Lavender in a moist but well-drained soil, and give it room as the plants do not handle competition well. It seems incongruent, but these plants of the marsh are prone to crown and root rot if the soil is too wet and heavy under cultivation. Not surprisingly, they are among the most salt-tolerant of wildflowers, and I suspect that many of the common fungal pathogens found in gardens cannot survive in such saline environments, and accordingly Sea Lavender has not developed resistance to them.

USES: Borders, seashore gardens, naturalizing in appropriate habitat.

PROPAGATION: Moderately difficult from seed. See p. 257.

Limonium carolinianum (nashii)

(lim-OWN-ee-um)
Plumbaginaceae
Sea Lavender

Limonium carolinianum

ZONES: 3–9; sun
SOIL: moist, sandy but with a high water table
NATIVE TO: salt marshes along the coast; Labrador south to northern Mexico
SIZE: 8–16 inches (12 inches)
COLOR: violet; **BLOOMS** in summer

A drift of Sea Lavender in bloom is an ethereal sight; the broccoli-shaped heads of tiny flowers are too small to see from afar but color the air over the salt grass with a gentle violet haze. In the wild they grow in distinct bands just above the upper reaches of the tides in coastal salt marshes and estuaries—certainly a specialized habitat that fortunately it does not require in cultivation. Sea Lavender is popular as a dried flower, though the heads are finer in appearance than the widely grown annual, German Statice (*Limonium sinuatum*) which hails from the Mediter-

Limonium carolinianum. *The fine hazy flowers of Sea Lavender are so popular among flower arrangers that some owners of coastal marshland post signs asking people, "Please don't pick the Statice."*

Linnaea borealis

Linnaea borealis (lynn-AY-ah)
Caprifoliaceae
Twinflower

(LEFT): Linnaea borealis. *You need to view Twinflower from chipmunk level to appreciate it. In the wild, Linnaea is most luxuriant on open, east- or north-facing slopes where the soils are acidic and never dry severely. I remember one recently burned forest in central Washington where it formed nearly unbroken carpets among the blackened stumps.*

(RIGHT): Linum perenne var. lewisii. *Like many western species, our native variety of Blue Flax is named after Meriwether Lewis, leader of the 1804 Lewis and Clark expedition that, among other things, first brought many of our native plants to the attention of botanists in Europe and the United States. It would have been a species the explorers encountered again and again on their trek to Oregon.*

ZONES: 2–6; part sun, shade
SOIL: moist to moderately dry, acid
NATIVE TO: moist to dry, cool woods and bogs, circumpolar; in North America from near the Arctic Circle south to New Jersey, West Virginia, Indiana, Minnesota, and California
SIZE: 1–3 inches (12 inches)
COLOR: white tinged with pink; **BLOOMS** in spring

I have grown very fond of Twinflower over the years. This little plant in the Honeysuckle family quietly trails its little stems through damp, cool forest throughout much of the Northern Hemisphere. Oval, evergreen leaves smaller than a dime grow in pairs every ½ inch or so along the stem, and in spring wire-thin 3-inch stems of paired, almond-scented bell flowers float above them (though you will have to get down on all fours to appreciate them). At its best, this diminutive creeper will form a thick carpet of shining leaves, rooting deeply into moss and old logs as it goes. Given its delicate appearance, I expected an equally fragile constitution, but I have been pleasantly surprised by how well it takes to cultivation. With a little fertilizer and a moist soil, the stems can grow 2 feet in all directions in a season, and the plant is so low-growing that it just works itself around its larger companions like a two-year-old at a cocktail party.

CULTURE: Plant in a moist, acid, humus-rich soil in light shade or partial sun. The plants will grow in heavy shade, but will look sparse and crestfallen. They also survive in full sun, though the exposed leaves will bronze in the strong light. If you have a mossy log that needs a friend, Twinflower could be the answer. I have even used it in large planters, where it trails ivylike over the edge and roots in the ground below. *Linnaea* is a plant for the cooler, damp areas of North America. In the South, it is happy only in the mountains.

USES: Evergreen ground cover.

PROPAGATION: Difficult from seed; easy from cuttings. See p. 257.

Linum perenne

Linum perenne var. *lewisii* (LINE-um)
Linaceae
Perennial Flax

ZONES: 4–9; sun
SOIL: dry, well drained
NATIVE TO: dry prairies and gravelly mountain slopes; North Dakota to British Columbia south to California and Texas
SIZE: 1–2 feet (12 inches)
COLOR: light violet-blue; **BLOOMS** in early summer

Flax has long been cultivated in Europe both for linseed oil and for linen. The annual flax plant, *Linum usitatissimum,* has been grown for so long that its origins are obscure. It was brought to this country by European settlers and is now naturalized along roadsides in old flax-growing regions of North America. There are perennial flaxes as well, and our native form of the blue flax, *L. perenne,* makes a fine addition to the rock garden or dry meadow. It has extremely fine, almost invisible leaves and stems growing in thick clumps, so the large, 5-petaled flowers appear from a distance to be suspended in midair. The sensuous flowers are of thin substance and each lasts only a day, but new ones continue to form for several weeks. The plants have a buoyant, carefree appeal to them when in bloom, and after the flowers fade, they recede into the background once again. Perennial Flax is a common and welcome sight from the Great Plains up to timberline in the western mountains.

CULTURE: Grow in a gritty, well-drained soil and full sun. The plants can be short-lived in heavy soils. They are difficult to divide, but will usually self-sow casually in the garden.

USES: Meadows, xeriscaping.

PROPAGATION: Easy from seed. See p. 257.

Lobelia cardinalis

Lobelia (low-BEAL-ee-ah)
Campanulaceae
Lobelia, Cardinal Flower

It is hard to describe the intensity of a Cardinal Flower bloom. It is as if the flowers catch sunlight inside some sort of secret crystal matrix and let it bounce around for a while until it has been stripped of all but the deepest, purest red imaginable. Then and only then is the light released to burn crimson into our corneas. I will never forget the first time I found one in the wild, just a single plant growing in a low area behind my house. I stood there stunned for about five minutes trying to fathom how such a mag-

ical thing had come there. I know now that the seed had probably been lying in the soil, dormant for years before being kicked up into the light by some worm or squirrel (or maybe a curious child's foot?). There are other lobelias in North America, all with flowers in shades of blue and purple, though only one, the Great Blue Lobelia, is commonly grown in gardens. It is a beautiful plant as well, perhaps not as luminous in color, but a lovely shade of blue-violet.

Lobelias are not true perennials, because the flowering stem and its associated roots die after setting seed. They are perennial in effect only because new offsets grow from the axils of the lowermost leaves and quickly put down their own abundant white roots. It is especially important, then, that these new offsets be coddled a little in the fall. Think of them as seedlings that must be kept free of debris and competition so that they will have a chance to establish roots before winter. With a little attention, the plants will come back indefinitely. They form low rosettes that remain semievergreen over the winter and begin to bolt in spring, sprouting leafy stems that yield to dense spikes of large mint-shaped flowers, which bloom sequentially up the spike. Both plants are also copious self-seeders, and in a wet, sunny spot they can become quite abundant in time.

CULTURE: Lobelias can tolerate very wet soils, even standing water temporarily, and they suffer from drought. The plants will grow well in average garden soils, but tend to self-sow only in wet areas, where they compete well with sedges and grasses as well as other wildflowers.

USES: Borders and meadows, naturalizing in swamps, streamsides, pond shores.

WILDLIFE: Excellent nectar plants. Both are very attractive to hummingbirds.

PROPAGATION: Easy from seed or cuttings. See p. 257.

Lobelia cardinalis

(Cardinal flower)

ZONES: 3–9; sun to light shade

SOIL: moist to wet

NATIVE TO: wet meadows, streambanks; New Brunswick to Minnesota south to Texas and Florida

SIZE: 2–4 feet (12 inches)

COLOR: crimson, occasionally white or pink; **BLOOMS** in late summer

If you are fond of red and have a moist open spot, you owe it to yourself to grow this plant. There is a Mexican species, *L. fulgens*, which is very similar, but hardy only in Zone 9. Its flowers are somewhat broader and fuller, and the leaves pick up a burgundy cast in sun. A bronze-leaved, large-flowered hybrid between the two has been popular in Europe (usually listed as 'Queen Victoria'), and recently a flood of

Lobelia cardinalis. The crystalline intensity of Cardinal Flowers shines through even on film. A healthy plant can produce about 5,000 seeds per stem, so Cardinal Flowers will easily naturalize in a damp meadow. The small seeds are able to sense the presence of light because they contain a special light-sensitive pigment called phytochrome. Full sunlight converts the chemical into a form that promotes germination, while darkness or dim, far red light preserves phytochrome in a form that inhibits growth. The ability to sense light is important for small seeds, as it signals that they are in a well-lit place at or near the soil surface. Small seeds lack the resources to struggle through deep layers of soil, and they are easily overshaded by larger plants when young. Consequently, Lobelias and other small-seeded species (like many weeds, unfortunately) germinate especially well on damp open ground.

(LEFT): Lobelia siphilitica. *Though antibiotics have lessened the impact if not the frequency of syphilis on the human population, in the 1700s it was a common and debilitating chronic infection. Great Blue Lobelia was promoted for a time as a sure cure for the disease, both here and in Europe. Though eventually proven completely ineffective as a treatment, this legacy lives on in the Latin name for the plant. Like its relative, the weedy little Lobelia inflata (Indian Tobacco), this species does contain powerful, poisonous alkaloids, including lobeline, that are similar in effect to nicotine. Herbalists have carefully employed Lobelia to treat respiratory problems such as asthma, among other things.*

(RIGHT): Lupinus perennis. *Whether or not you agree with my fanciful description of lupine flowers, it is hard to argue with their beauty. Sundial Lupine is a grassland species, relying on occasional fires to create the open habitat it needs to grow. Like Fireweed, it is abundant in the few years after a fire has passed, and the heat of the blaze may help scarify its thick seeds, allowing them to germinate. Lupine seeds are long-lived, many remaining dormant in the soil for years or even decades until conditions are favorable for growth.*

new cultivars with all three species in the background have become available. These are very ornamental, but most inherit *L. fulgens'* tenderness so are perennial only in Zones 7–9. Hybrids between *L. cardinalis* and *L. siphilitica* are hardy and very attractive as well, with flowers in the purple, pink, and magenta range.

Lobelia siphilitica
(Great Blue Lobelia)

ZONES: 3–9; sun, part sun
SOIL: moist to wet
NATIVE TO: wet meadows, commonly over limestone; Maine to Manitoba south to Colorado, Texas, and North Carolina
SIZE: 2–3 feet (12–16 inches)
COLOR: blue; **BLOOMS** in late summer

Great Blue Lobelia holds its flowers in thick spikes that grow in solitary or branched inflorescences. It seeds prolifically in moist, open soils, almost becoming a weed.

Lupinus perennis

Lupinus (lew-PINE-us)
Fabiaceae
Lupine

Lupines are consummate wildflowers, festooning countless acres with their regal, multicolored spires,

and moving only reluctantly into the easier life of the cultivated garden. The individual flowers look like a clutch of jabbering beaks gathered together for some important argument. There are hundreds of annual and perennial species through the West and down into the Andes of South America, ranging from dwarf, tufted alpines to towering perennials and woody shrubs. Only a few are grown widely in gardens, and these tend to be the large, herbaceous perennial types. Even more common are garden hybrids developed in England between *Lupinus polyphyllus*, *L. perennis*, the only eastern species, and the tender, yellow-flowered *L. arboreus*. They are impressive affairs in bloom, with flowers in all colors of the rainbow on thick 2-foot coon-tail spikes. There is also an interesting story involving these hybrids that holds a lesson for cavalier horticulturists everywhere.

L. perennis grows naturally in pine barrens and sandy prairies in the East and is the only food for the larvae of the lovely little Karner Blue butterfly (*Lycaeides melissa samuelis*). A combination of fire suppression and habitat loss have made both the Lupine and the butterfly less common, and now the Karner Blue is nearly extinct over much of its range. Things have been further complicated by the introduction of the Washington Lupine and its hybrids into New England, where it thrives in the cool climate and has widely naturalized. It readily interbreeds with the native Sundial Lupine, and the resulting offspring are unsuitable hosts for the Karner Blue—in effect the butterfly's food is being hybridized out of existence in some areas. So common are these *L. polyphyllus* hybrids that they have

become strongly identified with the rugged Maine coast, and few people realize they represent one of the few instances of a plant native to one part of the continent becoming a concern in another.

CULTURE: Grow lupines in a gritty, well-drained soil. They are nitrogen-fixing legumes, thriving in poor soils and summer drought. The herbaceous types emerge fairly early in the spring and quickly grow up and bloom, after which they set seed and fade into dormancy. This, combined with their proclivity for attracting aphids and mildew, makes them hard to incorporate into formal designs in which one relies on foliage as well as flower. They are better used as meadow plants, where close companions can hide their midsummer disintegration. Annuals like the much loved Texas Bluebonnet are best sown directly in a gritty spot in full sun, and these are the best option for gardeners in the humid Southeast where other lupines fear to tread. They will self-seed copiously if conditions are to their liking. In the western mountains and especially along the California Coast grow woody shrub lupines with silver or gray foliage and flowers of violet or yellow. These make wonderful landscape specimens for gardeners along the Pacific coast, but they suffer elsewhere. A number of alpine and dryland species are equally good plants for growers in the Rockies and Great Basin and rock gardeners elsewhere.

USES: Meadows, xeriscaping, rock gardens.

WILDLIFE: In addition to the Karner Blue and its relatives, the following butterflies rely on lupines as larval hosts: The West Coast Lady *(Vanessa annabella)*, Elfins *(Callophrys irus)*, Mountain Blue *(Phaedrotes piasus)*, and a Skipper, *Erynnis afranius,* that is closely related to the Wild Indigo Duskywing. The flowers are excellent for nectar and the seeds have value for birds and mammals.

PROPAGATION: Easy from seed. See p. 257.

Lupinus arboreus

(Tree Lupine)

ZONES: 7–9; sun
SOIL: well drained
NATIVE TO: coastal chaparral and sandy bluffs; southwestern Oregon to California
SIZE: 2–6 feet (3 feet)
COLOR: yellow or lilac; **BLOOMS** in spring

One of a bewildering number of lupines from California and Oregon. The plants could be the subject of a separate book, and I know I cannot do them justice here. This is a beautiful species, with small leaves on branched, woody stems and small racemes from the branchlet tips. The leaves are more or less covered with silvery hair, giving some of the shrubs a silvery appearance. Needs a cool, Mediterranean climate and well-drained soil. One of the parents of the Russell hybrids, though it is hard to see its influence except in flower color.

Lupinus argenteus

(Silvery Lupine)

ZONES: 4–8; sun
SOIL: dry, well drained
NATIVE TO: dry pine forest to subalpine ridges; Alberta to British Columbia south to northern California and New Mexico
SIZE: 8–24 inches (12 inches)
COLOR: blue-violet; **BLOOMS** in summer

One of many dryland/subalpine species and notable for the intensely silver down that covers all parts of the plant. It is a herbaceous type in habit, with flowers in small racemes. Needs an open, dry-in-summer location. This is a common plant in the mountain meadows of the Rockies, and fields of the blooming plants are a breathtaking sight.

Lupinus lepidus

(Prairie Lupine)

ZONES: 3–8; sun
SOIL: dry, well drained
NATIVE TO: dry soils, alpine to subalpine meadows and slopes; Wyoming to British Columbia south to Colorado and California
SIZE: 3–14 inches (4–12 inches)
COLOR: blue-violet; **BLOOMS** in summer

A wide-ranging and variable plant very common in the Cascades. The best forms are low, tufted alpines with 1-inch silvery leaves and little, rounded flower heads—so cute you could just hug them if they weren't so low to the ground!

Lupinus perennis

(Sundial Lupine)

ZONES: 3–9; sun, part sun
SOIL: well drained, acid
NATIVE TO: sandy, acid soils and barrens; Maine to Minnesota south to Indiana and Florida
SIZE: 14–30 inches (12 inches)
COLOR: blue-violet; **BLOOMS** in early summer

The most adaptable for gardeners in the East, with medium gray-green leaves and thin spikes of flowers. It goes into dormancy quickly after flowering. Typically lives for two to three years, though self-sown recruits will perpetuate a stand. In prairie ecosystems, it is one of the first species to flourish after a fire.

Lupinus polyphyllus

(Many-leaved Lupine, Large-leaved Lupine)

ZONES: 6–9; sun
SOIL: moist
NATIVE TO: meadows along the coast and foothills; Alberta to British Columbia south to California and Colorado
SIZE: 1–4 feet (14–20 inches)

COLOR: violet to reddish purple; BLOOMS from spring to summer

Robust herbaceous perennials or biennials with large leaves and flowers in dense spikes. *L. nootkatensis* (Nootka Lupine) is a related plant from farther north, so it is more winter-hardy, but equally short-lived.

Lupinus texensis
(Texas Bluebonnet)

ZONES: 6–9; sun
SOIL: well drained, alkaline
NATIVE TO: dry prairie over limestone; central Texas
SIZE: 1–2 feet (8–12 inches)
COLOR: blue-violet to white; BLOOMS in spring

A fast-growing annual species endemic to limestone soils in central Texas but found often in dryland wildflower seed mixes. It is becoming more widespread in its native range because it is left alone by cattle and so spreads quickly through range land. *L. subcarnosus* is closely related. The seed of both germinates in the fall and spends the winter as a rosette. To naturalize well, it needs a snowless climate and alkaline soils that dry in summer. In the Andes of Ecuador I was surprised to see lupines remarkably similar to Texas Bluebonnets in appearance growing in the dry inter-Andean valley that extends north from Quito to the Colombian border.

(LEFT): Lupinus texensis. *Many lupines, including Texas Bluebonnet, have spring-loaded anthers that fire pollen onto the lower abdomen of bees landing on the keel (the lower "beak" of the bloom). Notice that only the upper flowers on each spike of both this and Sundial Lupine in the photo on page 140 have a prominent white blotch on the upper petals. This is a signal to bees that the flowers are receptive and loaded with pollen. The blotch turns to red when the flowers are fertilized, making them less visible to bees so they don't waste their time.*

(RIGHT): Lysichiton americanum. *Contrary to its common name, Western Skunk Cabbage produces luminous, sweet-smelling blooms with a faint hint of citrus.*

Lysichiton americanum

Lysichiton americanum
(lye-sick-KYE-ton)
Araceae
Western Skunk Cabbage

ZONES: 5–8; part sun, shade
SOIL: wet, mucky
NATIVE TO: swamps, watercourses, and seeps; Montana to British Columbia and north to Alaska, south to California
SIZE: 2–3 feet (3 feet)
COLOR: yellow with a hint of green; BLOOMS in early spring

The remarkable flowers of the Western Skunk Cabbage emerge just before the leaves. They are a far cry from the fetid, red and green plastic inflorescences of its eastern cousin, *Symplocarpus*, and really the only family resemblances are found in the spathe and spadix arrangement of the flowers and the bold, swamp-loving foliage. *Lysichiton* begins growth in early spring, sending out thin, pointed buds that unfurl to opaque, soft yellow spathes curling around a green spadix like a parent sheltering a child from the wind. Soon huge leaves begin to grow in earnest. They are up to 3 feet in length, narrowly lance-shaped in outline, and covered with a Gore-tex–like, waterproof coating that lends a muted blue-green hue. Obviously these are large plants, as even one rosette can take up considerable real estate when mature. They grow from a thick, fleshy crown and make quite a statement in the bog garden.

CULTURE: Western Skunk Cabbage thrives in fertile, mucky soils and spring sun and summer shade. Standing water in spring is certainly tolerated, but summer drought is not and will force the plants reluctantly into early dormancy. They are native to a large area of the Pacific Northwest, but I think most of the plants available commercially originated from coastal stock so are less hardy. They can be damaged by late frosts and excessive summer heat, but are otherwise very long lived in the garden. A topdressing of aged manure in spring will help the leaves reach their fullest potential.

USES: Bold specimen in the bog or swamp garden.

PROPAGATION: Moderately difficult from seed. See p. 257.

Maianthemum canadense

Maianthemum
(my-ANTH-eh-mum)
Liliaceae
Canada Mayflower, Deerberry

Like most people, I am attracted to the siren's song of the new, rare, and different. It is hard to continually see the commonplace wildlings around me with the same sense of wonder and pulse-racing excitement fostered by the newest herbaceous infatuation from afar. Just as the mundane buildings and roads along my drive to work take on a drab monotony, so too do the ubiquitous plants that line my paths, fading into the background of my life like a worn living room carpet I no longer notice. I believe, though, that the practice of wildflower gardening provides us the perfect antidote, fostering a sensitivity for the richness of life that seethes and teems around us in all of its warm, muddy complexity. To catch a glimpse of this churning, odorous symphony, we need turn no farther than the nearest puddle or log, and to feel that transcendent shiver of joy that comes from somewhere deep and sacred, we must only open ourselves to the little mysteries abounding within these small microcosms.

One of my best teachers in this respect has been the little Canada Mayflower, without a doubt the most common woodland wildflower in the Northeast, forming bright green carpets anywhere there is a patch of trees thick enough to cast a bit of shade. It is a plant of modest dimensions—1 or 2 teardrop leaves with heart-shaped bases that wrap slightly around a short, upright stem. The plants form spreading patches from brittle, blanched rhizomes that weave gingerly through the humus a few inches down. Many of the mayflowers in a colony are merely a single leaf; only a chosen few put up another leaf and a little raceme of lacy white flowers. It is easy to overlook these plants, even though it is hard to walk through a wood without stepping on dozens. They seem oblivious to soil conditions, growing equally as well in bogs and rocky knolls, sand as well as clay. They can grow in deeper shade than just about any other wildflower, but will also stand considerable sun. For a long time I resisted growing Canada Mayflower, feeling it just too common, but it has patiently outlasted my insolence, drifting on its own quietly into my gardens and finally my wandering heart. I feel humbled and connected to this small plant in a way that is grounded and authentic—a true friend I share this community with. So while I still willingly make the acquaintance of some rare new treasure from far away, I know it will never be more than a passing indulgence, unconnected to the deeper currents of life and this place I am part of.

The False Solomon's Seals (*Smilacina*) have now been lumped into *Maianthemum* as well. While this makes perfect sense to me botanically, I am leaving them as a separate genus for horticultural clarity.

CULTURE: Mayflower will grow in most any situation where it is not too crowded by its companions. Except for alkaline soils and hot sun, it is easily accommodated. It is not a plant for the warmest areas of the United States, preferring moderate summers and cooler soils. Transplant sods containing the brittle rhizomes at any time, but ideally in late summer as the foliage is withering. They are quite rapid spreaders, making good companions for taller plants, but too aggressive for delicate plants of similar size.

Maianthemum canadense. The delicate blooms of Canada Mayflower create a frothy icing over the mats of foliage in spring. Each spike will ripen a few red berries about the size of a pickled caper (yes, I just ate at an Italian restaurant), that are dispersed by birds.

Marshallia grandiflora.
Barbara's Buttons are
rare plants in the south-
eastern United States,
but they grow readily in
cultivation. The intri-
cate flowers unfurl one
by one from the center
knot of buds, adding a
spot of color to our
pondside plantings in
late spring.

USES: Deciduous ground cover.

PROPAGATION: Difficult from seed; easy from division. See p. 257.

Maianthemum canadense
(Canada Mayflower)

ZONES: 3–8; part sun to deep shade
SOIL: wet to dry
NATIVE TO: moist to dry woods; Labrador to Manitoba south to North Dakota and Maryland and in the Appalachians to North Carolina
SIZE: 2–4 inches (12 inches)
COLOR: white; **BLOOMS** in spring

Maianthemum dilatatum
(Deerberry, May-lily, False Lily-of-the-Valley)

ZONES: 4–8; part sun to deep shade
SOIL: moist to dry
NATIVE TO: coastal to montane moist woodland; Alaska to British Columbia and south to California and Idaho
SIZE: 3–5 inches (14 inches)
COLOR: white; **BLOOMS** in spring

The northwestern counterpart of Canada Mayflower, with larger, broader leaves and a bit more aggressive nature. Grows under similar conditions and spreads rapidly.

Marshallia grandiflora

Marshallia
(mar-SHALL-ee-ah)
Asteraceae
Barbara's Buttons

Barbara's Buttons are a unique group in the Aster family, readily recognizable when in bloom. The flowers lack rays — the "petals" of a daisy — and instead have only disk flowers, but these are enlarged and have 5 small twisted petals of their own that are fused halfway up into a narrow tube. They follow the typical bloom pattern of the family, with new buds formed in the center of the disk and blooming flowers migrating toward the edges as they develop, the way a shark grows new teeth. From a distance, these blooming flowers look like ray petals that are exquisitely cut and shaped and give the bloom an intricate, lace-doily quality. *Marshallia*s seem, at least in appearance, to represent some transitional evolutionary stage within the Asters, on the way to the true ray/disk daisy inflorescence. They are attractive though not dramatic, the complex blooms rising singly on tall stems above a clump of neat, glossy basal foliage. You are fortunate if you find them in

the wild, as most are uncommon or rare inhabitants of the Southeast coastal plain. They adapt well to cultivation and are sometimes offered by native plant nurseries.

CULTURE: *M. grandiflora* is the most commonly grown, and it, like the other wetland species, prefers a wet to boggy, sunny spot, though it will grow in average soils with supplemental water. *M. caespitosa* will grow well in a dry meadow if the soil is not too acid. Transplant in spring.

USES: Watersides, naturalizing, borders.

PROPAGATION: Easy from seed. See p. 257.

Marshallia caespitosa
(Barbara's Buttons)

ZONES: 5–9; sun, part sun
SOIL: well drained, alkaline
NATIVE TO: limestone balds; Missouri and Oklahoma south to Texas and Louisiana
SIZE: 12–20 inches (12 inches)
COLOR: white to light pink; **BLOOMS** in late spring

A pretty species that deserves wider use in limestone

regions (I have not grown it myself, so I cannot say how it would fare in acid soils). The flowers appear atop long stems either singly, in var. *caespitosa,* or in bunches, in var. *signata.* The foliage is fine and narrow, in dense basal rosettes.

Marshallia graminifolia
(Grass-leaved Barbara's Buttons)

ZONES: 6–9; sun, part sun
SOIL: moist to wet
NATIVE TO: wet pine barrens, mostly near the coast; North Carolina to Florida
SIZE: 2–3 feet (12 inches)
COLOR: pink; **BLOOMS** from late summer to fall

A distinctive plant, with long, narrow basal leaves and tall, branched, finely leaved flowering stems topped with large ball-shaped heads (they look to me like exploding fireworks). *M. tenuifolia* (Narrow Barbara's Buttons) is a related species from wet, acid soils along the coast from Georgia to Texas.

Marshallia grandiflora
(Appalachian Barbara's Buttons, Large-flow-ered Marshallia)

ZONES: 5–9; sun, part sun
SOIL: moist to wet
NATIVE TO: scattered bogs and wet meadows; mostly in the Appalachians from southern Pennsylvania to Tennessee
SIZE: 10–14 inches (12 inches)
COLOR: rose pink to lavender; **BLOOMS** in early summer

A neat grower, with glossy, narrow, paddle-shaped leaves that send up dozens of single-flowered stems. This plant reminds me of an English Daisy, *Bellis perennis*, when not in bloom.

tubes of violet flaring to a 2-lobed white lip lightly spotted purple. The lip has a peach fuzz beard down the middle that I suppose gives overstuffed bumblebees a foothold while they attempt to squeeze inside. The flowers are huge for the size of the plant and grow in upright 3-inch racemes from short side branches. The flowers and foliage are a bit incongruous, the one plain, the other lavish and ornate, and even after years of growing the plant, I am still taken aback that this is a wild plant and not the product of some breeder's imagination.

Meehania is a relatively uncommon sight in the Appalachian Mountains, and this may help to explain its rarity in cultivation. It blends well with other rich woodland species and deserves wider use. There is a Japanese species, *M. urticifolia*, which is larger but otherwise similar.

CULTURE: I have grown *Meehania* in full sun and dry soils, but it suffers there. Give it a moist, humus-rich soil with filtered or morning sun and it will spread about happily; never, in my experience, has it become invasive or a pest. The layered stems can be dug and moved easily.

USES: Woodland ground cover.

PROPAGATION: Easy from seed or cuttings. See p. 257.

Meehania cordata. Creeping Mint in full regalia. The plants go about unnoticed when not in bloom, which makes the vernal appearance of these throaty little creatures all the more remarkable.

Meehania cordata

Meehania cordata
(me-HAN-ee-ah)
Lamiaceae
Creeping Mint

ZONES: 4–9; part sun, light shade
SOIL: moist, fertile
NATIVE TO: rich mountain woods; Pennsylvania and Ohio south to Tennessee and North Carolina
SIZE: 3–6 inches (16 inches)
COLOR: violet to white; **BLOOMS** in spring

Meehania is a low, creeping mint, similar in foliage and habit to the aggressive garden thug *Lamiastrum galeobdolan* but thankfully of a much kinder, gentler nature. The plants send out long trailing stems punctuated occasionally by pairs of triangular, coarsely toothed leaves that root along the way. Creeping Mint has a common, uncomplicated appearance that allows it to go about unnoticed in the damp, shaded spots it prefers until, miraculously, it erupts into bloom. The exquisite flowers are 1-inch

Mertensia virginica

Mertensia (merr-TENSE-ee-ah)
Boraginaceae
Bluebells

Mertensia virginica.
Pale blue is a difficult
color to capture on film,
so these Bluebells appear
more violet than azure.
This is one of the easier
woodland wildflowers to
raise from seed, provid-
ed you handle the plants
early in the season when
they are still vigorously
growing or wait until
well after they are dor-
mant.

As best I can determine, *Mertensia*s are not plants at all, but delicate clumps of sky, thinly disguised and sent here for a few weeks each year to bring us earthbound folks briefly closer to heaven. I, for one, am grateful for the gift. The flowers are the same ethereal blue as a cloudless spring day and hang like little long-handled bells on arching stems incorporated within the uppermost leaves. The broad, thin foliage is lightly brushed with this same glorious pigment, giving it a soft blue-green glow.

Bluebells are early risers in spring, barely able to contain themselves long enough for the snow to melt and the ground to thaw. They emerge stained a deep midnight purple — soft leafy stems with the beginnings of flower buds coiled up inside. The flowers follow the pattern of many in the family, like *Pulmonaria* and Borage, soft pink in bud fading to light blue as they open. The flowers open sequentially over several weeks, gradually getting farther and farther above the leaves. Hardly have the last blooms faded, though, when the plants quickly yellow and plunge into dormancy, patiently sleeping until the next spring warms the ground and they can briefly lighten our hearts once again. A thick, grizzled rootstock packed with food reserves makes this long slumber possible. When the plants are dormant, the tubers look like a piece of dead wood and can easily be dug and transplanted — a fact that has made *Mertensia*s prey to unscrupulous wild collectors who dig the plants by the thousands for the horticultural trade.

CULTURE: The eastern woodland species are easily grown in moist, well-drained soil with spring sun and summer shade. They tolerate a fair amount of drought in summer. The plants are best moved in early fall, as the tubers put out a flush of roots when the soils cool. You can break up older clumps as you move them, but try to keep track of which end is up as it is sometimes hard to tell once the roots are lying in a heap. Self-sown seedlings are usually available as well. There are several closely related bluebells in the western mountains; in habit they could be described as smaller versions of the Virginia Bluebells. All are beautiful species that thrive in the gritty soil of the rock garden, though they often prove short-lived at low elevations. *M. maritima* is a striking species, but difficult to grow in anything but pure sand.

USES: Woodland garden or rock garden, depending on species.

PROPAGATION: Moderately difficult from seed. See p. 258.

Mertensia alpina
(Alpine Bluebells)

ZONES: 3–6; sun
SOIL: moist in spring, gritty, well drained
NATIVE TO: moist alpine scree fields in the Rockies; Montana to Idaho south to Colorado and New Mexico
SIZE: 4–8 inches (6 inches)
COLOR: light to dark blue; **BLOOMS** in spring
Resembles *Myosotis* (forget-me-nots) in habit, with thin basal leaves and short-tubed, widely flaring flowers. This a beautiful plant for the specialist outside its native haunts.

Mertensia ciliata
(Broad-leaf Bluebells)

ZONES: 3–8; part sun, light shade
SOIL: moist (can be wet in spring)
NATIVE TO: moist areas, streamsides in mountain woodland; South Dakota to Oregon south to California and New Mexico
SIZE: 10–20 inches (12 inches)
COLOR: pink turning light blue-lavender; **BLOOMS** from spring into early summer
A robust species, very similar to Virginia Bluebells in appearance and requirements (albeit with smaller flowers). *M. paniculata* (Northern Bluebells) is a boreal species that grows through much of Canada and dips down into the northern United States. It is similar to Broad-leaf Bluebells with slightly smaller flowers still.

Mertensia maritima
(Seaside Bluebell, Oyster Plant)

ZONES: 3–6; sun
SOIL: very well drained, sandy but moist
NATIVE TO: sandy areas along the seacoast; in North America from Greenland to Massachusetts and also Alaska to British Columbia
SIZE: 4–8 inches (8 inches)

COLOR: pink changing to blue; BLOOMS from late spring to early summer

A remarkable plant with wavy, steel blue leaves that form loose, succulent rosettes above the tideline along northern beaches. The flowers sprawl out from the clump on pale stems. Requires perfect drainage and cool conditions. The closely related *M. asiatica* is easier to grow and more commonly available.

Mertensia virginica
(Virginia Bluebells)

ZONES: 3–9; part sun, shade
SOIL: moist in spring
NATIVE TO: moist woods; New York to Wisconsin and Kansas south to Missouri and Alabama
SIZE: 14–20 inches (12–16 inches)
COLOR: pink changing to light blue, occasionally remaining pink; BLOOMS in spring

An easy species that is luckily also the largest flowered and most robust and the primary one suffering from wild collection. This is the best choice for gardeners east of the Rockies.

Mertensia viridis
(Green Bluebells)

ZONES: 3–7; sun, part sun
SOIL: well drained; moist in spring, dry in summer
NATIVE TO: dry, rocky slopes near or above timberline; Montana to Oregon south to California, Nevada, and New Mexico
SIZE: 6–12 inches (8 inches)
COLOR: blue-purple; BLOOMS in spring

A lovely little plant with sparsely hairy, narrow leaves and short stems for the rock garden scree. *M. oblongifolia* (Leafy Bluebells) is a taller relative from the same areas.

out your glasses. The blooms are large and brightly colored, so although the plants are often short-lived (at least in colder climates) it is worth trying to naturalize some of these long-flowering wildflowers if you have a damp, open spot. All of the species have opposite leaves and weak stems growing from a thin root system and spreading rhizomes. Only *M. ringens* produces a hefty crown to guarantee its winter survival. The plants are more or less covered in viscid hairs that make them sticky to the touch (the slime they produce stays on your fingers for a while like slug mucus—yuck). All the monkey-flowers seed prolifically and grow quickly, so it is possible to have a large blooming patch in just a few seasons. There are a number of species in the western United States that are lovely to glimpse in the wild but more difficult to establish permanently, so I will cover only a few of the more readily cultivatable types.

Breeders have created hybrids using some of the species that are sold as annual bedding and container plants. These include the rose red *Mimulus × bartonianus* (*M. cardinalis × lewisii*) and the multicolored *M. × hybridus* (*M. luteus × guttatus*).

CULTURE: Establish container-grown plants in rich, moist soils and sun, preferably with little competition as the next generation needs a damp, open place to germinate.
USES: Naturalizing near water.
PROPAGATION: Easy from seed. See p. 258.

Mimulus cardinalis
(Scarlet Monkey-flower)

ZONES: 7–9; sun, part sun
SOIL: moist to wet
NATIVE TO: damp open areas in the mountains; Oregon south to California and Nevada
SIZE: 1–2 feet (8 inches)
COLOR: red to red-orange with yellow in the throat; BLOOMS from spring to summer

Mimulus cardinalis. A patch of brilliant Scarlet Monkey-flower looks more like a flock of cardinals than a tribe of monkeys. The yellow flowers in the background are Mimulus moschatus. *Both plants thrive in the low ground at the fringe of a swampy wetland at Garden in the Woods.* M. cardinalis *is not winter-hardy in Boston, but self-sown recruits perpetuate the colony. In some years they can be inexplicably abundant in the garden, even after several years of scarcity.*

Mimulus cardinalis

Mimulus (MIM-you-luss)
Scophularaceae
Monkey-flower

The monkey-flowers are colorful, long-blooming wildflowers making their home in damp mud banks scoured by streams and wet, mossy rocks bathed in a waterfall's mist. Carl Linnaeus, the father of modern taxonomy, saw in the lines of color patterning the flower's throat and the keels of its lip the face of a monkey and named the plants *Mimulus,* the Latin for mimic. It is a stretch as far as I'm concerned, but you might be able to make it out if you examine the flowers closely in a dimly lit room with-

Mitchella repens. *This Partridgeberry will be equally as colorful in February as it is here in late August. Heavy accumulations of leaves are the main enemy of this low woodlander, smothering it and producing weak and patchy growth. Here it has found refuge in the crook of a pine, elevated somewhat above its surroundings. The fine needles of pines and spruce are easier for the little plant to cope with, and under them it can form broad patches. In the garden, keep it clean of leaves in the fall or lightly mulch it with pine needles, and you will be rewarded with luxuriant swaths of green and red.*

A bushy, long-flowering species often available from seed. The spectacular flowers narrow to a tube as if pinched by an invisible hand—a ready invitation to roaming hummingbirds. It acts as a self-seeding annual in colder regions.

Mimulus lewisii
(Great Purple Monkey-flower)

ZONES: 5–9; sun, part shade
SOIL: moist to wet
NATIVE TO: mountain streambanks; Montana to Alaska south to California and Colorado
SIZE: 1–3 feet (12–16 inches)
COLOR: bright pink; BLOOMS in summer

A spectacular species with large open-faced flowers the size and shape of cultivated snapdragons. Given its range, this species should be hardier than it has proven to be in our gardens, and this may be a question of provenance. The habit is bushy and upright, with 2–3-inch oblong leaves and flowers on long petioles from the axils of the new growth.

Mimulus ringens
(Allegheny Monkey-flower)

ZONES: 4–9; sun, part sun
SOIL: moist to wet
NATIVE TO: swamps, wet meadows, and marshes; Nova Scotia to Saskatchewan south to Oklahoma, Louisiana, and Georgia
SIZE: 2–4 feet (1 foot)
COLOR: light violet; BLOOMS in summer

Allegheny Monkey-flower is a tall, narrow plant with flowers that are rather small and pale for its size when compared to the likes of *M. lewisii*. However, it is more reliably perennial in cold climates and naturalizes very well in wet meadows and watersides. The plants have little of the viscid slime so characteristic of the genus.

Mimulus tilingii
(Large Mountain Monkey-flower)

ZONES: 4–7; sun, part sun
SOIL: moist to wet
NATIVE TO: wet, alpine streambanks; Montana to British Columbia south to California and New Mexico
SIZE: 1–2 feet (12–16 inches)
COLOR: vibrant yellow; BLOOMS in summer

M. tilingii sports lovely, large canary yellow blooms on tall stems. It grows at fairly high elevations so needs a cool climate to thrive. *M. guttatus* (Common Monkey-flower) is also yellow, with a bit of red patterning in the throat. It is a widespread plant in the West, acting as an annual or short-lived perennial in the garden and easy to accommodate if you have a

moist open spot. We have large patches of it at Garden in the Woods along the border to a swamp, and the foot-high plants bloom much of the summer. *M. moschatus* (Musky Monkey-flower) is even smaller, forming creeping mats with starry, upward-facing yellow flowers over a long season. It ranges through much of northern and western North America.

Mitchella repens

Mitchella repens
(mitch-EL-ah)
Rubiaceae
Partridgeberry

ZONES: 3–8; part sun, shade
SOIL: moist to dry
NATIVE TO: woodland; Nova Scotia to Minnesota south to Texas and Florida
SIZE: 1–2 inches (12–16 inches)
COLOR: white; BLOOMS from spring to summer

In the depths of a northern winter, there are few signs of green on the woodland floor. Many of the semievergreens such as Wood Fern and Foamflower have a withered, ruddy look, and even the hardiest mosses become shriveled, sallow, and gray. It is during these times that the resolute Partridgeberry really shines, its leaves a deep, satisfying summer green even on the coldest February day. The plants form low, creeping carpets of paired, rounded leaves each with a distinctive gray midvein stripe. Scarlet fruits nestle among the leaves, the children of sweetly scented flowers that bloomed the previous spring.

Curiously, the paired flowers are fused at the base into one unit (their hypanthia are united, in the mystical language of botany) and as a result produce only one fruit between them. The berries must be unpalatable to most animals, because they remain on the plant until the following spring or summer.

CULTURE: In the wild, *Mitchella* forms scattered patches in moist, shady spots, looking fullest on banks where competition is low and few leaves accumulate. Because they are so low, Partridgeberries are easily smothered by a heavy buildup of tree leaves, so if kept free of debris in the garden, they will with time form a thick, substantial ground cover. They are somewhat slow to get established, but are otherwise trouble-free plants for shade or morning sun. They seem indifferent about acidity, as I have seen them growing as well in the cold, acid soils of New Hampshire's White Mountains as in the fertile, neutral loam along a river bottom in central Georgia. It is best not to disturb established plants, but you can tuck a few of the trailing stems under the soil and dig the rooted layers the following year.

USES: Evergreen ground cover for shade.

PROPAGATION: Difficult from seed; easy from cuttings. See p. 258.

Monarda didyma

Monarda (mon-ARE-da)
Lamiaceae
Bee Balm, Wild Bergamot

Gardeners have a love-hate relationship with the *Monarda*s. The brilliant, tousled flower heads range in color from soothing lilac to shocking pink and electric red, but the foliage easily succumbs to powdery mildew in a humid climate, which discolors and defoliates the plants by the time they bloom. In the wild or meadow garden this is not too much of a problem, as the flowering stems die back to low, running shoots soon after blooming anyway. However, in the perennial garden they become a midseason eyesore that even when cut back leave large gaps that are hard to overlook. Recently there has been a great deal of work in Canada and the United States to develop mildew-resistant cultivars, and we now have access to these resilient bee balms. While they are an improvement, they still die back after flowering and must be planned for accordingly. I do not mean to discourage you from growing them, for in many ways, *Monarda*s are trouble-free wildflowers that should be on every gardener's list. They are moderate spreaders, making them ideal for naturalizing and for informal plantings. The ragged flower heads are composed of clusters of curved tubular blooms that quickly attract the attention of hummingbirds and butterflies (especially Fritillaries). Wild Bergamot has an odor similar to the true Bergamot that flavors Earl Grey tea (a species of citrus from the Mediterranean) and was used as a substitute for it as well as in medicinal infusions. There are several self-sowing annual species including *M. citriodora*, *M. pectinata*, and *M. austromontana* that can be easily established in an open site.

CULTURE: For the most part, bee balms are happiest in moist, fertile soil, where they will spread to form substantial colonies. The shallow rhizomes are fairly easy to pull up, but give them room. *M. punctata* is slower to spread and needs drier soils. Unless you want to encourage self-sowing, cut the plants back to the ground after flowering. They are very easy to divide in the spring or fall, and they grow in full sun or light shade, though they will be more sparse in the latter.

USES: Borders, meadows.

WILDLIFE: A premiere butterfly nectar plant.

PROPAGATION: Easy from seed; generally easy from cuttings. See p. 258.

Monarda clinopodia
(Basil Bee Balm)

ZONES: 3–9; sun to light shade
SOIL: moist
NATIVE TO: openings and moist thickets; Connecticut to Ohio and Missouri south to Alabama and North Carolina
SIZE: 2–4 feet (18 inches)
COLOR: white; **BLOOMS** in summer

Very similar in habit to *M. fistulosa*, but with white flowers. To be honest, while drifts are very pretty in the wild, it is not too impressive in the garden as the plants are weak growers and the flowers quickly brown and look muddy.

Monarda didyma
(Oswego Tea)

ZONES: 3–9; sun to light shade
SOIL: moist

Monarda didyma. A blaze of Bee Balm in all its glory reminds me why I put up with its eccentricities. Blend two or three shades of Monarda together in a mass planting for a show-stopping burst of color.

Oenothera macrocarpa *ssp.* macrocarpa. *Missouri Evening Primrose is one of the most well-mannered Oenotheras in the garden, though you will have to visit them late in the afternoon or early in the morning to see the sumptuous 4-inch blooms fully unfurled. A beautiful silvery-leaved cultivar of its western subspecies fremontii, 'Lemon Silver', has recently become quite widely available, and if given a gritty soil and full sun, it is a very satisfying little camper.*

NATIVE TO: openings and moist thickets; Maine to Michigan south to Ohio, West Virginia, and down the Appalachians to northern Georgia
SIZE: 3–4 feet (2–3 feet)
COLOR: crimson to scarlet; BLOOMS in summer

A fantastic plant in flower and extremely easy to grow.

Monarda fistulosa
(Wild Bergamot)

ZONES: 3–9; sun to light shade
SOIL: moist
NATIVE TO: woods, thickets, prairies; Quebec to Manitoba and British Columbia south to Arizona and Georgia
SIZE: 3–4 feet (18 inches)
COLOR: violet; BLOOMS in summer

An adaptable and lovely wildflower, with rounded habit, sweetly aromatic foliage, and spreading stems. *M. media* (Purple Bergamot) is basically a royal purple- to magenta-flowered phase of the species and quite lovely mixed with *M. fistulosa*. They bloom at the same time as many of the yellow-flowered Composites, providing some needed contrast in the meadow garden.

Monarda menthifolia
(Western Wild Bergamot)

ZONES: 4–9; sun, part sun
SOIL: moist to moderately dry
NATIVE TO: open or wooded slopes, prairies; Saskatchewan to Alberta south to Arizona and Texas
SIZE: 1–3 feet (16 inches)
COLOR: violet; BLOOMS in summer

A common western wildflower, with narrow, pointed and deeply toothed leaves and smallish heads on unbranched stems. It is an important nectar plant, especially favored by many of the western Fritillary butterflies.

Monarda punctata
(Horsemint, Dotted Mint)

ZONES: 4–9; sun, part sun
SOIL: moist to dry, well drained
NATIVE TO: dry sandy soils; Vermont to Minnesota south to New Mexico and Florida
SIZE: 2–3 feet (2 feet)
COLOR: pink, green, beige and brown-purple; BLOOMS in late summer

Horsemint has flowers that are an unusual combination of colors, with large pink-tipped green bracts below the flowers, which are pale yellow spotted with dark brown-purple (the same color scheme as the kitchen of my last house—yes, that bad). The nar-

row, toothed leaves have a gray cast. Reputably short-lived in rich soils, and I have noticed this myself (longevity may be partly a function of genotype, with more western strains acting like annuals).

Monarda russeliana
(Russell's Bee Balm)

ZONES: 4–9; sun to light shade
SOIL: moist to moderately dry
NATIVE TO: openings and forest edge; Indiana to Kansas south to Texas and Alabama
SIZE: 16–28 inches (1–2 feet)
COLOR: white to pale violet; BLOOMS in late spring

A smaller, shade-tolerant species notable for its very early bloom. It is a weak grower though, best used for naturalizing. *M. bradburniana* (Bradbury Bee Balm) is similar, but at least in the material I have grown, the flowers are darker, the foliage glossier, and I find it the better of the two for gardens. It too blooms about a month earlier than other bee balms.

Oenothera macrocarpa ssp. *macrocarpa*

Oenothera (owe-NOTH-er-ah)
Onagraceae
Evening Primrose, Sundrops

The evening primroses produce such sumptuous, impossibly large flowers in shades of yellow, white, and pink that it is easy to be drawn in by their charms, but be forewarned—some are very aggressive and tenacious, tripling in size every season and soon overtaking areas of the garden entirely. Sundrops (*O. fruticosa* and *O. tetragona*) have been popular garden plants for many years, and I think their gregariousness has tainted the genus in the minds of many gardeners. There are species that are more civilized in their behavior, and these make wonderful subjects for a dry sunny spot, especially west of the Mississippi, as they resent too much summer moisture. The large 4-petaled flowers each last only a day or two, but are produced in succession so that the plants bloom on and off for much of the summer. They are interesting because the calyx forms a long floral tube or hypanthium that raises the flowers far above the ovaries nestled snugly in the axils of the leaves. The flowers of many species have the habit of opening late in the day and closing at sunrise the following morning. That, combined with the structure of the long floral tubes, leads me to believe they are pollinated by night-flying moths, though I have never seen this documented anywhere. The following species (except for *O. triloba* and *O. biennis*) are all perennial, but there are many annual and biennial species in the flora as well.

Calylophus is a genus of small shrubby evening primroses that are excellent long-blooming plants for a warm dry spot and well-drained soil. They range through much of the Great Plains and down into Mexico. The plants form multistemmed, sprawling clumps from a woody caudex. The stems continue to lengthen and bloom for most of the summer. The 2-inch flowers are bright yellow, shaped like a typical *Oenothera*, and nestle amongst the leaves. Species to look for include *C. lavendulifolius* (Lavender-leaved Primrose), with gray-purple foliage on 1-foot plants, *C. berlandieri* (Texas Primrose), and *C. serrulatus* (Plains Primrose), probably the best garden plant, with dark green leaves, slightly smaller flowers, and a tighter habit.

CULTURE: For the most part, the plants covered here are happiest in a moderately fertile, well-drained, sunny spot. They can take considerable drought, but this will temporarily put a halt to blooming. The spreading types need a fair amount of real estate or they need to be confined by pots or sunken edging. These spreaders are easy to divide and transplant in spring. In my opinion the best garden plants are *O. macrocarpa* and *O. caespitosa*, as they are nonspreading and large flowered, but they will suffer a bit in humid climates and need to be sited in a well-ventilated spot. Because of their deep taproots, it is best not to disturb them once they're established. Sundrops are adaptable plants that will grow in a range of soils, but excessive fertility will make them too lush and aggressive.

USES: Borders, rock gardens, xeriscaping.

PROPAGATION: Easy from seed or cuttings. See p. 258.

Oenothera caespitosa
(Rock-rose, Desert Evening Primrose, Butte Primrose)

ZONES: 4–9; sun
SOIL: dry, well drained
NATIVE TO: prairies, bare slopes, and openings; North Dakota to Washington south to Arizona and New Mexico

SIZE: 6–12 inches (12–16 inches)
COLOR: white to pink with bright yellow anthers; BLOOMS in summer

Rock-rose is yet another beautiful wildflower that deserves more attention from gardeners in dry climates. The plants form loose rosettes of long, deeply toothed leaves coated with beautiful silvery hairs. Three- to four-inch night-blooming flowers emerge from the center of each rosette over much of the summer. The plants will occasionally send up a few root suckers, but are for the most part strongly clumping. I usually sleep too late to see the blooms at their most pristine in early morning. Best in dry soils and full sun.

Oenothera fruticosa
(Southern Sundrops)

ZONES: 4–9; sun, part shade
SOIL: moist to dry
NATIVE TO: meadows, roadsides, open woods; Massachusetts to Indiana south to Louisiana and Florida
SIZE: 16–30 inches (3 feet)
COLOR: yellow; BLOOMS in summer

A spreading species, though not quite as aggressive as *O. speciosa*, with tall leafy stems and rounded leaves. The saucer-shaped flowers, which open in the morning and last a few days, appear from the tops of the stem for a long period in the summer. *O. tetragona* (Northern Sundrops) is very similar and often confused in the trade. It hails from farther north, ranging up to Nova Scotia and Quebec. Both plants have a buttercup cheerfulness about them if you have room to accommodate their wandering ways.

Oenothera macrocarpa (missouriensis)
(Missouri Evening Primrose, Ozark Sundrops)

ZONES: 4–9; sun
SOIL: moist to dry, well drained
NATIVE TO: dry prairies, mostly on limestone; Illinois and Missouri to Nebraska and south to Colorado and Texas
SIZE: 8–14 inches (14–18 inches)
COLOR: light to dark yellow; BLOOMS in summer

Missouri Evening Primrose is a wonderful plant. The short sprawling stems lengthen over the season from a single crown and taproot, so it is not invasive. The thin, strongly veined leaves are covered with a silky gray pubescence (which does tend to attract powdery mildew in humid weather), and immense trumpet-shaped, golden yellow flowers opening singly in the fading heat of late afternoon. Only a few flowers open at any one time, but their size easily makes an impact. Plant in neutral, well-drained soil and full

Opuntia macrorhiza. *The fleshy stems of prickly pears survive northern winters by pumping out most of their water when the first frosts arrive. The stems lay shriveled and sunken on the ground in winter, then plump up again in spring. This adaptation produces a sprawling, trailing growth habit very different from the erect, tree-like form of more tropical Opuntias.*

sun. There are two subspecies sometimes listed in catalogs—ssp. *incana* with wider, more densely silvery pubescent leaves and ssp. *fremontii* from Nebraska and Kansas, with smaller flowers.

Oenothera speciosa

(White Evening Primrose, Showy Evening Primrose)

ZONES: 4–9; sun
SOIL: moist, well drained
NATIVE TO: rocky prairies, openings, roadsides; Missouri to Nebraska south to Texas and Louisiana
SIZE: 10–20 inches (2–3 feet)
COLOR: white or blushed pink with bright yellow anthers, var. *childsii* is medium to dark pink; **BLOOMS** in summer

A very showy species with blooms up to 4 inches wide opening in the afternoon, and small, deeply toothed, narrow leaves. *O. speciosa* spreads by root suckers from a shallow root system, so it is particularly aggressive and best reserved for large gardens, massing, or naturalizing in well-drained soils. Var. *childsii* (often listed in catalogs as *O. berlandeiri*) is a smaller, tetraploid, dark pink form more common in the southern part of its range (it is subsequently less hardy in the North).

Oenothera triloba

(Stemless Evening Primrose)

ZONES: 4–9; sun
SOIL: dry, well drained
NATIVE TO: rocky prairies, roadsides, often on limestone; Virginia to Indiana and Kansas south to Texas and Alabama
SIZE: 8–14 inches (12 inches)
COLOR: pale yellow or white to pink; **BLOOMS** in summer

One of a number of biennial species, this is much like *O. caespitosa* in its tufted habit and dandelion-like leaves. It will naturalize in the garden. *O. biennis* (Evening Primrose)—also biennial—is a frequent roadside weed, forming large rosettes of long narrow leaves the first season and a tall, leafy stem the second, with successive flowers blooming for a month or more in late summer. It ranges through most of southern Canada and the United States.

Opuntia macrorhiza

Opuntia (oh-PUNT-ee-ah)
Cactaceae
Prickly Pear, Cholla

Prickly pears are certainly not for everyone, but if you love the resolute, don't-mess-with-me charac-

ter of cacti, they are certainly among the easiest to accommodate, and the huge, many-petaled, satiny flowers are an exquisite bonus in the late spring or summer. I love the *Opuntia*s, but I do not relish having to weed around them, as the stems are covered in little barbed spines called glochids that grow in tufts around the base of the larger spines. These enter the skin at the slightest brush and cause an irritating itch or mild stabbing pain. They are hard to see unless you silhouette them in the light, but they can be easily pulled out with tweezers or rubber cement that is brushed over the area and allowed to get semihard before it is removed.

Like all cacti, the prickly pears have forsaken leaves to cut down on water loss and instead rely on swollen, water-storing stems for photosynthesis. (The leaves of *Opuntia*s are present on new growth as small, fleshy, needlelike structures that quickly fall before the stems mature.) With most of the *Opuntia*s, these stems are flattened into rounded pads that are jointed or constricted where a new growth begins. The plants produce one to several of these jointed pads a year, which form lengthening chains that either grow upright or more commonly trail heavily over the ground. The pads are easily dislodged at the joints, and these will root were they fall to form a new clump. Prickly pears are common dryland plants throughout the deserts of subtropical and tropical North and South America, with a few dozen ranging into temperate areas of the United States and Canada. These species have adapted to cold winters by withdrawing most of the water from their pads in autumn so that they are shriveled and less likely to suffer freeze damage. They look pretty bedraggled in the winter, but quickly plump up and recover when the weather warms.

CULTURE: Grow prickly pears in well-drained, sandy soils, though many will grow in heavy clay soils in drier climates. They require little care and can be easily spread by removing (with gloves on!) a pad or two by severing it at the joint, letting it air dry for seven to ten days to callous the wound, and burying it severed end down halfway in the ground. This

is best done in spring before new growth begins. They are certainly the most moisture-tolerant cacti, so they make good subjects even in the East and Pacific Northwest.

USES: Rock gardens, xeriscaping.

PROPAGATION: Moderately difficult from seed; easy from cuttings. See p. 258.

Opuntia humifusa
(Eastern Prickly Pear)

ZONES: 4–9; sun
SOIL: sandy, dry
NATIVE TO: sandy prairies, beaches, and dunes; Massachusetts to Minnesota south to Texas and Florida
SIZE: 8–14 inches (12–18 inches)
COLOR: yellow with or without a blood red throat; **BLOOMS** in summer

The only cactus native to the Northeast, and a very easy garden plant for poor soils. The sprawling, oval pads typically lack large spines, or if present they are scattered along the upper margin, but the plants are well-armed with glochids. Interestingly, it has found a desertlike niche in the scattered dunes and barrens of a normally high rainfall region.

Opuntia imbricata
(Chain-link Cactus)

ZONES: 5–9; sun
SOIL: dry, well drained
NATIVE TO: gravelly and sandy soils on plains and deserts; Kansas and Colorado to Arizona south to Mexico and Texas
SIZE: 2–8 feet (2–3 feet)
COLOR: magenta or purple; **BLOOMS** in summer

The most widespread cholla or *Cylindropuntia,* with long, thin cylindrical pads forming shrubs or even small trees through much of the southern Rockies and plains. It is one of the plants that produces the cactus skeletons popular with tourists. The plants droop and sag in the winter, but are very cold-hardy, and while never getting very large in the East, they do survive. The 3-inch flowers, produced sporadically for a month or so, are noticeable even at 75 miles per hour. The stems are extremely spiny and were used in initiation ceremonies by Native Americans. The young initiates would grind the stems under their armpits as a test of strength and manhood.

Opuntia macrorhiza
(Plains Prickly Pear)

ZONES: 4–9; sun
SOIL: dry, well drained
NATIVE TO: sandy or rocky grasslands; Minnesota to Idaho south to Arizona and Louisiana

SIZE: 4–8 inches (12–18 inches)
COLOR: yellow, often with a red throat; **BLOOMS** in summer

A fierce-looking, sprawling plant with 2-inch spines gathered near the tops of each pad. The pads are basically rounded in outline narrowing at the joint. It is closely related to *O. humifusa* and grades into it in the East. In the West it grades into the widespread *O. phaeacantha,* a variable plant typically with large pads well armed with long spines.

Opuntia polyacantha
(Starvation Cholla)

ZONES: 3–9; sun
SOIL: dry, well drained
NATIVE TO: sandy or gravelly soils; South Dakota and Saskatchewan to British Columbia south to California, Mexico, and Texas
SIZE: 4–8 inches (12–18 inches)
COLOR: yellow, occasionally pink or red; **BLOOMS** in early summer

Much like *O. macrorhiza* in pad shape, but the spines are much denser and more evenly distributed over the plants. In fact the spines are so dense on some varieties that the plant takes on a hairy, gray appearance from a distance. Like most of the hardier prickly pears, it forms sprawling chains of jointed pads because the older growths never regain the vertical after winter dehydration. This species is notable for the lovely pink- and red-flowered forms that are available from specialty growers, and this, combined with the large pads and copius spines, makes it my favorite.

Opuntia tunicana var. *davisii*
(Sheathed Cholla, Abrojo)

ZONES: 6–9; sun
SOIL: dry, well drained
NATIVE TO: sandy or gravelly soils, hillsides or dry river beds; Oklahoma to New Mexico and Texas
SIZE: 8–16 inches (12–16 inches)
COLOR: yellow to greenish yellow; **BLOOMS** in spring

The Abrojo is one of a group of small cholla or chain cacti with the cylindrical pads of *O. imbricata* and a sprawling, low shrubby habit. This species is a fairly rare denizen of the western plains, but is popular in cultivation for its numerous golden yellow spines that make the plants glow radiantly in the sun. *O. whipplei* is a more common cousin, growing as either a sprawling mass of interwoven stems or elegant 6-foot shrubs in ideal locations. It has proven very hardy though slow growing for me in the East.

❧ Controlling Invasive Plants ❧

We often see or hear about invasive exotic species that have been introduced as ornamentals and become pests. The Purple Loosestrife (*Lythrum salicaria*) is a well-known example that has spread unchecked through much of the East. Researchers have begun to introduce several insects that feed exclusively (we hope) on the plants to attempt to control them. There are also many instances, however, of our natives becoming noxious weeds in other countries where they had no natural predators, and one of the most striking is the story of *Opuntia stricta* in Australia. *O. stricta* is a tall, nearly spineless subtropical cactus found in sandy soils and beaches along the southern Atlantic and Gulf coasts from South Carolina to Florida. It was introduced into Australia in 1839, and by the 1920s it had covered millions of acres in western Australia in impenetrable thickets that made the land useless for grazing and displaced the native flora. In desperation, in the mid 1920s researchers released a species of moth from Argentina, *Cactoblastis cactorum,* whose larvae feed on *Opuntia.* It had dramatic effects: by the 1930s, the plants had been nearly eliminated. They now occur only as infrequent, scattered plants.[5] It was one of the first successful planned biological controls involving a plant, and it has proved an important precedent for ongoing research to this day.

Orontium aquaticum

Orontium aquaticum (or-ON-tee-um)
Araceae
Golden Club, Never Wets

Orontium aquaticum.
More like some aquatic mushroom than the flowers of a plant, the naked spadixes of Golden Club are as strange as they are beautiful.

ZONES: 5–9; sun to light shade
SOIL: wet to inundated
NATIVE TO: coastal swamps and pools; Massachusetts to New York, south to Louisiana and Florida
SIZE: 8–12 inches (2–3 feet)
COLOR: golden yellow; **BLOOMS** in spring

Golden Club takes the waterproofing prize for the plants covered in this book. This aquatic arum has remarkable 12-inch dark blue-green leaves that are like the best of raincoats — water simply beads up on and rolls off (the name Never Wets is popular in the South). The leaves float on or partially below the surface of shallow water in swamps and pools along the coastal plain from Massachusetts to Florida, forming great patches in the hot, humid swamps like the Okefenokee in Georgia. The deep golden yellow flowers are produced on curved, club-shaped spadixes that are quite lovely floating in a ring beyond the emerging leaves in spring. (Unlike most arums, this lacks a prominent spathe around the flowers, so the bright spadix is clearly visible.) Golden Club is a fascinating addition to the garden, provided you have the right habitat for it.

CULTURE: The plants can be established in mucky soils and shallow water (less than 12 inches deep), where they slowly spread to form thick clumps. You may need to pin plants in place with stout wire until they're established or grow them like water lilies in containers. They are long-lived and essentially trouble-free.

USES: Water gardens.

PROPAGATION: Moderately difficult from fresh seed. See p. 258.

Pachysandra procumbens

Pachysandra procumbens

(pack-ee-SAN-dra)

Buxaceae
Allegheny Spurge

ZONES: 4–9; shade
SOIL: moist, fertile (can tolerate some drought once established)
NATIVE TO: rich woods; West Virginia to Kentucky south to Louisiana and Florida
SIZE: 6–10 inches (18–24 inches)
COLOR: white tinged with burgundy; **BLOOMS** in spring

For gardeners in the northern states, the word *Pachysandra* is synonymous with the resilient plasticity of the Japanese Spurge (*Pachysandra terminalis*), that vinyl siding of ground covers that carpets great areas of suburbia. Our indigenous species is a completely different animal, metaphorically more similar to cedar shingles than vinyl siding. The Allegheny Spurge produces whorls of semievergreen leaflets clustered near the top of short, clumping

stems in a tea rose sort of arrangement. The leaves have a muted blue-gray background overlaid with an irregular silver venation that varies in intensity fromplant to plant and even from stem to stem. It grows in tight clumps, not spreading mats, with a flush of new leaves appearing just after the delicious, cinnamon-scented blooms, which are arranged like bottlebrushes with male flowers above and females below.

Allegheny Spurge is a patient woodlander from rich forests in the southern mountains. It is occasionally still found as well in Florida and Louisiana, likely pushed to the edge of the Gulf of Mexico by advancing glaciers and still remnant there today. It forms broad mounds of foliage with the outermost stems sprawling down and the center ones more upright (about twice the size of Japanese Spurge in all respects). Allegheny Spurge is not a rapid grower, only doubling in size every year, so it takes a few seasons to become a substantial clump. This has its advantages in the shade garden, because it will not overtake its neighbors and makes an outstanding, well-behaved counterpoint to fine-textured ferns and wildflowers. If winters are mild the leaves will remain tattered but undaunted in spring, and like so many evergreens preparing for winter, they hunker down and stain dark burgundy at the approach of cold.

CULTURE: Grow in a rich, organic, acid soil in dappled shade for best effect. In my experience, Allegheny Spurge can handle brief summer droughts with little trouble; it also tolerates considerable shade. It is tempting to cut off tattered leaves in spring, but I would recommend leaving them, as they help get the plants going, and you may inadvertently remove some of the flower buds, which appear partway up the stems. New foliage will quickly grow up and mask any temporary vernal indecencies. It is rarely troubled by pests and diseases.

USES: Best scattered or massed in the woodland garden as a ground cover around taller plants.

PROPAGATION: Moderately difficult from seed and division. See p. 259.

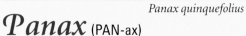

Panax quinquefolius

Panax (PAN-ax)

Araliaceae
Ginseng

It is difficult to speak of ginseng outside of its medicinal context. *Panax* has been revered in China for at least 7,000 years as a restorative tonic that helps the body cope with stress, cold, hunger, and exhaustion. It contains steroidal compounds called ginsenosides similar to human stress hormones that may help explain its therapeutic effects.[6] The Chinese species had become quite rare in the wild by the

(**TOP**): Pachysandra procumbens. *A nest of spicy-scented flowers appears from the base of last season's stems just before the new leaves begin to expand. All the flowers visible in this image are male; the ruddy red female flowers hide at the base of the stems nearly buried in the ground. My suspicion is that these are pollinated by crawling as opposed to flying insects, who dust pollen on the female stigmas on their way down the stem. Although a bit tattered by spring, Allegheny Spurge's mottled evergreen foliage gives it a jump on the season.*

(**BOTTOM**): Panax quinquefolius. *In the central part of Wisconsin, ginseng farming provides valuable supplemental income for farmers. The rich, nearly neutral soils and moderate climate are perfect for ginseng, which is grown mostly in raised beds under 70 percent shade cloth or wooden lath. The beds are seeded and the plants grown for three seasons before the valuable roots are harvested. Because the fungus diseases that plague ginseng build up in the soil over the course of the three years, it can never be grown there again. The shade houses are moved to a new spot and the old field goes back to corn and soybeans. Harvested roots are cleaned and the majority are sent to China for grading and packaging.*

Penstemon digitalis.
Tall White Beardtongue is one of the easiest Penstemon *species for eastern gardeners.*

eighteenth century, so when American Ginseng was discovered to have similar properties, it sparked a collecting boom likened to the California Gold Rush. Collectors (mostly Native Americans) were paid to scour the forests to collect huge quantities of the strange, human-shaped roots for export to China, and the plants were nearly eliminated over much of their range. The plants are now rare in the wild, and biologists try to keep known colonies secret to prevent even these from being wiped out. Wild collection has fortunately been replaced by cultivation, and in this country, Wisconsin growers produce tons of the roots annually for export to Asia and, increasingly, for domestic consumption as well. The plants are grown in prepared beds under shade cloth and harvested after three growing seasons.

As a garden subject, ginseng is a rather unremarkable plant, with 1-foot stems that split into 3 sets of leaves, each with 5 palmately compound leaflets and an umbel of small greenish flowers in the center. It is often confused with its relative, the common Wild Sarsaparilla *(Aralia nudicaulis)* but this differs in having pinnate leaves and a flower stalk that emerges separately from the crown. The flowers are followed by a few berries that turn bright red when ripe and are quickly consumed by birds. It is grown more for the folklore surrounding it than its beauty, but the toothed leaflets and distinctive architecture are interesting in a mixed woodland planting.

CULTURE: American Ginseng is a bit difficult to grow, and it suffers from leaf and root diseases that require considerable applications of fungicides to control in commercial operations. It is found commonly in limestone regions and sulks if the soil becomes too acid. A topdressing of dolomite every fall greatly improves its vigor and color if your soil is naturally acid. The roots require a moist but well-drained soil to prevent the root rots that plague the species. The plant also needs the dappled shade of deciduous trees to flower and fruit. Start with container-grown material, not roots bought from a commercial supplier, as these will often be diseased, and plant in spring or fall.

USES: Woodland-shade garden.

PROPAGATION: Difficult from seed. See p. 259.

Panax quinquefolius
(American Ginseng)

ZONES: 3–9; shade
SOIL: moist, neutral
NATIVE TO: rich woods, often on limestone; Quebec to Minnesota south to Louisiana and Georgia
SIZE: 8–16 inches (12 inches)
COLOR: greenish white; **BLOOMS** in spring

Panax trifolius
(Dwarf Ginseng)

ZONES: 3–8; shade
SOIL: moist
NATIVE TO: rich woods, commonly along streambanks and floodplains; Nova Scotia to Minnesota and Iowa south to Illinois, Pennsylvania, and northern Georgia
SIZE: 2–4 inches (6 inches)
COLOR: white; **BLOOMS** in early spring

A low, spring ephemeral that is easy to overlook when not in bloom. Dwarf Ginseng is much smaller than American Ginseng, with leaflets in pairs of 3 on short stems. It grows typically on the moist banks of woodland streams and goes quickly to seed and then dormant by early summer. It is not known to have medicinal properties and is really too small and inconspicuous to be of use in the garden, but I mention it because a number of people have asked me about it over the years.

Penstemon digitalis

Penstemon (pen-STEM-on)
Scrophulariaceae
Beardtongue

*P*enstemons are sometimes heralded as the largest genus of plants native solely to North America, a title now in dispute after the discovery of one species that has migrated over the Aleutians into northeast Asia. Semantics aside, though, virtually all of our 250-odd species are wonderful plants, with flowers that range in size and color from the spectacular to the sublime. By far the largest diversity can be found in the western mountains and Great Basin, each mountain range and valley often containing at least several endemic species. These have long been favorite rock garden subjects, and many are very easy to grow in scree conditions in drier climates. There is a small group of taller plants from the East that is easily accommodated in the perennial border, and these are by far the easiest all-around garden plants for moist climates. Mexico and the desert Southwest offer still others that have become popular plants in the warmer parts of the United States. Basically, there is a *Penstemon* for every climate, providing the wildflower enthusiast with immense variety that it would be impossible to do justice here, though I will try to cover some of the representatives from each area. Every year I discover half a dozen more to add to the garden, and I have grown only a mere 50 or so species, so far. There is a Penstemon Society and there are several good books on the genus that I would refer you to for a more complete synopsis.

All beardtongues share several things in common, most notably showy, brightly colored tubular flowers that flare open to reveal an intricately colored and spotted throat. The 5 petals that fuse to form this tube are free at their tips, forming 2 upper lobes and 3 lower lobes that jut out a bit farther to form a lip or tongue. This lip has a prominent beard in its center that I suspect is there to lure bees and give them a place to grab on to when they land. It is also obviously the source of the suggestive and vaguely unsettling common name. The plants all have strongly opposite leaves, typically with flowers in tiered inflorescences from their tips. In habit they can be anything from tall, multistemmed clumps or woody subshrubs to low creepers and tufted buns.

CULTURE: It is hard to generalize too much about such a large group that is fairly easy to grow provided some attention is paid to a particular species' natural habitat. The majority of the western and southwestern species require a gritty, well-drained soil and full sun to prevent root rot that can be a problem in wet weather. The eastern species like *P. digitalis* are suited to a range of average soils in sun to light shade. Shrubby and evergreen types will often be killed back to the crown in severe winters, but usually regrow come spring. *Penstemon*s are hollow-stemmed, and care must be taken when pruning back the taller types after flowering as water can enter the stem like a straw and rot out the crown. A particularly industrious gardener I know seals the cut ends with a dab of white glue to prevent this. The creeping types will get rangy and sparse after five years or so and are best started anew from rooted layers or cuttings. All the species I have grown certainly appreciate a fertile soil, which encourages heavy blooming. I suppose the biggest drawback to beardtongues as garden plants is their short season of bloom (one to two weeks) and subsequent awkward period as they die back and set seed. It is therefore wise to plant a range of species to extend blooming and to incorporate them into mixed plantings as well.

USES: Myriad—borders, meadows, xeriscaping, woodland, rock garden, massing.

PROPAGATION: Easy from seed. See p. 259.

Penstemon ambiguus
(Phlox Beardtongue)

ZONES: 5–8; sun
SOIL: well drained, sandy
NATIVE TO: sandy soils, sagebrush; New Mexico
SIZE: 12–28 inches (12 inches)
COLOR: white with violet to lavender on reverse;
   BLOOMS in summer

The perfect plant for a hot, sandy spot, with needle-like leaves and a shrubby habit. The flowers are flat and wide-petaled like a phlox and bloom over a long period in early summer.

Penstemon campanulatus
(Mexican Beardtongue)

ZONES: 7–10; sun
SOIL: well drained but moist

Penstemon eatonii. *Firecracker Beardtongue is a spectacular plant for a gritty soil and full sun.*

NATIVE TO: moist to dry soils from low elevation to montane; northern Mexico

SIZE: 1–2 feet (12–16 inches)

COLOR: purple through violet to red; **BLOOMS** in summer

A very beautiful plant for gardeners in mild, warm climates, with narrow, shiny evergreen leaves and large open flowers appearing over a long period. In habit it is a lax, low shrub. Plants in cultivation probably represent a hybrid swarm of this and related plants, such as the red-flowered *P. hartwegii* (*P. gloxinioides* is a horticultural name for hybrids of this later species). *P. gentianoides* is a dark blue-purple relative with similar habit and requirements. More and more hybrids are being produced by crossing these with hardier northern species (often listed as × *mexicana* hybrids) and most make excellent garden plants even in drier areas of Zone 5. Recently I have also seen the less hardy types being sold as annual bedding plants, their long bloom and large flowers in a range of colors mixing well with more traditional annuals.

Penstemon digitalis

(Tall White Beardtongue, Foxglove Beardtongue)

ZONES: 3–9; sun to light shade

SOIL: moist

NATIVE TO: moist forest gaps, bottomlands, and prairies; Nova Scotia to Minnesota south to Texas and Virginia

SIZE: 2–4 feet (14–18 inches)

COLOR: white; **BLOOMS** in spring

Penstemon fruticosus. *There are many excellent penstemons for the rock garden, including* P. fruticosus. *Though it needs a gritty soil, Bush Penstemon will suffer under droughty conditions.*

A tall, robust, multistemmed species for the border, with wide lance-shaped leaves and tiers of many small flowers above. Dies back to a clump of basal leaves after flowering. The burgundy-leaved cultivar 'Husker Red' is commonly available and a superior plant.

Penstemon dissectus

(Cut-leaf Beardtongue)

ZONES: 5–9; sun, part sun

SOIL: moist, well drained

NATIVE TO: rock outcrops; Georgia

SIZE: 1–2 feet (12 inches)

COLOR: violet purple; **BLOOMS** in summer

A very unusual eastern species endemic to Georgia and becoming rare in the wild. The stiffly upright stems are clothed in soft, finely dissected foliage and support clusters of 1-inch flowers. It reminds me more of many of the western species in habit and flowering. Cut-leaf Beardtongue is surprisingly hardy in the North, but needs a well-drained location to thrive.

Penstemon eatonii

(Firecracker Beardtongue, Eaton's Firecracker)

ZONES: 5–9; sun, part sun

SOIL: dry, well drained

NATIVE TO: sagebrush and open pinyon woodland; Utah and California to Arizona

SIZE: 2–3 feet (12 inches)

COLOR: orange-red to scarlet; **BLOOMS** in summer

A classic hummingbird plant, with narrow, brightly colored tube-shaped flowers on tall, willowy stems above mostly basal, gray-green foliage. Easy in well-drained soil, though it tends to be short-lived. *P. barbatus* is a taller version and a well-grown, 5-foot clump in full bloom is a remarkable sight.

Penstemon fruticosus

(Bush Penstemon, Shrubby Penstemon)

ZONES: 5–8; sun, part sun

SOIL: moist, well drained

NATIVE TO: rocky openings from foothills to higher elevations in the Cascades and Rockies; Montana to British Columbia south to Oregon and Wyoming

SIZE: 8–16 inches (2 feet)

COLOR: violet to lavender or pink; **BLOOMS** in late spring

An easy and lovely rock garden subject forming low, semievergreen, spreading shrubs with small toothed leaves and masses of large flowers in few-flowered racemes just above. *P. subserratus* is similar.

Penstemon grandiflorus

(Large Beardtongue, Large-flowered Beard-tongue)

ZONES: 3–9; sun

SOIL: dry

NATIVE TO: dry prairies; Wisconsin to Wyoming south to Texas and Missouri

SIZE: 2–5 feet (16 inches)

COLOR: blue-violet to gray-violet; BLOOMS in late spring

An imposing though short-lived species sometimes sold in prairie seed mixes. It has large, oval, blue-gray leaves and large open flowers. Self-sows. *P. cobaea* is similar in range and life span, with a smaller habit and pale violet flowers with darker stripes in the throat.

Penstemon hallii

(Hall's Penstemon)

ZONES: 3–7; sun

SOIL: moist, well drained

NATIVE TO: scree soils near timberline; Colorado

SIZE: 4–8 inches (6 inches)

COLOR: violet; BLOOMS in spring

One of a number of stunning alpine species, Hall's Penstemon seems to be fairly amenable to rock garden culture, forming low clumps of long narrow leaves and large flowers on short stems just above. The wide, bell-shaped flowers have a ring of lighter color around the opening to the throat.

Penstemon heterophyllus

(Foothill Penstemon)

ZONES: 7–8; sun

SOIL: dry, well drained

NATIVE TO: dry hillsides and chaparral; California

SIZE: 12–20 inches (12 inches)

COLOR: rose-violet with lighter lobes; BLOOMS in late spring

Not extremely hardy, but widely grown as a rock garden plant for its large vibrant flowers, neat habit, and narrow leaves.

Penstemon hirsutus

(Northeastern Beardtongue, Hairy Beard-tongue)

ZONES: 3–9; sun, part sun

SOIL: moist to dry, well drained

NATIVE TO: upland woods, dry or sandy meadows; Quebec to Wisconsin south to Kentucky and Virginia

SIZE: 12–18 inches (12 inches)

COLOR: violet to pale rose with yellow on the lobes;

BLOOMS in early summer

A carefree, almost weedy plant that naturalizes in dry, open spots. The foliage is lance-shaped and sparsely covered with long bristly hairs. Deadhead after flowering. The strain 'Pygmaeus' is a well-mannered 5-inch-high form for the rock garden.

Penstemon pinifolius

(Pine-leaved Beardtongue)

ZONES: 5–8; sun

SOIL: moist to dry, well drained

NATIVE TO: mountain slopes and ridges; New Mexico to Arizona and Mexico

SIZE: 3–7 inches (12–16 inches)

COLOR: red-orange, occasionally yellow; BLOOMS in summer

Considering its native habitat, this is a surprisingly easy plant for a well-drained, sunny spot. The 1-inch, extremely narrow flowers are produced over a long period. The soft, needlelike light green foliage clothes scandent stems. *P. linarioides* ssp. *coloradoensis* is similar though smaller in appearance, with blue-gray leaves and violet flowers. It is more challenging to grow but very beautiful where it succeeds.

Penstemon rupicola

(Rock Beardtongue, Cliff Penstemon)

ZONES: 5–8; sun

SOIL: moist, well drained

NATIVE TO: crevices in rock faces and alpine screes; Cascades, Washington to northern California

SIZE: 2–8 inches (8 inches)

COLOR: lavender to pink and red-purple; BLOOMS in spring

A stunning rock garden species forming low mats of small, rounded, blue-green leaves and short-stemmed, comparatively large blooms. Evergreen but burns back in hard winters. *P. davidsonii*, with green leaves and violet or purple flowers, is very similar and also forms low mats. It extends from British Columbia south to California in the mountains and hybridizes with *P. rupicola* where their ranges overlap.

Penstemon serrulatus

(Coast Penstemon)

ZONES: 5–8; sun, part sun

SOIL: moist

NATIVE TO: moist meadows and gaps; western Cascades of Oregon and Washington

SIZE: 2–4 feet (12–18 inches)

COLOR: blue to violet; BLOOMS in early summer

A tall plant with serrated, oval basal leaves that are glossy deep green above and reddish underneath. Upright, lightly branched stems are clothed at their tips with staggered whorls of small flowers that in some forms are a clear deep blue. Coast Penstemon is an easy garden plant for a moist spot. Self-sows.

Penstemon smallii
(Small's Beardtongue)

ZONES: 5–9; part sun
SOIL: moist to dry
NATIVE TO: forest openings, hillsides, and lightly shaded cliffs; Southern Appalachians from North Carolina to Tennessee and Georgia
SIZE: 18–28 inches (12–16 inches)
COLOR: rose fading to white on the petal lobes; **BLOOMS** in late spring

Much like *P. digitalis* in habit, with large rounded leaves and tiered inflorescences. It is an adaptable garden plant for borders or woodland edge. *P. australis* (Southern Beardtongue) is similar, differing in its darker flowers and shorter stature. It is found along the southeastern coastal plain in sandy, acid soils, though it grows well in the average garden soil.

Penstemon strictus
(Rocky Mountain Beardtongue)

ZONES: 4–9; sun
SOIL: dry, well drained
NATIVE TO: sagebrush grasslands and pinyon-juniper woodlands, mostly in the Rockies; Wyoming to Utah south to Arizona and New Mexico
SIZE: 18–30 inches (12–16 inches)
COLOR: deep violet blue; **BLOOMS** in early summer

Rocky Mountain Beardtongue is one of the best of a large group of taller, large-flowered plants from the Rockies and Great Basin. The plants have 2–3-inch-long narrow leaves in pairs up the flowering stems and dense spikes of gorgeous, 1½-inch flowers. It needs a dry rest in summer.

Phlox bifida

Phlox (FLOX)
Polemoniaceae
Phlox

The phloxes are a favored tribe, blessed with the three priceless gifts of beauty, grace, and proportion. Though their size and habit are quite variable, these always seem in scale with the enchanting, fragrant, 5-petaled blooms that are the hallmark of the genus. The flowers radiate the same uncomplicated optimism that makes us smile at puppies, babies, and panda cubs. Whether it is the flatness of the blooms, the central eyespot opening to the nectar tube, or their soft, luminous color, they are certainly among the most gently charming wildflowers one could hope to find. We are also fortunate that they are matched in this beauty by an ease of culture that has made them one of the premier natives for garden use.

There are basically three horticultural groups in the genus: woodland, border, and rock garden. Woodland species are typically creeping or mounding, ground-covering plants that bloom in the spring and are one of the backbones of the shade garden. The border phloxes include *P. paniculata* and *P. caroliniana,* among others. These are tall, multi-stemmed perennials with dense rounded heads of brightly colored flowers in summer. They have long been popular both in this country and in Europe, and a vast number of cultivars are available. However, the inbreeding that was necessary to produce these fancifully colored varieties has come at a price, and most of the hybrids have a weak constitution that predisposes them to fungus diseases that are much less troubling to wild stock. The rock garden

(**LEFT**): Penstemon strictus. *Rocky Mountain Beardtongue is an adaptable plant that is simply exuberant in flower. It is an excellent choice for massing in sunny, rather dry situations.*

(**RIGHT**): Phlox bifida. *The cut and arrangement of Sand Phlox's luminous, deeply lobed petals suggest violet snowflakes settled on mounds of needled foliage. It is the largest flowered of the moss phloxes and proves an easy and adaptable ground cover for difficult areas.*

phloxes are another wonderful group composed of the moss phloxes, like the carefree *P. subulata, P. douglasii,* and *P. nivalis,* which form carpets of needlelike leaves frosted with vibrant flowers in spring, and the cushion or microphloxes, a large group of western alpine species. These are exquisite miniatures that are basically compressed moss phloxes for rock gardeners to pamper.

CULTURE: The woodland species are best in a moist, organic, acid soil (of course, you say) with dappled shade. They typically form upright flowering stems that die after setting seed and spreading, evergreen leaves that persist until the following spring. For the sake of appearances you may want to clip off the ragged seed heads in early summer. They are easy to lift as layers or mats and transplant to a new location in early spring. Foliar nematodes, which get transmitted from plant to plant by rainwater or careless propagation, are a problem with many perennials but seem particularly fond of phlox. Many of the common cultivars are infected, and the symptoms are irregular yellow or black patches on older or stressed leaves. It usually will not kill the plants, but efforts should be made to propagate disease-free plants.

The border phloxes can be accommodated in similar soils in full or part sun. If, like me, you do not like to spray fungicides, select cultivars that are mildew-resistant or casually breed them yourself by selecting the best of the self-sown seedlings that invariably pop up in a mixed planting. (This sort of heresy may be unacceptable to the serious collector, but I prefer to let subtle natural selection replace frequent chemical intervention.) Both the woodland and border phloxes appreciate fertilization in the spring and water during drought.

The rock garden phloxes are best in sun and well-drained soils of moderate fertility. The moss types are more adaptable and very easy to grow, while the microphloxes require more attention to drainage and are difficult in a high summer-rainfall climate.

USES: Woodland, border, rock garden.

PROPAGATION: Easy from seed or cuttings. See p. 259.

Phlox adsurgens

(Periwinkle Phlox, Woodland Phlox)

ZONES: 6–8; dappled shade
SOIL: moist
NATIVE TO: moist organic soils in coniferous forests; Oregon to northern California
SIZE: 8–12 inches (18 inches)
COLOR: pink to apricot; **BLOOMS** in spring

Lincoln Foster considered this among the finest of the genus, with clear, pastel flowers and a faint center stripe on each petal. The plants are western cousins of the familiar *P. stolonifera,* but the flowers are car-

ried in larger, denser, rounded heads. Unfortunately, like many plants from the favored temperate rainforests of the western Cascades, it is a challenge to grow outside of the Pacific Northwest.

Phlox bifida

(Sand Phlox)

ZONES: 4–9; sun
SOIL: dry, well drained
NATIVE TO: dry, sandy soils and outcrops; Michigan to Wisconsin south to Kansas and Tennessee
SIZE: 2–6 inches (12–16 inches)
COLOR: luminous pale blue-violet; **BLOOMS** in spring

A lovely moss phlox with petals deeply cleft into 2 narrow lobes. Adaptable and easy for a dry, sunny site.

Phlox caespitosa

(Tufted Phlox, Clumped Phlox)

ZONES: 5–8; sun
SOIL: dry, well drained
NATIVE TO: dry limestone outcrops and slopes; Montana to Washington south to Oregon and California
SIZE: 2–6 inches (12 inches)
COLOR: pink through lavender and violet to white; **BLOOMS** in spring

A western counterpart of *P. subulata* that has been hybridized with it to produce a range of garden cultivars. The true species is less often sold and more difficult to grow. Tufted Phlox is a larger mat-forming version of plants like *P. caespitosa,* and many of the cushion phloxes have been lumped in as varieties of *P. douglasii.*

Phlox divaricata. *The heady aroma of Forest Phlox is as welcome in the nursery as it is in the garden. It is a staple of our spring displays, seeding and weaving around the woodland plantings and providing a unifying background of violet. Consequently, it is one of the most popular items produced in our nursery. Garden in the Woods is a source of inspiration for visitors, and our nursery has grown exponentially in response to public demand for the wildflowers used in garden plantings.*

Phlox divaricata
(Forest Phlox, Wild Blue Phlox)

ZONES: 3–9; part sun, shade
SOIL: moist
NATIVE TO: rich woods; southern Quebec to Minnesota south to Texas and Georgia
SIZE: 12–14 inches (12–16 inches)
COLOR: violet or lavender blue; **BLOOMS** in spring

An indispensable spring ephemeral for eastern shade gardeners. The plants loft clouds of 1-foot flowering stems with narrow, pointed cauline leaves that die after blooming and in the summer spread low stems of more rounded, dark green foliage. They will usually begin to self-sow and create great drifts that blend well with other woodlanders in successional plantings. It blooms a week or two earlier than *P. stolonifera*, so plant both for longer bloom. Var. *laphamii* is a more western form with unnotched petal tips.

Phlox maculata
(Meadow Phlox, Wild Sweet William)

ZONES: 3–9; sun, part sun
SOIL: moist
NATIVE TO: moist woods and damp meadows; Quebec to Minnesota and Iowa, south to Missouri and the southern Appalachians
SIZE: 2–3 feet (2 feet)

COLOR: bright pink to lavender; **BLOOMS** in summer

A carefree, spreading species for a moist, open site that will form dense stands in time. This is one of the border phloxes, with pointed, lance-shaped, opposite leaves; elongated, cylindrical flower heads; and red-spotted, stiff stems. *P. caroliniana* (Carolina Phlox) is very similar and often confused with it, but has unspotted stems and flowers in a tighter, dome-shaped cluster. It is native throughout much of the Southeast and blooms a few weeks earlier than Meadow Phlox. Another southeastern and central species, *P. galberrima* (Smooth Phlox), is also very similar but blooms a few weeks earlier still. They will all grow in light shade, but growth is weaker and flowers few.

Phlox missoulensis
(Cushion Phlox)

ZONES: 4–7; sun
SOIL: moist, well drained
NATIVE TO: rocky, gravelly slopes; Montana and Wyoming south to Colorado and New Mexico
SIZE: 2–5 inches (6–8 inches)
COLOR: lavender-pink; **BLOOMS** in spring

Cushion Phlox can be imagined as a reduced moss phlox that has adapted to harsh conditions by developing a tight cushion growth and tiny awl-shaped leaves that minimize water loss and conserve heat. What gives it its charm though, is that the flowers have remained full-size or even larger than its

Phlox paniculata.
Lavender pink is the "wild" color of Summer Phlox, and self-sown seedlings usually bloom this shade. Because these seedlings are often more vigorous than inbred cultivars, naturalized plantings often revert to this color eventually. This is not, as is mistakenly believed, because the cultivars revert to the wild type themselves, but simply that they are overtaken and shaded out by their more vigorous progeny.

cousins from more moderate climes. It has long been neglected by garden books produced in Europe and the eastern United States, where wet summers and snowless winters make its cultivation difficult to impossible. But for gardeners in the western plains and mountains, it is easy to accommodate and should be treasured. There are a number of other equally beautiful cushion phloxes between the Rockies and Sierras, including *P. hoodii* (lavender flowered, from dry prairies and mountains through the West), and *P. austromontana* (pink or violet flowered, from the Cascades and Rockies at moderate to high elevations). All have a tufted habit and deep taproot.

Phlox paniculata
(Summer Phlox)

ZONES: 3–9; sun, part sun
SOIL: moist
NATIVE TO: fertile bottomlands and meadows; New York to Illinois south to Missouri, Arkansas, and Georgia
SIZE: 3–5 feet (2–3 feet)
COLOR: pink to lavender or white; **BLOOMS** in mid-summer

The giant of the genus and for many years a staple in the summer perennial border. Selections are available in all shades of pink, lavender, white, and even violet-blue, as well as candy-striped and banded types, even some with variegated foliage. The plants form stiff clumps of tall stems heavily clothed in pointed, broadly lance-shaped leaves arranged in an opposite and strongly overlapping manner. The terminal, rounded flower heads are very showy. Some work has been done recently to reverse the effects of inbreeding on disease resistance, and cultivars are now available that are nearly mildew-free. Summer Phlox thrives in evenly moist, very fertile soils but suffers in drought. Self-sown seedlings usually revert to pink and lavender but are usually more vigorous than the cultivars.

Phlox pilosa
(Prairie Phlox)

ZONES: 4–9; sun to light shade
SOIL: moist to moderately dry
NATIVE TO: prairies and open woods, usually in drier soils; Connecticut to Manitoba south to Nebraska, Texas, and Florida
SIZE: 1–2 feet (12–16 inches)
COLOR: bright pink to lavender; **BLOOMS** in late spring

A close relative of *P. divaricata*, but differing from it in the taller, downy flowering shoots, flowers ranging more into the red than the blue side of purple. It also lacks the persistent evergreen nonflowering shoots. Since Prairie Phlox blooms a week or two later than Creeping Phlox, it is useful for extending the woodland bloom into early summer.

Phlox stolonifera
(Creeping Phlox)

ZONES: 4–9; part sun to shade
SOIL: moist
NATIVE TO: moist mountain woods; Pennsylvania to Ohio south to Tennessee and Georgia
SIZE: 6–10 inches (2 feet)
COLOR: violet-blue to lavender or white; **BLOOMS** in midspring

Creeping Phlox (or as I was once misquoted in a local newspaper "Creepy Phlox") is as it sounds, a ground-covering evergreen woodlander with paddle-shaped leaves that form 1–2-inch mats in moist, acid soils. The flower spikes shoot up above these mats on thin 8-inch stems for a wonderful effect. There are a number of cultivars on the market with different bloom colors and spread rates. The most vigorous, like 'Sherwood Purple', can quickly cover an area, but because of its low growth it is not a problem for companions. I have noticed some plants for sale in garden centers (several different cultivars) that were infected with what I believe is a mosaic virus that causes chlorotic streaks in the leaves and a decrease in vigor.

Phlox subulata
(Moss-pink, Moss Phlox)

ZONES: 3–9; sun
SOIL: well drained
NATIVE TO: sandy soils and open, lightly forested ridges; New York to Michigan south in the Appalachians to Georgia

Phlox subulata. Moss-pink can easily be naturalized in lawns to lovely effect. It blazes brilliantly for several weeks then blends in with the turf grass. Establish the plants in a sunny spot in spring and try to wait two or three weeks after blooming to mow (with the mower deck raised to its highest setting). Of course you will have to avoid using broadleaf herbicides on the lawn, which will eliminate the Phlox along with the dandelions and clover.

*Physosfegia virginiana.
A bee carefully rear-
ranging the two-ranked
flowers of Obedient
Plant into a more suit-
ably tousled display.*

SIZE: 2–6 inches (14–18 inches)

COLOR: lavender to pink or white; **BLOOMS** in spring

An iron-clad constitution and early, colorful blooms have made Moss Phlox a staple "supermarket perennial" for many years, but this should not diminish its beauty or value in the garden. Granted, some of the cultivars display colors that are painful to the eyes, but it is possible to find a shade to fit everyone's fancy. It will establish easily in a range of dry and poor soils and even thrives in rough lawns. The plants form spreading mats of needle or awl-shaped evergreen leaves with flowers on short stems just above, typically so heavy as to obscure the plants when in bloom. *P. nivalis* (Piney Woods Phlox) is a close, violet-flowered southern relative found on the coastal plain and Piedmont from Virginia to Florida. It is a less hardy plant with flowers a bit larger and the same needlelike leaves, and it as well as *P. bifida* have been hybridized with Moss Phlox to bring out violet colors.

Physostegia virginiana

Physostegia virginiana
(fie-zoe-STEE-gee-uh)
Lamiaceae
Obedient Plant

ZONES: 3–9; sun, part sun

SOIL: moderately dry to wet

NATIVE TO: open meadows and prairies; Quebec to Manitoba south to New Mexico and Florida

SIZE: 2–5 feet (3–4 feet)

COLOR: light to dark pink or white; **BLOOMS** in late summer

Obedient Plant gets its name from the pliable quality of the pedicels, which allows the individual flowers to be twisted or bent at any angle and remain there as if wired by a florist. It is certainly no obedient little angel in the garden, for it produces free-wheeling, colonial rhizomes that carry the plant hither and yon, either as scattered individual stems or large stands. Interestingly, the plants from the southern part of its range, var. *arenaria,* are well-behaved, clumping plants that are also adapted to drier sites, but most of the garden material is of the northern, spreading type or somewhere in between.[7] They produce tall, vertical stems lined with narrow, jaggedly toothed leaves in two ranks up their length. As the plants prepare to bloom, the leaves give way to terminal racemes that carry on the strongly two-ranked arrangement of the leaves. The showy, tubular flowers bloom successively up the stalk, and even the unopened blooms are ranked and colored like blushing Brussels Sprouts waiting their turn to dance.

There are a dozen species in the genus, all native to eastern North America, and all fairly similar to *P. virginiana*, which is the only one grown and really the showiest in flower. It is happiest in moist to wet soils, but better behaved if the soil is a bit drier. There are several cultivars on the market selected for height and color. Some appear to be closer to var. *arenaria* as they are less invasive in the garden ('Vivid' is especially good, with later flowers and a compact, less aggressive habit).

CULTURE: Easily transplanted in spring or fall and a carefree and beautiful wildflower for moist meadows, streamsides, and large gardens. The plants will tolerate a range of soils as long as it is not terribly dry. Deadhead after flowering as the tiny seeds are produced in huge quantities and can quickly self-sow otherwise. Move the plants by digging sections of rhizome in spring.

USES: Borders, meadows, naturalizing.

PROPAGATION: Easy from seed or cuttings. See p. 259.

Podophyllum peltatum

Podophyllum peltatum (poe-doe-FILL-um)

Berberidaceae
Mayapple

ZONES: 3–9; part sun, shade

SOIL: wet to dry

NATIVE TO: moist woods, streambanks; Massachusetts and southern Quebec to Minnesota south to Texas and Georgia

SIZE: 8–16 inches (4–6 feet)

COLOR: pearly white; **BLOOMS** in spring

I used to imagine that the paired leaves of Mayapple formed broad parasols to protect the pale, aristocratic flower that huddles beneath, sheltering it from inclemency and the harsh effects of the sun. While this may be the case, a more likely explanation for the broad, flat design of the leaves is that this is the most efficient angle for collecting the weak light that penetrates the upper canopy of its forest home. Mayapple is a spreading, colonial plant, advancing 6–12 inches a year on stiff, forking rhizomes that lie a few inches down in the soil. Over several years they can form large patches that shade out smaller plants, so they are hard to integrate into small gardens. If you have a larger space or a bit of low woods that could use some company, it is an excellent bold and carefree ground cover. The plants will remain fresh and green early into fall if the soil remains moist, but will go dormant earlier in drought.

The common name refers to the plum-sized yellow fruit that develops by late summer. Because Mayapple is self-sterile and most patches are clonal, few fruits are usually produced, and the ones that do grow are mostly small and free of seeds. Occasionally though, a flower will get cross-pollinated and a pendulous yellow plum will result. The ripe fruit has a musky, insipid flavor and a juicy pulp like that of an overripe peach. They are relished by Box Turtles, among other animals, who consume them with gusto and thus distribute the seeds. They are edible, but be careful to eat only the ripe, soft, yellow fruit—unripe fruits as well as all other parts of the plants are poisonous. (There are some reports that even the fully ripe fruits contain small levels of toxin and should be avoided or eaten in small quantities.) You would have to really go out of your way to become seriously poisoned, though, as the toxin podophyllin is extremely bitter and foul tasting and causes violent vomiting and (to use the words of one Dr. Millspaugh) "an urgent call to stool" if ingested.[8] The plants have a long history of medicinal use as an emetic and deworming agent, and most likely the few poisonings on record resulted from overdoses in a medicinal context. When cultivating the plants, take care to handle the rhizomes with gloves on, as exposure to the sap can cause irritation of the eyes and dermatitis on the skin. The plants are no longer considered safe to be used medicinally, but cancer research on synthetic derivatives of podophyllin have shown promise for their ability to selectively kill tumor cells.

CULTURE: Easily grown in wet to dry soils. Mayapple is extremely tough and once established can grow in poor, droughty conditions where most woodland wildflowers fail. In rich, fertile soils they are truly at their best, forming tall stems with leaves up to a foot in diameter. The rhizomes can be dug as the plants go dormant, cut into 8-inch lengths, and replanted horizontally. Even the eyeless pieces will regrow eventually. Give the plants plenty of room or save them for rough areas of the garden as they will spread quickly (though it is not too much trouble to spade out rhizomes that have crept too far).

USES: Deciduous ground cover for large areas and tough locations.

PROPAGATION: Moderately difficult from seed; easy from division. See p. 259.

Podophyllum peltatum. The alabaster flowers of Mayapple look shy beneath their leafy parasol. The blooms have the same overripe melon fragrance as the soft fruits. Podophyllum will quickly form large solid colonies in dappled shade, a valuable attribute if you have a lot of ground to cover.

LEFT): Pogonia ophioglossoides. *Aside from a single, narrow leaf, there is not much to the Rose Pogonia other than its intricate flower. Henry David Thoreau found its fragrance to be just like that of a snake —hence the alternative name Snakemouth. I can't say as I've ever made the close acquaintance of a serpent with halitosis, but the flowers have a pleasantly sweet smell to me. Sometimes I wonder what old Henry D. was doing out in those woods.*

(RIGHT): Polemonium reptans. *Spreading Jacob's Ladder is a soft plant, both in the color of the flower and the substance of its brittle stems. It is the most commonly available of the woodland group, and it will spread and seed easily in a damp, dappled spot. The flowers of Polemoniums vary little in color and shape from species to species, but the genus ranges widely in overall form, size, and growing requirements.*

Pogonia ophioglossoides

Pogonia ophioglossoides
(poe-GOWNE-ee-ah)
Orchidaceae
Rose Pogonia, Snakemouth

ZONES: 3–9; sun, part sun

SOIL: wet

NATIVE TO: bogs and wet shores; Newfoundland to Minnesota south to Texas and Florida

SIZE: 5–12 inches (6–12 inches)

COLOR: rose pink to yellow; **BLOOMS** in early summer

The **Rose Pogonia** is one of the easiest native orchids to cultivate, and provided you can give it a boggy, acid spot this little jewel will cheerfully send up a single waxy, oblong leaf and a ramrod straight flower stem topped with a leaflike bract and one exquisite bloom that looks much like a miniature corsage with a yellow bearded lip. They grow from wandering rhizomes that resemble those of Canada Mayflower or Wild Oats—blanched and brittle with a few thick roots and an inconspicuous pointed bud. In time they form loose patches in sphagnum mats or mucky soils and are barely noticeable when not in bloom.

It is certainly not easy to come by nursery-propagated plants currently, but I know of several growers propagating the plants from rhizome divisions, so I am optimistic that they will soon be more widely available.

CULTURE: It is best to seat dormant rhizomes or

container plants a few inches down in live sphagnum moss or a consistently damp, acid soil like that described for *Sarracenia*. Once the plants have rooted in, they require no care as they will migrate around to find a spot that suits them.

USES: Bog garden, waterside.

PROPAGATION: Difficult from seed; moderately difficult from division. See p. 260.

Polemonium reptans

Polemonium
(pole-eh-MOAN-ee-um)
Polemoniaceae
Jacob's Ladder

Jacob's ladder is named for the fancied resemblance of the leaves to the ladder from heaven that appeared in a vision to the Old Testament's Jacob, son of Isaac. The pinnate leaflets are vaguely runglike in arrangement, but I do not know who first dreamed up this obscure Biblical association. A common European species, *P. caeruleum*, has been used as a medicinal herb since ancient times, most likely for the expectorant effects of the saponin compounds it contains. It also has the most stiffly ladder-like foliage of any in the genus, and so undoubtedly it is the source of the common name. Enough about the foliage though, for it is the clouds of pale blue flowers centered with yellow that really inspire reverie. The plants are related to phlox and share a familial proclivity toward beauty. Typically Jacob's ladders are clumping plants, producing mounds of soft-textured foliage that are a good foil for the delicate, 5-petaled bells that decorate the tips of leafy flower stems in spring. There are basically two types of *Polemonium:* lush woodlanders that prefer, damp, humusy soils and partial shade; and dwarf, tufted alpines that need more sun and excellent drainage to prosper. As a group they are not difficult to grow if you can satisfy these requirements, and they provide lovely impressionist splashes in the spring garden. Most of the species are semidormant in summer, so it is best to integrate Jacob's ladder with late-rising companions that can take up where they leave off. Though individuals may live only a few years, they often seed lightly (especially the woodlanders) and so make excellent subjects for naturalizing.

CULTURE: All Jacob's ladders begin growing early in the season from a woody, branching crown or brittle rhizome. The flower stems of the alpine species can often be seen poking out of the melting snows as the spring sun warms the soil. The alpines need moisture in the spring—and a bit of fertilizer as well—but also sharp drainage and a pronounced dry rest in summer to prevent insidious crown rot from creeping in. They are at home in the scree garden or planted in the crevices of a sunny wall. The woodland species are best in a moist, fertile soil in dappled shade or morning sun and will also do well with a brief summer rest. All the plants can be sheared back hard after the seeds have shed, which will neaten them up, help reduce mildew, and encourage a new flush of foliage.

USES: Woodland, border, rock garden.

PROPAGATION: Easy to moderately difficult from seed and division. See p. 260.

Polemonium carneum

(Salmon Polemonium, Salmon Jacob's Ladder)

ZONES: 5–8; part sun, light shade
SOIL: moist
NATIVE TO: moist soils in grassy areas and openings in mountain woodlands; western Cascades from British Columbia to Oregon
SIZE: 10–14 inches (12–14 inches)
COLOR: light blue to salmon and apricot; BLOOMS in spring

A sumptuous plant in flower, especially the pastel forms that are more common in cultivation. It is of the woodland type, with sprawling flower stems, large full blooms and a reputation for being temperamental in cultivation, though I have not personally found this to be the case. Granted, it may be short-lived as many in the genus are, but I think problems may stem from keeping it too damp in summer or exposed in winter.

Polemonium chartaceum

(Papery Polemonium)

ZONES: 5–7; part sun
SOIL: moist, well drained, and dry in summer
NATIVE TO: alpine ridges and screes; from 6,000–14,000 feet in the Siskiyou, White, and Trinity Mountains of northern California
SIZE: 3–8 inches (6–8 inches)
COLOR: blue; BLOOMS in early spring

One of the lovely, specialized, high alpines, with the leaflets whorled around the petiole like a foxtail and covered in sticky, viscous glands. The petioles form papery sheaths where they attach to the stem, hence the common name. The flowers appear in tight, ball-like heads. A choice plant endangered in the wild. For the specialist and best grown in a trough or gravelly scree. *P. viscosum* (Sky Pilot) is a closely allied species growing in alpine areas through much of the middle Rockies and into the Cascades.

Polemonium foliosissimum

(Leafy Jacob's Ladder)

ZONES: 4–8; part sun
SOIL: moist in spring, dry in summer, well drained
NATIVE TO: sagebrush grasslands, subalpine forest; Wyoming to Utah, south to Arizona and New Mexico
SIZE: 2–3 feet (12–16 inches)
COLOR: pale to dark violet, blue, or white; BLOOMS in early summer

A delicate, fernlike appearance and long bloom period make this a valuable garden plant. In habit, *P. foliosissimum* is tall and narrow, as if to get up above competing grasses, with mostly cauline or stem leaves and bunched clusters of blooms at the top. A slowly spreading species more like the woodland types in appearance but needing a well-drained soil. It is very drought-tolerant after blooming.

Polemonium occidentale

(Western Jacob's Ladder, Western Polemonium)

ZONES: 5–8; part sun, light shade
SOIL: moist to wet
NATIVE TO: bogs and wet meadows at low to moderate elevations in the mountains; Alaska to Idaho south to California (the rare var. *lacustre* grows occasionally as far east as Minnesota)
SIZE: 2–3 feet (18 inches)
COLOR: light blue; BLOOMS in late spring

A close relative of the European *P. caeruleum* (Jacob's Ladder), with spreading rhizomes that form colonies in damp places. It is a tall woodland plant that looks a bit unkempt because of its running habit, but it is

One plausible explanation for the name Solomon's Seal comes from its ancient use as a poultice to aid in wound healing. A piece of the root would have been applied to a wound overnight to "seal" it. The root was also a powerful totem used to ward off evil among practitioners of voodoo in the southeastern United States. It was called John the Conqueror, explaining the meaning of a blues lyric that has always puzzled me: "Got my John d'Conqueror root . . ."

easy to grow and good for naturalizing if you can provide sufficient moisture.

Polemonium pulcherrimum
(Skunk-leaved Polemonium, Showy Polemonium)

ZONES: 4–7; part sun
SOIL: well drained
NATIVE TO: rocky slopes, dry or moist soils in the mountains; Wyoming north to Alaska, south to California, Nevada, and Utah
SIZE: 5–10 inches (8 inches)
COLOR: light blue to white; **BLOOMS** in spring

One of the easiest alpine species for the rock garden, not quite as tufted and refined as *P. chartaceum* and its clan, but still a diminutive plant. The leaves are pinnate, not whorled; pubescent but only lightly sticky; and the flowers are in looser, branched clusters more like those of the woodland species.

Polemonium reptans
(Spreading Jacob's Ladder)

ZONES: 3–8; part sun, light shade
SOIL: moist
NATIVE TO: moist woods; New York to Minnesota, south to Oklahoma and Alabama
SIZE: 10–16 inches (12–14 inches)
COLOR: light blue; **BLOOMS** in spring

A vigorous, sprawling species that easily naturalizes. The plants form much-branched flower stems that hold the blooms in loose sprays over the foliage. The flower stems are easily broken, so care must be taken when handling them at this time. Var. *villosum* (Furry Jacob's Ladder) is a superior plant horticulturally, found in a small area of southern Ohio and Kentucky. The leaves are attractively covered with soft downy hair, and the flowers, although a bit smaller, bloom on shorter, stronger stems so the plants have a neater appearance.

Polemonium van-bruntiae
(Appalachian Jacob's Ladder)

ZONES: 3–8; part sun, light shade
SOIL: moist
NATIVE TO: moist to wet woods, along streams, swamps; Quebec to Vermont and New York south to West Virginia
SIZE: 2–3 feet (12–16 inches)
COLOR: medium blue; **BLOOMS** in early summer

A close relative of *P. occidentale* and *P. caeruleum* with a scattered distribution throughout the Northeast. Although widespread, it is never common, and in fact is considered either rare or endangered throughout its range. The plants form tall,

unbranched stems from slowly spreading rhizomes with clusters of small open flowers at the top. It is not hard to grow provided the soil is damp, and because it is one of the last to bloom, Appalachian Jacob's Ladder is a valuable addition to the woodland garden.

Polygonatum biflorum

Polygonatum
(pol-ee-gon-AT-um)
Lilaceae
Solomon's Seal

There are few woodland wildflowers more statuesque and unmistakable than Solomon's seal. Their tall, arching stalks carry alternating leaves in two ranks that orient themselves relentlessly to the horizontal no matter what the angle of their particular section of stem. To further emphasize this foliar equilibrium, bell-shaped white flowers dipped in leprechaun green hang down like earrings or plumb bobs from the base of each leaf. Large, showy blue fruits follow the flowers in fall. These refined, indispensable plants provide elegance and height to shade gardens; the stems carry themselves loftily above ground covers and ferns but never so densely that they shade out their vertically challenged companions. The plants get their common name from the shape of the leaf scars along the rhizome, which look a bit like the 5-pointed, interlaced star that became a religious symbol in the Middle Ages (I think the "seal" is easier to see on the European species).

Polyploidy

Polyploidy is an uncommon but widespread phenomenon in the plant kingdom that has several repercussions for horticulturists. You may hear the word polyploid or tetraploid thrown around in gardening books, but there is a bit of confusion about what these actually mean. When cells divide during mitosis, the normal double set of chromosomes in a diploid cell splits into two matching sets, one for each resulting daughter cell. Sometimes mistakes occur during division, so that the cells divide but the nucleus containing the chromosomes does not, and one of the daughter cells gets the nucleus and both new sets while the other gets none. This results in what is called a tetraploid. (*Ploid* means literally "having chromosome sets," so *tetraploid* means having four chromosome sets. *Polyploidy* is a generic term indicating anything more than the normal two sets. Triploid and hexaploid plants are polyploids with three and six sets respectively.) If a tetraploid cell originates in a developing embryo, it can lead to a tetraploid plant, which usually differs from its normal siblings in certain ways. Tetraploids are often larger in size and flower, with more substance and vigor, at least in the best case scenario. Since these are qualities valued by gardeners, many naturally occurring tetraploids have been selected by horticulturists or even induced by treating seeds with colchicine, a toxic chemical found in the Autumn Crocus that prevents normal cell division during mitosis.

More important, as far as evolution is concerned, polyploidy has a central role in creating new species. Every species has a particular number of chromosomes that may or may not be the same as its near relatives. When two related species with different chromosome numbers cross to form a hybrid, the hybrid will usually be sterile because the pairs do not match up properly during sexual division (much like the well-known example of the mule—a sterile hybrid of the horse and donkey). Incompatible chromosome numbers is one of the key ways that related species prevent interbreeding and homogenization. However, a polyploid hybrid with double the chromosomes circumvents this problem and can lead to a new, fertile hybrid species that stabilizes as a separate race in time. (Think of it like this: two species with 30 and 32 pairs of chromosomes respectively hybridize to produce a plant with 31 chromosomes—a number that cannot be divided in half evenly, so it is sterile. Should a tetraploid hybrid develop, with a count of 2×31 or 62, then it can divide evenly and so is fertile.) One of the most famous examples of this is what we all know as Wheat (*Triticum aestivum*), but, remarkably, about half of the plant species alive today originated as such polyploid hybrids that have continued to evolve.

Rudbeckia hirta *var.* pulcherrima *(right and rear) and its tetraploid cultivar, 'Indian Summer' (left). In a side by side comparison of Common Black-eyed Susan and its tetraploid form, it becomes immediately apparent how markedly an extra set of chromosomes can affect an individual. Breeders have taken advantage of the superior substance and huge size that results in some polyploid Black-eyed Susans to create the immensely popular Gloriosa Daisies. Like their wild relatives, these are short-lived plants often treated as annuals readily grown from seed.*

Porteranthus trifoliatus. *The name Bowman's Root may refer to a bow man, or a man who uses bows and arrows, as this species was widely used as a medicinal by Native Americans in the East. The plants are easy to raise from seed collected in fall and stratified over the winter.*

There are two species widespread in the eastern half of North America that are hard to tell apart except by minor features of the leaf and numbers of flowers. They grow from jointed white rhizomes as thick as a big man's thumb, with the distinctive upward-facing leaf scars that form shallow depressions regularly along their length. The rhizomes can creep fairly rapidly (6–8 inches a year) in a spot that is to their liking, so the plants will sometimes form large stands, though more often they make scattered smaller clumps.

CULTURE: Easily established in moist woodland soil. Move as container plants in spring or dig and divide the plants in fall as they begin to yellow. Solomon's seals require little care other than dividing every five years or so. Occasionally the rhizomes can become infected by soft rots or borers.

USES: Specimen or massing in the woodland or shade garden.

PROPAGATION: Slow and moderately difficult from seed; easy from division. See p. 260.

Polygonatum biflorum
(Small Solomon's Seal)

ZONES: 3–9; shade
SOIL: moist
NATIVE TO: moist woods; New Hampshire to Minnesota, Manitoba, and North Dakota, south to northern Mexico and Florida
SIZE: 1–3 feet (16–24 inches)
COLOR: white edged with green; **BLOOMS** in spring

The typical form averages about 18 inches in height, but *P. biflorum* is occasionally found as a rare tetraploid form known as var. *commutatum* (Giant Solomon's Seal) that is truly spectacular. Its arching canes can, with time, grow 7 feet high in a rich moist soil, soaring effortlessly above the rest of the understory.

Polygonatum pubescens
(Downy Solomon's Seal)

ZONES: 3–9; shade
SOIL: moist
NATIVE TO: moist woods; Nova Scotia to Manitoba, south to Indiana, Maryland, and the southern Appalachians
SIZE: 12–28 inches (16 inches)
COLOR: white edged with green; **BLOOMS** in spring

A more northern species than *P. biflorum* but with considerable range overlap. Usually a bit smaller and with a downy pubescence on the small veins on the underside of the leaf.

Porteranthus trifoliatus

Porteranthus (Gillenia) (Por-ter-AN-thus)
Rosaceae
Indian-physic

The two species of Indian-physic have a rich tradition as medicinals, but they have been inexplicably neglected as garden plants. This is unfortunate as they are outstanding ornamentals for a wide variety of garden situations. *Porteranthus* are shrubby perennials in the Rose family, with zigzagging stems of toothy 3-parted leaves adorned in early summer with a weightless cloud of starry flowers that float above the foliage on invisible stems. The flowers have 5 narrow, pointed petals that array themselves unevenly, giving the plants an unmistakable, charming informality. They remind me quite a bit of shadbush (*Amelanchier*) flowers in this way. After the blooms fade, the leaves remain in good condition all summer and then in fall are set ablaze in glorious autumnal oranges and yellows. *Porteranthus* are tough, long-lived, and drought-tolerant plants, with a thick woody crown that never needs dividing.

American colonists learned from the Native Americans to use the bark from the roots as a powerful emetic, explaining the common name American Ipecac.

CULTURE: Transplant as container plants in spring. They will grow in a variety of soils, from moist and fertile to dry and poor, in full sun or light shade, and need little else than cutting back in fall and a bit of fertilizer in spring. Indian-physic's neat, shrubby habit makes it valuable for massing, though the plants also look good as individual specimens.

USES: Borders, slopes, woodland edge.

PROPAGATION: Easy from seed. See p. 260.

Porteranthus stipulatus
(Western Indian-physic, American Ipecac)

ZONES: 4–9; sun to light shade
SOIL: moist to dry
NATIVE TO: dry to moist woods; New York to Illinois and Kansas, south to Texas and Georgia
SIZE: 2–3 feet (2–3 feet)
COLOR: white tinged reddish pink; **BLOOMS** in early summer

This is the more refined and delicate of the two in appearance, with leaves deeply cut like shaggy green lace and flowers about two-thirds the size of Bowman's Root.

Porteranthus trifoliatus
(Bowman's Root, Mountain Indian-physic)

ZONES: 4–9; sun to light shade
SOIL: moist to dry
NATIVE TO: dry to moist woods, mostly in the Appalachians; Ontario to Michigan, south to Kentucky, Alabama, and Georgia
SIZE: 2–3 feet (2–3 feet)
COLOR: white tinged pink; **BLOOMS** in early summer

Bowman's Root has proven to be a bit more robust in our gardens, and the larger flowers make more of an impact. Both species have dark red peduncles supporting the flowers, and this bleeds into the unopened buds as well, a nice contrast with the snow white blooms.

Potentilla (Poe-ten-TILL-ah)
Rosaceae
Cinquefoil

Potentilla tridentata

Potentillas are a hardy lot, making their home primarily in the colder reaches of the Northern Hemisphere. I had debated including them in this text, for most walk that delicate—some would say imaginary — line between wildflower and weed. Certainly the shrubby *P. fruticosa* is a fine woody species that has become a staple of the landscaping industry for its long bloom and ruggedly adaptable nature. There is another fine species, Three-toothed Cinquefoil, which falls more comfortably within the scope of this book, and I encourage you to consider it for a difficult spot in your garden. It is a running ground cover from dry, poor soils along the seashore and in the mountains of the East, with small, 3-parted leaves notched at the tips with 3 small teeth. The leaves are a dark, glossy green in summer but turn blood red in fall, some persisting in this colorful condition until spring. *P. tridentata* is gregarious but not domineering, forming informal, low mats or scat-

tered patches that blend well with other ground covers in rocky or sandy soil. Branched spikes of small white flowers casually decorate the carpets in summer.

CULTURE: Easily grown in a range of soils. Three-toothed Cinquefoil looks particularly lovely emerging from the cracks between paving stones or boulders. The individual crowns with a length of rhizome attached are easy to separate and distribute in spring.
USES: Rock garden, edging.
PROPAGATION: Easy from seed or division. See p. 260.

Potentilla hippiana
(Woolly Cinquefoil)

ZONES: 4–8; sun
SOIL: dry, well drained
NATIVE TO: sagebrush meadow and open aspen-fir woodland to above the treeline; Saskatchewan to British Columbia, south to Nevada and New Mexico
SIZE: 12–18 inches (12 inches)
COLOR: yellow; **BLOOMS** in early summer

Of the many yellow-flowered, clump-forming species found in the West, this is one of the most ornamental. The sharply toothed, pinnate leaves are

a beautiful cool gray above and covered with white fur below. The branching panicles of ¾-inch butter yellow flowers form a dome above the low mound of foliage for several weeks in early summer. Others

Potentilla tridentata. *Three-toothed Cinquefoil can grow in the barest seams of soil between windswept boulders, an ability that serves it well in the Far North. It ranges into the tundra within the Arctic Circle, where thin, cold soils offer scant nourishment and a very brief growing season. The conditions at the summits of New Hampshire's White Mountains (where this photograph was taken) are very similar to those in the high Arctic, and many of the same plants can be found in both places.*

Pycnanthemum muticum. The unique velvety gray bracts surrounding Broad-leaved Mountain Mint's tiny flowers distinguish it from others in the tribe and make it my first choice for gardens. It spreads quickly by stolons that remain close to the surface, so it can be headed back in spring with the aid of a well-aimed spade.

worth looking for include *P. brevifolia,* an alpine from the Rockies and Cascades with pinnate leaves that look retracted, giving the plants a ruffled look. It is rarely over 6 inches high, forming clumps or mats in rocky soils. *P. nivea* (Snow Cinquefoil) is another yellow-flowered alpine from the western mountains. It has 3-lobed leaves dark green above and densely white woolly beneath — a lovely contrast.

Potentilla tridentata
(Three-toothed Cinquefoil)

ZONES: 2–7; sun, part shade
SOIL: acidic, well drained
NATIVE TO: sandy or rocky shores and mountaintops; Greenland to the Northwest Territories, south to Iowa and Connecticut and in the Appalachians to Georgia
SIZE: 2–4 inches (1–2 feet)
COLOR: white; BLOOMS in summer

Pycnanthemum muticum

Pycnanthemum (pick-NAN-thuh-mum)
Lamiaceae
Mountain Mint

In my mind there are few better nectar plants than the mountain mints, and they bloom at a time when many of the most voracious predatory wasps are active, providing these beneficial insects with great quantities of sugar to fuel their ceaseless hunting (for harmful pests, of course). The flowers are also friends to butterflies, day-flying moths, flower flies, and just about anyone else who needs a little of the sweet stuff now and then. As an added bonus for your olfactory delight, the foliage has a strong, clean fragrance somewhere between peppermint and oregano. *Pycnanthemum* flowers are bunched in flat-topped heads or balls at the tips of tall, leafy stems. Some have fine, narrow foliage; others, leaves that are

broad and oval. My favorites have modified leaves or bracts surrounding the flower heads that turn a beautiful frosted, downy gray as flowering begins, transforming the tops of the plants into a silver blanket for a month or more in summer.

To this unabashedly enthusiastic description I must add a caveat, however, for these are mints true to the core, spreading aggressively on long rhizomes. So please consider their placement in the garden carefully. Ideally, naturalize them in a sunny meadow or wildlife garden, but if you want to risk mountain mints in a more formal area, head them back around the edges with a spade every spring to keep growth in check.

CULTURE: Mountain mints are easily grown in a sunny spot with enough room to ramble. They will adapt to lightly shaded situations as well, but flowering will be much reduced. Most are native to dry soils, so are very tough and drought-tolerant. Sods containing the shallow rhizomes are moved easily in spring, or if the flowering stems are cut back hard, even in summer.

USES: Meadows, naturalizing, butterfly gardens.
WILDLIFE: Excellent nectar plants.
PROPAGATION: Easy from seed or cuttings. See p. 260.

Pycnanthemum incanum
(Hoary Mountain Mint)

ZONES: 3–9; sun, part sun
SOIL: moist to dry
NATIVE TO: dry woods and meadows; Vermont and Illinois, south to Tennessee and North Carolina
SIZE: 3–4 feet (2–3 feet)
COLOR: white-mottled violet; BLOOMS in mid- to late summer

Similar to *P. muticum* in habit, but the leaves are coated in a fine pubescence and the flower heads have fewer bracts. The plants grow in much drier habitats as well.

Pycnanthemum muticum
(Broad-leaved Mountain Mint, Blunt Mountain Mint)

ZONES: 3–9; sun, part shade
SOIL: moist
NATIVE TO: moist woods and meadows; Massachusetts to Michigan, south to Louisiana and Florida
SIZE: 3–4 feet (2–3 feet)
COLOR: white to violet; BLOOMS in mid- to late summer

This is my favorite species, with oval, pointed, deep green leaves and large, well-developed silvery bracts that cast a beautiful haze over the plants in midsummer. It is less drought-tolerant than the others listed here, however, and wilts quickly if the soil becomes too dry.

Pycnanthemum tenuifolium
(Narrow-leaved Mountain Mint, Slender Mountain Mint)

ZONES: 3–9; sun, part shade
SOIL: moist to dry
NATIVE TO: dry, upland woods and prairies; Maine to Minnesota and Kansas, south to Texas and Florida
SIZE: 12–18 inches (2–3 feet)
COLOR: white; **BLOOMS** in mid- to late summer

A fine-textured plant lacking much of a fragrance, but producing copious flowers and nectar for wildlife. The main stems put out short side branches along most of their length, clothed in narrow, almost needlelike leaves; the upper ones form a domed flower head without colored bracts.

P. virginianum (Common Mountain Mint) is similar, but typically twice as tall and with wider leaves. It ranges throughout the eastern United States as well.

Ratibida pinnata

Ratibida (rah-TIB-eh-duh)
Asteraceae
Prairie Coneflower

Among perennial growers, the prairie coneflowers fall under the heading of "just another DYD!" (damn yellow daisy), a term of derision applied to any num-ber of the yellow- and gold-flowered composites including *Arnica, Coreopsis, Helianthus, Helenium, Hymenoxys,* and *Rudbeckia.* The reality is that plant shoppers gravitate to blues, reds, and purples more than to yellow, especially in the spring, when all we have to go by is a brief description or a small picture on the label. It is unfortunate, though, because there are a number of DYDs that would make fine garden plants if given a chance, and I encourage you to give them a try and prove those marketing experts wrong!

The prairie coneflowers are long-blooming, care-free, clumping plants that send up tall, branched flower stems each crowned with a bloom shaped like a badminton shuttlecock, with drooping rays and a tall central cone. Their handsome pinnate leaves line the lower half of the flower stems and form a bushy clump at the base of the plants. They mix well in the perennial border or meadow, and the flowers are a good nectar source for butterflies.

CULTURE: *Ratibida*s are easy plants for a sunny, open spot in the garden. They will grow well in moist to dry soils, but cannot tolerate a heavy, wet situation. The southwestern *R. columnifera* var. *pulcherimma* (Mexican Hat), sold extensively in seed mixes and as a container plant, seems especially sensitive about wet feet. I believe the reason the genus has a reputation for being short-lived has more to do with bad siting and crowding than any genetic predisposition. The plants will often self-sow, and it is best to move these seedlings rather than attempt to divide the heavy, woody crowns of established plants.

USES: Borders, meadows.
PROPAGATION: Easy from seed. See p. 260.

Ratibida columnifera
(Columnar Coneflower, Prairie Coneflower, Mexican Hat)

ZONES: 3–9; sun
SOIL: dry to moist, well drained

(**LEFT**): Pycnanthemum tenuifolium. *Slender Mountain Mint is not as showy as some of the others, but its flowers soften mixed meadow and prairie plantings dominated by the mid-summer yellows and purples of the Daisy family.*

(**RIGHT**): Ratibida pinnata. *I would describe the color of Prairie Cone-flowers as a soft yellow, easy on the eyes. The drooping rays of this consummate grassland species flutter delicately in each passing breeze.*

Rhexia virginica. Meadow Beauties enclose their seeds in urn-shaped capsules. When the seeds are ripe, the opening in the neck of the urn dilates, so the seeds can shake free in the breeze. The distinctive little pitchers remain dried at the stem tips to make identification easier when the plants are out of flower.

NATIVE TO: dry prairies and meadows; Minnesota to Montana, south to New Mexico and Texas

SIZE: 1–3 feet (16–20 inches)

COLOR: light yellow (or chocolate) rays and a green turning to dark brown cone; **BLOOMS** in summer

Generally this is the smaller of the two species, with finely cut foliage and very long cylindrical cones which give it an appealing, Pinocchio-like character. The var. *pulcherimma* has rays either banded with or entirely chocolate brown or dark purple and grows only half the size of the typical species (12–18 inches). Its gaily colored flowers and sombrero shape explain its common name.

Ratibida pinnata

(Globular Coneflower, Gray-headed Coneflower)

ZONES: 3–9; sun

SOIL: dry to moist, well drained

NATIVE TO: dry prairies and meadows, often on limestone; Ontario to South Dakota south to Oklahoma, Louisiana, and Florida

SIZE: 2–4 feet (18–24 inches)

COLOR: light yellow rays and a green cone changing to brown; **BLOOMS** in summer

Gray-headed Coneflower has a stiffly erect to rounded outline, with drooping flowers 2½ inches across and short rounded cones. As with *R. columnifera*, the individual flowers are very long lasting, the cones gray before the disk flowers open and dark brown as the seeds are set.

venturing well westward. Their crowns may die off each autumn, but *Rhexia*s have become perennial in colder climates by forming sweet potato–like tubers along the roots that are covered in adventitious buds. These overwinter safe in the ground and sprout vigorously in spring, producing square, branched stems of opposite, oval leaves with 3 prominent, parallel veins and flowers produced sequentially from the stem tips. Since the tubers form a few inches from the current season's crown, the plants tend to migrate around somewhat from year to year.

CULTURE: Transplant in spring to a moist to wet, acidic spot without too much competition (they also respond well to fertilization). The plants tend to seed into disturbed, moist spots along pathways and among mosses. One of my friends planted *R. virginica* in a standard perennial border that was irrigated but certainly not wet, and the plants performed beautifully, forming dense, low mounds that bloomed heavily for weeks on end. *R. mariana* and its relatives are less hardy and grow from a creeping rhizome that is more easily cold-damaged. They can be separated in spring or transferred as self-sown seedlings.

USES: Waterside, bog gardens.

PROPAGATION: Moderately difficult from seed and division. See p. 260.

Rhexia (REX-ee-ah)
Melastomataceae
Meadow Beauty

Rhexia virginica

Rhexias, like *Hibiscus* and *Spigelia*, are brave northern pioneers of mainly tropical families that have managed to adapt to our seasonal climate without losing the vibrant, sumptuous flowers that characterize their respective tribes. The magnificent Melastomas reach an incredible diversity in the cloud and rain forests of South America, but here in the North, they are represented by only a dozen or so species in the one genus *Rhexia*. Though few in number, our meadow beauties are lovely plants, with 4-petaled, crepe paper blooms with a bright cluster of yellow stamens in the center. They remind me of miniature, single-flowered peonies or camellia blooms, albeit with fewer petals.

Meadow beauties inhabit wet shores, meadows, and bogs along the Atlantic coastal plain, with a few

Rhexia mariana
(Dull Meadow-pitchers, Maryland Meadow Beauty)

ZONES: 6–9; sun, part sun
SOIL: moist to wet, acid
NATIVE TO: moist, open meadows, wet ditches; Massachusetts to Florida along the coastal plain
SIZE: 1–3 feet (12–18 inches)
COLOR: rose pink, lavender, or white; **BLOOMS** in late summer

A robust plant, perhaps a bit rank for formal areas. The related *R. interior* (Showy Meadow-pitchers), which ranges west to Louisiana, Oklahoma, and Kansas, is a neater plant, with wider leaves covered in bristly hairs and more intensely colored flowers with pointed petal tips.

Rhexia virginica
(Virginia Meadow Beauty)

ZONES: 3–9; sun, part shade
SOIL: moist to wet
NATIVE TO: wet meadows, bogs; Nova Scotia to Wisconsin, south to Texas and Florida
SIZE: 8–28 inches (12–16 inches)
COLOR: rose pink; **BLOOMS** in late summer

Over its wide distribution, this species varies quite a bit in size, with northern populations barely a foot or so and southern ones up to 3 feet. The plants can be single stemmed or, more commonly, clumping or mounded, with beautiful, crinkled flowers and stiff little leaves.

insects, and when in bloom look as if draped in a quilt of chocolate and gold.

Orange Coneflower has become one of the top-selling perennials in the United States, and it is no wonder, for this is a superlative plant for massing, meadows, or the border. If the highway yellow color is hard on your eyes, try Green-eyed Coneflower, a larger, more informal species with soft yellow blooms.

CULTURE: Very easily transplanted when not in flower. Most will grow well in a range of soils but are best in moderately fertile, well-drained loam and full sun. The perennial species need occasional dividing to keep them neat and flowering well, and this is best accomplished in spring. Unless they're deadheaded, all will self-sow, which is especially important for maintaining the biennial types.

USES: Borders, meadows, massing.
WILDLIFE: Favorites of butterflies, seeds for birds.
PROPAGATION: Easy from seed. See p. 261.

Rudbeckia fulgida var. sullivantii
(Orange Coneflower)

ZONES: 3–9; sun, part sun
SOIL: moist
NATIVE TO: moist meadows, clearings, and swamps; Michigan and Illinois south to Missouri and West Virginia
SIZE: 20–30 inches (18–24 inches)
COLOR: bright golden yellow; **BLOOMS** in midsummer

One of the best all-around summer-blooming natives, producing leafy clumps of dark green quilted leaves on long petioles and stiff, branched stems

Rudbeckia fulgida *var.* sullivantii. *A stand of long-blooming Orange Coneflower is a rolling sea of golden yellow. It's consistent height, vigor, and overall reliability, combined with sheer knock-your-socks-off color make this an excellent choice for massing and formal gardens. It will grow in a meadow as well, but the plants look a bit manicured and uncomfortable in such a naturalized setting.*

Rudbeckia fulgida var. *sullivantii*

Rudbeckia
(ruhd-BECK-ee-ah)
Asteraceae
Black-eyed Susan

Black-eyed Susans need little introduction, for whether lining the roadside or the garden path, they are some of our most cherished and recognizable wildflowers. They offer an award-winning combination of bold, eye-catching flowers and an easy disposition that has made the genus popular here and abroad. These are true meadow and prairie plants that are perfectly at ease with ornamental grasses, blazing stars, and coneflowers, among others, and they have helped to popularize a new trend in gardening based on a prairie aesthetic, characterized by bold sweeps of grasses intermixed with colorful drifts of late-blooming perennials. They are good nectar plants visited by a host of butterflies and other

of 3-inch flowers. It is a slowly spreading species that will eventually crowd out the less stalwart. The old German seed strain 'Goldsturm' has virtually replaced the species in the trade, but I see no differ-

Rudbeckia hirta *var. pulcherrima. Common Black-eyed Susan is often included as a component of meadow seed mixes because it grows quickly from seed and blooms reliably the first year, when many of the perennial wildflowers in the blend are still just establishing their root systems. Though it provides welcome color for the first year or two, this short-lived Rudbeckia is gradually replaced by more permanent species.*

ence between the two and suspect that this is merely a marketing gimmick. Var. *speciosa* (sometimes listed as *R. newmanii*) is a more understated version, with smaller leaves and flowers in greater numbers. In some ways I prefer it to var. *sullivantii*—the flowers are long-lasting and the effect of the plant is more restrained.

Rudbeckia grandiflora
(Large Black-eyed Susan)

ZONES: 5–9; sun, part sun
SOIL: moist to dry
NATIVE TO: open, dry woods; Missouri to Kansas south to Louisiana and Texas
SIZE: 2–3 feet (2 feet)
COLOR: yellow and brown; BLOOMS in summer

I do not have much experience with this plant, but it is a showy, large-leaved, coarse species with basal foliage up to a foot long and 6 inches wide (like a large Orange Coneflower in habit). The flower rays droop as in *Echinacea*, and they are big—up to twice the size of *R. hirta*.

Rudbeckia hirta var. *pulcherrima*
(Common Black-eyed Susan)

ZONES: 3–9; sun, part shade
SOIL: moist to dry
NATIVE TO: open, typically disturbed habitats; New-foundland to British Columbia, south to Mexico and Florida (originally native to the Midwest, but naturalized elsewhere)
SIZE: 2–3 feet (12–16 inches)

COLOR: gold and brown; BLOOMS in summer

People have helped the Black-eyed Susan spread far and through the entirety of North America. This is an opportunistic biennial or short-lived perennial that easily colonizes disturbed habitats along roads and old fields. The plants have thin, lanceolate leaves covered with prickly hair and large flat flowers with tousled ray petals and a dark brown disk. Tetraploid garden strains called Gloriosa Daisies with huge 5–6-inch flowers and dark central blotches are popular but short-lived as well (see Tetraploid, p. 305).

Rudbeckia laciniata
(Cutleaf Coneflower)

ZONES: 3–9; sun, part shade
SOIL: moist
NATIVE TO: moist open places; Quebec to Montana south to Arizona and Florida
SIZE: 3–6 feet (3–4 feet)
COLOR: light yellow-green disk; BLOOMS in summer

A stately perennial with deeply cut leaves and tall stems of drooping, informal blooms. This species, like most of the others, will slowly spread, but the double flowered, old-fashioned cultivar 'Golden Glow' is for some reason as rampant as bamboo. A related species, *R. nitida* (Green-eyed Coneflower) is often confused with this species, but *R. nitida* is a marginally hardy plant from the southern coastal plain and plants in cultivation are really *R. lacinata*.

Rudbeckia maxima
(Great Coneflower)

ZONES: 5–9; sun, part sun
SOIL: moist
NATIVE TO: moist prairies and forest openings; Mis-souri to Oklahoma and south to Texas and Louisiana
SIZE: 3–4 feet (3 feet)
COLOR: yellow and brown; BLOOMS in summer

A very unusual plant as *Rudbeckia*s go, with flat, 1–2-foot glaucous leaves that form big basal clumps and tall, leafless stems of drooping flowers with fat coni-cal disks. It is an excellent plant for the border, com-bining the qualities of a large, bold ground cover with an airy verticality. Likes hot summers.

Rudbeckia occidentalis
(Western Coneflower)

ZONES: 5–8; sun, part sun
SOIL: moist
NATIVE TO: moist woods and streambanks; Washing-ton and Idaho to Oregon
SIZE: 2–6 feet (2–3 feet)
COLOR: yellow to brown-black; BLOOMS in summer

This species has short drooping rays and an enor-

SIZE: 2–3 feet (12–16 inches)

COLOR: yellow with a chocolate disk; **BLOOMS** in late summer

This plant has a girl-next-door friendliness to its little gold flowers centered in brown. Maybe it is the pleasantly unsophisticated look of the ragged 3-fingered leaves and the dozens of flat-faced flowers that I find so appealing. It is an accommodating plant that, though short-lived, will continue to seed, making it ideal for naturalizing in a meadow or prairie.

mous, missilelike cone that can reach 3 inches in length by the time seeds are set. The leaves are ovate with pointed tips and cover the tall stems.

Rudbeckia subtomentosa

(Sweet Coneflower, Sweet Black-eyed Susan)

ZONES: 3–9; sun, part sun

SOIL: moist to wet

NATIVE TO: moist prairies and bottomlands; Michigan and Wisconsin south to Oklahoma, Louisiana, and Tennessee.

SIZE: 3–5 feet (3–4 feet)

COLOR: yellow and brown; **BLOOMS** in summer

A tall, leafy species that looks more like a *Helianthus* than a Black-eyed Susan at first glance. Its gray-green, sweet-scented leaves form large bushy clumps liberally laced with black-centered daisies. Sweet Coneflower can be lightly tipped in late spring to keep it compact and less likely to lean.

Rudbeckia triloba

(Three-lobed Coneflower, Brown-eyed Susan)

ZONES: 3–9; sun, part sun

SOIL: moist

NATIVE TO: moist meadows and open woodland; Connecticut to Michigan and Nebraska south to Texas and Florida

Sabatia angularis

Sabatia (sab-AY-sha)
Gentianaceae
Sea-Pink, Marsh Pink

At first glance, the sea-pinks might be mistaken for a particularly colorful *Coreopsis* or daisy, as they have a whorl of raylike petals surrounding a darker center. They are gentians, though, and sublimely beautiful ones at that. *Sabatia*s produce flowers that are at the same time soft and vibrant, the pigments strong, but also muted—like a flamingo through the fog. They are unlike any other wildflowers I know, but for some reason they are rarely cultivated. I suppose this is in part because many are annuals or biennials, and also because they need fairly wet, open ground to thrive. However, if you have a suitable spot, sea-pinks are not hard to establish, and the perennial types are particularly satisfactory and lovely in the garden.

(**LEFT**): Rudbeckia maxima. *The exaggerated, skirted cones of Great Coneflower develop far above the leaves. When not in bloom, the blue-gray, paddlelike foliage held in stiff, vertical array is unusual and certainly unique—flattened cabbage leaves come to mind, as does the strongly vertical arrangement of Prairie Dock.*

(**RIGHT**): Sabatia angularis. *Maybe it's just a personality quirk, but I tend to shy away from biennials, especially those that are reluctant to naturalize and require my annual intervention to perpetuate in the garden. There are always exceptions, though, like the magnificent Fringed Gentian and this, the charming Rose Pink, Sabatia angularis. Sabatia seed germinates easily in the nursery, and if repotted gingerly when the plants are the half the size of a penny, by autumn they will form lusty mounded rosettes of deep green leaves slightly curled under along the edges. Place these in a damp, sunny spot, and the following year they'll be bedecked with muted soft pink blossoms for a month or so before turning the last of their resources to the production of seed. If the spot you choose is fairly open and damp, they may even begin to self-sow with abandon.*

In habit the species are very similar—opposite, lance-shaped leaves in low clumps that erect straight wiry stems displaying the upward-facing flowers in loose panicles. The biennial and perennial species overwinter as a dense leafy rosette that needs to remain free of smothering fallen leaves and debris, and all the plants produce hundreds of tiny seeds that will naturalize in a spot to their liking.

CULTURE: *Sabatia*s are opportunists that tend to colonize in open, moist or wet ground that has been disturbed by flooding, fire, or human activity. The tiny seeds germinate best on the surface of mud or moss, and the plants can form dense stands in ditches or along pond shores where the water has receded. The annuals and biennials can be introduced as seed of young plants set out in spring, and if the area is kept free of heavy competition, they will amply reseed. The perennials are easier to handle, and rosettes set out in a similar situation in spring will bloom for many years, provided they are not crowded out. Areas such as the edge of a pond or pool, along a mossy path or drainage ditch, or even just a moist spot in the perennial border will do.

USES: Naturalizing on pond shores, bog gardens.

PROPAGATION: Moderately difficult from seed and division. See p. 261.

Sabatia angularis
(Rose Pink)

ZONES: 4–9; sun, part sun
SOIL: moist to wet
NATIVE TO: low woodlands, marshes, and fields; Connecticut to Michigan south to Texas and Florida
SIZE: 12–30 inches (12 inches)
COLOR: rose pink with a green center; **BLOOMS** in summer

A widespread, vigorous biennial that in its second year forms bushy plants producing numerous 1½-inch daisies of a lovely, soft pink. Not difficult to get established.

Sabatia campestris
(Western Marsh Pink)

ZONES: 5–9; sun, part sun
SOIL: moist
NATIVE TO: open, disturbed areas—moist to drier soils; Illinois to Missouri south to Texas and Mississippi
SIZE: 8–16 inches (6 inches)
COLOR: lilac; **BLOOMS** in summer

An annual species, so a bit more difficult to handle, but best sown directly in the garden. It has large, full flowers with pointed petal tips that make this worth the extra effort to establish.

Sabatia dodecandra
(Perennial Sea-Pink)

ZONES: 5–9; sun, part shade
SOIL: moist to wet
NATIVE TO: coastal marshes; Connecticut south to Florida and Louisiana
SIZE: 12–26 inches (8–12 inches)
COLOR: rose flushed white with red and yellow in the center; **BLOOMS** in summer

A wonderful perennial species, with twice the normal number of petals (10–12); thin, pointed leaves; and large luminous flowers on tall, thin stems.

Sabatia kennedyana
(Plymouth Gentian)

ZONES: 4–9; sun, part sun
SOIL: moist to wet
NATIVE TO: coastal pond shores; rare and scattered from Nova Scotia to South Carolina
SIZE: 16–26 inches (8–12 inches)
COLOR: rose pink and white with red and yellow markings in the center; **BLOOMS** in summer

The finest of the genus, in many respects similar to *S. dodecandra*, but with larger, flat flowers up to 2½ inches wide and marked in the center with hieroglyphs of red and gold. It is a slowly spreading perennial that succeeds in a moist soil in the garden.

Sabatia kennedyana. Unfortunately for the budget-minded plant conservationist in New England, few of the region's growing pantheon of rare plants qualify as the floral equivalent of "charismatic large mammals" (like the Bengal Tiger or Manatee) that garner so much public attention and most of the fundraising revenue as well. Plants such as Threadleaf Pondweed (Stuckenia filiformis) and Dwarf Mistletoe (Arceuthobium pusillum) may make a botanist smile but do not, alas, have the same effect on the average citizen. Fortunately there's the Plymouth Gentian, with a perfect combination of charisma and rarity to act as a lovely spokesflower for the equally important but often maligned BIOs (of botanical interest only).

Salvia coccinea

Salvia (SAL-vee-ah)
Lamiaceae
Sage

Although *Salvia* is a cosmopolitan genus with representatives throughout Asia and Europe, it is in the rocky soils and deserts from southern California and Mexico south to Argentina that the group blossoms in an unrivaled diversity of form and color. We have hummingbirds to thank for this optical feast, because the tubular flowers in brilliant shades of red, orange, yellow, white, blue, and purple are advertisements for their services. In fact it was a dark purple form of the South American *S. guaranitica* that exploded the myth I had always heard about hummingbirds visiting only red-orange flowers. Of all the plants in the garden, this midnight purple sage was the absolute favorite of our resident female Ruby-throated Hummingbird.

The 5 petals of sages are fused into a tube that diverges into an upper and lower lip. The upper lip is narrow and arches over the anthers like a claw-shaped umbrella, protecting them from the elements and forcing them up against the beak or head of the pollinator. The female stigma arches down from the claw so that it is positioned smack dab in the middle of the nectar tube—a nightclub bouncer waiting for her granular gratuity. The lower lip is large and bannerlike, variously ruffled and shaped like colorful prayer flags hung on a pole, and it is these that give the plants such a luminous appeal.

The New World *Salvia*s are mostly woody sub-shrubs that are only reluctantly herbaceous. They have strongly scented, opposite leaves in various shapes and sizes, with flowers produced in long-blooming, tiered racemes from the stem tips. Many of the subtropical species can be wintered over in the warmer parts of the United States provided the ground does not freeze. In the North they are becoming popular as annuals, and a few, like *S. splendens* from Brazil, have been popular bedding plants for many years. There are a few brilliantly colored species that range into the warmer parts of the United States beyond southern California, and these make excellent border plants in Zone 7 and south. The hardiest of all is *S. azurea*, which can easily survive a Zone 4 winter and reward you with glistening sky blue flowers late in the season.

CULTURE: The native sages are full-sun plants for well-drained soils of moderate fertility. A rich diet produces floppy stems and decreases winter hardiness. If given these conditions, they are carefree, drought-tolerant plants that will brighten up the border or large rock garden with their cheery blossoms. Since most grow from a heavy rootstock, they are difficult to divide, so start with seedlings or well-rooted cuttings set out in spring. Many of the New World *Salvia*s are short day bloomers, so plants overwintered in a greenhouse will put out a flush of flowers in spring and then again in fall. If you live in an area where the subtropical types are marginally hardy, try to site them out as soon as the danger of frost has passed in a protected spot such as near a building foundation where the ground is less likely to freeze. Alternatively, they are not hard to dig up and overwinter as houseplants.

USES: Borders, xeriscaping.

WILDLIFE: Hummingbirds, as well as bees and butterflies, find the flowers a very attractive source of nectar.

PROPAGATION: Easy from seed or cuttings. See p. 261.

Salvia azurea
(Blue Sage)

ZONES: 4–9; sun
SOIL: moderately moist to dry, well drained
NATIVE TO: limestone glades, rocky prairies, bluffs; Minnesota to Nebraska south to Texas, Arkansas, and Kentucky
SIZE: 2–3 feet (2 feet)
COLOR: medium to deep blue; **BLOOMS** from late summer to early fall

This is the hardiest perennial species, with fairly large flowers coming late in the season above narrow, gray-green 2–3-inch leaves. It survives the winter by dying completely back to a thick rootstock, and the new growth is slow to emerge in spring. The plants

Salvia coccinea. Though in my experience the red strains of Scarlet Sage are the most reliably perennial, the species also acts as a self-sowing annual, so soft pink and even occasionally white plants commonly appear in my garden every year.

Sanguinaria canadensis. *As fleeting as Blood-root's flowers are, they have naturalized so extensively around the Garden and its little microclimates that you can find plants in bloom somewhere here for nearly a month in early spring. The first to emerge are coaxed by the warm soil near buildings long before the ground has fully thawed in the shaded recesses of the lower woodland. Occasional plants in a colony are naturally slower to emerge from sleep than others (some would say that about me as well), further extend-ing the period of bloom.*

have a tendency to send up long stems that arch and flop, and this lax habit is its biggest drawback. If you tip-prune the plants in late spring and again in mid-summer, site them in full sun and do not overdo the fertilizer, they will form very satisfactory bushy clumps. For late-season color this is a tough, reliable plant that is hard to beat, but it seems rather seldom grown. There is some name confusion in the trade, so to set the record straight: *Salvia azurea* var. *gran-diflora* occurs in the western part of the range and has slightly larger flowers, among other minor differ-ences with the eastern *S. azurea* var. *azurea*. *S. pitcheri* (also listed as *azurea* var. *pitcheri*) is a syn-onym for var. *grandiflora*, not var. *azurea*. Because of its larger flowers and—in my experience—neater growth, the western variety is better for gardens and the one commonly sold.

Salvia coccinea

(Scarlet Sage, Mirto)

ZONES: 8–10; sun, part sun
SOIL: moist to dry, well drained
NATIVE TO: sandy soils, chaparral and open woods; South Carolina to Florida west along the Gulf Coast to Texas and Mexico
SIZE: 2–4 feet (16–28 inches)
COLOR: scarlet to crimson or occasionally pink or white; **BLOOMS** from summer to fall

Scarlet Sage lives up to its name, producing spikes of large brilliant flowers over a long season. In habit it starts out tall and narrow, with wide, pointed bright green leaves more or less covered in a fine downy pubescence. New flowering stems emerge from the axils of the leaves, so by season's end they become fairly bushy and dense. This is a justly popular bor-der plant in the Southeast, and if given a sandy soil that does not freeze, it will remain perennial. At the nursery in central North Carolina where I formerly worked, the plants would mostly winterkill, but self-sown recruits would more than take up the slack the following summer, blooming a mixture of white, pink, and red.

Salvia farinacea

(Mealy-cup Sage)

ZONES: 7–10; sun
SOIL: moist to moderately dry, well drained
NATIVE TO: limestone prairies, meadows and flood-plains; Texas and New Mexico
SIZE: 2–4 feet (2 feet)
COLOR: petals deep purple with 2 lines of white on the lower lip, calyx tube violet; **BLOOMS** from summer to fall

Mealy-cup Sage is a familiar bedding plant long sold as an annual in the North but reliably hardy in mild climates. It is an unbeatable, carefree and long-

blooming species, with a shrubby habit and flower spikes much like Lavender in effect. The calyx tube that surrounds each bloom is covered in a frosty lilac down that contrasts wonderfully with the blooms, and these remain colorful for a few weeks after the flowers fade. New spikes are produced continually over the season, so by fall the plants become quite large and robust. As with many of the others, it is perennial in a frost-free soil, even evergreen in Zone 9 and warmer.

Salvia greggii

(Autumn Sage, Texas Sage)

ZONES: 7–10; sun
SOIL: moderately moist to dry, well drained
NATIVE TO: rocky soils; Texas south into Mexico
SIZE: 24–30 inches (18–24 inches)
COLOR: orange-red to scarlet, also red-purple, yellow, and white; **BLOOMS** in fall

The flowers of Texas Sage are shaped much like those of *S. coccinea*, with a large rounded lip in shades of red and orange. It has small rounded leaves of a slightly grayish cast clothing branching stems, and in habit the plants make neat rounded mounds by sea-son's end. They do not start blooming until late in the year, but make up for it with a heavy flush of blooms over a three- to four-week period. Plants from Mexico exhibit more of a color range than the typically scarlet Texas phase, but they are less reliably perennial in Zone 7.

Sanguinaria canadensis

Sanguinaria canadensis

(san-gwen-AIR-ee-uh)
Papaveraceae
Bloodroot

ZONES: 3–9; part sun, shade
SOIL: moist, well drained
NATIVE TO: moist woods, floodplains, slopes; Nova

Ants and Seed Dispersal

An amazing number of woodland wildflowers have fleshy, fat-rich appendages called *elaiosomes* that serve to attract ants, who carry off the seed as they would a dead insect. Ants are really the perfect seed vectors for these woodlanders for several reasons. First of all, they typically produce fairly large seeds —too big for wind dispersal— that are necessary to provide the energy reserves needed to push through heavy leaf litter and compete with hungry tree roots. Ants are remarkably strong and incredibly numerous (one estimate is that there are a million ants for every human on the planet—but who's counting). They are relentless in their search for food, and when a source is discovered an ant will leave a chemical trail for its siblings to follow so all can be gathered. As far as the plants are concerned, ants are preferable to mammals or birds because they are not interested in the seed itself— they simply discard it, like they do with indigestible exoskeleton of an insect on waste piles or middens in some far corner of the nest once the elaiosome has been consumed. In effect the seed gets "planted" in the ants' compost pile, where it is protected from harm from the territorial colony and nurtured by the nutrients released from decaying waste. The constant tunneling must also create somewhat tree root–free zones. It is a beautiful example of mutualism, in which both the ants and wildflowers clearly benefit from the interaction.

The main disadvantage to this system is that the seeds are usually not carried very far from the parents. While 30 feet or more is not uncommon, a typical distance is more like 1–3 feet (or, if they're not carried away by insects, the heavy seeds will simply sprout beneath the parent). Accordingly, plants like Wild Ginger, Trillium, Bloodroot, and Twinleaf are slow to recolonize areas from which they have been displaced by glaciation or agriculture. Occasionally, though, a few seeds must be picked up by birds or migrating mammals, otherwise the plants would not have made it as far north as Canada in the short time since the last glaciation. Ant-dispersed seeds are also intolerant of desiccation, so they must be handled differently when collected (see hydrophilic seed in the propagation chapter on p. 241).

The large ripe seeds of Bloodroot clearly display the fleshy elaiosome that is so attractive to ants. When they fall to the ground, they look like a collection of juicy caterpillars. Within minutes, an ant had found the seeds and carried one off to its nest 25 feet away, and within thirty minutes, all the other seeds were carried off as well.

Sarracenia flava. The hoods of the Yellow Pitcher Plant have ingeniously evolved to intercept and channel rainwater and prevent it from entering the trap. When rain does get in to these tall pitchers, the weight topples them over and renders them useless as traps (a few prostrate examples can be seen in the left background). The interior of functioning traps remains fairly dry, wetted only by the digestive exudations of the plant and the liquid latent in its prey. We mulch our pitchers with a protective blanket of pine needles in late fall, and these remain as an attractive mulch through the following summer.

Scotia to southern Manitoba, south to Texas and Florida

SIZE: 5–12 inches (16 inches)
COLOR: white with yellow centers (stamens); BLOOMS in early spring

I have a special respect for the first rugged plants to struggle free from winter's lingering grasp, and there is none more deserving of this admiration than the humble Bloodroot. Its snow white flowers with propeller-blade petals spring from the unfolding leaves like doves from a magician's hat at the first sign of a permanent thaw. Like Twinleaf, the flowers last only a few days, the petals falling to the ground in confettiesque heaps before the leaves fully expand. They have a pure, crystalline quality so befitting one with a life so brief. Bloodroot's foliage is also beautiful—nearly round and notched like a sand dollar with 2 long lobes at the base that make them look as if attached in the center to a stiff 6-inch petiole disappearing into the ground. The leaves can be up to 10 inches across and stand at an angle to the ground as if to shed rain or capture the low vernal sun. They make a splendid ground cover once the flowers have gone, persisting in good condition all summer into fall.

Bloodroot has dark red, knobby, horizontal rhizomes that are filled with a thin crimson sap that does remarkably resemble blood oozing from a wound. The juice was used as rouge by Native Americans, and it contains several bitter compounds, including sanguinarin, that can be poisonous but taste so awful that it is unlikely a poisonous dose could be accidentally ingested. They have been used with caution medicinally as an expectorant and a topical disinfectant.

CULTURE: Bloodroot's brittle rhizomes are easy to handle when dormant in fall and can be dug and broken into 3–4-inch segments and replanted just below the surface in a moist but well-drained, lightly shaded place. The chief problem I have encountered is a stem rot that affects the petioles just below soil level, causing the leaves to wither and fall prematurely. This can be prevented by keeping the plants free of heavy mulch and planting them in a gritty soil. They are agreeable plants though, and with a little fertilizer and lime in spring, they will form a large patch after several seasons. *Sanguinaria* is a perfect woodland companion for a host of spring ephemerals, and its long-lasting foliage helps hide the bare spots created by more fleeting wildflowers.

USES: Massing, deciduous ground cover for shade.

PROPAGATION: Moderately difficult from seed; easy from division. See p. 261.

Sarracenia flava

Sarracenia
(sarah-SEEN-ee-ah)
Sarraceniaceae
Pitcher Plant

What macabre lives these *Sarracenia*s lead, gaining sustenance from the hapless insects that fall into their traps and are slowly eaten alive (Oh, the horror!). Pitchers are fascinating plants, both as elegant examples of evolution and as studies in form, function, and beauty. They are distant relatives of *Hibiscus* that have been able to take advantage of the harsh growing conditions of acidic, nutrient-poor bogs and savannas by supplementing their mineral diet through carnivory, or—more accurately—insectivory. It is not energy they gain from this feast, but nitrogen and perhaps other nutrients that are easily leached and hard to obtain from the poor soils where they make their homes. Their leaves have been modified over time into tall or squat pitchers that lure insects like trumpets playing a siren's song. (The pitcher is really a rolled up leaf that has been sealed together to hold liquid.) The colorful areas around the opening are patterned like flowers and heavily smeared with rich nectar to entice all manner of bees, wasps, beetles, ants, and moths, who crawl deeper into the trap and are prevented from going backward by downward-facing hairs that act like tire spikes should they attempt to reverse direction. A safe distance down the tube, the hairs give way to a waxy smooth surface, and the insects slide down into a digestible soup, releasing nutrients as they eventually decay.

The Common Pitcher Plant, a low plant of sphagnum bogs, has pitchers like open funnels that catch rainwater to drown its victims. The other eight species are mostly taller plants of sandy pocosins and savannas with high water tables found along the southeastern coastal plain. Here they grow in the company of wiregrass and native bamboo, and this necessitates taller traps to rise above the surrounding vegetation. If these were to fill up with water, they would topple over, so each is outfitted with a rain hood that sheds water from the opening. They secrete a weak digestive fluid to take the place of water, and old traps are jammed full of the chitin-rich exoskeletons of their prey. Many are becoming rare because fire prevention and short-rotation forestry combined with development are eliminating the low, open habitat they require.

Like *Hibiscus*, the *Sarracenia*s have exquisite flowers. They are borne on tall, thick stems that curve like a shepherd's crook so that the flowers hang down. The blooms have an ingenious device to prevent self-pollination that again relies on trapping insects. In this case, though, they are imprisoned only temporarily by the flowers and then released. The tip of the style (a portion of the female part of the flower) balloons out like an upside down umbrella that fits snugly around the petals to form a dome. Its has 5 trap doors that allow pollinators to crawl in and pass over the stigmas before reaching nectar, but then to exit the insect must drop down into the umbrella, which is loaded with fallen pollen. It gets liberally dusted before climbing out the bottom – avoiding the stigma this time and preventing self-pollination. The plants freely hybridize when growing sympatrically, and all conceivable intermediate forms can come from seed grown from a mixed garden collection.

CULTURE: Pitcher plants are surprisingly easy to grow if you can provide them a sunny, boggy spot with poor, acid soil. The tall species are most at home in the steamy summer climate of the Southeast United States. These will grow but not set much seed in the North (it is advisable to give them a winter mulch of pine needles in Zone 5). The stout, creeping rhizomes can be divided either in early spring or after the leaves have expanded in summer, but they rarely need dividing except for increase.

USES: Bog garden.

PROPAGATION: Difficult from seed; moderately difficult from division. See p. 261.

Sarracenia flava
(Yellow Pitcher Plant, Biscuit-flower)

ZONES: 5–9; sun
SOIL: evenly moist to wet, acid
NATIVE TO: sandy bogs and savannahs; Virginia to Florida and Alabama
SIZE: 1–3 feet (12–16 inches)
COLOR: greenish yellow; BLOOMS in spring
One of the most widespread, tallest, and most robust pitchers that easily adapts to culture. The pitchers are yellow-green-veined with red around the hood. They flare widely at the opening, and the hood itself is a stately, spade-shaped affair.

S. alata (Yellow Trumpets) is a related plant, rare in the wild, with a greener suffusion to the traps.

Sarracenia leucophylla
(White Trumpet)

ZONES: 5–9; sun
SOIL: evenly moist to wet, acid
NATIVE TO: wet pine savannas; Georgia, Florida, and Mississippi
SIZE: 1–4 feet (12–16 inches)
COLOR: deep red; BLOOMS in spring
The most striking of all, with creamy white and green traps heavily veined in dark red, especially around the fluted, wide opening and regal hood—an unforgettable site in the wild sadly becoming rarer each year. This *Sarracenia* attracts night-flying moths with its light coloration, and the traps quickly fill to the rim with hapless victims of one species in particular. It is easy in cultivation but needs a long, warm growing season to reach full potential.

Sarracenia minor
(Hooded Pitcher Plant)

ZONES: 5–9; sun
SOIL: evenly moist to wet, acid
NATIVE TO: wet pinelands and savannas; North Carolina to Florida
SIZE: 1–2 feet (12 inches)
COLOR: yellow; BLOOMS in spring
A hooded pitcher like a sock puppet with an overbite. This is another of the taller species, with a narrow round constriction for an opening that functions like a lobster trap. Translucent "windows" on the roof of the trap fool insects into crawling toward the light deeper in the trap. *S. psittacina* (Lobster-pot Pitcher Plant), from Georgia to Florida and Louisiana, is another of the constricted type. It forms white and green pitchers veined red, but they rest on the ground facing upward. It is the most challenging to grow.

Sarracenia purpurea
(Common Pitcher Plant, Sweet Pitcher Plant, Southern Pitcher Plant)

ZONES: 2–9; sun, part sun
SOIL: wet, acid
NATIVE TO: sphagnum bogs; Newfoundland and Labrador to Manitoba south to Minnesota, Illinois, and Maryland and along the coast to Florida
SIZE: 6–12 inches (12 inches)
COLOR: dark red; BLOOMS in spring
The only pitcher to venture north of the Mason-Dixon Line. It has taken advantage of the vast stretches of boglands formed in the wake of the last

(LEFT): Sarracenia pur-purea. *Unlike its taller cousins, the squat pitchers of Common Pitcher Plant are designed to collect, rather than shed, rain. They lay resting on the ground to support the weight of a pool of rainwater it accumulates to drown and help decompose hapless insects.*

(RIGHT): Saxifraga careyana. *I routinely keep stock plants in the nursery, both as an extra source of seed and as insurance against loss in the garden. These elegant sprays of Carey's Saxifrage are a prelude to the copious seed I can expect to collect from them. Because this species ripens and sheds its dustlike seed expediently, I find keeping a few plants in a prominent place helps remind me to collect it in a timely fashion. Most of the leafy clumps to the rear of the Saxifrage are pots of Indian Pink, another plant whose seed often escapes me if I am not diligent.*

Saxifraga careyana

Saxifraga (sax-eh-FRAG-ah)
Saxifragaceae
Saxifrage

glaciation. The low, fat pitchers are green on the outside and deep burgundy around the lip and interior. They recline open end up to catch water. It is a very easy plant to grow, especially for northern gardeners.

Sarracenia rubra
(Sweet Pitcher Plant)

ZONES: 5–9; sun
SOIL: evenly moist to wet, acid
NATIVE TO: shrub bogs and savannas; North Carolina to Florida and Mississippi
SIZE: 8–18 inches (12 inches)
COLOR: maroon (green on the inside); **BLOOMS** in spring

A diminutive trumpet pitcher with narrow traps ocher yellow and green with a suffusion of maroon around the small but unconstricted opening.

Subspecies *jonesii* (Mountain Pitcher Plant) is smaller still, standing 12 inches at maturity. It is a rare plant restricted to a few cold boggy streams in the southern Appalachians. It is better adapted to a short, cool season, so it grows and sets seed reliably in the North.

Saxifraga is a genus familiar to every rock gardener, but otherwise underappreciated (don't we all feel that way sometimes). They are primarily mountain plants, needing cool, sharply drained but not droughty soils and a climate free of heat and humidity. A number of dwarf, cushion-forming boreal and alpine species like *S. oppositifolia*, *S. tolemiei*, and *S. serpyllifolia* are absolutely charming but difficult to grow even for the specialist, so I will reluctantly exclude them here.

This leaves a group of more robust wetland and woodland species that form overwintering rosettes of stiff, evergreen leaves that bolt in spring to produce clouds of small starry flowers. The flowering rosettes die after setting seed, but new ones should form around the base. However, if the plants are weak (or, as in some cases, are naturally biennial or monocarpic) no rosettes form and the plants perish. All is not lost in this case, as mature capsules release thousands of tiny seeds which readily take root and grow as soon as they hit some moist, open ground or patch of moss.

These larger saxifrages are not as showy in flower as some of their more colorful alpine relatives, but in combination with the rosettes of succulent deep green leaves often blushed burgundy, the blooms have an appealing hazy quality. They are more adapt-

Bog Garden

Bogs are fascinating places, home to some of our most remarkable wildflowers. Rare orchids, carnivorous plants, mosses, cotton grasses, and a host of shrubs are among those that have adapted to the poor, acid soils because they provide ample moisture and freedom from competition. Bogs form in low pockets or ponds left after glaciation that slowly fill with sediments and, in the case of sphagnum bogs, the undecomposed remains of sphagnum mosses and sedges that form a mucky peat that slowly fills the depression. Bogs have a high water table, and this, combined with an extremely acid pH, prevents the breakdown and release of nutrients from organic matter. They are transitional ecosystems, for over thousands of years, they fill to the point that trees can enter and begin to convert the area to low forest.

It is not difficult to construct a small bog garden using a 30–40-mil rubber pool liner (also sold as a roofing material). Choose a spot that receives full sun and dig out an area of at least 25–50 square feet to a depth of 12–18 inches, line the hole with a 1-inch layer of sand (to help protect the liner from puncture from below) and spread out the liner. It is important that the water table remain at least 6 inches below the surface of the bog, as most of the plants cannot stand prolonged flooding. Make a small ditch leading from the lowest side that is 6–10 inches shallower than the deepest part of the bog, as this will allow excess water to leave. Fill the lined bog with a 50:50 mix of builder's sand and sphagnum peat that has been premixed and wetted. If the bog is big enough, try to mound up the center to create a small dome or raised area. Remember that the mix will settle, so it is a good idea to thoroughly hose it down and let it sit for a week or two then add some more mix to bring the level up to the top of the liner. I would recommend sinking a vertical section of 1-inch PVC pipe in an accessible spot near the edge. Leave the bottom end open and set down just above the liner and let the other end protrude 12 inches above the surface. By shining a flashlight inside, you can get an idea how high the water table is and add some water with a hose if necessary. Ideally, site the bog in a low area that will collect rainwater runoff. This will cut down on watering and avoid possible soluble salt problems encountered with some tap water. Plant the bog and then sprig in live pieces of sphagnum moss. (If you do not have any available, it will eventually come in on its own.) Because the bare, moist soil is a perfect place for weeds to germinate, establishing a good moss layer will cut down on maintenance and give the garden a more natural look. A spongy layer of moss is also the ideal place for bog plants to root.

Fens are bogs usually formed in limestone areas where mineral-rich groundwater has found a way into the wetland. Here the pH and fertility of the muck is higher, and it supports a completely different flora dominated by grasses and sedges instead of moss. Fens are the home of plants like the Showy and Small White Lady-slippers. To grow these successfully, fill your bog with compost, peat moss, and sand in a 25:25:50 ratio and lime the mix to raise the pH above 6.0. Yearly dustings of lime will also be necessary.

Scutellaria serrata. There is certainly nothing repulsive about Allegheny Skullcap— my apologies, really. In our gardens, it fills a critical color gap in early summer, when the woodland cacophony has faded to silent green and the summer sun-lovers are still warming up.

able in the garden and tolerate heat and humidity more easily as well. I will admit they are never destined to be staples of the nursery industry, but for those of a naturalistic bent, these are a perfect choice.

CULTURE: The plants covered here are best naturalized among wet rocks, moss, or hummocks in bogs, or grown in a moist, partially shaded place in the rock garden or border. Learn to recognize the small seedling rosettes to avoid weeding them out. Pick a spot free from heavy competition and keep them well watered in spring.

USES: Naturalizing in swamp, bog, or other mucky ground.

PROPAGATION: Easy from seed and division. See p. 261.

Saxifraga careyana
(Carey's Saxifrage)

ZONES: 5–9; part sun to light shade
SOIL: moist
NATIVE TO: moist and wet ledges and slopes in the southern Appalachians; Virginia to Tennessee
SIZE: 6–16 inches (8–12 inches)
COLOR: white; **BLOOMS** in late spring

One of my favorites, with glossy, thick leaves jaggedly cut along the margins that are dark green above and blood red underneath. In my experience this is the most reliably perennial of the southern Appalachian species, with rosettes the size of a small head of lettuce under ideal conditions.

S. *caroliniana* is similar, with larger, broader leaves, as is the western *S. occidentalis* (Redwool Saxifrage), a lovely species from the Rocky Mountains.

Saxifraga michauxii
(Claw Saxifrage)

ZONES: 4–9; part sun to light shade
SOIL: moist
NATIVE TO: moist slopes and ledges in the southern Appalachians; Virginia to Kentucky south to Georgia
SIZE: 6–16 inches (8–12 inches)
COLOR: white; **BLOOMS** in early summer

The leaves of Claw Saxifrage have long teeth along the margin set like the jaw of a sperm whale. The leaves and stems are covered in glistening crimson hair that catches the light in an eerie halo. Like its close relative *S. careyana*, the thick leaves are green on top, red beneath. *S. ferruginea* (Coast Saxifrage) is similar in appearance, growing in mossy spots and along streams in the western mountains north to Alaska. Individual rosettes are elegant but short-lived, though they produce bulbils among the flowers that fall and root quickly to perpetuate the colony.

Saxifraga oregana
(Bog Saxifrage, Oregon Saxifrage)

ZONES: 5–8; sun to light shade
SOIL: moist to wet
NATIVE TO: swamps and bogs, wet meadows and streambanks; Montana to Alberta and Washington south to California, Nevada, and Colorado
SIZE: 1–3 feet (12 inches)
COLOR: white; **BLOOMS** in early summer

A very robust, fleshy plant with densely flowered, short-branched spikes that can grow 3 feet or more from 6–12-inch rosettes. The leaves are paddle-shaped and either lightly toothed or entire. With good culture and moisture, this plant can become immense. *S. pensylvanica* (Swamp Saxifrage) is the eastern form of this species and nearly identical in height and spread. It grows in similar habitats from Maine to Minnesota south to Missouri and Virginia.

Scutellaria serrata

Scutellaria
(scoot-el-LAIR-ee-ah)
Lamiaceae
Skullcap

I have to respect the power of association. For years I was mildly repulsed by the skullcaps, simply because I associated the name with some skull and crossbones apocalypse, imagining their tissues laced with an odorless poison ready to strike me down for some casual insult. Let the truth be told, the name refers to an intricate protruberance of the calyx that protects the developing seeds. It is a hollow, convex structure that looks a bit like a silk skull cap or yarmulke worn for religious occasions. The cap cracks open like one of those oval rubber coin purses popular in the seventies that you squeeze to access your fortune. Skullcaps are lovely plants in the Mint family with tubular, violet, pink, or white flowers that have a flared lower lip and a hooded, protruding upper one. Mad-dog Skullcap (*S. lateriflora*) was once touted as a remedy for people bitten by drooling mad dogs, but its main effect is as a restorative and nerve tonic, with a mild sedative and calming action used to treat insomnia, anxiety, and depression. This is the primary medicinal species in use today. Many in the genus are vigorously spreading and can become weedy, but I have chosen a few as well that are clumping plants of exceptional beauty. *S. serrata* is especially fine, with opposite, oval, serrated leaves with the teeth dipped in burgundy, a refined, bushy habit, and large blue-violet flowers that bloom in early summer (typically a dull time in the shade garden).

CULTURE: Easily transplanted in spring or fall and adaptable to many soil types. The plants look a little ragged after flowering, but if you snip off the spent seed heads, everything will be right again. There is a tiny leaf roller moth that feeds on *Scutellaria*, and it can cause considerable though temporary disfigurement of the foliage. The adults are only ¼ inch wide, but they are intricately colored in brown and white, with hints of red and blue.

USES: Borders, meadows, woodland.

PROPAGATION: Easy from seed; moderately difficult from cuttings. See p. 261.

Scutellaria incana
(Downy Skullcap)

ZONES: 3–9; sun to light shade
SOIL: moist to dry
NATIVE TO: upland woods; New York to Wisconsin south to Kansas and Georgia
SIZE: 2–3 feet (12–16 inches)
COLOR: violet-blue; **BLOOMS** in mid- to late summer

One of the showiest species in flower, with branched spikes from the upper nodes. This is a lanky, clumping plant that blooms later than most of the others listed here.

Scutellaria integrifolia
(Hyssop Skullcap)

ZONES: 4–9; sun
SOIL: moist to dry, well drained
NATIVE TO: sandy soils, mostly along the Atlantic coastal plain; Massachusetts to Florida and Texas, also inland to Ohio and Tennessee
SIZE: 16–20 inches (8–12 inches)
COLOR: violet-blue, rarely pink; **BLOOMS** in midsummer

This species can become a bit weedy, but the flowers are very lovely and useful in a poor, sandy soil. The plants have small oval to lance-shaped leaves of a dusty gray-green and long unbranched spikes. In my experience, this plant has been annual or biennial, though I see no reference to that in the literature. It will self-sow abundantly.

Scutellaria lateriflora
(Mad-dog Skullcap)

ZONES: 3–9; sun, part sun
SOIL: moist to wet
NATIVE TO: rich bottomlands and low meadows; Newfoundland to British Columbia south to California and Georgia
SIZE: 1–2 feet (2 feet)
COLOR: violet to lavender; **BLOOMS** in late summer

An important species for herbalists, but it is a spreading, rank grower in the garden. The quilted, toothed foliage looks much like spearmint but lacks a strong fragrance. Best suited for naturalizing.

Scutellaria ovata
(Heart-leaved Skullcap)

ZONES: 4–9; sun to light shade
SOIL: moist to dry
NATIVE TO: open woods and sandy soils; Maryland to Kansas south to northern Mexico, Texas, and Tennessee
SIZE: 6–18 inches (16 inches)
COLOR: violet-blue; **BLOOMS** in early summer

S. ovata is another of the stoloniferous species that needs to be sited with caution, but the felted leaves and branching flower spikes are attractive. Drought- and shade-tolerant.

Scutellaria resinosa
(Resinous Skullcap, Shrubby Skullcap)

ZONES: 4–9; sun
SOIL: well drained
NATIVE TO: dry short-grass prairies on rocky or sandy soils; Kansas to Colorado, south to Arizona and Texas
SIZE: 4–10 inches (8–12 inches)
COLOR: violet-blue; **BLOOMS** from late spring to early summer

A charming little plant, very unlike the others here, but representing a type of dryland, subshrubby *Scutellaria* found in the West and Southwest into Mexico. They have a woody base giving rise to many short stems clothed in very small, thick, oval leaves covered in warty glands that give the plants a grayish cast. The small flowers bloom for a long period in early summer. It needs a well-drained soil, full sun, and some summer drought to thrive.

Scutellaria serrata
(Allegheny Skullcap, Showy Skullcap)

ZONES: 4–9; sun to shade
SOIL: moist to dry
NATIVE TO: mountain woods; Pennsylvania and Ohio south to Tennessee and North Carolina

SIZE: 14–20 inches (16–18 inches)

COLOR: violet-blue; BLOOMS in early summer

As I have already liberally indicated, this is one of my favorites. It has a neat, clumping habit, rock solid constitution, and is just lovely blooming in light shade.

Sedum spathulifolium

Sedum (SEE-dum)
Crassulaceae
Stonecrop

Sedum spathulifolium. *Broad-leaf Stonecrop exemplifies all that is great about this genus. Its tight whorls of fat blue-green leaves emerge dusted with a chalky bloom that wears away to reveal crimson highlights masked underneath.*

If only all plants were as easy to grow as *Sedum*s, then gardens would clothe the suburbs in unbroken chains of color and life. They pack considerable water reserves in their succulent, spongy leaves, which not only helps them in times of drought, but also makes them exceptionally easy to root from cuttings broken off the plants in summer and stuck anywhere you want a new plant to grow. Some of the small creeping species can even be crumbled up and cast about like seeds. They will sprout up quickly as a thick ground cover—what a heady feeling that can be for the underconfident gardener. There are several thick-crowned, clumping *Sedum*s in our flora, and a number of the low, creeping types that fill in spaces between larger plants or crevices in rocks or cliffs. They all produce broccoli-shaped or flat-spreading flower heads with upward-facing, starry-crystalline blooms that must be tireless nectar producers, for the flowers are covered with satisfied insects. They seem especially attractive to hoverflies, whose larvae are important aphid predators in the garden. Many of the creeping types are evergreen or semievergreen, with leaves of many shapes, sizes, and colors. They make adaptable low ground covers for the rock garden, ledge, or between paving stones.

CULTURE: As you may have gathered, *Sedum*s are easily grown in a well-drained soil in sun or light shade (depending on the species). You can lightly shear the creeping species back after flowering or admire the architectural dried stalks. Many go into a semidormancy in the heat of summer and rebound in the fall.

USES: Ground cover, rock gardens, massing, borders (depending on species).

WILDLIFE: Superb nectar plants.

PROPAGATION: Fairly easy from seed; easy from cuttings and division. See p. 261.

Sedum divergens

(Cascade Stonecrop, Spreading Stonecrop)

ZONES: 5–8; sun, part sun

SOIL: well drained

NATIVE TO: talus slopes and alpine ridges in the Casacade and Olympic Mountains; southwest British Columbia to Oregon

SIZE: 2–6 inches (8–12 inches)

COLOR: yellow; BLOOMS in early summer

A low, dark green plant with tiny, rounded cylindrical leaves that makes an attractive, spreading mat in the rock garden.

Sedum lanceolatum

(Lance-leaved Stonecrop)

ZONES: 4–9; sun

SOIL: well drained

NATIVE TO: shallow rocky soils and ledges; South Dakota to British Columbia and Alaska south to California and New Mexico

SIZE: 2–8 inches (8–12 inches)

COLOR: yellow; BLOOMS in summer

A vigorous creeper with fleshy little needlelike leaves tightly clustered on sterile shoots and more spread out on flowering ones. The flowers are borne in loose, rounded heads.

Sedum nevii

(Nevy's Sedum)

ZONES: 5–9; sun to light shade

SOIL: well drained, limestone

NATIVE TO: limestone or shale outcrops in the southern Appalachians; Virginia to West Virginia south to Alabama

SIZE: 2–6 inches (6–8 inches)

COLOR: white; BLOOMS in early summer

A rare, elegant species that forms low, creeping clumps of congested, spoon-shaped leaves that are dusky warm gray in color. Although restricted primarily to limestone, it has not proved to be too fussy about soil and has grown easily in our partially shaded rock garden. *S. glaucophyllum* (Cliff Stonecrop) is a very similar plant of a looser habit. It, too, is native to the southern Appalachians.

Sedum pulchellum
(Rock Moss, Widow's Cross)

ZONES: 5–9; sun to light shade
SOIL: moist, well drained
NATIVE TO: moist, rocky places and cliffs; Kentucky to Missouri and Oklahoma south to Texas and Tennessee
SIZE: 6–12 inches (6 inches)
COLOR: pale to dark violet or purple; BLOOMS in late spring

This is a biennial or short-lived perennial, but it is one of the best for flower effect, so worth trying to establish in the rock garden. The thin leaves are up to 1 inch long and clothe the stems like needles on a fir branch. The flowers are held in star-shaped, perfectly horizontal branching inflorescences above the leaves.

Sedum rosea
(Roseroot)

ZONES: 2–7; sun, part sun
SOIL: well drained
NATIVE TO: rocky mountainous areas, seepage cliffs, alpine meadows; along the coast from Greenland to Maine (var. *rosea*) and in the western mountains (var. *integrifolium*) from Manitoba to Alaska south to California and New Mexico
SIZE: 6–10 inches (6–8 inches)
COLOR: yellow to dark red; BLOOMS in spring

Roseroot is an unusual plant that is honestly more of a curiosity than a prized ornamental. It is dioecious, with flowers in tight, ball-shaped heads at the tips of stocky, leaf-covered stems. (Their shape reminds me of a miniature *Banksia* bloom.) The foliage gets gradually larger up the stems, which grow from a thick woody caudex and go quickly dormant after blooming. The eastern var. *rosea* grows on sea cliffs and has yellow flowers. Var. *integrifolium* is a common sight in the mountainous West, with flowers typically dark red.

Sedum spathulifolium
(Broad-leaf Stonecrop)

ZONES: 5–8; sun, part sun
SOIL: well drained
NATIVE TO: rocky cliffs and ledges; coastal from California to British Columbia and in the mountains of Oregon and Washington
SIZE: 1–5 inches (6 inches)
COLOR: yellow; BLOOMS in late spring

A lovely species that forms thick rosettes of flattened, paddle-shaped leaves that are blue-gray and burgundy with a white, waxy overlay. It grows in fall and spring and rests in summer, corresponding to the rainfall patterns in its native haunts.

Sedum telephioides
(Wild Live-forever)

ZONES: 4–9; sun, part sun
SOIL: moist, well drained
NATIVE TO: rocky outcrops and openings in the southern Appalachians; West Virginia to Tennessee, also in Indiana and Illinois
SIZE: 8–16 inches (8–12 inches)
COLOR: pale pink; BLOOMS from late summer to fall

A clumping, woody-crowned species that closely resembles the Asian *S. spectabile* (Everlasting) often cultivated in gardens. It forms fleshy clumps of upright to scandent stems with broad, paddle-shaped leaves with wavy margins and broccoli-like flower heads late in the season.

Sedum ternatum
(Wild Stonecrop)

ZONES: 4–9; sun to shade
SOIL: moist, well drained
NATIVE TO: ledges, mossy rocks, woods; New Jersey to Iowa south to Arkansas and Georgia
SIZE: 4–8 inches (8–12 inches)
COLOR: white; BLOOMS in late spring

Wild Stonecrop has 3-branched, horizontal inflorescences above sprawling, medium green, rounded leaves. The foliage grows in whorls of 3 with long internodes that shorten toward the tip. It is an adaptable, shade-tolerant species that I have seen growing everywhere from mossy boulders in the middle of a stream to rather dry limestone cliffs. The plants are best in partial sun but will bleach if it is too intense.

Sedum ternatum. Wild Stonecrop is one of the most shade-tolerant native sedums, though understandably, growth and flowering will be more prolific with some sun.

(**LEFT**): Senna hebecarpa. *The flowers of Northern Wild Senna bear little resemblance to lupines or False Indigo, but they are all members of the same family. A few pods are beginning to form in this photograph, and each will develop the constricted shape (like an overripe green bean) that helps distinguish it from its close relative.*

(**RIGHT**): Shortia galacifolia. *Rising like magnificent, ragged skirts from the sullen debris of winter, emerging Oconee Bells herald the return of spring.*

Senna hebecarpa

Senna (Cassia) hebecarpa (SEN-ah)
Fabaceae
Northern Wild Senna

ZONES: 3–9; sun, part shade
SOIL: moist to moderately dry
NATIVE TO: moist bottomlands, meadows and roadsides; Massachusetts and New Hampshire to Wisconsin south to Tennessee and North Carolina
SIZE: 3–7 feet (4–6 feet)
COLOR: yellow; **BLOOMS** in summer

The wild sennas surpass even *Hibiscus* in the rapidity with which they spring up each year like towering exclamations to the power of life. If you can close your eyes and imagine a cluster of massive, 7-foot stump-sprouts from a Honey Locust tree (*Gleditsia triacanthos*) with large golden flowers clothing the last foot or two, you have come pretty close to visualizing these imposing perennials in bloom. They have pinnate leaves like many in the Pea family, and the central stem or rachis of each leaf is lighter in color and held perpendicular to the main stem, which gives the plants a distinctively tiered yet vertical effect in the garden. The flowers grow in clusters from the axils of the upper leaves. They are 5-petaled and regular, not pea-shaped in design. Long thin bean pods follow the flowers and are also ornamental, but their weight tends to cause the tall plants to bend after heavy rains.

S. marilandica (Southern Wild Senna) is nearly identical, differing in its wider, unconstricted pods, fewer flowers, and a more southerly range.

CULTURE: These are dramatic plants, valuable for vertical effect in larger gardens. They grow naturally in fairly damp, fertile soils, and this explains their prodigious growth. In a drier soil, the plants top out around 3 feet and tend to be less floppy and unkempt overall. Cutting off the spent flowers will help keep taller specimens from leaning over. It is difficult to move or divide an established plant, so site them carefully.

USES: Screening, large borders.

PROPAGATION: Fairly easy from seed. See p. 261.

Shortia galacifolia

Shortia galacifolia
(SHORT-ee-ah)
Diapensiaceae
Oconee Bells

ZONES: 4–8; shade
SOIL: moist, acid
NATIVE TO: damp, acid soils and banks; Appalachian Mountains of North and South Carolina
SIZE: 4–8 inches (12 inches)
COLOR: white occasionally flushed pink or blue; **BLOOMS** in early spring

Oconee Bells is related to *Galax*, and the only other members of the genus are in temperate Asia. They grow from creeping rhizomes that produce one yearly flush of rounded, glossy green leaves with strong veins and a burgundy overlay, eventually forming low ruffled mounds in moist dappled shade. The lustrous evergreen leaves are reason enough to grow the plant, so the exquisite flowers seem almost a bonus. They peek out of the previous season's foliage on individual stems two weeks before the new leaves appear. The 1-inch blooms are bell-shaped but widely flaring, with raggedly cut edges and a soft yellow center. *Shortia* has a certain calm self-confidence, as if aware of its beauty with no need to boast.

I was aware of the imposing botanical and horticultural mythology that surrounds Oconee Bells long before I had the pleasure of making its acquaintance. Often called the Queen of the Eastern Woodlands by those who prefer monarchy over democracy, *Shortia* is a rare, beguiling jewel driven nearly to extinction by past glaciation and restrictive germination requirements that severely limit its natural range to a few watersheds in the Appalachian Mountains along the North and South Carolina border. There is a well-known story of its discovery by André Michaux, a French plant explorer who tramped those wild mountains in the late 1700s. The dried specimens that he sent to France lay unnamed and unloved for 50 years until the noted American botanist Asa Gray found them and described the plant in a Paris herbarium. The field notes on the herbarium specimen were vague, as the area was then poorly charted, and despite thorough searching by Gray and others, it was another 40 years before the plants were rediscovered in the wild by an herb collector at the headwaters of the Catawba River.

Lincoln Foster speculates that the plants were once much more common throughout eastern woodlands, but were driven south to the unglaciated areas of the southern Appalachians during the recent Ice Age.[9] The fine seeds dry out quickly and, except for short river travel, have a hard time dispersing beyond their present limited range. Oconee Bells will probably always have a rarified air about it, but the plants are such genuine treasures in the garden that I try to disperse them as widely as I can, as I hope you will do too.

CULTURE: *Shortia* grows in damp, peaty soils amid rhododendrons along the banks of rivers and demands an acid humus and light shade for best growth. They are not foolproof in the garden, but with a little care in siting and maintenance, they are very long-lived and improve each year. A mulch of crushed oak leaves or pine needles worked down around the plants in spring will help the new growth to root and keep the soil sour. The roots are at first thin and fine like in the Ericaceae, and they are prone to damage by drought and overfertilization. Eventually, deeper, woody roots will grow from the center of the plant, but it is important to site the plants in a place where they will not dry excessively. They are very cold-hardy, but suffer in excessive heat and drought. Set out well-rooted container plants in spring. Like *Galax,* they are happiest in larger drifts as they compete better with their own kind.

USES: Specimen, massing, evergreen ground cover for shade.

PROPAGATION: Difficult from seed; moderately difficult from cuttings and division. See p. 262.

Silene virginica

Silene (sigh-LEE-nee)
Caryophyllaceae
Catchfly, Wild Pinks, Campion

Silene is a large genus related to *Dianthus* (carnations) and many of them are coarse, small-flowered plants of a weedy and unreputable character that proper citizens like myself do our very best to ignore. We have a number of naturalized species from Europe that were introduced as agricultural weeds and ornamentals, and these have joined our indigenous, ragtag menagerie in fields, roadsides, and other neglected corners of our post-industrial landscape. All is not grim among the catchflys, though, as a few striking, richly colored natives offer a chance for horticultural redemption. (I am tempted to insert a bad joke here about carnations and a breakfast of campions.)

*Silene*s have opposite leaves and 5-petaled flowers enclosed at their base by an inflated skirt formed by the united sepals. The naturalized weed, *S. vulgaris* (Bladder Campion), takes this to an extreme, forming a large pouch that looks like a pair of puffy cheeks stubbornly trying to inflate the flower from below.

The following are the most ornamental species, and generally they are adaptable plants. These catchflys are all drought-tolerant and self-sow moderately where it suits them. The genus has a reputation for being short-lived, but Fire Pink is the only one of this group that can be fleeting in the garden. It is technically perennial, but it blooms so heavily, burning its candle from both ends if you will, that it depletes its reserves and is easily overcome by environmental stress.

CULTURE: Set out container plants in spring or move small self-sown seedlings that have not yet bloomed. It is best to leave the plants undisturbed

Silene virginica. *You will be doing Fire Pink a favor if you remove at least half of its spent flowers as soon as they fade. Less energy shunted toward seed production means it will have a better chance to form new crowns to survive the winter. Though the common name is probably a reference to the flaming red color of the blossoms, I have noticed that this species pops up frequently in recently cut and burned-over pine plantations.*

Silphium perfoliatum.
Cup Plant produces flowers on short stems from the axils of its uppermost leaves, perfect bouquets of yellow daisies stuck in a leafy vase. If you have room for such an imposing species, it makes a wonderful summertime screen. Sorry we don't have little Tommy in there for scale, but the plants pictured here are over 8 feet tall. On a biological note: Silphium *differs from most of the Aster family in that its ray—not* its disk *flowers—is fertile. This explains why you find seed in a ring around the outside of the inflorescence, not clustered in the middle.*

when established, for they have deep taproots that are easily damaged and difficult to divide.

USES: Rock gardens for the smaller plants, borders or meadows for the larger.

PROPAGATION: Easy from seed and cuttings. See p. 262.

Silene caroliniana
(Wild Pink)

ZONES: 4–9; sun, part sun
SOIL: moist to dry
NATIVE TO: rocky, often calcareous woods and outcrops; Kentucky to Ohio south to Alabama
SIZE: 4–8 inches (8 inches)
COLOR: light to dark pink; **BLOOMS** in late spring
A charming, long-lived plant with a low mound of dark, semievergreen leaves that curl and nestle with each other and thin-stemmed spikes of delicate flowers resembling Creeping Phlox in size and aspect. The petals are triangular and narrowest toward the center. My favorite forms have flowers colored a deep, rosy pink. Though it is native to limestone areas, it has been doing fine in an acid soil for years at Garden in the Woods.

Silene regia
(Royal Catchfly)

ZONES: 4–9; sun to light shade
SOIL: moist to dry
NATIVE TO: prairies and openings; Ohio to Missouri south to Alabama and Georgia
SIZE: 2–5 feet (16–18 inches)
COLOR: crimson; **BLOOMS** in summer
Admittedly, Royal Catchfly is a bit awkward out of flower, with stiff, lanky stems and large blue-green leaves that have the unfortunate habit of shriveling up prematurely along the lower half. The vibrant, thin-petaled crimson flowers all but forgive these eccentricities, and it is certainly worth a place in the meadow where companions will hide its bare legs. *S. laciniata* (Mexican Campion) is a close relative from the Southwest with a similar habit and flower.

Silene stellata
(Starry Campion, Widow's Frill)

ZONES: 4–9; sun to light shade
SOIL: moist to dry
NATIVE TO: moist to dry woods; Connecticut to North Dakota south to Texas and Georgia
SIZE: 1–2 feet (8 inches)
COLOR: white; **BLOOMS** in summer
Starry Campion produces intricate nodding flowers cut like a fine paper snowflake that is set in an inflated, lime green calyx. In habit, it is taller than it is wide, with flat, lance-shaped leaves progressively smaller up the stem and thin spikes that bloom

sequentially over several weeks. It is a rugged, undemanding and drought-tolerant plant that will casually naturalize along paths in the woods.

Silene virginica
(Fire Pink)

ZONES: 4–9; sun, part shade
SOIL: moist, well drained
NATIVE TO: outcrops, banks, and open woodland; New Jersey to Ontario and Michigan south to Oklahoma and Georgia
SIZE: 8–14 inches (12 inches)
COLOR: scarlet to crimson; **BLOOMS** in summer
Fire Pink is a wonderful plant for rock gardens and sandy banks. The dark green resinous, narrowly lace-shaped leaves form in dense low clumps that send out wiry stems of starry crimson flowers in rounded bouquets. The plants self-sow pretty well if a hummingbird or bee happens by to pollinate the blooms.

Silphium perfoliatum

Silphium (SILL-fee-um)
Asteraceae
Rosin Weed

In my overactive imagination, I can see *Silphium*s joining perennial sunflowers and the taller *Rudbeckia*s to form an unbeatable professional basketball team called the Big Yellow Daisies . . . oh if only they had legs, arms, and a central nervous system. Rosin weeds can be towering plants, with big bold foliage and large yellow-centered sunflowers held high in the air along the upper stems. Many are fire-adapted and all are long-lived, with amazing taproots that can travel down 20 feet or more searching for water. (*Silphium*s can also resprout from a broken root, so they are not easy to eliminate once established.) The flowers have many thin ray petals, which gives them a hula skirt texture. The disks of *Silphium*s are not as large and long-blooming as those of black-eyed Susan, but new flowers appear sequentially for two to three weeks.

CULTURE: Transplant as small container plants or first-year seedlings and give them a year or two to establish. The species listed here are best in a fertile, moist soil but will take drought once established. They are very difficult to divide once mature, though whole plants can be dug and moved.

USES: Borders, meadows, screening.

WILDLIFE: The seeds are a favorite of goldfinches.

PROPAGATION: Slow but easy from seed. See p. 262.

Silphium lacinatum
(Compass Plant)

ZONES: 3–9; sun
SOIL: moist to dry
NATIVE TO: prairies or abandoned agricultural land; Ohio to Minnesota south to Oklahoma and Alabama
SIZE: 3–8 feet (3–4 feet)
COLOR: yellow; **BLOOMS** in summer

A strongly vertical plant with large basal leaves that are beautifully cut and lobed and which orient themselves in a north-south direction. The cauline leaves are also cut, but reduced in size, and fine-petaled, 4-inch sunflowers grow on short branches out of the axils of the upper leaves. There is a dynamic presence to this species, a subtle interplay of broad strokes and delicate flourishes.

Silphium perfoliatum
(Cup Plant)

ZONES: 3–9; sun, part sun
SOIL: moist to dry
NATIVE TO: moist low ground; Ontario to South Dakota south to Louisiana and Georgia
SIZE: 3–8 feet (4–5 feet)
COLOR: yellow; **BLOOMS** in summer

Cup Plant is absolutely imposing when mature, forming broad clumps of ¾-inch-thick stems like sections of pipe that perforate the united leaves as you would spear paper with a stick. The cups formed by the leaves hold water for birds to wash down their meal of *Silphium* seeds—a happy accident of their curious design. The large flowers are borne proudly on 1-foot stems at the tops of the plants like a bouquet placed in a vase. Cup Plant needs room and will seed in if not deadheaded, but for a moist spot in the larger garden, it has an unmistakable vertical presence.

Silphium terebinthinaceum
(Prairie Dock)

ZONES: 3–9; sun
SOIL: moist to dry
NATIVE TO: prairies; Ontario to Minnesota south to Mississippi and Georgia
SIZE: 4–8 feet (3–4 feet)

COLOR: yellow; **BLOOMS** in late summer

This is a *Silphium* very unlike the others, with huge paddles for leaves that look like they have been pressed flat. The rough leaves are all basal, growing from a fat, thickened root on long petioles with blades 20 inches long and 10 inches wide. They look a bit alien in a fine-textured meadow, like they have been blown in by a storm from some forest giant in Central America. In summer, the plants send up soaring, naked stems for the flowers to hang on.

Silphium trifoliatum
(Rosin Weed, Whorled Rosin Weed)

ZONES: 3–9; sun, part sun
SOIL: moist to dry
NATIVE TO: woodland edge, prairies; southern Pennsylvania to Ohio and Indiana, south to Mississippi and Georgia
SIZE: 3–4 feet (2–3 feet)
COLOR: yellow; **BLOOMS** in midsummer

Whorled Rosin Weed sends up leafy stems with the foliage in sets of 2 to 4 to a node. The leaves are lance-shaped, 4 inches long, and rough hairy like most in the tribe. Because of its smaller stature, it is easier to accommodate, but I think it lacks the presence of the others mentioned here. Close in garden effect are *S. integrifolium* (Prairie Rosin Weed) with smooth, wider leaves in pairs and *S. asteriscus* (Southern Rosin Weed) with shaggy, alternate leaves.

Sisyrinchium angustifolium. *Flowers are delicate things. Most lack the waxy cuticle that surrounds leaves and helps prevent water loss. To slow transpiration, many flowers close up when their pollinators are not active. Blue-eyed Grass opens only in the sun, when bees and flies are likely to visit. Conversely, many evening primroses (Oenothera spp.) open only after dusk, when moths are active.*

Sisyrinchium angustifolium

Sisyrinchium (siss-sea-RINCH-ee-um)
Iridaceae
Blue-eyed Grass

have always loved the little blue-eyed grasses, but I am baffled when I try to tell them apart. If you place a few side by side, sure there are differences, but you need a hand lens to make accurate pronouncements, so really, who cares. There are at least one or two that grow in your own neck of the woods, prairie, or mountain, and they will not be embarrassed if we don't know their names. *Sisyrinchium*s are small relatives of iris and have similar, ribbonlike leaves in overlapping fans that grow by the dozen from a miniscule rhizome. The flowers worship the sun, remaining tightly closed until warmed by its rays, so you now have an excuse to call in sick on a glorious spring day ("I [*cough cough*] need to see the . . . *Sisyrinchium* . . . [*sniffle*]"—your boss will be concerned and sympathetic, I'm sure). The little blue or purple flowers squeeze out of slits in the stem like Kangaroo babies with their heads out of the pouch. Typically, the sepals are wider than the petals, giving them a thin-fat, thin-fat appearance that is very distinctive. The color tends to pool and intensify in the throat, then change abruptly to orange or yellow deep inside. The flowers give way to large rounded pods that dangle ponderously from the slits on inadequate stems. If the plants did not set seed, they might bloom continuously. As it is, they enter a much-needed rest after the pods have ripened but often rebound and rebloom sporadically late in the summer if conditions are right. The thin, grassy foliage is nice in itself, and it will usually continue to grow and look good through the summer and fall. Seedlings are common around the base of adults, so even though some are short-lived, they are self-perpetuating, and with time thick stands will develop.

CULTURE: Sun and an average to well-drained soil are all that is necessary. Moderate fertility and moisture in summer will encourage repeat bloom, and the plants look perfect nestled among rocks or very low ground covers. I always try to encourage them to self-sow, as they will form thick turfs this way, but if this is unwanted, give them a light haircut after blooming. I have tried growing some of the lovely far western species as well as those from southern South America (these are popular in Europe), but all are killed by damp winter cold. Several hybrids utilizing large-flowered, tender species crossed with hardier northerners can be successful, and because these are sometimes sterile, they bloom continuously.

USES: Rock gardens, low meadows, ground cover.

PROPAGATION: Easy from seed or division. See p. 262.

Sisyrinchium angustifolium
(Stout Blue-eyed Grass, Common Blue-eyed Grass)

ZONES: 3–9; sun, part sun
SOIL: moist
NATIVE TO: damp meadows, grassy openings; Newfoundland to Minnesota south to Texas and Florida

SIZE: 10–20 inches (6–8 inches)
COLOR: blue; BLOOMS from late spring to early summer
A widespread, robust eastern species with relatively broad leaves and small true blue flowers. Related species like *S. mucronatum* (Slender Blue-eyed Grass), *S. fuscatum* (Sand Blue-eyed Grass), and *S. montanum* (Mountain Blue-eyed Grass) are all thinner plants with flowers leaning toward violet.

Sisyrinchium bellum
(California Blue-eyed Grass, Western Blue-eyed Grass)

ZONES: 6–8; sun, part shade
SOIL: moist
NATIVE TO: moist meadows from the coast into the mountains; California to Oregon
SIZE: 8–16 inches (6–8 inches)
COLOR: blue to violet and lilac, occasionally white; BLOOMS from spring to early summer
S. bellum is a species complex in which *S. idahoense* is sometimes included. Some plants of *S. bellum* I have seen are very similar to those of *S. idahoense*, with glaucous leaves and large flowers, but there is a great range to the flower color and size of the plants. Although not extremely cold-hardy, it is one of the most ornamental species in our flora.

Sisyrinchium californicum
(Golden-eyed Grass)

ZONES: 7–9; sun, part sun
SOIL: moist to wet
NATIVE TO: moist grasslands and marshes near the coast; Northern California to southwest British Columbia
SIZE: 8–20 inches (6–8 inches)
COLOR: bright yellow; BLOOMS from late spring to early summer
I include this lovely species, even though it is fairly tender, as it is the only North American species with bright yellow flowers. The leaves are also very broad, and because of this the plants look much like a small iris when not in bloom.

Sisyrinchium capillare
(Slender Blue-eyed Grass)

ZONES: 6–9; sun, part sun
SOIL: moist, well drained
NATIVE TO: pine savannas along the coastal plain; Virginia to Florida
SIZE: 8–18 inches (4–6 inches)
COLOR: light blue-violet; BLOOMS from late spring to early summer
A delicate, thin-leaved plant with narrow leaves in little grassy tufts.

Sisyrinchium (Olnysium) douglasii
(Grass Widows, Purple-eyed Grass)

ZONES: 5–8; sun, part sun
SOIL: well drained
NATIVE TO: dry ridges and sagebrush scrub in the Sierras and Cascades; Northern California to British Columbia
SIZE: 6–12 inches (6 inches)
COLOR: blue through violet to lavender; BLOOMS in spring

An unusual and very pretty species that lacks the prominent wings on the flower stems that give most *Sisyrinchium*s a flattened look. The large flowers have petals and sepals about equal in size. It grows in areas with a pronounced summer dry season, so it blooms early then dies back completely to a tuberous rhizome. For this and other technical reasons, it has been segregated into its own genus, poor thing. It needs excellent drainage at all times.

Sisyrinchium elmeri
(Orange-eyed Grass)

ZONES: 6–8; sun, part sun
SOIL: moist
NATIVE TO: boggy areas in the Sierra and San Bernardino Mountains (4,000–8,500 feet); California
SIZE: 3–6 inches (4–6 inches)
COLOR: tan and orange with darker veins; BLOOMS in summer

A very small, tufted plant with wide blades for its size. *S. elmeri* is the longest-blooming species I have grown, but appears to be an annual (whether this is a hardiness problem I do not know). A cute little thing with tannish orange flowers, it reseeds abundantly.

Sisyrinchium idahoense
(Idaho Blue-eyed Grass)

ZONES: 4–8; sun, part shade
SOIL: moist
NATIVE TO: wet mountain meadows (4,500–10,800 feet); California to Washington and Idaho
SIZE: 4–16 inches (6–8 inches)
COLOR: violet; BLOOMS from late spring to early summer

Possibly the best all-around garden species, with large flowers, beautiful glaucous blue foliage that is fairly stiff and broad, and good cold hardiness. Plants in the trade are often mislabeled *S. bermudanum*, a tender, subtropical species.

Smilacina racemosa

Smilacina
(smile-ah-SEE-nah)
Liliaceae
False Solomon's Seal

Smilacina racemosa. *False Solomon's Seal fruits undergo a kaleidoscopic transformation as they ripen. After the ivory flowers fade, green fruits begin to swell and take their place. By midsummer, red marbling develops over the green background (the stage pictured here), and then eventually the green turns to an iridescent silvery white, still with an irregular overlay of red. Next, marbling gives way to a rich crimson that appears first as if through frosted glass. Finally, even the iridescence fades—a signal that the glowing red fruits are ripe and ready.*

Three species of false Solomon's seal grow in North America, finding a home almost anywhere there is a stretch of damp woodland or bog. *S. racemosa* is the largest and most widespread, with 10–20 wide, deeply veined, sessile leaves alternating on arching stems that terminate in cottony, off-white panicles of tiny blooms. The plants spread on thick rhizomes to form large patches with time, all the stems leaning the same way toward the light. Star Flower (*S. stellata*) is smaller in all respects, with narrower leaves and a slender raceme of starry white flowers. It too is a spreading plant, with individual stems well spaced from each other as they rise from the ground. The final plant, *S. trifolia*, looks more like a robust Canada Mayflower (and as I mentioned under *Maianthemum*, most taxonomists now lump *Smilacina* into this genus). It is a resident of damp woods and bogs and is rarely grown.

The *Smilacina*s, especially *S. racemosa*, are easy, handsome plants for the shade garden. Their traveling tendencies are not so strong as to make them invasive, and the arching stems have the same rhythmic quality found in the true Solomon's seal. They also produce some of the most interesting berries you are likely to find in the autumn woodland. False Solomon's seal has grapelike clusters that start off green then turn pearly white with irregular red speckles and finally all red when fully ripe. Star Flower has fewer berries, but they are as big as marbles, maturing from green to a shiny gold-green with a fanciful burgundy cross that divides the fruit into sections like a beach ball, and then to a uniform dark red. *S. trifolia* is much like Canada Mayflower in fruit as well, with small dark red berries.

CULTURE: Move as container plants in spring or bare-root divisions in fall to a moist, acid spot in shade or partial sun. (They will grow in nearly full sun as well but look bleached and tattered.) False Solomon's seals are trouble-free and adaptable plants excellent for naturalizing along woodland edge or massed in the shade garden. They are not hard to dig and divide in the fall (after the fruit has ripened) if their spread needs to be checked. The larger two are fairly drough- tolerant as well.

USES: Massing in the woodland or shade garden.

PROPAGATION: Slow and moderately difficult from seed; easy from division. See p. 262.

Smilacina racemosa

(False Solomon's Seal, False Spiknard, Treacleberry)

ZONES: 3–8; part sun, shade
SOIL: moist
NATIVE TO: moist woods; Nova Scotia to British Columbia south to California and New Jersey and in the mountains to Arizona and Georgia

Smilacina stellata. *Although Star-flowered Solomon's Seal flowers are not large or extremely showy, they release a strong, deliciously sweet perfume. It is not to be outdone by its larger cousin in fruit, either. Its berry's journey from green to burgundy and gold and finally red is one of my favorite little autumn dramas.*

SIZE: 1–3 feet (3–4 feet)
COLOR: creamy white; **BLOOMS** in spring

The western phase is more robust than the eastern, so it is sometimes segregated as *S. racemosa* ssp. *amplexicaulis* (Fat Solomon). The fragrant flowers of this species are very ornamental and a good nectar source for bumblebees, and I like the pleated look of the leaves.

Smilacina stellata

(Star-flowered Solomon's Seal, Star Flower)

ZONES: 3–8; sun to shade
SOIL: moist
NATIVE TO: moist, well-drained soils in woods and prairies and meadows; Newfoundland to British Columbia south to California and New Jersey and in the mountains to Arizona and Georgia
SIZE: 1–3 feet (2 feet)
COLOR: white; **BLOOMS** in spring

The spreading, open habit of this plant is harder to accommodate in gardens, but the fruit is very ornamental. Like False Solomon's Seal, the western form of the plant is much more robust, fully twice as tall as its eastern counterpart when well grown. The flowers have a sweet, Easter Lily fragrance, and the leaves are smooth, not pleated (more like a true Solomon's seal in appearance).

Smilacina trifolia

(Three-leaved False Solomon's Seal)

ZONES: 2–7; shade
SOIL: moist to wet
NATIVE TO: boggy ground and low woods; Newfoundland to the Northwest Territories south to British Columbia, Ohio, and New Jersey
SIZE: 4–14 inches (1–2 feet)
COLOR: white; **BLOOMS** in spring

A dainty plant that is not as ornamental as the others, but worth considering in naturalized settings. It has long, running rhizomes.

Solidago nemoralis

Solidago (sol-eh-DAY-go)
Asteraceae
Goldenrod

Convincing gardeners to grow goldenrods is a bit like trying to sell Toyotas in Detroit, but I will continue anyway. They are certainly ubiquitous in the fall landscape and are still wrongly accused of causing hayfever. Therefore, it bears repeating that goldenrods, like aster, Joe-Pye, ironweeds, and all the Composites, are insect-pollinated, so their pollen is heavy and sticky in order to facilitate transfer by our six-legged friends. It is the wind-pollinated plants like the grasses, ragweed, and many trees (I am allergic to the maples, for example) that produce the great quantities of light, airborne pollen that get into our noses and throats and cause the immune reaction known as hayfever. There are goldenrods for every situation, and if you avoid the aggressively weedy species like *S. canadensis* (my apologies to Canada) and *S. graminifolia*, they are agreeable garden subjects at home in the border, meadow, rock, or shade garden. Once I started to learn the different species, I became more and more aware of their subtle differences and convinced of their important role in native ecosystems as soil stabilizers and sources of food and shelter for wildlife. They are beautiful in leaf and flower, too, and no wildflower garden is compete without a few of our hundred or so species scattered around.

The Latin name is a combination of *solidus* and *ago*, meaning "I make whole," a reference to its long history as an herbal remedy. Goldenrod has antioxidant, diuretic, and astringent and antifungal properties and is said to be especially useful for treating urinary tract and yeast infections, as well as sore throats and diarrhea.

Goldenrods grow from clumping or spreading rhizomes ending in winter rosettes that bear tall, leafy stems crowned with tightly packed spikes, panicles, or cymes of little daisies. A famous German landscape architect once told me of an orange-flowered goldenrod he had seen in Europe, but after years of hopeful searching, I have concluded that there was something lost in the translation. All goldenrods except *S. bicolor* have flowers in the yellow to gold range (I suppose this comes as no surprise) that mix well with the purples and blues of their fall-blooming companions.

CULTURE: Extremely easy to grow in a range of conditions. I have listed plants from a variety of habitats so you can choose one to fit your specific situation. They can be divided in spring or early summer and establish easily from containers. Planting from midsummer on is more difficult, as the plants are weaker from flowering and may not root in well for the winter without careful attention to watering. They do suffer occasionally from rusts; badly infected plants should be removed.

USES: Borders, meadow, butterfly gardens.

PROPAGATION: Easy from seed or cuttings. See p. 262.

Solidago bicolor

(Silver-rod)

ZONES: 3–9; sun to light shade
SOIL: moist to dry
NATIVE TO: dry woods and openings; Nova Scotia to Wisconsin south to Louisiana and Georgia
SIZE: 2–3 feet (2 feet)
COLOR: silvery white; **BLOOMS** in fall

This is a rugged, drought-tolerant plant with tall narrow wands of white flowers. Not particularly showy, but I include it for comparison.

Solidago caesia

(Blue-stemmed Goldenrod, Wreath Goldenrod)

ZONES: 3–9; sun to shade
SOIL: moist to dry
NATIVE TO: woods; Nova Scotia to Wisconsin south to Texas and Florida
SIZE: 16–50 inches (16–20 inches)
COLOR: golden yellow; **BLOOMS** in fall

Blue-stemmed Goldenrod is one of my favorites. It is a forest dweller looking its best at the woodland edge

Solidago nemoralis.
The neighbor next to my family's house on Cape Cod dutifully mows the impoverished, sandy soil by the street even though it is little more than some scurfy Purple Love Grass (Eragrostis spectabilis) *set among patches of Gray Goldenrod. These survivors hunker down and bide their time during this summertime rug making. It is not until September, when the mower has been drained and stowed for the year, that they burst into bloom — the Love Grass a misty cloud of plum surrounding the stiff little wands of Goldenrod — a lovely duet made sweeter by its perseverance.*

in dappled shade. The flowers bloom in 2 ranks on short spikes from the axils of the thin, lance-shaped leaves. The clumping stems have an arching habit like that of Solomon's seal. *S. curtisii* (Curtiss' Goldenrod) looks much the same but blooms two weeks later. It is found in the southern Appalachians.

Solidago flexicaulis

(Zigzag Goldenrod)

ZONES: 3–8; sun to shade
SOIL: moist to dry
NATIVE TO: woods; Nova Scotia to North Dakota south to Arkansas, and the Appalachians to Georgia
SIZE: 1–4 feet (2–3 feet)
COLOR: golden yellow; **BLOOMS** in fall

Another woodlander, with stems noticeably zigzag-ging from leaf to egg-shaped leaf. They are moderate spreaders, commonly about 2 feet tall, but the west-ern forms tend to be larger, tetraploid plants to 3–4 feet.

Solidago multiradiata

(Alpine Goldenrod)

ZONES: 2–7; sun, part sun
SOIL: moist, well drained
NATIVE TO: rocky slopes and dry meadows (7,000–12,000 feet); Labrador to Alaska south in the mountains to California and New Mexico
SIZE: 6–20 inches (12 inches)
COLOR: golden yellow; **BLOOMS** in summer

Alpine Goldenrod is a common high-mountain species in the West, producing low, leafy mats of pad-dle-shaped leaves and short rounded spikes early in the season. A neat rock garden plant that needs a dry summer rest and excellent drainage. The eastern

Solidago sempervirens. Semper virens is Latin for always green, a refer-ence to the tough, leath-ery rosettes that carry Seaside Goldenrod through the winter. This is misleading, though, as most Solidago species have leafy rosettes that persist through the cold months. Seaside Gold-enrod is one of the few plants that can survive in the wave-tossed dunes along the Atlantic coast, often growing vigorously in pure beach sand.

strains are easier to handle in the garden if you can locate a source that differentiates them.

Solidago nemoralis

(Gray Goldenrod)

ZONES: 3–9; sun, part sun
SOIL: dry, well drained
NATIVE TO: dry, typically sandy soils in meadows, dunes, and upland woods; Nova Scotia to Alberta south to Texas and Florida
SIZE: 1–2 feet (12 inches)
COLOR: golden yellow; **BLOOMS** in fall

Gray Goldenrod makes an attractive low ground cover of dusky silver-green paddle-shaped leaves and narrow, curved flower heads on short stems in fall. It thrives in the poorest of soils but can be short-lived if the site is too rich.

Solidago odora

(Sweet Goldenrod)

ZONES: 3–9; sun to light shade
SOIL: moist to dry
NATIVE TO: dry, sandy open woods and fields; New Hampshire to Ohio and Missouri south to Texas and Florida
SIZE: 2–5 feet (2 feet)
COLOR: golden yellow; **BLOOMS** in early fall

One of the earlier blooming fall species, with attrac-tive, thin glossy foliage and broad, flattened panicles. The anise-scented leaves were once popular in teas. It has a loosely clumping, neat habit and good drought tolerance.

Solidago rigida

(Stiff Goldenrod)

ZONES: 3–9; sun, part sun
SOIL: moist to dry
NATIVE TO: sandy soils, prairies and dry meadows; Massachusetts to Alberta south to New Mexico and Georgia
SIZE: 2–5 feet (2 feet)
COLOR: golden yellow; **BLOOMS** in fall

Stiff Goldenrod is one of the best species for foliage effect, with large leaves covered in gray downy hair. The basal leaves make it look more like one of the asters than a goldenrod. Flowers are in a flattened, balled panicle at the tips of the stems. The western phase of the species is smaller (1–2 feet) than the tetraploid, eastern one.

Solidago rugosa

(Rough-stemmed Goldenrod)

ZONES: 3–9; sun, part sun
SOIL: moist to dry

NATIVE TO: fields, meadows, prairies; Newfoundland to Michigan south to Texas and Florida
SIZE: 2–6 feet (3 feet)
COLOR: golden yellow; **BLOOMS** in fall

Rough-stemmed Goldenrod is one of the most common eastern grassland species. It typically colonizes old fields and roadsides in a range of moisture conditions. It is too aggressive and weedy for all but naturalizing, but I mention it because the cultivar 'Fireworks' is an excellent plant with none of the brutish qualities of the species. It has inflorescences that are long and thin, like the trails of fading fireworks.

Solidago sempervirens
(Seaside Goldenrod)

ZONES: 3–9; sun, part sun
SOIL: sandy, well drained
NATIVE TO: sandy soils and dunes along the coast; Nova Scotia south into Central America
SIZE: 2–4 feet (2 feet)
COLOR: golden yellow; **BLOOMS** in fall

Seaside Goldenrod is a very distinctive resident of the dunes, with thick fleshy leaves noticeably keeled down the midvein and thick flower heads with curling side branches. It needs a poor, sandy soil to keep its figure, as rich soils lead to rank, floppy growth.

Solidago speciosa
(Showy Goldenrod)

ZONES: 3–9; sun, part sun
SOIL: moist to dry
NATIVE TO: fields and prairies; New Hampshire to Wyoming south to New Mexico and Georgia
SIZE: 2–5 feet (2 feet)
COLOR: light yellow; **BLOOMS** in fall

One of a group of goldenrods with candlestick-shaped blooms. This is one of my favorites as well, with broad paddlelike leaves down low and oval ones above. They have a leathery, almost glaucous appearance. It blooms a bit later in fall, and at least in the strains I have grown, the flowers are a soft yellow. Showy Goldenrod is a wide-ranging species that has several morphological forms; the robust eastern phase is tetraploid.

Solidago sphacelata
(Short-pappus Goldenrod, False Goldenrod)

ZONES: 4–9; sun to light shade
SOIL: moist to dry
NATIVE TO: calcareous woodland and rocky pasture; Virginia to Illinois south to Kentucky, Alabama, and Georgia
SIZE: 2–4 feet (2–3 feet)
COLOR: golden yellow; **BLOOMS** in fall

This goldenrod is unique, forming a spreading ground cover of heart-shaped, bright green leaves that send up thin wands densely packed with flowers. The cultivar 'Golden Fleece' is a more compact form, rarely growing above 16 inches.

Spigelia marilandica

Spigelia marilandica (spy-GEEL-ee-ah)
Loganiaceae
Indian Pink, Pinkroot, Worm Grass

ZONES: 4–9; part sun, light shade
SOIL: moist
NATIVE TO: moist woods and coves; North Carolina to Indiana south to Texas and Florida
SIZE: 12–18 inches (12–16 inches)
COLOR: crimson with light yellow interior; **BLOOMS** in summer

Indian Pink is one of the most striking wildflowers of the southern Appalachians and Ozarks. Its rarity in cultivation is unfortunate, as it makes a wonderful garden specimen. *Spigelia* forms bushy clumps of glossy, broadly lance-shaped sessile leaves in pairs up the stem. The top pair nurture a short inflorescence that grows from their center with the magnificent flowers developing vertically along it in a one-sided rank. The buds resemble bowling pins sharpened to a point. The bottom two-thirds of even the smaller buds blush crimson with darker tips that peel back like a banana to reveal a soft yellow interior. The flowers are best pollinated by hummingbirds, and this service will result in a 2-lobed, oval capsule set in the pointed crown of the calyx. The capsules mature sequentially and show no outward signs of ripening until they burst open and violently expel the seeds. This makes collecting them a challenge and may be part of the reason the plants are so rare in cultivation. I have taken my cue from the squirrels and check the capsules every few days, picking those that

Spigelia marilandica. Indian Pink *presents a dramatic contrast between inside and out. Each crimson bud peels open like a banana to reveal an incongruous soft yellow underbelly. Under good culture, the plants bloom a second time four weeks later from side branches that grow up from the uppermost leaf axils after the first blooms have faded.* Spigelia *takes two or three seasons to become substantial, so give it time and some room to grow.*

Spiranthes odorata.
The sweet scent of Fragrant Lady's Tresses is a bit sluggish and shy to release in the cool days of autumn when this diminutive orchid comes into bloom. It adapts surprisingly well to indoor terrarium culture, however, and a large clump can really perfume a room.

have ceased to swell and turned a faintly lighter shade of green with a blush of crimson.

The Loganiaceae are mostly tropical plants, many containing poisonous alkaloids used with caution by humans. Curare—the dreaded arrow poison of the American Tropics—is in this family. Indian Pink contains the powerful alkaloid spigeleine, which has strong anthelmintic, or worm expelling, properties used to advantage by Native Americans. Overdoses of spigeleine (which is related to strychnine) can be fatal, but when mixed with other herbs that function as laxatives to expel the toxin and the worms quickly, it can be effective against intestinal worms.

CULTURE: In rich mountain coves, Indian Pink can form an almost continuous ground cover in dappled shade, and in the garden it does equally well in a fertile, moist soil in partial sun or light shade. I have grown the plants in full sun, but they bleach along the leaf margins, and drought is not well tolerated. *Spigelia* grows from a tight crown, so division is nearly impossible. The plants are slow growing, taking two years to become sizable and then getting better and better each year thereafter. Under good conditions, Indian Pink blooms in a flush in summer, then again in early fall. I prefer to plant them in drifts as they compete better with their own, and the flowers have more of an effect this way.

USES: Specimen or massing in the border or wild garden.

PROPAGATION: Moderately difficult from seed and cuttings. See p. 262.

basal, emerging one after the next in a small evergreen rosette. Late in the season, the plants bolt, sending up a single flower stem wrapped in a few smaller leaves and tipped with the distinctive spiraling raceme. Most of our native species are easily overlooked in the damp, mossy places they call home and are too small or hard to find commercially to be of much garden interest. However, this garden-friendly species has become increasingly available in the trade as of late. *S. odorata* is a robust orchid (some consider it a variety of *S. cernua*, the Nodding Lady's Tresses), with strongly vanilla-scented blooms late in the fall. Mature specimens form numerous root sprouts that can be snapped off in late spring to form new plants, so it is one of the easiest orchids to propagate. In a damp or boggy, acid spot in the garden, it will form neat clumps of foliage slowly spreading to form colonies.

CULTURE: Grow Fragrant Lady's Tresses in a moist, open spot like a bog or low area. It is fairly adaptable, not appearing to have a strong mycorrhizal association when mature. Rabbits like to munch off the flower spikes, but otherwise it is not troubled by pests. Plants can be easily moved or divided in spring if you are careful not to damage the few brittle roots.

USES: Bog garden, pondside, moist borders.

PROPAGATION: Difficult from seed; easy from division. See p. 263.

Spiranthes odorata

Spiranthes odorata

(spy-WRANTH-ease)

Orchidaceae

**Fragrant Lady's Tresses,
Swamp Lady's Tresses**

ZONES: 5–9; sun, part sun

SOIL: moist to wet, acid

NATIVE TO: estuaries and marshes along the coastal plain; Pennsylvania to Tennessee south to Louisiana and Florida

SIZE: 1–2 feet (6–12 inches)

COLOR: crystalline white with green veins; BLOOMS in late fall

Lady's tresses are small late-flowering orchids with endearing, hooded flowers arranged in a perfect spiral staircase on stiffly vertical stems. The plants have fat, thickened roots that seem out of scale with their long thin leaves and diminutive flowers. They lack a well-developed rhizome, so the roots store food reserves for the plants and even send up root sprouts to increase the colony. Most of the leaves are

Stokesia laevis

Stokesia laevis
(STOKES-ee-ah)

Asteraceae
Stokes' Aster, Stokesia

ZONES: 5–9; sun to light shade

SOIL: moist, well drained

NATIVE TO: bottomlands and pine forests along the coastal plain; North Carolina to Florida and Louisiana

SIZE: 1–2 feet (12–16 inches)

COLOR: violet-blue to purple, occasionally soft yellow or white; **BLOOMS** in early summer

The **remarkable** flowers of Stokes' Aster are almost beyond description—up to 3 inches across with lacy, finely notched ray petals and a pincushion puff of feathery disk flowers in the center. Typically the flowers are violet, but blue, yellow, and white forms have been found and introduced. The developing disk flowers are pale, giving the center a creamy glow. The plants look like a cross between a thistle (*Carduus*) and a Bachelor's Button (*Centaurea*), to which they are related, with fierce-looking spines protruding from the unopened buds and bases of the upper leaves. The spines are all for show, though, and too soft to prick the skin. Stokesia has suffered from deceptive marketing in catalogs that display drooling closeups of true blue flowers and not a hint about the floppy habit of the plant. (I have never seen an actual sky blue Stokes' Aster—about the closest are more blue-violet.) The leaves are long and fleshy with a gray-green cast and a strong white midrib. They grow in basal clumps or fans, forming a loose 10-inch semievergeeen ground cover under ideal conditions. The flowers are borne on thick, branching stems that are weakly attached at the base so that the accumulated weight of blooms and stem often causes them to fall over like trees after a hurricane. If you can forgive this possibly lax habit, the flowers are really quite spectacular planted on a slope or the front of the border. A seed strain selected by the Atlanta Botanic Garden and called 'Omega Skyrocket' has taller, stronger stems that do not flop as easily.

CULTURE: Although it is native to the damp, acid soils of south coastal pine forests, Stokesia is fairly drought-tolerant, and well-drained soil actually improves its winter hardiness in marginal areas. (Certain cultivars are more cold-tolerant than others, some successfully negotiating a Zone 4 winter with adequate snow cover.) Other than removing spent flower stalks, these long-lived plants require little maintenance. They form multiple fans with fleshy roots that can be divided with a knife in spring.

USES: Borders, slopes.

PROPAGATION: Easy from seed or root cuttings. See p. 263.

Streptopus roseus

Streptopus
(strep-TOE-puss)

Liliaceae
Twisted Stalk

Twisted **stalks,** like their close cousins the fairybells, send up branched stems from a slender rhizome clothed in alternating, sessile leaves. The stems meander like a lazy river from leaf to leaf, especially in some forms of *S. amplexifolius*. Why grow them, you ask pointedly? It is true that they are very similar in appearance to *Disporum*s, and more finicky to cultivate, but the light green leaves have a crystalline quality like fresh iceberg lettuce, and the undersides

(LEFT): Stokesia laevis. *Stokes' Aster comes readily from root cuttings taken after the plants have had at least two or three months of winter dormancy. Two- or three-inch sections of the fleshy white roots can be inserted vertically just below the surface into dampened sand and kept somewhere warm and bright. New shoots will be visible in six to eight weeks.*

(RIGHT): Streptopus roseus. *The demure flowers and later the glossy red fruits of Rose Twisted Stalk hide under the leaves, so it requires a little detective work to find them.*

Stylophorum diphyllum. *Celandine Poppy is a glorious weed at Garden in the Woods. Its diaphanous flowers yield to pickle-shaped pods that peel open and drop a bomber load of seeds gathered quickly by ants. I would not be without this lovely woodlander, but I religiously cut them back after they've flowered to curtail their exuberant fecundity.*

are paler with a hint of blue. Rose Twisted Stalk has cute little pink flowers growing one to a node like Solomon's seal, but in this case on a long peduncle that holds the little bells away from the leaf. Pink is such a rare color in the woodland lilies that I delight in searching for the flowers among the leaves each spring. Both *Streptopus* species form soft, orange to blood red fruits as big as small cherries that hang heavily from the stems in late summer. These juicy berries are a favorite of birds fattening up for the coming migration, so they do not last long on the plants. Whether in your garden or on a walk in the great north woods, I encourage you to stop and admire these subtly unique wildflowers for their elegance and grace.

CULTURE: *Streptopus* are plants of the cool northern forests and prefer a damp, humusy spot and a climate that is not excessively hot and humid. In the wild, I typically find them near a stream or brook, high enough from water to avoid flooding, but still enjoying the evenly moist, fertile alluvial soil. In the garden, place them where they will be out of the strong sun and in a soil that never dries severely in summer.

USES: Naturalizing in the woodland garden.

WILDLIFE: Berries are food for birds and mammals.

PROPAGATION: Difficult from seed. See p. 263.

Streptopus amplexifolius
(Twisted Stalk, White Mandarin)

ZONES: 2–7; shade
SOIL: evenly moist
NATIVE TO: streambanks and floodplains—circumboreal; Greenland to Alaska south to California, Wisconsin, and Massachusetts and in the mountains to Arizona and North Carolina
SIZE: 16–40 inches (16 inches)
COLOR: white-veined green; **BLOOMS** in spring
The two species are difficult to distinguish out of flower, but this one has heart-shaped leaf bases with lobes that clasp the stem.

Streptopus roseus
(Rosybells, Rose Twisted Stalk, Rose Mandarin)

ZONES: 2–7; shade
SOIL: evenly moist
NATIVE TO: rich woods, streambanks, and floodplains; Labrador to Alaska south to California, Minnesota, and New Jersey and in the Appalachians to North Carolina
SIZE: 12–30 inches (12–16 inches)
COLOR: pale to bright rose with darker veins; **BLOOMS** in spring

Stylophorum diphyllum

Stylophorum diphyllum (stye-LOFF-for-um)
Papaveraceae
Celandine Poppy

ZONES: 4–8; part sun, shade
SOIL: moist
NATIVE TO: rich woodland; Pennsylvania to Wisconsin south to Arkansas and Tennessee
SIZE: 12–20 inches (12 inches)
COLOR: bright yellow; **BLOOMS** in spring

The **butter yellow** flowers of Celandine Poppy mixed with the sky blue of Virginia Bluebells, the white of Showy Trillium, and the unfurling crosiers of Ostrich Fern create a spectacular symphony of color and form in our woodland garden every spring. It is one of those triumphs of serendipity and planning that prove the old adage "the whole is greater than the sum of the parts." Certainly, all these plants are beautiful in their own right, but massed together in a natural setting, the effect is transcendent—transforming a dappled woodland into a place of wordless majesty and beauty for a few brief weeks in spring.

Celandine Poppy is an undemanding plant with medium green pinnate leaves with undulating margins that look like they were drawn by an unsteady hand. The flowering stems emerge early in the season from big leafy clumps and unfurl exquisite 4-petaled blooms 2 inches across with a crinkled paper substance. Like on most poppies, the center of the flower is a tickly bun of yellow anthers a shade darker than the petals. *Stylophorum* blooms for three to four weeks before turning its energy to seed production. Seeds form in long pickle-shaped pods that hang from the stems ready to peel open at the seams and disgorge their contents for ants to disperse. Disperse they will if you leave the pods to ripen, until soon the whole garden will be rife with Celandine. Therefore, it is a good idea to remove most of the seedpods before they mature (wear gloves, as the yellow sap will stain your skin)—the plants are long-lived and few recruits are needed each year. After flowering, *Stylophorum* goes dormant, retreating to a hard knoblike bud to await the next spring.

Stylophorum is sometimes confused with the weedy Eurasian Lesser Celandine *(Chelidonium majus)*, a coarse, small-flowered biennial naturalized in waste places and disturbed habitats, as well as with Welsh Poppy, *Meconopsis cambrica*.

CULTURE: It is easily grown in a variety of soils, but prefers rich, moist soils under deciduous trees. Plant out container-grown plants in spring, or transplant the distinctive self-sown seedlings in spring or fall (seedlings do not go dormant as readily as adults do). Interplant with ferns or taller wildflowers such as Solomon's seal to hide the bare spots when the plants go dormant.

USES: Naturalizing in the woodland or shade garden.

PROPAGATION: Easy from seed. See p. 263.

Symplocarpus foetidus

Symplocarpus foetidus (sim-ploe-CAR-puss)
Araceae
Skunk Cabbage, Polecat Weed

ZONES: 3–7; sun to shade

SOIL: wet to seasonally inundated

NATIVE TO: bogs, swamps, and floodplains; Nova Scotia to Minnesota south to Iowa and western North Carolina

SIZE: 18–30 inches (3 feet)

COLOR: maroon and white; **BLOOMS** from late winter to early spring

The brook down below my office is invisible in summer, cloaked thickly in a verdant, nefarious green. In early spring, though, it is possible to see 500 feet down to the water, making the first stage of its annual transformation readily apparent. The low, swampy ground along the brook is a perfect place for Skunk Cabbage, and one magical week in April the plants leaf out and the ground plane goes from muddy brown to an advancing, tropical green flowing like lava along the path of the stream.

Skunk Cabbage has magnificent leaves, 2 feet long and a foot wide with complex veination that puckers the surface like a quilt. The leaves grow from a huge crown and root thicker than a sweet potato and three times as long. In habit they are like hostas, with the rounded leaves in a circle on long petioles attached in the center to an undergound stem. While I love these big tropical leaves, the most bizarrely fantastic thing about *Symplocarpus* is its flowers. They consist of a fleshy, deep red spathe shaped like the hood of a sweatshirt that enfolds a ball-shaped spadix buried partially underground. The flowers actually metabolize at such a rate that they release surplus heat as we do, raising the temperature inside the spathe 5°F or more above the air outside—enough to melt the snow that may still lie around but designed to win the favors of precocious flies who have just emerged from hibernation. A fly happening by could easily mistake the foul odor and warm red flower for the body of a recently deceased mammal or bird. What a perfect place to lay some eggs. I do not know whether flies actually mate or lay eggs on the flowers but in tramping around excitedly on the spadix, they handily pollinate them. The flowers of Skunk Cabbage are the first to bloom in the woods of New England, and it was a yearly rite for me as a child to march out back to the swamp in March and hail these strange little beasts.

CULTURE: To look its best, Skunk Cabbage needs a mucky soil and deciduous shade (or if the area is very wet, even full sun). It is a common sight in swamps and floodplains in the Northeast and Great Lakes, but languishes in the heat and humidity of the South. Even in the best of situations, it goes dormant by midsummer as the canopy closes in and the trees siphon off most of the water. The huge roots are difficult to completely remove, so it is not a plant that is readily eradicated once established. It is best to start with seed sown directly in place in fall or small container-grown seedlings that can be put out in spring.

USES: Adds bold texture to bog or water gardens.

PROPAGATION: Slow and moderately difficult from seed. See p. 263.

Symplocarpus foetidus. In the eastern deciduous forests, excess winter precipitation accumulates in vernal pools—really just low areas that fill with water during the winter and dry up in summer as trees and the heat of the sun draw off moisture. Since these pools dry up every year, egg-eating fish cannot survive in them. Salamanders, toads, and frogs take advantage of this safe haven for their young, migrating down to the water to breed during the first warm rains of spring. We close off part of the road to the Garden for a couple of weeks toward the end of March to prevent cars from killing these migrating amphibians returning like salmon to the pool of their birth. Vernal pools are also host to a variety of plants such as Skunk Cabbage that begin growth early and go dormant as the water dries in summer.

Talinum calycinum

Talinum (tal-EYE-num)
Portulacaceae
Fame Flower

Talinum calycinum. If allowed an open, sunny spot and gritty soil, Fame Flower will seed itself agreeably about. Its sun-loving flowers all face toward the light, so position it to the north of a path to enjoy the little blooms in full frontal perpetuity.

Fame flowers are little succulents with long fleshy leaves on a short stem that give them the look of a bloated pine bough. They have cute 5-petaled blooms like their cousins Lewisia and Spring Beauty dangling on hair-thin, branching stems a few inches above the leaves. I do not know the origin of their common name, but of course I have come up with a possible explanation. The flowers open only in the sun, unfurling in the morning and each lasting just a day—like a Hollywood star they crave the spotlight, living fast and dying young.

*Talinum*s grow in poor, rocky soil in both the East and West, but the easterners are more tolerant of wetness and generally hardier and easier to grow. *T. calycinum* is the most commonly available, and it and three other, smaller-flowered relatives make up the eastern contingent. The fleshy stems bloom most of the summer then promptly go to mush at the approach of cold. All that remains in the winter is a thick, rusty crown with a ring of pointed buds around the surface waiting for spring. Because they flower for so long, fame flowers produce large quantities of seed in little oval capsules that take root and naturalize in open, stony ground. The plants are small, so these self-sown seedlings should not be a problem, and they are not too hard to pull if they become overabundant.

CULTURE: Grow in a well-drained soil and full sun. The plants require little maintenance other than occasional weeding. The Pacific Northwestern species need a dry summer rest and mild winters to thrive, but *T. calycinum* and its ilk are an easy lot.

USES: Rock gardens.

PROPAGATION: Easy from seed. See p. 263.

Talinum calycinum
(Rockpink)

ZONES: 4–9; sun
SOIL: well drained
NATIVE TO: poor, rocky soils; Illinois to Nebraska, Kansas, and Texas
SIZE: 4–10 inches (6 inches)
COLOR: bright pink with darker veins; BLOOMS in summer

This plains species has ¾-inch flowers. Its relatives, *T. rugospermum* (Sand Fame Flower), *T. teretifolium* (Appalachian Fame Flower), and *T. parviflorum* (Prairie Fame Flower), have progressively smaller flowers, with the last having blooms only ¼ inch across. In habit they all look pretty similar.

Talinum okanoganense
(Okanogan Fame Flower)

ZONES: 6–8; sun
SOIL: well drained, summer dry
NATIVE TO: rock outcrops; Washington to British Columbia
SIZE: 3–6 inches (4–6 inches)
COLOR: pale to dark red-pink; BLOOMS from spring to early summer

A neat little plant with fine needlelike leaves and short stems of bunched ¾-inch flowers. It is difficult in areas with summer rain, and the persistent fleshy stems can be damaged by excessive cold.

Talinum spinescens
(Spinescent Fame Flower)

ZONES: 6–8; sun
SOIL: well drained, summer dry
NATIVE TO: rock outcrops and sagebrush desert; central Washington and Oregon
SIZE: 4–8 inches (6 inches)
COLOR: white to pale pink; BLOOMS from late spring to early summer

Much like *T. okanoganense*, but the old leaf bases remain on the fleshy stems as stiff (but not sharp) spines. It bears its light ½-inch flowers on taller spikes more like the eastern species.

Tellima grandiflora

Tellima grandiflora (tell-EYE-ma)
Saxifragaceae
Fringecups

ZONES: 3–8; part sun, shade

SOIL: moist

NATIVE TO: streambanks and moist woods; Idaho to British Columbia north to Alaska and south to northern California

SIZE: 1–3 feet (12 inches)

COLOR: white blushing pink; **BLOOMS** in late spring

Fragrance is a gift more precious than flowers, carefully blended and tuned over the ages as an offering of welcome and an invitation to dine. Animals and insects have their individual olfactory tastes: carrion flies relish smells that we find unspeakably repulsive, beetles prefer the heady odor of overripe fruit, and male euglossine bees the musky-sweet perfume of vanilla and clove. Moths have a "nose" that seems closest to our own, as flowers advertising for their services include the sublimely redolent Honeysuckle, Jasmine, and Gardenia. I wonder if a moth experiences the same sweet intoxication that sweeps through me when I inhale a Gardenia blossom. Moths do have a powerful sensitivity to certain odors, but this ability developed first for reproduction, not foraging. One of my friends once brought home the chrysalis of a giant owl-wing moth she had been given at a butterfly day sponsored by the local natural history museum. The moth soon hatched in

her kitchen, and after a few hours admiring it she carried the ponderous, spectacular creature out to her deck and let it grab hold of a wall under the eve. It turns out this particular moth was a female, who quickly began to release her secret owl-wing pheromone into the still night air. By morning, a wild male owl-wing had been lured to her side from the darkness—all without the female moving an inch. In all my years of wandering the woods, I have never seen one of these huge, elusive insects, so it is all the more remarkable to me that a little of the proper perfume could lure one in so easily from the mysterious canopy.

As you may have gathered from this lengthy introduction, Fringecups have their own voluptuous fragrance reminiscent of the warm, spicy-sweet odor of Trailing Arbutus (*Epigea repens*). These coralbells relatives produce tall wands of delicate, bell-shaped flowers with flared little petals cut with an intricate, lacy filagree. In leaf and habit they are much like a clumping foamflower, and their semievergreen foliage and carefree constitution make them welcome garden companions. Certainly there is nothing spectacular about the plants, but perhaps this is the best endorsement I could give, as understatement makes the gift of their perfume all the more sublime.

There are several related genera that seem best to metion here. *Tellima* is an anagram of *Mitella* (Mitrewort), a genus of a dozen small woodlanders from temperate North America and east Asia. They are not spectacular plants, but their little rounded leaves and intricate flowers have a certain charm. Grow them under similar conditions as Fringecups on damp mossy logs or moist duffy soil, and they will lightly naturalize and blend with their bryophyte companions, producing their small snowflake flowers in red, white, or pink in spring. *Mitella diphylla* (Two-leaved Mitrewort) is a common easterner in limestone regions, with mapleleaf foliage in a small basal clump and a pair of sessile leaves up the thin flowering stem that act as a serving tray for the wispy white blooms. There are a number of species in the coniferous forests of the Northwest. *M. trifida* (Pacific Mitrewort) and *M. diversifolia* (Varied-leaved Mitrewort) are both white flowered, the last with lower leaves pointedly lobed. *M. pentandra* (Alpine Mitrewort) and *M. breweri* (Brewer's Mitrewort) are two of the greenish flowered species, the latter spreading as a low, evergreen mat of small round leaves in damp, moist woods.

Lithophragma (Woodland Star) is often included with *Tellima* in older texts, but they are very different in many ways. The woodland stars are small plants with deeply lobed and fringed basal leaves and large 5-petaled flowers. The best for gardens is *L. parviflora,* a diminutive, poorly named plant (*parviflora* means small-flowered) with large pure white flowers with 3-lobed petals bunched at the top of tall stems.

Tellima grandiflora.
The filigreed petals of the Northwest's Fringecups need to be appreciated up close, but their perfume will "hop the olfactory gate" from several feet away. Some of the plants produce flowers that age a delicate pink, and it is these I encourage in the nursery. Tellima is but one of a group of closely related species in the Saxifrage family all boasting intricate racemes of finely cut little flowers.

Tephrosia virginiana.
*Goat's Rue rivals some
of the showiest western
milkvetches with its
Daffy Duck flowers of
salmon and rose. Its fine
downy foliage is lovely
as well, and though the
plant is slow to establish,*
Tephrosia *is certainly
worth a few years'
investment in time and
in space.*

It grows in vernally moist gravelly soils in open or partially shaded areas from North Dakota to British Columbia south to northern California and Colorado.

CULTURE: Fringecups thrive in a damp, lightly shaded spot, so they are perfect plants for the woodland. They appreciate fertility, but this must be doled out carefully, as a rich diet can cause lush growth and floppy spikes. They are not very drought-tolerant in spring, but some summer dryness is par for the course in their northwestern home. The tiny seeds shake from small capsules on a gentle swaying breeze, and the plants will welcomely self-sow.

USES: Borders, massing, naturalizing in the woodland garden.

PROPAGATION: Easy from seed. See p. 263.

Tephrosia—what a lyical name that is, like ambrosia, food of immortality for the ancient gods of Greece. These cousins of *Baptisia* and *Astragalus* are tough plants—if not immortal then certainly very long-lived. However, their tough, woody roots are certainly no ambrosia—at least for luckless fish —for they yield a powerful and well-known fish poison used extensively by Native Americans. Most *Tephrosia*s are native to warmer climes, and some have had a long use as arrow poisons as well. Do not let this dissuade you from growing the plants, for in the garden they are mild-mannered perennials for the toughest dry sun or shade. Goat's Rue sends up zigzag, 1-foot stems of finely pinnate leaves covered in matted gray hair that lends them an attractive gray-green cast. The stems terminate in a dense cluster of lovely ¾-inch bicolored pea blossoms of cream and mauve. After the flowers fade, long thin pods begin to grow, and the foliage remains resolute, looking soft and fine until fall forces the clump back underground.

T. spicata (Southern Goat's Rue) is a southeasterner, with smaller white flowers fading to pink in loose racemes. It is native to similar habitats but not nearly as showy as its cousins.

CULTURE: Goat's Rue will grow in sandy or rocky soil and even in dry clay amid the roots of hungry trees. They are best in a sunny spot, but will adapt to light shade, though growth will be more scandent. It is best to introduce them as small container plants or directly sown seed innoculated with the proper rhizobium bacteria and then left alone, as the plants are impossible to divide and resent transplanting once established.

USES: Rock gardens, xeriscaping, banks.

PROPAGATION: Moderately difficult from seed. See p. 263.

Tephrosia virginiana

Tephrosia virginiana
(teff-ROSE-ee-ah)
Fabaceae
Goat's Rue

ZONES: 4–9; sun to light shade

SOIL: well drained

NATIVE TO: dunes, sandy prairies, dry open woods; New Hampshire to Wisconsin and Kansas south to Texas and Florida

SIZE: 8–20 inches (8–12 inches)

COLOR: pale yellow and mauve or faded purple; **BLOOMS** in early summer

Thalictrum pubescens

Thalictrum
(thul-LICK-trum)
Ranunculaceae
Meadow Rue

The meadow rues are high-rises in the garden, with straight, fluted stems like bamboo stakes and fine, pinnate foliage held out from them at right angles. The plants are certainly taller than they are wide, providing soaring vertical accent in tight spaces and gracing the spring or summer border with billowing, feathery clouds of petalless flowers. Many of our two dozen species are very similar in habit and flower, with identification depending on the shape and size of the seed and the leaf, so I have chosen a few of the most ornamental representatives to list here.

CULTURE: Meadow rues are most at home in moist, rich soils in woodlands, floodplains, swamps, and prairies. In the garden, a damp sunny or lightly shaded spot is ideal, though *T. pubescens* and *T. dasycarpum* have proven moderately drought-tolerant in my own garden. Provided there is moisture, they are easy to grow and long-lived, and the tall plumes or delicate tassels mix equally well with taller wildflowers in the meadow and shorter woodlanders in the shade.

USES: Borders, meadows, woodland edge.

PROPAGATION: Easy from seed. See p. 263.

Thalictrum alpinum
(Alpine Meadow Rue)

ZONES: 2–6; sun, part shade
SOIL: moist to wet, cool soil
NATIVE TO: alpine and boreal meadows and bogs and fens; Greenland and the Maritime Provinces as well as high peaks in the West and northern British Columbia and Alaska
SIZE: 2–12 inches (12 inches)
COLOR: yellow with a hint of pink; **BLOOMS** in spring

I include this species for comparison, as it is a widespread, rhizomatous alpine with lovely blue-green leaves that remind me of the little Oak Fern (*Gymnocarpium dryopteris*). The flowers consist mostly of anthers hung in a drooping raceme. Not too difficult for northern rock gardeners, but it hates hot weather.

Thalictrum dasycarpum
(Purple Meadow Rue)

ZONES: 3–9; sun to light shade
SOIL: moist, fertile
NATIVE TO: low woods, swamps, wet meadows, and prairies; Quebec to British Columbia south to New Mexico and Mississippi
SIZE: 3–7 feet (16 inches)
COLOR: pale to dark pink-purple; **BLOOMS** in early summer

A lovely dioecious species with delicate, colorful, rounded plumes and leaflets with 2–3 large teeth. One of the best ornamentals.

Thalictrum dioicum
(Early Meadow Rue)

ZONES: 3–8; part sun, shade
SOIL: moist, at least in spring
NATIVE TO: rocky woods, banks, and coves; Quebec to southern Manitoba, south to Missouri and Georgia
SIZE: 1–3 feet (16–18 inches)
COLOR: yellow-green; **BLOOMS** in spring

T. dioicum is the earliest to bloom, acting more like a spring ephemeral in its life cycle. The plants are either male of female, the males having showier flowers with pale purple sepals and anthers that hang down like the tasseled lampshades that were popular a hundred years ago. The females shed their seed by June, and the plants fade into the background. It makes a fine if understated accent in light shade, with a bushy shape as broad as it is tall.

Thalictrum pubescens. Big puffy clouds. King of the Prairie looks like big puffy clouds. Think of the potential these lofty plumes bring to borders and meadows — such transcendent, fantastic, vaporous things. Cumulonimbus refined.

Tiarella cordifolia.

Three years ago we were extremely fortunate to receive the gift of a garden, a garden of 2,000 trilliums no less, that were lovingly nurtured for half a century from a handful of original plants by our friend Evelyn Adams. Her garden was photographed by a number of people and even featured in Ken Druse's popular Natural Garden *series. When Evelyn had to move, her land was subdivided and the garden turned into a house lot. Luckily, a few of our members arranged for us to dig up the whole thing and bring it to Garden in the Woods, where the plants are now thriving in a wooded glen between our offices and nursery. This brings me to Foamflower. There was quite a bit of Running Foamflower mixed in the sods of assorted plants we relocated, and it has spread exuberantly in its new home. It has filled in the gaps between clumps of taller plants and looks absolutely charming blooming with thousands of Showy Trilliums in May.*

Thalictrum pubescens (polygamum)

(Tall Meadow Rue, King of the Meadow)

ZONES: 3–9; sun to shade

SOIL: moist to wet

NATIVE TO: woods, wet meadows, swamps, and streambanks; Nova Scotia to Ontario south to Illinois, Mississippi, and Georgia

SIZE: 3–10 feet (24 inches)

COLOR: white; **BLOOMS** in summer

King of the Meadow is aptly named, for the towering stems and soft white plumes are regal indeed. The foliage looks much like that of Purple Meadow Rue, but coarser. The plants are reasonably shade-tolerant but thrive in open wet areas, where they will naturalize easily.

Thalictrum venulosum

(Northern Meadow Rue)

ZONES: 2–8; sun to light shade

SOIL: moist to wet

NATIVE TO: wet meadows, streambanks, low woods; New York to the Northwest Territories south to Oregon, New Mexico, and South Dakota

SIZE: 1–3 feet (16 inches)

COLOR: green; **BLOOMS** in summer

One of a group of green-flowered species not very striking in bloom but possessing finely toothed, delicate-looking foliage.

is blotted with color. The leaves are semievergreen in cold winters, turning deep burgundy and slumping from the chill. However, they give the plants a boost in the spring, and removing them in your early-season cleanup can set back blooming by one to two weeks.

There are two species, one in the East and one in the Northwest. Both are variable plants with distinctive varieties often listed as separate species in horticultural references. They are easy plants for the shade garden, where their evergreen leaves and frothy flowers are especially valuable in drifts and as ground covers. Even the peculiar seedpods are attractive. They are constructed of 2 boat-shaped, papery wings —the upper overturned inside the lower. The ripe seeds are held inside like balls caught in a mitt until a raindrop hits the lower lip, catapulting the seeds skyward.

CULTURE: Plant in spring in a moist, fertile soil for best effect. They need little care except to be sheared back after seeding. My only problem has been from an unidentified maggot that tunnels into the crown of the plant, killing it off at the roots. A pesticide drench seems all that will stop them once established, though some individuals are more resistant than others. The eastern species appreciate a dusting of limestone but do not require it.

USES: Ground cover, massing.

PROPAGATION: Easy from seed. See p. 263.

Tiarella cordifolia

Tiarella (tea-ah-RELL-ah)
Saxifragaceae
Foamflower

Foamflowers are flawless combinations of delicacy and resilience with a wonderfully descriptive name that perfectly captures their essence in bloom. The flowers are borne on thin spikes shaped like the narrow, pointed spires of a Gothic cathedral. The knobby, unopened buds are often flushed pink, quickly fading to white as the petals spring open. The open blooms stretch out on the stems in a distinctive way, as if slowly settling downward away from the tips. This floral ballet takes place above rich green, maple-shaped leaves, heavily puckered and creased along the main veins. The channels formed in this way are lightly to heavily stained with burgundy or maroon, which pools in the cracks like printing plate ink. The red tones are affected by temperature—they are most intense on the leaves formed in spring and in fall. Some plants within populations of *T. cordifolia* are so heavily stained that nearly the entire new leaf

Tiarella cordifolia var. collina (wherryi)

(Clumping Foamflower)

ZONES: 4–9; sun to shade

SOIL: moist

NATIVE TO: rich woods, chiefly in the southern Appalachians; Virginia and Kentucky to Georgia

SIZE: 5–12 inches (12 inches)

COLOR: white flushed pink; BLOOMS in spring

Distinguished by its lack of stolons, this southern variety (usually listed as *T. wherryi* in catalogs) remains tightly clumped in the garden. The forms I have grown have leaves more sharply lobed and glossy than typical *T. cordifolia*. This is a wonderful plant, valuable en masse or in scattered, mixed plantings.

Tiarella cordifolia var. cordifolia

(Running Foamflower)

ZONES: 3–9; sun to shade

SOIL: moist

NATIVE TO: rich woods; Nova Scotia to Ontario and Wisconsin south to Alabama and Georgia

SIZE: 3–10 inches (18–24 inches)

COLOR: white sometimes flushed pink; BLOOMS in spring

One of our best shady ground covers, with sometimes heavily colored leaves and long trailing stolons produced during the summer. The leaves are typically lightly felted and rounded in outline, though cut-leaved forms exist in the trade.

Tiarella trifoliata var. trifoliata

(Trefoil Foamflower)

ZONES: 4–8; sun to shade

SOIL: moist, acid

NATIVE TO: rich, moist forests; Alberta to Alaska south to Oregon and Idaho

SIZE: 6–12 inches (12 inches)

COLOR: white flushed pink; BLOOMS in summer

Trefoil Foamflower is a small clumping plant with 3-lobed fuzzy leaves and flowers in loose, short-branched spikes that appear later and have a more delicate, ethereal quality than *T. cordifolia*. It is fairly easy in cultivation but not as vigorous and foolproof as the eastern species. *T. trifoliata* var. *unifoliata* (Sugar-scoop) has less deeply lobed leaves, like smaller versions of *T. cordifolia*. It also has a delicate airy look to it, with flowers on tall thin stems barely visible among the moss and duff of the forest floor. Var. *laciniata* (Cutleaf Foamflower) is a particularly finely toothed and divided form from coastal rain forests along the Northwest coast and, though beautiful, it is less hardy and adaptable in cultivation. However, breeders are crossing Cutleaf Foamflower with the eastern species to get some lovely lacy-leaved offspring with improved hardiness and vigor.

Tradescantia hirsuticaulis

Tradescantia (trad-ess-CANT-ee-ah)
Commelinaceae
Spiderwort

I am not sure why I feel compelled to make excuses for some of the plants I describe, especially those with vaguely unsettling names that I worry might rebuff rather than entice you. I suppose I want you to love them as I do—all their idiosyncrasies included—with an eye unbiased by a name or reputation. Spiderwort is one of those words that wriggles and resonates from the depths of the unconscious with hints of dark basements and foul witches' brew. However, in reality, nothing about these dayflowers suggests anything sinister, and my best guess is that the name refers to the delicate weblike filaments that decorate the anthers of each 3-petaled flower like a feather boa in minature. The lightly fragrant flowers pop out one or two at a time from the folds of a leaflike bract. They open broad and flat in the heat of the day, then wither and curl under to be replaced the next morning by a new batch of blooms. The foliage of spiderworts looks very similar to a daylily's, especially when it is first emerging. (I remember confusing the two on tests in my perennials class in college.) The basal fans elongate in flowering to become leafy stems with alternate foliage arranged like sweet corn and blossoms appearing out of the topmost bract leaves.

Most of the plants offered in nurseries are the *T.* × *andersoniana* hybrids, a large, long-flowering, and vigorous group derived from the closely related *T. virginiana*, *T. subaspera*, and *T. ohiensis*. These are rampant growers, with a tendency to produce both spreading stolons and seedlings that border on

Tradescantia hirsuticaulis. *I imagine that the name Spiderwort is a reference to the web of hairs that cloak each stamen's filament. Though there is quite a range in both size and gregariousness within this genus, the size and shape of the flowers remains fairly constant from species to species. Each bloom lasts only a day or rarely two, opening in the morning and closing again at dusk.*

weedy in rich soils. Still, for a wildflower garden there are few plants more carefree and happy in the sun or the shade where the soil is moist—at least in the spring. Some of the species, such as *T. hirsuticaulis, T. longipes,* and *T. rosea,* are smaller and less exuberant, making better subjects for smaller gardens, rock work, and formal plantings.

CULTURE: The thick fleshy roots of spiderworts store all of their food reserves, so in spring—or preferably early fall—divide the plants carefully to leave each fan with a tangled mass of roots. They are easy to establish when in active growth, preferring moist fertile soil but adapting to a drier site, which also curbs some of their aggressive tendencies. Most spiderworts naturally go into semidormancy after they have set seed during the heat of summer, with new fans appearing in the cooler days of fall and remaining through the winter. I think it is better to deadhead them and turn your attention elsewhere rather than try to keep them awake with extra fertilizer and water. Other than a haircut after flowering and fertilizer in spring, they require little maintenance.

USES: Borders, naturalizing, and rock gardens (for the smaller species).

PROPAGATION: Easy from seed, cuttings, or division. See p. 264.

Tradescantia hirsuticaulis

(Hairy Spiderwort)

ZONES: 4–9; sun to light shade
SOIL: moist to dry
NATIVE TO: outcrops and dry woods; North Carolina to Georgia and Alabama
SIZE: 4–12 inches (12 –18 inches)
COLOR: typically violet, occasionally lavender; **BLOOMS** from late spring to early summer

An excellent compact and drought-tolerant species from the southern Appalachians, with leaves and stems covered in long translucent hair. The plants are noninvasive and have a pronounced summer rest. *T. tharpii* is a closely related species from a bit farther west.

Tradescantia longipes

(Wild Crocus)

ZONES: 5–9; sun to light shade
SOIL: well drained
NATIVE TO: dry soils, ridges in acidic, pine-oak woodland; limited mostly to the Ozark region of Missouri
SIZE: 3–8 inches (12 inches)
COLOR: deep purple to violet, lavender, and rose; **BLOOMS** in early summer

A charming little plant even smaller than Hairy Spiderwort, with low trailing leaves that do not produce aerial flowering stems, instead flowering nearly at ground level. A good rock garden subject.

Tradescantia ozarkana

(Ozark Spiderwort)

ZONES: 5–9; part sun to shade
SOIL: moist
NATIVE TO: alluvial soils and rock woods; Missouri to Arkansas and Oklahoma
SIZE: 12–28 inches (16–20 inches)
COLOR: white through rose to lavender; **BLOOMS** in spring

A large spring bloomer that differs from *T. virginiana* in that the flowering stems produce many axillary branches that bloom as well, so the plants have a bushy, dense appearance. The leaves can be furry or smooth and have a wavy margin like corn.

Tradescantia (Cuthbertia) rosea

(Pink Spiderwort)

ZONES: 7–9; sun to light shade
SOIL: moist, well drained
NATIVE TO: sandy woods and openings in the Piedmont and coastal plain; Virginia to Florida
SIZE: 4–12 inches (8–12 inches)
COLOR: rose pink; **BLOOMS** in early to midsummer

A delightful little plant often listed in its own genus, with low tufts of waxy, bright green foliage and slender flowering stems of small rose pink flowers. The variety *graminea* is the more northern, with thinner leaves. It performs very well in the Southeast, but is not reliably winter-hardy where the ground freezes deeply. This is unfortunate, because it is one of the most ornamental species in the genus.

Tradescantia subaspera

(Wide-leaved Spiderwort)

ZONES: 4–9; part sun to light shade
SOIL: moist
NATIVE TO: rich woods; West Virginia to Illinois, south to Missouri, Alabama, and Florida
SIZE: 1–3 feet (2 feet)
COLOR: violet-blue to lavender; **BLOOMS** all summer (if moist)

This is one of the tallest species, with large wide leaves and small flowers that appear sporadically most of the summer. It gives size and substance to the × *andersoniana* hybrids.

Tradescantia virginiana

(Virginia Spiderwort, Common Spiderwort)

ZONES: 3–9; sun to shade
SOIL: moist
NATIVE TO: rich woods and moist prairies; Maine to

Pennsylvania and Michigan, south to Missouri and Georgia

SIZE: 1–2 feet (16–24 inches)

COLOR: ranges from blue-violet to purple, lavender, rose, and white; **BLOOMS** in spring

A vigorous species and one of the hardiest, though most plants listed as *T. virginiana* in the trade are really the × *andersoniana* hybrids. This is one of the true spring bloomers that rests in summer. *T. bracteata* (Sticky Spiderwort), *T. occidentalis* (Prairie Spiderwort), and *T. ohiensis* (Smooth Spiderwort) are all very similar, chiefly midwestern and plains species. Prairie Spiderwort is the most drought-tolerant of the four, Smooth Spiderwort has a glaucous blue-green color, and Sticky Spiderwort is a good choice for full sun, with a wide range of flower colors and a compact habit. There are also a few closely allied species in Texas, including *T. gigantea* and *T. edwardsiana*, with others extending south into Mexico.

Trientalis borealis

Trientalis borealis

(try-en-TAL-us)
Primulaceae
Starflower

ZONES: 2–8; part sun, shade

SOIL: moist to dry

NATIVE TO: woods and bogs; Labrador to Alberta south to Minnesota, Ohio, and Pennsylvania and down the coast to Virginia; also in the Appalachian Mountains to Georgia

SIZE: 4–6 inches (12–16 inches)

COLOR: white; **BLOOMS** in spring

There are definite patterns in nature—patterns set by the limitations of environment and genes. Most of the strong patterns in the plant kingdom develop from the most elementary anatomy. Monocots (grasses, palms, orchids, etc.) begin life with one cotyledon and forever after send out one leaf at a time. Plants absorb blue and red light and reflect green, so the living world takes on a verdant hue. Plants cannot pull water higher than 300 feet or so, so forests cannot grow taller indefinitely. There are numerical patterns as well. The majority of dicot flowers have sets of 5 or 6 petals, sepals, and anthers, while monocots more commonly have 3. There are 4- and 8-petaled flowers, but rarely 2- or 7-parted ones. It is as if the evolutionary dice were rigged early on, so it is interesting and unusual to find a plant like Starflower composed of sevens. It has 7 leaves, 7 sepals, 7 petals , and 7 anthers. Why this came to be remains one of the curious little mysteries of nature, but it certainly makes the little woodlander easy to identify even if its whorled leaves do casually resemble Cucumber Root *(Mediola)*, Trillium, and others.

Starflower is one of the most common spring ephemerals in eastern North America. A thin, creeping rhizome sends up scattered stems each crowned with a whorl of leaves with 1 or 2 little flowers on angled stalks from the center. They seem equally at home in dry, sandy soil or on hummocks in swamps and travel about innocuously amid the fallen leaves and tree roots of deciduous and coniferous forests. The plants go dormant in midsummer, the leaves yellowing and falling so that all that remains is a naked stem with 1 or 2 tiny round seed capsules ripening at the tip. *Trientalis* is not showy or seasonally permanent enough for many people, but it adds a note of diversity and authenticity to naturalized plantings and woodlands, and I think it looks lovely growing among mosses, wintergreen, partridgeberry, and others.

CULTURE: Transplant in spring from containers or in late summer as dormant rhizomes to an acid soil, preferably one that is moist in spring. The plants will spread around as it suits them and require absolutely no maintenance once established.

USES: Naturalizing in woodland or bog.

PROPAGATION: Difficult from seed; moderately difficult from division. See p. 264.

Trientalis borealis. The unique, 7-petaled flowers of Trientalis *make it easy to identify in the wild. Though the number of leaves in a whorl is more variable, it is most commonly 7 as well.*

Trillium grandiflorum.
White Trillium is among the largest and certainly most vigorous in the genus, favoring rich, deciduous woodlands and neutral soils. You can encourage it with a dusting of limestone every year or two if your soil is naturally acidic. Healthy rhizomes readily produce offsets, and I further help them spread by plucking the fruits as they ripen in summer, pulling off the calyx (which rips a hole in the bottom of the fruit) and then pinching and squirting the seeds down into some nearby soil. Each fruit contains 20–40 seeds, and if treated this way, most of these will germinate within a few years.

Trillium grandiflorum

Trillium (TRILL-ee-um)
Liliaceae
Trillium, Wake-robin

I have been taught many lessons by the plants I have lived with over the years, none more important than the lesson of patience. We live in an impatient world, where slowness is a weakness and speed a virtue. My occupation as a nursery manager really boils down to growing the most plants in the shortest time possible with an acceptable level of quality. It is hard to accommodate wildflowers whose calenders are blocked off in years, not months, and among the most difficult in this respect are the trilliums. Trilliums are woodland plants, and like most woodland wildflowers, they take advantage of the brief growing window in spring when the ground has thawed but the trees have yet to leaf out. In this short time it is not possible to do much growing, so seedlings are content to plod along for seven years or more before finally producing their first bloom. Seven years! (And that is when everything goes right.) Not satisfied with this slothfulness, I have tried every trick I know to hurry the seed and seedlings along, but they doggedly refuse. The best I can do is knock a year or two off the cycle, but with trilliums there is an extremely fine line between optimization and overkill, so I have set back as many plants as I have helped.

The message here is that quality cannot be rushed, and many of the finest wildflowers are so beautiful precisely because they take their time. The slow addition of rings on a Redwood or stems on a trillium are like the patina that builds on a fine antique or the handle of a favorite shovel worn smooth by long contact with the skin. I know you might say, "I don't have enough years left to raise a crop of trilliums!" But I have a friend who is still regularly sowing the seeds in his mid-eighties, and he stubbornly insists on being around to see them bloom. He has learned the value of patience.

The genus *Trillium* includes some of our most exquisite native plants, with elegant proportion and breathtaking flowers. In the garden they are extremely long-lived, going on for decades, perhaps centuries, and faithfully sending up their trademark whorls of 3-leaved and 3-petaled flowers every year. They grow from a slowly creeping knobby rhizome as big as your thumb, which under good conditions puts out a few offsets now and then so that eventually the plants can become sizable clumps. There are broadly two types: sessile and pedunculate. Sessile trilliums have stemless flowers that nestle in the center of the leaves. Often their leaves are irregularly blotched and spotted with elegant markings of silver, gray, and maroon. The sessile trilliums, like the genus as a whole, are at their most diverse in the southeastern United States, with a few in the Midwest and far West. The second group bears their flowers on peduncles or stems that lift the bloom up and away from the leaves. For the most part these have leaves of solid green and a wider distribution. While all the species are showy or at least interesting, many are rare or hard to come by. Therefore, I will cover some of the more common, vigorous trilliums, and refer you to several excellent books on the subject for further reading. (See Case's *Trilliums* in bibliography.)

Nearly all plants for sale in the United States are originally wild-collected plants that have been "laundered" and then sold as "nursery-grown" plants. Ask your supplier where they get their plants. Bare-root plants are a dead giveaway, as no grower would purposely subject the tender roots of trilliums to such abuse. Remember, it takes three to seven years to produce a salable plant, so a plant that costs the price of a decent bottle of wine is not making anyone rich. Any that cost less are almost certainly wild collected. Recently, much progress has been made in tissue culture, and some of the western species are available now as lab-raised clones.

CULTURE: As a rule, trilliums want a moist, well-drained soil and dappled shade. The rhizomes of older plants can be 6 inches deep or more, but plant container plants 2–3 inches deep and let them adjust themselves over time. Never damage the roots if possible, as this will severely stunt and set back the plants (I can say this from experience). They are slow to establish, but not difficult to grow provided you take care to site them well. Some species (*T. nivale* and *T. grandiflorum* in particular) are lime lovers and appreciate a dusting of dolomite in autumn. Other than water during drought and a bit of mulch and fertilizer in spring, they require little maintenance. Older plants can be dug and divided, preferably in the early fall as growth yellows. Break or cut the rhizomes so that each division will have a healthy crop of roots and a new growth bud or two. (Buds will form from eyeless sections, but it can take a few years.)

USES: Specimens or scattered clumps in the shade or woodland garden.

PROPAGATION: Slow and difficult from seed; moderately difficult from division. See p. 264.

Pedunculate Species

Trillium catesbaei

(Rosey Wake-robin, Catesby's Trillium)

ZONES: 4–9; part sun, light shade
SOIL: moist, acid
NATIVE TO: moist woods and riparian zones; Virginia to Tennessee and Alabama
SIZE: 6–12 inches (12 inches)
COLOR: nearly white to dark rose; **BLOOMS** in spring

Rosey Wake-robin is one of the most common trilliums in the southern Piedmont, growing in the clay soil woods around my house in North Carolina and proving to be easy and vigorous in cultivation there. Plants put up offshoots much more rapidly than most, and the nodding, brightly colored flowers with thin, dramatically recurved petals are very sweet. It is adapted to a hot summer climate and grows reliably but much less vigorously in the North.

Trillium erectum

(Purple Trillium, Stinking Benjamin, Wake-robin)

ZONES: 3–8; light shade
SOIL: moist, acid
NATIVE TO: rich woods; New Brunswick and southern Quebec to Michigan, south to Ohio and Pennsylvania and in the mountains to Georgia
SIZE: 6–20 inches (12–18 inches)
COLOR: maroon; **BLOOMS** in spring

Purple Trillium is one of the most common acid soil species in the East, and its deep red flowers, vigorous, clumping habit, and adaptability make it one of the best for gardens. The flowers have a fetid odor, but only if inhaled at short range. There is a lovely white-flowered form with the charateristic maroon red ovary in the center that is common in the southern Appalachians, and this species readily hybridizes with others like *T. flexipes* to produce some unusual color forms. *T. vaseyi* (Sweet Beth), from the southern Appalachians, is a spectacular relative, with 3-inch-wide deep red flowers of heavy substance that hang below the leaves and lack the fetid odor of *T. erectum*. It is the last eastern species to bloom, with flowers persisting until the end of spring. *T. simile* (Sweet White Trillium) is another outstanding relative from the same area, with large triangular, glistening white flowers with a maroon center. *T. flexipes* (Bent Trillium) can be distinguished from these by its white ovary and petals (the flower lacks the maroon center). It is primarily from the upper Midwest, with outlying populations in the Appalachians. Typically the recurved flowers nod below the foliage, but the best forms have large flat flowers held above the leaves.

Trillium grandiflorum

(White Trillium, Great White Trillium)

ZONES: 3–8; part sun, light shade
SOIL: moist, neutral
NATIVE TO: rich woods, typically on slightly acid to neutral soils; Quebec to Minnesota south to Indiana and Pennsylvania and in the mountains to Georgia
SIZE: 8–20 inches (12–18 inches)
COLOR: white, fading to pink; **BLOOMS** in spring

A magnificent plant that couples vigor and ease in cultivation with some of the largest, showiest flowers of any wildflower. White Trillium typically forms large stands in Sugar Maple-Beech woodlands, and a carpet of blooming plants streching as far as you can see is breathtaking. The huge flowers with overlapping petals are held well above the leaves on nodding stems and typically fade to a ruddy pink as the flowers age. Var. *roseum*, from the Blue Ridge Mountains, opens a clear pink that is truly wonderful. This is a plant I am particularly focused on propagating. F. *multiplex*, the Double Trillium, is also spectacular, with fully double flowers.

Trillium ovatum

(Western White Trillium)

ZONES: 6–8; part sun, light shade
SOIL: moist
NATIVE TO: moist woodlands, particularly in the rain forest belt of the Pacific Northwest; Montana to British Columbia south to California and Idaho and locally in the central Rocky Mountains
SIZE: 6–24 inches (16–20 inches)
COLOR: white fading to pink; **BLOOMS** in spring

This is the most widespread western species, basically the West Coast form of *T. grandiflorum*. It is a common sight in the mossy fir forests of the Cascades, growing from the leaf litter and even the moss-covered trunks of fallen firs and spruce. For

Trillium ovatum. *In the fir forests where Western White Trillium commonly grows, space on the floor is at a premium. However, when massive old conifers come crashing down, they provide a balcony often 3–6 feet above the ground for this and many other small seedlings that would otherwise be shaded out. Conifer logs rot from the outside in (as opposed to hardwoods, which rot from the inside out), so after a few years in a moist climate, these "nurse logs" develop a spongy outer layer that supports mosses and then ferns, tree seedlings, and woodland herbs like trillium. Over time, the logs gradually decompose, but the process can take centuries. Consequently, it is common to see colonies of blooming Trillium ovatum growing from the sides of these fallen giants.*

gardeners outside of its native range, *T. grandiflorum* is a better choice, but in the Pacific Northwest, *T. ovatum* is an excellent garden plant. (It is fairly winter-hardy, but begins growth too early in spring to escape the late frosts that occur in the East.) There is a form from Vancouver Island, var. *hibbersonii*, that is dwarfed in all respects from a life on the rocky shores of this fog-shrouded place. The University of British Columbia was kind enough to send us some seed, and the plants are the cutest little things you have ever seen, though too slow and specialized to be good general garden plants.

Trillium undulatum
(Painted Trillium)

ZONES: 3–7; light shade
SOIL: cool, moist, acid
NATIVE TO: damp woods and bog margins; Quebec to Ontario and Michigan south to Pennsylvania and New Jersey and in the mountains to Georgia
SIZE: 8–20 inches (12 inches)
COLOR: white with a red-purple center; BLOOMS in late spring

Painted Trillium is a striking species, with pure white, upward-facing flowers with a prominent triangle of red-purple in the throat that bleeds up along the veins of the petals to the tips. The fruit is a distinctive, smooth oval berry with a pointed tip. Painted Trillium is a common species in northern New England and southeastern Canada, but is very difficult to grow in cultivation, needing consistently moist, cool, acid soils and especially prone to rots in less than ideal conditions. I include it because this is a species often wild collected and sold as "nursery propagated," but you can be 99 percent sure that no

nursery is really successfully propagating it. Please enjoy it in the wild.

Sessile Species

Trillium chloropetalum
(Giant Trillium)

ZONES: 6–8; part sun, light shade
SOIL: moist
NATIVE TO: scattered woodlands, moist forests, and grasslands; Washington to California
SIZE: 8–28 inches (16–20 inches)
COLOR: burgundy and maroon to rose and copper; BLOOMS in early spring

Giant Trillium is well named, for this sessile species can get very large, with rounded, overlapping leaves that are green with a faint burgundy overlay and a flower reminiscent of three starched kerchiefs standing bolt upright in the center of the leaves. In grows in the cool, maritime Pacific Northwest and coastal California, so proves difficult in most of the United States. In western Europe, this is a commonly grown garden plant, forming huge drifts that are truly stunning. *T. albidum* (White Toadshade) is a superb, white-flowered form of Giant Trillium from northern California and the southern half of Oregon.

Trillium cuneatum
(Whippoorwill Flower)

ZONES: 5–9; part sun to light shade
SOIL: moist
NATIVE TO: acid to neutral, sloping soils in rich woodland; North Carolina to Kentucky south to Mississippi and Georgia
SIZE: 6–12 inches (12–16 inches)
COLOR: deep maroon; BLOOMS in early spring

Whippoorwill is one of the earliest eastern trilliums to bloom and is one of the most vigorous and easy of the southeastern sessile types. The leaves are beautifully marbled with silver-gray and ruddy green, and the plants easily form large clumps in the garden. The flowers have a faintly sweet aroma. There are many other maroon-flowered, mottled-leaved species in the Southeast, such as *T. decumbens*, *T. eastwoodii*, and *T. reliquum*. Most have restricted or scattered distributions and rarely do they grow as vigorously and easily as this species. *T. sessile* (Toad Trillium) is a lightly mottled plant with smaller flowers that grows through a wide region of the Midwest and is commonly cultivated. It is a reliable and easy plant with a chubbier appearance than Whippoorwill. The flower color ranges from reddish green to maroon.

Trillium luteum
(Yellow Trillium, Yellow Toadshade)

ZONES: 4–8; light shade
SOIL: moist, neutral
NATIVE TO: rich woodland, especially on limestone;
southern Appalachians from Virginia to Georgia
west to Tennessee and Kentucky
SIZE: 6–14 inches (12–16 inches)
COLOR: yellow to yellow-green; **BLOOMS** in spring

Yellow Toadshade has mottled leaves more heavily
silvered than *T. cuneatum* and a limited wild distribution that sits squarely within the major wildflower
collecting region of central Tennessee, so plants are
commonly available in the trade as purportedly
nursery-grown material. It is a lovely plant that is
easy to grow, and the citrus-scented flowers are a nice
contrast in a mixed planting. *T. viride* is a mottled
plant from Missouri and Illinois with very thin green
petals that match the form and color of the sepals.
Plants listed in the trade as *T. viride* var. *luteum* are
probably *T. luteum*.

Trillium recurvatum
(Prairie Trillium)

ZONES: 4–9; part sun, light shade
SOIL: moist to wet
NATIVE TO: floodplains and rich woods; Ohio to
southern Ontario and Minnesota south to
Louisiana and Alabama

SIZE: 4–12 inches (12 inches)
COLOR: maroon; **BLOOMS** in spring

Prairie Trillium is one of the most diminutive sessile
species, with thin, mottled leaves and narrow petals,
but it is a rapidly spreading plant, easy in the garden.
The rhizomes of this species are thin and long jointed, with stems spaced 2–4 inches apart in loose
colonies.

Trollius laxus

Trollius (troll-EE-us)
Ranunculaceae
Globeflower

Some plants are so vigorous and easy in cultivation that their rarity in the wild is a great mystery to
me. We have one species of globeflower in temperate
North America, *T. laxus*, that has an interesting natural range. The common white-flowered alpine *T.
laxus* var. *albiflorus* (or listed as just *T. albiflorus*)
grows exuberantly in damp alpine meadows and
beside rushing mountian streams in the central
Rockies and north into British Columbia, then
resurfaces far to the east as *T. laxus* var. *laxus*, a yellow-flowered version. This northeastern form is a
very rare fellow, found only occasionally in limestone regions growing in damp meadows and
swamps. There is not much limestone in the East,
and every year there are fewer open wetlands, so its
rarity there may be explained simply by lack of habitat. In cultivation, both are satisfying plants (though
the western form demands a cool climate), with

(LEFT): Trillium luteum.
*I know deer like to eat
trilliums. The burgeon-
ing deer herds in the
Northeast are wreaking
havoc on stands of these
slow-growing wildflow-
ers. So I wonder if the
patterning on the leaves
of many of the sessile
trilliums serves to cam-
ouflage them from these
doe-eyed goats. If you
photograph a stand with
black and white film (as
a deer would see them)
the leaves effectively
blend into the back-
ground. It's food for
thought, anyway.*

(RIGHT): Trollius laxus. *If
you look carefully into
the center of this globe-
flower, you will see two
kinds of stamens — long
thin ones with pollen-
bearing anthers and
squat, glossy ones called
staminodes, which are
modified to produce nec-
tar, not pollen. The But-
tercup family is one of
the most primitive
groups of flowering
plants, and these
staminodes are an early
adaptation for luring
pollinators with a sugar
reward. Insects such as
butterflies that would
rather consume sugar
than protein-rich pollen
are of obvious advan-
tage to the plant, which
needs its pollen trans-
ferred to other flowers.*

Uvularia sessilifolia.
Small tubular flowers decorate the developing stems of Wild Oats in the spring. It is one of the most common wildflowers of the eastern deciduous forests, growing in damp to fairly dry soils with equal abandon. Though Wild Oats spreads quickly, it is too slight to overpower its neighbors, and I like to let it creep about informal plantings.

mounds of vibrant green, deeply cut 5-parted leaves and large, open, 5-sepaled flowers with a big yellow-green puff of stamens in the middle. The flowers are borne on thick stems just above the neat mound of emerging foliage, with a heavy flush of bloom in spring and occasional flowers again in summer and fall.

CULTURE: Best in a damp, humusy soil with good fertility and some sun. *Trollius* have stringy roots and a small, woody crown that it is best not to attempt to divide. Fortunately they readily self-sow, and the little seedlings with distinctive 5-parted leaves are easy to find and move in spring. The plants prefer a spot without heavy competition and even moisture all year, and the eastern form should receive an annual dusting of limestone.

USES: Waterside or bog gardens.

PROPAGATION: Moderately difficult from seed. See p. 264.

Trollius laxus var. *albiflorus*
(White Globeflower)

ZONES: 3–7; sun, part sun
SOIL: moist to wet, acid
NATIVE TO: alpine meadows and streambanks; Montana north to Manitoba and British Columbia and south to Washington, Idaho, and Colorado
SIZE: 8–20 inches (12–16 inches)
COLOR: creamy white fading to light yellow-green; **BLOOMS** in early spring

Trollius laxus var. *laxus*
(Spreading Globeflower)

ZONES: 4–8; sun, part shade
SOIL: moist to wet, calcareous
NATIVE TO: alkaline fens and swamps; Connecticut to Ohio south to Pennsylvania and Delaware
SIZE: 12–20 inches (12–16 inches)
COLOR: light yellow with a hint of green; **BLOOMS** from early spring to early summer then sporadically in fall

Uvularia sessilifolia

Uvularia
(you-view-LAH-ree-ah)
Liliaceae
Merrybells, Bellwort

Merrybells have a curious way of emerging in spring. The flaccid stems looks as if they are being gradually inflated from below like a minature float for the Thanksgiving Day Parade. The flowers are the first to expand, looking elegant and fully functional

while the leaves and stems are still soft and continuing to bloom even after the plants have lengthened and become completely expanded and hard. They are related to fairybells and have the same elegant form — stiff stems rising from the ground and branching halfway up like a tiered, three-dimensional Solomon's seal. Like *Disporum* and many of the woodland lilies, the leaves lack petioles and look deftly skewered by the arching stems. They are some of my favorite woodland wildflowers, combining ease of cultivation with graceful architecture and soft, delicate foliage.

CULTURE: *Uvularia*s grow from a blanched rhizome and thick roots which can be divided in late summer as the plants die down. Be careful not to divide them too severely, leaving several pointed buds and a good cluster of roots with each piece. They are happiest in a moist, lightly shaded location and compete well with the roots of trees. Large Merrybells is a lime lover, and a yearly dusting of dolomite will bring out the richest leaf color.

USES: Specimen, massing, or ground cover in the shade or woodland garden.

PROPAGATION: Slow and moderately difficult from seed; fairly easy from division. See p. 264.

Uvularia grandiflora
(Large-flowered Bellwort, Large Merrybells)

ZONES: 3–8; part sun, shade
SOIL: moist, neutral

NATIVE TO: rich woods, especially over limestone; Maine and Quebec to North Dakota south to Oklahoma and in the mountains to Georgia

SIZE: 12–16 inches (12–16 inches)

COLOR: pale to medium soft yellow; **BLOOMS** in spring

Large Merrybells is a peerless plant for the shade garden, with strongly clumping stems and large sweetly fragrant flowers dangling from the upper leaf axils. The tepals are not united as in the other species, and they twist and twirl pendantly from the green cap of the ovary. The plants have a weeping appearance in bloom, but stiffen up to a vase shape when mature. *U. perfoliata* (Bellwort) is very similar in leaf, but the flowers are smaller and the tepals fuse into a narrow bell flared at the opening. Both of these species have soft blue-green foliage that turns a glowing soft yellow in fall.

Uvularia sessilifolia
(Wild Oats)

ZONES: 3–8; part sun, shade

SOIL: moist to moderately dry

NATIVE TO: woods; Nova Scotia to South Dakota south to Louisiana and Florida

SIZE: 4–12 inches (12–18 inches)

COLOR: creamy white; **BLOOMS** in spring

U. sessilifolia is the most common and widespread species, sending up its familiar little stems throughout woodlands east of the Rockies. Its rhizomes are long and jointed, with thornlike buds at regular intervals and roots in between. (The rhizomes remind me of large white greenbrier canes in their arrangement and shape.) It forms loose spreading colonies and is useful as a carefree, fairly drought-tolerant deciduous ground cover. We have been growing a lightly variegated form for years that is quite vigorous and distinctive. The flowers of this species are fused into long, narrow, downward-facing bells hung sparingly from the leaf axils. *U. puberula* (Mountain Bellwort) is a closely related species from the southern Appalachians.

Vancouveria hexandra

Vancouveria
(van-coo-VAIR-ee-ah)
Berberidaceae
Inside-out Flower

The **nearest** thing in our flora to the elegant Asian genus *Epimedium* are the *Vancouveria*s, fine-textured, spreading ground covers from the central Pacific Coast with thrice-divided leaves and stiff flower spikes growing separately from wandering rhizomes. Even though all three grow over much the same native range, only the deciduous *V. hexandra* is reliably hardy in much of the United States. It is a somewhat rampant plant, with foliage resembling *Thalictrum* and colored a matte, medium green. The flowers (which look like little parachutes or sprung umbrellas hung above the leaves) are interesting but not particularly showy from a distance. It is a valuable plant for covering larger areas in deep shade, and the colonies can be spaded around the edges once a year to control their spread. The other two are evergreen, with glossy, deep green, leathery leaves and a similar habit. The genus is named for the English explorer George Vancouver, not the island, as I used to believe.

CULTURE: Transplant in spring as either rhizome divisions or potted plants. They thrive in fairly deep, dry shade and require little maintenance other than occasional root pruning and fertilization in spring. *V. planipetala* will survive in Zone 6 with a fall mulching, but it does not really thrive in a climate where the ground freezes hard in winter.

USES: Evergreen or deciduous ground cover for shade.

PROPAGATION: Easy from division. See p. 264.

Vancouveria hexandra
(White Inside-out Flower)

ZONES: 5–8; part sun to shade

SOIL: moist to summer dry

Vancouveria hexandra. *Inside-out Flower is a rugged, carefree tall ground cover even for difficult, dry shady spots. It does respond magnificently to a dressing of compost or fertilizer in spring. Most of its leaves come in a spring flush along with the curious flowers, but under good conditions, new foliage continues to emerge sporadically through the season.*

Veratrum viride. *There is a beautiful symmetry about an emerging False Hellebore, with pleated leaves arranged in 3 ranks along a thumb-thick stem. I can tell by its size that this is a "blind" (nonflowering) growth, typical for eastern plants growing in deciduous shade. In the western mountains, Veratrum grows abundantly in wet, open mountain meadows, where abundant sunlight allows prolific flowering.*

NATIVE TO: shady, coniferous forests; coastal Washington to northern California
SIZE: 8–16 inches (18–24 inches)
COLOR: white; **BLOOMS** in late spring

Vancouveria planipetala
(Inside-out Flower)

ZONES: 7–8; part sun to shade
SOIL: moist
NATIVE TO: shaded Redwood forests; southern Oregon to central California
SIZE: 8–16 inches (18–24 inches)
COLOR: creamy white; **BLOOMS** in spring

This is one of the few plants that can survive in the deep shade and toxic mulch of the giant coast Redwoods, but it is less vigorous and cold hardy than *V. hexandra*. *V. chrysantha* (Siskiyou Inside-out Flower) is a yellow-flowered version from serpentine soils in the Siskiyou Mountains of California and Oregon.

Veratrum viride

Veratrum viride
(ver-AT-rum)
Liliaceae
False Hellebore, White Hellebore, Indian Poke

ZONES: 3–8; part sun, shade
SOIL: wet to seasonally inundated
NATIVE TO: swamps, floodplains, and (in the West) damp mountain meadows; Quebec to Ontario south to North Carolina and Alaska south to Oregon

SIZE: 2–4 feet (2 feet)
COLOR: chartreuse; **BLOOMS** in spring

Amid the verdant spring green of a Skunk Cabbage swamp or the slopes of a wet mountain meadow you will often find huge, pleated leaves spiraling languidly from thick, vertical stems—the unmistakable, resplendent growths of False Hellebore. Superficially the plants resemble large lady-slipper orchids or some tropical ginger in habit, and mixed with the bold foliage of Skunk Cabbage, they give the scene a distinctly primeval aura. They grow in scattered colonies in mucky soil, appearing soon after the thaw and going dormant by early summer. Flowering must be a real energy drain on these creatures, for usually only one plant out of fifty blooms each year. The flowers are closer to strange than beautiful: starry, 6-tepaled affairs dyed an eerie shade of lime green and possessed of a thick, waxy substance that makes them feel artificial to the touch. The leaves of nonflowering stems get progressively smaller and smaller up the stem until they just disappear near the top, while flowering ones continue to lengthen and send out stiff racemes from the terminus and the axils of the small upper leaves. *V. woodii* is a smaller plant with reddish flowers that ranges from Ohio to Missouri south to Oklahoma, and there are other green-flowered species in the western mountains that are nearly identical to *V. viride*.

Veratrum contains toxic alkaloids that were employed medicinally and as insecticides in the past, but the plants are highly poisonous if ingested and considered unsafe to use today. Some Native American tribes prescribed a three-week treatment of a tincture made from the root to induce permanent sterility in women.[10]

There are a number of closely related genera and a few are worth mentioning. *Melanthium*s are mainly southeastern plants, with a clump of whorled basal foliage that erects a huge branching spike of cream flowers. The sepals and petals are stalked, so the center of the flower has 6 round gaps around the ovary. *M. hybridum* (Broad Bunchflower) is my favorite, with 1½-inch strappy leaves that are creased along the midvein and magnificent stout inflorescences. The ovaries are burgundy, which gives the center a reddish cast and helps distinguish it from its close relative, *M. virginicum*. *M. parviflorum* (Varebell—also listed as *Veratrum parviflorum*), has oval leaves like a small False Hellebore and greenish flowers in thin spikes. *Stenanthium graminium* (Featherbells) is another in this group, with long straplike leaves like a daylily and tall candelabras of snowy white flowers late in the year. *S.* var. *robustum*, the one we grow, is about twice as large as the species. It is a lovely plant with sweet-scented blooms, but I have trouble convincing spring visitors that the clump of nondescript leaves in the pot they are holding will amount to anything by fall.

CULTURE: All these species grow in damp or wet soils in full or partial sun. (Shade is tolerated, but blooms will be few.) They are equally slow as *Veratrum* from seed, but unlike it, once they reach flowering size they bloom consistently from year to year.

USES: Watersides, low meadows and woods.

PROPAGATION: Slow and difficult from seed. See p. 264.

Verbena stricta

Verbena (ver-BEE-na)
Verbenaceae
Vervain, Verbena

The verbenas are a colorful lot—their 5-petaled flowers just slightly irregular in shape (the lowest petal is a bit longer—like the lip of a mint flower) and saturated with pigment that more than makes up in intensity what they lack in size. They are long-blooming plants as well, most with flowers in tall thin spikes closely set with pointed seed capsules below and unopened buds above, and a ring of open flowers in the middle that never quite seem to catch the tip. The taller plants are perennials of meadows and prairies, while the low, trailing species are shorter-lived denizens of open, rocky sites. The smaller species have spikes with flowers aggregated near the tip in a rounded head like a tropical lantana, which hides the seed capsules stretched out below.

The vervains most familiar to gardeners are the vibrantly colored, tender perennials grown as annual bedding plants and valued for drought and heat resistance. It is in the tropical areas of the continent that the tribe reaches its greatest diversity. Traditionally the most commonly available was *Verbena × hybrida* (Garden Verbena) which comes in a range of vibrant colors inherited from several South American species like the red *V. peruviana,* pale lilac *V. teucriodes,* red or purple *V. phlogiflora,* and pink *V. incisa.* Recently, trailing hybrids, many with *V. canadensis* in their ancestry, have become more widely available as bedding plants in the North. These have long been grown and traded among gardeners in the Southeast, as they are well suited to a life of heat and humidity and are typically perennial in Zones 8–10. Like all in the tribe, they are long-blooming and excellent nectar plants for butterflies and bees.

CULTURE: Vervains are easy to grow, most tolerating dry soils but blooming heaviest in a moderately fertile, well-drained site with ample sun. All produce thousands of small seeds that establish themselves here and there but rarely in enough abundance to cause problems. The trailing types root and layer as they go, so it is easy to dig sections after they begin growth again in spring. The tall species are best left alone and propagated from seed or self-sown recruits. Tony Avent of Plant Delights Nursery recommends placing a flat stone over a section of trailing stems in fall to help *V. canadensis* and its hybrids pull through the winter. The rock helps protect the stems from freeze damage in marginal locations.

USES: Meadows, prairies, borders, edging, rock gardens.

PROPAGATION: Easy from seed or cuttings. See p. 265.

Verbena bipinnatifida
(Dakota Vervain)

ZONES: 5–10; sun
SOIL: well drained
NATIVE TO: dry plains and open, rocky sites; South Dakota to Arizona and Louisiana
SIZE: 3–12 inches (12 inches)
COLOR: pink or purple; **BLOOMS** from spring to fall
This is much like *V. canadensis* in habit, but leaves are twice divided and quite beautiful in a lacy, paper snowflake way. The flowers are a bit smaller though also similar, and the plants are more reliably hardy in the North. It is not as vibrant and showy as most of the trailing hybrids, but its perennial nature makes it a good substitute in areas too cold for the tender species to survive.

Verbena canadensis
(Rose Verbena)

ZONES: 5–10; sun, part sun
SOIL: moist to dry, well drained

Verbena stricta. Hoary Vervain is a lovely, solidly perennial species at home in dry, sunny locations. This plant was photographed in a state park in southwestern Wisconsin, where a program of controlled burning is keeping the woody vegetation down and allowing prairie wildflowers to return. Occasional fire is necessary to maintain grassland vegetation in the eastern Great Plains, where rainfall is high enough to otherwise support deciduous forest.

Vernonia noveboracensis. New York Ironweed mixes with other giants such as Swamp Sunflower, Flat-topped Aster, and Swamp Aster around the pond at Garden in the Woods for a dramatic show late in the season.

NATIVE TO: open, disturbed sites; Pennsylvania to Illinois and Colorado south to Texas, Tennessee, and Florida

SIZE: 3–12 inches (12–16 inches)

COLOR: blue-violet, purple, or white; **BLOOMS** from summer to fall

Rose Verbena is a valuable low border or edging plant with a loose, trailing habit and large flat flower heads produced over a remarkably long period. The lax stems are set with pairs of more or less triangular leaves that have irregular, deeply toothed margins. It is an unpredictable perennial north of Zone 7, with sections of a patch dying out in some years and coming through fine in others. They will also come from seed so that the plants usually persist one way or another in a scattered, informal way. In the South and far West it remains truly perennial, starting to bloom very early in the season with occasional breaks to regroup before beginning another flush. A hybrid of *V. canadensis* discovered by Michael Dirr and Alan Armitage around an old home site in Georgia and named *Verbena* × 'Homestead Purple' has proven to be a superior garden plant, with large blooms of a deep royal purple from spring to fall. It is unreliably hardy north of Zone 7, but can be used as a bedding plant in the North.

Verbena hastata
(Blue Vervain)

ZONES: 3–9; sun, part sun

SOIL: moist to wet

NATIVE TO: moist to wet meadows and prairies; Nova Scotia to British Columbia south to Arizona and Florida

SIZE: 2–4 feet (12–16 inches)

COLOR: dark blue-violet; **BLOOMS** from summer to early fall

A tall perennial of wet places with lance-shaped, toothed leaves and well-branched, strongly vertical spikes from the upper axils that bloom and lengthen much of the summer. I think of Blue Vervain as a companion plant in mixed, informal plantings and meadows as it is a little coarse to stand alone. The dark color of the small flowers mixes well with the yellows and golds of the summer prairie.

Verbena stricta
(Hoary Vervain)

ZONES: 3–9; sun

SOIL: moderately moist to dry

NATIVE TO: dry prairies and meadows; Ontario to Wyoming south to New Mexico and Texas and naturalized east to Massachusetts and West Virginia

SIZE: 2–3 feet (12–16 inches)

COLOR: strong violet; **BLOOMS** in summer

V. stricta is yet another wonderful wildflower that needs to be more widely grown. It is a tough, drought-tolerant perennial with strong stems and a narrowly vertical habit. The stiff, oval 2-inch leaves are jaggedly toothed and covered with a white pubescence that gives the plants a gray-green cast. They form in overlapping pairs that are pressed up against the stem like scales of a fish. Flowers are borne on tall, vertical spikes from the upper axils over much of the summer. They are fairly large and intensely colored, and the plants have a refined appearance on the whole that lends them to use in borders as well as naturalizing.

Vernonia noveboracensis

Vernonia (ver-KNOWN-ee-ah)
Asteraceae
Ironweed

The name ironweed has a nice ring to it, a diehard, rock-solid toughness. The ironweeds are a rugged lot, to be sure, but the name was inpired by the rusty brown color of the seeds' pappus or parachutes, not some implied metallic obstinacy. Most members of the genus are tall, clumping plants with medium green leaves alternating up thick stems crowned in late summer and fall with flattened panicles of rich purple blooms. They have an undeniable vertical presence in the meadow or border, especially in the moist rich soils that the larger species prefer. Admittedly, the plants are a little coarse in appearance, and the flowers vary little in color and shape from one species to the next, but for ease of culture and stature they are hard to beat.

There are an incredible number of ironweeds worldwide (over 1,000 by some estimates), with twenty or so in our flora. They are often difficult to tell apart, and frequent natural hybrids compound the problem further. New York Ironweed is the most commonly grown, but I have listed some of the others that are distinct enough to merit a closer look.

CULTURE: Ironweeds are easily cultivated in a sunny garden. And even though the majority are wetland plants, they will take some drought once established and require little care. Pinching back the tips in early summer will yield bushier specimens that are less likely to lean. Ironweeds readily self-sow, so deadhead after flowers fade. The plants form large deep-rooted clumps that are difficult to divide or move (broken roots will readily sprout if left behind), but seedlings or container plants can be set out in spring.

USES: Screening, large borders, naturalizing in meadows or prairies.

PROPAGATION: Easy from seed or cuttings. See p. 265.

Vernonia angustifolia

(Ironweed)

ZONES: 6–9; sun, part sun
SOIL: moist to dry
NATIVE TO: moist sandy soils along the coastal plain; North Carolina to Florida and Mississippi
SIZE: 2–4 feet (2 feet)
COLOR: deep reddish purple; **BLOOMS** in late summer
The true *V. angustifolia* is very easy to recognize, with long, almost needlelike leaves ⅛-inch wide and 2–4 inches long. The flower heads are more open and distinctly V-shaped in outline. The species is not particularly winter-hardy, and even hybrids with much larger leaves I received as *V. angustifolia* have proven unreliable in Zone 5. It is an attractive plant for gardeners in the South.

Vernonia fasciculata

(Smooth Ironweed)

ZONES: 3–9; sun
SOIL: moist to wet
NATIVE TO: wet prairies and marshes; Ohio and Minnesota to Manitoba south to Texas, Missouri, and Kentucky
SIZE: 3–5 feet (2–3 feet)
COLOR: deep reddish purple; **BLOOMS** in late summer
This species is distinctive because the flowers are bunched in broccoli-shaped heads rather than loose, open panicles.

Vernonia lettermannii

(Ironweed)

ZONES: 4–9; sun
SOIL: dry
NATIVE TO: dry meadows and banks; Kentucky to Arkansas
SIZE: 16–30 inches (12 inches)
COLOR: purple; **BLOOMS** in early fall
This is an unusual species with very narrow leaves

heavily clothing short stems. It looks *exactly* like Hubricht's Bluestar (*Amsonia hubrichtii*) when not in bloom. The flowers are fairly small, but the foliage is quite beautiful and the plants are very deep-rooted and extremely drought-tolerant. Last year I tried hybridizing this with New York Ironweed without success, though I am trying to spread the word by distributing the species to nurseries as much as I can.

Vernonia noveboracensis

(New York Ironweed)

ZONES: 3–9; sun, part sun
SOIL: moist to wet
NATIVE TO: low woods, ditches, and marshes, mainly near the coast; Massachusetts to Pennsylvania south to Tennessee, Alabama, and Florida
SIZE: 4–8 feet (3–4 feet)
COLOR: deep reddish purple; **BLOOMS** in late summer
This is a robust clumping perennial with 4–6-inch deep green lance-shaped leaves densely alternating up thick stems. The flowers are borne on short branching stems from the axils of the upper leaves, in effect a rounded or flat-topped crown of purple. In drier soils the plants remain shorter than 4 feet. *V. arkansana (crinita)* (Ozark Ironweed) is very similar, differing in its slightly narrower leaves and the curly bracts at the base of the flower. It hybridizes easily, and rarely do I get consistent seedlings from cultivated plants. *V. baldwinii* (Western Ironweed) is about half as tall, with wider, stiff gray-green leaves and smaller heads. It is a drought-tolerant plant, primarily of the Great Plains.

(LEFT): Veronicastrum virginicum. *The light pink form of Culver's Root caught in a breeze. It is one of the classic tallgrass prairie wildflowers, sending its wispy racemes above the tops of its companions in midsummer.*

(RIGHT): Viola canadensis. *The beautiful violet striations in the throat of Canada Violet are nectar guides that act as "landing lights" to lure and direct pollinators. Many flowers have patterns that function as pollinator guides, but often we cannot see them, as they are visible only in ultraviolet light. These have evolved to take advantage of insects' ability to see colors beyond violet, which is the spectral limit of human vision.*

Veronicastrum virginicum

Veronicastrum virginicum
(ver-on-eh-CAST-rum)
Scrophulariaceae
Culver's Root, Bowman's Root

ZONES: 3–9; sun, part sun

SOIL: moist

NATIVE TO: clearings, moist meadows and prairies; Vermont to Manitoba south to Louisiana and Georgia

SIZE: 3–6 feet (2 feet)

COLOR: typically white, though light pink forms are popular in gardens; **BLOOMS** in mid- to late summer

Culver's Root has the head of a Veronica and the body of a lily grafted together in an elegant combination of lightness and vertical strength. These durable meadow plants send up straight stems clothed their length with whorls of narrow leaves in sets of 3–6. By midsummer, the plants turn their attention to flowering, and the last few sets of leaves send out graceful spires of delicate flowers from their axils. The flower spikes have the general size and shape of the common garden Speedwell *(Veronica spicata)*, with a more sinuous quality, as if painted by Van Gogh.

The boiled, dried roots of the plant are a powerful emetic that was commonly employed by Native Americans in the Midwest and later by European settlers. One explanation for the common name is that Culver was a eighteenth-century doctor or herbalist who popularized the use of the plant. In smaller doses, it helps with digestive problems and constipation.

CULTURE: Easily grown in a moist to wet location. The plants are strongly clumping, and their vertical presence combines well with meadow companions like asters, ironweeds, and goldenrods. The thick roots are possible to divide in spring before the plants resume growth (*Veronicastrum* is a bit late to emerge in spring), and division every three to five years will keep the plants growing vigorously. Rarely do the strong stems need to be staked, and pinching back the plants will corrupt their beautiful architecture.

USES: Borders, meadows, watersides.

PROPAGATION: Easy from seed or cuttings. See p. 265.

Viola canadensis

Viola (vye-OH-la)
Violaceae
Violet

One afternoon last May when the air was heavy with the musky-sweet symphony of spring, I decided to count all the species of violets I could find at Garden in the Woods. I was amazed to discover that I easily found 23 species growing amid cold frames in the nursery, garden plantings, even in the parking lot gravel. I am hard-pressed to think of any other genus in the Garden with this much diversity. Violets are a bit like those Magic Eye 3-D posters that were popular a few years ago (the ones with a design that you held a foot from your nose and stared at cross-eyed until a three-dimensional image suddenly appeared magically before you). At first, a violet is a violet, but then you notice that this one has yellow flowers, that one has long narrow leaves, another sports a coating of downy hair. Pretty soon you'll notice myriad species growing in all conceivable habitats from swamps to ledges to misty mountain woods.

Violets are by nature a migratory group. While an individual plant can live for years, its offspring are being constantly and violently ejected from their seed capsules and will begin to grow around it in any spot that suits them. Thus many gardeners have a love-hate relationship with violets and decry their inability to stay put. This method of seed dispersal is of obvious evolutionary value, however, as it allows the plants to leapfrog around and colonize newly disturbed areas.

The seeds are small, usually a buff or brown color when ripe. They form in rows within 3-sided capsules that ripen two to four weeks after pollination. Each boat-shaped side of the capsule contains 1–2 rows of seeds. When the seeds are mature, the capsule splits open much as a flower would, revealing the 3 boats with their cargoes of seed. As the capsules dry and shrink, the sides put a great deal of pressure on the seeds, which are eventually squeezed so hard that they are ejected from the split capsule.

Violets are well known for their habit of producing small, closed, self-pollinating—or cleistogamous—flowers after the initial flush of open, petaled flowers in spring. Since the self-pollinating flowers do not depend on the vagaries of weather and insects, seed set is assured, but these seeds are necessarily inbred and lacking genetic diversity. The open flowers of spring allow out-crossing, but seed set is often erratic because of inconsistent pollinator activity. Seeds collected from the closed, summer flowers will come true to the parent, but those collected from the early flowers can sometimes yield surprises. We often have plants come up near our patch of *V. brittoniana* which are obviously hybrids between it and other species like *V. sororia*.

CULTURE: Since violets tend to self-sow, offspring can be easily dug from near the parent plants and moved to another area of the garden. I prefer to move violets in spring as this is when most are in active growth, but they are not too fussy. There are species for just about every garden niche, and if they are unhappy where you have placed them they will usually move. Some species are especially prone to thrip damage. The insects feed on the new leaves in summer, rasping away tissue so that the foliage develops scarring and malformation. I usually cut back affected plants and they recover well by spring. The same can be said for powdery mildew as well.

USES: Ground cover for woodland or rock garden; naturalizing.

PROPAGATION: Easy from seed. See p. 265.

Viola adunca
(Hook-spurred Violet)

ZONES: 3–9; sun to light shade
SOIL: moist to dry
NATIVE TO: sandy soils, alpine ravines; Greenland to Alaska south to California, Minnesota, and New York
SIZE: 3–6 inches (6–12 inches)
COLOR: violet; **BLOOMS** in spring

Hook-spurred Violet is one of a number of low-bunching species that begin the season as a neat tuft of leaves and flowers but continue to grow and lengthen over the season so that by late summer they are sprawling ground covers or loose clumps. *V. adunca* is a common northern species with dark green leaves of heavy substance. It is a cute little plant for gardeners in cool climates, with ¾-inch flowers as large as the leaves. Similar species include *V. rostrata* (Long-spurred Violet) and *V. conspersa* (Dog Violet), both more heat-tolerant eastern woodlanders with lighter flowers and larger leaves.

Viola appalachiensis
(Appalachian Violet)

ZONES: 4–8; part sun, shade
SOIL: moist
NATIVE TO: moist woods and cliffs; West Virginia to Tennessee and North Carolina
SIZE: 3 inches (12 inches)
COLOR: violet or white; **BLOOMS** in spring

This is one of my many favorites and a true ground cover. The round ¾-inch leaves are light green and produced on trailing stems that can spread a foot or more in a season. The little flowers appear in abundance on top of the leaves for three weeks in spring. Our original plants came from long-time friend and consummate plantsman Richard Redfield, who has admired these plants in his garden for many years.

Viola canadensis
(Tall White Violet, Canada Violet)

ZONES: 3–8; part sun, shade
SOIL: moist
NATIVE TO: fertile woods; Newfoundland to Alaska south to Arizona and Arkansas
SIZE: 10–16 inches (12 inches)
COLOR: pale violet in bud, opening white with violet striations on the lip; **BLOOMS** in spring

This is a robust, mounding species with lovely white flowers that are tinged violet on the reverse so they appear darker in bud. It blooms for most of the spring, with successive flowers scattered among the large heart-shaped leaves. The eastern form is strongly clumping, but the western var. *rugulosa* spreads by creeping rhizomes to form large colonies.

Viola fimbriatula
(Ovate-leaved Violet)

ZONES: 3–9; sun, part sun
SOIL: moist to dry
NATIVE TO: drier soils, upland woods, slopes and clearings; Nova Scotia and Maine to Minnesota south to Louisiana and Florida
SIZE: 3–6 inches (6 inches)
COLOR: violet; **BLOOMS** in spring

This is a distinctive plant with downy gray-green leaves that are longer than they are broad. It blooms in a flush before the leaves are fully emerged and forms tight, nonrunning clumps through the summer. Ovate-leaved Violet has also been lumped in with Arrow-leaved Violet *(V. sagittata),* which has smooth leaves shaped just like an arrowhead. Both are good choices for dry, poor soils and gravelly spots.

Viola labradorica
(Labrador Violet)

ZONES: 2–8; sun to shade
SOIL: moist to dry
NATIVE TO: moist open sites; Labrador and Ontario south to Maine
SIZE: 3–6 inches (8–12 inches)
COLOR: dark violet purple; **BLOOMS** in spring

Labrador Violet is a perennial favorite at Garden in the Woods, notable for its wonderful leaves that open burgundy and fade to dark purple-green. It is con-

Viola pedata. *A well-grown clump of Bird's-foot Violet is a breathtaking sight. The plants prefer sandy, disturbed sites in the wild, and I used to collect seed at a nearby landfill that would cap great mountains of garbage with poor, sandy fill. This particular dump hosted the largest population I've ever seen, and the gate attendant got a kick out of my collecting seed on top of Trash Mountain amid the stench, seagulls, and blowing plastic. I am sure I was the brunt of some pretty good lunchroom jokes. Oh, the travails we must endure.*

sidered by some to be a variety of *V. adunca* and shares its bunching then scandent growth habit. Considering its northern range, it is easy and adaptable in the garden, making a dense ground cover in good sites by midsummer.

Viola pedata
(Bird's-foot Violet)

ZONES: 3–9; sun, part sun
SOIL: well drained
NATIVE TO: dry, rocky or sandy slopes, fields and open woods; Maine to Minnesota south to Texas and Florida
SIZE: 3–5 inches (6 inches)
COLOR: violet, or in variety *bicolor,* with upper 2 petals dark purple and lower 3 violet; **BLOOMS** in spring

This is perhaps our finest species, and very different from most of the others covered here. Bird's-foot Violet grows from a fat caudex that sends out a tuft of leaves and flowers in spring. It does not produce any stems or cleistogamous seeds later in the season, only reluctantly producing another flush of leaves if conditions are especially favorable. The leaves are finely lobed and dissected, like the foot of a bird with about 5 extra toes. The exquisite var. *bicolor* occurs sporadically but more commonly south, with dark purple on the upper petals and violet below. To thrive, Bird's-foot Violet needs a well-drained spot to prevent crown root and full sun to encourage heavy flowering. It can withstand considerable drought as well. *V. palmata* (Wood Violet) is a variable plant, but many forms have a palmately lobed leaf much like *V. pedata.* It can be distinguished by its larger size, cleistogamous flowers in summer, and preference for shadier habitats.

Viola pubescens
(Yellow Forest Violet, Downy Yellow Violet)

ZONES: 3–9; part sun to shade
SOIL: moist
NATIVE TO: rich woods; Nova Scotia to Manitoba south to Texas, Louisiana, and Georgia
SIZE: 8–16 inches (12 inches)
COLOR: yellow; **BLOOMS** in spring

V. pubescens is one of the most common yellow violets in the East, growing into large bushy clumps with heart-shaped leaves up to 3 inches long. The flowers appear in a flush as the new growth expands, then sporadically for a few weeks thereafter. Unfortunately it is one of the most attractive to thrips and mildew. *V. glabella* (Pioneer Violet) is a relative from the mountainous West with hairless leaves. *V. nuttallii* (Prairie Violet), a widespread Great Plains species, is also yellow flowered but otherwise quite different. It is only half the size, with smaller flowers flushed violet on the reverse and long narrow, lance-shaped leaves.

Viola sororia (papilionacea)

(Dooryard Violet, Woolly Blue Violet)

ZONES: 3–9; sun to shade
SOIL: moist
NATIVE TO: moist to wet soils, disturbed areas; Newfoundland to British Columbia south to California, Texas, and Florida
SIZE: 8–18 inches (12 inches)
COLOR: violet to purple or white; **BLOOMS** in spring

Dooryard Violet is one of the most commonly encountered, weedy *Viola*s in gardens and around houses. It is a robust plant, with dark green heart-shaped leaves up to 5 inches long but more commonly 2–3 inches. The flowers are large and showy, and the plants make large bushy clumps, but it has aggressive creeping rhizomes and copious seeds that make it too invasive for all but the wild garden or naturalizing. Confederate Violet (*V. sororia* var. *priceana*) is a pale blue-gray form (the color of the Confederate Civil War uniform).

Viola striata

(Creamy Violet)

ZONES: 3–9; sun to light shade
SOIL: moist
NATIVE TO: wet areas, streambanks; Massachusetts to Wisconsin south to Oklahoma, Arkansas, and Georgia
SIZE: 8–12 inches (8 inches)

COLOR: white with violet striations in the throat; **BLOOMS** in late spring

Creamy Violet has a habit like that of Canada Violet, with bushy stems and heart-shaped leaves that are attractively furrowed along the veins. The flowers appear a week or two later than many, and they are a pretty shade of off-white with 5 distinct lines of purple on the lower petal. *V. blanda* (Sweet White Violet) is a smaller, creeping plant, with a habit like its relative *V. appalachiensis*. It prefers damp, mossy woods and ravines.

Waldsteinia fragarioides

Waldsteinia fragarioides

(walled-STEEN-ee-ah)
Rosaceae
Barren Strawberry

ZONES: 3–8; sun to shade
SOIL: moist to dry
NATIVE TO: woods; Maine and Quebec to Minnesota south to Indiana, Pennsylvania, and down the Appalachians to northern Georgia
SIZE: 3–6 inches (12 inches)
COLOR: bright yellow; **BLOOMS** in spring

Without a doubt, Barren Strawberry is one of our finest evergreen ground covers (evergreen to 15°F). As you may have guessed from the name, it is related to the true strawberry, with similar running growths terminating in tufts of 3-parted leaves. Unlike strawberries, though, *Waldsteinia* travels

(LEFT): Viola pubescens. *Downy Yellow Violet is one of our largest species, at home in dappled shade or sun.*

(RIGHT): Waldsteinia fragarioides. Waldsteinia fragarioides *is the most common Barren Strawberry, but several others bear mentioning as well. W. idahoensis is a rare species from the mountains of central Idaho and Montana with small 3-parted, glaucous leaves that remind me of Three-toothed Cinquefoil. It forms low mats of deciduous foliage with small yellow flowers appearing in a flush with the leaves. W. lobata is another uncommon and elegant plant native to streamsides in the Carolinas and Georgia. It has soft, downy leaves that are larger than the others, suggesting a Coralbell's in shape and arrangement. I saw it used very effectively as a ground cover at the University of Georgia, but it is a bit tender for us in Massachusetts.*

Wyethia amplexicaulis.
Amplexicaulis is a mouthful of a word meaning simply that the leaf bases clasp or nearly encircle the stem. The unmistakable leaves of Mule's Ears can be seen commonly in mountain pastures. Cattle do not like to eat them, and this gives them an advantage over more palatable competitors.

underground, forming a dense mat of roots and rhizomes below and a thick carpet of foliage above. The plants leaf out early, the foliage a light green that matures to a deep, glossy hue much like that of English Ivy or *Pachysandra*. Five-petaled bright yellow flowers on short branching stems mix with the leaves for a few weeks in spring, and these are followed by small woody (and sadly, not edible) capsules.

CULTURE: Easily established in a range of soils but at its best in a fertile, humusy place with some sun and a topdressing of fertilizer in spring. The plants spread 8–12 inches a year and form a fairly impenetrable, weed-smothering mat. They are fairly drought-tolerant once established, but require regular watering the first year. Rooted sections are easy to grub out and replant in spring after the flowers have faded.

USES: Evergreen ground cover.

PROPAGATION: Easy from division. See p. 265.

Wyethia amplexicaulis

Wyethia (WHY-thee-ah)
Asteraceae
Mule's Ears

Mule's ears is a perfect common name for these cheerful sunflowers with their large, stiff, mule-sized leaves arising in clumps from a deep, carrotlike taproot. They combine with lupines and paintbrushes to light up the high meadows of the West in spring with barely nodding 3-inch daisies on leafy stems just above the leaves. Most of the species grow in Cal-

ifornia, but a few are more wide ranging and make excellent perennials for the large rock garden or low meadow.

Balsamorhiza is a related genus with similar habit and needs. *B. saggitata* is a fairly common sight in the sagebrush steppes of the West. From a huge root come a clump of arrow-shaped leaves on long petioles and glistening yellow daisies. *B. hookeri* (Hooker's Balsamroot) has finely dissected pinnate leaves.

CULTURE: Mule's ears are adapted to the low humidity and intense sun of the mountainous West, and outside their range perfect drainage and strong sun are imperative. It is best to start from seed as they resent disturbance. Seedlings take a few years to reach full size as they focus on producing a sizable root when young. A soil that is moist in spring and drier in summer is ideal.

USES: Large rock garden, naturalizing, xeriscaping.

PROPAGATION: Moderately difficult from seed. See p. 265.

Wyethia amplexicaulis
(Northern Wyethia, Mule's Ears)

ZONES: 3–8; sun
SOIL: moist in spring
NATIVE TO: moist to drier meadows and prairies at moderate elevations; Montana to Washington south to Nevada and Colorado
SIZE: 1–2 feet (12–16 inches)
COLOR: bright yellow; **BLOOMS** in spring
The large yellow blooms are very showy over the varnished-looking, stiff leaves with prominent veins. A meadow full of this and Silvery Lupine (*Lupinus argenteus*) is a breathtaking sight. *W. mollis* (Woolly Mule's Ears) is also yellow flowered, but has leaves covered in a thick white down that wears off through the season like a winter coat shed by a wolf. It ranges from southern Oregon through the California Sierras to Nevada.

Wyethia helianthoides
(White-rayed Wyethia, White-head Wyethia, White Mule's Ears)

ZONES: 3–8; sun
SOIL: moist to wet
NATIVE TO: moist to wet meadows at low to moderate elevations; Montana to Oregon south to Nevada
SIZE: 1–2 feet (12–16 inches)
COLOR: white with yellow center; **BLOOMS** in spring
Prefers wetter spots than its yellow-flowered cousin, *W. amplexicaulis*. The leaves are finely hairy but otherwise similar to the preceding plant. A lovely species to be sure.

Xerophyllum asphodeloides

Xerophyllum

(zer-OFF-ill-um)

Liliaceae

Bear Grass, Turkey Beard

The tousled clumps of Turkey Beard and Bear Grass are composed of hundreds of stiff grasslike blades that arch away from a central growing point then curl back again when they hit the ground. A colony of the plants has a wave-tossed look about it and a wonderfully fine texture that is distinctly its own. They are slow-growing, requiring time to establish a large underground rhizome and deep roots before beginning to send up their annual display of glorious flowers. The flower stems are ½-inch thick and 3 feet high, clothed their length with progressively smaller leaves that finally yield to a densely flowered raceme of cream-colored blooms. The developing stems reorient themselves to the vertical after being bent by rain or wind, so the spikes often meander and curve like Fourth of July fireworks with a mind of their own. Each small flower is a perfect 6-parted lily, and a single spike has hundreds of flowers opening sequentially toward the nipplelike top.

CULTURE: *Xerophyllum*s take time to establish, and they resent root disturbance. Container-grown plants should be sited in a well-drained but not droughty spot with at least some sun. New roots are continually produced from the expanding crown, and they have contractile properties to pull the crown deeper and deeper so that the plants basically grow down rather than up and never form an above-ground stem. Turkey Beard grows in damper soils than Bear Grass, but it suffers from crown rot if the spot is too sodden. Once they are settled, these are very long-lived plants, gradually forming larger and larger clumps each year. Give them room and an acid soil, and have patience—for they are worth it.

USES: Truly specimen plants for rock gardens or heaths.

PROPAGATION: Difficult from seed. See p. 265.

Xerophyllum asphodeloides

(Turkey Beard)

ZONES: 5–9; sun, part sun
SOIL: moist, acid, well drained around the crown
NATIVE TO: pine barrens and balds; scattered along the coast from New Jersey to North Carolina and in the Appalachians from Virginia to Tennessee and Georgia
SIZE: 1–3 feet (18 inches)
COLOR: creamy white; **BLOOMS** in spring

Turkey Beard is a rare plant, so the first time I saw it on top of Grandfather Mountain in the Blue Ridge, I was baffled. The old withered flower stalks were lily-like, but the plants themselves looked more like a stiff blue-gray sedge. We have a number of them growing in the Garden, and they are naturalizing well in a damp sandy area with other pine barren species. Unfortunately, we may be the only nursery selling them at this point, a situation that must be remedied, for they are treasures.

Xerophyllum tenax

(Elk Grass, Bear Grass, Indian Basket Grass)

ZONES: 5–8; sun, part sun
SOIL: well drained
NATIVE TO: open woods and clearings mostly at middle elevations; Montana to British Columbia south to California, Oregon, and Idaho
SIZE: 1–3 feet (18 inches)
COLOR: creamy white; **BLOOMS** in spring

Bear Grass is a much more common plant than its eastern cousin, growing abundantly in the mountains of the Pacific Northwest, where it forms large patches in open pine and fir forest. It has leaves that are more green than blue and a fatter, drumstick flower head terminating in a distinct nipple—it resembles a baby bottle full of creamy milk. They are much more drought-tolerant and quite fire-tolerant as well, blooming heavily after forest fires sweep an area. This is a much harder species to grow in the East, and I suspect they are resentful of the damp winters and hot muggy summers.

Xerophyllum asphodeloides. It is fitting that I first encountered Turkey Beard on ancient Grandfather Mountain in North Carolina—it's slow to mature but just keeps getting better with age. I collect fresh seed from our garden plants in fall and sow them immediately in flats placed in a cold frame. They germinate like fine grass the following spring, each seedling a small tuft of 5–7 leaves by the end of the season. The seedlings are best left alone for their first year, then transplanted to individual containers the second spring. Turkey Beard also seeds itself into mats of sphagnum moss in the garden. The moss provides the evenly moist but well-aerated conditions the seedlings require, and we have a nice patch of it now in our pine barren display.

Yucca glauca. *Soapweed is the most widespread of a group of nearly stemless, thin-leaved yuccas native to the western deserts and steppes. It is one of the most cold-hardy species and helps to give the high intermountain deserts their distinctive character.*

Yucca glauca

Yucca (YUCK-ah)
Agavaceae
Yucca, Soapweed, Spanish Bayonet

Even though some yuccas grow well in cool, moist environments, their spine-tipped, dagger leaves immediately suggest the desert to most gardeners. They are unquestionably some of the boldest foliage plants available for a temperate climate, and they make wonderful exclamation marks in a bed of ground covers or softer wildflowers. Yuccas are also extremely tough and resilient, with huge underground taproots that can hold water reserves against times of scarcity and the food reserves necessary to erect towering spires of their distinctive, bell-shaped blooms. There are a number of trunk-forming species in our flora, among them the regal Joshua Tree (*Yucca brevifolia*) from the desert Southwest, and a host of trunkless, rosette-forming plants that can form large mounds with dozens of crowns over time. Yuccas bloom like a monocarpic or biennial plant: the huge inflorescence is the transformed growing tip of the plant, so after flowering, the crown has to produce a new leader or leaders and in this way the plants fork and multiply.

In this genus we find one of the most famous and remarkable plant-insect mutualisms—the story of the yucca and the Yucca Moth (*Tegeticula yucasella* and related species). The small white moths are about the size and shape of a common leafhopper and are found wherever yuccas grow naturally. (I am not sure whether they feed on all the species, but I have seen them on *Y. glauca* in New Mexico and *Y. aloifolia* along the coast of North Carolina.) The adult female is attracted to the nighttime fragrance of open flowers and feeds on the nectar, then rolls some of the sticky pollen into a large ball three times the size of her head, which she carries to another flower. She uses her long ovipositor to lay some eggs in the immature ovary of the flower before securing the pollen ball on the flower's stigma, pollinating the flower and assuring that her developing larvae will have food to eat. She lays few enough eggs in each capsule that only 20–50 percent of the seeds are usually eaten, assuring the plants can reproduce as well and provide food and shelter for future generations. The heavy pollen and shape of the flowers has co-evolved with the moth, so without it, the plants are rarely pollinated. It is easy to see the eaten seeds in the wild, as they remain in the open pods. They have small pinholes in their centers like a string of beads and dustlike frass scattered around them, but the larvae mature and drop to the ground to pupate before they make it down the end of a row of seeds so there are always some viable ones on the ends.

Y. aloifolia (Spanish Bayonet) from the southeast coastal plain rivals *Y. brevifolia* in size. Both are magnificent plants for gardeners in Zones 7–10, but they can become substantial 25 foot-trees with massive, branching trunks, really beyond the scope of this work.

CULTURE: Yuccas are extremely long-lived, drought-tolerant plants with monstrous, fleshy rootstocks that are difficult to dig without a backhoe once the plants are mature. (If you break a root off, it will usually resprout again from below.) Accordingly, site container-grown plants where they can remain indefinitely. They are not too particular about season, but keep them well watered the first year until they set down their roots. It takes a few years for seedlings to reach blooming size, and even then, many individuals, especially if they are in marginal conditions, will not bloom reliably every year. (The older and larger the plants, the more frequently they bloom.) The flowers are lovely, but short-lived, so they're really a bonus rather than the primary reason to grow yuccas. Full sun and a well-drained soil are important for the plants to look their best.

USES: Borders, rock gardens, xeriscaping.

PROPAGATION: Slow but easy from seed. See p. 265.

Yucca baccata

(Spanish-bayonet, Banana Yucca, Blue Yucca)

ZONES: 5–9; sun
SOIL: dry, well drained

NATIVE TO: dry slopes and outcrops; Colorado to Nevada and California south to Arizona and Texas

SIZE: 2 feet (3–6 feet)

COLOR: reddish brown or purple on the exterior, white on the interior; **BLOOMS** in spring

I first saw this species when I was exploring some of the Anasazi cliff dwellings in Bandolier National Monument near Santa Fe, New Mexico. It is a unique-looking plant with 1–2-foot-long leaves that are very dark green or strongly blue-green and that curve or cup upward so as to appear rounded. It gives them a succulent appearance akin to an agave. Banana Yucca is a clump-forming species, eventually forming large colonies up to 10 feet across and composed of dozens of crowns. I later obtained some seed of a blue-leaved strain that has been prospering in the rock garden of Garden in the Woods, but after three years they are still a ways from blooming. The very large flowers hang on dense branched stalks nestled among and barely longer than the leaves. These yield to long gnarled pods reminiscent of green bananas suffering from exposure to radiation. These were prized by the Native Americans of the Southwest who boiled or baked the sweet pods or ate the flesh raw.

Yucca elata

(Soaptree Yucca)

ZONES: (6) 7–10; sun

SOIL: dry, well drained

NATIVE TO: sandy deserts; New Mexico to southern Utah south to Arizona, northern Mexico, and Texas

SIZE: 2–6 feet (3–5 feet)

COLOR: creamy white to greenish white often tinged purple or pink; **BLOOMS** from spring to early summer

I fell in love with this plant after spending some time in New Mexico. The narrow 2-foot leaves form a dense, perfectly round pincushion ball on ever-lengthening stems clothed in a skirt of the old dried up foliage. Older plants usually have one or several pups coming from the base of the taller trunks—it gives them a nuclear family look. It is a plant of the barest of soils, tolerating even the blinding white, shifting dunes of White Sands National Monument. Flowers are borne in tall branching panicles up to 6 feet taller than the crown, and like many in the tribe, the leaf margins are heavily filamented so the plants have a shaggy appearance. These fibers prove a strong and durable cord for bow strings and fabric, and many species were valued by Native Americans for these and other purposes. *Y. baileyi* is a stemless cousin with similar, narrow leaves and short spikes of large flowers. It ranges mostly through the southern and central Rockies.

Yucca filamentosa

(Adam's Needle, Needle Palm)

ZONES: 4–10; sun, part sun

SOIL: moist to dry, well drained

NATIVE TO: dunes and dry, sandy soils along the coast; from Maryland to Florida and Louisiana

SIZE: 1–4 feet (18–36 inches)

COLOR: creamy white; **BLOOMS** in early summer

This and the following species are the most adaptable garden plants, tolerating more cold and wetness than the others. Adam's Needle has fairly broad, 1–1½-foot-long leaves that are typically gray-green and a bit shaggy along the margins. Older plants can produce multiple crowns, but rarely does it form the large colonies of *Y. baccata* or *Y. harrimanae*. Flower stems are 3–4 feet or more—branching panicles of pendent, creamy bells like a few dozen eggs hung on a limb.

Yucca glauca

(Soap Plant, Soapweed)

ZONES: 4–10; sun

SOIL: dry, well drained

NATIVE TO: dry prairies, plains and sagebrush grasslands; Iowa to Montana south to Arizona and Texas

SIZE: 1–3 feet (2–3 feet)

COLOR: greenish or creamy white, sometimes streaked purple-brown; **BLOOMS** from late spring to early summer

Soapweed is the primary yucca species used to make a type of soap called amole, which was used by Native Americans and later European settlers as well. The plants are very hardy and small-statured and carry rounded crowns of stiff, narrow leaves that lend a finer texture than the more common Adam's Needle. The foliage ranges from gray-green to a lovely blue-green that is more common in cultivation. Plants eventually form multicrowned, stemless colonies. Flowers are borne on short scapes in and just above the foliage. *Y. harrimaniae* and *Y. neomexicana* are more robust cousins from the Southwest that can form dramatic, stiff-leaved colonies with time. *Y. harrimaniae* has proven reliably hardy in Zone 5, and the flowers typically have a bronzy purple tinge that contrasts nicely with the blue-green leaves.

Zauschneria californica. *I must have been a hummingbird in a former life, because I am inexplicably drawn to tubular, hot-colored flowers. In North America, hummingbirds are most abundant and diverse in the Southwest and along the coast of California, so, not surprisingly, this is where we find the greatest diversity of plants with fiery blooms. California Fuchsia is a perfect case in point—the largest flowered of a group of stunning Fireweed relatives distributed along the Pacific coast.*

Zauschneria californica

Zauschneria
(zowssh-NAIR-ee-ah)
Onagraceae
California Fuchsia

California fuchsias are brilliantly colored, late-blooming plants of great garden merit that should be more widely grown. I think part of the reason they are neglected is that they perform poorly in cool, wet maritime Europe—still the epicenter of gardening haute couture. Granted, in their native haunts they are a bit aggressive like many in the Evening Primrose family, sending out parachute-equipped seeds like their close relative fireweed and establishing easily in open, stony ground. Elsewhere, where colder winters moderate their enthusiasm, the plants are much better behaved, forming rounded mounds of opposite, light green, sticky-hairy foliage that clothe the weak, spreading stems. From late summer into fall they are covered with spikes of 1-inch tubular flowers in the hummingbird colors of red, orange, and yellow. A well-grown clump makes a stunning floral display that rivals many *Salvia*s for sheer brilliance. The taxonomy of the group is very confusing, as different authorities lump the various species in with each other or separate out subspecies and varieties. They have also been put into the genus *Epilobium*, which makes absolutely no sense to me. Depending on who you listen to, there are 2–7 closely related species ranging from southern Oregon throughout California to Arizona and Mexico with one (*Z. garrettii*) that extends farther east into Wyoming and Utah.

CULTURE: *Zauschneria*s perform best in full sun and well-drained, warm soils. They are evergreen in mild winters but die back to a few soil-level branch stubs when temperatures fall below 20°F. I have seen both *Z. latifolia* and *Z. garrettii* growing well in Zone 5 if sited at the base of large rocks, which warm the ground and provide a nice foil for the blooms. The stems are brittle and easily damaged, so site them away from pathways. Division is best accomplished in spring as growth begins, and, once established, they are drought-tolerant and trouble-free.

USES: Rock gardens, xeriscaping, ground cover.

WILDLIFE: Hummingbirds love California fuchsias.

PROPAGATION: Easy from seed or cuttings. See p. 266.

Zauschneria californica
(California Fuschia)

ZONES: (7) 8–10; sun

SOIL: well drained

NATIVE TO: dry, gravelly soils up to 3,500 feet, chaparral, slopes, bluffs, and open woodland; California to Baja California

SIZE: 1–2 feet (12–18 inches)

COLOR: scarlet; **BLOOMS** from late summer to fall

This is the largest-flowered species, with rather narrow 1-inch leaves that, like the others, are more or less covered in gray-green pilose hair. The flowers flare open widely at the mouth of the tube, and the petals are rounded and notched as opposed to having pointed tips. The woody bases of this low-elevation species are easily damaged by cold, so it difficult to reliably overwinter even in Zone 7, but in a suitable climate it sends out underground stolons to form a dense, ground-covering colony.

Zauschneria cana
(Hoary California Fuchsia)

ZONES: 8–10; sun

SOIL: well drained

NATIVE TO: coastal chaparral; central California

SIZE: 1–2 feet (16 inches)

COLOR: scarlet to crimson; **BLOOMS** from late summer to fall

A striking plant where it can be grown, with small stiff leaves covered in matted gray hair. The plants have a powerful silvery cast and stiff branches that set off the flowers beautifully.

Zauschneria garrettii
(Garrett's California Fuchsia)

ZONES: 5–9; sun

SOIL: well drained

NATIVE TO: dry rocky soils, sagebrush and pinyon-juniper woodlands in the mountains; Wyoming and Utah to California

SIZE: 8–14 inches (12 inches)

COLOR: scarlet, occasionally pink-apricot; BLOOMS in summer

This is the hardiest species, with small but brightly colored flowers that appear a few weeks earlier than the others. The 1½-inch leathery leaves are oval and sharply toothed.

Zauschneria latifolia
(California Fuchsia)

ZONES: (5) 6–9; sun

SOIL: well drained

NATIVE TO: dry rocky soils and ridges in the mountains below 10,000 feet; southwest Oregon to California

SIZE: 8–14 inches (12 inches)

COLOR: scarlet, occasionally pink-apricot; BLOOMS from late summer to fall

Like *Z. garrettii*, *Z. latifolia* is completely herbaceous, dying back to underground crowns to survive the colder winters of its mountain home. It forms mounds of branching stems and rounded, hairy leaves that are sticky to the touch like some of the *Mimulus*. I have been impressed with its hardiness when it's given a warm spot and sharply drained soil. It does not spread like *Z. californica* and all in all is probably the best garden subject of the group.

Zizia (ZIZZ-ee-ah)
Apiaceae
Golden Alexanders

Zizia aptera

I have been writing this book alphabetically, so it is with some relief that I have finally arrived at *Zizia*. Although they are inevitably the last entry in every catalog I have produced and tend to get neglected for that reason, please do not overlook them as they are rugged, easy plants with lovely rich yellow flowers held in flat-topped umbels like Queen Anne's Lace. Heart-leaved Alexanders is the best garden plant, with leathery, dark evergreen basal leaves with a shape that reminds me of a round-point shovel toothed along the margins like a fine miter saw. The teeth have a distinct whitish cast that is echoed in the strong veins of the leaves. The plants bolt in late spring and the stem leaves are pinnately compound, with 3 to 5 leaflets like many in the family. Flowers give way to platters of round greenish capsules that slowly burnish purple like the foliage as fall approaches.

CULTURE: *Zizia*s are carefree plants that grow best in moist soils, but *Z. aptera* tolerates considerable dryness in summer. They can be set out in spring from containers, and usually self-sown

seedlings will reinforce them in a year or two to form a small colony.

USES: Borders, meadows, woodland edge.

WILDLIFE: *Zizia* is one of the larval food plants for the majestic Black Swallowtail butterfly (*Papilio polyxenes*) and its close cousin, Ozark Swallowtail (*Papilio joanae*).

PROPAGATION: Easy from seed. See p. 266.

Zizia aptera
(Heart-leaved Alexanders)

ZONES: 4–9; sun to light shade

SOIL: moist to moderately dry

NATIVE TO: moist meadows and clearings; New York to Manitoba and British Columbia south to Colorado, Missouri, and Georgia

SIZE: 1–2 feet (12–16 inches)

COLOR: bright yellow; BLOOMS in late spring

Zizia aurea
(Golden Alexanders)

ZONES: 4–9; sun, light shade

SOIL: moist to wet

NATIVE TO: moist meadows and low woods; Quebec to Saskatchewan south to Texas and Florida

SIZE: 1–3 feet (12–16 inches)

COLOR: bright yellow; BLOOMS in late spring

This is a coarser, sometimes weedy species best left for naturalizing in a wet meadow or open woodland. The bright yellow flowers are attractive, though the deciduous, compound leaves are not nearly as fine as those of *Z. aptera*. *Z. trifoliata* (Mountain Golden Alexanders) from the southern Appalachians is a similar plant with more coarsely toothed leaves with a bluish cast and open habit. I have placed the two side by side before and they are very distinct when you see them together but otherwise easy to confuse.

Zizia aptera. *Except for the umbels of flowers, Heart-leaved Alexanders is a very uncarrot-like member of the Carrot family. The glossy, evergreen leaves are very attractive en masse as a bold ground cover. It is a long-lived plant in a family of biennials. A patch at the base of a tree in the nursery has been there for fifteen years now despite drought, shade, and rather poor soil.*

Propagation

Growing plants from seeds or cuttings is a tremendous source of satisfaction for me—an opportunity to learn about a particular species and to grow many plants otherwise unavailable in the trade. It is also the best way to bring local plants into your own garden. Plants "want" to grow and reproduce, and have been doing so without my help for millions of years. What we do or don't do to aid them may help determine their eventual success, but the overwhelming desire for life burns as bright in the smallest seed as it does in us. However, there is something vaguely parental about plant propagation—nurturing a fragile new life into adulthood—that connects you to the plant far more profoundly than just buying a blooming specimen at the local garden center. I think of myself as a facilitator—providing optimal growing conditions for the plants under my care to vastly increase their relative success over what it would be in the wild. If an oak tree produces 100,000 acorns over ten years (a number I am pulling out of my hat), it would be doing well if one or two of those offspring reached adulthood. If I went out one fall and collected a few hundred nuts and grew them on, then planted them in a good sunny place, I would have probably just increased the tree's success rate by more than a hundred fold.

My approach in teaching plant propagation, like all horticulture, is to try and demystify and simplify the process as much as possible. As with any craft, there are tricks and shortcuts, but there is no substitute for experience and observation. So do not be discouraged if your first few attempts fail—you can learn as much from failures as from successes.

Seed

Most plants reproduce naturally by seed, and it is my method of choice for several reasons. First, seedlings retain a genetic diversity that is lost when one propagates things clonally. This allows you to select plants that are especially well adapted to your particular conditions. Out of a batch of 500 seedlings, there are always a few that grow more vigorously, bloom more colorfully, or resist disease more completely than the others. By choosing them, you are performing a gardener's brand of natural selection that will, over several generations, yield plants more amenable to your particular locale and its blend of soil, climate, and exposure.

In the wild, plants are constantly undergoing a similar selection, and this brings up the subject of provenance. Provenance, or place of origin, is becoming more of an issue in the field of habitat restoration and conservation biology, but is worth discussing in this context as well. A Goldenseal that originates from central Alabama has been selected over generations to thrive in the long warm season and short winter of the deep South, whereas a plant that originates in southeastern Minnesota has evolved in a much cooler climate with shorter growing season. Who is to say whether a plant of southern provenance would thrive in a northern climate or vice versa? Certainly place of origin must be taken into account. It is a fact that a *Trillium grandiflorum* from Lake Champlain that is adapted to a very long winter and cool summer will simply not thrive in the deep South even though it is within the natural range of the species; waning and losing strength over several years, it will then disappear altogether. A *Trillium chloropetalum* from northern California planted in Massachusetts will doggedly emerge within the first warm days of February and be promptly killed by frost, and a Yellow Pitcher Plant from Georgia may survive and grow well in Seattle, but without the long warm summer of its home, it will never ripen any seed. This is the strongest reason I can find for growing indigenous wildflowers whenever possible.

Seed Collection

Gardens are often a great source of seed, one, because they are accessible, and two, because (one hopes) the plants are growing vigorously and well, so the quality and quantity of seed is better than it would be in the wild. However, in a garden where different species are mixed together, it is easy for hybridization to occur, and often seed from cultivated plants can turn out to be different from its parent. Further, many plants are self-incompatible — that is, they cannot pollinate themselves and set viable seed. If you have only one clone of a particular species, you may never get seed. I sometimes have had to borrow a plant from a friend to act in stud service so that I could obtain viable seed. Self-incompatibility actually exacerbates the problem of hybridization in gardens. If you have one Fringed Bleeding Heart and one Western Bleeding Heart (both self-incompatible) the only viable seed that either will produce will be of hybrid origin and the resulting plants will have characteristics somewhere in between the parents (in this case not such a bad thing, as the hybrids can be superior garden plants). If you are planning to collect seed from garden plants with a reputation for promiscuity, collect from plants that are isolated from other related species or hand-pollinate the flowers to prevent unwanted hybridization.

Wild-collected seed is another option and has the advantage of likely being true to type and from plants with a local provenance. However, there are several disadvantages as well. Many seeds ripen within a very short window of time, and it is hard without experience to time your visits just right so that you do not miss the seed. There is also an ethical question regarding wild-collecting seed that must at least be considered. Theoretically, harvesting seed from a wild population lessens the chances of that population's long-term success. In reality, it would be very hard in most cases to collect enough seed from a population that you would be seriously

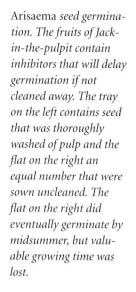

Arisaema seed germination. The fruits of Jack-in-the-pulpit contain inhibitors that will delay germination if not cleaned away. The tray on the left contains seed that was thoroughly washed of pulp and the flat on the right an equal number that were sown uncleaned. The flat on the right did eventually germinate by midsummer, but valuable growing time was lost.

threatening its survival, but as a precaution, *never collect seed from rare plants* and, for other species, take only a few seeds from each plant when possible. There is a big difference between taking 1 percent of the available seed and 75 percent. Never collect seed without the landowner's permission (remember—it is a crime to collect anything on state or federal land without a permit). Ideally, use wild-collected seed to establish cultivated stock that can be the source of future seed, and *never wild-collect the plants themselves.*

I remember as a child being fascinated with a gelatin capsule toy that you dropped in a glass of water and watched as it dissolved and out popped a sponge shaped like a giant animal cracker. The little sponge animal lay patiently in its gelatin cocoon waiting for the waters to set it free. I think of seeds in a similar way. Although they don't spring up fully formed, they do emerge from something that hardly resembles a plant as little copies of their parents. Little piles of beads or fluff transform almost magically into delicate flowers or forest giants. A friend once gave me a seed as big as a chestnut with a coat like polished turquoise. He had plucked it from a lugubrious leguminous vine that grew near his Peace Corps home in Brazil. It had journeyed around with him in pockets and boxes and writing desk drawers through 10 years of winters and springs by the time he gave it to me. After admiring it for a while, I nicked the seed coat with a file and ceremoniously dropped it in a glass of water overnight then planted it. Sure enough, three days later 2 huge cotyledons sprung triumphantly from the soil and grew into something resembling a giant bean plant.

Of course, most seeds would not have survived this sort of careless storage. A mature seed contains an embryonic plant, usually complete with a rudimentary leaf or leaves and root surrounded by food reserves in the form of fats, proteins, and starches. After fertilization, there is a period of maturation when the embryo develops to a certain size and the parent fills the seed with the food reserves necessary to allow the embryo to survive dormancy and then germinate and become established enough to begin to photosynthesize on its own. Seed that is collected prematurely often will be be insufficiently prepared and never germinate. Fortunately, most seeds give clues to help us determine when they are ripe. Seed coats—the protective jacket that surrounds most seeds—typically turn from green or white to gold, brown, or black when ripe. If a seed is contained within a fleshy fruit as with cherries and baneberries, ripening of the fruit can be taken as a clue that the seeds inside are ready to harvest. Seeds that ripen in pods or capsules will be ready when their container begins to yellow, split, and dry. If you are unsure, pull open a fruit or pod and examine the seeds. Are some or all the seed coats darkened (it helps to have some immature seeds for comparison)? Split one of the seeds open with your nail or a knife. Is the inside white and plump, filling the shell and appearing firm not milky? Then chances are the seeds are ripe and viable. (It is usually a good idea to split open a few seeds to make sure they are filled with viable embryos, as sometimes a plant will produce empty seeds that otherwise appear viable but will never germinate.) Most ripened seed should be harvested and allowed to dry in the open air (see the exception below). Drying does several things. First, it lowers the moisture content of the seed, making it less easy for pathogens to attack it in storage. Drying also triggers physiological changes in the seed, slowing down its metabolism and readying it for dormancy, and some seed will germinate well only after a period of dry storage (usually two to three months is sufficient).

Remember that a seed is a living, functioning plant which continues to burn energy in storage—energy it needs to germinate and grow. Slowing down the rate that the seed metabolizes this energy will greatly increase both its life in storage and its vigor and success when germinating. Immature seed still developing in the parent has a moisture content near 100 percent. As the seed ripens and the seed coat dries, an abscission layer forms between the seed and parent, cutting off water and drying the seed. Drying should continue after harvest to (ideally) bring the seeds down to a moisture content of between 3 and 10 percent. Since the relative humidity of your home is rarely this low, desiccants such as silica gel (sold in hobby stores to dry flowers) are often employed by people serious about long-term storage of seed. However, if you plan on sowing the seed within a year or two, just letting it get completely dried under household conditions will usually be sufficient.

The other way to slow down the aging process of your seed is to refrigerate it. Metabolism involves chemical reactions that are greatly slowed as the temperatures are lowered to near freezing, and air-dried seed stored in paper envelopes in the refrigerator will stay viable five to ten times as long as seed kept at room temperature. Most of the seed I harvest is allowed to dry at room temperature for a week or two then cleaned to remove any chaff, leaf debris, and also any insects that may be present. There are several tools that make the job easier. An old rolling pin works well to crush woody capsules, and as long as you roll gingerly, you will not damage the seed. Screens of several mesh sizes are very handy, and you can make them out of window screen and hardware cloth fashioned into a wooden frame. Kitchen stores are a good source of finer sieve screens as well. Seeds that are round in shape can be effectively separated from chaff by gently shaking them on a tilted surface such as a manila file. Let the seeds roll down then fluff up the chaff to allow more to fall. It is sometimes difficult to distinguish the seed from the chaff. I have tried in the descriptions for each genus to give a brief description of the seed, but if you have difficulty with a particular species, sowing the whole lot —chaff and all—will probably do no harm. Seed that develops in fleshy fruits, such as baneberry, Jack-in-the-pulpit and False Solomon's Seal, must be extracted before drying or sowing. Many fruit pulps contain inhibitory chemicals that retard germination if not removed. These are usually flushed away as the fruits pass through the digestive system of animals that eat the fruits and disperse the seed in their droppings. Small amounts of seed can be mashed and washed in a strainer in the sink, but if you are planning to clean larger quantities, I would recommend investing in one of those handheld milkshake blenders that you keep only for the purpose of cleaning seeds. Get one that comes with several blades and test out a small batch of seed to make sure it does not suffer in the blending. The one we use has a disk blade that looks like a miniature cheese grater and is safe for most seed. Fill the blender cup half full with water and add some berries and blend for a minute or two. Since pulp and dead seeds float and good seed sinks, you can fill the cup all the way up after blending and gently pour off the floating debris. It may take several refillings and pourings to get all the pulp out, but you will be left with perfectly clean seed. This also works to quickly scarify large batches of seeds like *Baptisia*s or *Callirhoe*s if it's done right before sowing. A final technique for cleaning away pulp involves soaking the fruits in a dish or pail of water for a week or two. This results in a stinking, fermenting mess that should be confined to the garage or porch, but after being washed in a strainer under a jet of water, the seed is fairly clean. The fermentation process is particularly effective at destroying germination-inhibiting chemicals in the pulp. Once the seed is cleaned of pulp, it can be air-dried for storage or sown immediately.

With this in mind, I need to now point out that certain seeds are intolerant of drying out below a moisture content of 30–90 percent, needing instead to be sown immediately when ripe. The list of plants with what has been termed *ephemeral* (meaning short-lived or transitory) or recalcitrant seeds (meaning hard to deal with) includes most of the stars of our spring woodlands. Included are *Asarum* spp. (wild gingers), *Hepatica*, *Sanguinaria* (Bloodroot), *Trillium* spp., *Iris cristata* (Crested Iris), *Achlys* (Vanillaleaf), *Stylophorum diphyllum* (Celandine Poppy), *Jeffersonia* (Twinleaf), *Claytonia* spp. (Spring Beauty), *Podophyllum peltatum* (May Apple), *Shortia* (Oconee Bells) and *Galax* (Wandflower), *Uvularia* (Merry Bells), and *Dicentra* spp. (Bleeding Heart, Dutchman's Breeches, Squirrel Corn) to name a few.

The term ephemeral is not entirely accurate,

however, and I think it leads to misconceptions about handling the seeds correctly. Many of these species have seeds that are very long-lived if stored moist. (Trilliums, for example, can remain viable in the soil for at least five to six years.) I think a more accurate term would be *hydrophilic* or *hydrophile*, meaning needing or requiring the presence of water. In general, hydrophilic seeds are associated with stable temperate forest communities, and especially with species whose seeds ripen in the spring and early summer. The majority of these seeds have fleshy appendages called *arils*, or *elaiosomes*, which are gathered and consumed by ants or other insects, thus dispersing the seed. It is fascinating to me to see the convergent evolution of this structure among plants of very different families, such as Bloodroot in the Poppy family, Crested Iris in the Iris family, Gold-star in the Daisy family, and *Euphorbia purpurea* in the Spurge family. All of these are anomalous, in that the vast majority of their relatives have conventional, nonhydrophilic seeds, yet if you take the seeds of Bloodroot and Crested Iris and place them side by side, it is difficult to tell them apart. Other seed vectors (dispersers) include Box Turtle (May Apple), rain drops *(Shortia)*, and birds and mammals (Baneberry).

I believe that these seeds have lost their ability to withstand drying out for the same reason cave animals lose their sight—in a temperate climate, with even, reliable rainfall, there is no need to waste resources preparing for desiccation if it is not a threat. The seeds of these plants simply ripen, fall, and are dispersed among the leaf litter, never having to dry. Many of the western equivalents to eastern woodlanders, such as *Trillium petiolatum, Claytonia megarhiza,* and *Phlox douglasii,* live in areas where summers are drier, and thus have seeds that can withstand desiccation more readily. When working with hydrophilic species (indicated in the germination code column of the propagation section with an asterisk), it is important to never let them dry, ideally sowing them immediately after they are collected and cleaned. Alternatively, they can be stored in self-sealing plastic baggies in the refrigerator for up to a year and still remain viable. As a rule, if the hydrophilic seed in question has an elaiosome or matures in a fleshy fruit, I add a handful of dampened vermiculite to the bag before sealing it, as this ensures a very high moisture content.

Seed Sowing

The actual process of seed sowing usually goes quite quickly if you have the materials prepared. It is important to consider several things before beginning: containers, potting mix, and a place to put the flats.

Theoretically, anything that will hold soil can

work as a container. However, a container's shape and size greatly influence the way water drains through a soil mix. Flats that are much wider than they are tall will hold more water for a given volume of soil than a tall, narrow pot. You can see this for yourself using a kitchen sponge. Soak the sponge in water until it is saturated. Do not ring it out. Place it flat on a screen and let it drain until it stops dripping. In this position its shape is much like that of a low seed flat. Now tip it up so that it stands on a narrow end and watch all the extra water drain out — it now mimics the shape of a tall, narrow container. Low seed flats are handy for seed sowing, but you must use a freely draining mix for adequate drainage. Tall, narrow pots (with a height at least twice their width) are better for moisture-sensitive alpine and dryland species. Always use containers with large drainage holes in the bottom and do not use dirty, second-hand containers without at least washing them with soap or, even better, soaking them overnight in a 10 percent household bleach solution (9 parts water to 1 part bleach) and then thoroughly rinsing them to kill pathogens and weed seeds.

A good potting mix is key. It is worth paying the money for a commercial, bagged mix rather than trying to blend your own. I use a soilless, peat-based seed-starting mix that is about half peat and fine-screened bark and half fine perlite and vermiculite. There are quite a few brands on the market that are all very similar. If you have trouble finding a suitable mix, go to a good nursery in the area and see if they will sell you a bag. Mixes that substitute ground coconut fiber (coir) for some of the peat are excellent if you can find them. Avoid mixes that contain soil or compost, even if they are pasteurized, because they break down quickly and become sodden. A good, soilless mix will work for 90 percent of the plants covered here, with a couple of exceptions. I add in about 30 percent more peat to the mix when sowing acid-loving pitcher plants. The standard mix holds too much water for many dryland/alpine species, so I blend in 1 part filter sand, fine gravel (often called turkey grit, with particles ⅛ inch or so in diameter), or brown pumice stone for every 2 parts potting mix.

Commercial mixes come with what is called a starter charge of fertilizer in them, but you will have to regularly fertilize the plants with a liquid brand once they are up and growing. (Use it at half strength but apply it every week or two from spring to mid-summer.)

Seed flats can be set out on the open ground during the warmer parts of the year, but a screened table

A simple cold frame at Garden in the Woods. We build boxes out of 2 × 10 inch lumber held in place with 2 × 4 inch stakes to overwinter seed flats as well as potted plants. The frames can be covered with rigid Styrofoam insulation panels held in place with bricks when temperatures drop below 27°F. Seed flats are visible in the middle of the frame, covered with sand, as are small pots of individual seedlings ready to step up into larger containers or plant out in the garden.

will keep them away from weeds, cats, and other furry diggers. If you live in an area where temperatures routinely fall below 20°F in winter, it is best to provide some protection for the seed flats. A cold frame with a floor set below grade and walls of concrete block or pressure-treated lumber is an excellent solution. You can site it in shade (best if you are working with slow-growing woodlanders, and it also has the advantage of not heating up prematurely in late winter) or sun, but be sure to cover it at the beginning of winter with a reflective, insulating cover. This is not like the cold frames used to start vegetables—really minigreenhouses with transparent lids. You want something that will keep out the sun and keep the seeds (and container plants, for that matter) consistently cold or frozen. For small frames, pieces of rigid Styrofoam insulation available as ½–1-inch-thick sheets from building stores work well. Cut to size and set it over the top of the frame. Hold it down with ropes or bricks and uncover as soon as you can in late winter to prevent premature germination. Inevitably any covered spot full of plants and seeds will attract mice and other rodents. You can enclose individual flats or even the whole frame in hardware cloth mesh, which should provide some protection, but resorting to traps and poison baits is not out of the question.

As a rule of thumb, sow seeds about as deep as they are thick. Fill a container with moistened mix and lightly tamp the mix down, then sprinkle on the seeds and dust a light coating of more mix over them. I cover all my seeds with an additional ⅛-inch layer of #1 filter sand (see Germination Code H section, p. 241 for further explanation). Not only does this help protect small surface-sown seeds, it keeps rain and irrigation from floating off larger seeds and cuts down on damping off. Water the flats thoroughly and keep them well watered from now on. Once you have wetted the seeds and begun the germination process, drying out will kill or at least greatly set them back. For slow-to-germinate seeds (types C and D), I recommend covering the flats with spunbonded row cover—the white, permeable fabric sold for vegetable gardens—and placing them in the shade. It shades the flats, keeps out weeds, and discourages rodents. (It is not a substitute for winter insulation, though, as it provides only a few degrees of frost protection.) Be sure to remove the fabric when seedlings begin to germinate to prevent fungus problems.

Seed Bed or Garden

An alternative to growing in containers is to sow seeds directly in a prepared seed bed or open spot in the garden. A seed bed can be constructed like a raised bed used for vegetables, using concrete block or timber for the sides and filling it with good-quality topsoil. This is certainly a low-maintenance alternative, but expect more attrition through predation. Sowing directly in the garden can be as simple as just scratching seeds here and there. This is a good way to handle plants that are difficult to transplant, but you'll have more control and better success with others if you mark and reserve an area to raise seedlings and transplant them when they are large enough to fend for themselves.

Germination

Seed germination is a process that culminates in the emergence of the seedling from below ground—a process that began when the ripened seed fell from the parent. You have likely grown tomatoes or marigolds from seed. In the case of such warm-season or tropical annuals, all that was needed to complete the process of germination was moisture and warmth. The seeds of most temperate plants (species that grow in a climate where conditions are unfavorable for growth part of the year because of excessive cold, heat, or drought) have evolved mechanisms to prevent premature germination during periods unfavorable to growth, i.e., winter. Understanding these mechanisms and providing the conditions to overcome them is the critical skill that you must learn to grow native plants from seed. In the propagation table there is a column of lettered germination codes or seed treatments. For each genus I have listed the treatment(s) that have worked well for me and should provide good results if they are followed. Below is an explanation of these germination codes and any relevant information about seed biology that pertains to them. For the sake of convenience, I will refer to two temperatures—70°F and 40°F—in these explanations. This does not mean you need to keep the seed at exactly those temperatures for the proper results. Temperatures from 32°–42°F are adequate for chilling, and temperatures from 60°–80°F for warmth are fine.

GERMINATION CODE A: seed will germinate within four weeks if sown at 70°F.

This is a common pattern with tropical and annual plants, and a few hardy perennials fall into this category as well. Addition of water is the mechanism that allows the seed to germinate, so this pattern is more common with dryland and desert plants that must be ready to grow when the rains come (technically this is referred to as nondeep physiological dormancy). In order for many A-type seeds to germinate, they need a period of one to three months of dry storage (after ripening) prior to planting. Thus, seed collected in fall and sown immediately will germinate poorly, while seed that has been cleaned and stored dry (preferably at 40°F) for three months will come up well. Still others, like many in the Aster family, will germinate with an A treatment, but emergence is erratic and slow. Cold stratification (B) will lead to more uniform germination in this case, and for that reason, I treat most of the A-type seeds I sow as B. Partly this is because the length of dry storage or after-ripening necessary to overcome dormancy can take much longer than cold stratification. (*Asclepias* seed may require a year of dry storage to germinate well, but just 60 days of moist, cold stratification will yield the same percentages.) A period of moist cold will generally have no ill effects, and it makes the process less complicated.

GERMINATION CODE B: seed will germinate upon shifting to 70°F after 90 days of moist, cold stratification at 40°F.

This is by far the most common germination pattern among the temperate wildflowers. It is vital that the seed be sown and well moistened before being exposed to cold. Water "activates" hormone and enzyme systems in the seed that block germination and allow the embryo to measure the length of cold that it is receiving. Dry, cold storage will not usually substitute for moist stratification if the seeds are truly type B germinators. The easiest way to germinate seeds of this type is to sow them outdoors in fall —either directly in the garden or in prepared beds or pots kept in a cold frame or crawl space that does not get too cold. Natural temperature changes are often much more effective than those you might achieve by placing the flats in a refrigerator. However, if you receive your seeds late in the winter, live in an area where winter temperatures do not stay regularly below 50°F, or do not have a place to keep them outdoors, you can sow them in pots and place them inside a plastic bag in the refrigerator (not the freezer). A method that takes even less space is to mix the seed with some damp vermiculite in a self-seal baggie and put them in the cooler this way. After cold treatment, sow the lot in a container just as you would any seed.

GERMINATION CODE C: seeds germinate only after multiple cycles of warm and cold, typically 40°-70°-40°-70°F.

Multicycle germination is common in the Lily family and woodland forbs. It is a slow process that discourages many beginning propagators, but it is really not too difficult. Long germination times are necessary for several reasons. First, many plants, such as trilliums, Solomon's seal, and twinleaf, are two-stage germinators—that is, after their first cold period they germinate underground to form a rudimentary rhizome or bulb and root system, but must be exposed to another cycle of cold and warmth to send up the cotyledon, or in the case of hypogeal species like *Jeffersonia*, the first true leaves. Secondly, plants like

Goldenseal have embryos that are not fully developed when the seed is ripe and need a full growing season to mature the embryo and prepare for germination. Others, like Blue Cohosh, have extremely hard seed coats that need time to weather away so that water can permeate. In all cases where the seed is both hydrophilic (*) and a C-type germinator, germination may be enhanced by collecting the seed when it is immature and sowing it immediately outdoors. Roughly this means collecting the seed three to four weeks early, but you may have to experiment with a particular genus to get the timing right. Seed

Trillium grandiflorum seed needs to be stored moist to retain viability. Mix the cleaned seeds with dampened vermiculite in a self-sealing bag, then put the bag in the refrigerator. Seeds of many hydrophilic species have remained viable for up to three years for me when stored this way.

Caulophyllum thalic-troides seed sowing. The procedure I use to sow large seeds is to fill a container to within 1 inch of the top with a clean, pasteurized seed mix, tamp it down, then sprinkle on the seeds. I cover the seeds with a thin layer of the same mix (about as deep as the seeds are thick), followed finally by a ⅛-inch layer of filter sand and water the flat thoroughly. These Blue Cohosh seeds may need to sit in the cold frame for three years before germinating, so a good, stable mix is important.

should be plump and full size, but still green or white without a hardened and darkened seed coat. I have had success with *Actaea, Trillium, Clintonia, Hydrastis,* and some *Disporum* using this method but it does not always work. Furthermore, most C germinators need exposure to the cycling or fluctuating temperatures and long warm and cold seasons (four to six months) that you find outdoors, and germination under artificial conditions of refrigeration or greenhouse is hit or miss. Seed that is sown in beds or cold frames and kept watered and allowed to go through the natural seasons will give the best results.

GERMINATION CODE D: seed needs a period of warm, moist stratification followed by cold stratification and will germinate after shifting back to warm (70°-40°-70°F).

This is a common cycle with early-ripening, hydrophilic species, such as Bloodroot, that naturally experience this pattern when they fall to the ground in early summer. Since I sow most of the hydrophilic species immediately outdoors, they get the proper treatment as a matter of course. However, when we sell seed of plants like Bloodroot that has been stored

moist at 40°F since collection, it will not germinate until it receives three to four months of warm then three to four months of cold temperatures, so typically it will not emerge until the second spring if sown outdoors in February or March. Some hypogeal species, like many of the true lilies, form a bulb and roots at 70°F then send up a cotyledon after three months at 40°F. There are others, such as Black Cohosh, that have immature embryos that require three months of moist warmth to develop before shifting to cold. Since both the lilies and *Cimicifuga*s ripen late in the year, I usually sow the seed in flats in a warm greenhouse (or on top of the refrigerator, near a radiator—any warm place) and leave them for at least three months before shifting them to a cold frame or the refrigerator for three months. In this way they come up well the following spring instead of waiting an additional year.

GERMINATION CODE G: chemical inhibitors.
Many if not most seeds that ripen in fleshy fruits must be well washed of all pulp to remove germination-inhibiting chemicals they contain. See seed cleaning (p. 236).

GERMINATION CODE H: seed requires light to germinate.

Small seeds that lack the resources to germinate deep underground are sensitive to light and will germinate only when a certain minimum intensity of light hits the seed coat. This is a cue that they are positioned at or near the soil surface. As a rule of thumb, I treat any seed smaller than a grain of salt as a type H, because they need to be sown shallowly anyway, whether light is important or not. There are also a few large-seeded species that require light, but these are rare. The easiest way to handle H seeds outdoors is to sow them over the surface of a tamped and dampened seed mix and cover them with a ⅛-inch layer of washed, coarse quartz sand. Quartz sand transmits some light just as glass does, yet provides some protection from drying and weather. I use #1 filter washed filter sand, available at swimming pool supply stores, as it is uniform and coarse, but you can make your own by screening regular builder's sand though a window screen then washing what remains in the screen to remove dust. It will have a few large pebbles that can be picked out, but is otherwise a good size — really a fine gravel.

Alternatively, you can sow the seed on the surface of a moistened flat of seed mix and enclose the whole thing in a large self-sealing bag. If the seed is type A, H, put the bag under grow lights at 70°F. (You can put it on a windowsill, but it is hard to find a spot with enough sunlight for most plants that will not at the same time heat up the bag too much.) Seedlings can be left in the bag for up to a year, but check them regularly for water and fertilize every month with half-strength liquid fertilizer when they are actively growing. Wean them out of this saturated environment slowly when they are large enough to transplant by first opening up the bag partway for a week or two. B, H seed can be treated the same except that the flats should be put in the refrigerator for three months prior to being set out in the light.

A final procedure that is an excellent way to start small-seeded acid-loving species like *Galax, Shortia, Epigaea,* and *Gaultheria* is moss-sowing. If you have a damp spot in the yard where moss grows well and stays fairly damp through the growing season, you can shake the seeds into the moss carpet and carefully water them in. You may have to supplement watering to keep the moss damp, but this method can work remarkably well. Alternatively, you can establish a moss carpet in a container by transplanting some tufts of moss. The tight-growing, carpeting types like fern-leaf moss are easiest to get going. (A mix of 1:1 peat and sand is good for acid-loving mosses, but others grow well on the surface of regular potting mixes, as anyone who grows plants in containers can attest.) Sphagnum works well, and certainly use it if you have some growing wild because it usually stays evenly moist. You can grow it by burying some of the long strands almost to their tips in a partially submerged container of 1:1 peat and sand, but it needs a season to become thick and established. All mosses are best watered with rain or distilled water.

GERMINATION CODE I: seed requires scarification because of an impermeable seed coat.

Many plants in the Bean and Mallow families have hard seed coats that will not let water into the embryo. Mechanical abrasion of the seed coat is necessary for imbibition and germination. Many legumes will germinate almost immediately after scarification but can take a year or more otherwise. I have used several methods. Placing a pile of seeds between two pieces of fine sandpaper and grinding the top piece back and forth quickly with your palm is easy and effective. It is not necessary to remove much of the cost, and typically 15–30 seconds of grinding is sufficient. Some people swear by the hot water method, in which near-boiling water is poured over a pot of seeds and they are allowed to cool and soak overnight before planting. The soaking allows the seeds to imbibe all the water they need. I have had mixed results with this treatment. It works well with *Baptisia*s and prairie clovers, but not so well with lupines. The milkshake blender method of cleaning seeds I describe on p. 236 also helps scarify them and is an easy way to treat species like Blue Cohosh. Sowing the seed outdoors in fall will also weather the seed coat by spring, and for *Baptisia*s, a combination of sandpaper scarification and cold stratification in a cold frame gives me consistent results.

GERMINATION CODE *: seed is hydrophilic, intolerant of dry storage (see seed collection p. 236).

This category includes all the ant-dispersed woodland species as well as a number of others that do not take desiccation very well. Freshly collected seed should be sown immediately or alternatively stored in sealed plastic bags at 40°F. Seed that ripens in fleshy fruits or has an attached elaiosome is best stored with a handful of slightly damp vermiculite mixed in. This maintains a consistent saturated atmosphere for the seeds. Small seeds as well as seeds that ripen in dry capsules and lack elaiosomes can be stored without the vermiculite, which will discourage molds.

Potting On

Getting the seed to germinate is only half the battle, but I think it is the tougher half. Once you have a flat of healthy seedlings, keeping them healthy is pretty straightforward. Seedlings have more plasticity than adults — that is, they are often more tolerant of transplanting damage and, if conditions are right,

Trillium flexipes divisions. Slow-growing species like trilliums can be stepped up over the course of several seasons into larger pots. If you use a good, freely draining mix, faster-growing species can go right from the seed flat or plug tray into a large container. The open structure of the potting mix will keep the roots aerated until they have filled the container.

will often continue growing and getting larger much more quickly than they would in the wild. For example, Red Baneberry seedlings are easy to transplant from the seed flat to small individual pots after their cotyledons are fully expanded. In the wild, first-year seedlings rarely put up more than 1 or 2 leaves before going dormant. However, with adequate fertilizer and water (I usually fertilize transplants every two weeks with liquid fertilizer mixed as directed on the label) they will continue to put out new leaves and after a month are large enough for a 4½-inch container. Repotting the healthy plant further encourages it, and it will grow through the summer and usually even bloom. Growth from seedling to adulthood would take two to three years in the wild, but in cultivation, it can be shortened to three months.

Propagating plants in pots has a number of advantages over garden beds, such as faster growth, portability, sanitation, and ease of transplant. I always try to transplant seedlings at the cotyledon stage or just after the first few true leaves have emerged because their root systems are small and less easily damaged. We grow most of our fast-growing seedlings in plugs—1–1½-inch-diameter containers that come in trays like the six-pack pots bedding plants and tomatoes come in (egg cartons work, too). The pots are small enough not to swamp the

seedlings, and after a month the seedlings can be popped out and stepped up into a 4–6-inch pot. Slow-growing plants like *Trillium* are best left in the seed flat for a couple of years and fertilized a few times during the spring until large enough for the garden or intermediate-sized containers (2–3-inch diameter). We use the same mix for plugs and small pots as we do for seeds. To bring seedlings up to saleable or plantable size, transfer them to 4–8-inch containers in early to midsummer (any later and they will not have time to establish before winter). Use a coarser mix for the larger pots as it will provide the necessary drainage. Do not add garden soil to your container mix, and compost only with caution. Water should pass quickly through the finished blend, not pool on top even for a few seconds. Addition of rotted pine bark or perlite to the seed mix will accomplish this, or you can blend your own, I have developed a blend that works well for most plants we grow that includes the following:

3 parts aged pine bark (the consistency of pine bark mulch and dark brown-black in color)
1 part baled peat moss
1 part coarse perlite

Blend and add ¾ cup of powdered dolomite lime, ⅓ cup wetting agent (optional but helpful), and 1 cup coated, balanced, time-release fertilizer for every cubic foot of bark, and blend again.

Cuttings

Every seed that germinates is a small miracle of sorts, but roots forming on a stem cutting is, to me, an event even more miraculous. Stem cuttings are sections of stem, usually with attached leaves that are forced to initiate roots and become new plants. Many perennials are very easy to root from stem cuttings, even without fancy equipment if you follow some basic rules. The basic principle involved in this bit of horticultural wizardry is *cell plasticity.* All developing cells, be they human or carrot, have a certain potential to be anything the organism needs them to be. Undifferentiated cells in the growing tip of a plant are "told" by specific hormones that they should become leaves, flowers, roots, etc. These undifferentiated cells can also be found in wound tissue that forms after cells have been damaged. The hormone messenger responsible for, among other things, initiating these cells to become root cells is IAA (Indole-3-acetic acid) or its less expensive synthetic equivalent Indole-3-butyric acid (IBA), found in commercial rooting powders and liquids. When you expose a stem cutting to IBA, the hormone persuades cells in either the dormant bud within each leaf axil or the wound tissue (callus tissue) that begins to form over the cut surface to become roots.

Cuttings offer certain advantages over seed, namely speed and the ability to produce exact duplicates of a special plant. Some species, like *Shortia galacifolia,* for example, are much easier to produce from cuttings as well. Obviously, by cloning plants you are not getting the genetic diversity you would from seed, and you need a little more equipment and practice to root cuttings well. Stem cuttings are the most common type of vegetative or clonal propagation, and the principles are the same as those used in tissue culture. Tissue or cell culture involves isolating undifferentiated cells in a sterile environment then exposing them to various hormones as well as nutrients and carbohydrates for energy to promote rapid cell growth or proliferation. Proliferating callus cell cultures can be divided and re-divided indefinitely so that large numbers of undifferentiated cells are produced. Then the balance of hormones is altered to encourage shoot and finally root formation so that the end result is a rooted cutting. While tissue culture can produce huge quantities of a particular clone, it is not without its problems. First of all, it takes a great deal of research and experience to determine the best ratio of different hormones and other factors to get a particular species to respond well. The time and equipment needed to run a lab make them prohibitive for even most nurseries. Second,

rapidly dividing cell cultures exposed to strong hormones can easily mutate, so that the finished plants are genetically different than the original material tissue-cultured. Characteristics such as variegation, which are often genetically unstable to begin with, can be lost in culture. Accordingly, the only garden perennials that are produced in tissue culture these days are valuable clones of species that are difficult to propagate by stem cuttings (hostas, lilies, coralbells, etc.).

Remember that when you sever a growing stem from its root system, you are not only cutting off its water supply, you are severely hampering its ability to manufacture energy and absorb nutrients. It becomes a race against time to get the cutting to root before its meager nutrient and energy reserves are exhausted. Always take cuttings from healthy, vigorous plants as these will have proportionately more reserves. Avoid drought-stressed or nutrient-deficient specimens. Plants shunt reserves to the growing tips, and the cells in rapidly growing tissue are more plastic, so always take tip cuttings (from the top 3–6 inches of stem) that are actively growing and show no sign of flowering (these "softwood" cuttings should flex or bend easily between your fingers without breaking). Late spring to early summer is the best time to root most wildflowers, though I have indicated exceptions in the propagation table. Repeatedly shearing back your stock plants and keeping them well fertilized will encourage additional flushes of juvenile growth for a second or third round of cuttings, but keep in mind that unless you have a greenhouse, plan on providing rooted cuttings at least two months of the growing season to mature and form crown buds to carry them through the winter. Herbaceous perennials naturally form dormant crown buds at or just below the soil line in late summer to fall, and these are the source of the following year's growth. One problem with stem cuttings is that while they may root and continue to grow though the summer, the adventitious roots that grew from the stem cells may not form a normal crown and crown buds. Such cuttings never come out of winter dormancy, even if the root system is large and healthy. You can increase the odds of success by making sure you set at least one leaf node or axil well into the rooting medium.

It is best to take cuttings on a cloudy, humid day and prepare them immediately. If you cannot, keep the material in sealed plastic bags in a refrigerator or ice chest to slow degradation. Stem cuttings should have at least 2 leaf nodes supported by a section of stem. Unless I am really short on material or the stems are very long, I usually try to leave 3–6 nodes per cutting. Strip or cut off the leaf or leaves from the lowest nodes and dip this freshly cut lower end into rooting hormone. (Powdered IBA, which is hormone mixed with talc, is available at most garden centers.) Most of the plants I have listed will root with concentrations of .01 percent IBA, the level sold for softwood cuttings. Liquid IBA is harder to find, but allows you to control [by diluting the liquid concentrate] the strength of the treatment. Cuttings are usually "quick dipped" in liquid IBA for 10–30 seconds, but otherwise the procedure is the same as for powdered hormone. Then place the cut end an inch or two deep into the rooting medium. For rooting medium, I usually use a mix of 2 parts commercial peat-lite seed-starting potting mix and 1 part coarse perlite. Acid-loving plants root well in a 1:1 mix of peat moss and coarse perlite or 1:1:1 peat moss, aged pine bark, and sand. You can use any sort of growing container to root cuttings, but remember that the larger the pot, the coarser the mix needs to be. I prefer either 16-by-16-inch by 3-inch-deep flats unless I am rooting under mist in a greenhouse, in which case 50- or 72-cell "plug" trays are best.

The key to success is keeping the cuttings in a humid environment to cut down on or eliminate water loss. The stem can absorb some water just as a rose can in a vase, so if the air is saturated, the cutting can still grow and manufacture energy at a much reduced rate. Remember that rooting is a race against time, and repeated moisture stress will usually lead to failure. Light is also important. Shade plants can be rooted successfully without much light, but most cuttings take better in strong light. Commercial propagators typically use greenhouses equipped with mist or fog systems that keep cuttings bathed in moisture and strong light. If the air temperature falls below 65°F, heat mats or circulating warm water are used to keep the root zone warm. The home propagator can approximate these conditions by placing cuttings and container in a sealed plastic bag and putting it in a window that receives morning sun or under grow lights set for 16-hour days. Alternatively, slow-to-root shade plants like Trailing Arbutus can be stuck in flats and covered with a spun-bonded row cover and placed in a shady spot that is regularly watered.

Check your cuttings after two to three weeks by gently tugging on them. If you feel resistance, take them out of the bag, row cover, or mist and give them a light fertilizing. Transplant once leaf growth recommences and the root systems are well developed.

Root Cuttings

Fleshy-rooted wildflowers such as bluebells, Stokes' Aster, shooting stars, and Bird's-foot Violet can be propagated by root cuttings. Basically root cuttings are the opposite of stem cuttings, inducing stem buds to form from root cells. Since root systems store energy for the plant in winter and shunt it to the aboveground parts in spring, the best time to take these cuttings is before growth begins in late winter or early spring, when root reserves are high. There is not a hormone preparation readily available that promotes shoot induction from roots, so this procedure works only on species that have the natural ability to regenerate from the root system. Typically, 1–3-inch sections of the largest roots are removed and stuck either vertically or at a 45° angle in a coarse, sterile medium like builder's sand or vermiculite. Try to keep track of the top and bottom ends of the roots when you cut them and orient them in the tray in the same direction. Keep the flat watered and warm and new shoots should emerge within six to eight weeks. An even easier method that often works is to dig down around a healthy plant in early spring and sever some of the larger roots from the crown, leaving them in place, then relocating the resulting plants in fall.

Aconitum   Monkshood p. 33   LATE SUMMER   **B***

SEEDS: Collect the follicles that contain the seeds as they begin to brown (usually 4–6 weeks after flowering). Allow them to dry for several days, until the tips split open, and the small fuzzy seeds will shake out easily. Sow immediately or keep the seeds in a plastic bag in the refrigerator. Seedlings grow quickly with good care and bloom the second season.

CUTTINGS/DIVISION: *A. uncinatum* forms daughter tubers from its rootstock that can be removed and grown on, but this is a slow method, and care should be taken as the tubers contain the highest concentrations of alkaloids. Some plants of *A. columbianum* (var. *viviparum*) form bulbils in the leaf axils, which can be removed and will grow into new plants.

Actaea   Baneberry p. 34   MID- TO LATE SUMMER   **B or C*, G**

SEEDS: *Actaea* seeds should be collected as soon as the fruits begin to color. There are 4–8 of the brown flattened seeds in each fruit. If cleaned and sown immediately outdoors, a good crop of seedlings will germinate the following spring, with half or more waiting an additional year to sprout. However, I have found that the less mature seeds found in newly ripened berries will germinate nearly 100 percent after one winter. Seed that is allowed to dry will take 2 or 3 years to germinate. The seedlings will grow quickly in containers, often flowering and setting a late crop of fruit in their first season.

Agastache   Wild Hyssop p. 35   LATE SUMMER TO EARLY FALL   **A**

SEEDS: All species come easily from seed collected 3–4 weeks after flowering. Peer inside the calyx cup and harvest when the seeds developing at its base begin to darken. Dry the heads in a paper bag until the seeds can be shaken free.

CUTTINGS/DIVISION: One- to two-node softwood cuttings root quickly.

Allium   Wild Onion p. 36   SUMMER TO FALL, DEPENDING ON SPECIES   **A, D or C**

(SEED RIPENS 3–6 WEEKS AFTER BLOOM)

SEEDS: The characteristic shiny black seeds are usually produced in abundance. Collect them when the capsules have dried to a papery husk. There is some variety in the germination patterns of different species. Many of the western plants are D-type germinators, but there are exceptions (*A. validum* for example). Most from the East are A-type seeds, but *A. tricoccum* is treated as a C-type. If unsure about a particular species, leave the seed flats in a cold frame for two full seasons before giving up. Flowering takes place in the second or third year from germination.

CUTTINGS/DIVISION: The more vigorous types can be easily divided by teasing apart the clusters of bulbs when dormant.

Amsonia   Bluestar p. 38   EARLY FALL   **B**

SEEDS: The seeds form in long capsules reminiscent of French filets-verts string beans. After the flowers fade, the plants put out secondary branchlets from just below each inflorescence which eventually hide the capsules amidst the foliage. Harvest the capsules when they have turned yellow in early fall and let them dry. The curious, cylindrical seeds are sometimes difficult to extract from the dried pods, which have a habit of rolling closed like a window blind when you tease them open. Seedlings sprout vigorously and will continue to grow strongly under good culture, blooming the second or third season. The plants will self-sow, and small plants can be dug and moved in spring.

CUTTINGS/DIVISION: Three-inch stem cuttings taken just before flowers fade will root easily, but not all will form the necessary crown buds to sprout the following spring. Seed is more reliable and consistent.

Anemone   Windflower p. 40   EARLY SUMMER TO FALL, DEPENDING ON SPECIES   **B or C***

SEEDS: The rhizomatous types are hydrophilic (B or C*) and should be sown as soon as they come loose easily from the plants. At least with *A. quinquefolia*, the plants grow in large clonal colonies that appear to be self-sterile, so seeds are seldom seen. *A. caroliniana* (B*) seeds should also be sown fresh, as soon as the cottony heads begin to disintegrate. The caudex types (B) can be harvested when the heads begin to disintegrate and stored dry until sown, though some loss in viability will occur after 6 months in storage. *A. patens* will germinate within 4 weeks if fresh seed is sown when ripe in late spring. Plants of this type will flower in their second season from seed.

CUTTINGS/DIVISION: *A. canadensis* is easy to divide—the individual crowns can be dug and moved any time during the growing season. Division of the brittle rhizomes is by far the easiest method to multiply the woodland species, and this is best done after the plants have gone dormant in summer or fall. Older, eyeless sections of rhizome should also be replanted.

Anemonella   Rue Anemone p. 42   EARLY SUMMER   **D***

SEEDS: It is best to harvest the seed and sow as soon as ripe. The seeds are enclosed in a green papery husk that need not be removed before sowing. There is little indication when the seeds are ripe other than that they fall easily away from the plant when brushed with a finger. Seed can be stored dry, but viability drops off quickly after 3–4 weeks. Under container culture, the seedlings will grow quickly and bloom the first season, but care must be taken to leave the crowns just at the surface when transplanting to avoid rot.

A: seed will germinate within 4 weeks if sown at 70°F; **B**: seed will germinate upon shifting to 70°F after 90 days of moist, cold stratification at 40°F;
C: seeds germinate only after multiple cycles of warm and cold, typically 40°-70°-40°-70°; **D**: seed needs a period of warm moist stratification followed by cold stratification and will germinate after shifting back to warm (70°-40°-70°); **G**: chemical inhibitors; **H**: seed requires light to germinate; **I**: seed requires scarification because of an impermeable seed coat; *****: seed is hydrophilic, intolerant of dry storage.

CUTTINGS/DIVISION: The tubers can be carefully dug and detached from the crown, either after they are dormant in summer or in early spring. Not all tubers will have a viable eye, so take only a few of the largest from each crown. This is an efficient way to multiply the very attractive, sterile double forms.

Antennaria   Pussy-toes p. 43   **EARLY SUMMER**   **A or B**

SEEDS: When ripe, seeds burst out of the heads in a froth of downy white. Collect them and store dry in the refrigerator until needed. Dividing is the easiest method, but seedlings germinate fairly well and grow quickly to flowering size.

CUTTINGS/DIVISION: The mat-forming types are easy to divide into single rosettes with attached, rooted stolons anytime during late spring or summer. These can be treated as cuttings or replanted directly in the garden.

Aquilegia   Columbine p. 44   **EARLY SUMMER**   **B**

SEEDS: Seed is the standard method of propagation. Collect it after the upright capsules have dried. Seeds can be shaken into an envelope and stored dry until needed. Our standard outdoor treatment has worked with all the species listed (plants bloom the second season from seed). GA3 treatment worked splendidly with the recalcitrant *A. jonesii*. Alternatively, you can help them self-sow by slapping the dry capsules several times with the back of your hand (pretend they have insulted you), catapulting the seeds all over the area.

Arisaema   Jack-in-the-pulpit p. 46   **EARLY FALL**   **A or B, G**

SEEDS: Seeds can be collected when the berries begin to color. As the berries can develop even without seeds, choose only fat, smooth fruits. Mash and wash the seeds to remove all pulp, which contain inhibitors that give irregular germination. All parts of the plants contain tiny crystals of calcium oxalate which imbed themselves in the skin and cause an irritating, tingly burning for 24 hours or so. Wear a pair of latex gloves when cleaning the fruits. Once the seeds are clean and dry, they are safe to handle. Either store dry in the refrigerator and sow in spring or sow outdoors in fall. Seedlings germinate easily and form a single round leaf the first year, putting all their energy into the developing corm. Plants take 2–3 years to bloom.

CUTTINGS/DIVISION: Divide the corms after the plants have withered in fall.

Aruncus   Goat's Beard p. 47   **EARLY FALL**   **B, H**

SEEDS: The tiny seed ripens in early fall. Clip the heads when small thin pods turn from green to yellow tinged red. Let the heads air dry, then crush them gingerly with a rolling pin and screen the seeds. Surface-sow and stratify the seeds. Seedlings are small at first, but a liquid fertilizing will quickly get them to a workable size. Blooms the second or third season. Division of the woody crown is possible, but hard on the plants. Self-sown plants can be moved in spring.

Asarum   Wild Ginger p. 48   **EARLY SUMMER**   **D*, G**

SEEDS: Seed ripens inside of a mealy fruit that basically splits and turns inside out when ripe. Ants pick up the seeds from the mushy pulp and carry them to their nests, but many fall around the base of the plant and germinate in small clusters the next spring. Harvest the fruits as the first begin to split. It is easier to clean the seeds if the fruit is a bit unripe. Fresh seed should be sown outdoors as soon as it is thoroughly cleaned, and it will germinate the following spring. In the wild, only the pair of fat cotyledons appear the first season, but with the extra water and fertilizer of container culture, the seedlings will eventually form a few true leaves and a strong rhizome as well. If transferred several times from plugs to larger containers, a near-flowering size plant can be produced in one season.

CUTTINGS/DIVISION: The gingers are easily divided in late spring or early fall, and this is the easiest way to produce mature plants rapidly. It is best to wait until the new growth has fully expanded and has had a chance to form some roots before splitting up the clumps.

Asclepias   Milkweed p. 49   **LATE SUMMER**   **(A), B, H**

SEEDS: Seed is the preferred method. Collect the pods as they yellow and begin to split. There are several weevil larvae that prey on the developing seeds, so look for frass and signs of damage, including small entry holes in the pod exuding latex. Usually most of the seeds in an affected pod will be dead. It is easier to pull heathy pods open immediately and dislodge the rows of seed from the wet down (ripe seed is brown). Dry down has a buoyancy that would make helium jealous, so if you let the pods dry and split, I recommend you clean them outdoors. Most of the species germinate easily if surface-sown and given a cold period. Seed germinates without a cold period, but it is slow and sporadic. The young plants grow robustly and will flower the first or second season.

CUTTINGS/DIVISION: It is possible to propagate milkweeds by stem or root cuttings, and some of the color forms of *A. tuberosa* are produced this way. However, the plants are reluctant to form adequate crowns and despite seeming robust in fall, they may never emerge in spring.

A: seed will germinate within 4 weeks if sown at 70°F; **B**: seed will germinate upon shifting to 70°F after 90 days of moist, cold stratification at 40°F; **C**: seeds germinate only after multiple cycles of warm and cold, typically 40°-70°-40°-70°; **D**: seed needs a period of warm moist stratification followed by cold stratification and will germinate after shifting back to warm (70°-40°-70°); **G**: chemical inhibitors; **H**: seed requires light to germinate; **I**: seed requires scarification because of an impermeable seed coat; *****: seed is hydrophilic, intolerant of dry storage.

Aster   Aster p. 51 — **LATE SUMMER TO LATE FALL** — **A or B**

SEEDS: Asters are very easy to raise from seed, and one of the plants I always recommend to beginners to try. Furthermore, the seeds are easy to harvest. Wait until the parachutes have begun to dry and expand to collect the seed. Store it dry in the refrigerator until it can be sown. Most species will germinate well when sown directly in warm temperatures, but I have had equal success sowing them outdoors in fall with germination the following spring. Many if not all of the plants are self-incompatible, so you will need at least 2 individuals of a species to get fertile seed. (As an experiment I sowed thousands of seeds of an isolated *A. concolor* over 3 years without a single one germinating. The following year, I placed another individual next to it and had hundreds of seedlings the following spring. The same was true of *A. oblongifolius, A. ericoides,* and *A. vimineus.*)

CUTTINGS/DIVISION: Stem cuttings taken in late spring are very effective, as long as the rooted cuttings are quickly potted on so as to have time for their crowns to mature.

Astragalus   Milkvetch p. 55 — **MID- TO LATE SUMMER** — **A, I**

SEEDS: Seed develops in round or oval inflated pods. The pods dry when the seed is ripe, but remain intact on the plant for several weeks, making collection easy. The small hard seed takes up relatively little room inside the pods, but should be tan or brown and firm. Stored dry in the refrigerator, it will stay viable for a number of years. Scarified seed will germinate in a few days when sown in warm soil, and the young plants immediately send down a deep taproot in search of water. Sixteen-ounce paper milk cartons opened up on top and with their four bottom corners snipped off make good containers for starting Milkvetch seedlings. Fill with a gritty mix and plant one or two of the nicked seeds in each. If you plan to sow the seed directly, wait until the weather has warmed in spring and scarify it first and soak it overnight in water, then plant it ½ inch deep in your prepared location. It should come up within a week.

Baptisia   Wild Indigo p. 57 — **LATE SUMMER TO EARLY FALL** — **A or B, I**

SEEDS: The sticky brown seeds are ripe when the inflated pods turn brown or black in late summer. Because the foliage continues to grow after flowering, you have to hunt around in it to find the pods. Common wisdom stresses the need to scarify before sowing, but simply sowing dry seed and placing in a cold frame over winter has worked for all the species covered here. The plants can be transplanted fairly easily when young, but do not overpot them as they grow slowly the first year. They take 2–3 years to bloom from seed.

CUTTINGS/DIVISION: Three- to four-node stem cuttings taken from the developing branch tips in late spring to early summer will root readily and continue to branch and form substantial root systems, but up to 75 percent of the cuttings fail to form crown buds. It is exasperating to toss out hundreds of pots with healthy root systems that have failed to re-sprout in spring, so I now grow all the plants from seed.

Boltonia   False Aster p. 58 — **FALL** — **B**

SEEDS: Seed can be collected as for aster, but cross-pollination is required for seed set. Since only a few cultivars are widely grown, garden seed is rarely viable. Good seed germinates easily after a period of moist cold, and the plants often bloom their first fall.

CUTTINGS/DIVISION: Two- to three-node stem cuttings taken in midspring are very effective, and this is the most common method used. Early spring division of older clumps into individual crowns will yield many new plants.

Calla   Water Arum p. 59 — **LATE SUMMER** — **B***

SEEDS: The berries ripen and are easily seen in late summer (though given the mucky conditions, not always easy to collect). Clean the dark brown seeds of all pulp and sow them immediately. They will germinate and grow well in a standard mix provided it remains evenly moist. The seedlings are best left until the second spring to transplant.

CUTTINGS/DIVISION: Spring or summer rhizome cuttings are easier. The thick, jointed rhizomes can be severed at every other node and replanted in pots kept in a shallow pan of water. Most will re-sprout and quickly fill the container.

Callirhoe   Poppy-mallow p. 60 — **LATE SUMMER** — **B, I**

SEEDS: The distinctive comma-shaped seeds are produced like wedges of an orange in the woody capsule. *C. involucrata* is gynodioecious, that is some plants have all female flowers while others have perfect flowers, so if you have only one plant, you may not get seed. Harvest the seeds when they brown and begin to split. The seeds have a hard seed coat which must be thoroughly scarified for uniform germination. The plants will bloom their second season.

CUTTINGS/DIVISION: Three-node stem cuttings taken well before flowering root well.

Calopogon   Grass Pink p. 61 — **LATE SUMMER** — **A, H**

SEEDS: Difficult — see "Cypripedium Seed Germination," p. 85.

CUTTINGS/DIVISION: The primary way to propagate Grass Pinks for those of us without access to a lab is through multiplication of

---

A: seed will germinate within 4 weeks if sown at 70°F; **B**: seed will germinate upon shifting to 70°F after 90 days of moist, cold stratification at 40°F; **C**: seeds germinate only after multiple cycles of warm and cold, typically 40°-70°-40°-70°; **D**: seed needs a period of warm moist stratification followed by cold stratification and will germinate after shifting back to warm (70°-40°-70°); **G**: chemical inhibitors; **H**: seed requires light to germinate; **I**: seed requires scarification because of an impermeable seed coat; *****: seed is hydrophilic, intolerant of dry storage.

the corms. I have used Carson Whitlow's courageous technique quite successfully.[11] I grow the plants in containers in our standard bog mix of 1:1 peat moss and builder's sand. During the growing season, the pots sit in a shallow pan of water is drained before they are covered for the winter. In early spring, I tamp them out of their pots and inspect the acorn-sized corms to find a place where they can be cut in half vertically, leaving two sections each with a small eye which will be the next growth Following Whitlow's advice, I then towel off the cut surfaces and spread a film of instant adhesive (glue) over one side and then quickly squeeze the halves back together just as they were and replant them in fresh mix. Severing induces both eyes to form healthy corms which can be dug out the following spring and either severed or planted in the garden. In this way, large numbers of the plants can eventually be obtained.

Caltha   Marsh Marigold p. 62   LATE SPRING TO EARLY SUMMER   **D***

SEEDS: The shiny, green-brown seeds of Marsh Marigold ripen quickly in crescent-shaped follicles arranged in a circle on lengthened stems. I have missed the seeds many times because they are quickly shed when ripe—unfortunately during the busiest part of late spring. The follicles will go from green through yellow to brown-black when ripe, splitting open like a pea pod along the upper margin. Carefully tip these into a plastic bag and shake out the seeds. Sow immediately and place in an outdoor cold frame; they will germinate the following spring. Like many wetland plants, marsh marigolds will grow quite happily in a standard perennial container mix provided they never dry out. With good culture, seedlings will not go dormant, continuing to grow all summer to bloom the second spring.

CUTTINGS/DIVISION: With cultivars, thick crowns can be dug and cut apart, preferably in earliest spring just as growth begins or when dormant in summer.

Camassia   Camas Lily p. 63   SUMMER   **B**

SEEDS: Seeds germinate readily after a moist stratification, but like many lilies, produce only one thin leaf the first year, which dies back to a ¼-inch bulb in midsummer. The large black seeds are easily collected when the pods begin to brown in summer. The seedlings take 4–5 years to bloom so are best sown around the parents or in a seed bed prepared for the purpose.

CUTTINGS/DIVISION: Under ideal culture, some species produce offsets that can be separated in the fall and replanted. They will bloom in 1–2 years. However, even though I usually like to propagate things myself, in this case I think it is much easier to buy mature bulbs.

Campanula   Harebell p. 64   MIDSUMMER TO FALL (4 WEEKS AFTER BLOOM)   **A or B, H**

SEEDS: The fine seed is a bit tricky to collect, as the capsules ripen quickly and crack open like a salt shaker. Collect the capsules when they are plump and green with a few turning brown and let them ripen in a paper bag. Because harebells ripen sequentially, you'll be guaranteed at least some seed this way. Plants are self-incompatible, so plant at least two for seed set. Shake and sieve through a screen. Dry seed germinates easily at warm temperatures, and the seedlings will usually begin blooming the first season.

CUTTINGS/DIVISION: Four- to six-node, softwood stem cuttings taken in spring just as the stems begin to bolt can be slow to root, but are an effective alternative if you do not have seed.

Castilleja   Paintbrush p. 65   SUMMER TO FALL (4–6 WEEKS AFTER FLOWERS FADE)   **B (D?)**

SEEDS: Seed is the only viable method. Of the dozen or so species I have grown, most come up well after outdoor stratification, although sometimes seedlings will not emerge for another year, suggesting they may also be type D germinators. The fine seed is produced in oval capsules that release it as they dry. Collect the seed as the pods begin to dry if you can, but usually some seed can be found even in older capsules. Sow in a gritty mix (except *C. coccinea,* which should be grown in a standard mix) and cover lightly with gravel. Fertilize the growing seedlings every 2–3 weeks with a liquid fertilizer. I have grown several paintbrushes in pots of *Penstemon fruticosus* (both were sown at the same time), but did not notice much difference in growth over plants sown without a host. The biennial *C. coccinea* can be moved from the seedflat to individual 3-inch pots when the rosettes are ½ inch in diameter andplanted out among Little Bluestem grass in late summer. They will bloom the following year.

Caulophyllum   Blue Cohosh p. 67   LATE SUMMER TO EARLY FALL   **C*, G, (I?)**

SEEDS: The plants each produce relatively few of the large seeds, which should be harvested when they begin to turn blue in late summer. Interestingly, the thin blue flesh covering the seed is not a fruit but technically an extension of the seed coat, which can be removed by cleaning in a blender or by fermentation soaking. The washed seed is best sown immediately in flats kept in an outdoor cold frame. Germination is hypogeal, and it is the first true leaf that emerges the second or third spring. Blue Cohosh is reportedly difficult to germinate, but we have grown countless plants, and I suspect the problem others encounter may be a combination of using dry (and therefore probably dead) seed and not washing or soaking to remove possible inhibitors then exposing it to natural temperature fluctuations outdoors. The seed coat is very hard and cleaning in a blender may have some

A: seed will germinate within 4 weeks if sown at 70°F; B: seed will germinate upon shifting to 70°F after 90 days of moist, cold stratification at 40°F; C: seeds germinate only after multiple cycles of warm and cold, typically 40°-70°-40°-70°; D: seed needs a period of warm moist stratification followed by cold stratification and will germinate after shifting back to warm (70°-40°-70°); G: chemical inhibitors; H: seed requires light to germinate; I: seed requires scarification because of an impermeable seed coat; *: seed is hydrophilic, intolerant of dry storage.

scarifying effect. The first-year seedlings are 4–6 inches tall, with a single compound leaf and a tangle of wiry yellow roots. These can be transplanted directly into the garden or into quart or larger containers. No further top growth will appear during the season, but the plants will form extensive roots and several crown buds. They flower in 3–4 years from seed.

Chamaelirium Devil's Bit p. 68   **LATE SUMMER**   **B, H***

SEEDS: The light, papery seed ripens in small capsules like many of the Liliaceae. Collect the capsules when they begin to brown and let them dry until they split and the seed can be shaken free. Although I have stored seed dry for several months before sowing, I suspect that *Chamaelirium* seed, like the related Swamp Pink *(Hellonias bullata)* is short-lived in storage. I have had excellent results sowing the seed in a cold frame in the fall, covered only with a layer of coarse sand. The seedlings are very small at first, forming a ¼-inch rosette the first season, so they are best left alone until the following season. If transplanted to individual pots by early summer, they will put out one or two additional flushes of growth and be ready for the garden the following spring. They take 3 years to bloom from seed.

CUTTINGS/DIVISION: Healthy older plants will form offsets that can be separated in spring, but I hesitate to divide them as clumps are much more effective in the garden.

Chelone Turtlehead p. 68   **FALL**   **B, H**

SEEDS: The thin, papery brown seeds ripen in large pointed capsules late in the year. Harvest when the capsules brown, and shake out the seeds. I have had mixed results germinating the seeds, and I suspect that they need some light to germinate well.

CUTTINGS/DIVISION: Two-node stem cuttings taken in late spring root easily, and this is the method I prefer.

Chimaphila Spotted Wintergreen p. 69   **EARLY FALL**   **?**

SEEDS: I have never successfully germinated the seed of any *Chimaphila*. It is suspected that like orchids, they need a fungal partner to germinate, and this may explain my failures. Quantities of the fine seed are produced in woody capsules, and the plants will readily self-sow under appropriate conditions.

CUTTINGS/DIVISION: Fortunately, they are easily propagated from cuttings taken in midsummer, and this is the method I use. The plants grow like rhododendrons, with a whorl of new foliage coming from the center of older nonflowering stems as well as from the rhizome. Clip the whorl of new growth with a section of stem after the leaves have fully expanded. The rooted cuttings should be left in the flat and potted or placed directly in the garden the following spring.

Chrysogonum Gold-star p. 70   **EARLY SUMMER**   **B***

SEEDS: Each black seed is enclosed by several bracts, which fall with it when ripe. The bracts have a fleshy cap or crown at one end, which may be an ant attractant. Collect seed heads when they begin to brown (there are usually only a few good seeds in each head, so be thorough). The seeds will fall out as the heads dry. I usually store seeds in plastic bags as I have had trouble germinating dry seed and suspect it may be moderately hydrophilic.

CUTTINGS/DIVISION: Flowering rosettes will send out offshoots that begin to form their own roots in early summer. These can be treated as cuttings or, if well rooted, replanted immediately.

Chrysopsis Golden Aster p. 71   **MIDSUMMER TO FALL (3–5 WEEKS AFTER BLOOM)**   **B**

SEEDS: Collect seed as for asters. It germinates easily after a cold period, and the seedlings are easily transplanted when young.

Cimicifuga Bugbane p. 72   **LATE SUMMER TO FALL**   **D***

SEEDS: All the species are classic D type germinators. The seed ripens in early to late fall in small crescent-shaped pods that can be picked when they yellow (split open a few first to see if the seed has turned brown). *C. racemosa* has smooth seeds, but the rest have seeds that are flattened and covered on their narrow edges with coarse auburn hairs (they look a little like small insects). I have always treated *Cimicifuga* seed as hydrophilic and usually sow it immediately in flats that I leave in a heated place for 3 months before putting them in the cold frame in February. In this way I usually get good germination the first spring. The seedlings are fast growing and best moved to individual pots when the third true leaf shows. They will usually bloom their second year from seed if treated in this way. Self-sown seedlings move easily in spring.

Claytonia Spring Beauty p. 74   **EARLY SUMMER**   **D***

SEEDS: The small, shiny black seeds are produced in a series of little pods that each sit between the 2 fused segments of the calyx (the whole reminds me of a string of duck bills all open and sticking out their tongues at me for some obviously graven but undisclosed offense). The seed ripens and is shed very quickly within a month of flowering, so you have to be observant. Since the plants bloom sequentially though, it is likely that you will at least be able to gather some seed if you collect the stalks about the time the plants are yellowing. Let the pods dry for several days, then sow them immediately and let them go through a summer and winter outdoors—they will emerge in spring. The plants are fairly slow from seed, however, taking a few years to reach

---

A: seed will germinate within 4 weeks if sown at 70°F; **B**: seed will germinate upon shifting to 70°F after 90 days of moist, cold stratification at 40°F; **C**: seeds germinate only after multiple cycles of warm and cold, typically 40°-70°-40°-70°; **D**: seed needs a period of warm moist stratification followed by cold stratification and will germinate after shifting back to warm (70°-40°-70°); **G**: chemical inhibitors; **H**: seed requires light to germinate; **I**: seed requires scarification because of an impermeable seed coat; *****: seed is hydrophilic, intolerant of dry storage.

blooming size (and the flats of dormant seedlings are a magnet for weeds all summer), so I usually let them self-sow and dig up sections as I need to.

Clematis   Virgin's Bower p. 75   **B, D or maybe protracted A***

SEEDS: When *Clematis* seed is ripe, the downy hairs that cover each seed's beak fluff out like the tail of a frightened cat and turn a gray or buff color. At this stage the seeds should fall easily from the stalk under gentle pressure. The germination patterns of the genus are somewhat confusing to me. *C. virginiana* is a straightforward type B germinator, but many of the others seem to need a long period of warm temperatures before emerging. I have sown *C. ocroleuca* and *C. viorna* outdoors as soon as they are ripe in midsummer and the cotyledons began to emerge late in that same season. If stored at 40°F under moist conditions until fall and sown in a cold frame, the seedlings emerge only near the end of the following summer—what really seems like a protracted A type pattern. With *C. occidentalis* and *C. reticulata,* the plants followed either a B or D pattern. This may be dependent on the maturity of the seeds at the time of sowing or whether they were stored dry or not. I suspect that *Clematis* seed, like many in the Ranunculaceae, resents dry storage and drying may prolong its dormancy requirements.

Seedlings tend to be slow-growing, but can be encouraged to continue growing by careful potting on first into small pots then larger containers their second year. They bloom the second or third season.

CUTTINGS/DIVISION: I have been fairly successful rooting 1- or 2-node stem cuttings taken from green wood in mid- to late spring. The cuttings are slow to root, but 2–3,000 ppm liquid IBA quick dip results in 50–80 percent success, and the plants are flowering size by the following spring.

Clintonia   Bluebead Lily p. 77   **B or C*, G**

SEEDS: Before reading any further, let me warn you that *Clintonia*s are one of the slowest wildflowers I have grown from seed—taking up to 7 years to mature. Harvest the seeds when the berries turn blue in fall and clean them thoroughly of all pulp. The seeds are hydrophilic and should be sown immediately. *C. umbellulata* requires two seasons to germinate, but the others will usually come up after only one winter outdoors. The first year, only thin cotyledons emerge, and it is best to leave them alone for another year or two before transplanting them to individual containers, taking care to keep them moist and shaded.

CUTTINGS/DIVISION: If you have some stock to work with, you can cut the rhizomes of older clumps into segments each containing a growing lead in fall. Replant even the eyeless sections, as they will usually re-grow as well. We have experimented with tissue culturing *C. umbellulata,* using sterilized, one-year seedlings. I was amazed at how quickly the plants proliferated and grew in culture given my experience with them conventionally, and I think this is a very viable alternative for this particular plant.

Conradina   Wild Rosemary p. 78   **B, I**

SEEDS: Seed ripens about a month after flowering, each calyx tube containing 1–2 seeds. Light scarification aids germination.

CUTTINGS/DIVISION: Seeds germinate easily enough, but 2–4-node softwood cuttings root so readily that I have rarely grown them from seed. Cuttings potted on in a gritty mix will form large flowering-size plants by the end of the season.

Coptis   Goldthread p. 79   **D***

SEEDS: Since the seed dries naturally while it awaits dispersal, I am not sure how long it can tolerate dry storage, but I have had the best success with fresh seed sown outdoors in summer. It requires some patience and diligence to find and collect the seed, as the daisywheel capsules blend in with the background colors of the forest litter. Break off a cluster of the capsules and gently squeeze them over an envelope. If there is any seed left, it will fall out. Seedlings will be ready for the garden after one season in containers.

CUTTINGS/DIVISION: If you have some stock, it is easy to divide *Coptis* by gently lifting individual rosettes along with an inch or two of rhizome in spring before new growth starts, or in summer after it has hardened.

Coreopsis   Tickseed p. 80   **A or B**

SEEDS: Seed of the perennial species germinates best after a cold spell, and the seedlings are vigorous and easy to handle. They bloom the first or second season from seed. Harvest when heads yellow. Ripe seed is usually gray-black in color.

CUTTINGS/DIVISION: Softwood stem cuttings taken in spring are very easy to root, but not all the tickseeds form leafy stems. You can also cut up the wiry rhizomes in spring before growth has commenced and obtain quite a few plants in this way.

Cornus   Bunchberry p. 82   **B, G**

SEEDS: Each berry contains a few hard seeds surrounded by a clinging, fibrous pulp that is virtually impossible to entirely remove. I soak the seeds for a week or so and then mash, rinse, and towel dry them. I then grind the dried pemmican-like mass betwixt my fingers, which gets them fairly clean (and leaves my skin silky smooth). Seed flats left in the cold frame for the winter germinate very well in spring, and I usually transfer the seedlings to 2-inch pots for a season before potting them on for sale

---

A: seed will germinate within 4 weeks if sown at 70°F; **B:** seed will germinate upon shifting to 70°F after 90 days of moist, cold stratification at 40°F; **C:** seeds germinate only after multiple cycles of warm and cold, typically 40°-70°-40°-70°; **D:** seed needs a period of warm moist stratification followed by cold stratification and will germinate after shifting back to warm (70°-40°-70°); **G:** chemical inhibitors; **H:** seed requires light to germinate; **I:** seed requires scarification because of an impermeable seed coat; ***:** seed is hydrophilic, intolerant of dry storage.

in larger containers the following year. With moisture and fertilizer, the seedlings continue to grow much longer than they normally would, and bloom the second or third season from seed.

CUTTINGS/DIVISION: Heel cuttings taken after the new growth hardens in summer that have a small piece of rhizome attached are another option, but seed is very reliable and easy.

Cypripedium   Lady-slipper p. 83   **FALL (USUALLY JUST AFTER THE FIRST FROST)**   **A or B**

SEEDS: I have elaborated on seed germination separately (see p. 85). As I haven't the patience for it, I leave the lab work to others and buy 1-year-old seedlings ready to be transplanted into nonsterile containers. Potted into 3-inch pots and fertilized lightly with a complete soluble fertilizer, they grow fairly quickly and, depending on the species, bloom after an additional 2–6 years.

CUTTINGS/DIVISION: Mature plants can be divided by digging the plants (preferably in early spring) and shaking off all the soil to expose roots and fat, pointed buds the size of a ballpoint pen cap. Carefully tease the crowns apart (you may have to sever a rhizome or two with a sharp knife), leaving 1–3 buds per division and a healthy tangle of roots all around.

Dalea   Prairie Clover p. 86   **LATE SUMMER**   **A, I**

SEEDS: The small, hard seed ripens in tiny pods packed together in the head. Pluck a few heads a month or so after flowering has finished and crunch them over a screen. If the dark seeds fall free, you will know they are ripe. Soak or scarify the seeds prior to sowing. The plants need a sunny, well-drained site to do well in containers. You may find it easier to just direct-sow them where you plan for them to grow. It takes a year or two for the plants to establish a good root system and look like anything.

Darmera   Umbrella Plant p. 87   **LATE SPRING TO EARLY SUMMER**   **A, H***

SEEDS: I suspect that seed is short-lived because while it has self-seeded into its neighbors' pots in the nursery, I have had poor germination with dry seed. It ripens in early summer as the two-sided capsules begin to split. I would recommend shaking some free and sowing it immediately on the surface of a wet mix. The seedlings do grow surprisingly rapidly, though you might want to keep them in a shallow water tray as they need copious amounts of water even when young.

CUTTINGS/DIVISION: Two- to three-inch sections of the dormant rhizomes can be cut and potted in early spring and most will sprout. We propagate the dwarf form of the species this way.

Delphinium   Wild Larkspur p. 88   **EARLY TO LATE SUMMER**   **B***

SEEDS: Seed ripens like *Aconitum* in 3-chambered pods that split along their margins when the seed is ripe. Collect the pods when they begin to yellow (3–6 weeks after bloom), let them dry for a week, and remove the seed. If sown immediately, it will germinate well the following spring. *D. tricorne* is very slow, requiring 3–4 years to reach flowering size, but the others will get there in a season or two.

Dentaria   Toothwort p. 89   **EARLY SUMMER**   **D***

SEEDS: I have rarely seen any seed set on *Dentaria*, but the narrow pods are easy to find above the foliage. Check a few that look particularly swollen to see if they contain seeds.

CUTTINGS/DIVISION: Toothworts are easy to propagate vegetatively, and I suspect that many colonies may be self-sterile clones too far from neighbors to be cross-pollinated. It is best to mark the location of your patch in spring and then dig up and pot some in late summer when the cooler weather spurs a late flush of rooting. Use 1–2-inch sections with at least one eye for best results.

Dicentra   Bleeding Heart p. 90   **LATE SPRING TO EARLY SUMMER**   **D***

SEEDS: *Dicentra*s are ant-dispersed, and each shiny black seed has a fleshy elaiosome attached. The plants produce quantities of seed in fat pods that rupture in two and curl back to release the seeds. Pop open one or two and if the seeds are black, remove the seeds and sow immediately, as viability drops off quickly under dry storage.

CUTTINGS/DIVISION: Squirrel Corn and Dutchman's Breeches multiply vegetatively more than by seed, forming numerous shallow bulblets that are best dug when dormant in summer and potted or replanted. *D. culcullaria* has a bulb with scales like a lily, and *D. canadensis* has smooth, round ones about as big as a marble. They both resume root growth in fall with the onset of cooler weather and are easily damaged if moved then.

Diphylleia   Umbrella Leaf p. 92   **LATE SUMMER**   **B*, G**

SEEDS: Fresh seed is imperative for good germination. The seedlings put up 2 large cotyledons the first spring, but can be coaxed with a little liquid fertilizer to send up a true leaf as well, which will greatly hasten the time to maturity. Transplant the second spring, and they will be near flowering size by the end of the growing season.

Disporum   Fairy-bells p. 92   **LATE SUMMER**   **B or C*, G**

SEEDS: Fairy-bells are slow but not difficult to grow from seed. If you harvest the large pearly white seeds when the fruits turn color and sow it immediately, there will usually be some germination the following spring, with the rest occurring a year later.

A: seed will germinate within 4 weeks if sown at 70°F; **B:** seed will germinate upon shifting to 70°F after 90 days of moist, cold stratification at 40°F; **C:** seeds germinate only after multiple cycles of warm and cold, typically 40°-70°-40°-70°; **D:** seed needs a period of warm moist stratification followed by cold stratification and will germinate after shifting back to warm (70°-40°-70°); **G:** chemical inhibitors; **H:** seed requires light to germinate; **I:** seed requires scarification because of an impermeable seed coat; ***:** seed is hydrophilic, intolerant of dry storage.

Germination is hypogeal, so the little plants emerge without a cotyledon as miniature versions of the adults. They can be transplanted the second spring, either into larger containers or directly into the garden.

CUTTINGS/DIVISION: Division is an indelicate procedure, but certainly possible (see culture section, p. 93). Certainly the easiest method is to dig the small seedlings that readily volunteer around an established planting.

Dodecatheon Shooting Star p. 93 EARLY SUMMER **B**

SEEDS: After the flowers are pollinated, down-turned pedicels reorient so that the developing seed capsules stand staunchly upright. The seeds are the size and color of coarsely ground coffee and are ripe when the capsules begin to crack open near the top. Carefully overturn them into an envelope and shake out the seeds. Seed germinates well, but the trick is to keep the seedlings growing vigorously through frequent light fertilization and consistent moisture. If you can keep the seedlings from going dormant at their normal time, you can grow a blooming-size plant in a year or two (in the wild it might take 3–5 years).

CUTTINGS/DIVISION: Shooting stars are very easy to produce from root cuttings taken before growth begins in spring. The brittle white roots break away easily from the crown when disturbed, and most will come away with a small dormant bud that will grow into a new plant. I will sometimes simply root around the crown of an established plant without digging it up to produce a plant with multiple crowns and more flowers.

Echinacea Coneflower p. 95 LATE SUMMER TO EARLY FALL **B**

SEEDS: Seed is readily available and easy to grow, but not all the species mature at the same rate. All the coneflowers are self-sterile, so plant at least two individuals for good seed set. The narrow-leaved types (*E. pallida, E. angustifolia, E. tennessensis, E. paradoxa*) are typically slower growing and demand a more well drained mix. Collect the seed by combing it from the dried heads (I would recommend gloves).

Echinocereus Hedgehog Cactus p. 96 LATE SUMMER **B**

SEEDS: Seed is produced in fleshy, fur-covered fruits that turn red or yellow when ripe. The small hard seeds will germinate well after a cold period, each first producing a pair of fleshy cotyledons that betray their leafy ancestry. Out of the center of these grows the barrel, at first a cluster of spines that takes the shape of a miniature cactus. They take 2–5 years to bloom from seed.

CUTTINGS/DIVISION: Some of the species readily form offsets, which can be carefully removed and treated like *Opuntia* cuttings (see. p. 258), but I prefer to let them form large clumps.

Epigaea Trailing Arbutus p. 98 LATE SPRING TO EARLY SUMMER **A, H***

SEEDS: The tiny seeds ripen on the outside of a pea-sized berry, much like a strawberry in this way (remember, plants are either male or female, so not all of them will have berries). When the seed is ripe, a papery capsule that encloses the fruit splits open, and the tasty berries are quickly scavenged by small mammals. Watch the capsules, and when they begin to yellow and crack, harvest the fruits. Separating the seeds from flesh is difficult. So I let the whole dry for a week or two then crush and screen them and end up with mostly the rusty seeds. *Epigaea* is slow and difficult, best surface-sown immediately and enclosed in a plastic bag under lights. They need a year of careful attention before they are large enough for life outside.

CUTTINGS/DIVISION: Stem cuttings are far easier than seed. Collect current season growths with a 1–2-inch length of stem and its associated leaves. I have found the best time to collect them is 8–10 weeks after bloom. I use a 1:1 peat and perlite mix, dip the cuttings in .01% IBA talc and keep them shaded and covered with Remay for the summer. After overwintering in a cold frame, the well-rooted plants can be potted on.

Epilobium Fireweed p. 99 LATE SUMMER **A or B**

SEEDS: Seeds form in very long, thin pods that rupture along the seams when ripe, releasing the cottony seeds in the wind. Seed germinates easily.

CUTTINGS/DIVISION: Softwood stem cuttings taken in late spring work well for *Epilobium* and *Zauschneria*.

Eriogonum Wild Buckwheat p. 99 SUMMER **B**

SEEDS: Seed is a hard, 3-sided, teardrop-shaped nutlet that is sometimes hard to find in the chaffy inflorescence. It germinates well after a period of cold stratification, though viability can be low.

CUTTINGS/DIVISION: I have not personally had much luck with cuttings, but semi-hard new growths with a length of rhizome attached are the recommended method.

Eryngium Rattlesnake Master p. 101 LATE SUMMER **B**

SEEDS: Seed is readily available and easy to grow. Collect your own when the heads have browned and dried.

Erythronium Trout Lily p. 101 LATE SPRING TO EARLY SUMMER **D or C***

SEEDS: Seed is formed in inflated pods, but seed set can be erratic from one year to the next. The plants are generally self-sterile,

A: seed will germinate within 4 weeks if sown at 70°F; **B**: seed will germinate upon shifting to 70°F after 90 days of moist, cold stratification at 40°F; **C**: seeds germinate only after multiple cycles of warm and cold, typically 40°-70°-40°-70°); **D**: seed needs a period of warm moist stratification followed by cold stratification and will germinate after shifting back to warm (70°-40°-70°); **G**: chemical inhibitors; **H**: seed requires light to germinate; **I**: seed requires scarification because of an impermeable seed coat; *****: seed is hydrophilic, intolerant of dry storage.

but they can interbreed, so seed raised from a mixed, cultivated planting can result in some interesting hybrids. It appears that some of the widely available cultivated plants such as 'White Beauty' and 'Pagoda' are hybrids of this type. I would not say trout lilies are difficult from seed, but they are certainly slow. I have had mixed results with dry storage, though I think in general the western species tolerate it and the eastern do not. Germination is two-stage, with roots and bulb forming in fall and the thin, grasslike cotyledon emerging the following spring. It is best to leave the seedlings undisturbed for a year or two, then transfer them in the fall to larger containers or a growing bed. They will take up to 5 years to reach blooming size.

Eupatorium   Joe-Pye Weed, Boneset p. 103   FALL   **B**

SEEDS: Seed ripens about a month after flowering and, like other Composites, should be collected when the heads split and dry and the fluffy seed begins to float away. They are all easily grown from seed, and *E. fistulosum* is one of the plants I recommend to beginners.

CUTTINGS/DIVISION: Two-node tip cuttings root very well. Many of the Eupatoriums develop hollow stems as the shoots mature, and these lower cuttings will root poorly, but if you keep pinching off just the tips, the plants will get very bushy over the course of the season and provide plenty of material to cut.

Euphorbia   Flowering Spurge p. 105   LATE SUMMER   **B**

SEEDS: The round black seed ripens 3–4 weeks after flowering in small oval capsules that go quickly from green to yellow before splitting. Collect them when they begin to turn color and dry. Seed germinates easily though the seedlings need a little care in transplanting not to damage the central taproot. If moved early they will usually flower the first season.

CUTTINGS/DIVISION: Cuttings are difficult but possible, the main problem being that the latex prevents uptake of powdered rooting hormone. I have had better luck with 2,000 ppm liquid dip (50 percent rooting in 4 weeks), taking only the top 4–6 inches of a stem for cutting. Do not trim back leaves, as damaged leaves will be quickly shed.

Filipendula   Queen of the Prairie p. 106   LATE SUMMER   **D**

SEEDS: The fine seed can be crushed out of the dry heads and should be sown immediately so that it will be exposed to a warm cycle before cold. The plants are fairly easy from seed, and the plants often self-sow as well.

CUTTINGS/DIVISION: Single-node cuttings taken from fresh growth in late spring root fairly well. Rhizome cuttings are another option, but I have not tried them.

Gaillardia   Blanket Flower p. 106   SUMMER   **A**

SEEDS: The seed ripens in midsummer. Blanket flowers are easy to raise from seed, although spring division is another option for *G. aristata*.

Galax   Wandflower p. 107   FALL   **A, H***

SEEDS: The tiny rust-colored seeds ripen late in the season. They are ready when the small capsules that line the flower spike begin to yellow. Dry the spikes for a few days and gently crush them with a roller to free the seeds. Sift through a fine screen. This is a slow plant from seed, best sown on the surface of a well-dampened mix and placed in a self-sealing freezer bag under lights set for 16-hour days. The seed will begin to germinate quickly and is best left in plastic until the plants are the diameter of a quarter (this may take a year or so). A dilute fertilizer every month will speed growth. In the wild they germinate mostly in moss carpets, and if you have a mossy spot, this is worth a try.

CUTTINGS/DIVISION: We have sizable patches in the garden, so I obtain large numbers of plants every year by lifting small sods here and there and potting up the individual crowns. They put out a fair amount of root and rhizome growth and yield good-sized plants the following spring. A final method is to dig sections of the thin, banded rhizomes before growth begins in spring and cut them into 1½-inch lengths stuck diagonally in peat/perlite trays. Most will produce a small rosette over the season. This is still a slow technique, but it saves at least a year over seeds.

Gaultheria   Wintergreen p. 108   LATE SUMMER TO FALL   **A, H**

SEEDS: The seed will germinate if cleaned from the fruit and surface-sown under lights. Seal the flats in plastic as described in the propagation chapter and fertilize lightly every 2–4 weeks. The plants are slow from seed, though, and cuttings and division are more practical.

CUTTINGS/DIVISION: Semi-hardwood cuttings taken in summer are the recommended method, but I have had mixed results. *G. hispidula* roots readily, but the others are slow, even at high hormone concentrations. Fall-winter cuttings should be tried. Rooted sections of rhizome with an attached whorl of leaves are easiest. Seperate them in spring before new growth starts.

Gaura   Gaura p. 109   LATE SUMMER TO FALL   **A**

SEEDS: Seed is an easy method of increase. Collect the long cylindrical pods as they begin to dry, and crush them to extract the seeds.

A: seed will germinate within 4 weeks if sown at 70°F; **B**: seed will germinate upon shifting to 70°F after 90 days of moist, cold stratification at 40°F; **C**: seeds germinate only after multiple cycles of warm and cold, typically 40°-70°-40°-70°; **D**: seed needs a period of warm moist stratification followed by cold stratification and will germinate after shifting back to warm (70°-40°-70°); **G**: chemical inhibitors; **H**: seed requires light to germinate; **I**: seed requires scarification because of an impermeable seed coat; *****: seed is hydrophilic, intolerant of dry storage.

CUTTINGS/DIVISION: Three-node cuttings taken on pre-flowering stems in spring take very well, and the rooted cuttings will begin to bloom the same season.

Gentiana	Gentian p. 110	**FALL**	**B, H**

SEEDS: The chaffy seed is produced in great quantities within pointed, grooved pods that develop within the withered flowers. They will begin to split when ripe (there is an insect—I believe a weevil—that infests the pods in the wild, often eating most of the available seed). I surface-sow the seed outdoors in flats that I cover with coarse sand, and the seedlings germinate in quantity the following spring. They are tiny plants at first, but liquid fertilizer speeds up growth so that by early summer they are ¼–½ inch across and ready to move into individual containers. By fall they are fat rosettes with a healthy root system, big enough for the garden or sale. Older wildflower books are full of lore regarding germinating and growing these plants but they are really not difficult.

Geranium	Wild Geranium p. 111	**EARLY SUMMER**	**B***

SEEDS: Given the projectile ability of the seed, you have to keep close watch on the carpel beaks and when they begin to turn a bit yellow pick the heads and let them dry in a bag until the seeds are ejected. It is best to sow the seed immediately, as it can be short-lived in dry storage (I have stored it in plastic for 4–6 months then sown it outdoors without problem, however). The seedlings can be encouraged to continue growing all summer with good container culture, and the plants will bloom the following spring.

Geum	Avens p. 113	**LATE SPRING TO EARLY SUMMER**	**B**

SEEDS: Collect the seed once the heads turn from red to brown. It is not necessary to remove the tails before sowing Prairie Smoke. Seed germinates easily, and the plants will bloom the following spring.

Helianthus	Sunflower p. 114	**FALL**	**A**

SEEDS: Seed ripens a month after flowering, provided the weather remains mild enough. As with most Asteraceace, plants are generally self-sterile, but they may form empty seeds anyway, so it is worth cracking a few open to look for embryos before you go to the trouble of collecting them.

CUTTINGS/DIVISION: Five- to seven-node cuttings taken from the top foot of growth in late spring root easily and will fill a gallon pot and bloom in season. The cuttings are sometimes reluctant to form new overwintering rhizomes and buds, but I have found that sticking deep cuttings with at least 3 nodes below ground greatly improves the percentages. The wetland species consume great quantities of water in containers.

Heliopsis	Oxeye p. 116	**LATE SUMMER**	**A**

SEEDS: Same as for *Helianthus*.

Helonias	Swamp Pink p. 116	**LATE SPRING**	**A or D, H***

SEEDS: The papery seeds develop in great quantities within small angled pods. The pods appear from within the dried tepals, and ripen fairy quickly, cracking open and disgorging the seeds. *Helonias* is slow to grow from seed. If sown immediately on a damp surface, some seed will begin to germinate in about a month, with the rest waiting until the following spring. The little rosettes should be left in their flats, set in a shallow tray of water for a year until they are ½ inch across, and carefully moved to larger containers. They bloom in 3–4 years from seed.

CUTTINGS/DIVISION: I prefer to propagate *Helonias* by division, as each mature rosette produces 2–5 offsets each year and, if divided every 2–3 years, can yield a steady supply of blooming-sized plants. They will grow very well in a regular container mix kept evenly moist.

Hepatica	Hepatica p. 117	**LATE SPRING**	**D***

SEEDS: The pointed, cylindrical seeds of *Hepatica* ripen in starry clusters wrapped by the persistent sepals. The seeds are green when ripe, so the only cue you have to collect them is the ease with which they dislodge from the stem. I begin to check them 4 weeks after blooming and if they come away easily, I collect and sow them immediately. The seedlings germinate well the following spring, but even with good culture only produce cotyledons and 1 or 2 true leaves. It is safer to leave them in the seed flat for a season and transplanting them the following spring.

CUTTINGS/DIVISION: Division of older plants after flowering is not difficult, but does not yield many plants. An intrepid propagator I know claimed that winter root cuttings are possible, but I have not confirmed it. We are researching tissue culture protocols, but we still have a way to go.

Heuchera	Alumroot, Coralbells p. 118	**SUMMER TO FALL**	**A or B, H**

SEEDS: The shiny black seed is very fine, but easy to collect from the capsules when they go from green to brown 3–4 weeks after flowering. Surface-sown seed will usually germinate sporadically at warm temperatures and more consistently if cold-stratified

A: seed will germinate within 4 weeks if sown at 70°F; **B**: seed will germinate upon shifting to 70°F after 90 days of moist, cold stratification at 40°F; **C**: seeds germinate only after multiple cycles of warm and cold, typically 40°-70°-40°-70°; **D**: seed needs a period of warm moist stratification followed by cold stratification and will germinate after shifting back to warm (70°-40°-70°); **G**: chemical inhibitors; **H**: seed requires light to germinate; **I**: seed requires scarification because of an impermeable seed coat; *****: seed is hydrophilic, intolerant of dry storage.

first. If you are growing several concurrently blooming plants near each other, you will likely get a range of hybrid offspring. They grow easily from seed and bloom the following season.

CUTTINGS/DIVISION: Named cultivars are produced primarily through tissue culture, but it is possible to root leaf cuttings provided you excise the small axillary bud along with the petiole (use a razor blade, slicing into the stem just under the bud and attached petiole). Without this bud, the leaf will root but never grow.

Hexastylis Evergreen Ginger p. 119   LATE SPRING TO EARLY SUMMER   **D*, G**

SEEDS: Same as for *Asarum*. Seed is rarely set outside its native range.

CUTTINGS/DIVISION: Division is slow, mainly because rhizomes don't form roots until the second year, so care must be taken to get rooted pieces. Unrooted divisions can be treated like cuttings and should establish roots in 6–8 weeks.

Hibiscus Rose Mallow p. 121   FALL   **B, I**

SEEDS: Seed ripens in fat pods that become woody as they split and dry. The seed remains inside for a while after the pods split, so I will usually wait for this to assure they are ripe. Norm Deno has found that fresh seed germinates well if sown at 70°F, whereas seed stored dry for 6 months germinates better with cold stratification.[12] I find that seed stored dry in the refrigerator until fall and sown outdoors germinated well if scarified before sowing. The seedlings can be transferred directly to large containers, as they put on a great deal of growth and will bloom the second season.

The root systems of both *H. coccineus* and *Kosteletzkya* seem to be particularly cold-sensitive in containers, even with some protection, but once in the ground they are much hardier. I have taken to overwintering them in a place that remains above freezing while in pots. *H. laevis, H. lasiocarpos,* and *H. moscheutos* are not a problem.

CUTTINGS/DIVISION: Softwood cuttings taken in early summer are effective.

Houstonia Bluets p. 123   SUMMER   **B, H**

SEEDS: The extremely fine seed ripens in small crownlike capsules that go from green to yellowish then brown when ripe. Wait until a few have browned and pick the rest, let dry in an envelope, then shake out the seeds through a sieve while muttering something like "Man, those are tiny!"

Hydrastis Goldenseal p. 124   LATE SUMMER   **B and C*, G**

SEEDS: I have found Goldenseal to be a fairly easy plant to grow from seed, provided one has the patience to wait the two seasons it takes for all the seed to germinate. It is important to use only fresh seed that should be harvested when the fruits first begin to blush with red. The fruit is inedible as far as people are concerned, but chipmunks and squirrels find it very tasty and will quickly strip the plants if the fruits are allowed to turn completely red. The large, shiny, black seeds sit in folds of the fruit, somewhat like magnolias. You can squeeze or carefully mash them free and give them a quick rinse before sowing them in flats outdoors. The plants germinate the second spring with 2 large cotyledons and can be moved at this stage to individual pots. As with many Ranunculaceae, the move to a fresh, fertile container soil will spur continued growth and the seedlings will produce 2–4 more leaves that season. By the following spring they are mostly blooming-size plants ready for the garden.

Hydrophyllum Waterleaf p. 125   LATE SUMMER   **B***

SEEDS: The large seeds can be collected as the heads begin to yellow in midsummer. If sown immediately, they will germinate well the following spring and grow quickly to flowering size. Inevitably, self-sown seedlings will appear that can be dug and moved when their first true leaf has expanded.

Hypoxis Yellow Star Grass p. 126   EARLY TO MIDSUMMER   **B**

SEEDS: *Hypoxis* seed is a bit challenging to collect, as each pod ripens individually and there are only a few of the salt-sized, black or brown seeds in each. The shriveled petals remain attached to the capsule, and when ripe the whole falls away to reveal a cluster of seeds clinging to the base of the pedicel. Usually by gathering a number of the withered flower stems you can be assured of at least some seed. The seedlings germinate easily after stratification, but should not be overpotted and are best grown for a time in plug trays or flats before potting on. They will bloom the first or second season.

CUTTINGS/DIVISION: Older plants produce many offsets wich can be carefully teased apart from the main bulb in summer and replanted.

Iris Iris p. 126   MIDSUMMER TO FALL   **B or C*, (H)**

SEEDS: Seed ripens in fat pods that can be really enormous on some of the wetland types. The seed itself is also often large and irregularly channeled. According to Deno,[13] the wetland species like *I. versicolor* need light to germinate, though a layer of coarse sand over the seeds has still produced good germination for me after stratifying them outdoors for a winter. The western species like *I. douglasiana* and *I. tenax* have been troubling unless I keep the seed flats in a pit house, so I suspect seed hardiness or maybe viability of cultivated seed is a factor with many of the Californicae series. Deno suggests a 4-week soak to

A: seed will germinate within 4 weeks if sown at 70°F; **B:** seed will germinate upon shifting to 70°F after 90 days of moist, cold stratification at 40°F;
C: seeds germinate only after multiple cycles of warm and cold, typically 40°-70°-40°-70°; **D:** seed needs a period of warm moist stratification followed by cold stratification and will germinate after shifting back to warm (70°-40°-70°); **G:** chemical inhibitors; **H:** seed requires light to germinate; **I:** seed requires scarification because of an impermeable seed coat; ***:** seed is hydrophilic, intolerant of dry storage.

remove possible inhibitory chemicals helps with this group. *I. cristata, I. lacustris,* and *I. verna* are unique in that they are ant-ispersed and have the familiar elaiosomes much like Bloodroot. These must be handled fresh or germination will be delayed an additional year (*I. cristata* is often not well pollinated naturally, so I must hand-pollinate the plants if I want seed). I have germinated the related *I. tenuis* from dry seed, but it took two seasons, so fresh seed may help with it as well. The seed of all the other species can be stored dry without harm. Seedlings are easy to transplant to larger containers once they have several leaves and bloom the second season.

CUTTINGS/DIVISION: While most irises can be grown from seed, division is so easy that most growers never bother with it except to produce new forms or hybrids. The plants are best divided when the new fans are just pushing out roots, typically early summer. If you are impatient, you can divided them earlier and treat them like cuttings.

Jeffersonia   Twinleaf p. 130   **EARLY SUMMER**   **C***

SEEDS: The seeds are easy and fun to collect. They are ant-dispersed and will quickly die if allowed to dry. Further, they germinate best after 2 years of natural temperature fluctuations, so plant them immediately and keep in the cold frame. The plants germinate vigorously if well treated, and you can move them quickly to individual containers (the seed germinates hypogeally the first season, forming a good root system, so that by the time the first leaves emerge, the seedlings are already well established). I would recommend clumping 3–5 seedlings together in a pot, as this makes for a better-looking plant the next season. You can also let the plants self-sow and obtain a number of seedlings this way.

Lewisia   Bitterroot p. 131   **EARLY SUMMER**   **B**

SEEDS: The small black seed ripens in little pods set inside 2 bracts that yellow and begin to shrivel before splitting. Some of the species, notably *L. tweedyi,* are reluctant to make seed in cultivation, though cross-pollinating these by hand may result in some. The seed germinates easily after a cold period, and small plants are easily handled when ½ inch across. Curiously, seedlings are often more rot-resistant than adults, but should be grown in a well-drained mix with regular fertilization. They bloom the first year from seed.

CUTTINGS/DIVISION: Leaf cuttings are possible with the evergreen types. Cut a leaf and dab the base in rooting hormone, then stick it vertically in moist sand and keep lightly shaded. A new plant should appear in a month if it is going to at all.

Liatris   Blazing Star p. 133   **FALL**   **A but I usually treat it as B**

SEEDS: Seed is readily collected and available. It ripens like most of the aster relatives within a bonnet of bracts, and when ripe the heads fluff out and are carried away on little parachutes (pappus). Because of the sequential blooming habit, it is easy to collect seed once you see the top bit start to dry. Seedlings emerge with a pair of cotyledons, but then put up a grasslike leaf or two before pausing to get some roots down. They are a little sensitive to root disturbance at this stage, but if carefully picked out and put into their own containers or a prepared bed, they will continue growing and often bloom the same season.

CUTTINGS/DIVISION: Two-inch-long softwood stem cuttings are possible, but seed is generally easiest. *Liatris* bulbs (or technically their cormlike roots) are possible to dig and separate when the plants are dormant in winter, and they are sold by mail-order bulb companies for this reason. Plant them roots down just below the surface.

Lilium   Lily p. 135   **EARLY FALL**   **D**

SEEDS: Lily seeds have an interesting hypogeal germination pattern. The large chaffy seed ripens in great quantities in large pods and can be harvested when they begin to dry toward the end of the growing season. If sown and kept warm for a month or two, the seed will swell and become a small bulb that must then have a cold period before the thin leaf emerges. As the seed ripens in the fall, it is worth keeping the seed flats indoors on top of the refrigerator or another warm place for 3 months before giving them a cold period. It will knock a year off germination time. I will be honest, lilies are not quick growers, though with good culture the seedlings can be pushed to produce two to three flushes of leaves a season. For this reason, few commercial nurseries bother growing them, and except for wild-dug material, growing the seed up yourself may be the only way to acquire many of the species. They are slow, yes, but not difficult, and you will, in a small way, be helping to take some collection pressure off the increasingly scarce wild plants.

CUTTINGS/DIVISION: If you are lucky enough to have plants already, you can propagate them from bulb scales by digging a bulb in the fall and carefully breaking off a couple of the kernellike scales before replanting it. Typically, the current season's bulb (with old stem hole in the middle) will be attached to a new bulb that has grown over the summer. Use the old bulb for propagating and replant the new bulb as is. Pot the scales or plant them in a holding bed, and they will sprout a leaf or two the following spring. It will take them a few years to reach flowering size, but it is twice as fast as seed.

Limonium   Sea Lavender p. 137   **LATE SUMMER**   **B**

SEEDS: The small seeds are ripe a month after bloom, when the chaffy heads brown. They can be teased out with fingers or by

A: seed will germinate within 4 weeks if sown at 70°F;   **B**: seed will germinate upon shifting to 70°F after 90 days of moist, cold stratification at 40°F;   **C**: seeds germinate only after multiple cycles of warm and cold, typically 40°-70°-40°-70°;   **D**: seed needs a period of warm moist stratification followed by cold stratification and will germinate after shifting back to warm (70°-40°-70°);   **G**: chemical inhibitors;   **H**: seed requires light to germinate;   **I**: seed requires scarification because of an impermeable seed coat;   *****: seed is hydrophilic, intolerant of dry storage.

rubbing the heads on a screen. The seed germinates well, and the plants will grow on and bloom the following summer provided they have a well-drained mix.

Linnaea   Twinflower p. 138   LATE SPRING TO EARLY SUMMER   **B, H**

SEEDS: Seed develops in tiny capsules (one seed per capsule) that are difficult, if not impossible, to find unless you have excellent eyesight. It is not hard to germinate, but the plants are so easy to propagate from layers or stem cuttings that I never bother with it. *Linnaea* grows vigorously in containers and can be lightly sheared in spring for fullness.

CUTTINGS/DIVISION: Three-inch sections of vigorous new growth root readily in early summer. It is easy to layer the plants by pinning some stems down and digging up the rooted plants the following spring.

Linum   Perennial Flax p. 138   SUMMER   **B**

SEEDS: Seedlings germinate readily, but should be thinned when small and potted individually or placed directly in the garden as they resent being transplanted.

Lobelia   Cardinal Flower p. 139   EARLY FALL   **A, H**

SEEDS: Lobelias produce great quantities of small brown seed in inflated pods that ripen and split 3–4 weeks after blooming. Usually there are still a few flowers at the top of the spike when the bottom pods are ripe. Dry them and shake out the seed. The seed germinates very well provided it has light, and the tiny rosettes can be transferred when as big as a penny (dilute liquid fertilizer speeds them up immensely). They will often try to bloom the first fall, but is better to clip these spikes off to encourage rosettes to form.

CUTTINGS/DIVISION: One- or two-node stem cuttings root well at any time, even when the plants are in flower, but they need time to establish rosettes to overwinter sucessfully, so take them as early as you can.

Lupinus   Lupine p. 140   SUMMER, THOUGH THE DRY PODS CONTAINING A FEW SEEDS   **A, I**
MAY HANG ON THE PLANTS MUCH LONGER

SEEDS: All lupines have an impermeable outer seed coat that must be filed or weathered away before sowing. A few passes between two sheets of sandpaper is usually all it takes. Ideally, treat seed with a rhizobium innoculant (see section on N₂ fixation, p. TK) before sowing them. It's best if they're sown directly in the garden in spring, as they are difficult to maintain in a container for long. If you wait until the soil has warmed in spring, scarify the seed and soak it overnight in water, then innoculate and plant it in situ, and the seedlings will emerge within a week or so. Once they're established, let the plants drop their hard seeds and self-sow naturally (weathering over winter will scarify them).

Lysichiton   Western Skunk Cabbage p. 142   EARLY FALL   **A*, G**

SEEDS: The pea-sized seeds mature in a thick, fleshy cone that turns to complete mush when ripe in early fall. It is pretty disgusting to handle in this state, but grit your teeth and throw one in an old strainer and blast away the pulp. If the flesh is not completely ripe, ferment soak the whole thing for a week (then it is *really* pleasant to work with). If you miss the fruits (they quickly rot away), seed may still be visible amidst the sunken, shriveled remains for a week or two. Plant it and keep it moist and warm for a couple of months, and the seed will germinate, grow some roots and a pointed bud, then be ready for a cold period. Transfer the husky little plants to individual pots or the garden in spring and keep them well watered (they do not need to be actually standing in water, though). They should fill a 6-inch container by fall.

Maianthemum   Canada Mayflower p. 143   LATE SUMMER   **B*, G**

SEEDS: *Maianthemum* produces several ⅛-inch fruits that turn from marbled silver and brown to red when the seed is ripe. Clean the seeds (there are 1–3 pearly white seeds in each fruit) and sow them immediately outdoors. The plants should be transferred in their second spring.

CUTTINGS/DIVISION: It is rarely necessary to grow the plants from seed unless to obtain some initial stock, as they divide readily, and rhizomes divided into small branched segments in early spring (try to get 2–3 leads on each division) will quickly fill a container with roots.

Marshallia   Barbara's Buttons p. 144   SUMMER TO FALL   **B**

SEEDS: Seed germinates readily and the plants will bloom the following season.

Meehania   Creeping Mint p. 145   EARLY SUMMER   **B**

SEEDS: Collect seed when the large papery calyx has browned. There should be 1 or 2 seeds in each.

CUTTINGS/DIVISION: Single-node cuttings taken from vigorous, nonflowering growth is the best method of increase.

Mertensia   Bluebells p. 146   LATE SPRING TO SUMMER   **B or D***

SEEDS: Seed ripens in open, inverted cups formed by the calyx and are clearly visible as a cluster of green changing to brown-

A: seed will germinate within 4 weeks if sown at 70°F; **B:** seed will germinate upon shifting to 70°F after 90 days of moist, cold stratification at 40°F; **C:** seeds germinate only after multiple cycles of warm and cold, typically 40°-70°-40°-70°; **D:** seed needs a period of warm moist stratification followed by cold stratification and will germinate after shifting back to warm (70°-40°-70°); **G:** chemical inhibitors; **H:** seed requires light to germinate; **I:** seed requires scarification because of an impermeable seed coat; ***:** seed is hydrophilic, intolerant of dry storage.

black. Pick the seeds as they begin to darken, or else they will be quickly shed and lost. I have germinated dry seed of the western species after a cold period, but *M. virginica* and *M. paniculata* are moderately hydrophilic, and I usually sow them fresh outdoors (D pattern); however, *M. virginica* seed that was stored for 8 months in moist vermiculite at 40°F also began to germinate, suggesting that simply cold stratification may suffice. *Mertensia* seedlings emerge very early and are easily transferred at the cotyledon stage to plug trays or small pots then stepped up to larger pots 4 weeks later. It is important to keep them watered and move them early, as they are easy to shock into premature dormancy once the weather warms. If transferred quickly and kept fertilized and growing, the seedlings will form husky rootstocks that will bloom the following spring. I see absolutely no reason, given their ease from seed, that growers need to resort to wild-collected bare-root material.

CUTTINGS/DIVISION: Roots can be broken apart and replanted during their summer dormancy, but a percentage will be lost to rot. It is a good idea to let the wounds air dry and callus for a week or so in a shady spot before replanting.

Mimulus   Monkey-flower p. 147   MID- TO LATE SUMMER   A, H

SEEDS: Seed germinates very easily and the plants will be stunted and bloom prematurely if the seedlings are held too long in a crowded container. They are heavy feeders, though this tends to make them lanky and weak—the price for heavy blooming.

CUTTINGS/DIVISION: Cuttings or layerings are possible, though seldom necessary if seed is available.

Mitchella   Partridgeberry p. 148   FALL OR SPRING   B and C*, G

SEEDS: Each berry contains about 8 small seeds that can be mashed from the pulp and cleaned. The seed should be sown fresh in the fall; some will germinate the following spring while the rest waits another year.

CUTTINGS/DIVISION: I prefer to root the plants from 2-inch fall stem cuttings of the current season's growth. These are remarkably easy to root and should be held in the flat until they can be potted the following spring. Ideally they should be grown for a season in small liner pots before being stepped into the finished size, as they are slow to fill out the first year.

Monarda   Bee Balm, Wild Bergamot p. 149   SUMMER TO LATE SUMMER   B

SEEDS: Seed is very easy to grow, but takes some patience to clean from the prickly heads. The heads—really a conglomeration of calyx tubes—turn from green to brown when ripe. Pick them and let them dry, them mash them over a screen to free the seeds located at the base of the tubes. Seedlings are easy to transplant and bloom their second summer.

CUTTINGS/DIVISION: Two- to three-node cuttings taken from soft growth are extremely easy to root, but use only the younger stem tips that have not become hollow. The hollow stems trap water and usually rot. *M. bradburiana* and *M. russeliana* do not winter over well from stem cuttings—why, I do not know—but they are reluctant to send out stolons.

Oenothera   Evening Primrose p. 150   SUMMER   A

SEEDS: Seed is easy to germinate, although the plants are mainly self-sterile, so you will need to plant at least 2. The seeds are produced in long winged or angled pods that split when ripe. There are usually a few ripe pods at any time in late summer.

CUTTINGS/DIVISION: The spreading types can be easily propagated by division, and all *Oenothera*s as well as *Calylophus* can be easily rooted from tip cuttings taken in spring.

Opuntia   Prickly Pear p. 152   LATE SUMMER TO FALL   B or C, G, I

SEEDS: The hard seeds are produced in large jelly-filled fruits (the edible cactus pears found in supermarkets are the fruits of the subtropical *Opuntia ficus-indica*). Harvest the fruits when they turn yellow, red, or burgundy, but be wary of their spines. The seeds are difficult to clean from the gelatinous mass, but fermentation works tolerably well. It is important to thoroughly wash the seeds of pulp, and I usually lightly scarify them as well before sowing. The seeds germinate after one or two winters, and the fat cotyledons quickly yield to the first fleshy pad. They will grow rapidly with light fertilizing and can be potted on when the first pad has expanded.

CUTTINGS/DIVISION: Cuttings are an easier and faster way of obtaining mature plants if you have the stock. Sever last year's pads at the joint in spring and let them air dry away from the hot sun for a week or so, then bury them halfway in a 2:1 mix of sand and potting mix. Roots will form in 4–6 weeks.

Orontium   Golden Club p. 154   SUMMER   A*

SEEDS: The seeds are very interesting, contained in what is technically a utricle or thin, inflated fruit which acts like a float so the seeds can disperse on the water like little coconuts. The marble-sized fruits are easy to spot among the leaves on the withered spadixes in late summer. They are green when ripe, but should easily break free. Many will have already germinated, and the spearlike shoot can be seen emerging. Plant them in a wet soil or container sitting in water, and they will root in and begin to grow in earnest, forming small plants by fall.

CUTTINGS/DIVISION: It is possible but very messy to divide established plants by separating pieces of the creeping rhizome.

A: seed will germinate within 4 weeks if sown at 70°F; **B**: seed will germinate upon shifting to 70°F after 90 days of moist, cold stratification at 40°F;
C: seeds germinate only after multiple cycles of warm and cold, typically 40°-70°-40°-70°; **D**: seed needs a period of warm moist stratification followed by cold stratification and will germinate after shifting back to warm (70°-40°-70°); **G**: chemical inhibitors; **H**: seed requires light to germinate; **I**: seed requires scarification because of an impermeable seed coat; *: seed is hydrophilic, intolerant of dry storage.

Pachysandra   Allegheny Spurge p. 155   **SUMMER**   **B***

SEEDS: The teardrop-shaped seeds ripen in strange, fuzzy little oval capsules that have 3 tails on top (they remind me of those old-fashioned money sacks cinched closed at the top with a piece of twine). The female flowers on each raceme are down low, barely noticeable under the more colorful males, so you have to look where the flower stems meet the leaf stems to find the ripe capsules. I like to imagine that the plants are pollinated by ants or beetles that crawl up and over the flowers and transfer pollen on their legs, though I have seen bumblebees work them as well. Collect the capsules when they go from green to buff. This is an indistinct change, so I would force open a capsule or two in midsummer to see if the seeds have turned black. Sow them quickly, and you will get germination the following spring.

CUTTINGS/DIVISION: Most growers produce the plants by cuttings, which is much faster. If you pinch off the topmost 4–5 leaves in fall and overwinter them in a shaded, cool greenhouse, the cuttings will root but are frustratingly reluctant to send up new shoots. The method recommended by the Mt. Cuba Center is much more successful. Grasp a new stem after it hardens in mid-summer, and tug. It should come up with a piece of rhizome and maybe a root or two. Treat these like cuttings and all should form healthy new plants by the following season.

Panax   Ginseng p. 155   **LATE SUMMER**   **B*, G**

SEEDS: Collect and clean the seed when the fruits color. They resemble large hot pepper seeds in shape and color, and there are 1 or 2 in each berry. They must be sown fresh or stored moist. Several of the commercial ginseng producers sell cleaned, moist seed of excellent quality, but soak it in a 10 percent bleach solution for 20 minutes and rinse before sowing to kill any fungus spores that may have come along with them. The seeds germinate hypogeally, with the cotyledons remaining below ground and one robust, 3-fingered leaf emerging in spring. Transfer these in bunches of 3 immediately to deep containers and they will be ready for the garden by fall with roots about ¼ inch across and 3 inches long. Some will bloom the following season.

CUTTINGS/DIVISION: Root cuttings seem like they would work, but after many trials, I gave up and now stick with the seeds.

Penstemon   Beardtongue p. 156   **MIDSUMMER TO FALL**   **B, H**

SEEDS: Penstemon seed ripens in urn-shaped, upright capsules that open at the top to let the mature seed shake free as wind sways the stems. It is therefore easy to collect by overturning and shaking the dry capsules over an envelope. Seed of many species is readily available from specialty nurseries. Beardtongues freely interbreed, so beware of open-pollinated garden seed as chances are it will produce as many hybrids as true species. This has made for much confusion horticulturally, so that plants sold in garden centers are commonly mislabeled or of ambiguous origin. For the most part, seed will germinate well after a cold period. Light appears necessary to germinate the eastern species, and I typically sow them with just a sand cover.[14] The plants take well to container culture and bloom the following season from seed.

CUTTINGS/DIVISION: Two- to four-node soft or semihard wood cuttings are usually easily rooted and the best way to ensure the plants stay true to type. Use nonflowering tip cuttings that have not yet become hollow.

Phlox   Phlox p. 160   **LATE SPRING TO FALL**   **B or C**

SEEDS: Ninety-eight percent of commercially produced phloxes are cultivars propagated asexually by cuttings, but seed is not difficult if you wish to select your own colors or grow the wild types that are generally hard to find in nurseries. The plants are self-sterile, so plant at least two different cultivars in close proximity for garden seed. Good capsules (light brown when seed is ripe) will contain a few hard, dark brown seeds that are best sown in an outdoor frame and left to germinate as they will. The woodland species can handle short-term dry storage, but I believe from experience that their viability drops off quickly if not kept in plastic. Seedlings are readily transplanted when they are big enough to handle.

CUTTINGS/DIVISION: Softwood cuttings should be taken from nonflowering shoots. With the woodland types, this means waiting until summer and rooting the evergreen shoots that form after flowering. The border phloxes can be rooted from 1- or 2-node cuttings taken in spring from the top 6–8 inches of stems. Establish cuttings early in containers to ensure they form crown buds for the next season. Rock garden species can be rooted from summer cuttings as well, but it is best to stick them in pure sand to minimize the stem rots that would otherwise be a problem. The cushion phloxes are especially difficult from cuttings, and seed is a better option if available.

Physostegia   Obedient Plant p. 164   **LATE SUMMER TO FALL**   **B**

CUTTINGS/DIVISION: Seed germinates readily, but plants in cultivation are mostly cultivars produced from 3-node softwood cuttings taken in late spring or rhizome cuttings taken in fall.

Podophyllum   Mayapple p. 165   **EARLY FALL**   **B*, G**

SEEDS: If you can find some filled fruits with viable seed, wait until the fruit yellows and squeeze out the large seeds from the center and let them ferment for a week to remove the remaining pulp. Sow them outdoors. They will germinate the following spring but take a few years to mature.

A: seed will germinate within 4 weeks if sown at 70°F; **B**: seed will germinate upon shifting to 70°F after 90 days of moist, cold stratification at 40°F; **C**: seeds germinate only after multiple cycles of warm and cold, typically 40°-70°-40°-70°; **D**: seed needs a period of warm moist stratification followed by cold stratification and will germinate after shifting back to warm (70°-40°-70°); **G**: chemical inhibitors; **H**: seed requires light to germinate; **I**: seed requires scarification because of an impermeable seed coat; *****: seed is hydrophilic, intolerant of dry storage.

CUTTINGS/DIVISION: Usually the plants are propagated by rhizome cuttings taken in late summer. If dug at this time, the rhizomes will have a joint where the current season's leaf was attached and beyond that 1–3 new branches each with a pointed bud and the beginnings of roots. Cut the rhizomes behind the joint, which will leave a forked piece that can be potted either horizontally or vertically in a suitable container. It will root in by winter and bloom in spring. Smaller cuttings will grow, but the growth will be stunted.

Pogonia   Rose Pogonia p. 166   **LATE SUMMER**   **?**

SEEDS: I am not aware of anyone yet growing this species from seed in the lab.

CUTTINGS/DIVISION: I propagate the plants by lifting a few rhizome pieces every other year in late summer just as the leaves begin to yellow. I sever them in two, potting up the lead section, which should have a joint where the current leaf was attached and a length of new growth ending in a small pointed bud with a bract wrapped around it. I replant the back section in the stockbed. Pot in a 1:1 mix of sand and peat and fertilize sparingly with liquid the following spring.

Polemonium   Jacob's Ladder p. 166   **EARLY SUMMER**   **A or D***

SEEDS: The calyx persists after the petals have been shed, providing a little basket for the developing oval capsule. Seed set is not always great (the plants are self-sterile), but when you see the calyxes turn from green to yellow, that is your cue to pick and dry the stems and gently crush out the seeds that may have formed. It is best to sow the woodland types immediately, as viability drops in storage and they need a period of cold stratification, but the alpines do not require this and can be stored and planted in spring.

CUTTINGS/DIVISION: Division of the crowns is possible after flowering, when new crowns form around the base of the old. These can be removed when they begin to form their own roots.

Polygonatum   Solomon's Seal p. 168   **EARLY FALL**   **C*, G**

SEEDS: Seed is slower but not difficult and a viable option. Collect the berries when they have turned fully blue-black and extract the copious large white seeds (the berries are favored by wildlife, so act quickly). Sown immediately and put in an outdoor frame, the seed will germinate hypogeally the first spring with the cotyledon emerging the second season. Transfer these to small pots and grow them one more season and they will be ready for full size pots or the garden the following year.

CUTTINGS/DIVISION: Solomon's seals are easily dug and handled, which has unfortunately led to quite a bit of wild collecting for sale to the trade. This is frankly quite unnecessary, for all one needs to do is spend a few years building up stock in beds to have a never-ending supply of rhizomes. Dig the rhizomes in early autumn and break off the lead sections (2–4 inches) along with the associated roots and pot these. The plants will be a bit stunted when they emerge the next spring, but will quickly re-establish. Replant the back sections in a stock bed and they will soon regrow. A 3-year rotation is enough to let the plants build up strength in between division.

Porteranthus   Indian-physic p. 170   **EARLY FALL**   **B**

SEEDS: The brown crescent-shaped seed is easy to germinate and grow. It ripens late in the season in small lobed capsules that brown and crack when ripe.

Potentilla   Cinquefoil p. 171   **SUMMER**   **B**

SEEDS: Seed ripens in small capsules that turn from green to yellow then brown when ripe. Collect the capsules when they yellow and dry—the fuzzy seeds should then tease out easily. Not difficult from seed.

CUTTINGS/DIVISION: *P. tridentata* is easy to propagate by dividing rooted pieces of rhizome with at least one fan of leaves attached in early summer. The others cannot be divided as easily and I would stick to seed.

Pycnanthemum   Mountain Mint p. 172   **LATE SUMMER**   **B**

SEEDS: Collect and handle seeds as for *Monarda*—they are small, but easy to grow.

CUTTINGS/DIVISION: Two-node stem cuttings taken in late spring root readily, though they do not always overwinter well for me.

Ratibida   Prairie Coneflower p. 173   **LATE SUMMER**   **A or B**

SEEDS: Seed is the best method of increase; collect and handle as for *Rudbeckia*.

Rhexia   Meadow Beauty p. 174   **FALL**   **B, H**

SEEDS: The tiny seed ripens in curious, pitcher or urn-shaped, upright woody capsules that open by way of a narrow constriction when ripe. If you invert these in late summer, the seed can be easily shaken out. Surface-sown seed germinates easily but the tiny seedlings require frequent, dilute fertilizing to get them started and are not large enough to move until midsummer. They make up time quickly, though, and bloom the following summer.

A: seed will germinate within 4 weeks if sown at 70°F; **B**: seed will germinate upon shifting to 70°F after 90 days of moist, cold stratification at 40°F; **C**: seeds germinate only after multiple cycles of warm and cold, typically 40°-70°-40°-70°; **D**: seed needs a period of warm moist stratification followed by cold stratification and will germinate after shifting back to warm (70°-40°-70°); **G**: chemical inhibitors; **H**: seed requires light to germinate; **I**: seed requires scarification because of an impermeable seed coat; *****: seed is hydrophilic, intolerant of dry storage.

Rudbeckia Black-eyed Susan p. 175 **LATE SUMMER TO EARLY FALL** **A or B**

SEEDS: The central cones brown and dry when the seeds are ripe, and the seed should dislodge easily with the twist of your forefinger and thumb. Like most daisies, *Rudbeckia*s are self-sterile, so plant at least 2 for seed (if in doubt, cut open a seed. It should be full of white endosperm). The seed will germinate at 70°F after 3 months of dry storage, but it can be sporadic, so I usually stratify it as a precaution.

Sabatia Sea-Pink p. 177 **LATE SUMMER** **B, H**

SEEDS: The tiny seed ripens in oval, 2-parted capsules harvested when they turn yellow. Surface-sow and chill. Lightly fertilize the small seedlings and transfer them when dime-size to bigger pots or the garden. Like all gentians, the seedlings are slow growing at first. They need 2 months or more in the seed pan before they're big enough to move, but after that they grow much more rapidly.

CUTTINGS/DIVISION: The perennial species can be readily divided by gently teasing apart individual rosettes in late spring.

Salvia Sage p. 179 **LATE SUMMER TO FALL** **A**

SEEDS: Collect seed as for *Agastache*. *Salvia*s are very easy to grow from seed, but some of the late bloomers fail to ripen it in marginal climates.

CUTTINGS/DIVISION: One- to three-node softwood cuttings are usually very easy to root if taken before any sign of flower buds. Strong light greatly enhances rooting in this group.

Sanguinaria Bloodroot p. 180 **LATE SPRING TO EARLY SUMMER** **D***

SEEDS: The beautiful red-brown seeds are easy to brush out of large boat-shaped pods when they begin to yellow and split open. Since the pods ripen and disgorge their seeds quickly, split one open and harvest others if its seeds are brown. Sow the seeds immediately outdoors and transplant at the end of the first growing season or beginning of the second.

CUTTINGS/DIVISION: Division of the rhizomes is an easy affair in early fall, and eyeless divisions will regrow in time.

Sarracenia Pitcher Plant p. 182 **LATE SUMMER TO EARLY FALL** **B, H**

SEEDS: Pitcher plants ripen great quantities of chalky brown seed in large pumpkin-shaped pods. The seeds have a waxy coating that allow them to float, which can be partially removed by soaking the seeds in a glass of water with a few drops of dish detergent added. Surface-sow in a mix of 50:50 peat moss and sand, then chill. The germinated seedlings begin immediately to form pitchers and should be allowed to grow undisturbed and evenly moist the first summer or at least until they are an inch tall. I prefer to leave them sealed in a plastic bag under grow lights until they are an inch or two in height. *Never* allow them to dry out, but do not keep them flooded either.

CUTTINGS/DIVISION: Division of older clumps can be accomplished after flowering by cutting the stout rhizomes with a knife.

Saxifraga Saxifrage p. 184 **EARLY SUMMER** **A, H**

SEEDS: Seed is tiny, but very easy to grow, the seedlings coming in so thickly that they need regular applications of liquid fertilizer to reach a size that they can be handled. Transfer nickel-sized seedlings to individual pots or the garden. They often bloom the first season. Harvest seed when capsules yellow.

CUTTINGS/DIVISION: Rosettes can be teased apart in summer after the new ones have formed their own root systems.

Scutellaria Skullcap p. 186 **EARLY TO LATE SUMMER (3–4 WEEKS AFTER FLOWERING)** **B**

SEEDS: Collect seed as the purses yellow (there are 1–2 round, dark brown seeds per capsule). Be alert, because seed ripens and is shed quickly. The plants bloom sequentially, so you may have to make several passes to get a quantity of seed. It germinates readily after a cold treatment and the plants often reach blooming size the first year.

CUTTINGS/DIVISION: Cuttings taken in spring will root, but not as easily as I would suspect.

Sedum Stonecrop p. 188 **SUMMER TO FALL (4–6 WEEKS AFTER FLOWERING)** **A or B, H**

SEEDS: Cuttings are so easy that seed is usually unnecesary, but it can be collected as the heads begin to turn from yellow to brown. It is extremely fine and should be surface-sown and stratified for best germination.

CUTTINGS/DIVISION: Stem cuttings root easily. Late-flowering species are best taken in late spring, and early flowerers in summer, but they will root fairly readily at any time. Individual leaves can also root if you sever them where they meet the stem and bury the cut end in sand. A new shoot should begin to form in a month or so.

Senna Wild Senna p. 190 **LATE SUMMER** **B, I**

SEEDS: Scarified, stratified seed germinates well, and the plants reach blooming size in a couple of years. Do not keep them in containers too long, as they form a heavy root system. Harvest when long pods yellow, and allow to dry and split them open.

A: seed will germinate within 4 weeks if sown at 70°F; **B**: seed will germinate upon shifting to 70°F after 90 days of moist, cold stratification at 40°F; **C**: seeds germinate only after multiple cycles of warm and cold, typically 40°-70°-40°-70°; **D**: seed needs a period of warm moist stratification followed by cold stratification and will germinate after shifting back to warm (70°-40°-70°); **G**: chemical inhibitors; **H**: seed requires light to germinate; **I**: seed requires scarification because of an impermeable seed coat; *: seed is hydrophilic, intolerant of dry storage.

Shortia   Oconee Bells p. 190   **LATE SPRING**   **A, H***

SEEDS: Fresh seed collected in early summer as the upright capsules burst open (you can see the cinnamon-colored seed emerging from the capsules as they split) will germinate quickly if surface-sown and placed under plastic in bright shade or, ideally, under lights, but the seedlings are very slow growing and easy to lose through under- or overwatering. With patience and luck, they will be silver dollar–sized seedlings ready for the garden after the second season. As an alternative, they can be sown directly in moss growing in a damp place.

CUTTINGS/DIVISION: Heel cuttings are my preferred method. Take them from the new growth 6 weeks after flowering. I use a 50:50 mix of perlite and peat moss and keep the flats covered with row cover fabric in the shade until rooted. They usually root within 6 weeks and can be immediately potted or held in flats over winter.

Silene   Catchfly p. 191   **EARLY TO LATE SUMMER (3–4 WEEKS AFTER BLOOM)**   **B**

SEEDS: Seed ripens in inflated capsules with tops that open up like bottles as they dry. You need to catch the pods when they are beginning to yellow and let them finish drying in a paper bag, as the seed quickly falls out and is lost once the capsules brown. Seedlings are a bit fussy about being moved, so try to minimze root disturbance and wait until they are an inch across to transplant. Once past this stage they are easy to grow.

CUTTINGS/DIVISION: Most of the plants covered here send out new growths on short stolons after flowering, and these can be taken as cuttings or allowed to layer on their own and treated as divisions (this is the way I propagate the *S. virginica* hybrids).

Silphium   Rosin Weed p. 192   **LATE SUMMER TO FALL**   **B**

SEEDS: The seed is surrounded by chaffy scales that are easy to mistake for the real thing (look for the ones with the swollen embryo at one end). Good seed is usually only around the outer edge of the dried head. The plants are partially self-sterile, so plant more than one individual for seed. Seedlings have huge cotyledons, so they are easy to handle and I prefer to transfer them to individual pots at this stage, before the roots get too long and intertwined.

Sisyrinchium   Blue-eyed Grass p. 193   **SUMMER**   **B or C**

SEEDS: Seed is simple to collect and grow. The pods turn from greenish yellow to dark brown or black when ripe, then split open in 3 sections like violets. Harvest when the pods have darkened and you can easily crush out the round black seeds. Most of the species germinate abundantly after a cold treatment, but *S. douglasii* and sometimes *S. campestre* wait 2 years to sprout. Seedlings bloom the first season.

CUTTINGS/DIVISION: Division of the fans at any time in the summer is very easy. You can routinely get 30–40 good divisions from one healthy stock plant.

Smilacina   False Solomon's Seal p. 195   **EARLY FALL**   **C*, G**

SEEDS: Collect and clean the seed from ripe berries and sow outdoors. They are all hypogeal germinators best handled as described under *Polygonatum*.

CUTTINGS/DIVISION: Rhizome division is a simple matter in fall. Handle like *Polygonatum*.

Solidago   Goldenrod p. 197   **FALL**   **B**

SEEDS: Seed is generally easy and germinates most consistently after cold stratification. Collect it when the heads brown and become fluffy as the pappus expands.

CUTTINGS/DIVISION: Four- to six-node softwood cuttings taken in late spring root nearly 100 percent. And many species can be divided by separating individual crowns with a length of rhizome before growth begins in spring.

Spigelia   Indian Pink p. 199   **SUMMER (4 WEEKS AFTER BLOOM)**   **B***

SEEDS: The plants are effectively pollinated by hummingbirds, and a larger patch will both help to attract the birds and provide flowers with enough ripe pollen and fertile stamens at any one time to ensure pollination. The 2-lobed capsules mature to about ¼ inch in diameter and turn from medium to lighter green when ripe. It is fairly hard to judge, so crack one open to make sure the seeds are turning dark brown. Seeds grow in a curious cluster resembling a soccer ball. Each cluster has between 5 and 10 seeds, and they can be lightly crushed to separate the individuals from the central core. Capsules ripen sporadically over several weeks. I have had mixed results with dry seed, so I prefer to sow it immediately and leave the flats outdoors. Seedlings bloom in their second season.

CUTTINGS/DIVISION: Given the difficulty collecting quantities of seed, I have experimented with stem cuttings and find that 2-node tip cuttings taken in late spring and treated with 2,000 ppm liquid IBA will root slowly but effectively (60–70 percent) and form decent plants by the following season. By constantly taking tip cuttings, I prevent flowering and keep the plants producing more juvenile growth for a second and even third round of cuttings in early summer. These later cuttings may need to be overwintered in a greenhouse to have time to set winter buds.

A: seed will germinate within 4 weeks if sown at 70°F; **B**: seed will germinate upon shifting to 70°F after 90 days of moist, cold stratification at 40°F; **C**: seeds germinate only after multiple cycles of warm and cold, typically 40°-70°-40°-70°; **D**: seed needs a period of warm moist stratification followed by cold stratification and will germinate after shifting back to warm (70°-40°-70°); **G**: chemical inhibitors; **H**: seed requires light to germinate; **I**: seed requires scarification because of an impermeable seed coat; *****: seed is hydrophilic, intolerant of dry storage.

Spiranthes Lady's Tresses p. 200 **LATE FALL** **B, H**

SEEDS: This is one of the few orchids I have grown that readily seeds into a standard peat-bark-perlite growing mix. I routinely find numbers of seedlings germinating in pots that were located near a blooming *S. odorata* the previous season. Whether the plants are less reliant on mycorrhizae or they can use some widely distributed fungus, I am not sure. But seedlings have germinated in everything from pots of coralbells to daylilies. I have failed to germinate seeds in an empty flat of fresh mix, so perhaps there is some fungal action that develops as the material breaks down.

CUTTINGS/DIVISION: The fleshy roots send out numerous sprouts that can be separated in early summer. The central clump easily splits into several crowns as well. A single, healthy clump in a 6-inch container can yield as many as 20 divisions.

Stokesia Stokes' Aster p. 201 **LATE SUMMER TO FALL** **B**

SEEDS: Good seed is large (the size of a small sunflower seed) and easy to collect from the dried bird's nest heads, but the plants are moderately self-sterile, so plant at least 2 cultivars. Often, 70–80 percent of the seed in a head is not viable.

CUTTINGS/DIVISION: Cultivars can be easily multiplied by 2-inch winter root cuttings taken from the larger, fleshy roots and stuck vertically.

Streptopus Twisted Stalk p. 201 **LATE SUMMER** **B*, G**

SEEDS: Collect and clean seed when fruit turns red. You have to search a bit because the fruits hide under the foliage. Clean and sow outdoors immediately. Long thin cotyledons emerge like grass in spring, but should be left an additional year in the flat before transplanting. Seedlings take 3–4 years to reach maturity.

CUTTINGS/DIVISION: Division as for *Disporum* and *Uvularia*.

Stylophorum Celandine Poppy p. 202 **LATE SPRING TO EARLY SUMMER** **D***

SEEDS: Seed is readily collected and should be sown immediately. The elaiosomes are small and not necessary to remove. Seedlings are vigorous and easy if kept watered and fertilized, blooming the second spring.

Symplocarpus Skunk Cabbage p. 203 **LATE SUMMER** **C*, G**

SEEDS: The marble-sized seeds are embedded in the swollen spongy spadix that ripens into a pleasant-smelling pulpy fruit which quickly ferments into a putrid mass when the seeds are mature. If you can manage to collect a few of the kiwi-sized fruits before they rot, break them open and carefully pry out the seeds. Soak the seeds for a week, then sow outdoors, either directly in the garden or in a flat. They are hypogeal, forming roots and a pointed bud the first year and a little 1–3-leaved plant the next.

Talinum Fame Flower p. 204 **SUMMER** **B, H**

SEEDS: Collect the tiny seed as capsules yellow. It germinates easily after a cold period, and the seedlings bloom the first year.

Tellima Fringecups p. 205 **MIDSUMMER** **A or B, H**

SEEDS: The tiny brown seed ripens in midsummer inside small capsules that open like bottles when the seed is ripe. It is easy to raise.

Tephrosia Goat's Rue p. 206 **LATE SUMMER** **B, I**

SEEDS: Seed is reputedly difficult to germinate, but I have found that thorough scarification coupled with outdoor stratification works pretty well (low seed viability may be the culprit as germination rates vary from year to year). The seed can be collected easily from the large ripe pods, but several plants are necessary for good pollination. Transfer the seedlings when young or sow in place, and be careful not to damage their thick taproot.

Thalictrum Meadow Rue p. 207 **EARLY TO LATE SUMMER** **B**

SEEDS: Like *Anemonella*, meadow rue seed ripens in a papery green husk that makes it difficult to tell when they are ripe. Collect them when the clusters of seed break away easily to the touch. I usually sow the seeds immediately outdoors (they lose viability moderately fast under dry storage) with germination the following spring. They are generally easy from seed.

Tiarella Foamflower p. 208 **LATE SPRING AND MIDSUMMER** **A or B***

SEEDS: Seed should be collected when the lowermost capsules on the stem get light brown and papery. Each contains a few shiny black seeds. If sown immediately, they begin to germinate within a month, but I usually store them in a plastic baggie then sow them outdoors in autumn. Viability drops off fairly quickly if the seeds are kept dry in a paper envelope. Seedlings are small at first and need frequent light fertilizing to get to a size that they can be handled.

CUTTINGS/DIVISION: *T. cordifolia* can be rooted in summer by treating the long stolons as cuttings. Each cutting should have at least one leaf. The other species can be rooted if you can carefully pull off single leaves or small side clumps with a small bud at the base. You can do this any time the plants are actively growing, but I prefer early summer. Stick the leaf base in a rooting mix and handle like a standard cutting.

A: seed will germinate within 4 weeks if sown at 70°F; **B**: seed will germinate upon shifting to 70°F after 90 days of moist, cold stratification at 40°F; **C**: seeds germinate only after multiple cycles of warm and cold, typically 40°-70°-40°-70°; **D**: seed needs a period of warm moist stratification followed by cold stratification and will germinate after shifting back to warm (70°-40°-70°); **G**: chemical inhibitors; **H**: seed requires light to germinate; **I**: seed requires scarification because of an impermeable seed coat; *****: seed is hydrophilic, intolerant of dry storage.

Tradescantia   Spiderwort p. 209   **EARLY SUMMER**   **B***

SEEDS: Division is so easy that I rarely grow this plant from seed. It ripens in round capsules wrapped in the sheathing calyx. The capsules splay open in 3 sections when the large brown or gray seeds are ripe, dropping them quickly. Therefore, you have to crack one open now and then about 6 weeks after flowering and look for ripe seeds. Based on poor success with dry seed, I suspect spiderworts are moderately hydrophilic and should ideally be sown immediately or stored in plastic.

CUTTINGS/DIVISION: Single-node stem cuttings taken as the plants begin to bolt are a reliable means of propagating cultivars. Insert the cutting up to the base of the leaf and a new fan will spring from the axil when fully rooted. Division is best accomplished in spring before the plants bolt. The heavy roots are difficult to disentangle, but the individual fans can then be easily separated.

Trientalis   Starflower p. 211   **MIDSUMMER**   **B***

SEEDS: The little waxy gray seed clusters are difficult to spot after the leaves have withered, so mark the plants with flagging. Collect and sow immediately.

CUTTINGS/DIVISION: Rhizome division is simpler than seed and best done in summer after the plants have yellowed.

Trillium   Trillium p. 212   **MID- TO LATE SUMMER**   **C*, G**

SEEDS: Trillium seed ripens in a fleshy capsule. The seed is ripe when the capsules color either red or yellow-green (8–10 weeks after flowering). These are typical ant-dispersed plants, with large elaiosomes and hydrophilic seed. Seed that is cleaned and sown immediately outdoors in late summer will send out a root the next spring and a long narrow cotyledon the spring after that. After a couple more years, the young plant should be large enough to plant in the garden. We leave the seedlings in their seed flats for their first year and then pot them indiviually in 2-inch containers for one season before transfering them to a 4-inch pot ready for sale or garden in 2 more years. A simpler method is to sow the seeds in a prepared seedbed or even around the base of the parents and let them proceed at their own pace.

CUTTINGS/DIVISION: Much has been written about various ways to wound mature rhizomes as a way of forcing the production of offsets. This is a very invasive procedure that puts the plants at great risk of infection, so I usually do not bother. Healthy plants often form offshoots on their own, which can be carefully removed in autumn if they have made their own roots. If you wish to try surgery, I would recommend partially excavating a healthy rhizome in summer and girdling it with a sharp knife just below the chocolate kiss–shaped white terminal bud. Cut shallowly enough that you don't sever the bud. Cover up the plant again and if sucessful, some offshoots will be ready to remove in another year.

Trollius   Globeflower p. 215   **LATE SPRING**   **B***

SEEDS: The shiny black seed ripens in boat-shaped pods arranged in a circle that split open along the upper seam so that the seeds can shake free. Sow immediately or store in plastic and sow in fall. They will produce a nice crop of vigorous seedlings the following year.

Uvularia   Merrybells p. 216   **MIDSUMMER**   **C***

SEEDS: Seed ripens packed in a lobed capsule that hides among the leaves. The capsules yellow slightly when ripe, but it is easy to miss them. Split one open and see if the large seeds have gone from translucent white to tan — their mature color. Capsules left to dry in a paper bag for 3–7 days will split open and disgorge the seed. Sow it immediately or store moist. The seedlings are hypogeal, so a nice little plant emerges the second spring that can be potted on or left for another season or two. I handle this like *Polygonatum*, transferring first-year seedlings to 2-inch pots for a year then stepping them up. They bloom the following spring and reach full size the year after.

CUTTINGS/DIVISION: Rhizomes can be divided into single growths in autumn. This is an easy task with wild oats, but the others have thick roots and a clustered rhizome that is difficult to divide cleanly, and I usually prefer to grow them from seed. (I have found that wild oats responds well to careful division and potting in the spring as well; even though no additional top growth will occur that year, the plants form an extensive rhizome system in the container by fall.)

Vancouveria   Inside-out Flower p. 217   **SUMMER?**   **B?**

SEEDS: I suspect the plants are self-sterile and I am working with single clones, as I have never been able to find seed on our garden plants. Sorry.

CUTTINGS/DIVISION: The rhizomes are tough and wiry, but not hard to cut apart, and if this is done early in the season and you are careful not to break the brittle leaves, the plants will send up some new foliage and unleash copious roots and rhizomes during the summer. In a mild climate, fall transplanting would probably work, but they tend to winterkill more easily when I have tried it.

Veratrum   False Hellebore p. 218   **EARLY SUMMER**   **B**

SEEDS: Harvest seed when the capsules yellow, the waferlike, tawny seeds germinate after one cold period, but form only cotyle-

---

A: seed will germinate within 4 weeks if sown at 70°F; **B**: seed will germinate upon shifting to 70°F after 90 days of moist, cold stratification at 40°F; **C**: seeds germinate only after multiple cycles of warm and cold, typically 40°-70°-40°-70°; **D**: seed needs a period of warm moist stratification followed by cold stratification and will germinate after shifting back to warm (70°-40°-70°); **G**: chemical inhibitors; **H**: seed requires light to germinate; **I**: seed requires scarification because of an impermeable seed coat; *****: seed is hydrophilic, intolerant of dry storage.

dons the first spring, then go dormant. It is best to leave them in the flat for their first year, then transplant. They are slow to bloom from seed, taking up to 6 to 7 years.

Verbena Vervain p. 219 SUMMER TO FALL **B, H**

SEEDS: Since seed ripens sequentially over a long season, the best thing to do is harvest some racemes in late summer, let them dry, and lightly crush the capsules to release what seed is ripe. Seedlings grow fairly rapidly and bloom the first or second summer.

CUTTINGS/DIVISION: The trailing species are extremely easy to root from nonflowering 2-node cuttings taken from active growth throughout the season. The tall plants can be rooted from spring stem cuttings as well, but I prefer seed, which yields a higher-quality plant.

Vernonia Ironweed p. 220 FALL **B**

SEEDS: Collect seed when the pappus dries and heads fluff out. The seed germinates easily and the plants grow rapidly, often blooming the first season.

CUTTINGS/DIVISION: Five- to seven-node softwood cuttings root fairly well, but as is typical with Composites, don't always overwinter well.

Veronicastrum Culver's Root p. 222 LATE SUMMER **B, H***

SEEDS: The tiny seed is produced in quantity within small woody capsules that yellow then brown when ripe. The seeds do not fall out easily, and I usually have to lightly crush the dried capsules with a rolling pin and run the seeds through a very fine screen. They germinate fairly well, and seedlings are large enough to move by midsummer.

CUTTINGS/DIVISION: Two- to three-node tip cuttings root readily in late spring, so I prefer them over seed.

Viola Violet p. 222 SPRING TO SUMMER **B***

SEEDS: The explosive quality of violet seedpods makes them a challenge to collect. The trick is to get them just before the capsule splits, when they have turned from white to brown. Usually pods that are almost ripe will uncurl and face upright, and their stems will lengthen in preparation for launch. Their color goes from green to a yellowish or mauve. Split one of these open and see if the seeds have darkened; and if they have, pick others of similar size and place them in a sealed paper bag to dry. You will hear the seeds popping like popcorn as they dry. Store in plastic bags and sow outdoors in fall.

CUTTINGS/DIVISION: For some reason, we rarely get any seed set on *V. pedata* (it is the only noncliestogamous species). Fortunately this plant is easy to propagate from root cuttings. The easiest method is to choose some healthy container plants and damage the fat crown bud in early spring by severing it off at ground level with a knife. Leave the plants alone for 6 weeks, and dozens of new sprouts should appear from the cut roots and dormant buds on the crown. These can be separated and potted on. This does not work well with other violets.

Waldsteinia Barren Strawberry p. 225 EARLY SUMMER **B?**

SEEDS: The small seed can be crushed out of the capsules after they have dried. Either we have only one clone that is on the whole self-sterile, or seed viability is just low, because I have not had good germination whenever I have tried. Division is so simple that it really has not mattered.

CUTTINGS/DIVISION: Division is the easiest method of increase. Pieces of the wiry rhizome with at least one crown attached can be gently separated and potted up. If done in midsummer, the plants will form husky, well-rooted clumps by the following spring.

Wyethia Mule's Ears p. 226 SUMMER **B**

SEEDS: Collect seed as for *Helianthus*. Seedlings have a deep taproot, so sow in place or grow in tall containers. The seedlings go dormant fairly quickly their first year, so be careful not to overwater them when they're sleeping.

Xerophyllum Bear Grass, Turkey Beard p. 227 LATE SUMMER **B (*)**

SEEDS: The crescent-shaped light brown seeds are produced in abundance within oval capsules that line the upper stems. I pick them just as the capsules begin to yellow and let them dry for a week or two before crushing out the seeds with a rolling pin. *X. asphodelioides* should be sown immediately or stored in plastic, but *X. tenax* grows well from dry seed. The plants germinate easily but are best left alone their first year and carefully potted in the spring of their second. By the end of the second season they are large enough for the garden, but still 3 to 5 years from blooming.

Yucca Soapweed p. 228 LATE SUMMER, OFTEN PERSISTING IN THE PODS UNTIL SPRING **B**

SEEDS: The waferlike black seeds of yuccas are packed into a 3-chambered pod like books on a shelf. Moth-eaten seeds will have a small pinhole drilled through them and should be discarded. Yuccas germinate well, with the cotyledon emerging tipped with the seed coat as if to protect the point. They can be transferred easily at this stage before the taproot becomes too large.

A: seed will germinate within 4 weeks if sown at 70°F; **B**: seed will germinate upon shifting to 70°F after 90 days of moist, cold stratification at 40°F; **C**: seeds germinate only after multiple cycles of warm and cold, typically 40°-70°-40°-70°; **D**: seed needs a period of warm moist stratification followed by cold stratification and will germinate after shifting back to warm (70°-40°-70°); **G**: chemical inhibitors; **H**: seed requires light to germinate; **I**: seed requires scarification because of an impermeable seed coat; *****: seed is hydrophilic, intolerant of dry storage.

Seedlings are fairly slow to mature and best grown in a small container and then stepped up for an additional season. **CUTTINGS/DIVISION**: Root cuttings are possible, but accessing the tremendous roots is another question. Easier is to damage or remove the main shoot tip with a knife and let side shoots develop until they can be severed and grown on. Tissue culture is now being used to produce some of the popular, variegated cultivars of *Y. filamentosa*.

Zauschneria   California Fuchsia p. 230   **LATE SUMMER TO EARLY FALL**   **B**

SEEDS: Seed ripens in long thin pods that split and release it on silky parachutes. Harvest when capsules split (they ripen sequentially, so there are usually some ready in season). Seedlings grow easily.

CUTTINGS/DIVISION: Softwood cuttings root very easily, but use a very well drained rooting mix as they tend to rot. Cuttings grow to blooming-sized plants in one season.

Zizia   Golden Alexanders p. 231   **SUMMER**   **B**

SEEDS: Large round seed capsules ripen slowly in flattened heads or umbels. They are green for much of the summer then gradually darken to burgundy and then brown, at which time they can be removed and crushed to release the dark brown seeds. The seedlings come up well and are easy to handle. Pot them in individual containers by midsummer and they will be blooming-sized by the following spring.

A: seed will germinate within 4 weeks if sown at 70°F; **B**: seed will germinate upon shifting to 70°F after 90 days of moist, cold stratification at 40°F; **C**: seeds germinate only after multiple cycles of warm and cold, typically 40°-70°-40°-70°; **D**: seed needs a period of warm moist stratification followed by cold stratification and will germinate after shifting back to warm (70°-40°-70°); **G**: chemical inhibitors; **H**: seed requires light to germinate; **I**: seed requires scarification because of an impermeable seed coat; *****: seed is hydrophilic, intolerant of dry storage.

Appendixes

WILDFLOWERS FOR VARIOUS SITES

Wildflowers Suitable for Sunny, Dry Locations

Agastache barberi (syn. *A. pallida*) (Giant Hummingbird's Mint)

Agastache mexicana (Mexican Hyssop)

Agastache rupestris (Sunset Hyssop)

Allium acuminatum (Tapertip Onion, Hooker Onion)

Allium brandegei (Brandegee Onion)

Allium brevistylum (Short-style Onion)

Allium cernuum (Nodding Onion)

Allium stellatum (Prairie Onion)

Amsonia eastwoodiana

Amsonia jonesii (Jones' Amsonia)

Amsonia tomentosa (Wooly Bluestar)

Anemone caroliniana (Prairie Anemone, Carolina Anemone)

Anemone (Pulsatilla) patens var. *multifida* (Pasqueflower)

Antennaria species (Pussytoes)

Asclepias cryptoceras (Pallid Milkweed)

Asclepias humistrata (Sandhills Milkweed)

Asclepias syriaca (Common Milkweed)

Asclepias tuberosa (Butterfly Weed)

Aster azureus (Prairie Heart-leaved Aster)

Aster concolor (Eastern Silvery Aster)

Aster fendleri (Fendler's Aster)

Aster sericeus (Western Silvery Aster)

Aster spectabilis (Showy Aster)

Astragalus species (Milkvetch)

Callirhoe species (Poppy-mallow)

Campanula rotundifolia (Harebell)

Castilleja chromosa (Desert Paintbrush)

Castilleja integra (Paintbrush)

Chrysopsis species (Golden Aster)

Conradina species (Wild Rosemary)

Coreopsis lanceolata (Longstalk Tickseed, Lance-leaved Coreopsis)

Coreopsis tinctoria (Plains Tickseed, Calliopsis)

Dalea species (Prairie Clover)

Delphinium bicolor (Little Larkspur)

Delphinium nuttallianum (Upland Larkspur)

Echinacea angustifolia (Purple Coneflower)

Echinacea pallida (Prairie Coneflower)

Echinacea paradoxa (Yellow Coneflower)

Echinocereus species (Hedgehog Cactus)

Eriogonum species (Wild Buckwheat)

Eryngium yuccifolium (Rattlesnake Master)

Eupatorium capillifolium (Dog Fennel)

Eupatorium hyssopifolium (Thoroughwort)

Euphorbia corollata (Flowering Spurge)

Gaillardia species (Blanket Flower)

Gaura species (Gaura)

Helianthus mollis (Ashy Sunflower)

Helianthus salicifolius (Willow-leaved Sunflower)

Heuchera cylindrica (Roundleaf Alumroot, Lava Alumroot)

Heuchera parvifolia (Small-flowered Alumroot)

Heuchera sanguinea (Coralbells)

Iris missouriensis (Western Blue Flag)

Lewisia species (Lewisia)

Liatris graminifolia (Grass-leaved Blazing Star)

Liatris punctata (Dotted Blazing Star)

Liatris scariosa (Northern Blazing Star)

Lilium philadelphicum (Wood Lily)

Linum perenne var. *lewisii* (Perennial Flax)

Lupinus argenteus (Silvery Lupine)

Lupinus perennis (Sundial Lupine)

Lupinus texensis (Texas Bluebonnet)

Monarda menthifolia (Western Wild Bergamot)

Monarda punctata (Horsemint, Dotted Mint)

Oenothera berlandieri (Mexican Evening Primrose)

Oenothera biennis (Evening Primrose)

Oenothera caespitosa (Rock-rose, Desert Evening Primrose, Butte Primrose)

Oenothera macrocarpa (Wing-fruit Evening Primrose, Ozark Sundrops)

Opuntia species (Prickly Pear)

Oxytropis species (Locoweed)

Penstemon eatonii (Firecracker Penstemon, Eaton's Firecracker)

Penstemon grandiflorus (Large Beardtongue, Large-flowered Beardtongue)

Penstemon hirsutus (Northeastern Beardtongue, Hairy Beardtongue)

Penstemon pinifolius (Pine-leaved Beardtongue)

Phlox austromontana (Desert Phlox)

Phlox bifida (Sand Phlox)

Phlox caespitosa (Tufted Phlox, Clumped Phlox)

Oxytropis lambertii.
Locoweeds are excellent plants for a dry, sunny location. They are best sown in place, as their deep taproot is sensitive to rot when confined in containers.

Phlox nivalis (Piney Woods Phlox, Trailing Phlox)
Phlox subulata (Moss-pink, Moss Phlox)
Pycnanthemum tenuifolium (Narrow-leaved Mountain Mint, Slender Mountain Mint)
Pycnanthemum virginianum (Common Mountain Mint)
Ratibida species (Prairie Coneflower)
Rudbeckia hirta var. *pulcherrima* (Common Black-eyed Susan)
Salvia species (Sage)
Scutellaria integrifolia (Hyssop Skullcap)
Scutellaria resinosa (Resinous Skullcap, Shrubby Skullcap)
Silene virginica (Fire Pink)

Sisyrinchium angustifolium (Stout Blue-eyed Grass, Common Blue-eyed Grass)
Sisyrinchium capillare (Slender Blue-eyed Grass)
Sisyrinchium douglasii (Grass Widows, Purple-eyed Grass)
Sisyrinchium elmeri (Orange-eyed Grass)
Sisyrinchium fuscatum (Sand Blue-eyed Grass)
Sisyrinchium idahoense (Idaho Blue-eyed Grass)
Solidago nemoralis (Gray Goldenrod)
Solidago odora (Sweet Goldenrod)
Solidago rigida (Stiff Goldenrod)
Solidago rugosa (Rough-stemmed Goldenrod)
Solidago sempervirens (Seaside Goldenrod)
Solidago speciosa (Showy Goldenrod)
Talinum species (Fame Flower)
Tephrosia species (Goat's Rue)
Tradescantia hirsuticaulis (Hairy Spiderwort)
Vernonia lettermannii (Ironweed)
Viola pedata (Bird's-foot Violet)
Wyethia species (Mule's Ears)
Yucca species (Soapweed)
Zauschneria species (California Fuchsia)
Zizia aptera (Golden Alexanders)

Wildflowers Suitable for Sunny, Wet Locations

Allium validum (Swamp Onion)
Asclepias incarnata (Swamp Milkweed)
Aster carolinianus (Climbing Aster)
Aster puniceus (Bristly Aster, Purple-stemmed Aster)
Boltonia asteroides (False Aster)
Boltonia decurrens (Decurrent False Aster)
Calopogon tuberosus (Grass Pink)
Caltha leptosepala (biflora) (Elkslip)
Caltha palustris (Marsh Marigold)
Camassia species (Camas)
Chelone species (Turtlehead)
Coreopsis integrifolia (Tickseed)
Cypripedium californicum (California Lady-slipper)
Cypripedium candidum (Small White Lady-slipper)
Cypripedium reginae (Showy Lady-slipper)
Darmera (Peltiphylum) peltatum (Umbrella Plant)
Eupatorium coelestinum (Mist Flower, Hardy Ageratum)
Eupatorium fistulosum (Hollow-stemmed Joe-Pye Weed)
Eupatorium maculatum (Spotted Joe-Pye Weed)
Eupatorium perfoliatum (Boneset)
Filipendula rubra (Queen of the Prairie)
Gentiana andrewsii (Prairie Closed Gentian, Prairie Bottle Gentian)
Gentiana clausa (Meadow Closed Gentian, Meadow Bottle Gentian)
Geum rivale (Water Avens)
Helianthus angustifolius (Narrow-leaved Sunflower, Swamp Sunflower)

Helianthus giganteus (Swamp Sunflower, Giant Sunflower)

Helianthus nuttallii (Swamp Sunflower)

Helonias bullata (Swamp Pink)

Hibiscus species (Rose Mallow)

Iris brevicaulis (Lamance Iris, Zigzag Iris)

Iris fulva (Copper Iris)

Iris prismatica (Slender Blue Flag)

Iris versicolor (Northern Blue Flag)

Iris virginica (Southern Blue Flag)

Kosteletzkya virginica (Seashore Mallow)

Liatris spicata (Marsh Blazing Star, Gayfeather)

Lilium canadense (Canada Lily)

Lobelia species (Cardinal Flower)

Lysichiton americanum (Western Skunk Cabbage)

Marshallia species (Barbara's Buttons)

Mimulus species (Monkey-flower)

Monarda didyma (Oswego Tea)

Monarda fistulosa (Wild Bergamot)

Orontium aquaticum (Golden Club)

Physostegia virginiana (Obedient Plant)

Pogonia ophioglossoides (Rose Pogonia, Snake-mouth)

Polemonium occidentale (Western Jacob's Ladder, Western Polemonium)

Pycnanthemum muticum (Broad-leaved Mountain Mint, Blunt Mountain Mint)

Rhexia species (Meadow Beauty)

Sabatia species (Marsh Pink)

Sarracenia species (Pitcher Plant)

Saxifraga oregana (Bog Saxifrage, Oregon Saxifrage)

Saxifraga pensylvanica (Swamp Saxifrage)

Scutellaria lateriflora (Mad-dog Skullcap)

Spiranthes odorata (Fragrant Lady's Tresses, Swamp Lady's Tresses)

Stenanthium (Melianthemum) gramineum (Feather-fleece, Feather-bells)

Symplocarpus foetidus (Skunk Cabbage, Polecat Weed)

Thalictrum dasycarpum (Purple Meadow Rue)

Thalictrum pubescens (syn *T. polygamum*)

Trollius laxus (Spreading Globeflower)

Trollius laxus var. *albiflorus* (White Globeflower)

Veratrum viride (False Hellebore, White Hellebore, Indian Poke)

Vernonia noveboracense (New York Ironweed)

Wildflowers That Can Tolerate Moderately Dry Soils and Shade in Summer

Actaea rubra (Red Baneberry)

Allium tricoccum (Ramps, Wild Leek)

Anemonella thalictroides (Rue Anemone)

Aquilegia canadensis (Canada Columbine)

Asarum canadense (Wild Ginger)

Asarum caudatum (Western Wild Ginger)

Aster cordifolius (Blue Heart-leaved Aster, Blue Wood Aster)

Aster divaricatus (White Wood Aster)

Aster macrophyllus (Big-leaved Aster)

Campanula divaricata (Southern Harebell)

Chimaphila maculata (Spotted Wintergreen, Pipsissewa)

Chimaphila umbellata (Prince's Pine, Pipsissewa)

Chrysogonum virginianum (Gold-star, Golden Star)

Claytonia lanceolata (Western Spring Beauty)

Clematis albicoma (Clematis)

Clematis ochroleuca (Curly-heads)

Cypripedium acaule (Pink Lady-slipper)

Dentaria species (Toothwort)

Epigaea repens (Trailing Arbutus)

Eupatorium rugosum (White Snakeroot)

Gaultheria procumbens (Checkerberry, Wintergreen)

Geranium maculatum (Wild Geranium)

Geranium oreganum (Western Geranium)

Hepatica americana (Round-lobed Hepatica)

Heuchera villosa (Maple-leaved Alumroot)

Hexastylis arifolia (Arrow-leaved Ginger)

Hexastylis virginica (Virginia Wild Ginger)

Hydrophyllum canadense (Maple-leaved Waterleaf)

Hydrophyllum occidentale (Western Waterleaf)

Hydrophyllum virginianum (Eastern Waterleaf)

Iris cristata (Crested Iris)

Iris douglasiana (Douglas Iris)

Maianthemum canadense (Canada Mayflower)

Maianthemum dilatatum (Deerberry, May-lily, False Lily-of-the-valley)

Mertensia ciliata (Broad-leaf Bluebells)

Mertensia virginica (Virginia Bluebells)

Podophyllum peltatum (Mayapple)

Sanguinaria canadensis (Bloodroot)

Sedum glaucophyllum (Cliff Stonecrop)

Sedum nevii (Nevy's Sedum)

Sedum ternatum (Wild Stonecrop)

Silene stellata (Starry Campion, Widow's Frill)

Smilacina racemosa (False Solomon's Seal, False Spikenard)

Smilacina stellata (Star-flowered Solomon's Seal, Star Flower)

Solidago caesia (Blue-stemmed Goldenrod, Wreath Goldenrod)

Solidago curtisii (Curtiss' Goldenrod)

Trientalis borealis (Starflower)

Uvularia sessilifolia (Wild Oats)

Vancouveria hexandra (White Inside-out Flower)

Vancouveria planipetala (Inside-out Flower)

Wildflowers Suitable for the Rock Garden

Agastache rupestris (Sunset Hyssop)

Allium acuminatum (Tapertip Onion, Hooker Onion)

Allium brandegei (Brandegee Onion)

Allium brevistylum (Short-style Onion)

Amsonia eastwoodiana

Amsonia tomentosa (Wooly Bluestar)

Anemone caroliniana (Prairie Anemone, Carolina Anemone)

Anemone (Pulsatilla) patens var. *multifida* (Pasque-flower)

Antennaria species (Pussytoes)

Aquilegia species (Columbine)

Asclepias cryptoceras (Pallid Milkweed)

Aster alpigenus (Alpine Aster)

Aster coloradoensis (Colorado Aster)

Astragalus species (Milkvetch)

Baptisia arachnifera

Baptisia perfoliata (Eucalypt Wild Indigo)

Campanula species (Harebell)

Castilleja chromosa (Desert Paintbrush)

Castilleja flava (Yellow Paintbrush)

Castilleja integra (Paintbrush)

Chrysopsis (Pityopsis) falcata (Sickle-leaved Golden Aster)

Chrysopsis villosa (Hairy Golden Aster)

Claytonia megarhiza (Alpine Spring Beauty)

Clematis hirsutissima (Sugar-bowls)

Delphinium bicolor (Little Larkspur)

Delphinium glaucum (Pale Larkspur)

Delphinium menziesii (Menzie's Larkspur)

Delphinium nuttallianum (Upland Larkspur)

Echinacea angustifolia (Purple Coneflower)

Echinocereus species (Hedgehog Cactus)

Eriogonum species (Wild Buckwheat)

Gaultheria humifusa (Alpine Wintergreen)

Geum triflorum (Prairie Smoke)

Heuchera bracteata

Heuchera parvifolia (Small-flowered Alumroot)

Heuchera rubescens (Red Alumroot)

Hypoxis hirsuta (Common Star Grass, Yellow Star Grass)

Lewisia species (Lewisia)

Liatris punctata (Dotted Blazing Star)

Linum perenne var. *lewisii* (Perennial Flax)

Mertensia alpina (Alpine Bluebells)

Mertensia maritima (Seaside Bluebell, Oyster Plant)

Mertensia viridis (Green Bluebells)

Mitella pentandra (Alpine Mitrewort)

Oenothera caespitosa (Rock-rose, Desert Evening Primrose, Butte Primrose)

Oenothera macrocarpa (Wing-fruit Evening Primrose, Ozark Sundrops)

Opuntia species (Prickly Pear)

Oxytropis species (Locoweed)

Penstemon davidsonii (Timberline Penstemon, Davidson's Penstemon)

Penstemon fruticosus (Bush Penstemon, Shrubby Penstemon)

Penstemon hallii (Hall's Penstemon)

Penstemon linarioides ssp. *coloradoensis*

Penstemon pinifolius (Pine-leaved Beardtongue)

Penstemon rupicola (Rock Beardtongue, Cliff Penstemon)

Phlox adsurgens (Periwinkle Phlox, Woodland Phlox)

Phlox austromontana (Desert Phlox)

Phlox bifida (Sand Phlox)

Phlox caespitosa (Tufted Phlox, Clumped Phlox)

Phlox hoodii (Hood's Phlox)

Phlox missoulensis (Cushion Phlox)

Phlox nivalis (Piney Woods Phlox, Trailing Phlox)

Phlox subulata (Moss-pink, Moss Phlox)

Polemonium chartaceum (Papery Polemonium)

Polemonium foliosissimum (Leafy Jacob's Ladder)

Polemonium pulcherrimum (Skunk-leaved Polemonium, Showy Polemonium)

Polemonium viscosum (Sky Pilot, Sticky Polemonium)

Potentilla tridentata (Three-toothed Cinquefoil)

Salvia species (Sage)

Sedum divergens (Cascade Stonecrop, Spreading Stonecrop)

Sedum glaucophyllum (Cliff Stonecrop)

Sedum lanceolatum (Lance-leaved Stonecrop)

Sedum rosea (Roseroot)

Sedum spathulifolium (Broad-leaf Stonecrop)

Silene caroliniana (Wild Pink)

Silene virginica (Fire Pink)

Sisyrinchium bellum (California Blue-eyed Grass, Western Blue-eyed Grass)

Sisyrinchium capillare (Slender Blue-eyed Grass)

Sisyrinchium douglasii (Grass Widows, Purple-eyed Grass)

Sisyrinchium elmeri (Orange-eyed Grass)

Sisyrinchium idahoense (Idaho Blue-eyed Grass)

Solidago multiradiata (Alpine Goldenrod)

Talinum species (Fame Flower)

Tephrosia virginiana (Goat's Rue)

Thalictrum alpinum (Alpine Meadow Rue)

Tradescantia (Cuthbertia) rosea (Pink Spiderwort)

Tradescantia hirsuticaulis (Hairy Spiderwort)

Tradescantia longipes (Wild Crocus)

Trillium ovatum f. *hibbersonii* (Dwarf Western White Trillium)

Viola pedata (Bird's-foot Violet)

Xerophyllum tenax (Elk Grass, Bear Grass, Indian Basket Grass)

Zauschneria species (California Fuchsia)

Woodland Wildflowers

Actaea pachypoda (syn. *A. alba*) (Doll's Eyes)
Actaea rubra (Red Baneberry)
Allium tricoccum (Ramps, Wild Leek)
Anemone oregana (Western Wood Anemone)
Anemone piperi (Piper's Anemone)
Anemone quinquefolia (Wood Anemone)
Anemonella thalictroides (Rue Anemone)
Arisaema dracontium (Green Dragon)
Arisaema triphyllum (Jack-in-the-pulpit)
Aruncus dioicus (Goat's beard)
Asarum species (Wild Ginger)
Aster cordifolius (Blue Heart-leaved Aster, Blue Wood Aster)
Aster divaricatus (White Wood Aster)
Aster macrophyllus (Big-leaved Aster)
Astilbe biternata (False Goat's Beard)
Callirhoe involucrata (Purple Poppy-mallow)
Caulophyllum thalictroides (Blue Cohosh)
Chimaphila maculata (Spotted Wintergreen, Pipsissewa)
Chimaphila umbellata (Prince's Pine, Pipsissewa)
Chrysogonum virginianum (Gold-star, Golden Star)
Cimicifuga species (Bugbane)
Claytonia caroliniana (Spring Beauty)
Claytonia lanceolata (Western Spring Beauty)
Claytonia virginiana (Spring Beauty)
Clematis albicoma (Clematis)
Clematis ochroleuca (Curly-heads)
Clematis viorna (Leather Flower)
Clintonia species (Bead-lily)
Coptis species (Goldthread)
Cornus canadensis (Bunchberry)
Cypripedium acaule (Pink Lady-slipper)
Cypripedium aretinum (Ram's-head Lady-slipper)
Cypripedium kentuckiense (Kentucky Lady-slipper)
Cypripedium parviflorum (Small Yellow Lady-slipper)
Cypripedium pubescens (Large Yellow Lady-slipper)
Dentaria species (Toothwort)
Dicentra species (Bleeding Heart)
Diphylleia cymosa (Umbrella Leaf)
Disporum species (Fairy-bells)
Epigaea repens (Trailing Arbutus)
Erythronium species (Trout Lily)
Galax urceolata (Wandflower, Galax)
Gaultheria hispidula (Creeping Snowberry)
Gaultheria ovatifolia (Slender Wintergreen, Oregon Wintergreen)
Gaultheria procumbens (Checkerberry, Wintergreen)
Hepatica acutiloba (Sharp-lobed Hepatica)
Hepatica americana (Round-lobed Hepatica)
Hexastylis species (Evergreen Ginger)
Hydrastis canadensis (Goldenseal)
Hydrophyllum species (Waterleaf)
Iris cristata (Crested Iris)

Iris douglasiana (Douglas Iris)
Iris lacustris (Dwarf Lake Iris)
Iris tenuis (Clackamas Iris)
Iris verna (Dwarf Iris)
Jeffersonia diphylla (Twinleaf)
Linnaea borealis (Twinflower)
Maianthemum canadense (Canada Mayflower)
Maianthemum dilatatum (Deerberry, May-lily, False Lily-of-the-valley)
Meehania cordata (Creeping Mint)
Mertensia paniculata (Northern Bluebells)
Mertensia virginica (Virginia Bluebells)
Mitchella repens (Partridgeberry)
Mitella breweri (Brewer's Mitrewort)

Jeffersonia diphylla. Twinleaf is well adapted to a life in the forest. Its large, upward-facing leaves are designed to efficiently capture the weak light that penetrates the tree canopy.

Mitella diphylla (Two-leaved Mitrewort, Bishop's
　Cap)

Mitella diversifolia (Angle-leaved Mitrewort, Varied-
　leaved Mitrewort)

Pachysandra procumbens (Allegheny Spurge)

Panax quinquefolius (American Ginseng)

Phlox divaricata (Forest Phlox, Wild Blue Phlox)

Phlox stolonifera (Creeping Phlox)

Podophyllum peltatum (Mayapple)

Polemonium carneum (Salmon Polemonium,
　Salmon Jacob's Ladder)

Polemonium occidentale (Western Jacob's Ladder,
　Western Polemonium)

Polemonium reptans (Spreading Jacobs Ladder)

Polygonatum species (Solomon's Seal)

Penstemon smallii.
*Penstemon smallii is one
of the tallest beard-
tongues, making it a fine
choice for mixed mead-
ow plantings.*

Sanguinaria canadensis (Bloodroot)

Sedum ternatum (Wild Stonecrop)

Shortia galacifolia (Oconee Bells)

Smilacina species (False Solomon's Seal)

Solidago caesia (Blue-stemmed Goldenrod, Wreath
　Goldenrod)

Solidago curtisii (Curtiss' Goldenrod)

Spigelia marilandica (Indian Pink, Pinkroot, Worm
　Grass)

Streptopus species (Twisted Stalk)

Stylophorum diphyllum (Celandine Poppy)

Tellima grandiflora (Fringecups)

Thalictrum dioicum (Early Meadow Rue)

Tiarella species (Foamflower)

Trientalis borealis (Starflower)

Trillium species (Trillium)

Uvularia species (Bellwort)

Vancouveria hexandra (White Inside-out Flower)

Vancouveria planipetala (Inside-out Flower)

Viola species (Violet)

Wildflowers for Meadow and Prairie

Agastache foeniculum (Lavender Giant Hyssop,
　Anise Hyssop)

Agastache nepetoides (Catnip Giant Hyssop, Yellow
　Giant Hyssop)

Agastache scrophularaefolia (Purple Giant Hyssop)

Agastache urticifolia (Nettle-leaf Giant Hyssop)

Anemone canadensis (Canada Anemone)

Aruncus dioicus (Goat's beard)

Asclepias exaltata (Tall Milkweed)

Asclepias purpurascens (Purple Milkweed)

Asclepias speciosa (Showy Milkweed)

Asclepias syriaca (Common Milkweed)

Asclepias tuberosa (Butterfly Weed)

Asclepias variegata (White Milkweed)

Aster azureus (Prairie Heart-leaved Aster)

Aster concolor (Eastern Silvery Aster)

Aster grandiflorus (Big-headed Aster)

Aster laevis (Smooth Aster)

Aster lateriflorus (Goblet Aster, Calico Aster)

Aster novae-angliae (New England Aster)

Aster novi-belgii (New York Aster)

Aster oblongifolius (Aromatic Aster)

Aster turbinellus (Prairie Aster)

Aster vimineus (Small-headed Aster, Small White
　Aster)

Baptisia alba (syn. *B. pendula*) (White Wild Indigo)

Baptisia alba var. *macrophylla* (syn. *B. leucantha*)

Baptisia australis (Blue False Indigo)

Baptisia australis var. *minor*

Baptisia bracteata var. *leucophaea* (Cream Wild
　Indigo)

Baptisia sphaerocarpa (syn. *B. viridis*) (Yellow Wild
　Indigo)

Baptisia tinctoria (Wild Indigo, Yellow Wild Indigo)

Boltonia asteroides var. *latisquama* (Showy False
　Aster)

Boltonia decurrens (Decurrent False Aster)
Callirhoe digitata (Finger Poppy-mallow)
Castilleja coccinea (Painted Cup)
Castilleja miniata (Great Red Paintbrush)
Chelone species (Turtlehead)
Coreopsis atkinsoniana (Columbia Coreopsis)
Coreopsis integrifolia (Tickseed)
Coreopsis rosea (Pink Coreopsis)
Coreopsis tinctoria (Plains Tickseed, Calliopsis)
Coreopsis tripteris (Tall Tickseed)
Dodecatheon amethystinum (Amethyst Shooting Star)
Dodecatheon meadia (Eastern Shooting Star)
Dodecatheon pulchellum (Few-flowered Shooting Star, Dark-throat)
Echinacea species (Coneflower)
Epilobium angustifolium (Fireweed)
Eryngium yuccifolium (Rattlesnake Master)
Eupatorium species (Joe-Pye Weed)
Euphorbia corollata (Flowering Spurge)
Filipendula rubra (Queen of the Prairie)
Gaillardia species (Blanket Flower)
Gaura species (Gaura)
Gentiana andrewsii (Prairie Closed Gentian, Prairie Bottle Gentian)
Gentiana clausa (Meadow Closed Gentian, Meadow Bottle Gentian)
Gentiana saponaria (Soapwort Gentian)
Gentianopsis crinita (Fringed Gentian)
Geum triflorum (Prairie Smoke)
Helianthus species (Sunflower)
Heliopsis helianthoides (Oxeye)
Iris missouriensis (Western Blue Flag)
Iris versicolor (Northern Blue Flag)
Iris virginica (Southern Blue Flag)
Liatris species (Blazing Star)
Lilium canadense (Canada Lily)
Lilium columbianum (Oregon Lily)
Lilium michiganense (Michigan Lily)
Lilium pardalinum (Leopard Lily)
Lilium philadelphicum (Wood Lily)
Lilium superbum (Turk's Cap, Turk's Cap Lily)
Linum perenne var. *lewisii* (Perennial Flax)
Lobelia species (Cardinal Flower)
Lupinus species (Lupine)
Monarda species (Bee Balm)
Oenothera biennis (Evening Primrose)
Oenothera fruticosa (Southern Sundrops)
Penstemon eatonii (Firecracker Penstemon, Eaton's Firecracker)
Penstemon grandiflorus (Large Beardtongue, Large-flowered Beardtongue)
Penstemon smallii (Small's Beardtongue)
Petalostemon species (Prairie Clover)
Phlox carolina (Carolina Phlox)
Phlox maculata (Meadow Phlox, Wild Sweet William)
Phlox paniculata (Summer Phlox)
Physostegia virginiana (Obedient Plant)

Pycnanthemum species (Mountain Mint)
Ratibida species (Prairie Coneflower)
Rudbeckia species (Black-eyed Susan)
Scutellaria lateriflora (Mad-dog Skullcap)
Senna species (Wild Senna)
Silene regia (Royal Catchfly)
Silphium species (Rosin Weed)
Solidago species (Blue-stemmed Goldenrod, Wreath Goldenrod)
Tephrosia species (Goat's Rue)
Thalictrum dasycarpum (Purple Meadow Rue)
Thalictrum pubescens (syn. *T. polygamum*)
Tradescantia occidentalis (Prairie Spiderwort, Western Spiderwort)
Tradescantia ohiensis (Smooth Spiderwort, Ohio Spiderwort)
Tradescantia subaspera (Wide-leaved Spiderwort)
Tradescantia virginiana (Virginia Spiderwort, Common Spiderwort)
Veratrum viride (False Hellebore, White Hellebore, Indian Poke)
Vernonia species (Ironweed)
Veronicastrum virginicum (Culver's Root, Bowman's Root)
Wyethia species (Mule's Ears)
Zizia aurea (Golden Alexanders)

Ground Covers

Antennaria species (Pussy-toes)*
Asarum species (Wild Ginger)*
Aster macrophyllus (Big-leaved Aster)
Aster spectabilis (Showy Aster)
Astragalus kentrophyta (Thistle Milkvetch)
Chimaphila maculata (Spotted Wintergreen, Pipsissewa)*
Chimaphila umbellata (Prince's Pine, Pipsissewa)*
Chrysogonum virginianum (Gold-star, Golden Star)
Claytonia caroliniana (Spring Beauty)
Claytonia lanceolata (Western Spring Beauty)
Claytonia virginiana (Spring Beauty)
Clematis ligusticifolia (Virgin's Bower, Pipestem)
Clematis virginiana (Woodbine, Virgin's Bower)
Clintonia species (Bead-lily)
Coptis species (Goldthread)*
Coreopsis auriculata var. *nana* (Dwarf Lobed Tickseed)*
Coreopsis rosea (Pink Coreopsis)
Cornus canadensis (Bunchberry)
Dentaria species (Toothwort)
Dicentra canadensis (Squirrel Corn)
Dicentra cucullaria (Dutchman's Breeches)
Epigaea repens (Trailing Arbutus)*
Eriogonum umbellatum (Sulphur Flower)
Galax urceolata (Wandflower, Galax)*
Gaultheria species (Wintergreen)*
Geum rivale (Water Avens)
Geum triflorum (Prairie Smoke)*
Helonias bullata (Swamp Pink)*

Hepatica acutiloba (Sharp-lobed Hepatica)*
Hepatica americana (Round-lobed Hepatica)*
Hexastylis species (Evergreen Ginger)*
Hydrastis canadensis (Goldenseal)
Hypoxis hirsuta (Common Star Grass, Yellow Star Grass)
Iris cristata (Crested Iris)
Iris lacustris (Dwarf Lake Iris)
Iris verna (Dwarf Iris)
Jeffersonia diphylla (Twinleaf)
Linnaea borealis (Twinflower)*
Maianthemum canadense (Canada Mayflower)
Maianthemum dilatatum (Deerberry, May-lily, False Lily-of-the-valley)
Meehania cordata (Creeping Mint)
Mitchella repens (Partridgeberry)*
Mitella breweri (Brewer's Mitrewort)
Mitella diversifolia (Angle-leaved Mitrewort, Varied-leaved Mitrewort)
Opuntia humifusa (Eastern Prickly Pear)*
Opuntia macrorhiza (Plains Prickly Pear)*
Pachysandra procumbens (Allegheny Spurge)*
Penstemon davidsonii (Timberline Penstemon, Davidson's Penstemon)
Penstemon pinifolius (Pine-leaved Beardtongue)
Penstemon rupicola (Rock Beardtongue, Cliff Penstemon)
Phlox adsurgens (Periwinkle Phlox, Woodland Phlox)
Phlox bifida (Sand Phlox)
Phlox subulata (Moss-pink, Moss Phlox)
Potentilla tridentata (Three-toothed Cinquefoil)
Rudbeckia fulgida var. *speciosa* (Wing-stem Meadow-pitchers, Meadow Beauty)
Sanguinaria canadensis (Bloodroot)
Saxifraga careyana (Carey's Saxifrage)*
Saxifraga michauxii (Claw Saxifrage)*
Sedum divergens (Cascade Stonecrop, Spreading Stonecrop)*
Sedum glaucophyllum (Cliff Stonecrop)*
Sedum lanceolatum (Lance-leaved Stonecrop)*
Sedum nevii (Nevy's Sedum)*
Sedum spathulifolium (Broad-leaf Stonecrop)*
Sedum ternatum (Wild Stonecrop)*
Shortia galacifolia (Oconee Bells)*
Silene caroliniana (Wild Pink)*
Sisyrinchium angustifolium (Stout Blue-eyed Grass, Common Blue-eyed Grass)
Sisyrinchium bellum (California Blue-eyed Grass, Western Blue-eyed Grass)*
Sisyrinchium mucronatum (Slender Blue-eyed Grass)
Solidago sphacelata (Short-pappus Goldenrod, False Goldenrod)
Stokesia laevis (Stokes' Aster)*
Talinum calycinum (Rockpink)
Tellima grandiflora (Fringecups)*
Thalictrum alpinum (Alpine Meadow Rue)

Tiarella cordifolia var. *cordifolia* (Running Foam-flower)*
Trientalis borealis (Starflower)
Uvularia species (Bellwort)
Vancouveria hexandra (White Inside-out Flower)
Vancouveria planipetala (Inside-out Flower)*
Viola appalachiensis (Appalachian Violet)
Viola labradorica (Labrador Violet)
Viola sororia (Dooryard Violet, Woolly Blue Violet)
Waldsteinia fragarioides (Barren Strawberry)*

(* INDICATES EVERGREEN)

Wildflowers Especially Good for Providing Food for Butterflies and Other Insects

Agastache species (Wild Hyssop)
Allium species (Wild Onion)
Amsonia species (Bluestar)
Antennaria species (Pussy-toes)
Aquilegia species (Columbine)
Aruncus dioicus (Goat's beard)
Asclepias species (Milkweed)
Aster species (Aster)
Astragalus species (Milkvetch)
Baptisia species (Wild Indigo)
Boltonia species (False Aster)
Callirhoe species (Poppy-mallow)
Campanula species (Harebell)
Castilleja species (Paintbrush)
Chelone species (Turtlehead)
Chrysopsis species (Golden Aster)
Cimicifuga species (Bugbane)
Conradina species (Wild Rosemary)
Coreopsis species (Tickseed)
Dicentra species (Bleeding Heart)
Echinacea species (Coneflower)
Eriogonum species (Wild Buckwheat)
Eryngium yuccifolium (Rattlesnake Master)
Eupatorium species (Joe-Pye Weed)
Filipendula rubra (Queen of the Prairie)
Gaillardia species (Blanket Flower)
Gaura species (Gaura)
Gentiana species (Gentian)
Geranium species (Wild Geranium)
Helianthus species (Sunflower)
Heliopsis helianthoides (Oxeye)
Liatris species (Blazing Star)
Limonium carolinianum (Sea Lavender)
Linum perenne var. *lewisii* (Perennial Flax)
Lobelia species (Cardinal Flower)
Lupinus species (Lupine)
Marshallia species (Barbara's Buttons)
Mimulus species (Monkey-flower)
Monarda species (Bee Balm)
Opuntia species (Prickly Pear)
Penstemon species (Beardtongue)
Petalostemon species (Prairie Clover)

Phlox species (Phlox)
Physostegia virginiana (Obedient Plant)
Polemonium species (Jacob's Ladder)
Polygonatum species (Solomon's Seal)
Pycnanthemum species (Mountain Mint)
Ratibida species (Prairie Coneflower)
Rudbeckia species (Black-eyed Susan)
Salvia species (Sage)
Scutellaria species (Skullcap)
Sedum species (Stonecrop)
Silphium species (Rosin Weed)
Solidago species (Blue-stemmed Goldenrod, Wreath Goldenrod)
Stokesia laevis (Stokes' Aster)
Tiarella species (Foamflower)
Vernonia species (Ironweed)
Viola species (Violet)
Yucca species (Soapweed)
Zauschneria species (California Fuchsia)

Silene regia (Royal Catchfly)
Silene virginica (Fire Pink)
Silphium species (Rosin Weed)
Smilacina species (False Solomon's Seal)
Solidago species (Blue-stemmed Goldenrod, Wreath Goldenrod)
Spigelia marilandica (Indian Pink, Pinkroot, Worm Grass)
Streptopus species (Twisted Stalk)
Symplocarpus foetidus (Skunk Cabbage, Polecat Weed)
Trillium species (Trillium)
Vernonia species (Ironweed)
Zauschneria species (California Fuchsia)

Lobelia cardinalis. *Cardinal Flower provides a rich nectar that is relished by hummingbirds and also many butterflies, including this Swallowtail.*

Wildflowers That Provide Food for Birds and Mammals

Agastache barberi (syn. *A. pallida*) (Giant Hummingbird's Mint)
Agastache rupestris (Sunset Hyssop)
Aquilegia species (Columbine)
Clintonia species (Bead-lily)
Cornus canadensis (Bunchberry)
Diphylleia cymosa (Umbrella Leaf)
Disporum hookeri (Hooker's Fairy-bells)
Disporum lanuginosum (Fairy-bells, Yellow Mandarin)
Disporum smithii (Fairy-lantern)
Echinacea species (Coneflower)
Epigaea repens (Trailing Arbutus)
Eupatorium species (Joe-Pye Weed)
Gaultheria species (Wintergreen)
Helianthus species (Sunflower)
Heuchera sanguinea (Coralbells)
Hydrastis canadensis (Goldenseal)
Liatris species (Blazing Star)
Lobelia species (Cardinal Flower)
Lupinus species (Lupine)
Lysichiton americanum (Western Skunk Cabbage)
Maianthemum canadense (Canada Mayflower)
Maianthemum dilatatum (Deerberry, May-lily, False Lily-of-the-valley)
Mitchella repens (Partridgeberry)
Monarda species (Bee Balm)
Opuntia species (Prickly Pear)
Panax quinquefolius (American Ginseng)
Penstemon species (Beardtongue)
Physostegia virginiana (Obedient Plant)
Podophyllum peltatum (Mayapple)
Polygonatum species (Solomon's Seal)
Rudbeckia species (Black-eyed Susan)

Wildflowers That Are Less Palatable to Deer and Other Herbivores

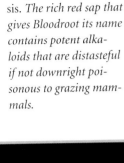

Sanguinaria canadensis. *The rich red sap that gives Bloodroot its name contains potent alkaloids that are distasteful if not downright poisonous to grazing mammals.*

Aconitum species (Monkshood)
Actaea species (Baneberry)
Allium species (Wild Onion)
Amsonia species (Bluestar)
Aquilegia species (Columbine)
Arisaema dracontium (Green Dragon)
Arisaema triphyllum (Jack-in-the-pulpit)
Aruncus dioicus (Goat's beard)
Asclepias species (Milkweed)
Aster species (Aster)
Astilbe biternata (False Goat's Beard)
Astragalus species (Milkvetch)

Baptisia species (Wild Indigo)
Campanula species (Harebell)
Caulophyllum thalictroides (Blue Cohosh)
Chelone species (Turtlehead)
Chimaphila maculata (Spotted Wintergreen, Pipsissewa)
Chimaphila umbellata (Prince's Pine, Pipsissewa)
Coreopsis species (Tickseed)
Delphinium species (Larkspur)
Dicentra species (Bleeding Heart)
Echinacea species (Coneflower)
Echinocereus species (Hedgehog Cactus)
Eryngium yuccifolium (Rattlesnake Master)
Eupatorium species (Joe-Pye Weed)
Euphorbia corollata (Flowering Spurge)
Geranium species (Wild Geranium)
Jeffersonia diphylla (Twinleaf)
Limonium carolinianum (Sea Lavender)
Lobelia species (Cardinal Flower)
Lupinus species (Lupine)
Maianthemum canadense (Canada Mayflower)
Mimulus species (Monkey-flower)
Mitchella repens (Partridgeberry)
Monarda species (Bee Balm)
Oenothera species (Evening Primrose)
Opuntia species (Prickly Pear)
Oxytropis species (Locoweed)
Petalostemon species (Prairie Clover)
Podophyllum peltatum (Mayapple)
Pycnanthemum species (Mountain Mint)
Rudbeckia species (Black-eyed Susan)
Salvia species (Sage)
Sanguinaria canadensis (Bloodroot)
Smilacina species (False Solomon's Seal)
Solidago species (Goldenrod)
Spigelia marilandica (Indian Pink, Pinkroot, Worm Grass)
Stenanthium (Melianthemum) gramineum (Featherfleece, Feather-bells)
Stylophorum diphyllum (Celandine Poppy)
Symplocarpus foetidus (Skunk Cabbage, Polecat Weed)
Talinum species (Fame Flower)
Tephrosia species (Goat's Rue)
Veronicastrum virginicum (Culver's Root, Bowman's Root)
Viola species (Violet)
Wyethia species (Mule's Ears)
Xerophyllum species (Turkey Beard, Elk Grass, Bear Grass)
Yucca species (Soapweed)

Wildflowers with Bold Foliage

Aconitum reclinatum (Trailing Wolfsbane)
Allium tricoccum (Ramps, Wild Leek)
Arisaema dracontium (Green Dragon)
Arisaema triphyllum (Jack-in-the-pulpit)
Asarum species (Wild Ginger)
Asclepias exaltata (Tall Milkweed)
Asclepias humistrata (Sandhills Milkweed)
Asclepias purpurascens (Purple Milkweed)
Asclepias speciosa (Showy Milkweed)
Asclepias syriaca (Common Milkweed)
Asclepias variegata (White Milkweed)
Aster macrophyllus (Big-leaved Aster)
Calla palustris (Water Arum)
Caltha palustris (Marsh Marigold)
Cimicifuga rubifolia (Appalachian Bugbane)
Clintonia species (Bead-lily)
Darmera (Peltiphylum) peltatum (Umbrella Plant)
Diphylleia cymosa (Umbrella Leaf)
Galax urceolata (Wandflower, Galax)
Helianthus maximiliani (Maximilian Sunflower)
Helianthus mollis (Ashy Sunflower)
Helonias bullata (Swamp Pink)
Hexastylis species (Evergreen Ginger)
Hydrastis canadensis (Goldenseal)
Hydrophyllum macrophyllum (Hairy Waterleaf)
Iris fulva (Copper Iris)
Iris versicolor (Northern Blue Flag)
Iris virginica (Southern Blue Flag)
Jeffersonia diphylla (Twinleaf)
Lysichiton americanum (Western Skunk Cabbage)
Mertensia maritima (Seaside Bluebell, Oyster Plant)
Mertensia virginica (Virginia Bluebells)
Opuntia species (Prickly Pear)
Orontium aquaticum (Golden Club)
Pachysandra procumbens (Allegheny Spurge)
Podophyllum peltatum (Mayapple)
Rudbeckia maxima (Great Coneflower)
Sanguinaria canadensis (Bloodroot)
Saxifraga oregana (Bog Saxifrage, Oregon Saxifrage)
Saxifraga pensylvanica (Swamp Saxifrage)
Silphium laciniatum (Compass Plant)
Silphium perfoliatum (Cup Plant)
Silphium terebinthinaceum (Prairie Dock)
Symplocarpus foetidus (Skunk Cabbage, Polecat Weed)
Veratrum viride (False Hellebore, White Hellebore, Indian Poke)
Wyethia species (Mule's Ears)
Xerophyllum asphodeloides (Turkey Beard)
Xerophyllum tenax (Elk Grass, Bear Grass, Indian Basket Grass)
Yucca baccata (Spanish-bayonet, Blue Yucca, Banana Yucca)
Yucca filementosa (Adam's Needle, Needle Palm)

Wildflowers with Fine-textured Foliage

Actaea pachypoda (syn. *A. alba*) (Doll's Eyes)
Allium species (Wild Onion)
Amsonia ciliata (Bluestar)
Amsonia hubrichtii (Hubricht's Bluestar)
Anemone multifida (Cut-leaved Anemone)
Anemonella thalictroides (Rue Anemone)
Aquilegia species (Columbine)
Aruncus dioicus (Goat's beard)
Asclepias verticillata (Whorled Milkweed)
Callirhoe digitata (Finger Poppy-mallow)
Campanula divaricata (Southern Harebell)
Campanula rotundifolia (Harebell)
Castilleja chromosa (Desert Paintbrush)
Chrysopsis (Pityopsis) falcata (Sickle-leaved Golden Aster)
Cimicifuga americana (American Bugbane)
Cimicifuga laciniata (Cut-leaved Bugbane)
Claytonia virginiana (Spring Beauty)
Clematis crispa (Blue Jasmine)
Clematis hirsutissima (Sugar-bowls)
Conradina species (Wild Rosemary)
Coptis asplenifolia (Spleenwort-leaved Goldthread)
Coptis laciniata (Oregon Goldthread, Cutleaf Goldthread)
Coreopsis atkinsoniana (Columbia Coreopsis)
Coreopsis rosea (Pink Coreopsis)
Coreopsis species (Tickseed)
Coreopsis tinctoria (Plains Tickseed, Calliopsis)
Coreopsis verticillata (Threadleaf Tickseed)
Delphinium species (Larkspur)
Dentaria laciniata (Cut-leaf Toothwort)
Dicentra species (Bleeding Heart)
Eupatorium capillifolium (Dog Fennel)
Helianthus salicifolius (Willow-leaved Sunflower)
Hypoxis hirsuta (Common Star Grass, Yellow Star Grass)
Liatris graminifolia (Grass-leaved Blazing Star)
Liatris microcephala (Small-headed Blazing Star)
Liatris pycnostachya (Prairie Blazing Star, Gay-feather)
Linum perenne var. *lewisii* (Perennial Flax)
Penstemon linarioides ssp. *coloradoensis*
Penstemon pinifolius (Pine-leaved Beardtongue)
Petalostemon species (Prairie Clover)
Phlox bifida (Sand Phlox)
Pycnanthemum tenuifolium (Narrow-leaved Mountain Mint, Slender Mountain Mint)
Senna species (Wild Senna)
Sisyrinchium species (Blue-eyed Grass)
Talinum species (Fame Flower)
Thalictrum dioicum (Early Meadow Rue)
Thalictrum venulosum (Northern Meadow Rue)
Vernonia lettermannii (Ironweed)
Viola pedata (Bird's-foot Violet)

SOURCES OF PROPAGATED
NATIVE PLANTS AND SEEDS

I realize that not all of the plants covered in this book are readily available, but there is a growing network of specialty mail-order nurseries out there, and you can find almost anything with a little searching. The power of the Internet is bound to only improve access to both information and plants in the coming years. I managed a mail-order nursery before coming to the Wild Flower Society, and at that time its Web site brought in only a couple hundred dollars a year in business. Now, five years, later it has grown exponentially and makes up a significant portion of the total sales.

The following list of nurseries was compiled by staff and volunteers of the New England Wildflower Society. This list, which emphasizes sources for nursery-propagated native plants, was last updated in January 2000. It is by no means complete, but it does offer a wide cross section of firms whose inventory is at least 25 percent North American native plants. We listed only respondents who stated that they do not sell wild-collected plants, or in the case of seed, wild harvest responsibly or buy from reputable collectors.

However, we cannot guarantee the truth or accuracy of the information reported by suppliers participating in this survey. The catalog prices are based on 1999 figures and are subject to change. Please note that some of the nurseries are wholesale only, and we include them as a service to those in the trade. I would like to extend special thanks to Kerry Norlin, Susan Dumaine, Lynn Luck, Sheila Magullion, and Laura Schaufeld for their help in compiling this list.

There are several good source listings available, including *Gardening by Mail,* by Barbara Barton (Boston: Houghton Mifflin Company, 1997) and *The Anderson Horticultural Library's Source List of Plants and Seeds,* published by the Minnesota Landscape Arboretum, 3675 Arboretum Drive, Box 39, Chanhassen, MN 55317-0039. Additionally, many of the local and regional native plant societies listed on the following pages have lists and other helpful information, and I encourage you to join the one nearest you.

Amanda's Garden

8410 Harper's Ferry Rd.
Springwater NY 14560
716-669-2275
efolts4826@aol.com
RETAIL/MAIL ORDER
PLANTS ONLY
Comments: 100% native: 98% nursery propagated, 2% from other nursery source. Specializes in woodland wildflowers. Plants are 1-year-old minimum. Garden planning advice available. Catalog cost: free.

Aquascapes Unlimited, Inc.

PO Box 364
Pipersville PA 18947
215-766-8151
wetland@comcat.com
WHOLESALE/MAIL ORDER
PLANTS AND SEEDS
Comments: 80% native: 50% nursery propagated and 50% from seed (1/2 collected, 1/2 other source). Specializes in container-grown ornamental hardy aquatic plants. Offers consulting services. Catalog cost: free.

Arrowwood Nurseries, Inc.

870 W. Malaga Rd.
Williamstown NJ 08094
856-697-6045
njplants@aol.com
WHOLESALE/MAIL ORDER
PLANTS AND SEEDS
Comments: 100% native: 75% nursery propagated and 25% seed from other nursery source. Specializes in grasses, sedges, and rushes of New Jersey coastal plain. Will contract grow. Mail-order seeds only, may ship small plant orders. Catalog cost: free.

Bitterroot Restoration, Inc.

445 Quast Ln.
Corvallis MT 59828
406-961-4991
sales@revegetation.com
www.revegetation.com
WHOLESALE/MAIL ORDER
PLANTS ONLY
Comments: 100% native: 100% grown from wild-collected seed. Specializes in restoration and revegetation of large dis-

turbed sites. Offers a range of services: consultation, native plants, project implementation. Catalog cost: free with $5.00 minimum order.

Bluestem Nursery

4101 Curry Rd.

Arlington TX 76001

817-478-6202

grassman@flash.net

WHOLESALE/RETAIL/MAIL ORDER

PLANTS ONLY

Comments: 95% native: 70% propagated from stock, 10% wild-collected seed, and 20% seed and liners from other nursery source. Specializes in native ornamental prairie grasses—sod (minimum order required) or container grown. Catalog cost: free.

Bluestem Prairie Nursery

13197 E. 13th Rd.

Hillsboro IL 62049

217-532-6344

RETAIL/MAIL ORDER

PLANTS AND SEEDS

Comments: 100% native: 100% propagated from stock. Special interest in tall-grass prairie restoration with a particularly extensive selection of plant species native to the Illinois prairie. Custom blended seed mixes. Catalog cost: free.

Bluestone Perennials, Inc.

7211 Middle Ridge Rd.

Madison OH 44057

800-852-5243

bluestone@bluestoneperennials.com

www.bluestoneperennials.com

WHOLESALE/RETAIL/MAIL ORDER

PLANTS ONLY

Comments: 50% native: 98% propagated from stock and 2% from other nursery source. Specializes in perennials and ornamental shrubs. Container-grown plants. Free shipping for large orders. Catalog cost: free.

Bobtown Nursery

16212 Country Club Rd.

Melfa VA 23410

757-787-8484

WHOLESALE/MAIL ORDER

PLANTS ONLY

Comments: 75% native: majority nursery propagated. Specializes in native shrubs and wetlands plants. Offers liners, rooted cuttings, seedlings, and bare-root transplants. Catalog cost: free.

Broken Arrow Nursery

13 Broken Arrow Rd.

Hamden CT 06518

203-288-1026

brokenarrow@snet.net

WHOLESALE/RETAIL/MAIL ORDER

PLANTS ONLY

Comments: 30% native: 85% propagated from stock and 15% from other nursery source. Specializes in *Kalmia* cultivars and many unusual ornamental shrub cultivars. Landscaping consultation provided. Catalog cost: $2.00.

Colvos Creek Nursery

PO Box 1512

Vashon Island WA 98070

206-749-9508

colvoscreek@juno.com

WHOLESALE/RETAIL/MAIL ORDER

PLANTS ONLY

Comments: 40% native: 100% propagated from stock. Majority of plants are Northwest natives. Container grown and shipped with rootballs enclosed in plastic bags. Catalog cost: $3.00.

Cultured Natives

36170 County 14 Blvd.

Cannon Falls MN 55009-5239

RETAIL/MAIL ORDER

PLANTS ONLY

Comments: 100% native: 100% propagated from stock. Specializes in field-grown native Minnesota flora. Shipped dormant and bare-root. Catalog cost: free.

Dean Swift Seed Co.

PO Box B

Jaroso CO 81138

719-672-3739

dswift@phone.net

WHOLESALE/MAIL ORDER

SEEDS ONLY

Comments: 98% native: 50% propagated from stock and 50% wild-collected seed. Specializes in select species of Aster, Columbine, and conifers. Catalog cost: free.

Doyle Farm Nursery

158 Norris Rd.

Delta PA 17314

717-862-3134

WHOLESALE/RETAIL/MAIL ORDER

PLANTS ONLY

Comments: 65% native: 75% propagated from stock and 25% from other nursery source. Specializes in native and unusual perennials and grasses. Catalog cost: $ 1.00.

Eco-Gardens

PO Box 1227

Decatur GA 30031

404-294-6468

eco-garden@mindspring.com

RETAIL/MAIL ORDER

PLANTS ONLY

Comments: 50% native: 100% propagated from stock including many *Trillium* species and orchids. Specializes in Southeast woodlanders. Catalog cost: $ 2.00.

Elixir Farm Botanicals

General Delivery
Brixey MO 65618
417-261-2393
efb@aristotle.net
www.elixirfarm.com
WHOLESALE/RETAIL/MAIL ORDER
PLANTS AND SEEDS

Comments: 50% native: 98% propagated from stock and 2% from other nursery source. Specializes in Chinese and native North American medicinal plants, seeds, rootlets, and books. Organic growing methods. Catalog cost: free (seed), $2 (growers guide).

Environmental Concern, Inc.

201 Boundry Ln.
PO Box P
St. Michaels MD 21663
410-745-9620
info@wetland.org
www.wetland.org
WHOLESALE/MAIL ORDER
PLANTS AND SEEDS

Comments: 99% native: 25% propagated from stock and 75% wild-collected seed. Offers wetland species only. Catalog cost: free.

F. W. Schumacher Co., Inc.

36 Spring Hill Rd.
PO Box 1023
Sandwich MA 02563
508-888-0659
treeseed@capecod.net
WHOLESALE/RETAIL/MAIL ORDER
SEEDS ONLY

Comments: 50% native: 80–90% wild-collected seed. Specializes in bulk seed sales of trees and shrubs for nurserymen and foresters. Catalog cost: free.

Fancy Fronds

PO Box 1090
Gold Bar WA 98251
360-793-1472
www.fancyfronds.com
RETAIL/MAIL ORDER
PLANTS ONLY

Comments: 10% native: 100% propagated from stock. Offers ferns only—wide selection. Fact-filled, educational catalog. Catalog cost: contact for information.

Forest Farm

990 Tetherow Rd.
Williams OR 97544-9599
541-846-7269
RETAIL/MAIL ORDER
PLANTS ONLY

Comments: 30% native: 100% propagated from stock. Specializes in ornamental and useful plants from around the world. Extensive offerings. Catalog cost: $ 4.00.

Gardens North

5984 3rd Line Rd. N.
North Gower, Ontario
Canada KOA 2TO
613-489-0065
garnorth@istar.ca
www.gardensnorth.com
WHOLESALE/RETAIL/MAIL ORDER
SEEDS ONLY

Comments: 50% native: 100% propagated from stock. Specializes in the production and sale of hardy perennial seed for northern gardens. Includes many woodland seeds. Organic growing methods. Catalog cost: $4.00.

Genesis Nursery, Inc.

23200 Hurd Rd.
Tampico IL 61283
815-438-2220
WHOLESALE/RETAIL/MAIL ORDER
SEEDS ONLY

Comments: 99% native: 100% propagated from stock. Offers specialized seed mixes for various soils, moisture regimes, and sun or shade. Contract growing and harvesting services. Catalog cost: free.

Hamilton Seeds and Wildflowers

16786 Brown Rd.
Elk Creek MO 65464
417-967-2190
hamilton@train.missouri.org
www.hamiltonseeds.com
WHOLESALE/RETAIL/MAIL ORDER
PLANTS AND SEEDS

Comments: 100% native: 100% propagated from stock. Specializes in midwestern species adapted to the higher rainfalls and prairie soils of the Midwest. Garden design consultation and seed mix ratings services. Catalog cost: free.

Heritage Seedlings, Inc.

4199 75th Ave. SE
Salem OR 97301
503-585-9835
jmkhsi@open.org
WHOLESALE/MAIL ORDER
PLANTS ONLY

Comments: 35-40% native: 100% propagated from stock. Specializes in unusual deciduous trees and shrubs from seed of North American and European-Asiatic origin. Greenhouse and field grown. Catalog cost: free.

Heronswood Nursery, Ltd.

7530 N.E. 288th St.
Kingston WI 98346
360-297-4172
heronswood@silverlink.net
www.heronswood.com
RETAIL/MAIL ORDER
PLANTS ONLY

Comments: 25% native: 90% propagated from stock and 10% other nursery source (has a "no resale of wild-collected plants" policy). Offers *Trillium*. Extensive selection of rare and unusual native and exotic plants. Catalog cost: $ 8.00.

Holland Wildflower Farm

290 O'Neal Lane, PO Box 328
Elkins AR 72727
501-643-2622
info@hwildflower.com
www.hwildflower.com
WHOLESALE/RETAIL/MAIL ORDER
SEEDS ONLY

Comments: 75% native: 85% propagated from stock, 10% wild-collected seed, and 5% from other nursery source. Specializes in wildflower plants and seeds. Nursery open by appointment. Catalog cost: free seed and information packet.

Hsu's Ginseng Enterprises, Inc.

T6819 County Hwy. W.
PO Box 509
Wausau WI 54402-0509
715-675-2325
info@hsuginseng.com
www.hsuginseng.com
WHOLESALE/RETAIL/MAIL ORDER
SEEDS ONLY

Comments: 100% native: 100% propagated from stock. Offers seeds and rootlets of ginseng and plants of goldenseal only. Field grown. Rootlets shipped within U.S. only. Catalog cost: free.

Intermountain Cactus

1478 North 750
East Kaysville UT 84037
801-546-2006
RETAIL/MAIL ORDER
PLANTS ONLY

Comments: 95% native: majority propagated from stock. Specializes in winter-hardy cactus. Catalog cost: free.

Ion Exchange

1878 Old Mission Dr.
Harpers Ferry IA 52146-7533
800-291-2143
hbright@means.net
www.ionxchange.com
WHOLESALE/RETAIL/MAIL ORDER
PLANTS AND SEEDS

Comments: 100% native: majority propagated from stock, some seed wild collected. Specializes in native wildflowers and grasses for praires, woodlands, and wetlands. Offers consulting and contract growing services. Catalog cost: free.

Joseph Brown Native Seeds & Plants

7327 Hoefork Ln.
Gloucester Point VA 23062
804-642-0736
RETAIL/MAIL ORDER
PLANTS AND SEEDS

Comments: 95% native: 95% propagated from stock, 5% other nursery source, and some seed wild collected. Uncommon selection of eastern U.S. native species. Catalog cost: $ 1.00.

Lamtree Farm

2323 Copeland Rd.
Warrensville NC 28693
336-385-6144
WHOLESALE/RETAIL/MAIL ORDER
PLANTS AND SEEDS

Comments: 98% native: 100% propagated from stock. Specializes in native rhododendron species. Field-grown stock. Catalog cost: $ 2.00.

Larner Seeds

PO Box 407
Bolinas CA 94924
415-868-9407
RETAIL/MAIL ORDER
PLANTS AND SEEDS

Comments: 100% native: 100% propagated from stock. Specializes in California natives. Mail-order seeds only. Catalog cost: $ 2.50.

Lazy K Nursery, Inc.

705 Wright Rd.
Pine Mountain GA 31822
706-663-4991
info@lazyknursery.com
www.lazyknursery.com
WHOLESALE/RETAIL/MAIL ORDER
PLANTS ONLY

Comments: 90% native: 100% propagated from stock. Specializes in native rhododendrons. Container grown. Catalog cost: $1.00.

Little Valley Farm

5693 Snead Creek Rd.
Spring Green WI 53588
608-935-3324
RETAIL/MAIL ORDER
PLANTS AND SEEDS

Comments: 100% native: 90% propagated from stock and 10% from other nursery source. Specializes in woodland and prairie wildflowers, shrubs, and prairie grasses. Catalog cost: free.

Lower Marlboro Nursery

PO Box 1013
Dunkirk MD 20754
301-812-0808
mssds@erols.com
RETAIL/MAIL ORDER
PLANTS ONLY

Comments: 75% native: 100% propagated from stock. Specializes in eastern U.S. natives with special interest in genetically diverse species. Catalog cost: $ 2.00.

Mary's Plant Farm

2410 Lanes Mill Rd.
Hamilton OH 45013
513-894-0022
RETAIL/MAIL ORDER
PLANTS AND SEEDS

Comments: 50% native: 100% propagated from stock. Specializes in ordinary and unusual selections including shade-loving perennials and flowering shrubs, understory trees, and shade trees. Catalog cost: $ 1.00 (refundable).

Midwest Wildflowers

Box 64
Rockton IL 61072
RETAIL/MAIL ORDER
SEEDS ONLY

Comments: 80% native: 50% propagated from stock, 40% wild-collected seed with permission on private lots, and 10% other nursery source. Specializes in midwestern wildflowers. Strictly seed mail order. Catalog cost: $ 1.00.

Missouri Wildflower Nursery

9814 Pleasant Hill Rd.
Jefferson City MO 65109
573-496-3492
mowldslrs@sockets.net
RETAIL/MAIL ORDER
PLANTS AND SEEDS

Comments: 100% native: 90% propagated from stock and 10% other nursery source. Seed is ethically wild collected from prairies in Missouri. Specializes in Missouri natives. Field and container grown. Catalog cost: $ 1.00.

Moon Mountain Wildflowers

PO Box 725
Carpinteria CA 93014
805-684-2565
ssseeds@silcom.com
www.ss-seeds.com
RETAIL/MAIL ORDER
SEEDS ONLY

Comments: 50% native: 13% wild collected and 87% from other nursery source. Specializes in native North American wildflowers. Offers wildflower mixes. Catalog cost: $ 3.00.

Native Gardens

Rt 1, Box 464
5737 Fischer Ln.
Greenback TN 37742
423-856-0220
meredith@native-gardens.com
WHOLESALE/RETAIL/MAIL ORDER
PLANTS AND SEEDS

Comments: 99% native: 97% propagated from stock and 3% from other nursery source. Specializes in native North American species. Catalog cost: free.

Native Seeds, Inc.

14590 Triadelphia Mill Rd.
Dayton MD 21036
301-596-9818
WHOLESALE/RETAIL/MAIL ORDER
SEEDS ONLY

Comments: 90% native: 40% propagated from stock and 60% from other nursery source. Specializes in native North American meadow wildflowers. Offers regional seed mixes. Price list: free.

The Natural Garden, Inc.

W. 443 Highway 64
St. Charles IL 60175
630-584-0150
WHOLESALE/RETAIL/MAIL ORDER
SEEDS ONLY

Comments: 33–42% native: 90% propagated from stock and 10% collected seed from private stockbeds. Many species native to Chicago region. Catalog cost: free.

New England Wild Flower Society

180 Hemenway Rd.
Framingham MA 01701
508-877-7630
newfs@newfs.org
www.newfs.org
RETAIL/MAIL ORDER
PLANTS AND SEEDS

Comments: 95% native: 90% propagated from stock and 10% from other nursery source. Specializes in northeastern woodland wildflowers. Mail-order seed only. Catalog cost: $2.50, free with membership.

Niche Gardens

1111 Dawson Rd.
Chapel Hill NC 27516
919-967-0078
mail@nichegdn.com
www.nichegdn.com
RETAIL/MAIL ORDER
PLANTS ONLY

Comments: 60% native: 95% propagated from stock and 5% from other nursery source. Sends large healthy plants. Garden consultation and design services available. Catalog cost: $ 3.00.

North Creek Nurseries, Inc.

388 North Creek Rd.
Landenberg PA 19350
610-255-0100
dale@northcreeknurseries.com
WHOLESALE/MAIL ORDER
PLANTS ONLY

Comments: 70% native: 100% propagated from stock. Specializes in the sale of shrubs, annuals, grasses, and perennials in cell packs or plugs. Custom-grown orders taken with adequate notice. Catalog cost: free.

Northplan/Mountain Seed

PO Box 9107
Moscow ID 83843-1607
208-882-8040
norplan@moscow.com
WHOLESALE/MAIL ORDER
SEEDS ONLY

Comments: 98% native: 60% wild-collected seed, 40% from various seed houses. Specializes in North American native seed. Supplier for land restoration projects. Catalog cost: $ 1.00 or #10 SASE.

Northwest Native Seed

4441 S. Meridian St. #363
Puyallup WA 98144
RETAIL/MAIL ORDER
SEEDS ONLY

Comments: 100% native: 100% wild-collected seed. Specializes in seed collected from the western U.S., including alpines from the northern Rockies and California. Catalog cost: free.

Orchid Gardens

2232 139th Ave. NW
Andover MN 55304
RETAIL/MAIL ORDER
PLANTS ONLY

Comments: 95% native: 100% propagated from stock. Uncommon selection of northern woodland natives. Field grown in northern Minnesota. Bare-root mail order. Catalog cost: $ 1.00.

Paradise Water Gardens, Ltd.

14 May St., Rt. 18
Whitman MA 02382
781-447-4711
pstetson@paradisewatergardens.com
www.paradisewatergardens.com
WHOLESALE/RETAIL/MAIL ORDER
PLANTS ONLY

Comments: 50% native: 60% propagated from stock, 20% wild collected, and 20% from other nursery source. Specializes in water gardening offering their own product designs, hybridized aquatics, and fish. Catalog cost: $ 3.00.

Plant Delights Nursery

9241 Sauls Rd.
Raleigh NC 27603
919-772-4794
office@plantdel.com
www.plantdel.com
RETAIL/MAIL ORDER
PLANTS ONLY

Comments: 25% native: 95% propagated from stock and 5% from other nursery source. Specializes in breeding hostas and offering as new and strange a listing of perennials as possible. Catalog cost: 10 stamps or box of chocolate.

Plants of the Wild

PO Box 866, Willard Field
Tekoa WA 99033
509-284-2848
kathy@plantsofthewild.com
www.plantsofthewild.com
WHOLESALE/RETAIL/MAIL ORDER
PLANTS AND SEEDS

Comments: 99% native: 99% propagated from stock and 1% wild-collected seed. Specializes in natives including woody, wildflowers, grasses, and wetland. Container grown. Will contract grow species not listed. Catalog cost: $ 1.00.

Prairie Moon Nursery

Rt. 3, Box 163
Winona MN 55987
507-452-1362
pmnrsy@luminet.net
www.prairiemoonnursery.com
RETAIL/MAIL ORDER
PLANTS AND SEEDS

Comments: 100% native: 95% propagated from stock, 5% other nursery source. Natives for wetland, prairie, savanna, and woodland. Organic methods. Plants shipped bare-root. Custom seed mixes available. Catalog cost: free.

Prairie Nursery

PO Box 306
Westfield WI 53964
800-476-9453
customerservice@prairienursery.com
www.prairienursery.com
WHOLESALE/RETAIL/MAIL ORDER
PLANTS AND SEEDS

Comments: 100% native: majority propagated from stock. Specializes in prairie wildflowers, grasses, and sedges, as well as customized seed mixes. Consultation and other services available. Catalog cost: free.

Prairie Restorations, Inc.

PO Box 327
Princeton MN 55371
612-389-4342
prairie@sherbtel.net
www.prairieresto.com
WHOLESALE/RETAIL/MAIL ORDER
PLANTS AND SEEDS

Comments: 100% native: 99% propagated from stock and 1% wild collected, including *Trillium* (seed from nursery-owned land). Mail-order seed only. Specializes in prairie natives. Offers prairie management consultation. Catalog cost: free.

Prairie Ridge Nursery

9738 Overland Rd.
Mt. Horeb WI 53572
608-437-5245
crmeco@chorus.net
WHOLESALE/RETAIL/MAIL ORDER
PLANTS AND SEEDS

Comments: 100% native: 90% propagated from stock and 10% from other nursery source. Specializes in native restorations. Offers wildflowers, grasses, sedges, and rushes. Consultation services available. Catalog cost: free (restoration guide $5).

Prairie Seed Source

PO Box 83
North Lake WI 53064
RETAIL/MAIL ORDER
SEEDS ONLY

Comments: 100% native: 100% propagated from stock. Dedicated to the preservation and proliferation of southeastern Wisconsin prairie genotype and related ecosystem members. Catalog cost: $ 1.00.

The Primrose Path

921 Scottdale-Dawson Rd.
Scottsdale PA 15683
724-887-6756
primrose@a1usa.net
www.theprimrosepath.com
WHOLESALE/RETAIL/MAIL ORDER
PLANTS ONLY

Comments: 25–30% native: 100% propagated from stock with the exception of *Trillium sessile,* which was rescued. Specializes in shade-tolerant plants, including unique selections of *Asarum.* Catalog cost: $ 2.00.

Raising Rarities

PO Box 405
Jacksonville VT 05342
802-368-7273
RETAIL/MAIL ORDER
PLANTS ONLY

Comments: Source for mature *Cypripedium*s (Lady-slippers): 100% propagated from stock. (The result of 15 years of laboratory work on artificial seed germination.) Catalog cost: free.

Russell Graham, Purveyor of Plants

4030 Eagle Crest Rd. NW
Salem OR 97304
503-362-1135
WHOLESALE/RETAIL/MAIL ORDER
PLANTS ONLY

Comments: 50% native: 100% propagated from stock. Specializing in Pacific Northwestern and North American native perennials and unique companion species. Bare-root shipping. Catalog cost: $ 2.00.

Seeds of Change

PO Box 15700
Santa Fe, NM 87506
888-762-7333
gardener@seedsofchange.com
www.seedsofchange.com
RETAIL/MAIL ORDER
SEEDS ONLY

Comments: Network of organic farmers growing all of their own seed. Primarily vegetables and herbs including some native selections. Catalog cost: free.

Shooting Star Nursery

444 Bates Rd.
Frankfort KY 40601
502-223-1679
sevans007@aol.com
RETAIL/MAIL ORDER
PLANTS AND SEEDS

Comments: 100% native: 95% propagated from stock and 5% from other source. Specializes in eastern U.S. natives of forest, prairie, and wetland, especially Kentucky. Container and garden grown. Design consultation. Catalog cost: $ 2.00 (refundable).

Siskiyou Rare Plant Nursery

2825 Cummings Rd.
Medford OR 97501
541-772-6846
www.wave.net/upg/srpn
RETAIL/MAIL ORDER
PLANTS ONLY

Comments: 30% native: 100% propagated from stock. Grows hard-to-find hardy perennials, shrubs, and smaller conifers, and alpine and rock garden plants. Container and garden grown. Catalog cost: $ 3.00.

Smith Nursery Co.

PO Box 515
Charles City IA 50616
515-228-3239
WHOLESALE/RETAIL/MAIL ORDER
SEEDS ONLY

Comments: 70% native: 50% propagated from stock, 5% wild collected, and 45% from other nursery source. Specializes in trees and shrubs including shade trees, fruit bearing, and ornamental. Catalog cost: free.

Spangle Creek Labs

21950 County Rd. 445
Bovey MN 55709
218-247-0245
www.uslink.net/~scl
RETAIL/MAIL ORDER
PLANTS ONLY

Comments: Source for *Cypripedium* (Lady-slipper) seedlings only: 100% propagated from stock. Catalog cost: free.

Sunlight Gardens

174 Golden Ln.
Andersonville TN 37705
800-272-7396
sungardens@aol.com
www.sunlightgardens.com
WHOLESALE/RETAIL/MAIL ORDER
PLANTS ONLY
Comments: 80% native: 75% propagated from stock and 25% from other nursery source. Specializes in eastern natives for retail through mail-order only. Shipped in 3½-inch pots. Catalog cost: free.

Sylva Native Nursery & Seed Co.

1683 Sieling Farm Rd.
New Freedom PA 17349
717-227-0486
plants@sylvanative.com
www.sylvanative.com
WHOLESALE/MAIL ORDER
PLANTS AND SEEDS
Comments: 100% native: 70% wild-collected seed or cuttings, and 30% from other nursery source. Offers wetland, riparian, and upland forest and meadow plant species, including trees. Bioengineering products. Catalog cost: free.

Van Engelen, Inc.

23 Tulip Dr.
Bantum CT 06750
860-567-8734
catalog@vanengelen.com
www.vanengelen.com
WHOLESALE/RETAIL/MAIL ORDER
PLANTS ONLY
Comments: 5% native: 100% propagated from stock. Specializes in bulbs, including *Camassia* and *Erythronium.* Catalog cost: free.

Virginia Natives

PO Box D
Hume VA 22639-0903
540-364-1665
vanatus@erols.com
WHOLESALE/RETAIL/MAIL ORDER
PLANTS ONLY
Comments: 70% native: 75% propagated from stock, 25% from other nursery source. Specializes in regional natives to eastern U.S.: wildflowers, ferns, grasses, shrubs, and trees. Catalog cost: $ 1.25.

WE-DU Nurseries

Rt. 5, Box 724
Polly Spout Rd.
Marion NC 28752
828-738-8300
wedu@wnclink.com
www.we-du.com

RETAIL/MAIL ORDER
PLANTS ONLY
Comments: 50% native: 95% propagated from stock, including *Trillium* and orchid, 3% wild collected, and 2% other nursery source. Specializes in natives and collector rarities of bulbs, perennials, and woody—also oriental counterparts. Catalog cost: $ 2.00.

Wetlands Nursery

PO Box 14553
Saginaw MI 48601
517-752-3492
jewelr@aol.com
WHOLESALE/RETAIL/MAIL ORDER
PLANTS AND SEEDS
Comments: 100% native: 100% propagated from stock. Specializes in wetland plant species native to Michigan. On-site project consulting services on wetland ecology. Catalog cost: free.

White Flower Farm

PO Box 50, Rt. 63
Litchfield CT 06759-0050
800-503-9624
custserv@whiteflowerfarm.com
www.whiteflowerfarm.com
WHOLESALE/RETAIL/MAIL ORDER
PLANTS AND SEEDS
Comments: 17% native: 92% propagated from stock. Offers wide range of annuals, bulbs, perennials, shrubs, and houseplants. Field and greenhouse grown. Catalog cost: free.

Wild Earth Native Plant Nursery

PO Box 7258
Freehold NJ 07728
732-308-9777
wildearthnpn@compuserve.com
WHOLESALE/RETAIL/MAIL ORDER
PLANTS ONLY
Comments: 98% native: 100% propagated from stock, including orchid. Specializes in eastern U.S. flora. Seed-propagated plant material whenever possible to maintain genetic diversity. Catalog cost: $ 2.00.

Wild Ginger Woodlands

PO Box 1091
Webster NY 14580
RETAIL/MAIL ORDER
SEEDS ONLY
Comments: 75% native: 80% propagated from stock and 20% other nursery source . Caters to the home gardener specializing in seeds of northeastern woodlanders. Catalog cost: $ 1.50 (refundable).

Windrose Nursery

1093 Mill Rd.
Pen Arlyl PA 18072-9670
610-588-1037
windrose@epix.net
RETAIL/MAIL ORDER
PLANTS ONLY

Comments: Offers a wide variety from perennials to shrubs to trees with an emphasis on providing material that may be used to reestablish natural ecosystems. Will contract grow wholesale to professionals. Catalog cost: $ 3.00.

Woodlanders, Inc.

1128 Colleton Ave.
Aiken SC 29801
803-648-7522
woodlanders@triplet.net
RETAIL/MAIL ORDER
PLANTS ONLY

Comments: 70% native: 85% propagated from stock and 15% from other nursery source. Specializes in southeastern U.S. natives, including trees, yuccas, palms, grasses, ferns, bulbs, tubers, and nursery-propagated endangered plants. Catalog cost: $ 2.00.

SELECTED NATIVE PLANT SOCIETIES
OF THE UNITED STATES AND CANADA

ALABAMA
Alabama Wildflower Society
c/o Caroline R. Dean
606 India Rd.
Opelika AL 36801
334-745-2494
www.auburn.edu/~deancar/

ALASKA
Alaska Native Plant Society
PO Box 141613
Anchorage AK 99514-1613
907-333-8212

ARIZONA
Arizona Native Plant Society
PO Box 41206
Sun Station
Tucson AZ 85717-1206
www.azstarnet.com/~anps/

ARKANSAS
Arkansas Native Plant Society
PO Box 250250
Little Rock AR 72225
501-460-1066
www.anps.org

CALIFORNIA
American Iris Society
PO Box 55
Freedom CA 95019
www.irises.org

California Botanical Society
c/o Herbarium, Life Sci. Bldg.
University of California
Berkeley CA 94720
http://ucjeps.herb.berkelee.edu/cbs/

California Native Plant Society
Allen Barnes, Exec. Dir.
1722 J St., Suite 17
Sacramento CA 95814-2931
916-447-2677
www.calpoly.edu/~dchippin/dev/cnps.
main.html

Southern California Botanists
Dept. of Biology
California State University
Fullerton CA 92834
714-448-7034

Theodore Payne Foundation
10459 Tuxford St.
Sun Valley CA 91352
818-768-1802

COLORADO
American Penstemon Society
1569 South Holland Court
Lakewood CO 80266

Colorado Native Plant Society
PO Box 200
Fort Collins CO 80522-0200
303-443-9365
http://carbon.cudenver.edu/~shill/conp
s.html

CONNECTICUT
Connecticut Botanical Society
Casper J. Ultee, pres.
55 Harvest Ln.
Glastonbury CT 06033
860-633-7557
www.vfr.com/cbs/

Connecticut Chapter
New England Wild Flower Society
Ellen Bender
25 Lanz Ln.
Ellington CT 06029-2310
860-871-8085
www.newfs.org/ct

DISTRICT OF COLUMBIA
Botanical Society of Washington
Dept. of Botany, NHB 166
Smithsonian Institution
Washington DC 20560
www.fred.net/kathy/bsw.html

FLORIDA
Florida Native Plant Society
PO Box 690278
Vero Beach FL 32969-0278
561-562-1598
www.fnps.org

GEORGIA
Georgia Botanical Society
Teresa Ware, Memberchair
2 Idlewood Court NW
Rome GA 30165-1210
706-232-3435
http://science.kennshaw.edu/org/gabot-
soc

Georgia Native Plant Society
PO Box 422085
Atlanta GA 30342-2085
770-343-6000
www.mindspring.com/~gnps/

HAWAII
Native Hawaiian Plant Society
PO Box 5021
Kahului HI 96733-5021
www.mrtc.org/~thomasp/nhps/

IDAHO
Idaho Native Plant Society
PO Box 9451
Boise ID 83707-3451
www.state.id.us/fishgame/inps.htm

ILLINOIS
Illinois Native Plant Society
Forest Glen Preserve
20301 E. 900 North Rd.
Westville IL 61883
www.vccd.org

INDIANA
Indiana Native Plant & Wildflower
    Society
Michael Stiffler, Treas.
2606 S 600W
Morgantown IN 46106
317-422-8914
www.inpaws.org

IOWA
Iowa Prairie Network
PO Box 516
Mason City Iowa 50402-0516
www.netins.net/showcase/bluestem/ipn
    app.htm

KANSAS
Kansas Wildflower Society
c/o R.L.McGregor Herbarium
University of Kansas
2045 Constant Ave.
Lawrence KS 66047-3729
913-864-3453
www.feist.com/~wichitacsj/kwsweb

KENTUCKY
Kentucky Native Plant Society
Dept. of Biological Science
E. Kentucky University
Richmond KY 40475
606-622-2258
http://www.biology.eku.edu/jones/knps.
    htm

LOUISIANA
Louisiana Native Plant Society
Jessie Johnson, Treas.
216 Caroline Dormon Rd.
Saline, LA 71010

MAINE
Josselyn Botanical Society
Rick Speer, Corr. Secty.
566 N. Auburn Rd.
Auburn ME 04210

Maine Chapter
New England Wild Flower Society
Ginger Carr, Pres.
RR 1, Box 79, Sawyer's Island
Boothbay ME 04537
207-633-4327

MARYLAND
Maryland Native Plant Society
PO Box 4877
Silver Spring MD 20914
www.geocities.com/RainForest/vines/
    2996

MASSACHUSETTS
New England Botanical Club
22 Divinity Ave.
Cambridge MA 02138
617-308-3656 (Ray Angelo)
www.herbaria.harvard.edu/nebc

New England Wild Flower Society
180 Hemenway Rd.
Framingham MA 01701-2699
508-877-7630
www.newfs.org

Cape Cod Chapter
New England Wild Flower Society
Lenore M. Clarke
33 Lakeway Ln.
Harwich MA 02645-2031
508-432-4188

MICHIGAN
Michigan Botanical Club
University of Michigan
Herbarium, North Univ. Building
1205 N. University
Ann Arbor MI 48109-1057
http://www.michbotclub.org

MINNESOTA
Minnesota Native Plant Society
220 Bio. Sci. Center
University of Minnesota
1445 Gortner Ave.
St. Paul MN 55108-1020
www.stolaf.edu/depts/biology/mnps/

MISSISSIPPI
Mississippi Native Plant Society
Ron Wieland
Mississippi Museum of Natural Science
111 N. Jefferson St.
Jackson MS 39202
601-354-7303

MISSOURI
Missouri Native Plant Society
P.O Box 20073
St. Louis MO 63144-0073
314-577-9522
http://web.missouri.edu/~umo_herb/
    monps/index.html

MONTANA
Montana Native Plant Society
PO Box 8783
Missoula MT 59807-8783

NEVADA
Northern Nevada Native Plant Society
PO Box 8965
Reno NV 89507-8965
775-852-0733
www.state.nv.us/nvnhp/nnnps.htm

NEW HAMPSHIRE
New Hampshire Chapter
New England Wild Flower Society
Anne Moore, Pres.
8 Boulters Cove
North Hampton NH 03862
603-964-1982
www.newfs,org/nh/nh.htm

NEW JERSEY
The Native Plant Society of New Jersey
PO Box 231
Cook College
New Brunswick NJ 08903-0231
908-671-6400

NEW MEXICO
Native Plant Society of New Mexico
PO Box 5917
Santa Fe NM 87502-5917
www.zianet.com/npsnm/

NEW YORK
Long Island Botanical Society
Eric Lamont, Pres.
Biology Dept.
Riverhead High School
Riverhead
Long Island NY 11901
http://pbisotopos.ess.sunysb.edu/molins
    /libs/libs.htm/

New York Flora Association
New York State Museum
3132 CEC
Albany NY 12230

Niagara Frontier Botanical Society
Buffalo Museum of Science
1020 Humboldt Parkway
Buffalo NY 14211

The Finger Lakes Native Plant Society of
    Ithaca
Cornell Cooperative Extension
615 Willow Ave.
Ithaca NY 14850

NORTH CAROLINA
North Carolina Wildflower Preservation
    Society
North Carolina Botanical Garden
PO Box 3375 Totten Center
Univ. of North Carolina
Chapel Hill, NC 27599-3375

Western Carolina Botanical Club
Elton & Aline Hansens
125 Far Horizons Ln.
Givens Estates
Asheville NC 28803
704-277-7486

OHIO
Central Ohio Native Plant Society
Sharon A. Treaster, Program Chair
1315 Kinnear Rd.
Columbus OH 43212
614-846-8419
www.-obs.biosci.ohio-state.edu/coplant.
    htm

Cincinnati Wildflower Preservation
    Society
Bill Eisele, Treas.
9005 Decima St.
Cincinnati OH 45242
216-761-2568

Native Plant Society of Northeastern
    Ohio
Tom Sampliner
2651 Kenwick Rd.
University Heights OH 44118
216-321-3702

OKLAHOMA
Oklahoma Native Plant Society
Tulsa Garden Center
2435 S. Peoria
Tulsa OK 74114-1350
918-496-2218
www.telepath.com/chadcox/onps/index.
    html

OREGON
Native Plant Society of Oregon
PO Box 902
Eugene OR 97440
www.npsoregon.org

PENNSYLVANIA
Botanical Society of Western PA
Loree Speedy, editor
5837 Nicholson St.
Pittsburgh PA 15217
412-521-9425

Delaware Valley Fern & Wildflower
    Society
Dana Cartwright
263 Hillcrest Rd.
Wayne PA 19087
215-687-0918

Muhlenberg Botanical Society
Franklin and Marshall College
North Museum
PO Box 3003
Lancaster PA 17604

Pennsylvania Native Plant Society
Robert M. Gruver, Treas.
PO Box 281
State College PA 16804-0281

RHODE ISLAND
Rhode Island Wild Plant Society
Deborah Poor, Exec. Dir.
PO Box 114
Peace Dale RI 02883-0114
401-783-5895

SOUTH CAROLINA
South Carolina Native Plant Society
Rick Huffman, Pres.
PO Box 759
Pickens SC 29671
864-868-7798
http://cufp.clemson.edu/scnativeplants/

Southern Appalachian Botanical Club
Charles N. Horn, Secty/Treas.
Newberry College, Biology Dept.
2100 College St.
Newberry SC 29108
803-321-5257

Wildflower Alliance of South Carolina
PO Box 12181
Columbia SC 29211
803-799-6889

SOUTH DAKOTA
Great Plains Native Plant Society
Cindy Reed
PO Box 461
Hot Springs SD 57747-0461

TENNESSEE
American Association of Field Botanists
PO Box 23542
Chattanooga, TN 37422

Tennsssee Native Plant Society
Dept. of Botany
University of Tennessee
Knoxville TN 37996-1100
423-974-2256

TEXAS
El Paso Native Plant Society
7760 Maya Avenue
El Paso TX 79912
915-584-8690

Ladybird Johnson Wildflower Center
4801 La Crosse Blvd.
Austin TX 78739
512-292-4200
www.wildflower.org

Native Plant Society of Texas
Dana Tucker, Coordinator
PO Box 891
Georgetown TX 78627-0891
512-238-0695
www.npsot.org

UTAH
Utah Native Plant Society
Pam Poulson
PO Box 520041
Salt Lake City UT 84152-0041
801-581-3744

VERMONT
Vermont Botanical and Bird Clubs
Deborah Benjamin, Secty.
Warren Rd., Box 327
Eden VT 05652
802-635-7794

Vermont Chapter
New England Wild Flower Society
Thelma Hewitt, Pres.
PO Box 307
Woodstock VT 05071
www.newfs.org/vermont/index.htm

VIRGINIA

Virginia Native Plant Society
Blandy Experimental Farm
400 Blandy Farm Ln., Unit 2
Boyce VA 22620
540-837-1600
www.vnps.org

WASHINGTON

Washington Native Plant Society
Catherine Hovanic, Admin. Assist.
PO Box 28690
Seattle WA 98118-8690
206-760-8022
www.wnps.org

WEST VIRGINIA

West Virginia Native Plant Society
PO Box 75403
Charleston WV 25375-0403

WISCONSIN

Botanical Club of Wisconsin
Wisconsin Academy of Arts,
Sciences and Letters
1922 University Ave.
Madison WI 53705

WYOMING

Wyoming Native Plant Society
PO Box 3452
Laramie WY 82071
www.rmh.uwyo.edu/wnps.html/

CANADA

North American Native Plant Society
Box 336, Postal Sta. F
Toronto ON M4Y 2L7
Canada
416-924-6807
www.acorn-online.com/hedge/
cws.html

Alberta Native Plant Council
52099 Garneau Postal Outlet
Edmonton AB T6G 2T5
Canada

Field Botanists of Ontario,
c/o W.D. McIlveen, RR.#1,
Acton ON L7J 2L7
Canada

Native Plant Society of British Columbia
Diane Gertzen
14275-96th Ave.
Surrey BC V3V 7Z2
Canada
604-255-5719

The Wildflower Society of Newfound-
land and Labrador
c/o the MVN Botanical Garden
Memorial University of Newfoundland
Saint John's NF A1C 5S7
Canada

Nova Scotia Wild Flora Society
Nova Scotia Museum
1747 Summer St.
Halifax NS B3H 3A6
Canada
www.navnet.net/~csensen/index.htm

Flora Quebeca
83 rue Chenier
Saint-Eustache PQ J7R 1W9
Canada

Selected Botanic Gardens and Arboreta Specializing in Native Plant Display Collections and/or Conservation

ARIZONA

Arboretum at Flagstaff
PO Box 670
Flagstaff AZ 86002
520-774-1442
www.flagguide.com/arboretum

Desert Botanical Garden
1201 North Galvin Pkwy.
Papago Park
Phoenix AZ 85008
480-941-1225
www.dbg.org

CALIFORNIA

Rancho Santa Ana Botanic Garden
100 North College Ave.
Claremont CA 91711-3157
909-625-8767
http://www.cgu.edu/inst/rsa/index.html

Santa Barbara Botanic Garden
1212 Mission Canyon Rd.
Santa Barbara CA 93105
805-682-4726
www.sbbg.org

University of California Botanical
Garden
200 Centennial Dr. #5045
Berkeley CA 94720-5045
510-642-0849

COLORADO

Denver Botanic Gardens
909 York St.
Denver CO 80206
303-331-4000
www.botanicgardens.org

DELAWARE

Mt. Cuba Center for the Study of the
Piedmont Flora
PO Box 3570
Greenville DE 19807-0570
302-239-4244
(visitors by appointment)

FLORIDA

Bok Tower Gardens
1151 Tower Blvd.
Lake Wales FL 33853-3412
941-676-1408
www.boktower.org

Fairchild Tropical Garden
10901 Old Cutler Rd.
Miami FL 33156-4299
305-667-1651
www.ftg.org

GEORGIA

State Botanical Garden of Georgia
University of Georgia
2450 S. Milledge Ave.
Athens GA 30605
706-542-1244
www.uga.edu/~botgarden

HAWAII

Harold L. Lyon Arboretum
University of Hawaii
3860 Manoa Rd.
Honolulu HI 96822-1254
808-988-0455
www.botany.hawaii.edu/lyon

National Tropical Botanical Garden
PO Box 340
Lawai HI 96765
808-332-7324
http://www.ntbg.org/index.html

ILLINOIS
Chicago Botanic Garden
1000 Lake Cook Rd.
Glencoe IL 60022
847-835-5440
www.chicago-botanic.org

Morton Arboretum
4100 Illinois Rte. 53
Lisle IL 60532-1293
630-968-0074
www.mortonarg.org

MASSACHUSETTS
Arnold Arboretum
Harvard University
125 Arborway
Jamaica Plain MA 02130-3500
617-524-1718
www.arboretum.harvard.edu

New England Wild Flower Society
Garden in the Woods
180 Hemenway Rd.
Framingham MA 01701-2699
508-877-7630
www.newfs.org

MINNESOTA
Minnesota Landscape Arboretum
University of Minnesota
3675 Arboretum Dr., Box 39
Chanhassen MN 55317
612-443-2460
www.arboretum.umn.edu/fall_index.
    htm

MISSOURI
Missouri Botanical Garden
PO Box 299
Saint Louis MO 63166-0299
314-577-5111
www.mobot.org

NEBRASKA
Nebraska Statewide Arboretum
PO Box 830715
University of Nebraska
Lincoln NE 68583-0715
402-472-2971

NEW YORK
Brooklyn Botanic Garden
1000 Washington Ave.
Brooklyn NY 11225-1099
718-622-4433
www.bbg.org

New York Botanical Garden
200 St. and Southern Blvd.
Bronx NY 01458-5126
718-817-8700
www.nybg.org

NORTH CAROLINA
North Carolina Botanical Garden
PO Box 3375, Totten Center
University of North Carolina
Chapel Hill NC 27599-3375
919-962-0522
http://ils.unc.edu/hiking/NCBOT.HTM

North Carolina Arboretum
100 Frederick Law Olmstead Way
Asheville NC 28806-9315
828-665-2492

OHIO
Holden Arboretum
9500 Sperry Rd
Kirtland OH 44094-5172
440-256-1110
www.holdenarb.org

OREGON
Berry Botanic Garden
11505 SW Summerville Ave.
Portland OR 97219-8309
503-636-4112
www.berrybot.org

PENNSYLVANIA
Bowman's Hill State Wildflower Pre-
    serve
Washington Crossing Historic Park
PO Box 685
New Hope PA 18938-0685
215-862-2924
www.bhwp.org

TEXAS
Mercer Arboretum and Botanic Gardens
22306 Aldine-Westfield Rd.
Humble TX 77338-1071
281-443-8731

San Antonio Botanical Gardens
555 Funston Pl.
San Antonio TX 78209
210-207-3255
www.sabot.org

UTAH
Red Butte Garden and Arboretum
University of Utah
18A deTrobriand St.
Salt Lake City UT 84113-5044
801-581-4747
www.utah.edu/redbutte

WASHINGTON, DC
U.S. National Arboretum
3501 New York Ave., NE
Washington DC 20002-1958
202-245-4523
www.ars-grin.gov/ars/beltville/na

WISCONSIN
University of Wisconsin Arboretum
1207 Seminole Highway
Madison WI 53711
608-262-2746
http://wiscinfo.doit.wisc.edu/arbore-
    tum/

CANADA
Memorial University of Newfoundland
Botanical Garden
St John's NF A1C 5S7
Canada
709-737-8590
www.mun.ca/botgarden

Montreal Botanical Garden
4101 Sherbrooke East
Montreal PQ H1X 2B2
Canada
514-872-1400
www.ville.montreal.qc.ca/jardin/en

Royal Botanical Gardens
PO Box 399
Hamilton ON L8N 3H8
Canada
905-527-1158
www.rbg.ca

University of Alberta Devonian Botanic
    Garden
Edmonton AB T6G 2E1
Canada
403-987-3054
www.discoveredmonton.com

University of British Columbia
   Botanical Garden
6804 SW Marine Dr.
Vancouver BC V6T 1Z4
Canada
604-822-3928
www.hedgerows.com

VanDusen Botanical Garden
5251 Oak St.
Vancouver BC V6M 4H1
Canada
604-257-8666
www.hedgerows.com/VanDusen

Related Organizations

American Association of Botanic
   Gardens and Arboreta
351 Longwood Rd
Kennett Square PA 19348
610-925-2500
www.aabga.org

American Horticultural Society
7931 East Boulevard Dr.
Alexandria VA 22308-1300
703-768-5700
www.ahs.org

Canadian Botanical Conservation
   Network
PO Box 399
Hamilton ON L8N 3H8
Canada
905-527-1158 x309
www.rbg.ca/cbcn

Center for Plant Conservation
Missouri Botanical Garden
PO Box 299
St. Louis MO 63166-0299
314-577-9450
www.mobot.org/CPC

Garden Club of America
598 Madison Ave.
New York NY 10022
212-753-8287
www.gcamerica.org

Lady Bird Johnson Wildflower Center
4801 LaCrosse Blvd.
Austin TX 78739
512-292-4200
www.wildflower.org

National Council of State Garden Clubs
4401 Magnolia Ave,
St. Louis MO 63110
314-776-7574

Native Plant Conservation Initiative
Bureau of Land Management
Fish, Wildlife, and Forest Group WO 230
1849 C St., NW, LSB-204
Washington DC 20240
202-452-0392
www.nps.gov/plants

Perennial Plant Association
3383 Schirtzinger Rd
Hilliard OH 43026
614-771-8431
www.perennialplant.org

Society for Ecological Restoration
PO Box 41626
Tucson AZ 85717
520-626-7201
www.ser.org

PHOTO CREDITS

Jean S. Baxter/NEWFS: 89, 137, 171, 198
Berry Botanic Garden: 217
Frank Bramley/NEWFS: 13 third from top, 40, 44, 191, 206, 218
Albert Bussewitz/NEWFS: 5 left, 12 second from right, 12 right, 53, 68 right, 70, 111, 156, 166 right, 168, 195, 203, 207, 233 bottom
Jeff Carmichael/NEWFS: viii–ix, xiv–1, 83
William Cullina/NEWFS: ix second from top, 23, 24 top, 24 bottom, 25, 26, 28, 29, 31, 43, 72, 75, 78, 90, 92 left, 99 right, 106 right, 119, 130 left, 145, 149, 150, 155 top, 160 left, 161, 169, 172, 181 right, 184 right, 186, 204, 209, 219, 232, 233 second from top, 234, 237, 239, 240, 270
R. Todd Davis Photography: 19, 118, 125, 160 right, 193
Steven Foster Photography: 47, 55, 155 bottom
Carol Fyler/NEWFS: 101 right
Catherine Heffron/NEWFS: 50
Hal Horwitz: 77, 200
Hal Horwitz/NEWFS: vii top, vii second from top, 6 top, 8, 9, 46, 82, 93, 126 right, 140 right, 196, 201 left, 211, 231, 233 third from top
William Larkin: 1 top left, 13 top right, 61, 85, 117
William Larkin/NEWFS: 12 left, 13 second from top, 20, 51, 71 right, 199, 224, 233 top right
Dorothy S. Long/NEWFS: ii–iii, iv–v, vii bottom, x–xi, xi second from top, 1 second from top, 2 right, 3, 4, 10, 13 top left, 14, 32 inset, 38, 48, 49, 54, 57, 64, 74, 84, 96, 104, 108, 110, 124, 126 left, 131, 132, 134, 135, 136 left, 138 left, 139, 140 left, 142 right, 146, 147, 163, 175, 178, 184 left, 201 right, 212, 220, 222 left, 227, 233 top left, 267, 277, 278

David R. Longland/NEWFS: 180
Cheryl B. Lowe/NEWFS: 182
John A. Lynch/NEWFS: vii third from top, ix bottom, xi top, xi third from top, 1 top right, 2 left, 7, 16, 30, 32, 33, 34, 36, 41, 58, 60, 62, 67, 69, 71 left, 79, 80, 87, 91, 95, 101 left, 103, 105, 106 left, 113 right, 114, 116 left, 129, 130 right, 133, 138 right, 144, 148, 152, 158, 162, 164, 165, 170, 173 left, 173 right, 174, 176, 177 left, 177 right, 190 left, 190 right, 192, 197, 205, 214, 215 left, 222 right, 225 left, 225 right, 242, 274
Charles Mann Photography: 5 right, 11, 13 bottom, 35, 45, 65, 86, 88, 107, 109, 128, 142 left, 157, 179, 188, 226, 228, 230
Lawrence Newcomb/NEWFS: 189
NEWFS: xi bottom, 123, 136 right, 181 left
Walt and Louiseann Pietrowitz/NEWFS: vi–vii, 1 third from top, 15, 59, 63, 202, 208, 273
Adelaide M. Pratt/NEWFS: ix top, 121, 143, 216
Willa Schmidt/NEWFS: 1 bottom, 92 right, 98
Steven Scrimshaw: ix third from top, 113 left, 116 right, 154
Anne Sears/NEWFS: 215 right
Paul Somers: 68 left
Arieh Tal: 166 left
Arieh Tal/NEWFS: 6 bottom, 12 second from left, 99 left
Lucien Taylor/NEWFS: 42

Hardiness Zone Map

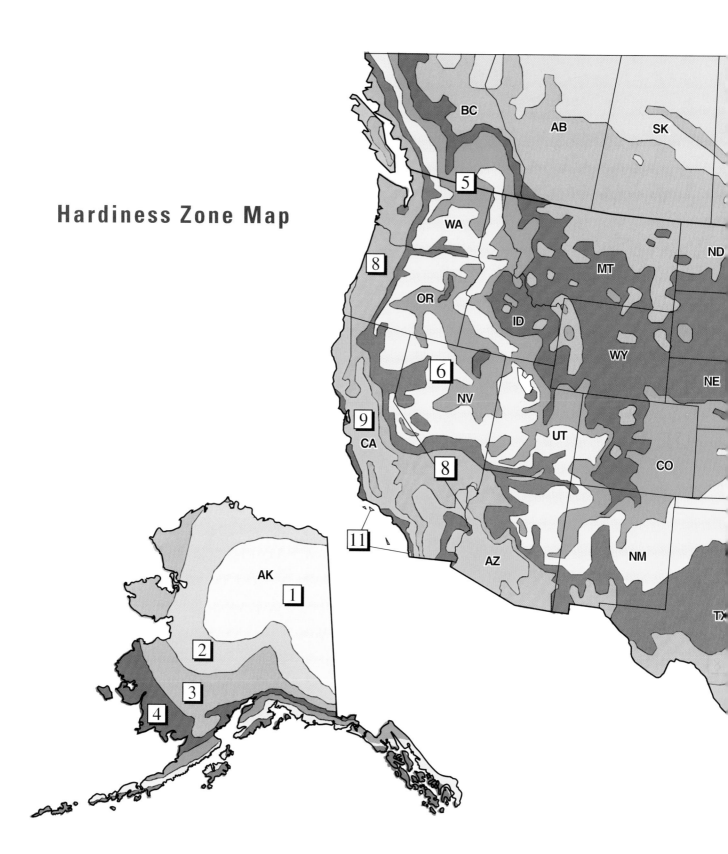

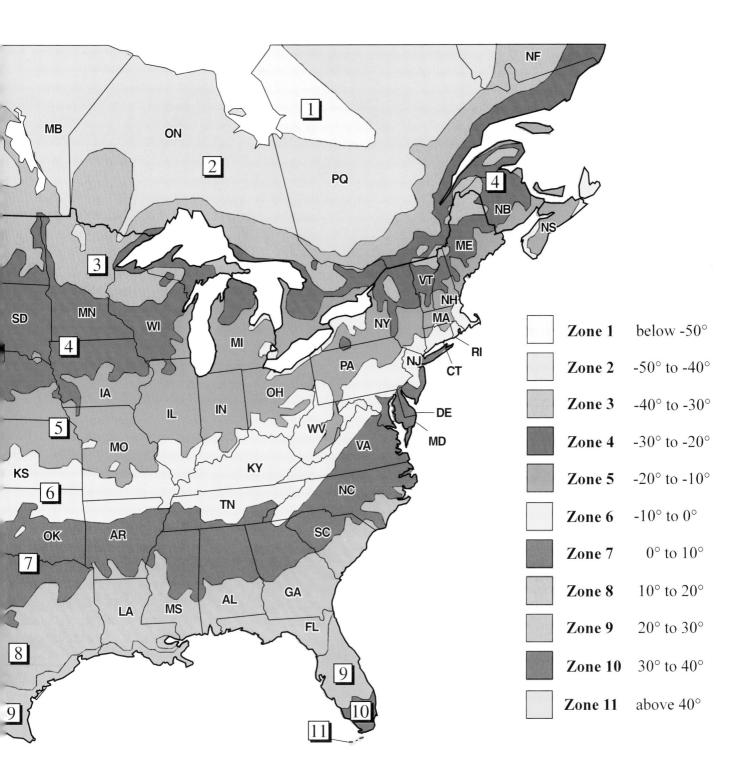

Zone 1   below -50°

Zone 2   -50° to -40°

Zone 3   -40° to -30°

Zone 4   -30° to -20°

Zone 5   -20° to -10°

Zone 6   -10° to 0°

Zone 7   0° to 10°

Zone 8   10° to 20°

Zone 9   20° to 30°

Zone 10   30° to 40°

Zone 11   above 40°

NOTES

1. (p. 8) Robert G. Bailey. 1995. *Description of the Ecoregions of the United States* (Miscellaneous Publication 1391), second edition. Washington: USDA Forest Service. pp. 3–88.
2. (p. 8) Michael G. Barbour and William D. Billings. 1988. *North American Terrestrial Vegetation.* Cambridge, England: Cambridge University Press.
3. (p. 34) A. Bacon. 1903. An Experiment with the Fruit of Red Baneberry. *Rhodora.* Vol. 5: 77–78.
4. (p. 126) Robert L. Dressler. 1993. *Phylogeny and Classification of the Orchid Family.* Portland, OR: Diosconides Press. pp. 60–61.
5. (p. 154) John Harper. 1977. *Population Biology of Plants.* London: Academic Press. pp. 501–502.
6. (p. 155) Andrew Chevallier. 1996. *The Encyclopedia of Medicinal Plants.* New York: DK Publishing. pp. 116, 241.
7. (p. 164) Henry A. Gleason and Arthur Cronquist. 1991. *Manual of Vascular Plants of the Northeastern United States and Adjacent Canada,* second edition. New York: New York Botanical Garden. p. 449.
8. (p. 165) L. H. Pammel. 1911. *A Manual of Poisonous Plants.* Cedar Rapids, Iowa: The Torch Press. p. 471.
9. (p. 191) H. Lincoln Foster. 1982. *Rock Gardening.* Portland, Oregon: Timber Press. pp. 307–326.
10. (p. 218) Chevallier. p. 279.
11. (p. 248) Carson Whitlow. 1989. Conference Proceedings from North American Native Terrestrial Orchid Propagation and Production. pp. 71–72.
12. (p. 255) Norman J. Deno. 1994. *Seed Germination Theory and Practice,* second edition. State College, Pa.: published by the author. pp. 153.
13. (p. 256) Deno. p. 160.
14. (p. 256) Deno. p. 187.

BIBLIOGRAPHY

Allen, Carol, editor. North American Native Terrestrial Orchids, Propagation and Production—Conference Proceedings 1996. Germantown, Maryland: North American Native Terrestrial Orchid Conference, 1996.

Bailey, Liberty H., and Ethel Z. Bailey, et al. *Hortus Third.* New York: Macmillan Publishing Company, Inc., 1976.

Bailey, Robert G. *Description of the Ecoregions of the United States* (Miscellaneous Publication 1391), second edition. Washington, USDA Forest Service, 1995.

Barbour, Michael G., and William D. Billings. *North American Terrestrial Vegetation.* Cambridge, England: Cambridge University Press, 1988.

Barkley, T. M., et al., editors. *Flora of the Great Plains.* Lawrence: University Press of Kansas, 1986.

Baskin, Carol C., and Jerry M. Baskin. *Seeds: Ecology, Biogeography, and Evolution of Dormancy and Germination.* San Diego: Academic Press, 1998.

Beckett, Kenneth, editor. *Alpine Garden Society Encyclopedia of Alpines,* volumes 1–2. Dorchester, England: Friary Press, 1994.

Benson, Lyman. *The Cacti of the United States and Canada.* Stanford, California: Stanford University Press, 1982.

Case, Frederick W., and Roberta B. Case. *Trilliums.* Portland, Oregon: Timber Press, 1997.

Chevallier, Andrew. *The Encyclopedia of Medicinal Plants.* New York: DK Publishing, 1996.

Clausen, Ruth R., and Nicolas H. Ekstrom. *Perennials for American Gardens.* New York: Random House, 1989.

Coffey, Timothy. *The History and Folklore of North American Wildflowers.* Boston: Houghton Mifflin Company, 1993.

Correll, Donovan S., and Marshall C. Johnston. *Manual of the Vascular Plants of Texas.* Richardson: University of Texas at Dallas, 1979.

Cronquist, Arthur, et al. *Intermountain Flora: Vascular Plants of the Intermountain West, U.S.A.* volumes 1–5. New York: New York Botanical Garden, 1994.

Deno, Norman C. *Seed Germination Theory and Practice,* second edition. State College, Pennsylvania: published by the author, 1994.

Dressler, Robert L. *Phylogeny and Classification of the Orchid Family.* Portland, Oregon: Diosconides Press, 1993.

Foster, H. Lincoln. *Rock Gardening.* Portland, Oregon: Timber Press, 1982.

Gleason, Henry A., and Arthur Cronquist. *Manual of Vascular Plants of the Northeastern United States and Adjacent Canada,* second edition. New York: New York Botanical Garden, 1991.

Harper, John L. *Population Biology of Plants.* London: Academic Press, 1977.

Haskin, Leslie L. *Wild Flowers of the Pacific Coast.* Portland, Oregon: Metropolitan Press, 1934.

Hitchcock, C. Leo, and Arthur Cronquist. *Flora of the Pacific Northwest.* Seattle: University of Washington Press, 1987.

Holmgren, Noel H. *The Illustrated Companion to Gleason and Cronquist's Manual.* New York: New York Botanic Garden, 1998.

Howe, William H. *The Butterflies of North America.* Garden City, New York: Doubleday and Company, Inc., 1975.

Jelitto, Leo, and Wilhelm Schacht. *Hardy Herbaceous Perennials,* volumes 1–2, Portland, Oregon: Timber Press, 1990.

Jolivet, Pierre. *Interrelationship Between Insects and Plants.* Boca Raton, Florida: CRC Press, 1998.

Kartesz, John T. *A Synonymized Checklist of the Vascular Flora of the United States, Canada, and Greenland,* second edition, volume 2—*Thesaurus.* Portland, Oregon: Timber Press, 1994.

Martin, W. C., and C. R. Hutchins. *A Flora of New Mexico.* Germany: J. Cramer, 1980.

Millspaugh, Charles F. *American Medicinal Plants.* New York: Dover Publications, Inc., 1974.

Morin, Nancy R., et al., editors. *Flora of North America,* volume 3. Oxford, England: Oxford University Press, 1997.

Munz, Philip A. *A California Flora.* Berkeley: University of California Press, 1968.

Newcomb, Lawrence. *Newcomb's Wildflower Guide.* Boston: Little, Brown and Company, 1977.

Opler, Paul A. *A Field Guide to Eastern Butterflies.* Boston: Houghton Mifflin Company, 1992.

Pammel, L. H. *A Manual of Poisonous Plants.* Cedar Rapids, Iowa: The Torch Press, 1911.

Phillips, Harry R. *Growing and Propagating Wildflowers.* Chapel Hill: University of North Carolina Press, 1985.

Radford, Albert E., et al. *Manual of the Vascular Flora of the Carolinas.* Chapel Hill: University of North Carolina Press, 1978.

Raven, Peter H., et al. *Biology of Plants,* fifth edition. New York: Worth Publishers, 1992.

Sawyers, Claire E., editor. North American Native Terrestrial

Orchids, Propagation and Production — Conference Proceedings 1989. Chadds Ford, Pennsylvania: The Brandywine Conservancy, 1990.

Scott, Richard W. *The Alpine Flora of the Rocky Mountains,* volume 1. Salt Lake City: University of Utah Press, 1995.

Steyermark, Julian A. *Flora of Missouri.* Ames: Iowa State University Press, 1975.

Still, Steven M. *Manual of Herbaceous Ornamental Plants.* Champaign, Illinois: Stipes Publishing Company, 1988.

Voss, Edward G. *Michigan Flora.* Ann Arbor: University of Michigan, 1985.

Welsh, Stanley L. *A Utah Flora.* Provo, Utah: Brigham Young University, 1993.

Westbrooks, Randy G., and James W. Preacher. *Poisonous Plants of Eastern North America.* Columbia: University of South Carolina Press, 1986.

GLOSSARY

Abscission layer. A zone of specialized tissue where two plant parts, such as leaf and stem, separate.

Acidic. Having a pH under 7.0, as related to soils, generally found in high rainfall regions without limestone-derived soils.

Alkaline. Having a pH over 7.0, as related to soils, generally found in low rainfall and/or limestone regions.

Alkaloid. A large group of nitrogen-based compounds produced by plants, many poisonous or otherwise pharmacologically active.

Alpine. Technically any plants growing above treeline in the mountains, but horticulturally used more broadly to refer generally to mountain plants with low, cushion-forming or otherwise compact habits that are useful for the rock garden.

Alternate. Having flowers and leaves attached one per node —not paired.

Anther. The pollen-bearing tip of the male part of the flower (stamen).

Apomictic. Capable of setting seed without fertilization.

Aerial. Aboveground.

Axil. The point or angle where the stem connects to the leaf.

Axillary. Arising from an axil.

Biennial. Living only two seasons and typically forming a low rosette of leaves the first year and a tall flowering stem the next.

Bolt. The flowering pattern seen commonly in biennials but not limited to them, in which a rapidly elongating flower stem emerges from a clump of leaves.

Boreal. Northern—typically referring to the cold temperate, coniferous forests of northern North America and Eurasia.

Bract. A modified leaf associated with but not part of a flower or inflorescence, often brightly colored and acting in lieu of petals to attract pollinators.

Bulb. An underground shoot with leaves swollen and modified to act as energy storage organs.

Caespitose. Densely tufted or tightly clumped.

Callus. Thickened tissue, often associated with wound healing.

Calyx. The sepals of a flower taken as a group.

Carpel. The modified, fertile leaf that surrounds the seeds.

Caudex. A swollen, perennial, woody stem or base at or below ground level.

Cauline. Leaves attached to an aboveground stem, not the base of the plant.

Circumboreal. Literally around the north, meaning a distribution in both northern North America and Eurasia.

Cleistogamous. A flower that is self-pollinating and never opens.

Clumping. A habit of growth characterized by tightly spaced stems and/or rhizomes/bulbs.

Colony. Plants that form spreading patches or loose clumps connected by underground rhizomes or roots.

Compound. A leaf composed of two or more leaflets.

Connate. Grown together or fused.

Cordate. Heart-shaped, typically referring to the leaf base.

Corm. A swollen, underground stem used for food storage.

Corolla. The petals of a flower taken as a group.

Cotyledon. The first or embryonic leaf or leaves of a seed-ling.

Cross. Shorthand for a hybrid between two species or the act of creating such a hybrid with controlled pollination. Represented in the Latin name as an ×.

Crown. The typically enlarged junction of the stem and roots, important in herbaceous plants as the source of new stem buds.

Cushion-forming. Having a tight bun or pillow-shaped habit.

Cyme. A flat-topped flower cluster with flowers opening in the center first.

Deciduous. A plant that loses its leaves at the end of the growing season.

Dicot. Short for Dicotyledons, the class of angiosperms characterized as having two cotyledons, net-veined leaves, and flower parts typically in fours and fives.

Dioecious. A species that bears male and female flowers on separate individuals.

Diploid. Bearing a normal double set of chromosomes per cell.

Disk. A term that describes the specialized, compound flower structure at the center of an Asteraceae inflorescence.

Disk flower. The central, fertile flowers in an Asteraceae inflorescence.

Dryland. Plants originating from or adapted to environments receiving an average of ten inches or less of rain yearly.

Elaiosome. A fatty, oil-rich appendage on some seeds designed to attract ants for seed dispersal.

Endemic. Having a small native range encompassing a particular geographical area or region.

Endosperm. Tissues surrounding the seedling embryo designed for food storage.

Filiform. Slender, threadlike.

Frass. The fecal remains of insects.

Fruit. A ripened ovary and any affiliated tissue containing seeds.

GA₃. Gibberellic Acid. An important plant growth hormone that induces stem elongation, flowering, and seed germination. It is used to overcome dormancy in seeds requiring a period of cold stratification.

Genera. Plural of genus.

Genus. A group of closely related plants. The first (capitalized) word of the binomial Latin name.

Glabrous. Smooth, hairless.

Glaucous. A waxy bloom that covers leaves or stems and imparts a bluish cast.

Gyno-dioecious. A species in which there are some individuals with female flowers and others with perfect flowers.

Head. A dense cluster of flowers.

Herbaceous. Lacking woody stems, usually indicating the plant dies back to the ground in the dormant season.

Hirsute. Covered in coarse, stiff hairs.

Hybrid. A plant with parents that are different species or even different genera.

Hydrophilic. Water-loving; refers to seeds that are intolerant of dry storage.

Hypogeal. Germination in which the cotyledons remain underground and the first true leaf or leaves emerge aboveground(opposite of epigeal). Many hypogeal germinators are also two-stage germinators, requiring more than one season to emerge aboveground.

Inflorescence. A cluster of flowers.

Lanceolate. Lance-shaped. Long and narrow, widest below the middle.

Legumes. A family of plants (Fabiaceae) characterized in part by the presence of nitrogen-fixing bacteria in special nodules on the roots.

Linear. Long and narrow with nearly parallel edges.

Lip. An enlarged or irregular segment, typically the enlarged lower petal of orchids or petals of mints.

Lobed. Leaf margins that are deeply indented but not divided into separate leaflets.

Lodge. To fall over.

Mallet cutting. A soft wood cutting with an attached heal of older wood or rhizome.

Monocarpic. Flowering once then dying. Many monocarpic plants are annual or biennial, but some, like *Agaves*, live for many years before finally flowering.

Monocots. Short for Monocotyledons, the class of angiosperms characterized as having a single cotyledon, parallel veination, and flower parts typically in threes.

Monoecious. A species that bears both male and female flowers or perfect flowers on the same plant.

Morphological. Regarding form and structure.

Mycorrhizal. Modified roots containing mycorrhizal fungi.

Mycorrhizae. Plural of mycorrhiza, a symbiotic association between certain fungi and the roots of higher plants.

Nitrogen-fixing. Organisms (typically bacteria in the genera *Rhizobium* and *Bradyrhizobium*) capable of converting gaseous nitrogen into the fixed or reduced form ammonium that can be used in biological processes.

Node. Place on a stem where a leaf or leaves attach.

Oblong. Rectangular with rounded corners.

Obovate. Generally egg-shaped, but wider toward the tip.

Open-pollinated. Opposite of hand-pollinated. When the pollen that fertilizes the ovary is free to come from any available source. In gardens, open pollination can lead to hybridization between related species typically separated geographically in the wild.

Opposite. Having two flowers or leaves attached at the same node—paired.

Ovary. The structure that contains the ovules or seeds.

Ovate. Egg-shaped.

Ovipositor. An extension of the abdomen of certain female insects through which eggs are deposited.

Palmate. A radially lobed or divided leaf in which all segments originate from a central point as in the fingers of a hand.

Panicle. A branched inflorescence.

Pappus. The modified calyx found in the Aster family that forms bristles, wings, or parachutes on the seed to aid seed dispersal.

Pedicel. The stalk of a single flower in a flower cluster.

Peduncle. The primary stalk attaching a flower or inflorescence to the stem.

Pedunculate. Borne on a peduncle.

Perennial. Any plant with a life span of two years or more.

Perfect flower. Flower that has functional male and female parts.

Perfoliate. A leaf that is fused along the margins and wraps around the stem so that the stem appears to pierce through its middle.

Perianth. The sepals and petals collectively.

Petal. A modified leaf surrounding the sexual parts of the flower variously colored, shaped, and patterned to attract pollinators.

Petiole. Leaf stalk.

Pilose. Covered with sparse, long and straight hairs.

Pinnate. A compound leaf in which the leaflets are arranged along either side of a central stalk or rachis.

Pistil. The female part of the flower, i.e., the stigma, style, and ovary as a unit.

Pollen. The male gametophytes or haploid cells that fertilize the female ovule.

Polyploid. Aberrant cells (or organisms) having more than the standard two sets of chromosomes.

Prostrate. Growing low or flat on the ground.

Pubescent. Hairy.

Raceme. An unbranched inflorescence of pedunculate flowers that is typically long and thin.

Rachis. The central stalk—typically of a pinnately compound leaf.

Ray flower. Modified (and often sterile) outer flower, typical of an Asteraceae inflorescence, in which the corolla has been fused together into one straplike super petal.

Reflexed. Abruptly bent backwards (more extreme than recurved).

Rhizome. An underground stem, typically prostrate and producing roots below and shoots or leaves above.

Rosette. A flattened, circular cluster of leaves, usually arising directly from the crown.

Scandent. Climbing, vining.

Scape. A leafless flower stem growing directly from the crown.

Scree. Substrate composed of various sizes of rock and grit with very little fine material or organic matter found in rock fall areas of mountain slopes. Scree soils in the garden can be blended using one part topsoil, two parts leaf compost, and eight parts grit and pea gravel.

Sepal. One of a set of modified, outermost floral leaves, typically green in color but, as in many lilies, colored similarly to the petals and nearly indistinguishable from them.

Serrate. Sharply toothed along the margin.

Sessile. Lacking a peduncle or petiole, attached directly to the base without a stalk.

Softwood. In the context of this book, plant stem tissue that has not fully matured or hardened.

Spadix. A crowded spike of small flowers on a fleshy stem. Typical of the Araceae.

Spathe. A large bract which surrounds or encloses the inflorescence. Typical of the Araceae.

Stamen. The male portion of a flower, consisting of the anther and filament (stalk).

Stigma. The section of the pistil (typically the tip) that is receptive to pollen.

Stolon. A long, creeping, aboveground stem. Sometimes also used to describe slender rhizomes that grow near the surface.

Stoloniferous. Producing stolons.

Style. The stalk that connects the stigma to the ovary.

Subalpine. Below alpine—plants that grow in the zone just below treeline in the mountains.

Symbiosis. The living together of two organisms in a close and mutually beneficial association.

Sympatric. Occupying the same place. Growing together.

Tepal. Sepals and petals that are indistinguishable from each other.

Tetraploid. Having four sets of chromosomes per cell, or a plant with four sets of chromosomes.

Tomentose. Covered in a dense, woolly hair.

Tuber. A thickened rhizome used for food storage. Tubers can also form on roots (tuberous roots).

Whorled. Having flowers or leaves attached three or more per node.

Xeric. Dry.

Xeriscaping. Landscaping with drought-tolerant plants for water conservation.

INDEX

Numbers in *italics* refer to pages on which photographs appear.

Starflower, *211*, 211, 264. *See also Smilacina stellata*

Star Grass, *126*, 126, 255

Statice. *See* Sea Lavender

Stenathium graminium var. *robustum*, 218

Stinking Benjamin, 213

Stokesia laevis (Stokes' Aster), *201*, 201, 263

    'Omega Skyrocket', 201

Stonecrop, *188*, 188–89, 262

Strawberry, Barren, *225*, 225–26, 265

Streptopus, 201–2

    amplexifolius, 201, 202

    propagation of, 263

    roseus, 201, 202

Stukenia filiformis, 178

Stylophorum diphyllum, *10*, 10, *202*, 202–3, 236, 263

Sugar-bowls, 76

Sugar-scoop, 209

Sulfur Flower, 100

Summer Phlox, *162*

Sundrops, 150, 152

Sunflower, *114*, 114–15, 116, 220, 254

Swallowtail butterfly, *277*

Swamp Aster, 220

Swamp Milkweed, *49*

Swamp Pink, *116*, 116–17, 248, 254

Swamp Saxifrage, 95

Swamp Sunflower, 114–15, 220

Swedish Cornel, 82

Symplocarpus foetidus, *142*, *203*, 203, 263

Syphilis, 140

Taiga (boreal forest), 23–24, 79

Talinum, 204

    calycinum, *204*, 204

    okanoganense, 204

    parviflorum, 204

    propagation of, 263

    rugospermum, 204

    spinescens, 204

    teretifolium, 204

Taxonomy, 7

Tegeticula yucasella moth, 228

Tellima grandiflora, *205*, 205–6, 263

Telluride, Colorado, 26

Temperature, 21, 23, 24, 88

Tephrosia virginiana, *206*, 206, 263

    T. spicata, 206

Texas Bluebonnet, *19*, 141, *142*, 142

Thalictrum, 207–8

    alpinum, 207

dasycarpum, 207

dioicum, 207

propagation of, 264

pubescens (polygamum), *207*, 207, 208

thalictroides, 42–43

venulosum, 208

Thimbleweed, 42

Thoreau, Henry David, 166

Thoroughwort, 104–5

Threadleaf Pondweed, 178

Thuja plicata, 26

Tiarella, 74, 118, 208–9

    cordifolia, 118, *208*, 208, 264

        var. *collina (wherryi)*, 118, 209

        var. *cordifolia*, 209

    propagation of, 264

    trifoliata

        var. *trifoliata*, var. *unifoliata*, var. *laciniata*, 209

Tickseed, *80*, 80–82, 250–51

Toothwort, *89*, 89–90, 251

Tradescantia, 209–11

    × *andersoniana*, 209, 210, 211

    bracteata, 211

    edwardsiana, 211

    gigantea, 211

    hirsuticaulis, *209*, 210

    longipes, 210

    occidentalis, 211

    ohiensis, 209, 211

    ozarkana, 210

    propagation of, 264

    (Cuthbertia) rosea, 210

        var. *graminea*, 210

    subaspera, 209, 210

    tharpii, 210

    virginiana, 209, 210–11

Trailing Arbutus, *98*, 205, 244, 252

Trailing Wolfsbane, 33

Treacleberry, 196

Trefoil Foamflower, 77

Trientalis borealis, *211*, 211, 264

Trillium, 77, 78, 181, 208, 212–15

    albidum, 214

    catesbaei, 213

    chloropetalum, 214, 234

    cuneatum, 214, 215

    decumbens, 214

    eastwoodii, 214

    erectum, 5, 213

    flexipes, 213

        division, *242*

    grandiflorum, 5, 31, 208, 212, 213, 214, 233

var. *roseum*, 6, 213

    seed storage, 239

    luteum, *215*, 215

    nivale, 213

    ovatum, 213, *214*

        var. *hibbersonii*, 214

    pedunculate species, 213–14

    petiolatum, 236

    propagation of, 236, 239, *239*, 240, 264

    recurvatum, 215

    reliquum, 214

    sessile, 214

    sessile species, 214–15

    simile, 213

    undulatum, 214

    vaseyi, 213

    viride, 215

Triticum aestivum, 169

Trollius, 215–16

    laxus var. *albiflorus*, *215*, 216

    laxus var. *laxus*, 215, *215*, 216

    propagation of, 264

Trout Lily, *101*, 101–3, 253

Tundra, *23*, 23, 171

Turkey Beard, *227*, 227, 266

Turk's Cap, 136–37

Turtlehead, *3*, *68*, 68–69, 249

Tweedy's Lewisia, *132*

Twinflower, *138*, 138, 257

Twinleaf, *130*, 130–31, 181, 236, 239, 256, *273*

Twisted Stalk, *201*, 201–2, 263

Umbrella Leaf, 29, *92*, 92, 251

Umbrella Plant, *87*, 87, 251

Uncompahgre Mountains, *43*

University of British Columbia, 214

University of Georgia, 225

University of Wisconsin Arboretum, *28*

Uvularia, 216–17

    grandiflora, *216*, 216–17

    perfoliata, 217

    propagation of, 236, 264–65

    puberula, 217

    sessilifolia, *216*, 217

Vaccinium angustifolia, 31

    V. vitisidaea, 23

Vancouver, George, 217

Vancouveria, 217–18

    chrysantha, 218

    hexandra, *217*, 217–18

    planipetala, 217, 218

    propagation of, 265